RICHELIEU AND REASON OF STATE

Richelieu AND REASON OF STATE

BY WILLIAM F. CHURCH

PRINCETON UNIVERSITY PRESS

PRINCETON, NEW JERSEY

PREFACE

THE ORIGINAL inspiration of this volume dates from a casual but profound remark by my beloved teacher, the late Professor Charles H. McIlwain, some thirty years ago when he said, "The end-product of divine right sovereignty was reason of state." Intermittent investigation of this proposition over many intervening years has merely served to confirm its accuracy. Research for this book was carried on during part of two years when I held Guggenheim Fellowships, and its writing was essentially completed during my tenure of a Senior Fellowship from the National Endowment for the Humanities. To both of these organizations, I owe a considerable debt of gratitude. They have enabled me to conduct research on a fascinating and significant topic and to present the findings that stem from one of the most fruitful suggestions that I ever received. In this way, the book serves as but another illustration of the fact that the teacher's influence never ends.

W. F. CHURCH

CONTENTS

CONTENTS

RICHELIEU AND REASON OF STATE

INTRODUCTION

IN THE HISTORY OF political thought, there is no more persistent theme than the relations between politics and morals. Indeed, the exact nature of their mutual relevance and the many problems that it presents have been primary concerns of political speculation since the beginning of western civilization. Predicated upon the assumption that human conduct should be guided not only by practical advantage but also by higher principles, the predominant canons of political thought have given rise to perennial tensions between the expedient and the ideal. Acts of government, because of their very nature, partake of both elements, and discussions of the role of the state in human affairs have usually turned upon the effectiveness of its policies and their justice according to the currently accepted system of values. Definition of the proper use of power is therefore crucial to the political experience of any age and must be a major concern of all rulers and political thinkers who would be guided by moral principles in an immoral world. The influence of Christianity has rendered the problem especially acute because of the obvious tensions between the concept of a higher law governing all human activity and the necessity of immoral policies to rulers who would guide and defend their states while dealing with others who know no such scruples. With the rise of modern states, the problem was further compounded by the growth of a political system in which each state claimed not only to be sovereign in its own right but also to enjoy quasi-autonomy from traditional values because its actions were vindicated by a special morality, that of the state itself. Reason of state provided the concomitant means-end rationality and went far to justify measures that were in themselves reprehensible but which benefited the state as a whole. Because it purports to accommodate morality to the demands of necessity, reason of state presents problems that are insoluble in absolute terms unless one adopts either higher law or practical expediency as one's sole criterion of judgment. In almost all periods of western history, however, political writers have succeeded in developing a casuistry with which to justify questionable but necessary acts of government.

INTRODUCTION

Although the phrase "reason of state" did not become current in
western Europe until well into the sixteenth century, experience
over the ages has shown that its central issue—the relations between
the expedient and the ideal in political affairs—has not only been
a perennial concern of governments and thinkers but also poses an
ideological dilemma that is impossible to resolve in universally acceptable terms. For this reason, the only valid method of studying
the history of reason of state is to examine the manner in which
the problem was handled in a given period, that is, the ways in
which statesmen and writers understood and grappled with the
issue in a particular time and place. On the basis of the record, it
seems that their approaches to the problem have invariably been
determined by the frame of reference, practical and ideological, that
was provided by the age itself. A strong case may be made for the
fact that political thought and experience evolve together and that
man, as a thinking animal, reacts to both in such a way that his understanding of political life on both levels is simultaneously enriched.
Indeed, in the growth of all political thought except the frankly
utopian, continual interaction occurs between prevailing ideals and
transitory circumstances, the latter frequently determining the focus
of attention and therefore the direction of growth.[1] It is not that
political speculation is completely derived from and dependent upon
the realities of the moment. Currents of thought undoubtedly have
lives of their own and may evolve along lines that are set by strictly
intellectual processes. There is, nevertheless, a large pragmatic element in almost all political thought, if only because of the nature
of its concerns and objectives. This is especially true of speculation
concerning reason of state, since its primary purpose, the delineation
of just and effective policy, would have little meaning for contemporaries apart from the realities of practical politics in their own time.

For this reason, this book generally follows the chronology of
political developments during Cardinal Richelieu's tenure of power
rather than any other pattern that might have been imposed upon
the relevant sources. It is my conviction that the subject of this study

[1] For a cogent discussion of this point, see E. Weil, "Philosophie politique,
théorie politique," *Revue française de science politique,* xi (1961), 267-94.

is a prime example of the manner in which the interaction of official policy and debate concerning the same may produce new insights and perspectives in political thought. In fact, it is my hope to demonstrate that the growth of the concept of reason of state in France during this period roughly paralleled and was inspired by the policies that Richelieu undertook for the benefit of the French state. This resulted in part, of course, from the fact that the Cardinal himself extensively publicized justifications of his actions, but not all writers who supported him did so for self-interested reasons. Rather it may be said that royal policy presented a large, disparate group of thinking men with a series of political developments to which they reacted in a variety of ways, thereby enriching contemporary thought concerning the proper role of government. The fundamental issue that they debated was by no means new, but the focus of their arguments was largely determined by the political experiences of the moment, that is, the Cardinal's policies and their impact upon the life of the realm.

The direct relevance of official policy to political discussion may be illustrated by a few examples. From 1610 to 1624, the problem of just government was widely debated in France, but the polemics were usually centered upon such issues as the extent and limits of royal power, the necessity of a strong monarchy to maintain order in society, the rights of the nobles, the royal virtues, and the dangers in the teachings of Tacitus and Machiavelli. Although the Spanish marriages were frequently criticized as contrary to French interests, so fundamental a problem as the divergence of foreign policy from moral and religious principles was rarely examined because during most of these years official policy favored cooperation with the Hapsburgs and advancement of the Catholic faith, while internal policy had little impact upon the rights and privileges of various powerful groups within the realm, even the dissident great nobles. When Cardinal Richelieu became First Minister, however, he undertook many newly strong measures against all elements of French society that he believed to be encroaching upon the royal prerogative, and embarked upon a much more aggressive anti-Hapsburg foreign policy, even at the expense of the interests of international

5

Catholicism. These developments presented the problem of just government in a Christian monarchy in much sharper focus and inspired widespread debate concerning the legitimate exercise of royal power in both foreign and domestic affairs. It may also be shown that such dramatic incidents as the Valtelline episode and the Day of Dupes extensively influenced the course of the controversy. In this way, the progress of events and the clash of opinion together accelerated and enriched the development of that increasingly fashionable concept, reason of state.

The scope of this book is determined by its purpose: to trace the growth of the idea of reason of state in France as it evolved in conjunction with the policies that Cardinal Richelieu undertook for the purpose of strengthening the French state system. To the extent that it involves examination of the Cardinal's motives and especially his justifications of his actions, our subject may be viewed as the intellectual counterpart of his program of state-building. The requisite treatment of the materials of intellectual history is both limited and extensive. Since Richelieu's policies embraced all important political affairs during his tenure of power, he directly or indirectly influenced an enormous amount of writing. Directly he enjoyed varying contacts with many historians, dramatists, academicians, jurists, archivists, administrators, and pamphleteers, not to mention his corps of secretaries who compiled many records and apologetic works for the benefit of his contemporaries and posterity. And indirectly his influence upon many other authors during his time, while impossible to measure precisely, was of great moment. It has even been stated that the Cardinal exercised at least indirect influence upon the entire literary production of his generation.[2] For this reason, it is superfluous to attempt to analyze all writings that touch upon his acts, even many that mention reason of state. Since much of the pamphleteering, both for and against his policies, is repetitive in the extreme, a carefully chosen selection of relevant tracts and treatises will suffice for our purposes. All purely literary works have been excluded because they are rarely concerned with specific matters of

[2] M. Deloche, *Autour de la plume du Cardinal de Richelieu*, Paris, 1920, Preface and p. 3.

policy. The treatises of certain great thinkers such as Descartes and Grotius have also been omitted since their influence lies outside the currents of thought that are examined in this book.

The materials through which I have attempted to trace the growth of reason of state in this period consist of a selection of sources regarding Richelieu's policies, the debates and apologetic works which they occasioned, and the final articulation of the concept under his aegis. This in itself is a substantial subject of investigation because of the varied nature and vast amount of pertinent evidence. It also presents in full force the problem of the value and reliability of the materials that are available to the historian. Generally I have taken the position that unless there are important reasons for discounting a given source, the view that it expresses should be taken at face value, at least in its essentials. The many treatises, tracts, memoirs, and documents that were either written by Richelieu, dictated by him, written under his supervision, or reviewed by him before publication may be regarded as accurate presentations of his view of himself, his motives and objectives, or at least that which he wished others to have of him. We can never completely fathom the depths of his amazingly rich and vigorous mind; these writings and the record of his life are the best evidence that we have of his ideological position. The works of his many supporters and apologists among men of letters are considerably more numerous and must also be carefully analyzed, since they developed positions that were central to the growth of reason of state. In fact, these tracts provide the most extensive evidence of the manner in which reason of state was articulated during this period and are therefore crucial to our investigation. Because many of these authors enjoyed varying degrees of intimacy with Richelieu and their works were often officially inspired, their publications are sometimes dismissed as mere propaganda in support of his policies. Interested and partisan they certainly were, but not necessarily specious. Although individual cases varied greatly, the relative independence of many of Richelieu's apologists from official controls is indicated by the wide diversity of their views and by their hesitations before some of the implications of reason of state, even in works whose purpose was to justify the

Cardinal's acts. Their writings are analyzed both for their contributions to the growth of reason of state and the extent to which they reflect the Cardinal's position. The great majority of these tracts were written in the heat of controversy and cannot be understood outside this context. It is therefore necessary to trace the course of the many debates concerning the justice and morality of official policy. These polemics frequently forced Richelieu's partisans to defend their positions with new types of argumentation which revealed many of the implications of reason of state and furthered the development of the concept. And finally, the whole is placed in the general context of Richelieu's many-faceted program of state-building, the true source of concern for reason of state among his contemporaries. By examining these diverse historical materials, it is our hope to elucidate Richelieu's understanding of reason of state and his contributions to its growth in his time.

In spite of the many recent advances in knowledge of Richelieu's place in French history, there remains a strong latent tendency to regard him as a mere man of power, a Machiavellian statesman in Cardinal's clothing.[3] Actually, the picture is much more complex. A man of power he undoubtedly was, but his ideals, objectives, and his conception of the good of the state were such that he was unquestionably a man of higher principle as well. The charge so frequently made that Richelieu secularized politics stems in large

[3] It would be superfluous to cite the many works by French, German, British, and American authors who take this position, although a number are included in the Bibliography at the end of this volume. One recent work, however, requires special mention: Etienne Thuau, *Raison d'État et pensée politique à l'époque de Richelieu*, Paris, 1966. Readers of Thuau's book will find it a very able, scholarly, systematic analysis of the many elements of reason of state during Richelieu's period. Thuau's treatment, however, is limited to reason of state as an intellectual phenomenon, and he makes no effort to relate it to Richelieu's policies which were the source of the concern of his contemporaries about reason of state and sparked the controversies which furthered its development. He also, for all the qualifications that he introduces, regards Richelieu as essentially Machiavellian in precept and motivation. Readers of his volume and mine will find that we adhere to fundamentally different views of Richelieu's understanding of reason of state.

measure from hindsight, that is, a knowledge of the fruits of his policies in later periods. We now know that his building of state power and some of his tactics opened the way for the growth of the modern state which eventually became a lawless and thoroughly secular affair, deliberately divorced from the religious phase of human experience. This crucial development in recent centuries, however, lay far in the future in Richelieu's time and was totally unknown to him and his contemporaries. It is therefore unwarranted to accuse him of fostering elements of the modern world of which he had no knowledge and which he would have deplored.

The view that Richelieu was a disciple of Machiavelli may be substantially refuted by placing the Cardinal in the context of his time and recalling the nature of the state whose first servant he became. Indeed, the fundamentally religious character of the French state for whose good he committed many high-handed acts suffices to indicate the great distance between Richelieu's ideology and the secularism of Machiavelli. The mentality of the early seventeenth century, in spite of great variation among individuals, was predominantly religious, and this fact was massively reflected in the almost complete fusion of religion and politics in the period. The functions, ideology, and objectives of the French state were shaped to a great extent by its Christian traditions, values, and purposes, while the religious trappings and attributes that it inherited from past centuries continued in full force and even received renewed emphasis during the reign of Louis XIII. Conclusive evidence concerning the religious nature and ends of the French state in the early seventeenth century is found not only in many functions of the monarchy and the writings of contemporaries but also, most significantly, in the lives and ideals of the men who were devoted to its service. The tradition of the Cardinal-minister was in full vigor, with complete papal approval.[4] The many courtier-clerics who haunted the royal

---

[4] Richelieu's appointment as royal minister was approved by Pope Urban VIII who agreed that the Cardinal might handle any matters that concerned the good of the French state. L. von Pastor, *The History of the Popes*, London, 1938, Vol. xxviii, 72.

court found it entirely appropriate to work for religious purposes while in the king's entourage.[5] Such outstanding religious leaders as Bérulle, Saint-Cyran, and Father Joseph supported Richelieu for years because they believed that his efforts on behalf of the French monarchy were for a religious good. And many administrators and jurists, for all their Gallicanism, demonstrated firm religious convictions and devoted themselves to religious causes.[6] Indeed, the *dévots* and *bons Français* were essentially agreed concerning the need to strengthen the French state as it stood. Their strife resulted from disagreement concerning means rather than ends. Bérulle and Saint-Cyran eventually broke with Richelieu because they feared, with some justice, that his more questionable policies were taking precedence over his objectives. Those who accused the Cardinal of Machiavellism during his lifetime were alarmed lest his ruthless methods of government degrade the French monarchy to the point where its Christian qualities might be extensively compromised. Father Joseph and many others, however, remained loyal to Richelieu but never lost sight of higher ends of a religious nature. As for the Cardinal himself, the sincerity of his religious beliefs is generally accepted,[7] and he was thoroughly convinced that they were in no

[5] Among the innumerable examples that might be listed, we may cite the Carmelite friar, Léon de Saint-Jean, whose career, politico-religious ideology, and support of Richelieu and Mazarin are well described in J.-P. Massaut, "Autour de Richelieu et de Mazarin. Le Carme Léon de Saint-Jean et la grande politique," *Revue d'histoire moderne et contemporaine*, vii (1960), 11-45.

[6] Many jurists, including magistrates in the Parlement of Paris, were members of the Company of the Holy Sacrament. R. Allier, *La Cabale des dévots*, Paris, 1902, pp. 39-40. An outstanding example of the religious minded administrator is René d'Argenson who was a nephew of Cardinal Bérulle, a jurist, councillor of state, and holder of various intendancies as well as a genuine Christian mystic. M. de Certeau, "Politique et mystique: René d'Argenson (1596-1651)," *Revue d'ascétique et de mystique*, xxxix (1963), 45-82.

[7] L. Cognet, "La Spiritualité de Richelieu," *Études franciscaines*, iii (1952), 85-91. Many more extensive studies might be cited. Although some authors are critical of his doctrinal position, they do not deny the strength and sincerity of his convictions. J. Orcibal, "Richelieu, homme d'église, homme d'État, à propos d'un ouvrage récent," *Revue d'histoire de l'église de France*, xxxiv (1948), 94-101.

way compromised by his policies for the good of the French state. The exigencies of politics often forced him to resort to many Machiavellian measures, but his fundamental ideals and objectives were utterly remote from those of the astute Florentine.

It may easily be demonstrated that the concept of reason of state was the most important contribution of Cardinal Richelieu's generation to the growth of political thought in France. The foundations of seventeenth-century absolutism had been laid during and immediately following the Wars of Religion with the development of divine-right sovereignty, and the final essential element was added with the formulation of reason of state. The latter concept was not new in that it concerned very old and continuing political problems, but the writers of Richelieu's period articulated new solutions and gave them a new rationale. Their individual contributions, however, were limited and rarely transcended the intellectual categories that they inherited from the past. Their enormous debt to earlier thinkers is everywhere apparent in their writings. For this reason, it is necessary to preface our analysis of intellectual developments under Richelieu with an extensive though summary treatment of their background during the preceding half-century. The apparent lack of originality among writers during Richelieu's period and their dependence upon earlier treatises reflect the fact that there appeared in his time no genuinely great thinker who was capable of synthesizing prevailing political concepts and advancing to new intellectual frontiers. Instead, political speculation was the work of many minds that made limited, specific contributions to the growth of the new concept. It was the hesitant method of men who accepted the intellectual tools at hand and pushed slowly and haltingly toward a justification of policies that they felt to be essential to the preservation and strengthening of the state. The procedure presented major difficulties, both because of the nature of the issues and the cogency of the opposition which the new means-end rationality inspired in Richelieu's critics. No one was more conscious of this than the Cardinal himself, and he keenly felt the need to justify the policies that he believed necessary to the continued success and development of the French state system. For this reason, he and his supporters embarked upon the first concerted effort in the history of French political thought to develop a viable concept of reason of state. The result was a new view of the justifiable use of power which was associated with the French monarchy, for better or worse, during the remainder of the Old Regime.

PART I

THE BACKGROUND

POWER, POLITICS, AND MORALS IN THE
FRENCH STATE SYSTEM

THROUGHOUT THE COURSE OF European history, the proper
definition of governmental policy has been the central and
most consequential issue that has forced its attention upon
rulers, statesmen, and political thinkers alike. The consolidation of
governmental power and the emergence of newly strong states during
the early modern period, far from providing ready-made solutions
to this perennial problem, added a new dimension, reason of state.
For the most part, the political theorists and statesmen of the age
attempted to resolve the increasingly difficult questions that confronted them in accordance with their understanding of the general
good, but in the process they invariably approached matters of policy
through the political realities and intellectual preconceptions of
their own time. In a book that attempts to analyze the place of
reason of state in French thought and practice during the ministry
of Cardinal Richelieu, it is essential to begin by indicating the political and ideological factors that impinged directly upon speculation
concerning this concept. Like all statesmen and political thinkers,
the Cardinal, his supporters, and critics were men of their time and
approached the problem of rightful governmental policy from the
standpoint of their generation's experience and needs. The institutional factor in their spectrum may be shown by sketching certain
major elements of the French state system, with special attention to
the prevailing view of governmental authority, its nature, purposes,
and limitations. It is significant that this key element of French
political life should crystallize at the opening of the Age of Absolutism. Also, it is necessary to examine the heritage of relevant ideas
of just government from preceding generations of French theorists
and to examine certain parallel currents of an international char-

13

acter. All these elements, particularly those in the French tradition, are important because they not only determined the framework within which Cardinal Richelieu and his contemporaries viewed the problem of reason of state but also provided the philosophical and practical tools with which they sought its solution. It is the purpose of these initial sections of the book to analyze the basic background factors, political and ideological, that determined in large measure the fundamental categories within which the Cardinal and his generation approached the concept of reason of state.

By the early years of the seventeenth century, the French state system had attained a significant degree of maturity and henceforth provided the most important framework of the life of the nation. To achieve this position had required centuries of effort on the part of the French kings, their jurists, and administrators, but in certain respects their work was now essentially complete. From the earlier medieval organization of society as a hierarchy of estates in which that of the king was but one, persistent expansion of royal power and institutions of government had extended the king's estate to the point where it had achieved predominance over all others and had, in certain respects, become synonymous with the state itself. Unfortunately for those who would trace the growth of the French state, the word *état* is ambiguous. Not only is the historic confusion between the king's "estate" and the "state" perpetuated by the single term for both; in this period it was also variously used to denote a territorial unit that was ruled by a single sovereign, the royal government with its vast apparatus of offices and powers, and the community or nation at large. The most frequent and important usage was undoubtedly the second, that is, the state as the governing organ that was animated and controlled by the sovereign power of the king. Be that as it may, it should be emphasized that all these meanings had one important element in common, their juridical basis. As it developed in the French tradition, the idea of the state was fundamentally a legal concept, since all major elements of the French state system ultimately rested upon and were perpetuated by accepted law. It is therefore crucially important to note that the categories of law which determined the rights and position of all elements of the state were largely complete during the early years of the seventeenth century. As the Age of Absolutism progressed, certain portions of the governmental system increased in importance and new mechanisms for the exercise of power were added, but these developments took place within an organization whose structure was essentially formed at the outset of the period. From this standpoint, reason of state was a political concept that was added to, and grafted upon, a mature juridical state system.

As a territorial unit, the French state of this period was a distinct, identifiable entity, quite different from the earlier feudal realm. Its frontiers with neighboring states were rapidly hardening, permitting a much clearer differentiation of French and non-French territory. Although border disputes remained to plague later generations, there occurred a noticeable tightening of royal control along the frontiers of the realm.[1] Within the borders, important changes were also taking place. With the accession of Henry IV to the throne and the incorporation of his patrimony into the domain of the crown in 1607, the last great feudal principality disappeared. Henceforth, with minor exceptions, the royal domain was coterminus with the realm.[2] In this sense, the territorial basis of the French state was largely complete, and royal agents were now able to penetrate into all portions of the realm without significant interference. As a result, royal institutions were by far the most important governing organs in the land. The ancient function of dispensing justice was effected by a series of Parlements and lesser royal courts, while administration proper, chiefly financial and military, was carried out by a vast army of officeholders and commissioners

[1] L. Mirot, *Manuel de géographie historique de la France*, Paris, 1948, pp. 248-49.

[2] P. Viollet, *Le Roi et ses ministres*, Paris, 1912, pp. 65-68. A possible exception is the Duchy of Nevers which survived until the Revolution. From the sixteenth century onward, however, the administration of the duchy was largely in the hands of royal agents. L. Despois, *Histoire de l'autorité royale dans le comté de Nivernais*, Paris, 1912. I use the phrase "royal domain" to denote the areas of the realm over which the king was feudatory and into which his subordinates penetrated, rather than the crown lands whose income supported the royal family and certain governmental activities.

15

scattered throughout the realm. This vast bureaucracy provided the vital instrumentality with which the royal prerogative was made effective throughout the length and breadth of the land. Although certain administrative and judicial bodies survived on ecclesiastical and baronial holdings, by far the most significant institutions of government were royal. They gave graphic meaning to the concept of the state as the organ of sovereignty, the state as the governing power.

The strength and permanence of the French governmental system during the early seventeenth century were such that it was increasingly acquiring the characteristics of a continuing, impersonal, administrative state. Although the French monarchy necessarily retained personalized power in the hands of the king, the governmental system was in effect a vast bureaucratic apparatus that was capable of carrying out many of its functions without specific royal instruction. The major defect of personalized power was, of course, the risk that the normal functions of government would be interrupted by the death of the ruler, particularly if his heir were a minor, but France had traveled far since the Middle Ages when government ceased with the death of the king. Because of the continuity of its all-important legal and institutional foundations, the French state continued intact without the person or policies of the sovereign. According to the fundamental laws of the French monarchy, the crown was not a heredity but a dignity that was conferred by law upon each ruler in turn and thereby enjoyed permanent legal existence apart from the transitory life of the king who merely exercised royal power during his reign.[3] Thus, although the king might die, the sovereign authority was immortal. From this position, it was but a short step to the assertion that "the king never dies."[4]

[3] J. Declareuil, *Histoire générale du droit français*, Paris, 1925, pp. 394-410. W. F. Church, *Constitutional Thought in Sixteenth Century France*, Cambridge, Mass., pp. 81-82, 317-20.

[4] Antoine Loisel's third maxim was: "Le Roi ne meurt jamais." *Institutes coustumières*, M. Reulos, ed., Paris, 1935, Vol. 1, 19. Declareuil, pp. 401-06. R. E. Giesey, *The Royal Funeral Ceremony in Renaissance France*, Geneva, 1960, Chap. 10.

Likewise, any interregnum was ruled out by the immediate transfer of power to the legally designated successor of the defunct ruler.[5] Although the king might be a minor and a regency might be required until he could assume the reins of government, all authority remained in the hands of the young king and the regent merely ruled in his name.[6] Even the coronation ceremony meant nothing regarding the transfer of power from one ruler to the next and was retained merely because of its religious and symbolic significance.[7]

The legal basis of royal authority and the immediate transfer of power from one ruler to his successor enabled many organs of government to continue to function without interruption. La Roche-Flavin, in his important work on the Parlements wrote that the courts' authority and their dispensing of justice continued although the king might be dead, captured, or absent.[8] Similarly, many administrative practices gave continuity to the state system. Although royal ordinances were in theory effective only during the life of the king who issued them, they were generally observed without express confirmation by succeeding rulers and constituted a large and growing body of public law which was evidenced by the appearance of many published compilations.[9] The status of the treaties and the debts that had been contracted by the dead king was less certain, but it became customary to observe treaties unless they were specifically repudiated, while loans were increasingly made in the name of the state rather than the king.[10] And the most important factor making for the continuity of government was the very exist-

[5] C. Loyseau, *Cinq Livres du droit des offices*, Bk. I, Chap. x, No. 58, in *Œuvres*, Lyon, 1701. Giesey, pp. 183-92.

[6] P. Dupuy, *Traité de la majorité de nos rois, et des régences du royaume*, Paris, 1655, pp. 1-2.

[7] *Ibid.*, p. 13. Many instances of this are cited in the sixteenth and early seventeenth centuries in M. Bloch, *Les Rois thaumaturges*, Paris, 1924, p. 356.

[8] B. de La Roche-Flavin, *Treze Livres des Parlemens de France*, Bordeaux, 1617, Bk. xiii, Chap. 88, No. 10.

[9] *E.g.*, A. Fontanon, *Les Édicts et ordonnances des Roys de France*, 2 vols., Paris, 1580. P. Guenois, *La Conférence des ordonnances royaux*, Paris, 1593.

[10] F. Olivier-Martin, *Histoire du droit français des origines à la Révolution*, Paris, 1948, pp. 327-28.

ence of a vast corps of royal officials, most of whom held their offices as property because of the prevailing practice of venality.[11] Such features of the French governmental system extensively facilitated the growth of a continuing, impersonal, administrative state with special characteristics and a life of its own.

Although major developments in France made for the establishment of an impersonal, bureaucratic state, personalized power remained central to the system and even increased in importance as the Age of Absolutism advanced. In a monarchy, especially one that claimed to be absolute, there was necessarily a profound personalization of power, since it was universally agreed that the king held all public authority and that all acts of government were done either by him in person or by others in his name. Sovereignty was indivisible according to the prevailing Bodinian concept with the result that all officials merely exercised authority as a temporary delegation, all right to rule remaining in the hands of the king. Charles Loyseau, one of the ablest French jurists in the early seventeenth century, stated the accepted view when he wrote that although an official in the royal administration might enjoy a proprietary in his office, the powers that he wielded belonged solely to the king.[12] This concentration of all public authority in the king, however, carried many more connotations than the merely legal and institutional. As born leader, ruler, and defender of the nation, the king was the object of the strongest loyalty in the state and the focal point of growing French patriotism. He was even believed to embody superior virtues and to set the ideal toward which his subjects should strive. Because he subsumed its values and purposes, he symbolized and personified the state and was identified with it in this sense. Statements to this effect are legion during the period and too numerous to list. This view of monarchy increased in strength throughout the century, reaching its historical climax under Louis XIV. These twin develop-

[11] R. Mousnier, *La Venalité des offices sous Henri IV et Louis XIII*, Rouen, 1945, Conclusion.

[12] Loyseau, *op.cit.*, Bk. ii, Chap. i, Nos. 20, 23. Cf. M. P. Gilmore, *Argument from Roman Law*, Cambridge, Mass., 1941, pp. 113-24. Mousnier, pp. 75-79.

ments, the growth of the impersonal, administrative state and increased emphasis upon the pivotal role of the king, were crucial to the development of the French state system during the Age of Absolutism. Together they combined to strengthen the view that the state was a newly significant reality in the life of the French people and possessed a value and ethic of its own.

In its broadest sense, the word "state" in the early seventeenth century signified the nation or human community at large. Not only was it a territorial unit with a well-organized system of government; it was also a human collectivity, a living organism that was possessed of uniquely French features and values. Since the late Middle Ages, there had occurred a strong growth of a cultural nationality and patriotism which endowed the French kingdom with special attributes and set it apart from all other political units in Europe. If a nationality is defined as "a group of people who speak either the same language or closely related dialects, who cherish common historical traditions, and who constitute or think they constitute a distinct cultural society,"[13] all requisite elements were present in France during the early seventeenth century in large measure.[14] The French language was rapidly evolving into its modern form, and the tradition of literature in the vernacular was firmly established. Likewise, the historical traditions of the realm were widely known among its inhabitants. The mere fact of living under a common sovereign in a realm with a distinct set of laws, institutions, and traditions contributed strongly to a sense of pride in the French heritage. And the whole was placed on a high intellectual plane by being infused with a sense of religious values and purposes,

[13] C.J.H. Hayes, *Essays on Nationalism*, New York, 1928, p. 6.
[14] For various interpretations of French nationality and patriotism in this period, see H. Hauser, *Le Principe des nationalités: ses origines historiques*, Paris, 1916. H. F. Stewart and P. Desjardins, *French Patriotism in the Nineteenth Century*, Cambridge, 1923, Preface. A. Aulard, *Le Patriotisme français de la Renaissance à la Révolution*, Paris, 1921. L. Zanta, *La Renaissance du Stoicisme au XVIᵉ siècle*, Paris, 1914. M. Vanel, *Histoire de la nationalité française d'origine*, Paris, 1945. J. Barzun, *The French Race*, New York, 1932. R. Johannet, *Le Principe des nationalités*, Paris, 1923. J. Lestocquoy, *Histoire du patriotisme en France*, Paris, 1968.

particularly since the work of Jeanne d'Arc who effectively combined the ancient tradition of crusading monarchy with the concept of national patriotism. In the literary world, perhaps the most specific evidence of the widespread acceptance of this position was the appearance of many histories of France that were implicitly predicated upon the unique significance of the French past. This school of historians acquired a degree of maturity in the late sixteenth and early seventeenth centuries, and the popularity of their works is ample evidence of widespread interest in specifically French traditions.[15] Their writings even included the most potent ingredient of modern nationalism, a concept of the French race.[16]

During the upheavals of the late sixteenth century, French cultural patriotism was strengthened by a revival of Roman Stoicism in which many educated men, while continuing to adhere to essential Christian doctrines, found consolation in ancient Stoic morality.[17] Admirably suited to this purpose, this best of pagan philosophies provided a fully developed lay ethic and a noble sentiment of virtuous patriotism which French thinkers easily fused with their thought concerning the state. For our purposes, the best example of this union of precepts is found in the writings of the Christian Stoic patriot, Guillaume Du Vair. A jurist, man of letters and of action, Du Vair supported the position of the *politiques* during the rebellion of the Catholic League and exhorted his countrymen to remain steadfast in their traditional loyalties. His brief *Exhortation à la vie civile* argued against withdrawing from the harsh realities of civil strife and maintained that all Christians were obligated to endure the hazards of life in a period of social disruption.[18] The

[15] L. André, *Les Sources de l'histoire de France: XVIIᵉ siècle*, Paris, 1913, Vol. i, 265-70. W. H. Evans, *L'Historien Mézeray et la conception de l'histoire en France au XVIIᵉ siècle*, Paris, 1930, Introduction. D. R. Kelley, *Foundations of Modern Historical Scholarship: Language, Law, and History in the French Renaissance*, New York, 1970.

[16] Barzun, *passim*.

[17] Zanta; Stewart and Desjardins; F. Strowski, *Pascal et son temps*, Paris, 1922, Vol. i.

[18] *Exhortation*, p. 250. Printed with the *Traité de la constance et consolation és calamitez publiques*, J. Flach and F. Funck-Brentano, eds., Paris, 1915.

man of ability should actively contribute all his resources to the preservation of society, the most precious thing on earth, and willingly assume the risk of failure.[19] In his more important *Traité de la constance*, Du Vair lamented the calamities that the League had inflicted upon Paris, his native city, the capital of the most beautiful realm on earth and the common temple of all France.[20] His ideal was embodied in the words that he placed in the mouth of the dying de Thou who exhorted his countrymen to remember that they were French, to go down with their weapons in hand, and to sacrifice all for the defense of the state and the preservation of the *patrie*.[21] The key word *patrie* is used with sufficient frequency in the literature of the period to indicate widespread acceptance of the concept of the fatherland as applied to the realm at large.[22]

All these factors, both substantive and ideological, combined in such a way that the state in its various connotations acquired new meaning in the life of the French people. The most potent influence in this direction, however, was the widespread belief that strong monarchy was the only instrument that was capable of maintaining order among the turbulent French populace. During the early seventeenth century, all thinking Frenchmen were haunted by the memory of the anarchy and bloodshed that had been visited upon their land during the Wars of Religion. More destructive than any other wars in recent centuries, the religious struggle had caused unparalleled economic and social disruption, brought hordes of foreign invaders to French soil, and reduced the state to the point where the king was merely the leader of one warring faction. The work of restoration undertaken by Henry IV and Sully was cut short in 1610, and during the subsequent regency all the evils of the earlier period threatened to reappear, causing a crisis of confidence of the first order. Furthermore, in a broader sense, the seventeenth century in

[19] *Ibid.*, p. 252.
[20] *Traité*, pp. 57-58. Cf. R. Radouant, *Guillaume Du Vair, l'homme et l'orateur*, Paris, 1907, Chap. 12.
[21] *Traité*, p. 238.
[22] G. Dupont-Ferrier, "Le Sens des mots 'patria' et 'patrie' en France au moyen âge et jusqu'au début du XVIIe siècle," *Revue historique*, CLXXXVIII (1940), 89-104.

France may be called an age of permanent crisis because of the very nature of contemporary social dynamics. New and generally misunderstood economic changes were bringing distress to the masses and major dislocations to the privileged classes. The hierarchical social structure itself was fragmented by the existence of innumerable privileged units—great families and all manner of social, professional, and administrative "corporations"—which fiercely defended their favored status and often showed greater loyalty to their own fellow members and interests than to the crown. In addition, the propensity of many powerful men—particularly great nobles, high-ranking administrators, and even members of the royal family —to develop clienteles of followers gave rise to factions which often warred to the death. It seemed that all levels of French society were plagued by a variety of frictions and disorders that ranged from chronic peasant uprisings to intense factionalism at the royal court.[23] To the disruptions that stemmed from an extended and destructive civil war were added the chronic unrest and insecurity of a society torn within itself by permanent imbalances in many key areas. This condition of continuing ferment arose from inherent and insoluble difficulties within the French social and economic system. It meant that order and stability were the greatest needs of the age, and all who prized them realized that strong monarchy alone was capable of bringing them about. Hence the widespread, almost eager willingness to submit to increased royal power and to support the view that loyalty to the state should supersede all others.

The generally accepted reasons for the supremacy of the state over all individuals were cogently argued in an early work by the young Jean Duvergier, who later became the Abbé de Saint-Cyran and one of the founders of Jansenism. Henry IV, it seems, raised in his entourage the question whether a subject should willingly sacrifice his life for his king, and Duvergier set forth his answer in a

[23] The "permanent crisis" in French society during the seventeenth century is most extensively analyzed in R. Mousnier, *Les XVIe et XVIIe siècles*, Paris, 1954. See also R. Mousnier et al., *Problèmes de stratification sociale: Deux cahiers de la noblesse pour les états généraux de 1649-1651*, Paris, 1965, Introduction. R. Mousnier, ed., *Problèmes de stratification sociale: Actes du Colloque International (1966)*, Paris, 1968.

book whose success surprised even its author.[24] All persons, he argued, are subject to three types of government on three different levels, those of self, family, and the king or the *chose publique*. Each represents a different type of authority and is characterized by a corresponding law and morality.[25] In case of doubt, the highest authority, that of the state, must be obeyed because every man who lives in organized society under the rule of a king has become part of the community and is obligated to act, suffer, live, and die for the state.[26] In case the state is threatened with ruin, should not the individual be sacrificed for its preservation, since the good of all is the aim of each of its parts and the common good the objective of each person in the community?[27] Duvergier discussed at length the example of Socrates who avoided possible flight and preferred to submit to the laws and judgment of the state, sacrificing himself for the whole of which he was but a small part.[28] If such were the case with Socrates, is it not much more imperative to sacrifice one's life to preserve that of the ruler (Henry IV) from whom France has received life itself?[29] Duvergier concluded that citizenship in the state obliged its members to assume the burden of the most austere religion on earth, the confraternity of the dying, which bound each and all to sacrifice themselves for the prince and the good of their fellow citizens.[30] Such statements evidently evoked a very sympathetic response at the time they were published.

Taken together, all these factors—territorial, governmental, and ideological—indicate that the French state system of the early seventeenth century had acquired a marked degree of maturity and had become a major reality in the life of the nation. Although the state was governed and symbolized by the sovereign, it was a permanent, continuing entity and rested upon solid foundations that were independent of the transitory existence of the ruler. Furthermore, the state was endowed with powers, purposes, and values that were

---

[24] *Question royalle et sa decision*, Paris, 1609. On this work see J. Orcibal, *Les Origines du jansénisme*, Paris, 1947, Vol. II, 159-67.

[25] *Question royalle*, pp. 19v-20r.

[26] *Ibid.*, p. 34r.   [27] *Ibid.*, p. 34r.   [28] *Ibid.*, pp. 37-41.

[29] *Ibid.*, p. 43r.   [30] *Ibid.*, p. 56v.

superior to those of any individual or group and gave it meaning. It was even quasi-autonomous in the sense that it represented a good in and of itself, and thinkers were beginning to view its actions from the standpoint of a special ethic. The vital consequence was that statesmen and writers were increasingly conscious of the good of the state as the major objective of political thought and action. It is not surprising that there soon appeared a massive literature concerning the interests of the French state and the ways in which they might legitimately be implemented. This concept of the good of the state in terms of its special values and purposes was an essential prerequisite to any well articulated theory of reason of state.

Central to any concept of the rightful use of governmental power is a precise definition of such power. This was no longer a problem for French thinkers during the years when Cardinal Richelieu guided royal policy because the doctrine of divine right sovereignty had won general acceptance not only in official circles but throughout the realm. During the two previous generations, the jurists and other writers had developed this all-important view of monarchy which was to provide the theoretical basis of seventeenth century absolutism. In reaction to the turmoil and devastation of the Wars of Religion, many writers sought an extension of royal power as the only means of meeting the crisis of their time. This approach to the problem was most apparent among the members of the *politique* party, and it was their spokesmen who were chiefly responsible for this crucial development in French political thought. Through redefinition of the royal prerogative and expansion of the competence of legitimate royal discretion, they succeeded in developing a concept of royal authority that was seized upon by contemporaries as providing the needed theoretical basis of increased royal power. With the accession and triumph of Henry IV, the doctrine became quasi-official and was associated with the French monarchy throughout the Age of Absolutism. Because divine right sovereignty provided the core of French thinking about royal power and its legitimate applications, a knowledge of its formation and exact connotations is

essential to an understanding of reason of state in Cardinal Richelieu's period.

Any analysis of the growth of seventeenth century absolutism
must begin with a brief examination of the theory of sovereignty
that was set forth a generation earlier by Jean Bodin. As the most
important political theorist to support the *politiques*, Bodin not only
sought to meet the crisis of civil war by a marked expansion of legitimate royal power but also developed a universal system of politics
which he thought valid for all states. In the process, he drew upon
an immense body of learning and succeeded in articulating a concept of royal power with which he hoped to solve the pressing
problem of effective government in France.[31] His major contribution
was his crucially important theory of royal sovereignty. Instead of
following earlier writers who defined the royal prerogative as a
series of marks of sovereignty, Bodin developed the concept of sovereignty as an undifferentiated body of legitimate power that was
found in all true states. As fundamental as the power of the father
over the family, that of the sovereign over his subjects was an
ineluctable fact of nature with a firm basis in natural law. The exact
locus of sovereignty in any given state determined the nature of the
constitution; in a monarchy it was held solely by the king and was
therefore indivisible. His specific definition of sovereignty was brief
and clear: sovereignty is the absolute and perpetual power in a republic.[32] Regarding the "absolute" nature of sovereign power, Bodin
hastened to add that it was not absolute in the sense of suffering no
limits whatsoever, since all are subject to the laws of God, of nature,
and the laws common to all peoples.[33] The sovereign was absolute
only in that he was not subject to the commands of others and was
above the civil law which he might change according to need. Bodin

---

[31] The bibliography on Bodin is very scattered and extensive. A recent, comprehensive bibliography is contained in the English translation of Bodin's
work, *The Six Bookes of the Commonweale*, K. D. McRae, ed., Cambridge,
Mass., 1962.

[32] *Les Six Livres de la République*, Paris, 1578, p. 89.

[33] *Ibid.*, p. 95.

was clear that the laws and commands of the sovereign were synonymous and were the most important expression of his supreme
power.[34]

It was in this manner that Bodin was moved to define royal power
in terms of legislative sovereignty. The concept was a milestone in
the development of French political thought, since heretofore the
royal prerogative had been defined merely as a series of marks of
sovereignty that were essential to administration and adjudication.
To these, Bodin added a third element, legislation. The import of
the addition as an extension of the traditional powers of the ruler is
evident. In analyzing the nature of sovereignty, Bodin stated that
its first mark was the power to give law to all in general and each
in particular.[35] Moreover, he insisted, the authority of legislation
embraced all others since the making of law was the primary manifestation of sovereign power.[36] In this way, Bodin not only expanded
the area of legitimate royal power but changed its nature.

Within this frame of reference, the purposes of royal legislation
and its ultimate sanction assume major significance. In explaining
the authority of royal laws, Bodin stated that such legislation might
and should embody the principles of justice but ultimately it was
binding because it represented the will of the sovereign. In support
of this position he cited the terminal clause of all royal edicts and
ordinances: *car tel est notre plaisir*.[37] The element of will was therefore crucial to Bodin's concept of royal sovereignty. His decision to
place the king above civil law undoubtedly resulted from his desire
for a strong ruler who could control the social and political upheavals attendant to civil war. In the midst of change, he wrote, it
is necessary for the sovereign to alter the laws according to the dictates of circumstance, as a pilot governs the course of his ship.[38] For
this reason, the prince must be supreme over civil law so that he
may change it according to necessity.[39] In essence, therefore, Bodin
proposed a concept of royal power as the will of the ruler that was
to be exercised above the limitations of civil law and according to
the ever-changing needs of the state. The position necessarily em-

[34] *Ibid.*, p. 96. [35] *Ibid.*, p. 161. [36] *Ibid.*, p. 163.
[37] *Ibid.*, p. 97. [38] *Ibid.*, p. 104. [39] *Ibid.*, p. 106.

bodied a large measure of legitimate discretionary power whose primary purpose was the preservation of the general welfare. In this fashion, the appearance of Bodinian sovereignty represented a major advance toward a concept of reason of state.

It should be emphasized that Bodin placed important restrictions on the exercise of royal power, thus defined. Although his theory of sovereignty paved the way for seventeenth century absolutism, his handling of these limitations on the royal discretion differentiated his thought from the later position. The limits of divine and natural law were fundamental in Bodin's system, since sovereignty for him was a fact of nature and could hardly be exercised in a manner contrary to its foundation in natural law. His definition of the republic itself stipulated rule according to the principles of *droit gouvernement*.[40] This phrase, which denotes rightful governmental processes, indicates that for Bodin legitimate royal policy might not contravene right and justice. In the opening pages of the *République*, he stated that a group of thieves and brigands might never be a true republic since they lacked laws, justice, and right, and *droit gouvernement*.[41] And he did not hesitate to assert that since justice was the end of the law, law the work of the prince, and the prince the image of God, the laws of the prince should be modeled on those of God.[42] Clearly, the legitimate commands of the king must be tempered by natural and divine law. Likewise the fundamental laws of the realm, such as the Salic Law, lay outside the royal prerogative since these laws were annexed to the crown and the sovereign power was founded upon them.[43] Civil or man-made law, however, was necessarily subordinate to the prince-legislator. This included the laws of his predecessors[44] and all customary law which existed only on royal sufferance.[45] All civil law was therefore subject to the will of the prince although he was limited by divine, natural, and fundamental law.

The problem that is immediately suggested by the supremacy of the king over civil law is the precarious position of popular rights which were protected by that law. Bodin, however, solved this issue

[40] *Ibid.*, p. 1. [41] *Ibid.*, p. 3. [42] *Ibid.*, p. 118.
[43] *Ibid.*, p. 100. [44] *Ibid.*, p. 96. [45] *Ibid.*, pp. 104, 106.

to his satisfaction by giving the subjects' property rights a basis in natural law that the sovereign might not violate. Indeed, the degree to which the ruler observed the principles of natural law determined for Bodin the character of the monarchy itself. Bodin classified monarchies as royal, seigneurial, and tyrannical. In royal monarchy, the subjects obeyed the laws of the prince and the prince the laws of nature, leaving natural liberty and property rights to the subjects. In seigneurial monarchy, the prince was lord over the lives and goods of his subjects, while in tyrannical, he treated them as slaves.[46] In the French monarchy, which Bodin defined as royal, he found a clear distinction between the legal rights of the sovereign and those of the subjects. The latter should contribute taxes to the common good and in case of necessity the prince might confiscate property, although with just compensation,[47] but as a general rule the king should not take a subject's property without his consent.[48] Bodin's sharp differentiation between public power and private property is evident, and the inviolable foundation of both was natural law. In consequence, he urged the prince to resort to extraordinary taxation only as a last resort and then only with the consent of the Estates General.[49] In royal monarchy, he insisted, the citizen was merely the free subject under another's sovereignty. He was free not only in that he was not a slave but also because he enjoyed rights that were permitted to him by society: he might enter into groups, assume office, and above all hold property.[50] Similarly, Bodin held that many social and professional groups enjoyed special rights and privileges. In discussing "estates, colleges and corporations," he maintained that these were natural and necessary social organizations and that they possessed rights that might be defended, especially those pertaining to property. The king, he urged, should govern so as to preserve the harmonious proportion that existed between the crown and the social estates.[51] In this fashion, Bodin reduced all citizens to the position of subjects under the king but at the same time preserved inviolate their natural freedom and

[46] *Ibid.*, p. 200. [47] *Ibid.*, pp. 114-15.
[48] *Ibid.*, p. 115. [49] *Ibid.*, Bk. vi, Chap. 2.
[50] *Ibid.*, pp. 53, 68, 69. [51] *Ibid.*, Bk. iii, Chap. 7.

rights which should not be touched even by the sovereign who wielded very extensive powers and whose will was supreme.

Bodin's definition of sovereignty was without doubt one of the most successful ventures in the history of political thought, if this may be judged by the rapidity with which his views were adopted by his contemporaries. In the late sixteenth century, particularly with the triumph of Henry IV and the *politique* party, Bodin's concept of sovereignty won general acceptance and thus became a milestone in the growth of political ideas. The explanation of this phenomenon seems to be that a large majority of political writers of the period found in Bodin's redefinition of royal power an important solution to the crisis of the age.[52] The exact concept that he set forth, however, was inevitably altered in the hands of later writers. This mutation initially took place because of the universal tendency to place Bodinian sovereignty in the framework of the divine right of kings. Bodin himself had made the usual statements concerning the divine authorization of royal power, but he preferred to regard sovereignty simply as a fact of nature. His contemporaries, however, understandably combined his concept with the traditional religious sanctions of monarchy. The resulting conception of divine right sovereignty was of momentous significance since it provided the ideological foundation of seventeenth century absolutism. Furthermore, this union of concepts gave rise to intellectual trends that increased even further the power and majesty of the king, and correspondingly weakened the limitations upon his discretion. In this way, divine right sovereignty provided the fundamental basis from which reason of state was later developed.

It was inevitable that French political thinkers of the early seventeenth century should place Bodinian sovereignty in the framework of divine right. The long-established tradition of religious monarchy was so thoroughly ingrained in French thought that any other frame of reference was out of the question.[53] Since time im-

[52] Evidence of the rapid adoption of Bodin's theory of sovereignty is given in Church, pp. 243ff.

[53] On the subject of religious monarchy in France, see Bloch, *passim*. P. E. Schramm, *Der König von Frankreich*, Weimar, 1939, 2 vols. Thuau, Chap. 1.

memorial, the King of France had been the arm and defender of the Church, crusader, persecutor of heretics, and Most Christian King. At his coronation he was anointed with holy oil from the sacred ampula and became a semi-divine being who was endowed with miraculous attributes such as the power to cure through the royal touch.[54] From this position it was but a short step to the assertion that the king was a miniature god on earth and enjoyed corresponding power. Assertions of this nature are legion during the early seventeenth century; a few examples will suffice to indicate their tenor. The pamphleteer Du Boys, writing in 1604, stated that the king was the image of God and his powers a gift of God who transferred them to the king as a special grace.[55] Slightly later, the historian Duchesne wrote that kings were gods on earth and children of the Most High whose image they represented in all splendor. Royal power was therefore sacrosanct, ordered by the Divinity, the principal work of his providence and proportionate to his grandeur.[56] And early in the reign of Louis XIII, Louis Roland, a professor in the arts faculty of the University of Paris, addressed his young sovereign in this vein: "Your reign, Sire, is of God .... The king is the true image of the God of heaven and earth, Father of all .... As God is in heaven, so is the prince on earth .... If there is a question of the safety of God or one's father, it is preferable to die for Your Majesty rather than to save one's own father, since the king is the god common to all."[57]

Innumerable pamphlets illustrating this tradition are listed in André, *Sources*, Vol. IV, Chap. 8, Pt. I, and Vol. VII, Chap. 13, Pt. I.

[54] Cf. J. Barbier, *Les Miraculeux Effets de la sacrée main des Roys de France, pour la guerison des malades, et pour la conversion des hérétiques*, Paris, 1618. S. Faroul, *De la Dignité des Roys de France, et du privilège que Dieu leur a donné de guerir les écrouelles*, Paris, 1633. T. Godefroy, *Le Cérémonial français*, Paris, 1649, Vol. I, 411-12, 417, 457. Also many citations in Bloch, pp. 347, 360-61.

[55] H. Du Boys, *De l'Origine et autorité des Roys*, Paris, 1604, p. 35.

[56] A. Duchesne, *Les Antiquitez et recherches de la grandeur et maiesté des Roys de France*, Paris, 1609, pp. 124-26.

[57] *De la Dignité du Roy*, Paris, 1623, pp. 17-18. Cf. La Maunyaie, *Panégyrique au Roy*, Paris, 1622; *Le Prince absolu*, Paris, 1617. For examples in the late sixteenth century, cf. Church, pp. 245-50, 263-67. Also Bloch, *loc.cit.*

Proceeding from such assumptions, it is not surprising that many contemporaries believed the king to have received from God a knowledge of government superior to that of all other mortals. This concept of the "royal science" was well presented by the royal secretary Pierre de La Mare in a book that he published in 1618.[58] All men have their vocations, stated La Mare, but the king is born to the greatest perfection attainable on earth and understands the highest and noblest elements of nature.[59] Among men, he is a celestial soul sent by God for the governing of men and raising them above the level of beasts.[60] The royal science causes men to live in concord, is synonymous with good government, and ensures obedience. As the king excels among men, so is the sun resplendent in heaven; the king's commands should be so excellent that they contain nothing but pure perfection.[61] Such statements occur with sufficient frequency in the early seventeenth century to indicate their widespread acceptance. They clearly combine the twin concepts of divine appointment of the king and the divine inspiration of his mind.

Although works of this type represent royalism in its most extreme form, they illustrate a key aspect of the political thought of the period, namely, a strong tendency to regard the acts and policies of the king as *ipso facto* just. When the Bodinian concept of sovereignty which combined the authorities to make law and enforce its execution was placed in the framework of divine right, its adherents inevitably tended to regard the king as a living law, superior to all other mortals, and one who could do no wrong. The relevance of this view of royal competence to the problem of just policy and reason of state is obvious. Discussion of the issue is frequently found in commentaries on the jurist Antoine Loisel's first maxim, the will of the king is law.[62] When stated without qualification, this meant simply that the ruler's will had the force of law, but such an inter-

---

[58] *Discours sur la justice et science royalle*, Paris, 1618. The same idea is found in La Maunyaie, F. Marchant, *La Science royale*, Saumur, 1625, *Discours de la Prudence, au Roy*, Paris, 1611, and *Manifeste pour le public au Roy*, Paris, 1620.

[59] *Op.cit.*, fol. 3a.   [60] *Ibid.*, fol. 3b.   [61] *Ibid.*, fols. 4a-4b.

[62] "Qui veut le Roy, si veut la loy." A. Loisel, *Institutes coutumières*, No. 1. First published in Paris, 1607.

pretation ignored the existence of higher values that few believed the king might violate. Duchesne presented the dilemma when he said that the king's power is so great that whatsoever pleases him is licit and whatever he says is law, but Duchesne quickly added that although the king may do anything, only that which is just and praiseworthy is permitted to him.[63] Louis Roland carried the argument further but likewise left the issue unresolved in a more extensive examination of the question. After initial statements concerning divine authorization of the ruler, he said that the will of the king is law because the king, like God, may do anything, and Roland urged that the sovereign's actions always be presumed to be just since even the most burdensome were for the public good.[64] However, Roland then added the important qualification that all properties in the realm belonged to the king only in the sense that they were under his protection and jurisdiction; they might be taken only for legitimate cause.[65] Furthermore, laws should be made after consultation with royal officials and should conform to the principles of justice, after which Roland cited the *digna vox* which required voluntary submission of the ruler to established law. Such statements clearly illustrate the dilemma of the royalists who upheld divine right sovereignty but continued to believe that universal, higher values were binding upon all men, including the king.

A considerably more sophisticated treatment of the king's will as law was given by a number of jurists of the period. Although they fully accepted divine right sovereignty, they were loath to admit that the king's supremacy over all earthly laws and institutions permitted him to rule arbitrarily and to override the laws that formed the basis of organized society, particularly since civil law for them was by no means divorced from the higher values that the prince should not violate. The absolute authority of the ruler in matters of civil law and government undoubtedly permitted him to override this law if he chose, they held, but such hardly seemed consonant with the justice and equity that should guide royal policy. As a partial solution to this problem, the jurists developed the distinction between the "absolute" and "ordinary" power of the king.

[63] *Op.cit.*, p. 149.   [64] *Op.cit.*, pp. 26-30.   [65] *Op.cit.*, pp. 30-31.

On the basis of the former, he was superior to all earthly laws (save the fundamental laws of the French monarchy), but in his more accustomed role when he exercised ordinary power, he should, according to the precepts of the *digna vox*, submit voluntarily to established law. In discussing this question, the provincial jurists such as Pierre de Lancre of Bordeaux and La Roche-Flavin of Toulouse lagged behind those of the capital in accepting the implications of absolutism. La Roche-Flavin's important book on the Parlements essentially reiterated the views of the sixteenth century jurists from whom he extracted most of his statements. Making no effort to hide his dislike of *puissance absolue*, he insisted that the French monarchy was not absolute in the sense that the king's will was law, because all that he did must accord with the will of God. Only Asiatic tyrannies were of that nature. And he stated that the rule of princes should suffer two basic limitations, those of religion and justice.[66] Lancre, who wrote his very lengthy work for the express purpose of combatting the influence of flatterers at the royal court, urged that it was extremely dangerous to persuade the king that he might do anything because he was above the law. He decried the presumption and arrogance that accompanied princely sovereignty when the ruler felt himself superior to all others and refused to submit to the limitations of ordinary justice that bound the common people.[67] The importance of Lancre's insistence upon a single standard of justice for all was apparent when he explicitly denied that princes might allege reasons of state to justify policies contrary to divine and human law.[68]

The jurists in the capital were less reluctant to recognize the *puissance absolue* of the ruler, although they often hesitated before some of its more absolutistic implications. The very able Charles Loyseau urged that although sovereignty (*seigneurie publique*) embodied the *puissance absolue*, it should be exercised with justice because the sovereign ruled over free men and his power was limited by divine, natural, and fundamental law.[69] Of these, Loyseau found that only the latter involved specific restrictions, since he was clear

[66] *Op.cit.*, pp. 704-05.
[67] *Le Livre des princes*, Paris, 1617, p. 423.
[68] *Ibid.*, p. 445.
[69] *Traité des seigneuries*, Chap. II, No. 9.

that natural law did not include positive law. On the other hand, he carefully distinguished between the king's *puissance absolue* and his *puissance réglée* which he should normally use and did not violate private rights. As an illustration, Loyseau stated that the ruler's use of the *puissance réglée* permitted nobles free exercise of their traditional rights over local administration and jurisdiction, even though he might abolish these at any time by using his *puissance absolue*.[70] The distinction seems to be that the king should normally use only his *puissance réglée* without touching the rights of the subjects, but that he might, under certain circumstances, use his *puissance absolue* and override all but divine, natural, and fundamental law. The jurist Pierre de L'Hommeau, however, showed no such scruples in accepting the absolutistic implications of divine right sovereignty. In discussing Loisel's first maxim, L'Hommeau applied the Roman legal doctrine, "what pleases the prince has the force of law," to the French monarchy. Since the king, he said, holds his authority and power from God, he may make laws entirely on his own. Thus law depends strictly on his will and pleasure. And L'Hommeau cited as proof the terminal clause of all royal edicts, *car tel est notre plaisir*.[71] Such statements by a responsible jurist demonstrate the lengths to which the strongest royalists might go in representing the acts of the king as *ipso facto* just.

The debate concerning the exact limits of the royal discretion remained unresolved. It should be noted that the major area of disagreement concerned the relevance of higher values to royal policy rather than any limitations of substantive law. When Bodin placed the sovereign authority above all customary law and grounded property rights merely in natural law, he took a major step toward absolutism since natural law proved an ineffective barrier to growing royal power. The best evidence of this is the rapid disappearance in the early seventeenth century of all insistence upon consent to taxation.[72] The lengths to which the royalists might go in attributing

[70] *Ibid.*, Chap. IX, No. 12; Chap. XIV, No. 23.

[71] *Les Maximes géneralles du droict françois*, Rouen, 1614, pp. 19-21.

[72] This current was already strongly operative in the late sixteenth century. Church, *op.cit.*, pp. 255-60, 270, 332. The original version of Loyseau's *Traité*

the force of law to the royal will is dramatically illustrated by the book of Jean de Baricave, a lesser theologian of Toulouse. Since the laws of the king, he stated, are issued with the phrase *car tel est notre plaisir*, who can doubt the justice of the royal intentions? Princes are not judged by mortals and are accountable only to God.[73] The *puissance absolue* that places the prince above civil law is not tyranny, for tyranny is merely the usurpation of power without just title. Limitations of divine and natural law upon the prince are sufficient, and only God may punish transgressions against them.[74] Since kings are the images of God on earth, their laws are as oracles and should be obeyed in all matters of government; such is the will of God.[75] Thus, Baricave reached the conclusion that the king was the *source* of right and wrong in all temporal matters. Aside from the truths of divine and ecclesiastical law, he said, nothing is inherently just or unjust. Since the king is a just king, his laws establish the standard of temporal justice not only because they are inherently just but because he made them. Whatever he orders is just because he orders it.[76] Quite simply, the king's actions conform to the law because he made it.[77] It is apparent that in Baricave's thought we find the ultimate implications of divine right sovereignty in justifying any policies that the king might undertake. That Baricave had far outdistanced the majority of his contemporaries who feared the implications of the *puissance absolue* is evident in the remonstrance that the Parlement of Paris submitted to the Regent in 1615. One provision of this important document protested against counselling the young Louis XIII to initiate his reign with so many acts

---

des seigneuries (1608) maintained the necessity of consent to taxation, but this was removed in the official text of the first edition of the work. M. P. Gilmore, "Authority and Property in the Seventeenth Century: The First Edition of the *Traité des seigneuries* of Charles Loyseau," *Harvard Library Bulletin*, IV (1950), 258-65. After the Estates General of 1614-1615, the issue of consent to new taxes was essentially dead in French political thought.

[73] *La Defence de la monarchie françoise et autres monarchies, contre les detestables et execrables maximes d'estat d'Etienne Junius Brutus, et de Louys de Mayerne Turquet, et leurs adherans*, Toulouse, 1614, pp. 480-81.

[74] *Ibid.*, pp. 498-500.

[75] *Ibid.*, p. 502.   [76] *Ibid.*, p. 505.   [77] *Ibid.*, p. 511.

of *puissance absolue,* since good kings used it but rarely. Although royal power was absolute, it should be used with caution and moderation in order that it might long endure.[78] Such statements demonstrate that many persons close to the royal administration were at once familiar with divine right sovereignty and fearful of its implications.

On the basis of the foregoing, the view of monarchy that was upheld by the more advanced royalists early in the seventeenth century may be summarized as follows. The state was governed by a divinely appointed and inspired sovereign whose will was superior to all substantive laws, save the fundamental laws of the French monarchy. His sovereignty was absolute in that he alone held all governmental power and was subject to no human limitation. He enjoyed an expanded discretionary power that included the authority to make laws and enforce their execution. Although he recognized the limitations of divine and natural law, he was superior to customary law, and the property rights of his subjects were held on an increasingly precarious basis. Thus the sovereign was raised to great heights above his subjects and was superior to them in all ways. The state, in the sense of monarchical government, had acquired a distinct value of its own. It was below God but supreme in temporal matters and consequently enjoyed a quasi-autonomy in human affairs. There was a strong tendency to regard the acts of the king as self-justifying since they were for the good of the whole and reflected the will of the divinely appointed and inspired sovereign. The major remaining limitations upon the royal discretion lay in the realm of intangibles, that is, natural and divine law. The exact nature of royal subordination to these higher values remained uncertain, however, and was to be of crucial significance in later discussions of justifiable royal policy and reason of state.

General acceptance of the doctrine of divine right sovereignty meant that the theoretical foundations of absolutism had been laid

[78] Mathieu Molé, *Mémoires,* A. Champollion-Figeac, ed., Paris, 1855, Vol. I, 31. Also in La Roche-Flavin, p. 8.

before Cardinal Richelieu was called to the royal council in 1624, but the problems of practical politics during the early seventeenth century were such that it was impossible to adhere strictly to abstract principles in the formulation of day-to-day policy. Admittedly, the concept of divine right sovereignty implied certain fundamental canons of just government and the legitimate exercise of royal authority, but this was far from meeting all the requirements of political necessity that confronted the rulers and statesmen of the era. The permanent crisis in French domestic affairs plus the lawless conduct of foreign relations presented many problems that were not to be solved by mere definition of royal power and abstract ideals of just government. The king and his ministers were under enormous pressure because of their responsibility for the preservation of the state and often felt obliged to adopt any and all measures, however questionable, that were conducive to that end. Because of the force of circumstances and the various challenges of the age, those in charge of governmental policy were frequently compelled to sacrifice the lives and goods of individuals and groups and even to violate the canons of law and morality when seeking to advance the general welfare. Increasingly, thinkers of the period asked whether the good of the whole might imply a special morality of politics which differed from that among individuals. Might not the superior interests and unique concerns of the state justify a means-end rationality that would render legitimate all measures that were undertaken for the general good? Clearly there were tensions between the ideal of just government and the exigencies of contemporary political life. For this reason, the most pressing problem of political thought after the development of divine right sovereignty lay in the definition of policy that was at once acceptable in theoretical terms and sufficiently effective to meet the demands of political necessity.

It should be noted that the problem of defining justifiable royal policy was fundamentally different in foreign and domestic affairs. The concept of divine right sovereignty chiefly concerned relations between the ruler and his subjects but implied little regarding those between states except that all were equally sovereign and recognized no earthly superior. In domestic matters, divine right sovereignty, as understood by the absolutists, authorized more than sufficient competence to enable the ruler to fulfill his normal responsibilities. In addition to the doctrine of emergency powers which had been accepted for centuries,[79] the expansion of the king's discretion, his authority to make law and tax at will, his superior knowledge of government, and his responsibility only to God went far to justify any measures that he might undertake. Within this framework, reason of state appeared simply as the science of government that the sovereign, in his wisdom, might freely utilize for the general good.[80] More conservative views of the justifiable exercise of royal power persisted in certain quarters, however, especially among the nobles whose traditional influence in government and feudal prerogatives frequently ran counter to Richelieu's program of state-building, not to mention their attitude that submission to the king was voluntary and might be shifted from one ruler to another. Richelieu's policies in dealing with the nobility often violated tradition, but he was usually able to demonstrate their legality according to the prevailing idea of royal sovereignty. Although he was hated as arbitrary and tyrannical and his critics frequently feared that his policies ran counter to the best interests of France, he was rarely criticized as exceeding the legitimate sphere of governmental power. The result was that discussion of his domestic policies revolved less around their legality than around their potential benefits to the nation and ethical soundness relative to well-established tradition. Their legitimacy according to the increasingly prevalent view of royal authority was a potent asset to the Cardinal's program, and this seems to have been realized in his own time. In consequence, domestic policy was discussed less than foreign in the literature on reason of state that appeared during Richelieu's ministry. The explanation seems to be that the theoretical foundations of absolutism and reason of state in internal affairs were already widely accepted

[79] G. Post, "The Theory of Public Law and the State in the Thirteenth Century," *Seminar*, VI (1948), 55-57. Reprinted in his *Studies in Medieval Legal Thought: Public Law and the State, 1100-1322*, Princeton, 1964.
[80] Declareuil, p. 446; Olivier-Martin, p. 341.

and were sufficiently comprehensive to provide ready-made justifications for the many measures that he believed to be required by political necessity.

Foreign policy, on the other hand, was subject to no generally recognized principles, legal or moral. The basic fact, which the kings of Europe and their ministers knew only too well, was that "Machiavellian" relations between states were the order of the day with the result that any canons of accepted conduct were quite lacking and political necessity largely governed actions in this area. Although a few far-sighted writers were developing the principles of international law, they had no appreciable influence upon the handling of foreign affairs in the capitals of western Europe. In fact, divine right sovereignty which emphasized the total independence and self-sufficiency of each state merely worsened the problem by seeming to legitimize any measures that might be undertaken for a given state's benefit. The absence of any effective legal principles in this area, however, did not mean that rulers and diplomats viewed the interests of their states in purely secular terms, followed practical advantage as their sole guide, and had abandoned all other principles. Such was out of the question, since the secular state that was deliberately divorced from religious considerations lay far in the future. During the early seventeenth century, the religious position and commitments of every state in Europe were well known in its chancelleries and continued to exercise important influence on the conduct of inter-state relations. Religious principles, therefore, were intimately associated with statecraft and frequently gave diplomats pause, particularly when their policies bore directly upon the fate of a given religious faith or institution. This was especially true in France because her secular interests often ran counter to those of international Catholicism. The spectacle of the Catholic monarchy of France pursuing the interests of the French state at the expense of organized Catholicism disturbed many loyal French Catholics and presented the problem of justifiable royal policy in the sharpest possible focus. Where did the religious obligations of Catholic France and the Most Christian King end and the good of the French state begin? Or, if it was impossible to separate the two, might not the interests of both be served by a properly articulated foreign policy? In a nation that was experiencing a major resurgence of reinvigorated Catholicism, such questions assumed formidable proportions. They go far to account for the preponderant attention that was given to foreign affairs in the literature on reason of state under Richelieu.

Although French intellectual life during the first half of the seventeenth century ranged from extreme libertinism to mystical Christianity, its most important element in determining the "climate of opinion" was the so-called Catholic Renaissance, the final flowering of the Counter Reformation that was centered in France and was of great moment in shaping the mentality of the nation. It was a deep and many-sided movement that not only revitalized many segments of the French Church, often in cooperation with the crown, but sought and won the conquest of souls by widespread teaching, preaching, and example. The elements of the movement were many, extending from Christian mysticism and "devout humanism" to institutional regeneration and social action. New religious orders were founded and many old ones were rejuvenated; Bérulle's *Oratoire* wrought extensive reforms among the clergy and in educational institutions; the adoption of the precepts of the Council of Trent was general among the French clergy; lay groups of spontaneous origin devoted their efforts to charitable and religious purposes, and extensive missionary work was conducted among the Calvinists and the heathen of the new world.[81] This rich and varied

[81] The extent of the movement may be gathered from the following. J. H. Mariéjol, *Henri IV et Louis XIII (1598-1643)*, (*Histoire de France*, E. Lavisse, ed., Paris, 1911, Vol. VI²), 86-100, 203-9, 369-81. F. Strowski, *Pascal et son temps*, 3 vols., 1906-1908, and *Saint François de Sales: Introduction à l'histoire du sentiment religieux en France au XVIIᵉ siècle*, Paris, 1928. H. Bremond, *Histoire littéraire du sentiment religieux en France depuis la fin des guerres de religion jusqu'à nos jours*, Paris, 1916-1936, 12 vols. L. Cognet, *Les Origines de la spiritualité française au XVIIᵉ siècle*, Paris, 1949. M. D. Poinsenet, *La France religieuse au XVIIᵉ siècle*, Paris, 1952. L. Prunel, *La Renaissance catholique en France au XVIIᵉ siècle*, Paris, 1921. G. de Vaumas, *L'Eveil missionnaire de la France au XVIIᵉ siècle*, Paris, 1959. "Missionnaires catholiques à l'intérieur de la France pendant le XVIIᵉ siècle," *XVIIᵉ siècle*, No. 41, 1958.

movement touched all levels of French society and was paralleled by the character of the royal court which was unusually sensitive to, and sympathetic with, the new religious currents. At no time since the reign of Louis IX were matters of religion treated with greater respect by the sovereign.[82]

Such developments ensured that the canons of religious morality would occupy an important position in the intellectual climate of the age and would be of major significance in shaping any acceptable definition of just rule. Unfortunately for the interests of the French state, it had become traditional during the course of the Counter Reformation that the Spanish Hapsburgs were the recognized leaders of the forces of international Catholicism. The potency of this factor in shaping relations between the Catholic powers was demonstrated during the period, 1610-1624, when French policy was preponderantly oriented toward cooperation with the Hapsburgs and the advancement of Catholicism. Cardinal Richelieu, however, returned to the anti-Hapsburg policy that had prevailed before 1610 because he believed it essential to the protection and advancement of French interests. Earlier French kings, notably Francis I, Henry II, and Henry IV, had been vigorously anti-Hapsburg in both diplomacy and war, but none was subjected to such massive criticism as greeted Louis XIII's reorientation of French foreign policy under Richelieu's guidance. The explanation seems to be that the Cardinal directed French affairs during a period of resurgent Catholicism which was stronger than any similar religious movement in the three earlier reigns. When he sought the alliance of the Protestant powers and even took France into the Thirty Years' War with their support against the Hapsburgs, he was inevitably accused of placing the interests of the state above those of

---

L. Febvre, "Aspects méconnus d'un renouveau religieux en France entre 1590 et 1620," *Annales: Economies, Sociétés, Civilisations*, XIII (1958), 639-50. P. Chaunu, "Le XVIIᵉ siècle religieux: Reflexions préalables," *ibid.*, XXII (1967), 279-302.

[82] G. Goyau, *Histoire religieuse* (*Histoire de la nation française*, G. Hanotaux, ed., Vol. VI), Paris, 1922, 395.

Catholic Christianity. He believed, however, that he was the servant of both causes and strove to develop a convincing justification of his policies in these terms.

So extensive and virile a movement as the Catholic Renaissance was certain to influence contemporary thought concerning just rule. The strength of the conviction that religious principles should serve as the standard of judgment for *all* mundane things, including governmental policy, may be illustrated by examining two books that were published in the 1620's by ecclesiastics who were close to the royal administration, Etienne Molinier and Claude Vaure. Molinier was a doctor of both laws, renowned for his eloquence in the pulpit, and enjoyed considerable favor at court, preaching before the young Louis XIII at his coronation. His book on Christian politics was consistently oriented *"contre les Machiavelistes"* and was a veritable *politique tirée de l'Ecriture sainte.*[83] At the outset, Molinier admitted that he had no experience in governmental affairs but insisted that he was qualified to discuss them because theology provides knowledge of first causes and guides all things.[84] Categorically he asserted that political science concerns the earth and the regulation of civil affairs but should take its rule from heaven and its reasons from the eternal decrees of divine wisdom, since human knowledge and experience are imperfect if divine law does not give them being and perfection. Human affairs are the matter, but divine truth should give it form. And he argued vigorously against all who deny that God is not the God of the state as well as that of the Church.[85] God is the first cause and alone may protect our judgment from error. The true and wise statesman does not accommodate God to worldly affairs and justice to the times but regulates temporal matters according to God and molds the times to justice.[86] In a lengthy discussion of political prudence, Molinier defined it simply as the facility to apply higher truths to governmental problems. Purely human prudence, he maintained, availed nothing since it brought only death and destruction to in-

[83] *Les Politiques chrestiennes: ou Tableau des vertus politiques considerées en l'estat chrestien*, Paris, 1621.
[84] *Ibid.*, pp. 1-4.   [85] *Ibid.*, pp. 24-26.   [86] *Ibid.*, pp. 44-46.

dividuals and states alike. Rulers and subjects should equally submit to the truths of God who is the Ultimate for both men and states.[87] And he concluded that "the law of God is the sacred school of true political prudence. Instruct yourself, says God; O you who judge the earth, serve God in fear."[88]

Claude Vaure was even closer to the seats of power since he was one of Louis XIII's chaplains and a member of the royal household. His book is more practical than Molinier's in that it reveals a greater awareness of the many problems that confronted statesmen, and it devotes more attention to such fashionable subjects as dissimulation and reason of state.[89] Its viewpoint, however, is quite similar. Vaure's stated purpose was to combat the false reason of state of Machiavelli and the libertines by deducing all essential political truths from Scripture. After setting forth at length the current theory of divinely authorized and inspired royal government, he drew the logical conclusion that since the king is the image of God, he should rule strictly according to God's *bon plaisir* and the laws that He prescribes. Otherwise the king would be guilty of divine *lèse-majesté*.[90] Pursuing the argument, Vaure insisted that religious principles and reason of state are inseparable, and nothing is more dangerous than divergence between them. Only when they are united does God permit the successes that are falsely ascribed to fortune.[91] Vaure was similarly uncompromising in discussing the diplomatic practices of the period. All dissimulation and fraudulent appearance of virtue, he said, all deceit and falsehood are both inherently evil and self-defeating; their fruits are only temporary.[92] Likewise, the prince and all others are bound to observe their oaths, promises, treaties, contracts, and other sworn obligations because such is required by the principles of Christianity. The devious maneuvers that many use to circumvent their promises are even worse than outright denial.[93] For Vaure, therefore, true reason of state was simply the

[87] *Ibid.*, Chaps. 9-11.   [88] *Ibid.*, p. 93.
[89] *L'Estat chrestien, ou Maximes politiques, tirées de l'Escriture; contre les faulses raisons d'estat, des libertins politiques de ce siècle*, Paris, 1626.
[90] *Ibid.*, p. 242.   [91] *Ibid.*, pp. 160, 234-35, 253.
[92] *Ibid.*, Chap. 11.   [93] *Ibid.*, Chap. 16.

knowledge and rigorous application of Christian principles to all matters of government.

This uncompromisingly theocentric view of politics was by no means generally accepted in France. All who held to even the basic rudiments of Catholic Christianity, however, believed that religious morality should in *some* degree determine the fitness of governmental policy. The apparent divergence between the interests of international Catholicism and Cardinal Richelieu's foreign policy inevitably gave rise to extensive discussion of the relations between politics and morals in the international sphere. The strength of contemporary religious conviction was reflected in this literature and strongly influenced the Cardinal's role in the controversy. Richelieu was thoroughly aware of the necessity of presenting the literate world with a well-articulated concept of reason of state that would successfully answer his critics who argued from the primacy of religious principle and would be acceptable to a majority of Catholic believers. Any justification of foreign policy that was set forth in strictly secular or Machiavellian terms would utterly fail to satisfy the thinking public and was out of the question. A majority of the writers who supported the Cardinal therefore sought to develop a concept of reason of state that was grounded upon the religious nature and purposes of the French state and attempted to demonstrate that one of the objectives of royal policy was the benefit of universal Christendom and the religious life of the people. Far from divorcing the interests of the state from organized religion, they defined the aims and ends of official policy partially in religious terms and endeavored to show that the good of the state coincided with that of religion. The result was a concept of reason of state that purported to justify Richelieu's policies as serving both the religious principles and secular interests of the French nation.

THE DEVELOPMENT OF REASON OF STATE

Because of the complexity of the problem, the writers who discussed reason of state under Richelieu made extensive use of approaches and suggestions that were readily available in the works of earlier authors. In fact, in its broader context, the controversy during Richelieu's ministry appears as a late phase of a protracted literary debate that had its beginnings in the sixteenth century and continued into the seventeenth, although sharply modified by changed conditions in the later period. That it originated during the sixteenth century is not surprising, since it was in large measure a direct offshoot of the great struggles of the age, especially the Wars of Religion. The very nature of these wars presented in stark relief the problem of means and ends. For observers and participants alike, the religious wars represented a clash of thousands of men who were battling not only for political causes but also for religious principles, both elements being inextricably intertwined. In many years, the fate both of states and religious truths hung in the balance. Under these conditions, all parties did not hesitate to use every weapon, good or bad, to achieve their objectives. Europe became more than ever aware of the central issue of reason of state, the legitimacy of violent and immoral means in the service of higher ends. And the nature of the warfare was such that the role of the state acquired new significance in human affairs. This convergence of trends caused many observers to ask whether politics might be fundamentally different from other human activities and might require a special rationality and ethic.

The idea that politics are characterized by an exceptional morality and rationale not only lies at the heart of reason of state but also seems to be indicated by the phrase itself. It is therefore not surprising that the growing awareness of the problem of political morality among French writers coincided with the appearance of the term in the French language. The phrase *raison d'état* or *raison d'estat* first appeared in French usage in the late sixteenth century and became increasingly prevalent in the early seventeenth.[94] The

---

[94] The following are early instances. *Procès-verbaux des États Généraux de 1593*, A. Bernard, ed., Paris, 1842, p. 203. Several instances before 1600 in d'Ossat's letters, cited in n. 119. (I use this form for cross-references to other parts of this volume.) Mathurin Régnier, Satire X (1609). The second edition of Antoine de Laval, *Desseins de professions nobles et publiques*, Paris, 1612, contains a section on *raison d'état* which is lacking in the first edition, Paris,

French *raison d'état* was undoubtedly an imitation of the Latin *ratio status* and the Italian *ragion di stato*, themselves inventions of the sixteenth century.[95] The phrase therefore originated and gained currency in Italy, the land of Machiavelli and ruthless political practices, and was originally intended to provide the thoroughly secularized politics of the peninsula with a certain rationale. As its use became more widespread, however, Europe's disputes assumed a religious character and the problem of means and ends was increasingly examined in this context. The issue became the exact definition of governmental policy which was rendered legitimate not by its own nature but by the religious ends that it was intended to serve. If it is admitted that political affairs in this world may neither be entirely consonant with the highest Christian principles nor allowed to sink to the level of purely mundane expediency in which anything goes, the problem becomes the exact relevance of policy to each extreme. Certain writers attempted to determine the precise position of legitimate governmental policy between morality and amorality as a matter of *degree*. Others sought to identify the specific *occasions* when rulers who normally followed the dictates of conscience might justifiably violate moral precepts in the common interest. Still others studied the problem from the standpoint of the different *levels* of morality that were associated with the individual and the state respectively. But in all cases the central issue was the same: the exact relevance of politics to morals in a world where men habitually use all manner of means to attain and defend higher ends.

Throughout the sixteenth century, the more sophisticated discussions of reason of state were produced not by Frenchmen but

---

1605. These disprove the legend that Cardinal Richelieu was the first to use the phrase, *raison d'état*.

[95] R. de Mattei, "Il Problema della 'Ragion di Stato' nel Seicento," *Rivista internazionale di filosofia del diritto*, xxvi (1949), 187-210, and "Il Problema della 'Ragion di Stato' nei suoi primi affioramenti," *ibid.*, xxxxi (1964), 712-32. Mattei shows that "ratio status" was lacking in the Latin of the ancient world and that while Machiavelli may have had the idea of *ragion di stato*, he did not use the phrase. It first appeared in Della Casa and Guicciarcini and rapidly became current later in the sixteenth century.

by writers in Italy, Spain, and the Low Countries. The reasons for the indifference of French observers to the more subtle elements of the problem may be traced to the special nature of the wars that ravaged the French nation. Combining civil and religious warfare, the successive outbursts of violence increased in intensity until the monarchy itself was reduced to the level of one faction among several and the fate of the French state hung in the balance. Under these circumstances, French thinkers were absorbed with the problem of sheer political survival and found few occasions to discuss such refinements as a special ethic of politics and its rationale. When such matters were considered, they usually appeared in commentaries on Machiavelli whose ideas lent themselves well to the unsubtle and thoroughly partisan polemics during the religious crisis. The simplest approach to the problem of politics and morals is, of course, to deny the relevance of the latter in the definition of legitimate policy. Early in the sixteenth century, Machiavelli had stated this position in its classic form, and subsequent debate concerning reason of state could never be entirely divorced from his precepts. Although his ideological position was rejected by all major French writers of the period, there is considerable evidence that his works were widely read and well known. Three different translations of the *Prince* and one of the *Discourses* were published in France before 1600,[96] and the more popular editions of both were frequently reprinted. Machiavelli was repeatedly referred to by many authors and whole books were written to combat his views, not to mention the widespread belief that Catherine de Medici and her sons habitually followed his teachings. It should be stressed, however, that French writers did not know the historic Machiavelli whom we know today: Machiavelli, the republican patriot, the champion of ancient civic virtue, the formulator of a political science. Instead, he was viewed simply as the progenitor of Machiavellism, a scheme of politics that was totally secularized and sanctioned any methods that might contribute to the preservation of the state and its power. If this Machiavellism were synonymous with reason

[96] W. H. Bowen, "Sixteenth Century French Translations of Machiavelli," *Italica*, xxvii (1950), 313-19.

of state, the task of tracing its growth and development in Europe would be simple indeed because the Machiavellian version ignores its central problem, the relations between politics and morals, simply by denying the relevance of the latter. That such a view of legitimate royal policy was contrary to French tradition may easily be demonstrated by examining its rejection by all major parties during the Wars of Religion.[97]

Although the Huguenots published many tracts for the purpose of justifying their illegal rebellion and use of force, the strength of their religious convictions was such that they never borrowed support from Machiavelli and were among the most vehement in denouncing his teachings. La Noue, d'Aubigné, and the author of the *Vindiciae contra Tyrannos* inveighed against any and all of Machiavelli's ideas,[98] and the pamphleteers of the party did not hesitate to disseminate the idea that Catherine de Medici and her sons followed his precepts to the letter, as evidenced by the Massacre of St. Bartholomew's Eve.[99] The most important work of this type to be

[97] Since the place of Machiavelli in French thought has been extensively studied, it is superfluous to analyze it in detail. The following are among the better works on the subject. A. Cherel, *La Pensée de Machiavel en France*, Paris, 1935. J. R. Charbonnel, *La Pensée italienne au XVIᵉ siècle et le courant libertin*, Paris, 1919. L. A. Burd, ed., *Il Principe by Niccolò Machiavelli*, Oxford, 1891. O. Tommasini, *La Vita e gli scritti di Niccolò Machiavelli nella loro relazione col Machiavellismo*, 2 vols., Rome, 1883, 1911. P. Janet, *Histoire de la science politique dans ses rapports avec la morale*, 2 vols., Paris, 1913. F. Chabod, "Del 'Principe' di Niccolò Machiavelli," Pt. VII: "Il Principe et l'antimachiavellismo," *Nuova Rivista Storica*, IX (1925), 445-73. (Reprinted in F. Chabod, *Scritti su Machiavelli*, Turin, 1964, pp. 108-35.) A. M. Battista, "Sull'antimachiavellismo francese del secolo XVI," *Storia e Politica*, I (1962), 413-47. G. Procacci, *Studi sulla fortuna del Machiavelli*, Rome, 1965, Pt. II, Secs. 1-3.

[98] F. de La Noue, *Discours politiques et militaires*, Lyon, 1595, Sixth Discourse. See the treatment of D'Aubigné in Charbonnel, p. 34, and Tommasini, Vol. I, 12. *Vindiciae contra Tyrannos*, n.p., 1579, Preface.

[99] *Le Reveille-matin des françois, et de leurs voisins*, 1574, reprinted in *Archives curieuses*, Iᵉʳ série, L. Cimber and F. Danjou, eds., Paris, 1834-1837, Vol. VII, 202. *Discours merveilleux de la vie, actions et déportemens de la Reyne Catherine de Medicis*, 1574, in *ibid.*, Vol. IX, 7. This view of Catherine's policy was even accepted by the *politique* historian, J. A. de Thou, *Histoire universelle*, The Hague, 1740, Vol. IV, 566.

produced by a Huguenot was the *Anti-Machiavel* of Innocent Gentillet which not only crystallized opinion concerning Machiavelli but exercised decisive influence in shaping the concept of Machiavellism as it was understood by all parties.[100] Rarely has a more complete and effective denunciation of Machiavelli's political ideas been written. It may be noted that this uncompromising condemnation of Machiavelli by the Huguenots continued into the seventeenth century in their discussions of the legitimacy of rebellion.[101]

The spokesmen for the Catholic League were equally vehement in their denunciation of Machiavelli and in their insistence upon the supremacy of religious principle. The author of the *Dialogue d'entre le maheustre et le manant* put their case succinctly when he said that it was blasphemous to subordinate religion to the state; such was the position of Machiavelli. It could end only by allocating God to one small corner of the state, an idea so devoid of reason as to merit no answer.[102] The fiery preacher Boucher asserted that Henry III habitually carried a copy of the *Prince* in his pocket and sought to introduce Machiavelli's infamous precepts into France.[103] The international character of the Catholic League as well as the official position of the Roman Church were reflected in the condemnations of Machiavelli by the Jesuits Possevino and Ribadeneyra.[104] Both authors not only agreed with the criticisms of Machiavelli in the *Anti-Machiavel* of Gentillet but actually made use of the latter's work.[105]

The fundamentally religious motivation of both Huguenots and Ligueurs rendered inevitable their rejection of Machiavellism. Much more controversial was the position of the *politique* party which

---

[100] *Discours sur les moyens de bien gouverner et maintenir en bonne paix un royaume, ou autre principauté . . . Contre Nicolas Machiavel Florentin,* n.p., 1576. The key position of this work in the growth of the idea of Machiavellism is noted by many authors. C. E. Rathé, "Innocent Gentillet and the first 'Anti-Machiavel,'" *Bibliothèque d'Humanisme et Renaissance,* xxvii (1965), 186-225.

[101] *Mercure français,* Vol. viii, 180-84.

[102] *Dialogue d'entre le maheustre et le manant,* n.p., 1594, p. 8.

[103] *De Iusta Henrici tertii abdicatione,* Paris, 1589, p. 122v.

[104] Tommasini, Vol. i, 20-22; Burd, pp. 56-57.

[105] Burd, pp. 57-58.

expanded into a position of strength during the reign of Henry III and attempted to bring about peace through increasing royal power and a compromise solution of the religious warfare that had devastated France. The problem of interpreting the *politiques'* position is not resolved by their acceptance or rejection of Machiavelli, since their statements invariably echoed the general hostility to all that he advocated. Louis Le Roy,[106] Pasquier,[107] and de Thou,[108] to mention three representative writers, all vehemently denounced the Florentine's precepts as pernicious. And Jean Bodin, for all his desire to strengthen the monarchy, specifically rejected Machiavelli's view of princely power.[109] Although the Ligueurs repeatedly accused the *politiques* of Machiavellism because they refused to subordinate political considerations to the interests of international Catholicism,[110] the *politiques* replied in kind that the Ligueurs were using religion to cloak their true objective, personal aggrandizement at the expense of the general good.[111] It would seem, therefore, that all parties in the Wars of Religion rejected Machiavellism as a justification of effective governmental policy and supported a concept of the state and legitimate rule that was conceived in very different terms.

Considerably more important is the question whether the *politiques*, in spite of their rejection of Machiavellism, did in fact subordinate religious principles to the interests of the state, thereby opening the way for the predominance of political expendiency and

[106] *Les Politiques d'Aristote*, Paris, 1568, pp. 788-89.

[107] *Œuvres*, Amsterdam, 1723, Vol. II, 231-38.

[108] *Op.cit.*, Vol. VIII, 325; Vol. IV, 566.

[109] Bodin's reaction to Machiavelli has been extensively studied. The works cited by Cherel, p. 59, and by P. Mesnard, *L'Essor de la philosophie politique au XVIe siècle*, 2nd edn., Paris, 1951, pp. 538-43, give ample evidence that Bodin rejected Machiavelli's ethic of government. The most elaborate study of the subject is G. Cardascia, "Machiavel et Jean Bodin," *Bibliothèque d'Humanisme et Renaissance*, III (1943), 129-67. Cardascia gives extensive evidence of Bodin's rejection of Machiavelli but argues that while this was true in theory, Bodin was in fact very similar to Machiavelli in advocating government based on force. It is impossible to accept this interpretation.

[110] E.g., *Exhortation à la Sainte Union des Catholiques de France* (1589), in *Mémoires de la Ligue*, Amsterdam, 1758, Vol. III, 511.

[111] E.g., G. Coquille, *Œuvres*, Bordeaux, 1703, Vol. I, 230.

the triumph of the secular state in modern times. Although the *politique* party was a large, heterogeneous group with varied interests and attitudes, it members essentially agreed that royal power must be strengthened in order to restore peace to the war-torn land and that toleration of the two religions should be permitted insofar as necessary to achieve that end. In this sense it may be said that the *politiques* were willing to sacrifice religious orthodoxy for the more mundane interests of the state and the community generally, and it was for this reason that the Ligueurs accused them of Machiavellism. Although this view of the *politiques* is consistent with that of the Ligueurs, it is more surprising to find a number of modern authors asserting that the *politiques* in effect separated the state from religious doctrine and were therefore the secularists of their day.[112] Such statements seem to ignore the fact that no party during the Wars of Religion abandoned the religious nature and objectives of the state and embraced outright secularism. With considerably greater historical accuracy, a subtler and more convincing case has been made to the effect that the *politiques* did in fact represent an important turning point in the history of political thought because their precepts contributed to the partial abandonment of the supremacy of religious morality in political affairs, heretofore intact, and the substitution of incipient statism. Because of their insistence upon stronger royal authority, their close alliance with Gallicanism, and their willingness to resort to compromise in the sphere of religion, they tended to justify all measures that would benefit the state, even at the expense of religious principle, and made religious affairs a subordinate part of royal policy.[113] In addition,

[112] F. De Crue de Stoutz, *Le Parti des politiques*, Paris, 1892, pp. 4-5. J. N. Figgis, *Studies of Political Thought from Gerson to Grotius*, Cambridge, 1907, Chap. 4. V. Martin, *Le Gallicanisme et la réforme catholique*, Paris, 1919, Chap. 9. F. Meinecke, *Machiavellism* (English trans.), New Haven, 1957, p. 152. W. J. Stankiewicz, *Politics and Religion in Seventeenth-Century France*, Berkeley, 1960, p. 43. A modified version of this position is found in J. Lecler, *Toleration and the Reformation* (English trans.), London, 1960, Vol. II, 99-111.

[113] R. Pintard, *Le Libertinage érudit dans la première moitié du XVIIe siècle*, Paris, 1943, Vol. I, 10-14. P. Mesnard, *Essai sur la morale de Descartes*, Paris, 1936, pp. 195-98.

two recent American studies have examined the question at length and have demonstrated that although the *politiques* supported divine right of kings, were generally strong Gallicans, and adocated toleration as far as necessary to maintain peace, they never abandoned the religious nature of monarchy and the state. They transferred their frame of reference from the *Respublica Christiana* to the national state, but they retained the medieval idea of the cooperation of church and state, now redefined according to the principles of Gallicanism and divine right of kings, and they never denied the traditional concept that government enjoyed religious sanctions and was for religious ends.[114] In other words, the *politiques* may have deviated from traditional religious and political concepts as far as necessary for the restoration of royal authority and the pacification of the realm, but they did not abandon the religious purposes of royal government in favor of a policy of pure expediency and secularized reason of state. Innumerable statements by their leading spokesmen—Bodin, Pasquier, Belloy, Servin, Barclay, Pithou, Coquille, de Thou and many others—might be cited in support of this interpretation.

For our purposes, the major question is the *degree* to which the *politiques*, in striving for royalism, Gallicanism, toleration, and incipient statism, opened the way for a policy in which the practical advantage of the state took precedence over all else, thereby anticipating the theory of reason of state. An answer may be found in their major contribution to political ideology, divine right sovereignty. This all-important concept provided for a marked expansion of royal discretionary power but retained the religious nature and purposes of the state. The tradition of cooperating king and papacy and the exclusive adherence of the French monarchy to Roman Catholicism were compromised only as far as necessary to establish religious toleration. In fact, the brand of royalism that the *politiques*

---

[114] W. Givan, "The Politiques in the French Religious Wars (1560-1593): Advocates of Religious Toleration and Strong Monarchy," Ph.D. dissertation, Yale University, 1950. E. M. Beame, "The Development of Politique Thought during the French Wars of Religion (1560-1595)," Ph.D. dissertation, University of Illinois, 1957. Beame's work is superior to that of Givan. In this discussion of the *politiques*, I have borrowed a few citations from these theses.

championed placed increased emphasis upon the religious attributes and trappings of monarchy as the most effective answers to the theocratic arguments of the Huguenots and the Ligueurs. In developing their position, the *politiques* did not hesitate to make use of various religious postulates that had traditionally been used to justify papal absolutism. The idea of divine right itself, when applied to the secular ruler, represented this transfer of concepts. The resulting position placed great emphasis upon the king's responsibility to God and his obligation to rule according to higher law. This was anything but secularism. The *politiques* did not seek to strengthen royal power by denying the ruler's responsibility to govern in accordance with Christian justice; instead, they sought to accomplish this by expanding his sphere of legitimate power *within* the traditional framework of law and morality.

In the process, however, the *politiques* not only enlarged the sphere of royal competence but partially altered its attributes. Because of their great sense of urgency when faced with the collapse of royal power, they stressed the king's divine authorization and responsibility solely to God, accorded him legislative sovereignty which placed him above customary law and property rights, and abandoned doctrinal rigidity as far as necessary to permit the peaceful coexistence of two brands of Christianity within the realm. To the extent that religious toleration was established by royal edict and the principles of Gallicanism were followed in the government of the French Church, religious affairs were brought within the competence of the crown. Since the primary purpose of most of these changes was to restore the realm to its former condition of well-being, the criterion of just government partially shifted to a more utilitarian concept of the good of the state: order, peace, and prosperity. All this caused the more extreme *politiques* to support the idea that the state enjoyed a sphere of competence that was independent of theological determinations and in which the good of the state was the sole criterion. Hence the marked tendency among some of the strongest absolutists to regard many elements of royal policy as self-justifying. To this extent, the *politiques* prepared the way for reason of state. For them, this position was in no sense revolutionary since it merely represented a redefinition of the time-honored concept that the king was absolute within his sphere of authority but suffered limitations from legal, moral, and religious principles that were beyond his control. They also believed that the fundamentally religious nature and purposes of the state remained intact. That there were unresolved tensions within the position is clear, but these persisted in French political thought throughout the seventeenth century. It was within this framework that Cardinal Richelieu and his supporters fashioned their ideas concerning reason of state.

While French writers of all parties were rejecting Machiavelli's ideas and the *politiques* were developing the concept of divine right sovereignty, the debate concerning reason of state assumed a more advanced and sophisticated form in other areas of Catholic Europe. In Italy, Spain, and the Low Countries, a number of authors appeared who wrestled with the problem and whose analyses were considerably more searching than any that were produced in France. French writers, as has been mentioned, were thoroughly absorbed with the problem of national survival, but many other political thinkers in Catholic Europe found occasion to go further and examine the legitimate use of political power in more theoretical terms. The major issues that they faced stemmed directly from the problems that were inherent in the political aspects of the Counter Reformation. Of these, by far the most important was the legitimacy of questionable means in the service of the highest possible good in their eyes, the preservation of the Roman Church and the Catholic faith. For a great many rulers, administrators, and political theorists who were loyal to Rome, the very shape of the religious crisis posed the problem in unmistakable terms. The resulting analyses of reason of state became known in France chiefly after the restoration of peace in 1598 and provided important elements in the debate that revolved around Cardinal Richelieu's policies.

Unfortunately, the political practices of the papacy itself contributed nothing to the solution of the problem since many of the popes unhestitatingly acted upon the time-honored assumption that any measure which benefited the Church was entirely justified. For centuries, the popes had proceeded on this basis and the sixteenth century witnessed dramatic confirmation of this view of papal policy, whether the measures in question were the wars of Julius II or the political maneuvers of the popes of the Counter Reformation. All Europe understood when Paul IV and his successors sought to nullify the Peace of Augsburg,[115] Pius V approved the execution of Egmont and Hoorn,[116] Gregory XIII celebrated the Massacre of St. Bartholomew's Eve,[117] and when Gregory XIV sent papal troops to France to augment the armies of the treasonable Catholic League.[118] In the face of its greatest challenge, the Italianate papacy of the Counter Reformation inevitably adopted this means-end rationality. Machiavelli's works, to be sure, had been placed on the Index of Prohibited Books, but the popes did not hesitate to support the widespread view that Catholic princes, both lay and ecclesiastical, were justified in resorting to very Machiavellian measures for the benefit of both their states and the Church. Instructive examples are found in the diplomatic dispatches of Cardinal d'Ossat, the capable French emissary to Rome at the close of the century. In his audience with Clement VIII on January 24, 1597, which was devoted to discussing the newly ratified treaty of alliance between France and England, the pope showed his dislike for the treaty and maintained that Henry IV was not bound to observe it since his oath to do so had been given to a heretic, Queen Elizabeth. Clement then went on to assert that if a mere nobleman broke his word, he would be dishonored and criticized by all, but sovereign princes might, because of reason of state, make and break treaties and alliances, lie, betray, and follow other such practices. "I knew very well," added the Cardinal, "what to reply to all this, but I did not feel obliged to consider such a slippery and reprehensible matter and proceeded to take up others."[119] At the end of the dispatch, d'Ossat added that

[115] L. von Pastor, *History of the Popes*, London, 1924, Vol. XIV, 341ff. Cf. C. C. Eckhardt, *The Papacy and World Affairs*, Chicago, 1937, Chap. 3.

[116] B. de Meester, *Le Saint-Siège et les troubles des Pays-Bas, 1566-1579*, Louvain, 1934, pp. 61-62. Pastor, Vol. XVIII, 99.

[117] Pastor, Vol. XIX, 500.   [118] *Ibid.*, Vol. XXII, 368ff.

[119] *Lettres du Cardinal d'Ossat*, A. de La Houssaye, ed., Amsterdam, 1708,

Clement meant no offense, but his hatred of heretics was such that he allowed pernicious maxims, unworthy of an upright man, to escape his lips. In any case, the popes of the Counter Reformation consistently held to the position that error (that is, heretic princes) had no rights and that the policies of the papacy were self-justifying. Such an approach to the legitimate exercise of power accurately reflected the popes' concept of their unique role in Christendom, but it did little to solve the problem of international morality.

Catholic writers, on the other hand, could not ignore the problem of means and ends, even if the policies in question were for religious objectives. This was particularly true of those authors whose concern was the legitimacy of Catholic princes' policies, whether for the good of their states or the Church. From both the practical and theoretical standpoints, in the struggle for men's minds there was a clear need to justify the deeds that resounded throughout Europe over several decades. It might always be argued that a given act of violence was beneficial to the preservation of the faith, but princes were laymen and, like many of the authors who wrestled with the problem, were conscious of traditional limits of law and morality upon the exercise of power. The result was a widespread search by Catholic authors for a rationale that might enable princely actions to meet simultaneously the requirements of effectiveness and justice. The effort was not a coordinated movement since it embraced many thinkers who adopted a variety of approaches to the problem, but all had one important objective in common. Having rejected Machiavellism in politics, they laboriously sought to develop a *good* reason of state that would enable Catholic princes to meet the challenge of political necessity in a ruthless world and yet remain within the bonds of Christian morality.

Vol. ii, 357-68. Henry IV answered d'Ossat's dispatch with another, dated March 7, 1597. In it, Henry respectfully but emphatically indicated that he would under no circumstances break his oath to observe the treaty. Printed in A. Poirson, *Histoire du règne de Henri IV*, Paris, 1865, Vol. ii, 299-302. Other instances of Clement VIII's recommending such tactics are found in d'Ossat's accounts of audiences held on September 17, 1596 and February 19, 1599 in the same collection of letters.

Although all the Catholic writers who wrestled with the problem of reason of state were loyal to the Roman Church, they were strongly influenced by a variety of intellectual traditions and assumed very divergent positions concerning the relationships between faith and reason as well as their applications to political matters. The great variety in the precepts of individual authors and the innumerable crosscurrents in the intellectual life of the period notwithstanding, the writers with whom we are concerned may roughly be assigned to one of two categories whose differences on key issues stemmed largely from the tensions within their combined Christian and classical heritage.[120] The first group may be called humanistic. Their position was greatly strengthened by the revival of Stoicism in the sixteenth century and they were especially numerous among the jurists and men of affairs.[121] They generally preserved their reverence for religious truths but exhibited extensive confidence in man's capabilities, especially his reason, and therefore came to regard reason not only as an instrument of knowledge but also a means of achieving virtue, even a rule of life. In spite of their Catholic orthodoxy, they tended to separate faith from reason and to attribute a significant degree of autonomy to the latter when it was applied to human concerns. The other group was more exclusively Christian and was extensively influenced by the revived Augustinianism which was the most powerful force in molding the Catholic Renaissance. Here the emphasis was upon human sinfulness and ignorance, relieved only by man's love of God which in practice assumed various forms ranging from charitable works to mystical union with the Diety. For this group, who were predominantly religious leaders and their adherents, reason was but a means of approaching God and virtue was achieved through faith. The two positions inevitably gave rise to very different views of political prudence and justifiable

[120] This classification is suggested in A. Adam, *Sur le Problème religieux dans la première moitié du XVIIᵉ siècle*, Oxford, 1959. A. Levi, *French Moralists*, Oxford, 1964, shows that there were innumerable exceptions to this grouping, but an examination of his analyses show that it is generally valid. Cf. R. Bady, *L'Homme et son 'institution' de Montaigne à Bérulle, 1580-1625*, Paris, 1964.
[121] Levi, pp. 55-56.

policy. All writers were familiar with Aristotle's dictum, repeated by St. Thomas Aquinas, that true prudence is inseparable from virtue and if so separated would be mere cleverness,[122] but their implementation of the concepts of prudence and virtue varied according to the respective roles that they assigned to reason and religious values. The humanists understandably emphasized secular knowledge, reason, and experience in political affairs and tended toward a rational and even utilitarian view of prudence which was partially independent of religious principle. The Augustinians, on the contrary, insisted with equal vehemence upon the direct relevance of divine knowledge to human conduct and implemented both prudence and virtue in religious terms. Innumerable combinations of these positions appeared in the writings of the Catholic authors, but none, it is to be noted, reached Machiavelli's purely secularized, mechanistic concept of *virtù*.[123] The more complex position was that of the humanists who attempted to preserve their Christianity while allowing extensive latitude to partially autonomous human reason and will. The resulting dichotomy presented difficulties which many failed to resolve but which, nevertheless, had important bearing upon the problem of an independent political ethic.[124]

One of the most important writers of the humanist group was Justus Lipsius, a Flemish scholar of vast erudition and international renown. Lipsius was a convinced devotee of Stoicism, believing that virtue was found through living according to the laws of the supreme Good in nature and that man's reason was the source of his ability to do so. Although he outwardly conformed to a variety of creeds and had intermittent difficulties with the ecclesiastical authorities, his Christianity seems genuine and he urged the study of Stoicism as an aid to belief in Christian truths. His political thinking was influenced by his reading of Tacitus whose works he edited,

---

[122] *Nicomachean Ethics*, Bk. vi, Chap. 13. *Summa Theologica*, Pt. ii, Q. 47, Art. 13.

[123] Machiavelli's *virtù* is ably discussed from this standpoint in C. S. Singleton, "The Perspective of Art," *Kenyon Review*, xv (1953), 169-89.

[124] Bodin's confusions on this score are clearly demonstrated in T. N. Tentler, "The Meaning of Prudence in Bodin," *Traditio*, xv (1959), 365-84.

writing an extensive commentary on the *Annals*. For many writers of the period, Tacitus served as a convenient substitute for the condemned Machiavelli because both discussed the expediency of lawless means of securing and retaining power. Although the ideas of the two authors were far from identical, commentaries on Tacitus served to raise issues that could only offend when associated with Machiavelli. Specifically, it was Tacitus' description of the artifices, stratagems, and utterly lawless reign of power politics at the Roman imperial court that fascinated European scholars and moved them to examine the fitness of such measures in their own time. Discussions of Tacitus invariably centered upon the necessity of unscrupulous policy, and his name was usually associated with such.[125] In France, both Casaubon and Pasquier warned against his precepts as pernicious,[126] but Lipsius did not hesitate to derive inspiration from them. In the preface of his most important work on politics, the *Politicorum Sive Civilis Doctrinae Libri Sex* which was published in 1589, he called Tacitus the fountain of political prudence and even praised Machiavelli's abilities, although not his moral position. When Lipsius was accused of outright Machiavellism, his denials were apparently sincere.[127] The work was quickly translated into French, repeatedly republished, widely read, and exercised considerable influence on later discussions of reason of state.[128] Lipsius

[125] The following are among the more important works on Tacitus in this period. G. Toffanin, *Machiavelli e il "Tacitismo,"* Padua, 1921. F. Ramorino, *Cornelio Tacito nella Storia della Coltura*, Milan, 1898. G. Ferrari, *Histoire de la raison d'État*, Paris, 1860, Pt. II, Sec. 3, Chap. 3, and *Corso sugli scrittori politici italiani*, Milan 1863, Chap. 18. B. Croce, *Storia della età barocca in Italia*, Bari, 1929, pp. 82-85. Thuau, Chap. 2. E.-L. Etter, *Tacitus in der Geistesgeschichte des 16. und 17. Jahrhunderts*, Basel, 1966. A. Momigliano, "The First Political Commentary on Tacitus," *The Journal of Roman Studies*, XXXVII (1947), 91-101.
[126] I. Casaubon, *Ephemerides*, Oxford, 1850, Vol. II, 786. E. Pasquier, *Œuvres*, Amsterdan, 1723, Vol. II, 543-44.
[127] Burd, p. 42.
[128] *Politicorum Sive Civilis Doctrinae Libri Sex*, Leiden, 1589. This work passed through twenty-three editions between 1589 and 1641. I have used the Frankfort edition of 1590. A French translation by Charles le Ber, *Les Six Livres des politiques, ou Doctrine civile de Iustus Lipsius*, was published at La Rochelle in 1590 and again in 1594 at Tours. In 1594, Simon Goulart made

may be classified as a Catholic scholar of partially secularized views who sought in ancient learning the solutions to current problems.

Lipsius' political ideas represent an interesting combination of the old and the new. His treatises on politics consistently reiterated the traditional concept of Christian monarchy in which the ruler was characterized by religious faith, virtue, and respect for higher law. Specifically, Lipsius insisted that the ruler preserve his treaties inviolate and never break his word under any circumstances.[129] However, Lipsius was exceedingly conscious of the divergence between his ideal of just government and the realities of his age. Willingly, he said, he would prefer the teachings of the idealists who judge all according to the highest principles, but these writers are as far removed from reality as Plato's *Republic* and ignore the dangers and malice of the world in which we live.[130] The solution to this dilemma he found in his concept of political prudence which was not entirely novel but occupied a major place in his works on politics and influenced many later writers. Lipsius defined prudence as "an intelligence and discretion concerning public and private things that one should seek or avoid," and he explained that while intelligence sees all, discretion "chooses among things, distinguishes the honest from the sordid and the useful from the injurious."[131] Clearly, Lipsius allowed the ruler a large measure of discretion in which rea-

---

a new French translation which was published in that year and in six later editions. Lipsius' *Monita et Exempla Politica* was first published in Antwerp in 1605 and was republished nine times before 1650. I have used the first edition. Nicolas Pavillon's French translation, *Les Conseils et les exemples politiques de Iuste Lipse*, was published in Paris, 1606. A second translation was published by Jean Baudoin in Paris, 1653. On Lipsius, see C. Nisard, *Le Triumvirat littéraire au XVIᵉ siècle: Juste Lipse, Joseph Scaliger, et Isaac Casaubon*, Paris [1864]. J. L. Saunders, *Justus Lipsius: The Philosophy of Renaissance Stoicism*, New York, 1955. Toffanin, pp. 170-78. A. M. Battista, *Alle Origine del pensiero politico libertino: Montaigne e Charron*, Milan, 1966, pp. 229-41. G. Oesterich, "Justus Lipsius als Theoretiker des Neuzeitlichen Machtstaates," *Historische Zeitschrift*, CLXXXI (1956), 31-78. F. van der Haeghen et al., *Bibliographie Lipsienne*, 3 vols., Ghent, 1886-1888.

[129] *Politicorum*, Bk. II, Chap. 14. *Monita*, Bk. II, Chap. 13.
[130] *Politicorum*, p. 147.
[131] *Ibid.*, p. 37. Cf. *Monita*, Bk. I, Chap. 8.

son would be his sole guide. The primary purpose of prudence was the application of virtue, Lipsius insisted, but he did not hestitate to admit that the nature of politics required the ruler to temper his prudence with frauds, ruses, and the like.[132] Do not the public utility and the laws of reason and nature permit the ruler to make use of measures that are necessary for the safety of all?[133] As a solution to the dilemma, Lipsius proposed a mixed prudence which, while adhering to the general rules of upright conduct, would mingle the useful with the honest and permit a limited degree of deceit and treachery according to necessity.[134] Virtue would remain intact, he argued, since prudence is still prudence even when mixed with trickery for a good end. The prince should combine the courage of a lion with the cunning of a fox, and should recognize that in this life it is necessary to make use of honest deceit.[135]

Having opened the door to this Procrustean doctrine, Lipsius at once attempted to limit its application by determining the exact nature of permissible frauds and ruses. For this purpose he posited three categories: light, medium, and great. The first did not depart seriously from virtue and included deceit and dissimulation; the second was mid-way between virtue and open vice, while the third broke entirely with virtue and law, resulting in perfidy and injustice. The first Lipsius advised; the second he tolerated, while the third he condemned.[136] In implementing these categories, Lipsius argued that in simple frauds and ruses, the fault lay not with their author but the victim; they were therefore acceptable within the Christian frame of reference.[137] Middling ruses included the corruption of another ruler's emissaries and agents, the sending of spies abroad, and the spreading of false information.[138] The third category included perfidy, such as the willful breaking of treaties and other sworn agreements, and injustice contrary to the highest legal and moral principles.[139] The latter Lipsius prohibited entirely, arguing

---

[132] The subject of the important thirteenth and fourteenth chapter of Book IV of the *Politicorum*. Cf. *Monita*, Bk. II, Chap. 5.

[133] *Politicorum*, pp. 147-48.

[134] *Ibid.*, pp. 148-49.   [135] *Ibid.*, p. 149.   [136] *Ibid.*, p. 150.

[137] *Ibid.*, pp. 151-53.   [138] *Ibid.*, pp. 153-56.   [139] *Ibid.*, pp. 156-58.

that most of Europe's ills resulted from princely violation of the canons of just government.[140] In this fashion, Lipsius attempted to define the relationship between necessity and conscience and to indicate the limits of justifiable policy. His concept of civil prudence permitted extensive use of unscrupulous measures according to the dictates of reason and circumstance, thereby allowing the ruler wide discretionary powers, yet throughout his book he maintained the fundamental tie between morals and politics and consistently denied the autonomy of the latter from higher values. In this way, Lipsius' view of royal competence paralleled that of the *politique* jurists, although they reached the position by a different route. His solution to the problem of just government, however, was merely one of rhetoric and compromise and lacked a firm basis in law or principle. For this reason it was more ingenious than persuasive and in other hands was easily altered to vindicate measures of which he disapproved.

The Italian writers of the late sixteenth and early seventeenth centuries were understandably the most active in seeking a respectable reason of state that would not conflict with Christian morality. During the late Counter Reformation, they found themselves in an ideological position that made them peculiarly sensitive to the problem of politics and morals. Their religious orthodoxy and their reiterated condemnation of Machiavelli caused them to place great emphasis upon the supremacy of religious values, but the chaotic nature of Italian politics and their own intellectual traditions caused them to view the problem of government essentially in practical terms.[141] They consequently produced a very extensive literature in their quest for a morally sound reason of state. Especially after the appearance of Botero's *Ragion di Stato* in 1589, the discussion rapidly expanded and eventually included a large number of authors with a wide variety of views. Many of their works were known in France,

---

[140] *Ibid.*, p. 160.

[141] F. Chabod, *Giovanni Botero*, 1934, p. 52. This work was first published without appendices in *Nuovi Studi di Diritto, Economia e Politica*, IV (1931), 250-83, 341-68, and V (1932), 29-57, 154-78. Also reprinted in *Opere di Federico Chabod*, Turin, 1967, Vol. II, 271-458.

in some cases through French translations. Because the Italian writers were very repetitive and ultimately failed to develop a generally acceptable theory of reason of state, only a few of the most important will be examined here.[142]

The *Ragion di Stato* of Botero occupies an important place in the history of Italian political thought because it gave great impetus to discussion of reason of state.[143] Botero was educated by the Jesuits and was a member of the order for a time. He subsequently became secretary to Charles Borromeo and still later was tutor to the children of Duke Charles Emmanuel of Savoy. The express purpose of his book was to develop a Catholic reason of state, and this largely accounts for its popularity and influence, since it partially filled the void left by the condemnation of Machiavelli. Unfortunately, the virtue of Botero's book lies in its intent rather than its success. He genuinely sought to associate morality with political policy rather than merely to justify the latter through laudable ends, and he duly denounced Machiavelli and Tacitus for advocating measures that were impious and opposed to divine law.[144] Throughout the work, he attempted to adumbrate a true Christian politics but was only partially successful because of the narrow focus of his treatment.

---

[142] On this very extensive literature, see Meinecke, Chap. 5, Croce, Chap. 2, and Ferrari, *Corso*, Chap. 16. The best treatment is R. de Mattei, "Il Problema della 'Ragion di Stato' nel Seicento," *Rivista Internazionale of Filosofia del Diritto*, xxvi (1949), 187-210; xxvii (1950), 27-38; xxviii (1951), 333-56, 705-23; xxix (1952), 406-24; xxx (1953), 445-61; xxxi (1954), 369-84; xxxiii (1956), 439-49; xxxiv (1957), 166-92; xxxv (1958), 680-93; xxxvi (1959), 517-43; xxxvii (1960), 553-76; xxxviii (1961), 185-200. An interesting interpretation of the relation of this school to later French thought is presented in R. Maspétiol, "Les Deux Aspects de la 'raison d'État' et son apologie au début du XVIIᵉ siècle," *Archives de philosophie du droit*, x (1965), 209-19.

[143] *Della Ragion di Stato*, Venice, 1589. A French translation with parallel columns in French and Italian was made by Gabriel Chappuys and published under the title, *Raison et gouvernement d'estat*, Paris, 1599. Because Botero has been extensively studied, it is superfluous to give details concerning his position. On Botero, see C. Gioda, *La Vita e le opere di Giovanni Botero*, Milan, 1898-1895, 3 vols. Chabod, *Giovanni Botero*. Meinecke, Chap. 3. The article by Mattei cited in the previous note, *Rivista* . . . , xxvii (1950), 27-38; xxviii (1951), 333-56.

[144] *Ragion*, Dedicatory Epistle.

Since he was neither a jurist nor an able theologian, he could only stress the practical aspects of politics, returning to the terrain of Machiavelli. The result was that most of the work was little more than trite, specific advice to princes regarding the many problems which confronted them, much of it reminiscent of Machiavelli, and Botero's criterion of judgment was often mere expediency.[145] He even recommended piety and the sanctity of treaties on utilitarian grounds and found Christianity superior to other religions because it was more effective in ensuring the obedience of the subjects.[146] Much of the work was oriented toward the interests of the prince rather than those of the state.[147] In both its general qualities and specific suggestions, therefore, it contained strong echoes of Machiavellism. The most that can be said for Botero is that he insisted that the means whereby governments seek to attain their objectives should continually be weighed in the light of Christian morality and that true prudence should embody the honest as well as the useful, but he was incapable of bridging the gap between necessity and principle.

Three years after the publication of the works of Lipsius and Botero on reason of state, there appeared a tract on the same subject by Girolamo Frachetta whose importance seems not to have been realized by modern scholars.[148] Frachetta was in the service of

[145] In a famous passage of the *Aggiunte*, first published in 1598, he stated that reason of state is little more than reason of interest.

[146] *Ragion*, Bk. v, Chap. 1; Bk. 11, Chaps. 14, 15.

[147] Chabod, *Giovanni Botero*, pp. 55, 64-67.

[148] *Discorso della ragione di stato*, in *L'Idea del libro de governi di stato et di guerra con due discorsi, l'uno intorno la Ragione di Stato, & l'altro intorno la Ragione di Guerra*, Venice, 1592. L. Melliet translated the second part of this work (the two discourses on reason of state and reason of war) into French, gave them the title, *Curieux Examen des raisons d'estat et de guerre*, and published them as Bk. xii, Discourse 12 in the second edition of his translation of Ammirato, Lyon, 1628. (The first edition is cited in note 155.) Frachetta's tract was not available to Meinecke. Other modern authors usually neglect it for Frachetta's later and more extensive works. Cherel, p. 101, and Maspétiol, pp. 210, 212 erroneously attribute it to Melliet, whereas he merely translated it and added it to his second edition of his translation of Ammirato because he felt that it had relevance to events in France, notably the Huguenot rebellion. On Frachetta, see the article by Mattei, cited in note 142, *Rivista . . .*, xxx (1953), 447-49.

Cardinal d'Este and later Cardinal Gonzaga while he wrote the work in which this piece appears, and he therefore seems to have been the first writer who was close to high ranking members of the Catholic hierarchy to give a clear definition of good and bad reason of state. His entire treatise is an effort to combat the widely accepted Machiavellian connotation of the term and to indicate the view of reason of state that was acceptable in Catholic circles. At the outset he took the position that "reason of state is of two types, one, the true, which . . . I have called civil prudence and is separated neither from moral virtue nor religion, and is therefore the true reason and rule of government. The other is only its counterfeit and is concerned only with the advantage of him who uses it, with no consideration for God or duty."[149] The latter, he admitted, was the more widespread meaning of the phrase and it was that which he would combat. In discussing knowledge of governmental affairs, he argued that while this may be increased by the study of ancient writers, the lessons of history and the teachings of experience, ultimately true prudence should never be separated from moral virtue.[150] For this reason, true reason of state might never be used by the ruler merely to further his personal interests, apart from the precepts of religion and justice, for in that case he degenerates into a tyrant and becomes worse than a savage beast.[151] Because the prince is called by God to the throne, he should never assume that he may legitimately employ any measure whatsoever for the preservation of the state and should constantly be aware of his great obligation to rule according to God's dictates and his duty. In this, he may use a great number of just and legitimate expedients but none that is iniquitous or illicit. And Frachetta repeatedly warned that princes who fail to follow true reason of state will suffer from divine wrath.[152] His position was epitomized by his maxim, "Princes should use reason of state in such manner that it conforms to divine and human laws, that is, subordinate to justice and religion, and not otherwise."[153] Through this rigid but simple reasoning, Frachetta equated

[149] *Discorso*, pp. 37b-38a.
[150] *Ibid.*, pp. 39a-42b.
[151] *Ibid.*, pp. 44a-44b.
[152] *Ibid.*, pp. 45a-45b.
[153] *Ibid.*, p. 46a.

true civil prudence with good reason of state and thoroughly subjected both to religious principles. The distance between his position
and Botero's is manifest, and it is not surprising that Frachetta criticized his compatriot's book as demonstrably unacceptable.[154]

Fundamentally similar although differently implemented was
Scipione Ammirato's concept of reason of state in his commentary
on Tacitus which appeared two years after Frachetta's tract.[155] Ammirato was an able professional writer, widely known in the literary world. In his book on Tacitus, he approached the problem
of reason of state through an ingenious analysis of the levels of
reason and value in human society. In the state of nature, he said,
there was only one reason, natural reason. But with the growth of
civilization, there appeared civil reason, reason of war, and reason
of peoples. Each has its place and content, but each derogates from
the other. Thus civil reason is a reality with its own nature and
limits even though it partially derogates from natural reason; likewise reason of war derogates from civil reason.[156] He therefore defined reason of state as a contravention of ordinary reason for the
good of the state or out of respect for higher reason.[157] Reason of
state has its rights and its sphere, but if the ruler goes beyond its
confines and commits injustice and iniquity, he becomes a tyrant.
Reason of state should always be subservient to divine reason. As
the good of the individual is subordinate to that of the whole and
the personal interests of the prince are inferior to those of the state,

---

[154] Frachetta's letter of March 22, 1594, to Botero criticizing his *Ragion di
Stato* unfortunately does not make his objections clear, but the evident differences between the two men's views and the fact that Botero was forced to
leave Rome later in 1594 seem to indicate that his political ideas were unacceptable to the ecclesiastical authorities. Chabod, *Giovanni Botero*, Appendix IV.
Mattei, article cited in note 142, *Rivista . . .* , XXX (1953), 335.

[155] *Discorsi sopra Cornelio Tacito*, Florence, 1594. Two French translations
of this work appeared in the same year. J. Baudoin, *Discours politiques sur
les œuvres de C. Cornelius Tacitus, tirez de l'Italien de Scipion Amirato*,
Paris, 1618. *Discours politiques et militaires sur Corneille Tacite, traduits,
paraphrasez, et augmentez par Laurens Melliet*, Lyon, 1618. Melliet's translation is much superior to Baudoin's. On Ammirato, see R. de Mattei, *Il
Pensiero politico di Scipione Ammirato*, Milan, 1963.

[156] *Discorsi*, pp. 228-30.   [157] *Ibid.*, p. 231.

so reason of state must yield to religion.[158] Not even the survival of the state justifies contravention of religion; if necessity and principle do not concur, religion must take precedence regardless of circumstances.[159]

In this fashion, Ammirato would limit reason of state to what he considered its proper sphere in human affairs. Although he insisted that its scope was wide and that it was superior to private rights,[160] he never compromised its strict subordinance to higher values. These he interpreted as including religion, equity, and all that was grounded in them. Thus he was adamant that the prince must always keep faith and observe his sworn promises,[161] that punishments should be tempered with justice and mercy,[162] and that a mask of religion should never be used to conceal one's true ambitions.[163] Ammirato clearly placed severe limitations upon princely discretion, and his complete anti-Machiavellism is obvious. Reason of state for him was merely reason of rule, and it was good or bad depending upon the prince's use of it.[164] The crux of the matter is Ammirato's insistence that the ruler should *never* violate higher values which lay outside his competence, for any reason whatsoever. Many other writers readily adopted Ammirato's definition of reason of state as a derogation, but their systems varied directly with the rigidity of the limits that they placed upon the ruler's rightful sphere of action.[165] Ammirato's analysis of the relations between politics and morals did not answer all the problems of political necessity, but it had the virtue of defining distinct levels of value in human affairs and the limits that they placed upon official policy.

For our purposes, the three interpretations of reason of state that were developed by Botero, Frachetta, and Ammirato respectively may serve to represent the essential contributions of the Italian school to French thought. Although the three works that we have examined were but the earliest in a very extensive literature on the subject by a large group of Italian authors, their later writings were

---

[158] *Ibid.*, pp. 232., 241.
[159] *Ibid.*, pp. 233-34.
[160] *Ibid.*, pp. 236-37.
[161] *Ibid.*, Bk. xiv, Discourse 8.
[162] *Ibid.*, Bk. ii, Discourse 9.
[163] *Ibid.*, Bk. iii, Discourse 10.
[164] *Ibid.*, p. 240.
[165] Mattei, *Scipione Ammirato*, Chap. 7.

very repetitive and frequently did little more than develop earlier positions.[166] Even when Campanella presented his highly personalized view which condemned both the terminology and the concept of reason of state as mere subterfuges and cloaks for iniquity, this was merely another way of insisting upon the unqualified supremacy of justice and religious principles.[167] Essentially, little fundamental progress was made by the Italian school until the publication of Zuccolo's work in 1621.[168] Zuccolo argued that reason of state is merely the type of rule that is necessary to preserve and benefit the state in its present form and that the nature of the state determines the means to be used toward that end. Since reason of state for him was simply what the established state required, the issue of justifications was shifted from policy to the state itself. This different approach placed the problem of politics and morals in a new perspective but seems to have had little influence in France because French writers were thoroughly occupied with their own special problems during the years immediately following the appearance of Zuccolo's work.

As final examples of authors produced by the Counter Reformation, we may choose two Spanish ecclesiastics, Pedro de Ribadeneyra and Juan Marquez. Ribadeneyra was the older and more important. A friend of Ignatius Loyola and early member of the Jesuit order, he served extensively as missionary in the Low Countries and Spain. His work on reason of state appeared in 1595 and may be regarded

---

[166] E.g., Giovanni Antonio Palazzo, *Discorso del governo e della ragion vera di stato*, Naples, 1604. French trans. by A. de Vallières, *Discours du gouvernement et de la raison vraye d'Estat*, Douai, 1611. Palazzo developed the idea that true reason of state is merely rule according to established law which embodies religious truths.

[167] Tommaso Campanella, *Città del sole*, written in prison in 1602. On Campanella, see Meinecke, Chap. 4, and R. de Mattei, *La Politica di Campanella*, Rome, 1927.

[168] Ludovico Zuccolo, *Della Ragione di stato*, in *Considerazioni politiche e morali sopra cento oracoli d'illustri personaggi antichi*, Venice, 1621. The importance of Zuccolo's position in the Italian school is noted by Croce, *Storia*, pp. 93-97, 165-67, and *Politici e moralisti del seicento*, Bari, 1930. Also the article by Mattei, cited in note 142, *Rivista . . .* , xxviii (1951), 705-23.

as the classic statement of the Spanish position.[169] This was continued in the book of Marquez who was an important Spanish theologian and high-ranking official in the Augustinian order.[170] Ribadeneyra wrote his treatise for the express purpose of combatting the doctrines of Machiavelli, Tacitus, and various *"Politicos"* of his own time such as La Noue, Du Plessis-Mornay, and Bodin,[171] while Marquez likewise inveighed against Machiavelli and Bodin.[172] As might be expected, both men maintained the complete supremacy of religion over politics and all other earthly matters, but they also recognized that government presents special problems which are invariably handled according to reason of state. The issue therefore was to define an acceptable reason of state. Ribadeneyra set forth his views on the matter in an important formula which was echoed by many later writers. Princes, he said, are not obliged to reject all reason of state and rules of prudence that are necessary to government and should constantly be mindful of these precepts when shaping their policies. There are, however, two types of reason of state, "one false and unreal, the other sound and true; one deceitful

---

[169] *Tratado de la religión y virtudes que deve tener el Príncipe Christiano, para governar y conservar sus Estados. Contra lo que Nicolas Machiavelo y los Politicos deste tiempo enseñan*, Madrid, 1595. French trans. by A. de Balingham, *Traité de la religion que doit suivre le prince chrestien et des vertus qu'il doit avoir pour bien gouverner et conserver son Estat, contre la doctrine de Nicolas Machiavel et des politiques de nostre temps*, Douai, 1610. The work of Ribadeneyra was strictly a Jesuit production, since both the author and the translator were Jesuits and the translation was made at the Jesuit school at Tournai. On Ribadeneyra and Marquez, see J. A. Maravall, *La Philosophie politique espagnole au XVIIe siècle*, translated and presented by L. Cazes and P. Mesnard, Paris, 1955.

[170] *El Governador Christiano, deducido de las vidas de Moysen y Josue*, Salamanca, 1612. French trans. by D. Virion, *L'Homme d'Estat chrestien, tiré des vies de Moyse et Iosué Princes du Peuple de Dieu*, Nancy, 1621.

[171] *Tratado*, Preface, Bk. II, Chaps. 4, 5, etc.

[172] *El Governador*, Bk. II, Chaps. 22, 24, 25, 34. On the Spanish reaction to Machiavelli in this period, see the following. G. Fernández de la Mora, "Maquiavelo, visto por los tratadistas políticos españoles de la Contrarreforma," *Arbor*, XIII (1949), 417-49. D. W. Blesnick, "Spanish Reaction to Machiavelli in the Sixteenth and Seventeenth Centuries," *Journal of the History of Ideas*, XIX (1958), 542-50.

and diabolical, the other certain and divine; one that accommodates religion to the state, the other that accommodates the state to religion; one taught by politicians [*Politicos*], the other taught by God, based upon God himself and the means that He reveals to princes with his paternal providence, giving them strength to use well, as the Lord of all states."[173] Ribadeneyra's intent was to reveal the differences between these two positions and to show all persons in authority that God alone founds states, gives them to whom He pleases, and renders the preservation of the state dependent upon the observation of his rules which should never be separated from religion. This statement may be said to summarize completely the Spanish view of good and bad reason of state.[174]

In spite of their rigidity concerning the supremacy of religious values, both Ribadeneyra and Marquez recognized that in the play of politics certain occasions must arise which require the use of questionable means. In an effort to allow Christian princes a degree of elbow room in the conduct of policy, both authors permitted certain deceits which they called dissimulation. Since princes move among enemies, Ribadeneyra said, it is necessary that they be armed and dissimulate, but they must be aware of how far they may go with these artifices without becoming disciples of Machiavelli.[175] Outright falsehood must be avoided, but this does not preclude keeping silent concerning important matters, maneuvering so as to appear ignorant of known facts, and informing few persons when giving the impression of informing many—all in an effort to confuse the enemy and cause him to draw false conclusions. It is also permissible to speak the truth in such an equivocal way as to deceive others by meanings that are apparent but not real. Likewise, one's actions may be so handled, especially in time of war, that the enemy may be confused as to one's true intent. All this is not falsehood; it is merely prudent handling of policy for the good of the state.[176] Ribadeneyra evidently would allow the ruler considerable latitude in the measures that he might adopt. Marquez took essentially the same position, since he too would permit de-

[173] *Tratado*, Preface, pp. 20-21.   [174] Maravall, pp. 302-03.
[175] *Tratado*, pp. 234-35.   [176] *Ibid.*, pp. 237-38.

ception by giving false impressions but forbade outright untruths.[177] This was as far as both men would go. Their recognition of the political realities of their time and the exigencies of religious proselytizing caused them to permit the use of many questionable means, but they stopped short of clear violation of moral principle, insisting vehemently and at length that princes are bound to observe their treaties and all sworn promises regardless of their interests.[178] Marquez even added that treaties with heretics must not be broken, and he criticized the burning of John Hus as a breach of faith.[179] In this way, Marquez was more rigid than the popes themselves in applying religious morality to politics.

This cursory examination of a limited number of works by non-French Catholic authors is sufficient to indicate important patterns of thought. In the late sixteenth and early seventeenth centuries, fashion decreed that dissimulation, ruses, and the like be closely scrutinized, both because of the practices in vogue at many princely courts and because of widespread concern for the rightful conduct of political affairs in a morally distraught world. This in turn focused attention upon the concept of political prudence which rapidly became one of the major topics of discussion. Although by no means new, the concept of prudence in governmental affairs acquired a new importance because of its clear relevance to the problems of justifiable policy and reason of state. In fact, a given writer's view of the latter often turned on his implementation of political prudence. Writers such as Lipsius who would allow a major area of competence to autonomous human reason tended to relax the limitations upon the ruler's discretion and permit many questionable measures for a utilitarian good. On the other hand, many who insisted upon the strict subordination of policy to religious principle were less inclined to allow reason free play but were willing to permit limited questionable means if they were used for religious ends. In the name of prudence, both groups found themselves justifying acts that were intrinsically immoral and were de-

---

[177] *El Governador*, Bk. ii, conclusion of Chap. 14.
[178] *Tratado*, Bk. ii, Chaps. 15-17. *El Governador*, Bk. ii, Chaps. 22-25.
[179] *El Governador*, Bk. ii, Chap. 24.

nied to private individuals. Writers of such different complexion as Lipsius, Botero, Ammirato, and Ribadeneyra all reached this position although by different routes and while insisting that clear limits be placed upon such practices. All maintained that religious morality must be the ultimate guide of princes, but their stipulations did little to solve the practical problems of political necessity. And all continued to focus their attention upon the legitimacy of means while assuming the validity of the ends to be served. Although the concept of reason of state had become a highly fashionable topic of discussion and had been analyzed from various standpoints by many able writers, they had done little more than examine different approaches and assume different positions. This was the pattern of the debate when it was transferred to France and carried further in the context of French political experience.

To return to the intellectual currents that were native to France, the growing rationalism and skepticism of the late sixteenth and early seventeenth centuries should be examined as far as they impinged upon reason of state. These currents are best represented by the pertinent works of Montaigne and Charron. Since the main concern of both men was the development of a personalized ethic, political considerations were secondary in their intellectual systems, yet both were sufficiently perceptive to realize the relevance of political morality to their ethical problems. In many ways, their general outlook paralleled that of Lipsius and the *politique* jurists. All passionately desired order and stability, placed confidence in human reason, and were willing to allow the ruler a large measure of discretionary power for utilitarian ends. Although they implemented this position in very different ways, all contributed to the growth of the idea that the state possessed an independent morality.

Montaigne's viewpoint was that of a strict moralist who placed himself at the center of his personal spectrum and, despite his doubts and hesitations, was confident that his reason would lead him in his search for truth.[180] Through study, observation, and introspection,

[180] On Montaigne's political ideas, see G. Lanson, *Les Essais de Montaigne*, Paris, 1930, Chap. 9; F. Strowski, *La Sagesse française*, Paris, 1925, Chap. 4,

he developed a personalized ethic that was characterized by rigorous obedience to conscience. He always claimed to be a Christian and insisted upon submission to God, but the universal morality of which he was so thoroughly aware was that of nature rather than Revelation. Reason was his guide and criterion of judgment. The result was an essentially independent morality within the framework of nature, a personalized ethic that was intended to serve only his individual needs. As for the human society in which all men are forced to live, Montaigne regarded it simply as an organic construct which evolved according to natural principles, that is, the spirit of the people and their needs. As a result, laws and customs differed greatly from time to time and place to place. Established law should be obeyed, not because it was right in a moral sense but because it had proved useful to society and the individuals that composed it. The justice of human affairs therefore varied enormously according to transitory circumstances and to that extent was independent of

---

and *Montaigne*, Paris, 1931, Chap. 6; V. E. Alfieri, "Politica e morale in Montaigne," *Studi in onore di Vittorio Lugli e Diego Valeri*, Venice, 1961, Vol. I, 1-12. A different viewpoint is presented in the following articles. C. Aymonier, "Les Opinions politiques de Montaigne," *Actes de l'Académie nationale des sciences, belles-lettres et arts de Bordeaux*, 6e série, XI (1937-1938), 213-37. A. Nicolaï, "Le Machiavélisme de Montaigne," *Bulletin de la société des amis de Montaigne*, 3e série, No. 4, Oct.-Dec., 1957, pp. 11-21; No. 5-6, Jan.-June, 1958, pp. 25-47; No. 7, July-Sept., 1958, pp. 2-8; No. 9, Jan.-March, 1959, pp. 18-30. These studies, especially that of Nicolaï, not only insist that Montaigne separated morals and politics but go so far as to maintain that this separation was total, that Montaigne accepted the argument of political necessity without qualification, and that he would allow the ruler any expedient policy whatsoever after the manner of Machiavelli. In view of Montaigne's explicit statements and the fundamental cast of his thought, it is impossible to accept this interpretation. A recent examination of this problem is in Ch. 1 of A. M. Battista, *Alle Origini del pensiero politico libertino: Montaigne e Charron*, Milan, 1966. This was originally published in a slightly different form as "Montaigne e Machiavelli," *Rivista Internazionali di Filosofia del Diritto*, XL (1963), 526-63. Although the author finds that Montaigne separated morals and politics except on the level of the ruler's conscience, she maintains that this resulted from Montaigne's method and personal spectrum rather than any influence of Machiavelli. Generally I would agree with her interpretation, except that she seems to underrate the important, latent affinities that Montaigne found between political policy and higher values.

higher principle. It followed that the state was a positive reality that should be accepted as it stood. Its objective was not absolute justice but betterment of the human condition, and its justice was relative to the demands of the people and the times. Deviation from the principles of universal morality Montaigne believed to be wrong, yet his recourse was to reduce the matter to a problem of conscience rather than face the arduous task of defining acceptable policy.

Montaigne, the recluse, instinctively sought to avoid entanglement in the world's affairs and prided himself on maintaining complete personal integrity during his brief ventures into politics, yet he was sufficiently astute to recognize the problems that face the man of intelligence and principle in a position of public responsibility. In his famous essay, *"De l'utile et de l'honneste,"* he attempted to grapple with the central issue, personal morality *versus* the compromises that are forced upon one who participates in active affairs. Recognizing that public and private relationships are in fact full of iniquity, Montaigne found this to be the result of human nature and therefore ineradicable.[181] In consequence, he said, there are in practice two standards of justice, one natural and universal, the other practical and necessary.[182] Reluctantly he admitted that circumstances required the ruler to dissimulate and even to break his word and resort to violence. Such acts were not vice because they were forced upon him by factors beyond his control, but they were great misfortunes which he should regret if he were to be right with his conscience.[183] Surely it was with genuine misgiving that Montaigne recognized the necessity of these departures from universal morality and the existence of two standards of justice. In a later addition to this essay which he inserted toward the end of his life, he explicitly advised the prince in great adversity to stand firm and follow the dictates of his conscience for he could go down no more worthily. He should consign protection of his vessel to heaven, for where would he find more binding necessity? His faith and honor should be dearer to him than his personal safety and even that of his

---

[181] *Essais*, Bk. iii, Chap. i, 3-4, in *Œuvres complètes*, A. Armaingaud, ed., Paris, 1927, Vol. v.

[182] *Ibid.* pp. 19-20.　　　　　[183] *Ibid.*, pp. 6, 14, 20-22, 27-28.

people. With arms folded, he should appeal to God who would surely reward a ruler whose hands were clean.[184] Such statements suggest that Montaigne had examined the doctrine of reason of state and found it wanting.

While Montaigne recognized the existence of a special ethic of political action but urged princes to restrict and deplore the inequities that necessity thrust upon them, no such scruples were exhibited by his friend and popularizer, Pierre Charron. The divergence between the two men on this score may partially be explained by Charron's thoroughly eclectic manner of composition. In his most important work, *De la Sagesse*, Charron openly relied upon the works of others, among whom the most important were Montaigne, Du Vair, Bodin, and Lipsius.[185] In the portions where he discussed the problem of justifiable royal policy, Charron closely followed Lipsius, repeating his definition of political prudence[186] and adopting all his major positions. The result was that Charron went much further than Montaigne in permitting immoral measures for the general good. The relative ease with which Charron, Montaigne's disciple, adopted the more permissive views of Lipsius, sometimes even outdoing the latter, demonstrates the flexibility and precariousness of any essentially egocentric morality. In any case, Charron's work succeeded in introducing Lipsius' ideas to a host of French readers and extensively influenced French thought during the early seventeenth century.[187]

The most important feature of Charron's treatise was his complete secularization of wisdom, and in this his position clearly illustrates the potentialities of rationalism, skepticism, and Stoicism. Al-

[184] *Ibid.*, pp. 28-29.

[185] Charron's *De la Sagesse* was first published in Bordeaux, 1601. My references are to the edition edited by A. Duval, Paris, 1820-1824, 3 vols. On Charron's sources, see J. B. Sabrié, *De l'Humanisme au rationalisme: Pierre Charron*, Paris, 1913, Chap. 11. For his concept of wisdom, see E. F. Rice, *The Renaissance Idea of Wisdom*, Cambridge, Mass., 1958, Chap. 7. Battista places Charron's political ideas in the intellectual currents of the period.

[186] *De la Sagesse*, Vol. II, 283.

[187] Sabrié, Pt. III. H. Busson, *La Pensée religieuse française de Charron à Pascal*, Paris, 1933, Chap. 4.

though he paid his respects to divine wisdom, he found that it differed from human wisdom in every essential. The latter for Charron
was achieved through perfection of natural man and was a moral
virtue whose qualities were purely human, practical, and active. It
was acquired by developing one's innate faculties and living according to nature; in this way man became truly wise and virtuous.
Prudence was acquired through observation and experience, and
justice was consonance with universal natural values.[188] For this
reason, Charron experienced little difficulty in attributing an independent ethic to things political. Like Lipsius, he grounded his
argument upon the undeniable fact that politics are more amoral
than the affairs of individuals and therefore necessitate occasional
violations of official morality for the safety of the whole: *salus populi
suprema lex esto.*[189] Thus it was the obligation of the prince who
would protect his subjects to meet dastardly attacks with countermeasures of similar nature; otherwise he would betray his trust.[190]
But after opening the gates in this fashion to all manner of Machia-
vellisms, Charron immediately added in the same paragraph that
the prince should use such measures with the greatest caution, never
breaking with virtue and honesty. All things were not permitted
to the sovereign by the requirements of expediency; he might practice only minor immoralities and deviations from the straight and
narrow.[191]

In explaining and implementing this utterly elastic position,
Charron explicitly relied upon Lipsius' three categories of political
misconduct. Silent or covert measures such as prudent distrust of
all men and dissimulation of the truth he found not only justified
but necessary in politics.[192] His list of permissible overt actions was
very long and included the bribing of foreign agents, false promises,
multiple missions and other diplomatic devices, and even such
serious matters as secretly executing suspected persons without trial,
reducing the power and property of any subject who might chal-

[188] Sabrié, Chap. 13. Rice, Chap. 7.
[189] *De la Sagesse*, Vol. ii, 302-03.   [190] *Ibid.*, Vol. ii, 303-04.
[191] *Ibid.*, Vol. ii, 304-05.   [192] *Ibid.*, Vol. ii, 305-07.

lenge the royal authority, and seizing a neighboring city or province to keep it from a potential enemy.[193] Charron advised caution in the use of these measures, but he outdid Lipsius in the boldness with which he approved of them when they were needed for the general good. Like Lipsius, he believed that the prince might preserve his virtue intact even when resorting to such extremes. Lipsius' forbidden third category, the outright breaking of treaties and sworn promises, Charron also prohibited, insisting that justice was inherent in royal rule and that the prince's word might be broken only when the agreement involved clear injustice or was impossible to execute. This applied even to treaties with heretics.[194] And he closely paraphrased Bodin to the effect that violation of sworn promises was worse than atheism since the perjurer openly mocked God and denied the very foundation of justice.[195]

In this way, Charron attempted to delineate the rightful competence of the sovereign who would remain virtuous while meeting the challenges of necessity. His view of political prudence, however, was not that of Lipsius who retained the essential tie between politics and morals even while allowing wide discretion to the ruler. Instead, Charron developed a secularized concept of prudence which allowed a purely autonomous ethic of state action. That he envisaged a separate morality of the state is evident from his categorical denial of similar precepts to private individuals in other portions of his work. It is clear that he was considerably in advance of his time, both in his secularized concept of wisdom and the extent to which he would allow immoral policies for the good of the state. This may easily be demonstrated by comparing his views with those of the other authors whom we have considered. It is not surprising that Charron's work was unacceptable in official Catholic circles,[196] but it at least bore witness to the fact that even the proponents of an

---

[193] *Ibid.*, Vol. II, 309-13.
[194] *Ibid.*, Vol. III, 16-20.   [195] *Ibid.*, Vol. III, 21-22.
[196] Charron's *Sagesse* was placed on the Index of Prohibited Books in 1605, apparently because of its Machiavellism. J. Dagens, "Le Machiavélisme de Charron," in *Studies aangeboden aan Gerard Brom*, Utrecht-Nijmegen, 1952, pp. 56-64.

autonomous "natural" ethic believed that universal values placed some limitations upon royal policy.

Charron's concern for the nature and limits of just rule was shared by large numbers of French authors during the first generation of the seventeenth century, but they ordinarily expressed their ideas on the matter in different terms. The subject was usually touched upon in works that dealt with the nature of the royal authority, the legal foundations and limits of the prerogative, the roles of various institutions, the royal virtues, the qualities of effective rule, and the like. A representative cross-section of such works that appeared during the fifteen years before 1624 would include those of the jurists Charles Loyseau, Pierre de L'Hommeau, Jérôme Bignon, Jean Savaron, Pierre de Lancre, and such professional writers as André Duchesne, Nicolas Faret, and Louis Roland.[197] All were concerned with the problem of rightful policy, but it is noteworthy that none discussed it specifically in terms of reason of state. Instead, they followed the traditional and less sophisticated approach which centered upon the definition of sovereignty and the qualities that should characterize just and effective government.

The vogue of examining rightful policy through the concept and terminology of reason of state was nevertheless gaining currency in France. An interesting illustration of this, plus the fact that it stemmed largely from Italian sources, is found in Antoine de Laval's *Desseins de professions nobles et publiques*.[198] Laval was a man of considerable knowledge in civil and religious affairs and held the post of royal geographer. His book is a long, rambling analysis of the learning that was required in the various vocations which he

[197] Jérôme Bignon, *De l'Excellence des Roys, et du Royaume de France*, Paris, 1610, and *De la Grandeur de nos Roys, et de leur souveraine puissance*, Paris, 1615. Jean Savaron, *Traité de la souveraineté du Roy, et de son Royaume*, Paris, 1615, and *De la Souveraineté du Roy*, Paris, 1620. Nicolas Faret, *Des Vertus nécessaires à un prince pour bien gouverner ses sujets*, Paris, 1623. For representative works of Loyseau, L'Hommeau, Lancre, Duchesne, and Roland, see notes 5, 56, 57, 58, 67, 69, 71, 72.

[198] *Desseins de professions nobles et publiques, contenans plusieurs traictés divers et rares*, Paris, 1605, 1612.

regarded as ennobling. The first edition which appeared in 1605 made no mention of reason of state, but in the second, dated 1612, he added a *"Dessein des problèmes politiques"* which included a section on the subject.[199] After stating at length the traditional arguments that a knowledge of *"science politique"* was essential to rulers, that it might be increased by the study of history, and that informed counsel was essential to good government, he capped these by analyzing reason of state. The concept, he said, had been introduced into France by Italians whose books were full of it, and so fashionable had it become that it was a favorite topic of discussion among great and small alike.[200] No published treatment entirely satisfied him, he continued, although he found Ammirato's commentary on Tacitus the best because it showed that reason of state should always be subordinate to religion.[201]

Having taken this position, Laval reiterated Ammirato's categories of reason that adhered to human activity on various levels and agreed with him that true reason of state was simply just government according to accepted law and morality.[202] Laval admitted that the Machiavellian connotation of the term was the more widespread, but he proceeded to condemn "this reason without reason" outright. Reason of state thus defined was merely a departure from justice for the good of the state. Utility rather than right was its guide, and modern writers frankly called it fraud, deceit, and treachery contrary to virtue and law. The usual justification, the good of the state, did *not* remove the stain of injustice. For this reason, he said, it should never be used by a Christian prince; he should avoid all that might tarnish his honor and should conduct himself as a lion rather than a fox.[203] Machiavelli, the atheist, understandably taught such doctrines but no worthy ruler followed them, and Laval cited Louis XII, Francis I, and Henry IV as examples of kings who steadfastly refused to violate their sworn promises.[204] Such a com-

---

[199] Pp. 313a to 348b in the edition of 1612.
[200] *Desseins*, 2nd edn., pp. 338a, 339b.
[201] *Ibid.*, pp. 340a-340b.   [202] *Ibid.*, pp. 338a-340a.
[203] *Ibid.*, pp. 339a-339b.   [204] *Ibid.*, pp. 339b, 342b-344b.

mentary on reason of state vividly illustrates the difficulties that many French writers experienced in accepting what they regarded as an alien doctrine that was contrary to the traditions of the French monarchy.

On the basis of such evidence, it seems clear that the vogue of reason of state was increasingly prevalent in France during the first quarter of the seventeenth century but had not yet become the accepted frame of reference within which to justify royal policy. A variety of interpretations of reason of state were known in France but none had won widespread acceptance. The hostility of predominant opinion, the contrary nature of the traditions of the French monarchy, and the difficulty of accepting what many regarded as an Italianate doctrine that stemmed from Machiavelli all go far to explain the reluctance of French writers to accept the canons of reason of state. Furthermore, the nature of official French policy during the years 1610-1624 was such that the issues were blurred for many observers. When the Regent and such ministers as Luynes conciliated the troublesome nobles and strengthened French ties with the Hapsburgs, they were operating within what many regarded as the natural relationships of the French monarchy with the nobility and the Catholic faith. They were criticized for not strengthening the monarchy, but this was because they did little to differentiate the interests of the state from those of the great nobles and international Catholicism. Subsequent efforts by other ministers seemed equally ineffective in strengthening the monarchy's position. Beginning in 1624, however, Cardinal Richelieu undertook to advance the interests of the French state, as he understood them, by such measures as repression of the rebellious nobility and an aggressive anti-Hapsburg foreign policy. These and other moves on his part reflected his intense desire to strengthen the French state vis-à-vis all potentially hostile social and political entities both within and without the realm, and dramatically posed the issue of the supremacy of state interests over all others. Only after this turn of events did the good of the state assume clear precedence and reason of state become a major consideration in French political thought and experience.

RICHELIEU BEFORE 1624

In retrospect, there seems to be a certain historical consistency in the fact that reason of state first acquired significance in French political ideology during Cardinal Richelieu's ministry, since his personal characteristics, policies, and ideals epitomized so much that was essential to the concept. Although he was thoroughly aware of the ways of the world, he was forced to devote the first half of his career to the long, tortuous climb toward his ultimate objective, supreme power in the royal administration. The route was long and painful and left its mark upon him. Originally mere Bishop of Luçon, he first won important recognition at the Estates General of 1614-1615 and was rewarded with an appointment as Secretary of State for five months during 1616-1617, only to be dismissed and exiled from the court after a turn of the wheel of fortune. His subsequent, extremely complex maneuvers within both the ecclesiastical and royal administrations were finally rewarded with a cardinalate and, in 1624, the position of First Minister. Since he was thirty-nine years of age when he received this appointment and had repeatedly been tested by innumerable obstacles that beset his path, his personal qualities had hardened and he had developed certain traits of character which stamped him as a man of determination, great ability, and one eminently fitted to wield supreme power. His personal ideals had crystallized and had been expressed, at least in fragmentary form, on a number of occasions but he had carefully avoided aligning himself with any faction. Although Richelieu's appointment as First Minister was momentarily pleasing to all, it is possible to demonstrate that during his early years he held to a consistent political and religious ideology, the main evidences of which are his writings, speeches, relations with other persons, and his policies during his first ministry.

Considerably before 1624, Richelieu's personal qualities clearly exhibited the characteristics of a man of power as they were conceived by the baroque era. His enormous ambition was coupled with an equally strong sense of his personal superiority and his destiny to achieve great things. Taking great pride in his noble blood, he was thoroughly imbued with a sense of honor and felt it to be both his obligation and his mission to serve his king and his state. Thus he deemed it his right as well as his duty to raise himself to the highest political levels and to participate in the mysterious *arcana imperii* that were incomprehensible to ordinary mortals. During his long, frustrating climb to power, he repeatedly demonstrated his ability to dominate men and situations, and in the privations of Luçon he spent many hours calculating the most expeditious means of winning royal favor. In a remarkable document which he penned during the final years of Henry IV's reign, Richelieu set forth with characteristic thoroughness and clarity his views of the most effective methods of gaining influence with the king.[205] Abundantly aware of the pitfalls that continually plagued the life of a courtier, he analyzed such stratagems as presenting himself at key moments, praising the royal virtues, and urging his indispensability, but the most effective he found in the fashionable art of dissimulation. Like many other writers of the period, he believed silent dissimulation to be entirely justified but had serious doubts concerning the advisability and morality of open, positive distortion of the truth.[206] His first major opportunity for self-advancement occurred during the Estates General of 1614-1615, when his closing oration was chiefly significant for its clever identification of himself with important causes and his successful recommendation of himself to the Regent. In all his early efforts, whether maneuvering for personal advantage, administering his bishopric of Luçon, writing his religious tracts, or experiencing a brief moment of political power, he was aided by a rich and powerful intellect. Its predominant characteristics were encyclopedic information, power of analysis, and reliance upon reason which was to be his guide throughout his entire career. In combination with his imperious mien, powerful will, and

[205] *Mémoire d'Armand du Plessis de Richelieu, évêque de Luçon, écrit de sa main, l'année 1607 ou 1610, alors qu'il méditait de paraître à la cour*, A. Baschet, ed., Paris, 1880. Richelieu gave this piece the title, "Instructions et maximes que je me suis données pour me conduire à la cour."

[206] *Ibid.*, pp. 21-22. Richelieu's discussion of various stratagems for self-advancement at court is remarkably similar to that in the later, very popular work of Eustache Du Refuge, *Traité de la cour*, Paris, 1616, Bk. II.

ability to govern others, these attributes produced a man of exceptional endowments in any age. The product was indeed a leader who possessed in abundance the personal qualities that are associated with effective use of political power.

Richelieu's temperament was clearly reflected in his political ideas which crystallized many years before 1624. At no time during his early career did he set forth a systematic statement of his ideological position, but various evidences indicate that he held to a consistent body of political principles and followed them throughout his life. The keynote of his early statements is their authoritarianism, and in this he clearly adhered to the well-established doctrine of divine right sovereignty. In fact, it may be said that an all-encompassing concept of authority provided the foundation of his entire political system. The social and institutional organization of society he viewed essentially as a great mosaic of units, each possessing a well defined competence and enjoying corresponding rights and privileges. In his most important early religious tract, the *Instruction du chrétien*,[207] he ultilized the fourth commandment of the Decalogue as a springboard for insisting upon the necessity of authority at every social level: that of the parents over the children, the husband over the wife, the elderly over the young, the clergyman over his flock, the magistrate over the subjects, the teacher over his pupils, and the master over his servants.[208] Similarly, the supremacy of the Church and the monarchy over the populace rested upon inviolable right, since both were instituted by God.[209] In his closing speech before the Estates General in 1615, Richelieu cleverly urged the Regent to preserve the Church both because of considerations of conscience and reason of state, since disrespect for the Church would surely undermine the foundations of God's other creation, the state.[210] And in his answer to the brochure of the four Huguenot

[207] Richelieu completed his *Instruction du chrétien* at Avignon in 1618. It was first published at Poitiers in 1621 and passed through many editions and translations. I have used the Paris edition of 1944, an exact reproduction of that of Paris, 1642.

[208] *Instruction*, p. 155. [209] *Ibid.*, pp. 157-58.

[210] Richelieu, *Mémoires*, Paris, 1907, Vol. 1, 353-54. In this passage, Richelieu uses the phrase, "raison d'Estat."

ministers of Charenton, he carefully refuted their claims that the Church of Rome supported various forms of resistance to sovereigns and added that the Huguenots were the chief offenders in this respect.[211] Such statements reflect a comprehensive view of well-defined, divinely ordained authority at all levels of society. It followed that the state, the highest element of secular society, enjoyed indefeasible supremacy over all subordinate units and should exercise controls appropriate to its mission.

Richelieu's condemnation of the revolts by the great nobles during his first ministry further illustrates his devotion to authoritarianism and legitimacy. In answer to the published complaints of the leaders of the rebellion that powerful persons near the king were denying security to others and ruining the realm with their mistaken policies,[212] Richelieu penned one of his most important early statements concerning the power and position of the monarchy.[213] How dare the rebels insist that there is no security near the king, he asked. Do they not know that kings are sure sanctuaries for all who repent their faults, that their word is inviolable, that their integrity is the hallmark of royalty, and that it is a crime to think otherwise?[214] The position of the rebels is intolerable. They demand justice with arms in their hands; they insolently accuse the king of breaking his word; they even attempt to coerce the king and to usurp royal authority.[215] Kings dispense favors to whomever they please, he said; others have no basis of complaint.[216] Only the king has the right to establish peace by force of arms; subjects have no weapons against the prince

---

[211] *Les Principaux Poincts de la Foy de l'église catholique, deffendus contre l'escrit addressé au Roy par les quatre Ministres de Charenton*, Paris, 1618, Chaps. 8, 9.

[212] *Lettre de M. le duc de Nevers au roi sur la déclaration publiée contre lui sous le nom de Sa Majesté*, in *Mercure français*, Vol. IV (1617), 36-42. *Manifeste des ducs et pairs de France, de Vendôme, de Mayenne, maréchal de Bouillon, marquis de Cœuvres et le président Le Jay*, n.p., 1617.

[213] *Déclaration du Roy sur le subject des nouveaux reüemens de son royaume*, in *Lettres, Instructions diplomatiques et papiers d'état du Cardinal de Richelieu*, Avenel, ed., Vol. I, Paris, 1853, pp. 301-16. Hereafter referred to as *Lettres*. Also in the *Mercure français*, Vol. IV (1617), 68-86. I have used the version in the *Lettres*.

[214] *Déclaration*, p. 303.   [215] *Ibid.*, pp. 304-08.   [216] *Ibid.*, p. 309.

but their prayers and depart from duty if they resort to others.[217] Kings, like fathers, are occasionally constrained to punish their rebellious children even while regretting the necessity of the act.[218] In the present circumstances, the king's only recourse is to punish the leaders of the rebellion. Through this means and with the protection that God affords kings and realms, peace will be reestablished and all subjects will make their accustomed contributions: the clergy through their prayers, the nobles with their arms in the service of the king, and the corporations and common people through continued obedience. The result will be peace for the state, prosperity for the king, and greatness for the monarchy.[219]

Clearly, Richelieu's view of government was that the royal authority was imposed upon the populace from above and must be obeyed regardless of all other considerations. For him, the monarchy was a divinely appointed instrument whose purpose was to maintain order in society and to ensure that all persons and groups remained in their stations and contributed to the life of the whole. Because the state had the special obligation of preserving the peace and the general welfare, he believed that its interests differed from those of individuals and that its punishments should be correspondingly more severe. A man who has lost an arm, he wrote in his *Instruction du chrétien*, should follow Christian charity and forgive the perpetrator of the deed, but he may not pardon the offense against the state which has the unique function of maintaining peace among its subjects and preserving them from injury. For this reason, the state should be as severe in its punishments as individuals should be lenient in their sentiments.[220] Even when mere Bishop of Luçon, Richelieu therefore held that the state, because of the special nature of its interests and purposes, was obliged to depart from the code of Christian ethics that prevailed among individuals and to operate on a different level. Such a position contained the seeds of reason of state.

Equally significant were Richelieu's religious convictions and the type of churchman that he became in his early years. Since he and

---

[217] *Ibid.*, pp. 312-13.   [218] *Ibid.*, p. 314.   [219] *Ibid.*, pp. 315-16.
[220] *Instruction*, p. 255, marginal note.

the great majority of his contemporaries viewed the problem of politics and morals in religious terms, it is essential to note the doctrinal positions that he assumed concerning religious matters. In spite of the limited nature of his religious education, Richelieu succeeded in amassing extensive theological learning at an early age, largely through personal application. He also became Bishop of Luçon at the uncanonical age of twenty-two. When he took up residence at Luçon, he continued his theological studies and rapidly became an efficient, energetic administrator, achieving considerable success in putting the affairs of his poverty stricken bishopric in order. He also keenly felt his obligations as guardian of souls and made extensive efforts to revive local religious devotion. There seems no doubt concerning the strength of his religious convictions along orthodox lines. His more important religious tracts, such as the *Instruction du chrétien*, present their arguments with logic and sincerity and give ample evidence of considerable religious fervor. He may therefore be regarded as a theologian of the orthodox, tradition-oriented type, the professional ecclesiastic rather than the mystic or contemplative. These characteristics caused him to be largely untouched by the more ascetic elements of the Catholic Renaissance, but this does not mean that his convictions were any less genuine. He devoutly believed in the Roman Church's great mission and repeatedly sought to improve its institutional functioning and to abet its religious purposes.

Furthermore, his concept of his role as high churchman markedly affected his view of the state, church-state relations, and his service of the two institutions. In spite of his many disagreements and frictions with Rome as First Minister, he consistently regarded the Church and the state as correlative, interlocking institutions that were divinely authorized to lead and control humanity in their respective spheres. From his early religious tracts to his *Testament politique*, he maintained that the rule of the Church and the state was of God, that they shared many functions, especially in religious matters, and that it was possible for him to serve the best interests of both. Neither strictly Gallican nor ultramontane, he developed a program that was considerably richer than that of either faction.

As Bishop of Luçon, he achieved notable success in administrative reforms, spiritual guidance, and religious proselytizing, the natural functions of an able, energetic, and devout churchman. Later as First Minister he attempted much of the same in a new context and on a national scale but for similar ends. Because of the religious sanctions, nature, and purposes of the French monarchy, Richelieu felt it to be entirely appropriate to work for religious objectives through the instrumentality of the state. That a prince of the Roman Church might serve the cause of Catholic France by exercising the power of the crown seemed to him to be in the nature of things. Like the Church, the state was a divinely established institution through which God made known his will in the world. "When justice punishes a crime," he wrote, "it is God who is avenged, since men punish only by virtue of the authority of God who commands them."[221] Such a statement signally reveals his belief in the religious qualities and purposes of the French monarchy. It is not surprising that he defined the good of the state to a large extent in religious terms and attempted to give his policies a religious justification even while resorting to highly questionable means.

Richelieu's belief in the religious attributes of monarchy even appears obliquely in his views concerning the thorniest doctrinal issue facing the Most Christian King and his future Cardinal-Minister, the toleration of heresy within the realm. Briefly, Richelieu hated the Huguenots as heretics and sought by various means to effect their return to the Roman fold but was willing to tolerate them and allow them to live unmolested as long as they remained loyal subjects of the crown.[222] He also opposed the use of force to bring about their restoration to Catholicism. In his closing oration before the Estates General, he stated that Calvinists who lived peacefully under the royal authority should be converted to Catholicism only by such temperate means as example, instruction, and prayer.[223] In assuming

---

[221] *Ibid.*, p. 257, marginal note.

[222] E.g., *Les Principaux Poincts de la Foy*, p. 20. In his posthumous treatise on converting the Huguenots to Catholicism, Richelieu moderated his evident antipathy toward heresy. *Traité qui contient la méthode la plus facile et la plus asseurée pour convertir ceux qui se sont separez de l'église*, Paris, 1651.

[223] *Mémoires*, Paris, 1907, Vol. I, 355-56.

this position, he merely followed official policy as determined by the Edict of Nantes. None of his statements showed a genuine, willing acceptance of toleration on any grounds other than expediency. Like so many of the earlier *politiques*, Richelieu was forced by past events and present circumstances to accept the fact that the king was sovereign over all persons in the realm regardless of their religious beliefs, but he was adamant that differences in religion should in no way lessen their subordination. In his declaration against the rebel princes during his first ministry, he accused them of speciously attempting to stir up trouble among the people by pitting Catholics against Calvinists, forgetting that the king cherished both equally and kept his promises to both without discrimination.[224] His major problem in Germany at that time was to allay the fears of friendly German princes that the Spanish marriages and the pro-Catholic policies of various French ministers had aligned France too closely with Spain and Rome. To counteract this impression, he instructed Schomberg, the able French ambassador to the German states, to argue that while Frenchmen were divided in their religious beliefs they were united in their loyalty to the crown and the interests of France rather than those of Spain or Rome. In matters of state, no French Catholic was so blind as to prefer a Spaniard to a Huguenot.[225] As for royal policy against the rebellious Huguenot nobility, this was not a question of religion but of pure rebellion. The king would treat all his subjects equally regardless of religion, merely requiring all to remain in their stations as reason required.[226]

These statements by Richelieu during his first ministry might be taken to imply that he already divorced many political matters from religious considerations and therefore held to a partially secularized ethic of state policy. Upon closer examination, however, they merely indicate that certain concerns of the French government were now handled apart from the theological determinations because of prevailing circumstances. The Edict of Nantes had ended the crown's ancient function of forcibly extirpating heresy within the

---

[224] *Lettres*, Vol. I, 311.
[225] *Ibid.*, Vol. I, 210, 224.   [226] *Ibid.*, Vol. I, 226.

realm and to this extent the relationships between the king and his subjects had been secularized. The ties binding all Frenchmen to their ruler were now chiefly legal and emotional, and the maintenance of order within the realm was increasingly for such secular purposes as peace and prosperity. As for alliances with friendly but heretic foreign princes, there were ample precedents for this in the sixteenth century. All these features of French foreign and domestic policy resulted from changed religious circumstances across the face of Europe. Accommodation to these facts necessarily detached certain matters of policy from rigid adherence to Catholic doctrines. It did little, however, to alter the prevailing concept of monarchy itself. Like the vast majority of his contemporaries, Richelieu believed that the monarchy was divinely instituted, enjoyed many religious attributes, and should work for the general welfare which was partially defined in religious terms. The unresolved tensions within the position resulted more from the necessary adaptations of policy to circumstances in a world that had lost its religious unity than any alteration of the concept of monarchy. Richelieu and the great majority of Frenchmen continued to regard the Roman Church and the French monarchical state as the two great, coordinate, interlocking, divinely instituted agencies for the government and guidance of the people in their respective but closely allied spheres.

These elements of Richelieu's thought were little more than personalized versions of concepts that were accepted by most of his contemporaries, but it should be noted that his position in matters of Catholic doctrine placed him outside the more virile religious currents of his time.[227] As a professional ecclesiastic, he combined administrative expertise and extensive theological learning with a large measure of genuine devotion, but his worldly orientation is evident in his choice of precepts within the broad spectrum of Catholic tradition. His religious tracts demonstrate a certain limited affinity

[227] Richelieu's religious views have been examined by many authors. J. Orcibal, "Richelieu, homme d'église, homme d'état, à propos d'un ouvrage récent," *Revue d'histoire de l'église de France*, xxxiv (1948), 94-101. L. Valentin, *Richelius, Scriptor Ecclesiasticus*, Toulouse, 1900.

for the spirituality of the Catholic Renaissance,[228] but they do not require a rigorous personal morality. Instead, his writings are marked by a strong desire to accommodate the spiritual to the human and make extensive concessions to man's imperfections and entrenched custom. The result was that he consistently supported positions that were intimately allied with the probabilism of the period and leaned toward an easy morality which made salvation available to all who would fulfill minimum requirements. The instructions for confessors that were issued in his diocese of Luçon under his authority showed a marked willingness to compromise with contemporary usage in lascivious dress, usury and other commercial matters, as well as an unmistakable leniency toward questionable conduct when carried on in secret.[229] And his important *Instruction du chrétien* repeatedly stressed the sufficiency of a far less rigorous route to salvation than was required by many contemporary religious leaders. In introducing his discussion of the Decalogue, he made the revealing statement that the law of God is easy to obey and far from burdensome, and he cited such unspectacular persons as Zachariah and St. Elizabeth as entirely justified in the sight of God.[230] Most important was his discussion of the sacrament of penance and his acceptance of a very liberal interpretation of attrition rather than the more exacting contrition.[231] In the debate concerning attrition as stemming from love of God or mere concern for self, Richelieu went far toward the latter position when he allowed the sufficiency of repentance which originates in fear but may partially lead to love.[232] This was the most liberal interpretation that he could adopt while remaining within the Canons and Decrees

---

[228] L. Cognet, "La Spiritualité de Richelieu," *Etudes franciscaines*, III (1952), 85-91.

[229] *La Briefve et Facile Instruction pour les confesseurs composée par Maistre Jacques de Flavigny Docteur en théologie, et grand-vicaire de Monseigneur l'Evesque de Luçon, par commandement de mondit Seigneur*, Fontenay, 1613. Cf. M. Deloche, *Autour de la plume du Cardinal de Richelieu*, Paris, 1920, pp. 28-56. Deloche notes that this was the first of Richelieu's lifelong efforts to reconcile the spiritual and the temporal.

[230] *Instruction*, pp. 116-17. After this statement, Richelieu goes on to denounce Calvin for requiring the impossible.

[231] *Ibid.*, pp. 295-96.   [232] *Ibid.*, p. 78.

of the Council of Trent.[233] He added that remission of sin was complete even without the performance of the prescribed act of penance, provided that confession was made with the intention of carrying out the act,[234] and at the close of the book he listed a series of daily exercises that would render salvation easier to attain.[235] Richelieu held this approach to the problem of personal morality throughout his entire career and reiterated it more extensively in his *Traité de la perfection du chrétien*, his final and most comprehensive work on religious doctrine. His position is not susceptible to the charge of religious insincerity; rather, it represents a significant willingness to accommodate religious teachings to human capabilities and to allow maximum autonomy to human nature and will.

In retrospect, it seems both fitting and necessary that the future architect of reason of state in France should adopt this position in the religious ideology of his time. As it developed in the seventeenth century, reason of state was predicated upon the partial autonomy of political affairs from theological determinants, and it was possible for a given thinker to uphold this view only if he accepted a relatively loose application of religious morality to temporal affairs generally. Richelieu's tendency toward laxism and his willingness to accommodate religious principles to practical, human reality represented this position. On the basis of the record, we know that many of the proponents of reason of state among his contemporaries tended this way in their religious thinking. Indeed, acceptance of a special ethic of politics and adherence to religious liberalism seem but twin aspects of a single ideological pattern, given the predominance of religious categories in so many elements of French thought.

---

[233] J. Périnelle, *L'Attrition d'après le Concile de Trente et d'après Saint Thomas d'Aquin*, Le Saulchoir, 1927, Pt. I, Chaps. 2 and 3 elaborately examines the position taken at Trent. Orcibal (article cited in note 227, p. 98) holds that Richelieu in this passage exceeded the limits set by the Council. However, because the Canons and Decrees of the Council of Trent do not give a specific definition of attrition, because Richelieu's language is not entirely clear, and because he always claimed to adhere to doctrinal orthodoxy as determined at Trent, I prefer to regard him as going as far as possible in a liberal direction when taking this position.

[234] *Instruction*, p. 304.

[235] *Ibid.*, pp. 308ff.

Those who held to a more rigorous religious posture and insisted upon the subordination of *all* temporal matters, political as well as personal, to a single standard of religious morality ruled out any special ethic of public policy and regarded reason of state as no more than good government according to the universal principles of justice. For this reason, among others, religious and political doctrines were intimately related and controversy in one field frequently foreshadowed disagreement in the other. Richelieu's critics eventually opposed him on both religious and political grounds, and he consequently regarded opposition to his religious views as politically dangerous. Much of this, however, was not evident until many years after his appointment as First Minister. Before the alternatives were made clear by extensive experience with his policies, he maintained good relations with many men who later became his bitterest enemies.

During the decade before 1624, Richelieu witnessed the sorry spectacle of a royal policy that seemed perennially unsuccessful in meeting the many needs of the nation. The inconsequential Estates General of 1614-1615 were followed by a violent quarrel between the Parlement of Paris and the royal administration which threatened to disrupt the basic processes of government. Intermittent rebellions by the princes and the Huguenots were followed by various "peace" settlements which remained inconclusive, while the court was riven by factions that found their leaders in members of the royal family itself and advocated a variety of divergent policies to meet the most pressing problems. In foreign affairs, the rise of hostilities in Germany at a time when the French government was strongly aligned with the Hapsburgs presented a dilemma of major proportions. Should the prevailing policy be continued, largely for the benefit of European Catholicism, or should the anti-Hapsburg interests of the French state prevail? Various ministers attempted to protect the latter by repeated but inconclusive thrusts into the Valtelline, the vital communications link between the Spanish and German Hapsburgs, but at the same time they maintained only indifferent relations with France's traditional Protestant allies, the English and the Dutch.

In the welter of pressures and frictions that accompanied these halting attempts to pursue various policies, two rival factions gradually began to take shape in the early 1620's. They were not well organized bodies but merely loose, temporary associations of important persons in both church and state who held reasonably similar views concerning foreign and domestic affairs. There was always considerable variation of opinion within both groups, and it was not unusual for individuals to pass from one to the other in accordance with changes in policy decisions and opportunities for self-advancement. The *bons Français*, who were essentially the heirs of the former *politiques* and were especially strong among the jurists, administrators and Gallicans, generally favored an aggressive anti-Hapsburg policy even though it might destroy the remaining political unity of Catholic Europe. They approved of the pending English marriage and the alliance with the Dutch, and they urged prosecution of the Valtelline affair regardless of possible friction with the papacy. In domestic affairs, they advocated adherence to the terms of the Edict of Nantes and even favored postponement of reforms, as far as necessary, in favor of an aggressive foreign policy. On the other hand, the *catholiques zélés* or *dévots* as they were called by the pamphleteers favored peace abroad and at least a *modus vivendi* with the Hapsburgs if not outright cooperation for the advancement of the Catholic cause. Many favored war against the Huguenots and would have drastically reduced the protection afforded them by the Edict of Nantes. This group was strongly represented at court and in the royal council, and eventually included such outstanding personages as Michel de Marillac and Pierre de Bérulle, both of whom cooperated with Richelieu for years but later became his bitter enemies. Even this brief sketch of the issues at stake in the early 1620's indicates the importance of religious considerations in the political life of the period and the impossibility of separating religion and politics in either foreign or domestic affairs.

It should be emphasized that both the *bons Français* and the *dévots* adhered to many similar concepts in both religion and politics. As strongly as any Gallican jurist, the leading *dévots* upheld the doctrine of divine right sovereignty. During the controversy that followed the assassination of Henry IV, Marillac bluntly wrote that royal power is from God. Kings rule by divine right and exercise the power and dominion of God who guides them. The highest human glory is that of kingship, the image of God's glory and majesty on earth. For this reason, he said, Christians even venerate the images of kings, the anointed of God.[236] Somewhat later, Bérulle published his important *Grandeurs de Jésus* whose dedication to Louis XIII contained ever stronger statements concerning the divine authorization of kings and their power. Kings, he said, hold their lives and crowns from God and are established on earth as images of his mercy, grandeur, and power. They therefore surpass all others in piety and dignity; they beatify the earth as God beatifies heaven.[237] Continuing, Bérulle used laudatory figures that anticipated the words of Bossuet two generations later. According to Holy Scripture, said Bérulle, a king is a god not in essence but in power, not by nature but by grace, not eternally but for a limited time, not in heaven but on earth, not subsistent but dependent upon him who is eternally subsistent and who creates kings to resemble his power and dignity as visible images of the invisible God.[238] Bérulle also cited the verses of Scripture that enabled Bossuet to assert that kings are gods and children of the Most High.[239] And like Bossuet, Bérulle concluded that since kings are the images of God, they should rule according to his dictates rather than their own interests and would be punished by divine wrath for their transgressions.[240] No writer in the century went further in his royalism.

The fact that the basic principles of absolutism were accepted by men who advocated very divergent royal policies graphically demonstrates that the general course of the Age of Absolutism was

---

[236] *Examen du livre intitulé Remonstrance et Conclusions des gens du Roy et Arrest de la Cour de Parlement du vingt-sixiesme Novembre MDCX . . . sur le Livre du Cardinal Bellarmin*, n.p., 1611, pp. 17-19.

[237] *Discours de l'estat et des grandeurs de Iesus, par l'Union ineffable de la Divinité avec l'Humanité*, Paris, 1623, pp. 4-5. It is noteworthy that Richelieu, eight other bishops, and many religious leaders approved this work. *Correspondance du Cardinal de Bérulle*, J. Dagens, ed., Paris-Louvain, 1937, Vol. II, 358-59.

[238] *Discours*, pp. 14-15.   [239] *Ibid.*, p. 15.   [240] *Ibid.*, p. 20.

by no means fixed early in the century. Or in different terminology, it indicates that the concept of absolutism did not logically require the type of policy that Richelieu embarked upon as First Minister. Richelieu is correctly described by historians as one of the chief architects of French absolutism, but this is because of the nature of his policies rather than any unusual political concepts on his part. The leaders of the *dévots* and the *bons Français* were similar in supporting the principles of absolutism, but they advocated very different means of achieving their objectives, largely because of their disagreements concerning the nature of the general good. The more important religious leaders of the 1620's, far from retreating from the world, were very conscious of its ways and its opportunities. It was characteristic of the period that Christian mystics and pious laymen could mingle at court and be simultaneously absorbed in religious devotion and the intricacies of intrigue and negotiation concerning both religious and political affairs. This combination of traits is found in such different personages as Bérulle, Father Joseph, Michel de Marillac, Duvergier de Hauranne (appointed abbé de Saint-Cyran in 1620), and many others. It is also clear that all were interested in protecting the interests, secular and religious, of the French state. All therefore fit the preponderant pattern of French political life which combined royalism, Catholicism, and statism. The implementation of their ideals and objectives, however, was another matter and gave rise to major disagreements concerning the best policy for the crown. As time advanced, all were forced to accept or reject Richelieu's policies, but the choice was not made clear to them until after many years of close association with the First Minister.

During his brief first ministry, Richelieu attempted to strengthen the French state at home and abroad by vigorous measures against the rebellious nobles and by reinforcing France's ties with her Protestant allies, especially in Germany. Although his efforts were largely abortive, the nature of his policies marked him as a proponent of state power and the defense of French interests. In the course of his subsequent tortuous maneuvers between the Queen Mother, Louis XIII, and various key personages in both church and state, he deliberately dissociated himself from any single faction and was especially careful to maintain contact with religious leaders of different views. With Father Joseph he had long been intimate before 1624. The two men cooperated in the complex negotiations between the Queen Mother, the princes, and the royal administration, and in the establishment of pious foundations. Father Joseph headed a secret but extensive faction at court and subtly influenced Louis XIII in Richelieu's favor.[241] In return, he was among the first whom Richelieu notified of his appointment to the royal council.[242] Between 1617 and 1624, Richelieu also maintained close ties with Saint-Cyran who arranged for the publication of his *Principaux Poincts de la Foy* and his *Instruction du chrétien*.[243] He likewise was in close touch with Michel de Marillac through their mutual involvement in the faction of the Queen Mother, and Richelieu immediately secured Marillac's appointment as Superintendent of Finance in 1624. With Bérulle, Richelieu's relations were somewhat more distant but equally significant. As Bishop of Luçon, he aided in the establishment of Bérulle's Oratory in his diocese during the first years of the organization,[244] and the two men remained in contact during the 1620's in spite of their differing views on foreign policy.[245] Actually, Richelieu's personal qualities were such that he experienced little difficulty in maintaining relations with this group which, like himself, combined religious devotion with concern for worldly affairs. Through these various means, Richelieu seemed to offer something to every shade of opinion. The record of his first ministry, his polemics against the Huguenots, his close association with various religious leaders, his cardinal's hat, and his evident abilities combined to convince many powerful persons and eventu-

[241] G. Fagniez, *Le Père Joseph et Richelieu*, Paris, 1894, Vol. I, 91-101.

[242] *Lettres*, Vol. II, 3-4.

[243] J. Orcibal, *Les Origines du jansénisme*, Vol. II: *Jean Duvergier de Hauranne, Abbé de Saint-Cyran et son temps*, Paris, 1947, pp. 477-83.

[244] *Correspondance*, Vol. I, 84-85, 632-33.

[245] On about January 17, 1620, Bérulle wrote to the Prince of Piedmont advocating cooperation with the Hapsburgs for the defense of Catholicism and the destruction of heresy, and urging the Prince to adopt this policy. *Ibid.*, Vol. II, 93-95.

ally Louis XIII himself that Richelieu alone could give royal policy the direction and sustained leadership that had been lacking.

The clash of opinion among various personalities and factions concerning the best policy for the crown was both reflected and stimulated by the intense debates in the pamphlet literature of the period. During the Wars of Religion and the early seventeenth century, the pamphleteers of all parties continually poured forth a stream of opinionated and ephemeral but often influential tracts which now provide valuable guides to the flux of opinion. Many were even collected and republished in special volumes, apparently for the purpose of perpetuating the memory of events and individual viewpoints.[246] During the years immediately before 1624, all major problems of foreign and domestic policy were subjected to searching scrutiny in this literature. The clash of principles was especially clear between those who advocated hostilities against the Hapsburgs and those who feared that this would severely damage the cause of resurgent Catholicism.[247] The spokesmen for all groups, however, manifested considerable frustration and uncertainty because of the evident inability of successive ministers to cope with the increasingly complex problems that confronted them. Even those writers who advocated war against the Hapsburgs realized that France was unprepared for a major military effort because of extensive social and economic disruption in the realm and the lack of a strong

[246] For this period, the best collection is *Recueil des pièces les plus curieuses qui ont esté faites pendant le règne du Connestable M. de Luynes*, n.p., 1622 and later editions. I have used the edition of 1628. Cited hereafter as *Recueil des pièces*. For foreign affairs, the best collection is *Recueil de quelques discours politiques écrits sur diverses occurrences des affaires et guerres étrangères depuis quinze ans en ça*, n.p., 1632. Cited hereafter as *Recueil de quelques discours*. The practice of publishing collections of pamphlets originated during the Wars of Religion.

[247] E.g., *Discours sur le sujet des troubles de Bohème* (1619), in *Recueil de quelques discours*, pp. 158-84, which argues against intervention because of the danger to the Catholic cause. On the other hand, a number of slightly later pamphlets urge intervention in the Valtelline but hesitate before outright war against the Hapsburgs. *Les Sentinelles au Roy ou Advertissement des dangereuses approaches des forces Espagnoles pour bloquer le Royaume de France*, n.p., 1621. *Discours sur l'état lamentable auquel sont réduites les trois ligues des Grisons*, n.p., 1622.

military establishment, not to mention the absence of firm leadership in high places.[248] And because of the widespread acceptance of divine right sovereignty, it was generally held that the chronic troubles at home and the discredit of France abroad might be remedied only by able and enlightened exercise of monarchical power.

For several generations, French statesmen had been aware of the power of the press to influence public opinion, but Richelieu was one of the first to use it systematically and effectively for promoting his views and himself. During the final years of his climb to power, he accomplished the delicate feat of gaining the support of both factions while simultaneously utilizing the services of pamphleteers whose opinions were anything but neutral. Of these, the most important was François Langlois de Fancan, canon of Saint-Germain-l'Auxerrois and expert pamphleteer.[249] Fancan's personal position was that of a highly partisan *bon Français*. His hatred of the Spanish, the Jesuits, and any religious influence in the French government was intense, and he favored alliances with the Protestant powers abroad and accommodation of the Huguenots at home. His views therefore differed materially from Richelieu's, but their common antipathy toward the several ministers of Louis XIII and their agreement on certain matters of policy enabled Richelieu to make use of Fancan's talents for his own purposes. Their precise relation-

---

[248] *Discours sur les Affaires et Guerres d'Allemagne, après l'élection de l'Empereur Ferdinand et celle de Frederic Comte Palatin à la Couronne de Bohème*, in *Recueil de quelques discours*, pp. 231-70. *Discours sur ce qui peut sembler estre plus expedient, et à moyenner au sujet des guerres entre l'Empereur et le Palatin*, in *ibid.*, pp. 300-48.

[249] The following studies, which are of varying value, may be consulted on Fancan and his relations with Richelieu. L. Geley, *Fancan et la politique de Richelieu*, Paris, 1884. T. Kükelhaus, "Zur Geschichte Richelieus. Unbekannte Papiere Fancans," *Historische Vierteljahrschrift*, II (1899), 18-38. C. Parrot, *Fancan et Richelieu: le problème protestant sous Louis XIII*, Montbéliard, 1903. E. Wiens, "Fancan und die französische Politik, 1624-1627," *Heidelberger Abhandlungen zur mittleren und neueren Geschichte*, XXI (1908), 1-141. G. Fagniez, "Fancan et Richelieu," *Revue historique*, CVII (1911), 59-78, 310-22, and CVIII (1911), 75-87. L. Delavaud, "Quelques collaborateurs de Richelieu," *Rapports et notices sur l'édition des Mémoires du Cardinal de Richelieu*, J. Lair and de Courcel, eds., Vol. II, Paris, 1907-1914, 84-108. Deloche, Chaps. 8, 9.

ships on both the personal and literary levels remain obscure, but there is no doubt that Fancan's tracts increasingly reflected Richelieu's views, supported him as the ablest available administrator, and had considerable influence upon his appointment as First Minister.

For our purposes, it is sufficient to note the contents of two of Fancan's most important pamphlets, *La France mourante*[250] and *La Voix publique*.[251] The former is a very effective dialogue in which Chancellor L'Hospital and Chevalier Bayard speak their minds around the sickbed of stricken France. After deploring the decline of traditional French virtues and the massive incursion of Spanish influence into French affairs (Fancan's strongest phobia), the two men recommend many desperately needed remedial measures. The tract is therefore one of Fancan's most significant regarding royal policy, and there is no doubt that his suggestions extensively reflect Richelieu's views. His proposals regarding domestic affairs are presented by L'Hospital. Eliminate from the royal councils, he said, all those of the Spanish faction. Control the financiers; reclaim the alienated royal domain; reform the finances and remove all sources of peculation so as to avoid mortgaging the *taille*. Suppress the factions among the great nobles. Avoid civil war at all costs, especially one based on religion. Maintain peace by establishing concord between the King and the Queen Mother. Control the pretensions of officials and the prevailing fashionable extravagance which is such a drain on the state. Do not allow any financial official to become too powerful. Train the nobles in military activity. Do not engage the King in unessential travels which only breed factious strife. Reward the deserving and hang the wicked.[252]

Regarding foreign affairs, Fancan placed his recommendations

---

[250] *Dialogue de la France mourante* n.p., 1623. In *Recueil des pièces*, pp. 489-535. I have used this version. While Richelieu's direct inspiration of this tract cannot be proved, its parallelism with many of his ideas and several contemporary statements concerning its authorship warrant this assumption. The fact that this and two similar pamphlets were used in compiling Richelieu's memoirs indicates collaboration between him and Fancan.

[251] *La Voix publique au Roy*, n.p., 1624. In *Recueil des pièces*, pp. 536-80.

[252] *Dialogue*, pp. 530-31.

in the mouth of Chevalier Bayard. While the royal army was besieging Montauban, he said, the Hapsburgs made great advances in Germany, seized the Valtelline, and established control over many new areas. Soon they will dominate Germany and Italy, and it will be impossible to resist them. The remedy, he said, was not to send emissaries to the Hapsburgs nor even to make outright war on them. At this juncture, the French should support their allies by sending them all men who seek to bear arms and by preventing their taking service with the Spanish. The ministers should give strict orders to their ambassadors and punish those who are delinquent, improve the reputation of France abroad, and eliminate from the royal councils all who favor Spain.[253] The parallelisms of many of these points with Richelieu's later policies is obvious. During the following year, Fancan rendered Richelieu a supreme service by publishing *La Voix publique* which decisively influenced opinion in his favor and was an important factor in bringing about his appointment as First Minister. This tract is almost entirely personal invective against La Vieuville. After cogently arguing the vital necessity of an able royal council, Fancan accused La Vieuville of devious machinations, inconstancy in pursuing any policy, and inability to accomplish anything—all of which struck home and had the desired effect.

None of these pamphlets, even those most clearly inspired by Richelieu, seeks to justify its recommendations concerning royal policy with any argument other than practical benefit. As long as Richelieu was merely an observer and critic, outside the seats of power, he felt no need to support his proposals in any other terms, and the subtleties of means-end argumentation in relation to higher values and reason of state might be ignored. Upon becoming First Minister, however, his role was significantly altered. Now his responsibilities for policy decisions, their effective implementation, and their impact upon the nation forced him to justify his acts more comprehensively to all interested persons from Louis XIII to the most hostile pamphleteer. Opposition was certain to be forthcoming. Not only was contemporary opinion so censorious that any

[253] *Ibid.*, pp. 533-34.

policy was inevitably subjected to severe criticism; the state of French society and institutions was such that almost any governmental act automatically touched the rights and interests of many persons and groups. Furthermore, the special relations of Catholic France with the Hapsburgs and the papacy enormously complicated the pursuit of French interests abroad. Upon assuming direction of royal policy, therefore, Richelieu found himself burdened with a new obligation, that of justifying his actions before all shades of opinion. It was not sufficient merely to work for the immediate benefit of the French state; his measures must be shown to have merit in terms of the nature and purposes of the state itself. This introduced the element of justice and higher values, their exact definition and their precise relevance to politics—questions of which Richelieu was thoroughly aware. For this reason, his massive program of state-building was accompanied by an unremitting effort to articulate the concept of reason of state.

PART II

THE CONTROVERSY OVER THE
VALTELLINE EPISODE, 1624-1627

RICHELIEU'S VALTELLINE POLICY AND
THE RESULTING POLEMICS

DURING Cardinal Richelieu's initial years as First Minister, foreign affairs occupied his attention almost exclusively because of the thoroughly unsatisfactory and precarious nature of French relations with neighboring powers. The many problems that Richelieu inherited from La Vieuville in this area and the rapidly evolving course of war and diplomacy on the European continent forced the Cardinal to grapple with the intricacies of foreign relations at the outset of his tenure of power. This meant that he was thrust into the most difficult and controversial area of royal policy at a time when his position as First Minister was anything but secure. Because of the intensity of religious rivalry in the developing Thirty Years' War and the crucial role of religion in the factionalism at the French court, any foreign policy that he might pursue was certain to be subjected to the sharpest scrutiny and criticism. As his moves unfolded and his method of strengthening the position of the French state in Europe became clear, his policies gave rise to a violent polemic, one of the most extensive and penetrating of his entire ministry. This in turn forced him to justify his actions before public opinion and served as a catalyst in the formulation of a viable concept of reason of state. Before analyzing this very fruitful controversy, it is necessary to examine the actual chain of events and the roles of key personalities in order to present the context within which Richelieu and his supporters developed their views.

Earlier ministers had set the pattern of French foreign relations but without significant benefit to France. The Brûlarts had arranged a league of France, Venice and Savoy but its immediate influence was negligible. La Vieuville had established an offensive-defensive alliance with the Dutch, entered into relations with Mansfeld, and sought to strengthen the ties between France and England by marrying Louis XIII's sister, Henrietta Maria, to the Prince of Wales, the future Charles I, but these contacts with Protestant powers were plagued in each case by religious considerations. All such moves, in fact, were subordinate to the one all-encompassing determinate, French relations with the Hapsburgs. To the north, east, and south, Hapsburg power loomed menacingly on the horizon and dominated all French thinking on matters of foreign policy. Being too weak to challenge the Hapsburgs directly, the French sought at least to cut the Valtelline, the vital communications link between the Spanish and German Hapsburgs through extreme south-east Switzerland, by maintaining ties with nearby Venice, Savoy, and the Protestant Grisons who were the local overlords of the valley, and by staging occasional thrusts into the area. Shortly before 1624, the Spanish had taken control over the Valtelline from the Grisons, nominally in support of the native Catholic Valtellins. After subsequent pressure from France, the Spanish agreed to give control of the local forts to the pope pending settlement of the question. When Richelieu became First Minister, therefore, the valley was occupied and protected by papal troops. Pope Urban VIII was not entirely pro-Spanish in sentiment but cooperated with the Hapsburgs by allowing the passage of Spanish troops and ensuring that control of the valley was kept from the hands of the Grisons. Richelieu was therefore confronted with the fact that the papacy itself supported the Spanish and protected the most vulnerable link in their military communications.[1]

During the summer of 1624, the problem of the Valtelline was extensively discussed in the royal council. At its session on July 11

[1] The bibliography on the various ramifications of the Valtelline question is extremely extensive. Instead of citing the many essential items, I refer the reader to the comprehensive listings in R. Pithon's two valuable articles, "Les Débuts difficiles du ministère de Richelieu et la crise de Valteline, 1621-1627," *Revue d'histoire diplomatique*, LXXIV (1960), 298-322, and "La Suisse, théâtre de la guerre froide entre la France et l'Espagne pendant la crise de Valteline (1621-1626)," *Schweizerische Zeitschrift für Geschichte*, XIII (1963), 33-53.

before the definitive fall of La Vieuville, Richelieu argued at length that the reputation of France was at stake because of the affront to her allies, the Grisons. She might therefore justifiably resort to force to protect her honor and her interests. Initial moves, he said, should include further aid to France's allies, Catholic and Protestant, and prodding them into action. This should be accompanied by diplomatic moves and a generally more belligerent though covert anti-Hapsburg policy.[2] On August 13, La Vieuville was arrested and Richelieu became First Minister. His policies rapidly triumphed, for on September 5 Louis XIII wrote to Philippe de Béthune, his ambassador to the Vatican, instructing him to demand restoration of control over the Valtelline to the Grisons (that is, the French) within three months and, if necessary, to threaten closer ties between France and her Protestant allies.[3] Needless to say, Urban VIII refused. The decision to force the issue in the Valtelline was therefore taken in spite of the many formidable obstacles that confronted Richelieu both at home and abroad: the uncertainty of France's allies, her undeniable financial and military weaknesses, the strength of the *dévot* faction, and the danger of a Huguenot revolt.[4] In combination, these were sufficient to give any statesman pause, but Richelieu doubtless believed, as he stated a year later in the royal council, that domestic problems could be dealt with in due course but foreign affairs demanded immediate attention according to the pressure of events.[5]

The resulting military and diplomatic activity in which Richelieu seized and attempted to hold the initiative lasted approximately eighteen months. Late in 1624, the Marquis de Cœuvres joined the Grisons with a sizable French army, occupied the Valtelline, expelled the papal troops in a series of sieges, and restored French control in a campaign that lasted throughout the following year. Meanwhile the league with Venice and Savoy was reactivated and

[2] *Mémoires*, Vol. IV, Paris, 1920, 218-28.

[3] *Lettres*, Vol. VII, 545-48.

[4] Pithon demonstrates the importance of these factors in the first article cited in n. 1.

[5] *Mémoires*, Vol. V, 187.

a diversionary action was undertaken against Genoa. A subsidy was sent to the Dutch and aid was extended to Mansfeld. Most important, the English marriage was concluded, largely through the efforts of Pierre de Bérulle who obtained the necessary dispensation in Rome, accompanied Henrietta Maria to England, and bent all efforts to succor the English Catholics. Most inopportunely for Richelieu, the Huguenot leaders, Rohan and Soubise, chose to revolt early in 1625 in spite of criticism of their actions by the major Protestant powers. More significant, however, were the negotiations between the French and the papacy concerning the Valtelline. After Father Joseph, Richelieu's personal envoy to Rome, failed to effect an agreement, Urban VIII dispatched his nephew, Cardinal Francesco Barberini, to Paris as papal Legate where he remained for three months during the summer of 1625. His instructions specified that he should emphasize the religious issue, thereby ensuring that control of the valley remained in the hands of the Catholic Valtellins and denying it to the Grisons at all costs. Regarding the sanctity of Louis XIII's oath to protect the Grisons, Barberini was instructed to argue that it had been given to heretics toward whom no Catholic ruler could have any obligations whatsoever.[6] Negotiations with the Legate in Paris were conducted partially by Father Joseph who returned from Rome and by Bérulle who arrived from England. In spite of their Catholic sympathies and their deference toward the Legate, both men supported Richelieu's position.[7] They consequently failed to reach an agreement with Barberini concerning the sovereignty of the Grisons or the passage of troops and his mission accomplished nothing. Early in 1626, after further negotiations made it clear that no mutually satisfactory terms were possible, Richelieu temporarily solved one problem by making peace with the Huguenot leaders.

These developments understandably caused a sensation within the

[6] A. Malvezzi, "Papa Urbano VIII e la questione della Valtellina," *Archivio storico lombardo*, vii (1958), 23.

[7] G. Fagniez, *Le Père Joseph et Richelieu (1577-1638)*, Vol. 1, Paris, 1894, Chap. 4. M. Houssaye, *Le Cardinal de Bérulle et le Cardinal de Richelieu, 1625-1629*, Paris, 1875, pp. 54-57.

dévot faction and throughout Catholic Europe. For the Most Christian King to marry his sister to a heretic prince, enter into an alliance with the Dutch, give aid to Mansfeld, and make peace with the Huguenots was scandal enough, but the greatest offense by far was the Marquis de Cœuvres' campaign in the Valtelline where French troops actually fired upon those carrying the papal banner. When Spada, the papal nuncio in Paris, upbraided Richelieu for this use of force, he pointed to the papal brief permitting him to handle all matters of public policy when he was appointed minister.[8] He knew, however, that he was vulnerable from the Roman standpoint and did all that he could to forestall ultramontane criticism. He ordered Cœuvres to give all possible aid to Catholic missionaries in the conquered areas and told Béthune to impress upon the pope the limited nature of French objectives.[9] In February 1625 he even showed Spada false dispatches in which Cœuvres was ordered to delay further sieges for two months. These were sent to Cœuvres accompanied by secret orders to proceed and then sue for pardon which would be granted![10] In Richelieu's memoir to the king in May when his efforts seemed most successful, he admitted that it was difficult to capitalize upon them without seeming to compromise the cause of religion, but he added that Louis XIII's zeal and piety would ensure eventual advantage to the faith.[11] One of his major reasons for urging Louis XIII to assemble the notables at Fontainebleau in September was to neutralize the calumny to which royal policy was being subjected.[12] At this assembly, Richelieu urged that France seek peace with honor in spite of the Legate's intransigeance, and since "the reputation of the state is to be preferred to all else," it was necessary to continue hostilities.[13] Subsequently, repeated reverses in various quarters weakened Richelieu's position and enabled the *dévot* faction to reassert its influence. At a meeting of the royal council early in 1626, Marillac marshalled powerful political

---

[8] L. von Pastor, *History of the Popes*, London, 1938, Vol. xxviii, 72.

[9] E. Rott, *Histoire de la représentation diplomatique de la France auprès des cantons suisses, de leurs alliés et de leurs confédérés*, Berne, 1906, Vol. iii, 825-26.

[10] *Ibid.*, Vol. iii, 833-35.

[11] *Lettres*, Vol. ii, 81.

[12] *Ibid.*, Vol. ii, 119-23.

[13] *Mémoires*, Vol. v, 120-21.

and religious arguments against Richelieu's policy and urged peace with Spain "*à quelque prix que ce soit.*"[14] Lengthy negotiations during which Richelieu gradually gave ground finally resulted in the Treaty of Monçon, a unilateral agreement between France and Spain, in May 1626. The treaty ostensibly restored the Valtelline to the Grisons but permitted only the exercise of Catholicism in the valley and so limited the Grisons' control as to render it purely nominal. France's allies deeply resented their lack of participation in the negotiations, but Richelieu attempted to meet their objections by arguing that it was not necessary to justify success since "the good of the state is the supreme law."[15]

Even this brief sketch of the course of events reveals much concerning the motivation of those in charge of royal policy and their view of just government. That political and religious considerations were completely intertwined is obvious. Although Richelieu's acts ran counter to the interests of international Catholicism as viewed by Spain and the papacy, this was counterbalanced by the fact that the men who were responsible for implementing royal policy did not regard the interests of the French state as antithetical to religious values. Richelieu's role in the affair was simply that of using the limited means at his disposal to strengthen the position of the French state vis-à-vis her most formidable neighbor. That he regarded his efforts as partially for moral and religious purposes—those embodied in the French monarchical state—will be indicated when we examine the polemics that surrounded the episode. As for Father Joseph and Bérulle whose personal piety and devotion to Christian principles were beyond question, both merged their religious convictions with their patriotism and believed that they could work for religious ends by making the most of their opportunities as servants of the crown. True, the Capuchin and the Oratorian had other motives. Father Joseph dreamed of a crusade against the infidel; Bérulle

[14] *Ibid.*, Vol. v, Appendix vi. The quotation is on page 325.

[15] Instructions to Bullion whom Louis XIII sent as extraordinary ambassador to the Duke of Savoy to mollify his anger. Richelieu, *Mémoires*, Vol. v, 253. For a recent reexamination of the Treaty of Monçon, see A. D. Lublinskaya, *French Absolutism: The Crucial Phase, 1620-1629*, Cambridge, 1968, pp. 278-81.

hoped to alleviate the sufferings of the English Catholics, and both needed Richelieu's support for the work of their respective orders. Even so, the nature of their royalism was such that they did not scruple, as men of religion, to give extensive support to Richelieu's foreign policy which they clearly believed to be in the best interests of Catholic France. In Paris and Rome they treated with papal representatives at great length and showed no hestitation to seek French advantage. In particular, the saintly Bérulle, when negotiating in Rome for the papal dispensation that was required for the English marriage, played the diplomatic game with extreme dexterity for French interests.[16] He and Father Joseph certainly regarded themselves as much more than mere pious, well-intentioned "front men" for a nefarious First Minister.[17] At this point in their careers, their combined loyalties to Christian principles and the French state caused them both to give full support to Richelieu's foreign policy and to defend it against the criticism to which it was subjected.

Because of the nature of the Valtelline episode, no person in authority, least of all Cardinal Richelieu, was surprised that it gave rise to a vigorous and at times violent polemic in the pamphlet literature of the period. As events unfolded and ultramontane opinion was further alienated, criticism of Richelieu's acts became correspondingly more penetrating. As we have seen, the Cardinal was thoroughly aware of the influence that the publicists exercised upon public opinion and had profited by it in his rise to power. After he was appointed First Minister, however, he instinctively developed an antipathy toward discussion and criticism of official acts by all and sundry. This attitude on his part is understandable not only because he now bore the responsibility for all major policy decisions but also, more significantly, because he believed that only he, the king, and a very few others among the initiate understood the mysteries of state. Those outside the seats of power should remain in their stations and forbear to discuss higher matters that they did

---

[16] M. Houssaye, *Le Père de Bérulle et l'Oratoire de Jésus, 1611-1625*, Paris, 1874, pp. 489-529.

[17] This accusation was repeatedly made by papal representatives. Fagniez, *Le Père Joseph*, Vol. I, 228.

not understand. For this reason, he occasionally attempted to discourage publication even by those who favored his policies because it might be as injurious as outright slander.[18] To stifle the expression of opinion, however, was a complete impossibility in Cardinal Richelieu's France, as he very well knew, and he therefore sought to channel its course in his favor by making extensive use of the talents of some of the ablest pamphleteers of his time. Their resulting publications, although thoroughly partisan, give valuable evidence concerning Richelieu's motivation and objectives in the crucially important Valtelline affair.[19]

The pamphleteers who supported Richelieu during this period were a numerous and disorganized group who enjoyed varying degrees of intimacy with the Cardinal. Although they were quite unlike the later body whose existence was partially formalized by the French Academy, they did yeoman's work in expressing Richelieu's justification of his policy and incidentally developed an important version of reason of state. At the center of the group stood Fancan,

---

[18] *Lettres*, Vol. II, 256.

[19] In addition to those listed in Pt. I, n. 249, the following are the major works on the pamphleteers during this period. G. Fagniez, "L'Opinion publique et la presse politique sous Louis XIII, 1624-1626," *Revue d'histoire diplomatique*, XIV (1900), 352-401. H. Nabholz, "Die öffentliche Meinung in Frankreich und die Veltlinerfrage zur Zeit Richelieus," *Jahrbuch für Schweizerische Geschichte*, XXVI (1901), 1-67. P. Pellisson, and d'Olivet, *Histoire de l'Académie française*, C. L. Livet, ed., Paris, 1858, 2 vols. R. Kerviler, *La Presse politique sous Richelieu et l'académicien Jean de Sirmond (1599-1649)*, Paris, 1876. C. Perroud, "Essai sur la vie et les œuvres de Mathieu de Morgues, abbé de Saint-Germain, 1582-1670," *Annales de la Société d'agriculture, sciences, arts et commerce du Puy*, XXVI (1863), 205-383. G. Fagniez, "Mathieu de Morgues et le procès de Richelieu," *Revue des deux mondes*, CLXII (1900), 550-86. Considerable information concerning the pamphleteers may be gleaned from the debate between Fagniez and Dedouvres, as follows. G. Fagniez, *Le Père Joseph et Richelieu*, 2 vols., Paris, 1894. L. Dedouvres, *Le Père Joseph polémiste; ses premiers écrits, 1923-1626*, Paris, 1895. Fagniez, "L'Opinion publique et la polémique au temps de Richelieu, à propos d'une publication récente," *Revue des questions historiques*, LX (1896), 442-84. Review of Fagniez and Dedouvres by E. Bourgeois, *Revue historique*, LXII (1896), 134-42. Dedouvres, "Le Père Joseph polémiste," *Revue des questions historiques*, LX (1897), 137-65. Dedouvres, "Le Père Joseph diplomate," *Revue d'histoire diplomatique*, XII (1898), 80-98.

canon of Saint-Germain-l'Auxerrois, who delighted in continuing his polemics against the Hapsburgs and was even sent by Richelieu on diplomatic missions to Germany. There was Mathieu de Morgues, abbé de Saint-Germain, who had received extensive theological training and had published in the field. Appointed *prédicateur ordinaire du roi* in 1615, he was also chaplain of the Queen Mother and easily found himself supporting Richelieu. Jean Sirmond, an able writer, was a nephew of the great Jesuit scholar, Jacques Sirmond, and had a brother who also entered the order and achieved a certain renown. Jacques Pelletier and Jérémie Ferrier were both ardent Catholics, converts from Protestantism, and were always ready to defend Catholicism and the monarchy. Such men formed the inner core of the group of publicists upon whom Richelieu relied to justify his policies to the literate world. Father Joseph, who enjoyed a continuing special relationship with Richelieu, contributed his part by assuming direction of the *Mercure français*, the most important annual publication on current political affairs.[20] In addition, Richelieu frequently sought the support of other writers as the occasion required, but those whom we have listed are representative of the most active. Almost all, it is to be noted, had extensive theological training, yet they were thoroughly in sympathy with Richelieu's foreign policy which was essentially that of the *bons Français*. This was true even of Mathieu de Morgues who later became Richelieu's most indefatigable critic. Once again it is clear that the combined royalism, patriotism, and religious convictions of these men enabled them to support and to justify the Cardinal's policies to their satisfaction.

Earlier generations had witnessed extensive efforts to influence public opinion by means of the printed word, but Cardinal Richelieu was the first royal minister of note to mount a massive publishing campaign in his own behalf. In this he enjoyed the substantial advantage of having a controlled press at his command because of

[20] Dedouvres' extremely extensive attribution of pamphlets to Father Joseph has not been accepted, but he gives reasonably convincing circumstantial evidence that Father Joseph directed the *Mercure français* from 1624 to 1638, the date of his death. *Le Père Joseph polémiste*, pp. 434-39.

the prevailing practice of censorship by the lay and ecclestiastical authorities. Such controls were nothing new in his period, but he succeeded in regularizing them and making them more efficient, at least on paper. The attempt was to be expected from those in power during this period of French history for a variety of reasons. In spite of the great diversity in its intellectual and religious life, French society still retained many characteristics of an ideological society with well-defined traditions, conventions, and beliefs which the authorities feared would be undermined by undue license in publication. Also, thinkers and governors alike keenly felt the need for increased order and control not only in social and political affairs but also in all phases of intellectual and cultural life. Indeed, Cardinal Richelieu's most comprehensive self-appointed task was to channel French energies and to discipline all elements of national existence. His attempts to strengthen official controls over publication were therefore much more than mere self-interested machinations for the purpose of stifling criticism and should be regarded as part of his program of state-building in its broadest sense.

During the sixteenth century, the official censors were chiefly concerned with theological works. These were subjected to a long series of regulations which roughly coincided with the religious upheavals of the period. The Ordinance of Moulins (1566) added prohibitions against the publication of defamatory works against individuals and equated this with disturbing the peace and public tranquility. The prescribed penalties for unauthorized publication were confiscation and corporal punishment.[21] In practice, the censoring authorities were the Faculty of Theology and the Parlements, especially that of Paris, which strove to suppress all publications that might disrupt the traditional religious and political ideology of the French state. The only break in this situation occurred with the Edict of Nantes (1598) which specified that Calvinist (that is, heretical) works might be published but only in those towns where Calvinism was legally permitted.[22] Otherwise the traditional restrictions ac-

[21] Isambert et al., eds. *Recueil général des anciennes lois françaises*, Paris, n.d., Vol. XIV, 210-11.
[22] *Ibid.*, Vol. XV, 178.

cording to official religious and political doctrine continued to hold sway. In principle, no book was published in the kingdom without royal permission, but the frequent reiteration of this requirement suggests that it was more honored in the breach than in the observance.[23]

In practice, the enforcement of censorship proved very difficult, and the year 1624 witnessed extensive efforts to increase the efficiency of the system. On July 10, while Richelieu was a member of the royal council but before the fall of La Vieuville, a royal edict forbade the printing of any "letters, memoirs or instructions concerning affairs of state" without permission signed by a Secretary of State and sealed with the great seal.[24] This presumably strengthened controls over seditious publications and gave supervision of them to the Chancellor, his legal aides, and the royal courts. In August an elaborate edict provided for the appointment of four doctors from the Faculty of Theology with annual salaries of 2000 livres to serve as permanent censors of religious works.[25] Subsequently, Richelieu attempted to strengthen the system even further. In the proposals that he framed for presentation to the Assembly of Notables of 1626-1627, he urged that all who published defamatory libels without permission be subjected to heavier penalties.[26] During the assembly, he equated such publishers with disturbers of the peace, and the notables approved without debate his recommendation of severe punishment in conformity with earlier ordinances.[27] This is doubtless why the resulting "Code Michaud" of 1629 contained an article that not only renewed the provisions of the Ordinance of Moulins but added the publication and dissemination of defamatory libels to the long list of crimes that were punishable as *lèse-majesté*.[28] No heavier penalty could be prescribed.

[23] Letters patent of September 10, 1563. Renewed in 1598, 1612, 1618, 1626, and 1630. *Ibid.*, Vol. xiv, 150; Vol. xv, 178; Vol. xvi, 26, 120, 164, 360.

[24] *Ibid.*, Vol. xvi, 146-47.

[25] A. Chevillier, *L'Origine de l'imprimerie de Paris*, Paris, 1694, pp. 398-402. Cited in D. T. Pottinger, *The French Book Trade in the Ancien Regime*, Cambridge, Mass., 1958, p. 62, which contains a good discussion of censorship.

[26] *Lettres*, Vol. vii, 323.

[27] J. Petit, *L'Assemblée des notables de 1626-1627*, Paris [1936], p. 198.

[28] Isambert, Vol. xvi, 275-76.

For our purposes, the major issues are the degree of freedom of expression that the publicists enjoyed and the value of their tracts as guides to contemporary opinion. That freedom in the modern sense did not exist is undeniable, and its absence should not be lamented if we are to judge the Age of Absolutism on its own terms. The regime of controls over all publications thoroughly coincided with the ideals of the period in which church and state continued to lead, guide, and indoctrinate the great majority of the subjects. Whether from the standpoint of religious and political ideology, the recognized need to discipline French cultural and intellectual life, or merely the veneration that was sought by and accorded the established authorities, controls over expression of opinion were accepted by contemporaries as part of the prevailing order. Many authors were subjected to severe penalties because their ideas were deemed subversive, but it is important to note that almost none criticized the system of censorship in principle. Like the monarchy whose authority the censors represented, their function was accepted as normal and necessary even by those who suffered from its operation. As for the practical application of censorship, it was haphazard, inefficient, and occasionally brutal in punishing authors and publishers alike. Writers feared its grasp and resorted to many stratagems, including emigration and publishing abroad, to avoid prosecution. Its functioning unquestionably favored the regime during Cardinal Richelieu's ministry—a fact that partially explains the preponderance of writings in his favor.

In spite of repeated royal edicts and intermittent persecution, however, critical opinion found extensive outlets in many clandestine presses and the thriving publishing houses in the Spanish Netherlands and the Dutch Republic. Official controls in France were severe but chronically inefficient, and there were a variety of opportunities for self-expression in print by those who opposed royal policy. Furthermore, the pamphleteers well knew that the reading public eagerly awaited their tracts, if only because of the lack of more formal sources of information. By apprising their countrymen of current developments, the pamphleteers not only performed an important service but aided in the creation of public opinion, thereby exercising considerable influence. Many of their pieces were thoroughly irresponsible and little more than personal invective; these may be discounted as historical sources. On the other hand, those that deal with ideas, causes, and justifications are vital evidences of contemporary opinion concerning major developments. Because of these several factors, it may be concluded that the system as a whole permitted a significant degree of intellectual freedom and that the pamphlet literature provides invaluable guides to the reactions of contemporaries to the events of their time.[29]

When analyzing the pamphlets that contributed to the growth of reason of state during the Valtelline episode, it is necessary to consider only a limited number of those that appeared in a given year since the large majority added nothing to the discussion. Many were purely informational; others were little but shallow, partisan invective, while still others merely repeated positions taken elsewhere. In almost every instance these may be reasonably ignored. It is sufficient to concentrate upon those that developed the major arguments for and against Richelieu's very provocative policies and to show how the exchange of ideas caused the Cardinal's supporters to build new positions from old, well-known precepts. Usually the more important tracts on both sides of the controversy were launched by spokesmen for a given faction—a consideration that enhances their historical significance as criticism or justification. Although our treatment will be limited to the more important and better known pamphlets, they are sufficient to indicate the intricacies of the debate in which Richelieu and his supporters groped their way toward a viable concept of reason of state.

Because the Valtelline episode resulted from the rivalry of two great Catholic powers, one might expect contemporary justifications of French policy to emphasize the secular interests of the French state and to neglect religious considerations. Early in 1624, shortly before Richelieu entered the royal council, one such treatise was

---

[29] This is the position taken by Louis André whose analysis of the value of the pamphlet literature is still one of the best. E. Bourgeois and L. André, eds., *Les Sources de l'histoire de France: XVIIᵉ siècle (1610-1715)*, Paris, 1924, Vol. IV, Introduction.

published in France, the *Discours des princes et états de la Chresti-enté plus considérables à la France, selon les diverses qualitez et conditions.*[30] The author of this lengthy anonymous tract was well versed in the intricacies of European politics and thoroughly conversant with French policy. Relations between states, he maintained, are determined by the internal condition and very nature of the states themselves; the well-governed will be strong and the chaotic weak. And since "there are no princes in the world that do not conduct themselves according to their interests,"[31] the strong will take advantage of the weak as occasions present themselves, one ruler's opportunity being another's undoing. He thereupon analyzed at great length the current relations between the various European states, treating all strictly from the standpoint of their respective interests and power. Throughout it is clear that he was viewing the European scene from the vantage point of France and thoroughly approved of what later became Richelieu's foreign policy. Entirely lacking is any discussion of religious matters except in relation to political power. Friedrich Meinecke, who first emphasized the importance of this treatise, correctly maintained that it was a very early attempt to survey all Europe from a thoroughly modern standpoint, the respective interests of states as defined in terms of the realities of power politics and without reference to any other values.[32] He was wrong, however, in his assertion that it was typical of the many pro-Richelieu publications that appeared in this period.

If there was any pamphleteer in Richelieu's entourage who was capable of presenting the case for the strictly secular interests of the French state, it was Fancan. His hatred of the Spanish, his sympathy with the Huguenots, his extreme Gallicanism, his equivocal religious views, and his burning patriotism caused him to evaluate

[30] Two slightly different versions of this work were published. The first appeared in 1624 and was reprinted in *Le Mercure d'Estat ou Recueil de divers discours d'Estat,* n.p., 1635. The second is in the *Mercure français,* Vol. x, and the *Recueil de quelques discours politiques, escrits sur diverses occurrences des affaires et guerres estrangeres depuis quinze ans en ça,* n.p., 1632. I have used the latter version. On this work, see Meinecke, Chap. 6, Pt. 1.

[31] *Discours,* pp. 357-58.

[32] Meinecke, 153-62.

all things political merely in terms of their practical benefit to France. Fundamentally, he regarded the religious frictions that accompanied the Valtelline episode as irrelevant to the central issue, the political rivalry of two great states, and he repeatedly claimed that the Spanish merely used religion to cloak their true design, territorial aggrandizement. His passions and limited views therefore enabled him to adopt a simplistic, secularized view of international affairs which differed markedly from that of Richelieu. Not only did the Cardinal realize the crucial role of religious motivation in the politics of the period; his temperament and convictions also caused him to be strongly motivated by religious principle.[33] The cooperation of the two men therefore depended strictly upon the circumstances of the moment and the orientation of royal policy. During the Valtelline episode, Richelieu found it to his advantage to have at least one spokesman who was thoroughly capable of arguing the benefits of his policy apart from relevant religious issues. This is why he made use of Fancan's talents as a pamphleteer and even sent him on diplomatic missions to the Archbishop of Cologne and Duke Maximilian of Bavaria for the purpose of driving a wedge between them and their Catholic overlord, the Emperor.[34] When Richelieu's policies and his position relative to the factions at court changed, Fancan was quickly disgraced and imprisoned.

Fancan's manner of argumentation may be illustrated by examining several of his more important publications during the Valtelline episode. In 1624, a partisan of the *dévot* faction, probably Pierre du Cugnet, published a brief, moderately argued piece in which he urged the Queen Mother to prevail upon Louis XIII to follow her earlier pro-Spanish policy.[35] Her friendly relations with Spain had provided a firm, lasting basis of much-needed peace, du Cugnet said, insisting that he was making a case for French interests rather than Spanish. France should protect her neighbors and allies, but

[33] The contrasting ideals of the two men are well analyzed in G. Fagniez, "Fancan et Richelieu," *Revue historique*, CVII (1911), 63-72.

[34] Wiens, *op. cit.* Fagniez, "Fancan et Richelieu," pp. 61-62. Richelieu, *Lettres*, Vol. VII, 941.

[35] *Le Véritable ou le mot en amy, de Messieurs les Princes, addressé à la Royne Mere*, n.p. [1624].

the causes of all such interventions should be just and entirely honorable.[36] France and Spain should negotiate concerning the Valtelline question and avoid war at all costs, thus continuing to enjoy the benefits of the policy that had been symbolized by the Spanish marriages. Only in this way might Louis XIII crown his acts with religion and avoid the untold dangers of war.[37] To this sober reasoning, Fancan replied with his *Cabale espagnole*,[38] a vituperative pamphlet which emphasized the risks of any pro-Spanish policy. The argument that peace depends on good relations with Spain, he said, merely serves to promote Spanish interests. The Spaniards are notorious for their trickery and dissimulation and resort to any means of self-advancement. They are not concerned with religion but merely use it to conceal their true selfish aims, Fancan insisted, citing examples of Spanish aggression against Catholic rulers.[39] Even when France and Spain are allied, the latter encroaches upon territories near France's borders.[40] He concluded that alliances and agreements with Spain benefited the French only as long as they remained perpetually vigilant and defended themselves against Spanish machinations.

Several other pamphlets, which may be ascribed to Fancan with varying degrees of certainty, illustrate Richelieu's willingness to allow his supporters to defend his policies by appealing to necessity of state. One such is the *Discours sur l'occurrence des affaires présentes* which dates from January 1625.[41] If it was not written by Fancan, it certainly was the work of someone close to Richelieu and his policies. The pamphlet is devoted to discussing "four reasons of state which oblige all kings to defend their allies." These are (1) the importance of kings' honor and reputation (2) the desire for gain and advantage which some princes view as the supreme law

---

[36] *Ibid.*, p. 7.   [37] *Ibid.*, pp. 14-15.

[38] *La Cabale espagnole entièrement descouverte, à l'avancement de la France et contentement des bons français*, n.p., 1625. Fancan's authorship of this tract is very likely but not entirely certain. Deloche, pp. 253-54.

[39] *La Cabale espagnole*, pp. 4-6.

[40] *Ibid.*, pp. 18-22.

[41] In *Mercure français*, Vol. xi, 56-94. This work has been assigned to various authors. Bourgeois and André, *Sources*, Vol. iv, 225. Deloche, p. 257.

in matters of state (3) evident necessity which forces the hands of rulers, and (4) the availability of means to carry out princely enterprises. Of these, he found the third to be the most compelling since it depends upon actual circumstances rather than principle. Evident necessity, he said, obliges the French to resist Spanish aggression even when it is not directed against France because Spanish power has been growing since the time of Charles V and must be arrested.[42] This position Fancan pushed to its logical conclusion in *La Ligue nécessaire*[43] in which he argued that France should form and lead a grand alliance of all the Hapsburgs' enemies. All who seek liberty should put their trust in France which will lead them to victory over the common enemy. Indeed, the league that he proposed consisted of a galaxy of states that had little else in common: England, Denmark, Sweden, the United Provinces, the Hanseatic cities, a majority of the Catholic and Protestant princes of Germany, the Swiss, Venice, Savoy, and Bethlen Gabor. Religious differences should cause no difficulty, he insisted, since all should realize that the league is a *fait d'estat* and not a *fait de religion*,[44] whereupon he attempted to show how such an alliance would benefit all its members and incidentally prevent the outbreak of religious warfare. This ambitious scheme had certain affinities with Richelieu's foreign policy, but its specific design was more Fancan's than the Cardinal's.[45] If the latter gained any advantage from the publication of the proposal, this was because of the pressure that it exerted on the papal representatives in the Valtelline negotiations.

Fancan followed the same line of argument even when he was engaged in controversy concerning the religious phases of the Valtelline affair. As we shall note when examining this aspect of the debate, Fancan's very effective *Miroir du temps passé* (1625) met the issue by arguing that religion and affairs of state should be kept

[42] *Discours*, pp. 67-68.

[43] N.p., 1625. Most of the authorities attribute this work to Fancan. Bourgeois and André, *Sources*, Vol. IV, 226. Deloche, using very limited evidence, ascribes it to Mathieu de Morgues. I find more to support the attribution to Fancan.

[44] *La Ligue nécessaire*, p. 11.

[45] Fagniez, "L'Opinion publique . . . ," p. 393.

entirely separate. And in the following year, when Richelieu sought to justify the Treaty of Monçon to the English who felt duped after aiding him to make peace with the Huguenot leaders, he again turned to Fancan who published his *Advis salutaire sur l'estat présent des affaires d'Allemagne*.[46] In this well-reasoned, straightforward piece, Fancan accused the Hapsburgs, especially the Spanish, of seeking universal empire, and extensively documented his charge. Pointing to the successive collapse of their enemies in Germany, he warned that if the northern portion of the Empire came under their domination they would be irresistible. Catholicism is no protection for France, he said, pointing to Philip II's support of the rebellious Catholic League. The English also have reason to fear the Spanish because of the latter's ambitions in Ireland. He concluded that the English should cooperate with their allies, especially the French, in the common defense against Spain. It was on such occasions as this that Richelieu, knowing Fancan's abilities and prejudices, made use of his talents. Whenever the Cardinal felt it advantageous to justify his policies by argument strictly from political necessity and without reference to any other values or considerations, he called on Fancan. This pamphlet, however, was his last important service to Richelieu whose policies changed sharply in 1627 with the siege of La Rochelle and his rapprochement with the *dévot* faction. Because Fancan had committed himself in favor of an accommodation with the Huguenots, had gone to extremes in criticizing the Jesuits and ultramontanes generally, was of questionable religious sincerity, and was too able and unscrupulous to be allowed to continue his pamphleteering, he was sacrificed to the *dévot* party whose views Richelieu momentarily favored. His services to Richelieu had been extensive, but his limited, secularized view of politics was ultimately inadequate to serve the Cardinal's purposes.

To return to the polemics of the year 1625, where we have hardly scratched the surface, it is necessary to examine the criticism of

---

[46] Paris, 1626. In *Mercure français*, Vol. XII, 731-42, and *Le Mercure d'estat ou Recueil de divers discours d'Estat*. In this case, Fancan's authorship seems certain. Deloche, p. 412.

Richelieu's policies by staunch Catholics who feared that his alliances with Protestant powers and his campaign in the Valtelline were damaging to the Roman Church and its faith. Because of the nature of his moves, Richelieu would have been happy to avoid this issue and to represent the episode merely as a function of international rivalry, but he knew this to be impossible given the strength of contemporary religious drives. It is important to note, however, that during his early years as First Minister, by far the most important criticisms of this nature came from abroad rather than from native Frenchmen. Throughout this initial period of Richelieu's diplomatic activity, he was supported not only by the so-called *bons Français* but by members of the *dévot* faction as well. Because of the strength of French patriotism, Richelieu's clever use of men of religion as his trusted agents, and the relative novelty of his policies, he had a broader spectrum of French opinion behind him than at any other time in his career. Not yet had positions polarized and forced large numbers of his compatriots to accept or reject his policies and their implications.

The intervention of Richelieu's foreign critics in the debate began harmlessly enough. Early in 1625, there appeared in Antwerp a tract entitled *Mysteria politica*, probably by Jacob Keller who was Rector of the Jesuit college in Munich and Maximilian of Bavaria's confessor.[47] Consisting of eight letters purportedly from "illustrious" persons, the piece sought to ridicule French foreign policy and defend the Hapsburgs by satirizing various French maneuvers which were both inept in themselves and inimical to the Catholic faith. The first letter showed the ambassadors of Venice, Holland, and England in Constantinople seeking to persuade the Sultan to attack the Hapsburgs but completely disagreeing as to the best means. The second criticized the marriage of Henrietta Maria to the Prince of

---

[47] *Mysteria politica, Hoc est: Epistolae arcanae virorum illustrium sibi mutuo confidentium lectu et consideratione dignae*, Antwerp, 1625. The attribution to Keller was widely accepted. *Mercure français*, Vol. XI, 94. C. Sommervogel, *Bibliothèque de la Compagnie de Jésus*, Paris, 1893, Vol. IV, 993. There are summaries of the *Mysteria politica* in the *Mercure français*, Vol. XI, 34-49, and in [J. Godefroy], *Le Mercure jésuite*, Geneva, 1626, Vol. I, 725-27. Only Vol. I of the latter work is cited hereafter.

Wales because of their different religions, while the third stated that this marriage would result in reestablishing Frederick in the Palatinate, opening France to invasion by the English, and destroying Catholicism in certain areas. The fourth showed the Venetian Secretary of State visiting the Protestant German princes and imperial cities and the Swiss cantons vainly trying to incite them to war against the Hapsburgs, and the fifth mocked James I for arming a fleet of ninety vessels for the invasion of Italy. The sixth showed how the Duke of Savoy feared that his lands would become a theater of war and urged entering the Valtelline through Venetian territory. The seventh, by far the longest, argued that France should not aid the Elector Frederick with arms because the English, Dutch, Venetians, and German Protestants all sought to foment war between France and the Hapsburgs merely for their own benefit and would abandon France at the first opportunity. The last letter criticized James I's government and attempted to incite division between himself and his son, his daughter (the Electress Palatine), the Lords, the Anglican clergy, and the Puritans.

Although relatively innocuous, this pamphlet could not go unanswered because it portrayed the Hapsburgs as the defenders of Catholicism against assaults by the French, a type of criticism to which Richelieu felt particularly vulnerable. The answers that were forthcoming from French sources—doubtless with official inspiration since they were printed in the *Mercure français*—met the charge in two ways. First, the *Parallèles du Roy Saint Louys et du Roy Louys XIII*[48] stressed certain similarities between the policies of the sainted Louis IX and those of Louis XIII. Louis IX sought peace with foreign rulers and restored lands to their rightful owners; Louis XIII is attempting to do the same in the Valtelline. Louis IX was called defender of the Church; Louis XIII has restored the Church in Béarn and seeks recovery of its property. Louis IX went on a crusade against the infidel; Louis XIII has sent missions to the Sultan of Turkey to secure restoration of the holy places to the Cordeliers. Such argumentation capitalized upon the well-known

---

[48] In *Mercure français*, Vol. XI, 96-115. The authorship of this work is uncertain.

personal piety of Louis XIII and implied that criticism of royal policy was unwarranted because of the sacrosanct qualities of the French monarchy which continued to adhere to its religious traditions. The other answer, a tract entitled *Discours sur les affaires de la Valteline*,[49] returned to the familiar charge that the Spaniards merely used religion to justify their expansion into various parts of the globe. Citing many examples of Spanish aggression and consequent "tyranny" in Europe and the New World, the author accused the Spanish of constantly adhering to Machiavelli's maxim, "*an appearance of religion is of great service in the affairs of kings.*"[50] This is why they claim to be protecting the Catholic Valtellins from religious and political oppression by the Grisons, a transparent excuse for Spanish penetration into the area. Neither tract, it is to be noted, specifically defended Richelieu's policy or denied that it was injuring the Catholic cause. Instead, the *Parallèles* stressed the religious sincerity and consequent unimpeachability of the reigning monarch, while the *Discours* attempted to shift the onus of hypocrisy to the Spanish.

Vastly more important than the *Mysteria politica* was another pamphlet, the *Admonitio ad regem*, which began to circulate in September 1625.[51] Although its authorship was much disputed, it may have been written by André Eudaemon-Johannes, a Jesuit theologian of Greek origin who accompanied Cardinal Barberini to Paris. In any case, its inspiration was certainly ultramontane. Like the *Mysteria*, the *Admonitio* was quickly translated into French and

---

[49] In *Mercure français*, Vol. XI, 127-81. This work was purportedly a French translation of an Italian tract which appealed to Philip III to cease his aggression in the Valtelline, but this was doubtless a subterfuge. Deloche, pp. 259-60. The tract has been assigned to various authors, including Fancan, but without foundation.

[50] *Discours*, p. 146. Italics in the original.

[51] G.G.R. *Theologi ad Ludovicum XIII Galliae et Navarrae regem christianissimum Admonitio* . . . . Augustae Francorum, cum facultate Catholic. Magistrat., 1625. In addition to the works cited above, the following should be consulted regarding the Latin pamphlets that were published abroad. G. Hubault, *De Politicis in Richelium lingua latina libellis*, Paris, 1856. J. M. Prat, *Recherches historiques et critiques sur la Compagnie de Jésus en France du temps du Père Coton*, Lyon, 1876, Vol. IV, Bk. 25, Chap. 4.

circulated widely, but the latter caused a much greater sensation because it was the first complete, cogently argued denunciation of Richelieu's foreign policy and its consequences. Whereas the *Mysteria* was chiefly concerned with political matters, the author of the *Admonitio* based his case squarely upon religion and the damage of Richelieu's policies to Roman Catholicism. Furthermore, the *Admonitio* attacked Richelieu directly by ascribing French policy to bad counselors and imploring Louis XIII to abandon their evil ways. As a "warning" which purportedly stemmed from a spokesman for international Catholicism, it was the more dangerous in that it appealed to Louis XIII's well-known piety and even touched upon the salvation of his soul.

The *Admonitio* opened with an explanation of the author's position. Assuming the posture of a native Frenchman, he said that heretofore he had not petitioned the king because of his inaccessibility, the great power of his ministers who stifled all criticism, and the risk of seeming to disparage the king's arms in time of war. But the peril of the present moment is great because of the certain misery and uncertain benefits of the war as well as its damage to the true faith. With all due humility, then, he would appeal not to Louis XIII's majesty but to his piety and clemency, the virtues that had given him the title, Louis the Just.[52] The primary evil of current French policy, he insisted, was Louis XIII's alliances with heretic powers. Such alliances are not only prohibited by Scripture; they are forbidden by God because they aid his enemies and work for the destruction of his Church. And the author cited examples of anti-Catholic actions by the English, Dutch, Venetians, and Gabor. As for France, the Most Christian King, protector of the faith, example of justice, and ornament of piety now taxes his people, impoverishes the Church, torments the nobility, and reduces cities to hunger for the sake of maintaining these alliances. God will punish their perpetrators as He has punished other states that removed themselves from his protection, for in spite of all that has been said the true aim of France's allies is the destruction of the

---

[52] *Admonitio*, pp. 1-2.

Catholic religion.[53] Already many inroads have been made throughout western and central Europe with fire and sword. This is not the work of Arabs but Europeans who are in the pay of France, he said, giving a satirical prayer for the success of French policies that made for reduction of the Catholic clergy, destruction of churches, devastation of provinces and cities, enslavement of loyal Catholics, and expansion of heresy.[54]

Your ministers, the *Admonitio* continued, have adopted the Machiavellian position that this war is merely a secular matter without relevance to religion. We preserve our state by reducing the power of Spain. If religion suffers, that is not our concern; the maintenance of states is not to be neglected for any reason whatsoever. The realm is governed by the king; only souls are ruled by Christ. If our confederates do evil, that is their affair; the crime will be imputed to them but the fruits will be ours. Thus speak atheists who think themselves Catholic but mock God under the guise of serving the public good, the author said, making one of the most telling thrusts in the entire tract.[55] In point of fact, he continued, a king who consents to and facilitates an action is responsible for its fruits. He who lets in the wolves must answer for their deeds. He may claim to have no ill will toward the Catholic faith but he is in alliance with those who do. It is the office of a Catholic king to protect the faith and exert all efforts to extirpate heresy in his realm because he took this obligation with his crown. To support and cooperate with Huguenots is evil but it is worse to spread heresy abroad and shed the blood of Christians. There is no pretext that justifies such crimes.[56]

Indeed, he continued, it is impossible to separate religion and justice because no law or right permits the violation of religion. Our war is unjust because it is against God and the Church; the cause of our enemies is just because no one has the right to force Catholics to submit to heretics. If this war had merely to do with riches and power, there would be room for argument, but since it concerns

[53] *Ibid.*, pp. 2-4.   [54] *Ibid.*, pp. 5-6.   [55] *Ibid.*, pp. 7-8.
[56] *Ibid.*, pp. 9-11.

faith and souls there is none. Catholic princes are bound to enter this war on the side of religion. Since this is true, the cause of our enemies is just and ours is unjust.[57] This sweeping condemnation he followed by asking what gave the French the right to intervene diplomatically throughout Europe and cited many instances in which they interfered in relations between states, always in favor of the enemies of the Hapsburgs.[58] Furthermore, by what right do we wage war against the Spanish? We wish to reduce them because they are too rich and powerful. If they engage in an unjust war, let us resist them with all equity, but prosperity and power are no justifications for war. One does not attack his neighbor because of his success. To do so would destroy society and cause chaos; force would reign and virtue would languish.[59] For this reason, our success is not assured, he said, reviewing the precarious military situation. The royal counselors are greatly to blame for placing the king in such a position. But the pope may be forced to act against the king himself by using the traditional arms of the Church and absolving his subjects from their oaths of allegiance to him. When a prince bears arms against religion, his subjects are bound not to follow but to resist him; they cannot aid him with arms or money because his commands are unjust and they would be aiding the persecution of the true faith.[60] The king's counselors are in fact excommunicate because of the evil nature of their advice. The author concluded by indicating his willingness to sacrifice his life for his king and his fatherland and appealing to Louis XIII to cast off the war, thus preserving his personal piety and the peace of Christendom.[61]

DEFENSES OF RICHELIEU'S VALTELLINE POLICY

This brief summary of the *Admonitio*, which is inadequate to indicate the vehemence and cogency of the original, suffices to show that it attacked Richelieu's most vulnerable position and in certain areas

[57] *Ibid*., p. 11.   [58] *Ibid*., pp. 15-18.   [59] *Ibid*., p. 19.
[60] *Ibid*., p. 20.   [61] *Ibid*., p. 21.

penetrated to the quick. With a single blow, the author of the *Admonitio* seemed to sweep aside all earlier justifications of Richelieu's policies. The Cardinal therefore exerted every effort to answer the tract and to combat its teachings which he knew to be very influential with thousands of his compatriots. To do so required action on several fronts, and Richelieu accordingly sought the help of several of his ablest pamphleteers. First he turned to Fancan whose *Miroir du temps passé*[62] was the first of a series of officially inspired defenses of French policy and contains considerable evidence that the Cardinal played a part in determining its contents.[63] Briefly, Fancan's thesis was that the *dévot* faction was identical with the former Ligueurs in placing religion first and seeking to subvert the state. The greater part of the pamphlet listed innumerable instances of treason by the Catholic League, interference in French political affairs by the Jesuits and papal envoys, and efforts to counter French diplomacy in various parts of Europe, not to mention the deeds of Châtel and Ravaillac. True to his earlier position, Fancan emphasized the practical dangers of ultramontanism to the state and denied that religion should assume priority over patriotism or interested policy. Instead, he said, one should be a "good Christian, Catholic Frenchman, and good patriot to live and die in the Church and under the obedience of our king."[64] His main purpose, however, was not to define the place of religion in human affairs but to denounce its use by the ultramontane faction which was seeking to destroy French independence and promote Spanish endeavors toward universal monarchy. As always, Fancan argued from the standpoint of political necessity and the justice of policies that were needed to preserve the integrity of the realm.

Although Fancan presented a strong case from the viewpoint of state interests and French patriotism, he did not meet the argument of the *Admonitio* that French policy was iniquitous because it aided heretics and seriously compromised the Catholic cause. For this purpose, Richelieu wisely turned to others in his entourage. The

---

[62] Fancan, *Le Miroir du temps passé*, n.p., 1625.
[63] Deloche, pp. 292-95.   [64] *Le Miroir*, p. 48.

result was the famous *Catholique d'estat*, one of the most important justifications of his policies to appear during this period.[65] The work is usually attributed to the converted Protestant minister, Jérémie Ferrier, under whose name it appeared, but it seems to have been a cooperative production by a group that Deloche calls Richelieu's *conseil de conscience* and included Ferrier, Father Joseph, Bérulle, and possibly several other high-ranking ecclesiastics.[66] That Richelieu should seek the aid of such men speaks volumes concerning his purposes and the nature of the resulting work. The tract also contains evidence that Richelieu himself supervised its composition and extensively retouched the finished product.[67] It was therefore one of his most significant efforts at this time to justify his policies on the basis of their inherent values and to develop an acceptable concept of reason of state.

The *Catholique d'estat* is a more complex work than the *Admonitio* primarily because Richelieu's ultramontane critics adhered to a simpler intellectual position, the unqualified supremacy of theological values over all human activity. In the debate concerning the relations between politics and morals, this posture gave its pro-

[65] Jérémie Ferrier, *Le Catholique d'estat ou Discours politique des alliances du roy très-Chrestien contre les calomnies des ennemis de son estat*, Paris, 1625. Also in Paul Hay du Chastelet, ed., *Recueil de diverses pièces pour servir à l'histoire*, Paris, 1635. My references are to the *Recueil*.

[66] Deloche, pp. 297-309.

[67] *Ibid.*, pp. 309-15. Some of Deloche's arguments are based upon phraseology and are therefore uncertain, as the case of Dedouvres illustrates. There is, however, substantial evidence that Richelieu guided the construction of this tract and retouched it before publication. Joseph Lecler, in his important article, "Politique nationale et idée chrétienne dans les temps modernes," *Etudes: Revue fondée en 1856 par les pères de la Compagnie de Jésus*, CCXIV (1933), 698, states that the *Catholique d'estat* takes a more secular position than that of Richelieu or Father Joseph. The authorship of the pamphlet and Richelieu's approval of it, however, indicate that he was entirely willing to see his position supported with its type of argumentation. Also, it is to be noted that a document which was largely based upon the *Catholique d'estat* was used in the compilation of Richelieu's memoirs. (Printed in *Mémoirs du Cardinal de Richelieu*, Paris, 1921, Vol. v, Appendix II.) Thus it would seem that the *Catholique d'estat* unquestionably embodied an officially approved justification of Richelieu's policies. All translations from this and other works in this book are mine.

ponents the substantial advantages of simplicity and universality. On the other hand, the Cardinal believed that affairs of state, particularly those of a Christian monarchy, were possessed of a special nature and significance of their own. His conception of coordinate church and state ascribed important common qualities to both, such as divine ordination and similar religious purposes and values, but at the same time he maintained that each was limited to its proper sphere and participated in unique activities according to the nature of its mission. He consequently believed the state to be endowed with special qualities which set it apart from ordinary human concerns, raised it in the scale of values, and permitted it to function according to a unique standard of justice. The position was more complex than that of the ultramontane theologians and required more diversified supporting argumentation. Furthermore, the *Catholique d'estat* bears the marks of a composite work, the product of many minds, and lacks the cogency of a single polished effort. There is, however, an inner consistency to its varied contents since all support the view that enlightened policy for the benefit of the French state was sanctioned by its religious nature and purposes.

This complexity of concepts is visible even in the dedicatory epistle of the *Catholique d'estat*, an extravagant eulogy of Louis XIII in which the divinity of kings, their inspiration from on high, and the necessity of obedience by the subjects are set forth in elaborate terms:

It is because of God's will and on his authority that kings reign. And whenever Your Majesty performs royal acts as you customarily do, you have the honor of lending your services to God and appearing as his associate in ordering the universe. You have the honor of having at your side God who urges you forward, causes you to act, and cooperates with you in such manner that you are never without God who is more present in the actions of kings than other men because He guides all others through them. It is a glory above the thoughts and speech of mortals that kings are the most glorious instruments of divine Providence in the government of the world. The ancients who were not flatterers called you *corporeal and living gods,* and God himself has taught men the same language and desires that you be called gods. And since he calls you this, he wishes that you be gods and detests all who seek to tie your hands, diminish your rights, decry your acts that should be venerated, and attempt to be judges and censors of Your Majesty in things where you have only God as your judge . . . . In your rule, Sire, you have nothing above you but God alone. There is no power on earth to which you must render an account for the government of your state. The ancient maxim of all your ancestors, which was born with the monarchy and will never be obliterated from the hearts of Frenchmen, is that you hold your realm from God alone and the strength of your arms. Even if this were not true, your love of justice is so great and you are so religious that there is no upright man anywhere who would not revere you, as there is none of your subjects who does not lower his eyes before your rule and revere your laws as made with the counsel, the will and the command of God.[68]

After applying this to Louis XIII's foreign policy, the author concluded on a different note:

In other states, as they grow in strength, things often occur whose justice is not immediately apparent. This cannot happen in France because the motives and reasons for decisions are not made public. Those who do not understand them should keep silent and recognize what is true everywhere, that the justice of realms has other laws than the justice that is in force between individuals . . . . The laws of realms are not contained in the books of jurisconsults but in the virtue, dexterity and diligence of kings. That is, force is the queen of the virtues and in affairs of state ordinary laws are not heard, and he has greater right on his side who has power over states. Nevertheless it is always safest to have God and right on one's side, as all know that Your Majesty has, and that you prefer justice to all the conquests in the world. For this reason you will not fail to gain what you wish, and we rightly believe that this will be a most honorable

[68] *Catholique d'estat*, pp. 85-86. Italics in the original.

peace with all, through which the dignity of your crown will be preserved and the protection of your allies assured.[69]

This emphasis upon will and force may seem to introduce a discordant note in a work that emphasized the consonance of royal policy with religious values, yet it was a fundamental component of divine right sovereignty and the view that kings, because of their superhuman endowments and unique position among men, were permitted to conduct their affairs according to a special standard of justice.

The opening section of the *Catholique d'estat* dwells extensively upon the concept of the "Catholic of state." Since it is the keynote of the entire tract and is presented in meaningful but complex terms it is best to allow the key passages to speak for themselves.

> In earlier times and for sixteen centuries ... it has been a sign of true religion, good life, and genuine piety to love kings and to pray to God for them, not only for their persons but also their decisions, the power of their arms, and the greatness of their states. And until this miserable time that has befallen us, it was never a source of blame for a Catholic to love the state in which he was born and to desire its preservation and aggrandizement. It is a monstrous thing for Christianity that it is now an insult to call a man a Catholic of state and *politique*, for whoever is not is a traitor to his country; he is a hypocrite and an enemy of God and his word. He is impious and an atheist who does not believe in the word of God or the practices of the Catholic Church during so many centuries; he does not even believe what he professes daily at mass where prayers for the king are always said.[70]

Here appears the crucial objective of the work: to associate the king and the state with God and highest religious values, all within the framework of Catholicism. The Christian subject, a Catholic of state, was bound to revere both God and the king because such was

[69] *Ibid.*, p. 86.
[70] *Ibid.*, p. 92. It is impossible to translate the French word *politique* accurately with a single English word or phrase.

required by his faith. After listing the prayers that were customarily said in many lands for their monarchs and citing the words of the coronation ceremony, the author concluded that "the enemies of our kings are the enemies of God; they should therefore be ours. And we are not upright men if we do not regard them as our enemies."[71] From the standpoint of the subjects, royal policy was just because it was the work of the divinely authorized and inspired monarch. Quoting St. Thomas to the effect that a war is just when it is ordered by a sovereign ruler, is for a just cause, and the intention is right, the author insisted that this fitted the French situation perfectly.[72]

The logical corollary of this exaltation of the king and his policies, of course, was complete submission to them without question.

> The true Catholic of state and *politique*, that is, an upright, god-fearing man who is not a limited, factious Catholic and a traitor to his country, obeys the law of God without examining the actions of kings. He knows that the power of states is from heaven. If wars occur to punish the universe, it is true that he does not desire them and ardently prays God for peace among Christian princes; it is true that he is afflicted in his soul and expresses his grief before the altar at mass, beseeching God through prayer to lessen his ire against Christendom, but for all that he does not cease to obey God by praying for his king and the success of his armies. In his uncertainty regarding public misfortune and his duty, he lowers his head, fills the air with lamentations, and leaves the outcome to God. For He alone protects states and gives them peace or war as He pleases. Subjects may not censor nor judge in order to determine the justice or injustice of the arms of their kings; their role is merely obedience and fidelity. The laws of the state differ from those of the casuists, and the maxims of the schoolmen have nothing in common with politics. Governments would be very distraught if their secrets, the force that moves them, were given over to the people for judgment and if they required approval

[71] *Ibid.*, p. 94.   [72] *Ibid.*, p. 95.

by empty minds and perverse self-seekers who would judge states in the classroom and the guidance of monarchies and the rules of government like those of grammar. Whenever this madness begins, all order in the universe is broken, states are destroyed, religion is despised, and because of imaginary ills that frighten the people they are sent headlong toward inevitable ruin. Kings generally make war to bring peace to their subjects and security to their states. In such times as these, the only way to succeed is not to encur the contempt of our neighbors because of weakness. If we do not threaten them, they will boldly advance; if we do not raise our hands, they will never lower theirs. This is why those who decry war often decry peace and destroy their own security when they criticize action. The remedy for this is for everyone to remain in his vocation without encroaching upon those to which he was not called. On this depends all order among men in all elements of society. In households, if this is not observed, families will be disrupted by horrible confusion. If the valet wishes to fill the role of the master and influence his decisions, if the wife seeks to dictate to the husband, if the children wish to encroach upon the authority of their father, all will go to ruin. In politics it is the same. If the physician attempts to judge theological controversies, if the lawyer seeks to determine matters of conscience, if the magistrate amuses himself with Aristotelian disputations, no theologian or monk of any order whatsoever would not criticize this as most pernicious confusion. Is it not the same and even worse for a theologian who is confined to his cell to seek to obtrude himself as a councillor of state? . . . And is it therefore not a source of horror to observe that some of them thrust themselves even into the sanctuary of the state, seek to penetrate the most important mysteries, and, with license punishable under all sorts of law, boldly seek to condemn, as the Scriptures say, those things that they do not understand?[73]

The authors of the *Mysteria politica* and the *Admonitio* could not

[73] *Ibid.*, pp. 96-97.

be Frenchmen, the passage continues, because "French blood does not flow in the veins of traitors. To be French and hate one's king, condemn him, excommunicate him, criticize his religion and that of his council, and seek to destroy his state . . . are things incompatible."[74]

These very pregnant pages of the work contain the essence of the position that Richelieu and his supporters adopted in the face of their most severe critics. The true Catholic of state or believing subject should submit to the will of God and the king's policies as a matter of faith. All persons regardless of their vocations should remain in their stations and refrain from criticizing royal actions which were beyond their comprehension. This injunction, it should be noted, was pointedly applied to the theologians when it was insisted that "the laws of the state differ from those of the casuists and the maxims of the schoolmen have nothing in common with politics." Having neither the responsibilities nor the experience of government, they were completely ignorant of the mysteries of state. This denial that theologians might evaluate the justice of royal policies would seem to establish a cleavage between religion and politics, divorcing the latter from religious criteria and leaving it entirely in the hands of the practitioners. It is true that Richelieu's idea of coordinate church and state went far toward denying that theologians might be experts in political matters, but this does not mean that he advocated the secularization of politics. Rather, it was Richelieu's conviction that the rulers of a Christian state, *because* they were Christian, were thoroughly capable of establishing just standards of political conduct in accordance with religious values.

This crucially important contention was developed at length in the remaining sixty pages of the work. After recalling Louis XIII's extensive efforts in behalf of Catholicism, the disruption caused by militant ecclesiastics during the Wars of Religion, and many instances of Spanish aggression under the guise of supporting religion,[75] the author returned to the charge that France was pursuing a purely secular policy. His answer he found in the king's *conseil de conscience* which was his constant guide.

[74] *Ibid.*, p. 98.   [75] *Ibid.*, pp. 98-108.

We know by God's grace the effects of the *conseil de conscience* that controls the states of princes . . . . For we do not desire the counsel of Machiavelli or the south for our kings. The counsel of God is always necessary, certain, useful, and followed by infinite blessings. The prince who not only is good but seeks good and just counsel is among other princes like the sun among the stars. How rare is the counsel held in good conscience that causes evil! When a king governs his state well, pities the afflicted, eases the burden on his people, aids his allies, and protects the weak against the strong, it is a praiseworthy effect of his *conseil de conscience*! When he protects himself against the snares of his enemies, preserves the laws of majesty, gives special favor to no man; when he loves his state so dearly that he forestalls all dangers that menace it; when he guards his frontiers and does not allow himself to be surrounded on all sides by powers that may devour him; when he severely punishes his perfidious and disloyal subjects if they continue in their malice, O God, how good is the *conseil de conscience*![76]

In illustration, the author pointed to the fact that all the major officers and institutions of the crown were Catholic and served as a great *conseil de conscience*.[77] And as proof of its efficacy, he proceeded to examine the Hapsburgs' alliances in order to determine whose *conseil de conscience* was the more influential. France is allied with the Turks and Spain with the Persians; France with the Palatinate and Spain with Saxony; France with Hesse and Spain with Darmstadt; France with England but only after breaking her ties with Spain. France protects Geneva; the Hapsburgs protect Wittenberg. Charles V legally recognized heresy in the Empire long before the Edict of Nantes and used Protestant soldiers in his armies long before Henry IV.[78] This section concluded with a remarkable paragraph from the pen of Bérulle himself:

I report these actions, alliances and histories not in order to blame these princes, whose influence is great in the universe and

---

[76] *Ibid.*, pp. 110-111.   [77] *Ibid.*, pp. 111-12.
[78] *Ibid.*, pp. 113-17.

whose acts are illustrious throughout Christendom, but to blame those theologians who would render them blameworthy by their theology if it were legitimate and canonical. These doctors are so blinded by their desire to injure us that they do not realize that in order to weaken us in one instance they betray their own princes and convict them in a hundred similar instances. While they injure them, I honor them for their exalted quality and their most commendable conduct, for they have been able to gain such advantage on certain occasions that Christendom benefited, or at least was not notably concerned. Their zeal has not been lessened by such alliances; their piety has in no way changed because of them. Without involving their religion or consciences, they entered into these relationships to preserve what they had acquired and to conquer what they judged necessary. I shall speak frankly, but I beg these good doctors and theologians to do us the kindness and courtesy to believe that our rulers are as good Christians and as intelligent as those of the House of Austria when it comes to using similar questionable means toward the same ends and advantages, and with the same conscience. I mean with a conscience sufficiently clear and strong to guide these untoward events and turn them to the benefit of the state, the Church and Christendom. I do not think they can deny us this favor, as I would also not wish to oblige them to defend according to their rules all the acts that history attributes to us. We and they should revere monarchies and not make ourselves judges of great kings. In particular, the author of the *Admonitio* would be ridiculous to my way of thinking if he did not honestly recognize that the states of the House of Austria adhere to a justice that is not measured by ordinary rules and that their councils follow laws other than those of the Universities of Louvain and Salamanca.[79]

This significant contribution by the saintliest servant of the French crown during this period demonstrates that he thoroughly accepted

[79] *Ibid.*, p. 117. The fact that Bérulle contributed this and the following passages to the *Catholique d'estat* is established by M. Houssaye, *Le Cardinal de Bérulle et le Cardinal de Richelieu*, Paris, 1875, pp. 63-66.

the basic proposition of the *Catholique d'estat*: that theologians had neither the right nor the competence to judge rulers and that the latter, as Christians, might legitimately conduct their affairs according to standards other than those of the schoolmen. Far from divorcing religion and politics, Bérulle was merely maintaining that Christian kings, because of the nature of their authority and obligations, enjoyed a certain autonomy under God and therefore might justifiably engage in practices that were not directly subject to judgment by theologians. Necessity, he maintained, frequently forced Christian princes, both French and Spanish, to indulge in practices that lay outside the sphere of religion or were questionable in themselves but which ultimately benefited Christianity because of the rulers' beliefs and their services to Christian states. For Bérulle, these measures included alliances with heretic powers, as he made clear in a second interpolation concerning the Valtelline episode:

I do not wish to enter into the essentials of this affair . . . . It suffices for me to state in a few words what I know and what, to my way of thinking, no one can deny or blame. It is that before their heresy, the Grisons were allies of France, as early as the time of King Louis XII. Heresy alone does not suffice to deprive them of their sovereignty or their right to protection and assistance. France, Italy, Savoy, and Venice are still good Christian and Catholic states and are more interested than the Grisons in the outcome of this quarrel. Even the Holy See will some day pay dearly for its role in the matter if this is not soon arrested. The very liberty of all Christendom is involved, a much greater consideration than the liberty of a single valley. The king undertakes to aid and protect the Grisons only while aiding and protecting the Catholic religion both among the Grisons and in the Valtelline, and even proclaims this to all Christendom. His piety is as pure, his pledge as good, and his protection as sure as that of the Governor of Milan even though he is not as nearby. In fact, before these events, His Majesty considered the matter and would have handled it by efficacious and peaceful means if trouble had not been started in the valley while our

137

armies were occupied in France taking from the Huguenots the cities and provinces that they had seized.[80]

This contribution by Bérulle is colored by his experience in negotiating with representatives of the papacy, but it demonstrates his belief that Richelieu's policy for the benefit of France, including his alliances with heretics, was just because it would redound to the benefit of Catholicism.

The remainder of the work reiterates at length the thesis that heretic princes are legitimate rulers and Catholic sovereigns may make alliances with them as circumstances require. This is supported by extensive examination of Biblical precedents and contemporary alignments.[81] In fact, the diplomatic position of France is the most innocent in Europe because "she has lost a part of her territory and does not hold an inch that belongs to any other ruler in the world. She has the allies that necessity of state, the malice of her enemies, and the prudence of her kings (the ancestors of him who is presently reigning) make necessary. But she does not base her security upon these secondary factors and human measures which divine Providence permits to men in need. Her hope is in God who has protected her for twelve centuries and will always be able to defend her in the future."[82] The danger is not that religion will suffer but that the Hapsburgs will dominate Europe; current French policy is her only salvation. Richelieu has given excellent guidance to the troubled realm and is admired by all upright Frenchmen. Criticisms of his policies are so much wind and smoke which will be dissipated. The best attitude is to distrust and ignore such writings, for in the end God will protect the king and scatter his enemies.[83]

[80] *Catholique d'estat*, pp. 126-27. [81] *Ibid.*, pp. 128-48.
[82] *Ibid.*, p. 148.
[83] *Ibid.*, pp. 149-56. The fact that Louis XIII himself regarded his foreign policy as justified by arguments such as those in the *Catholique d'estat* and wished this to be publicized may be clear from the following work. N. Rigault, *Apologeticus pro rege christianissimo Ludovico XIII adversus factiosae Admonitionis calumnias, in causa Principum foederatorum*, Paris, 1626. Rigault was a keeper of the royal library and a man of considerable learning. According to its privilege, the *Apologeticus* was authorized by the king who com-

Never before had Richelieu and his aides published so fundamental a statement of their ideological position. In the ferment of
a major crisis, the Cardinal sought the help of some of his ablest
and most trusted contemporaries and produced a document that
presented his fundamental political concepts to the literate world.
That the *Catholique d'estat* was in part a *pièce de circonstance* cannot be denied, yet its parallelisms with earlier and later statements by
Richelieu indicate that it incorporated his basic beliefs. Fundamentally, his theory of just government was built on his concept of the
unique rights, nature, and purposes of the Christian state. Louis
XIII and his First Minister alone understood the mysteries of state
and governed according to the special justice that adhered to divinely
established monarchies. If they deviated from the dogmatic positions of the theologians, this was because of their superior understanding of matters of government rather than any desire to violate
Christian principles. In fact, the divinely established relationships
between coordinate church and state decreed that in their sphere,
the king and his minister were more knowledgeable than all others
concerning the proper measures with which to guide France toward
her higher objectives. And since France was a Christian state under
the leadership of a devout monarch who would ensure that all official
acts accorded with Christian morality, policies that benefited France
served the cause of the Christian religion. This was Cardinal Richelieu's understanding of just government, his version of reason of
state. That it was widely accepted by men of deep religious convictions is evidenced by their continued support of him during the
first years of his ministry.

---

missioned Rigault to write and publish it as an answer to the *Admonitio*. In
many ways the *Apologeticus* is similar to the *Catholique d'estat*. By examining
French policy since Henry IV, Rigault attempts to demonstrate that every
development either aided the Catholic cause (action in the Valtelline, alliances
with the English, Dutch, and Turk) or did not concern religion and was
merely for purposes of protection which is permitted both by religion and
natural law. He concludes that this is sufficient to demonstrate the "piety, justice, and necessity" of the French alliances. It seems safe to assume that mention of royal authorization in the privilege would not have been made without the king's approval.

The Cardinal had stated his position but almost at once was forced to reiterate it with greater precision. In answer to the *Catholique d'estat*, a group of ultramontane theologians in the Netherlands published a pamphlet entitled *Christiano-politicus* which satirized and ridiculed the very idea of a Catholic of state. An immediate reply was required, and Richelieu quickly engineered the publication of the *Advertissement à tous les Estats de l'Europe* which restated the essentials of the *Catholique d'estat* in condensed form.[84] The *Advertissement* is usually ascribed to Ferrier, but this time there is ample evidence that Richelieu himself dictated large portions of the work, closely following the *Catholique d'estat*, and that Ferrier acted only as his scribe.[85] The only novel element in the *Advertissement* occurs in the introductory *Au Lecteur*, where Richelieu discussed and defended the concept of the Catholic of state. Various terms such as *Catholique d'estat, Catholique de cour*, and *Catholique du palais* are used as reproaches, he said, adding *Cardinal d'estat* to the list as a personal note. But in fact, Christianity requires subjects to love their king and to support the state. The phrase "*Catholique d'estat*" therefore distinguishes a true subject from a former Ligueur or enemy of the state and simply means *Catholique français*. "I would like to know whether it is worse to say *Catholique d'estat* than to say *Chrestien politique*, and whether it is not the same thing to say *Politique chrestien* and *homme d'estat Catholique*. For what is a *Catholique d'estat* but an *homme d'estat Catholique*?"[86] This was Richelieu's basic position: a loyal Catholic is a loyal subject, and a Christian statesman (such as himself) is loyal to both church and state. The body of the *Advertissement* consists of fifteen propositions of which all but the last recite the usual criticisms of Spanish policy from the *Catholique d'estat* as a "warning" to the various European states. He concluded on his favorite note that all subjects should faithfully support their king against all his enemies, includ-

---

[84] *Advertissement à tous les Estats de l'Europe, touchant les maximes fondamentales du gouvernement et des desseins des Espagnols*, Paris, 1625. The dedicatory epistle refers to the *Christiano-politicus* and indicates its nature.

[85] Deloche, pp. 349-52.　　　　[86] *Advertissement, Au Lecteur*, n.p.

ing those who would tamper with their loyalties, and that to do otherwise was to betray one's country and to sin against God.[87]

Because the *Mysteria politica* and the *Admonitio* were generally believed to have emanated from Jesuit sources abroad, it would have been surprising if the French Jesuits had not become involved in the debate. Richelieu, however, was well aware of the strength of ultramontane sentiment in France and had no desire to quarrel with the order. The *Catholique d'estat* refrained from criticizing them directly but extensively cited Jesuit authors, especially Mariana. Another work that assumed this position was Gabriel Le Guay's *Alliances du Roy avec le Turc* which appeared in November 1625, was written at Richelieu's request, and went even further in making use of Jesuit authorities.[88] This extensive treatise presented a massively documented case for the French alliance with the Turk from various standpoints. It was justified by Biblical precedents; the Spanish have done worse. It gives advantages to the Christians in the Near East and prevents the alliance of Spain and Turkey—the worst possible thing for Christendom. The king's word must be kept even to the Sultan. A crusade against the infidel is to be desired but until this happens the alliance must be preserved because of the danger to the state. And finally, it prevents the Spanish from achieving universal monarchy. These various arguments essentially justified the alliance on practical grounds, that is, the safety of the French state. Although Le Guay attempted to demonstrate that the alliance benefited Christianity, Richelieu, through him, was saying that the French tie with the infidel was rendered legitimate by pre-

---

[87] *Ibid.*, pp. 15-16.

[88] *Alliances du Roy avec le Turc et autres, justifiées contre les calomnies des Espagnols et de leurs partisans*, Paris, 1625. For Le Guay's relations with Richelieu and the Jesuits, see Deloche, pp. 326-28. On the question of French diplomatic relations with the Ottoman Empire, see G. Tongas, *Les Relations de la France avec l'Empire Ottoman durant la première moitié du XVIIᵉ siècle*, Toulouse, 1942, and C. D. Rouillard, *The Turk in French History, Thought and Literature (1520-1660)*, Paris [1939], Pt. I. The background of Richelieu's policy of allying France with the Turkish and Protestant powers and its implications concerning the secularization of governmental policy are discussed in J. Lecler, "Politique nationale et idée chrétienne dans les temps modernes," *Etudes*, ccxiv (1933), 385-405, 546-64, 683-702.

vailing conditions in European politics. In this instance, the argument was not extensively challenged, an indication that ultramontane opinion regarded alliances with the infidel as considerably less dangeous to the faith than those with Protestant powers.

Although Richelieu sought to avoid entanglement with the French Jesuits in the controversy over the *Admonitio*, they were unwilling to let sleeping dogs lie and felt that they must openly dissociate themselves from the book. For this purpose they persuaded Jacques Pelletier, a close associate of Richelieu, to publish an *Apologie ou Défense pour les pères Jésuites*.[89] In this labored tract, Pelletier did not refer directly to the *Admonitio* but merely attempted to show that the French Jesuits could not have written it because of their unfailing loyalty to the king. Because of widespread belief to the contrary and the fact that no official publication had accused the Jesuits of writing the *Admonitio*, the effort completely backfired and merely served to convince doubters that the book was of Jesuit origin. There soon appeared an officially inspired *Examen de l'Apologie du sieur Pelletier pour les pères Jésuites*[90] which scornfully rejected Pelletier's arguments but still attempted to spare the order by stating "it is not a question of the Jesuits but the authors of those damnable books,"[91] after which the usual charges against Spain were repeated. The episode benefited neither party but illustrated how Richelieu was able to keep a tight rein on the discussion of delicate and potentially dangerous issues.

During this inconsequential joust with the Jesuits, Cardinal Richelieu was engaged in a much more serious matter, the suppression of the offending tracts and their condemnation by the highest ecclesiastical authorities in the realm. Of these objectives, the former proved much easier to accomplish than the latter. On October 30, 1625, the *procureur du roi* secured a decree from the *lieutenant civil* of Paris condemning the *Mysteria politica* and

---

[89] *Apologie ou Défense pour les pères Jésuites contre les calomnies de leurs ennemys*, Paris, 1625. Also in *Mercure français*, Vol. XI, 29-65, second pagination.

[90] Paris, 1625. In *Mercure français*, Vol. XI, 65-79, second pagination.

[91] *Examen*, p. 70.

the *Admonitio* as "pernicious wicked and seditious, filled with false facts and containing many maxims and propositions contrary to the authority of kings established by God, the security of their persons, the people's repose, and attempting to incite them to rebellion under a false and simulated pretext of religion."[92] The books were forthwith burned by the hangman in the Place de Grève. The decree also forbade anyone "to read or keep them, on pain of death," and applied the same penalty to all "printers, booksellers, and distributors who printed, sold, or exhibited them." This action was within the royal prerogative and presented no problems. The Faculty of Theology at the Sorbonne was similarly cooperative. On November 26, the *Admonitio* (only) was denounced by the Syndic of the Faculty before the assembled members and a committee of seven doctors was appointed to examine the matter. Their report was received and approved by the Faculty on December 1 and condemned the *Admonitio* in essentially the same terms: it was pernicious and dangerous, disparaged the royal dignity, falsely used religion to foment sedition, undermined loyalty to the crown, broke the ties between ruler and subjects, and contained much that was contrary to the true doctrine of the Church.[93]

The Assembly of the Clergy proved to be much less tractable. In fact, the disputes within that body concerning the *Admonitio* vividly indicated the strength of ecclesiastical opposition to both the independence of the secular power and the existence of a special standard of justice in political affairs. To be sure, many high-ranking French ecclesiastics were strongly Gallican and patriotic, but the concept of papal supremacy over kings continued to be upheld in many quarters. Its potency was clearly recalled by all who had witnessed the quarrels over the first article in the *cahier* of the third estate a decade earlier during the Estates General of 1614-1615, an episode that Richelieu had no desire to repeat. While he hoped for condemnation of the offending pamphlets by the Assembly of the

---

[92] *Mercure français*, Vol. xi, 1062. The entire decree is printed on pp. 1062-63. Also in *Mercure jésuite*, 734-36.

[93] *Mercure français*, Vol. xi, 1066-67. *Mercure jésuite*, 744-46.

Clergy, the most prestigious ecclesiastical institution in France, he knew that he must treat the body with caution.[94]

On November 7, 1625, the Assembly discussed the dangers of the *Admonitio* and requested Léonor d'Estampes who was Bishop of Chartres and a close associate of Richelieu to frame a condemnation. At subsequent meetings, the Bishop was instructed to translate his statement into Latin and add consideration of the *Mysteria politica*. On December 13, during an overburdened session, he began to read the document, but when the delegates realized its length they approved it without a complete hearing. Within a fortnight, d'Estampes' *Déclaration* condemning the offending tracts was printed with official approval and was distributed to members of the royal administration.[95] It came to the attention of Spada, the papal nuncio, on December 28, and he at once realized that he had a serious problem on his hands because the document contained much that was contrary to the ultramontane view of papal supremacy over kings.

The specific criticisms of the *Mysteria politica* and the *Admonitio* in the opening pages of the Declaration were identical with those of the Faculty of Theology: irreverence toward the king, unjustified criticism of his alliances, and false use of religion to foment rebellion and destroy the realm.[96] It is likely that only this portion was read before the Assembly. The Bishop, however, merely used these statements to preface what became a sizable treatise eulogizing the majesty and power of the monarchy. So extravagant were his words

[94] The best account of the tortuous maneuvers of the Assembly relative to this matter is in P. Blet, *Le Clergé de France et la monarchie: Étude sur les Assemblées générales du clergé de 1615 à 1666*, Rome, 1959, Vol. I, Bk. II, Chap. 3. See also V. Martin, "L'Adoption du gallicanisme politique par le clergé de France," *Revue des sciences religieuses*, VII (1927), 181-205.

[95] *Cardinalium, Archiepiscoporum, Episcoporum caeterorumque qui ex universis Regni Provinciis, Ecclesiasticis Comitiis interfuerunt, de Anonyms quibusdam et famosis Libellis Sententia*: 13. Decembris 1625. *Déclaration de Messieurs les Cardinaux, Archevesques, Evesques, et autres ecclésiastiques, Deputez en l'Assemblée Générale du Clergé de France, tenue à Paris. Touchant certains Libelles, faicts contre le Roy et son Estat*, Paris, 1626. The Latin and French versions are in the *Mercure jésuite*, 746-97. The French version is in the *Mercure français*, Vol. XI, 1068-95. My citations are to the French version which was published separately.

[96] *Déclaration*, pp. 3-11

that he raised the sovereign to great heights and implicitly denied papal supremacy over the secular power. One of his initial statements, it is to be noted, seems to have been borrowed from no less a work than Bérulle's *Grandeurs de Jésus* which had been published two years earlier: "Not only are kings ordained by God; they are themselves gods . . . . It follows that those who are called gods are gods not by essence but by participation, not by nature but by grace, not for always but for a certain time, as true lieutenants of the all-powerful God and, by imitating his divine Majesty, represent his image here below."[97] Continuing, d'Estampes asserted, "There is no one who does not hold and believe that he [the king] is in no way mortal but instead is something very like the Deity and similar to Him. For those to whom God communicates his power are given part of his majesty which is the most salutary protection of the state, so that they do not constrain their subjects to obey through terror but gently confine them to their duties by means of their reverence for the divine majesty that is imprinted on their foreheads."[98] Complete, unquestioning obedience was the logical corollary which he spelled out in a passage that is reminiscent of others in the *Catholique d'estat* and Richelieu's *Instruction du chrestien* and need not be repeated here.[99] Such adulation of monarchy was fashionable in many quarters, especially among the jurists, administrators, and strongly Gallican clergy, but d'Estampes presented it in such extreme form that it was certain to arouse opposition in the Assembly.

Not satisfied with interpreting obedience merely as a matter of faith, d'Estampes advanced to the position that the king must be obeyed even if he turns wicked. Rebellion is for heretics and not Catholics, he insisted, citing the voluntary submission of Christ and the early Christian martyrs to the pagan secular power. All true Catholics refrain from criticizing the words, acts, and thoughts of their king like so many censors, for to do so offends God because

[97] *Ibid.*, p. 12. The passage in Bérulle's *Grandeurs de Jésus* from which this may have been taken is cited in Pt. I, n. 238. It is noteworthy that Léonor d'Estampes was one of the bishops who approved Bérulle's work.

[98] *Déclaration*, p. 13.

[99] *Ibid.*, p. 16. See n. 73 and Pt. I, n. 208.

He alone may judge kings. David who committed adultery and murder was guilty only before God and subject to no other law, for kings do not endure the penalties of the law because they are protected by the majesty of their rule.[100] This statement went much further than the great majority of absolutist tracts because it not only placed the king above the law but also absolved him of guilt even for the greatest crimes, except in the eyes of God. Few proponents of absolutism ventured to take such an extreme stand. Implicitly it removed the king from any papal jurisdiction over him, direct or indirect.

The remaining two-thirds of the Declaration reviewed French alliances with Protestant and anti-Hapsburg Catholic powers and gave the usual justifications but entered several new notes. To all criticism of royal policy, d'Estampes said, "one need answer with a single word: the king made the alliance because he willed it; he undertook war because it is just and reasonable, or better, such a war is just because he undertook it."[101] This statement reduced justice to a matter of will and echoed the extreme absolutists who maintained that the sovereign's acts were *ipso facto* just. The parallel idea that political affairs enjoy a special standard of justice also appears in the tract. In discussing the conduct of the early Christians, the Bishop said "the Romans fought against the Parthians and the Christians against Christians under a leader who was an enemy of the Christians, for they knew the difference between religion and the state and did not think they offended our Lord Jesus Christ if they rendered the Emperors what He himself had ordered to be given them."[102] Regarding the French alliance with England, "if this had been made merely for reason of state (which has no small importance in the realm) rather than any respect for religion . . . one could not condemn what has been confirmed by all the examples that we have cited."[103] As for French support of the Elector Palatine, we are in league with him as a legitimate prince. He may be a heretic but he is authorized by God. "Religion and the dignity of the state give each other mutual support and in agreement cooperate effec-

---

[100] *Ibid.*, pp. 17-25.   [101] *Ibid.*, p. 29.   [102] *Ibid.*, p. 39.
[103] *Ibid.*, p. 42.

tively. Both nevertheless have their distinct rights and each is confined within its own limits, for it is not permitted to the state to violate religion nor to religion to overthrow the state. Whoever denies this seems to criticize Jesus Christ who ordered that we render unto Caesar what is Caesar's and unto God what is God's."[104] Taken together, these statements indicate that Léonor d'Estampes went far toward an independent ethic of state policy that was free from theological determinations and whose justice depended solely upon the monarch's will.

The Declaration by the Bishop of Chartres was by far the most wide-ranging condemnation of the *Mysteria politica* and the *Admonitio* to be published with anything resembling official approval. Comparison of it with the *Catholique d'estat* and the *Advertissement* at once demonstrates that Richelieu, in the latter two tracts, assumed an essentially different position. Both he and the Bishop upheld the concept of coordinate church and state with the latter enjoying a certain independence of action in its sphere, but Richelieu emphasized the religious nature and the consequent justice of its policies whereas d'Estampes practically made the state a law unto itself. It is a mystery why the Bishop seized this opportunity to argue in such extravagant terms the divinity of kings, their immunity from the law and theological censure even when wicked, the inherent justice of any policy that they might adopt, and a unique criterion of justice in political affairs. Nothing like such an extensive case was required for the condemnation of the two tracts. Did he hope thereby to please Richelieu and others in his entourage with whom he was on familiar terms? This is possible but remains to be proved. In any event, the Declaration set forth an important and largely secularized version of reason of state, but it was not the Cardinal's. Some of d'Estampes' ideas paralleled those of Richelieu, but it is significant that neither he nor the Assembly of the Clergy approved the document.

On January 7, 1626, the Assembly was finally apprised of the contents of the Declaration and moved to reconsider it. Complex negotiations followed between Richelieu, Spada, d'Estampes, and

[104] *Ibid.*, p. 46.

Cardinal La Valette who presided over the Assembly. Within a matter of days, they agreed to a much shortened censure, a single paragraph that was similar to the statement by the Faculty of Theology.[105] This was accepted by the Assembly on January 12. The matter might have ended there had not the Parlement of Paris, always strongly Gallican, intervened by issuing a series of decrees in favor of the original Declaration.[106] Again there occurred complicated negotiations whose details are superfluous. Richelieu hoped that the dispute might be solved in such a way as to satisfy all parties, Spada, the Assembly, and the Parlement, and considered requesting d'Estampes to write a small book refuting the pamphlets.[107] The clergy took matters into their own hands, however, and a rump session of the Assembly, meeting in the Abbey of Sainte-Geneviève on February 26, framed a disavowal of d'Estampes' Declaration and approved the statement of January 12.[108] After continued friction between the Assembly and the Parlement, Richelieu directly entered the fray and caused the matter to be evoked to the royal council.[109] He also obtained a written retraction from d'Estampes which was couched in general language. Later in the year, the Bishop submitted to censure by Rome in the process of which papal supremacy over kings was specifically mentioned.[110] The episode is significant because it vividly demonstrates the strength of contemporary opposition to the immunity of states and their policies from theological judgment. It also indicates that among the proponents of reason of state, Richelieu held to a moderate position which combined the integrity of royal power with the supremacy of religious values.

Considerably before Richelieu completed his negotiations with the Assembly of the Clergy, he was inundated by a veritable flood

[105] In Blet, p. 345.

[106] On January 21, February 18, and March 3. *Mercure français*, Vol. XI, 99-107, second pagination. *Mercure jésuite*, 821-27, 830-31.

[107] *Lettres*, Vol. II, 194, 196.

[108] In Blet, pp. 352-53. *Mercure jésuite*, 827-29.

[109] Blet, p. 362. *Mercure français*, Vol. XI, 109, second pagination. *Mercure jésuite*, 834.

[110] Blet, p. 366.

of Latin pamphlets which arrived from abroad to plague him. His responses to the *Mysteria politica* and the *Admonitio* and their official condemnation seemed merely to call forth more strictures from ultramontane sources.[111] These works, many of which were quite ephemeral, began to circulate early in 1626 and continued the criticisms of Richelieu's policies that had appeared in the earlier tracts but with certain modifications. Now the satire and denunciation were directed toward Richelieu himself in unmistakable terms. There was also more objection to his relations with the Huguenots with whom he reached an accord early in February. But the fundamental criticisms of his foreign policy remained the same, as is illustrated by two of the most important tracts, the *Quæstiones quodlibeticæ*[112] and the *Sapiens francus*,[113] both of which set forth a series of penetrating questions for the Cardinal to answer. The *Quæstiones* is the more satirical and less ponderous of the two and particularly angered Richelieu, doubtless because of the aptness of its innuendo. "Are Richelieu and La Rochelle the same?" the author asked, making an obvious play on words and recalling the nickname "Cardinal de La Rochelle" that had been given Richelieu.[114] "Until now, has any Catholic writer praised our most illustrious lord [Richelieu] and any Calvinist criticized him?"[115] His seeming ambivalence toward his sacred and secular offices was satirized by such questions as "Can there be a man who is neither fish nor fowl? And if such a man were to die where would he go? To heaven or hell, to the fields of Saint-Germain-des-Prés or to the waters that are above the

[111] Lists of these pamphlets are given in the *Mercure français*, Vol. XII, 500-501, and in A. Aubery, *L'Histoire du Cardinal Duc de Richelieu*, Paris, 1660, pp. 39-40. Many are completely unobtainable today.

[112] *Quæstiones quodlibeticæ tempori præsenti accommodæ ad Illustrissimum S. R. E. Cardinalem de Rochelius seu de Rupella, Negotiorum Status in Regno Galliarum, Supremum Praefectum . . .* , n.p., 1626.

[113] *Sapiens francus G.G.R. Theologi et Admonitoris regii nuper propter nimiam suam sapientiam innocenter combusti discipulus . . .* , Paris, 1626.

[114] *Quæstiones*, question III. In the title of the work and in this question, Richelieu is spelled "Rochelieu"; La Rochelle is "Rochellanus." Aubery, p. 39, mentions the taunt, "Cardinal de La Rochelle."

[115] *Quæstiones*, question XIII.

149

skies?"[116] Richelieu's system of alliances was the object of many thrusts. "Have those who distributed royal moneys to the poor soldiers of Holland, Savoy, Lower Saxony, the Valtelline, and the English fleet achieved the sainthood of St. Lawrence, martyr and Cardinal-deacon of the Holy Roman Church?"[117] Using another figure, "Are they not obligated to work for an alliance of fire and water, heat and cold? Is there hope that they will establish peace between God and Belial?"[118] Richelieu found these serious pleasantries extremely annoying and had the *Quæstiones* condemned and burned.[119] The *Sapiens francus*, after making many of the same criticisms in a more serious vein, asked for an immediate, straightforward, and unencumbered answer.[120] Richelieu determined to oblige.

For this purpose he chose Mathieu de Morgues because of his demonstrated abilities as author of religious tracts and pamphlets. By training and instinct, Morgues was essentially a theologian. He had published controversial works combatting Calvinism,[121] and in 1620, at Richelieu's request, he wrote the *Véritez chréstiennes*[122] for the purpose of effecting a reconciliation between the Queen Mother and Louis XIII. Upon being rewarded with the post of chaplain to the Queen Mother, he seems to have demonstrated a certain eloquence in the pulpit. These factors explain why Richelieu chose Morgues to answer the charge that French policy ran counter to the interests of Catholic Christianity. For this purpose a theologian was needed, one who could reconcile Richelieu's policies with the supremacy of religious values, and Morgues had the necessary training and experience in polemical writing. To convince Catholic opinion that Richelieu's policies were justified on religious grounds, Morgues wrote his *Théologien sans passion* in answer to the flood

---

[116] *Ibid.*, question XVIII.
[117] *Ibid.*, question XV.
[118] *Ibid.*, questions XXVII, XXVIII.
[119] *Mercure français*, Vol. XI, 1122-23.
[120] *Sapiens francus*, Conclusion.
[121] *Déclaration de la volonté de Dieu sur l'institution de l'Eucharistie contre les erreurs de Pierre Du Moulin, ministre de la religion prétendue réformée,* Paris, 1617. *Le Droict du Roy sur les subjects chréstiens, à ceux de la religion prétendue réformée,* Paris, 1622.
[122] *Véritez chréstiennes au Roy très-chréstien,* n.p., 1620.

of critical tracts from abroad.[123] Furthermore, Morgues composed the work in close collaboration with Richelieu who provided notes and a detailed plan and corrected the finished product with his own hand.[124] The *Théologien sans passion* should therefore be viewed as a cooperative work which accurately expressed Richelieu's convictions concerning the justice of his policies and their relevance to religious values. That official circles regarded it as the most important official answer to the ultramontane pamphlets is indicated by its key position in the *Mercure français*.[125]

In the introductory pages of the *Théologien sans passion*, Morgues considered the origin and nature of the ultramontane tracts, claiming that all were published in Augsburg or Ingolstadt and were by a renegade Frenchman, a Bavarian, and an Italian living in Flanders. All pose as theologians, he said, but in fact they are "more carried away by passion than guided by reason." Christ did not indulge in calumny and one cannot serve God by criticizing kings and prelates who are his images. Morgues therefore proposed to answer the tracts as an "upright man and true Christian," that is, as a "theologian without passion." Actually, he continued, these authors have a political motive because they seek to create a block of Catholic states—France, Savoy, Venice, Bavaria, and certain other German principalities—as a third force between the Hapsburgs and the Protestant powers. France refuses to accept this Bavarian scheme because it would weaken her position in Europe; therefore its proponents color their political proposals with religion and denounce

---

[123] *Advis d'un théologien sans passion, sur plusieurs libelles imprimez depuis peu en Allemagne*, n.p., 1626. In Hay du Chastelet, *Recueil de diverses pièces pour servir à l'histoire*, Paris, 1635. My citations are to the *Recueil*.

[124] C. Perroud, "Essai sur la vie et les œuvres de Mathieu de Morgues, abbé de Saint-Germain," *Annales de la Société d'Agriculture, Sciences, Arts et Commerce du Puy*, XXVI (1863), 233-34. Fagniez shows that Richelieu chose Morgues because of his ability as a theologian. "Mathieu de Morgues et le procès de Richelieu," *Revue des deux mondes*, CLXII (1900), 555-56. Deloche, pp. 422-23.

[125] After listing eighteen Latin pamphlets that were published abroad and hostile to Richelieu, the *Mercure français* answers them by printing a shortened but substantially accurate version of the *Théologien sans passion*, Vol. XII, 501-21.

as unbelievers all who will not adopt them—a strange use of Christianity. With this clever thrust, Morgues showed that Richelieu's critics were as motivated by political considerations as the French and gave credence to the charge that they merely used religion to cloak their true designs. Vituperation, Morgues insisted at length, especially against kings and high-ranking prelates, is contrary to the spirit of true religion which teaches forgiveness rather than calumny. And he added, with Richelieu clearly in mind:

> A wise man is not afflicted by it and does not change his course; on the contrary he rejoices in public recognition that he disagrees with those who might cause him to be suspected of treason if they approved his intentions. He firmly believes that the decisions he makes are holy and good because the enemies of his king and his country would dissuade him from them. And finding themselves unable to do so, they pursue him with insults that cause all to realize the wisdom of him who despises them and the folly of those who write them.[126]

These "men without reason, Christians without conscience, theologians without knowledge of God, sanguinary priests, religious without religion,"[127] Morgues continued, even have the effrontery to criticize Louis XIII as an abettor and protector of heretics, whereas he among all Christian princes has pursued them most vigorously. After reciting Louis XIII's many actions against heresy (the restoration of Catholicism in Béarn and other places, his destruction of seminaries for training Huguenot preachers, and his taking of two hundred strong places from them, all at great cost in men and money and at considerable personal peril) plus the many evidences of Louis XIII's piety (his chastity, devotion, presence in processions, etc.), Morgues concluded that the ultramontane pamphleteers were "enemies of the best king on earth, envious of the glory of the greatest Christian prince, jealous of the honor of the most religious nation in the world."[128] With this simple but effective argument, Morgues associated the French state with Christian values through the poli-

[126] *Théologien*, pp. 667-68.   [127] *Ibid.*, p. 668.
[128] *Ibid.*, p. 670.

cies and character of her king. In an age when the king symbolized and personified the state, there was no more meaningful mechanism for demonstrating the Christian character of the state and the religious justification of policies that were undertaken for its benefit.

Regarding France's defense of her allies, some of which were Protestant, Morgues insisted that this was a matter of self-preservation and humanitarianism. Christianity permits self-defense and sanctions protection of the weak. Furthermore, the king includes clauses in all treaties for the protection of Catholicism and, unlike many other rulers, does not permit religious observances by heretics in his armies. If only his enemies would cease troubling him by attacking his allies, he might advance the work of reducing heresy in France, said Morgues in a telling passage.[129] The remainder of the tract is devoted to extensive praise of Richelieu's services to both church and state—a fitting climax of a treatise that sought to defend his political policies on religious grounds. As a Prince of the Church, Richelieu has distinguished himself in many capacities: as administrator while Bishop of Luçon and as author of religious tracts that are used throughout France and others that combat heresy. He is held in high esteem as a theologian in both Paris and Rome and has distinguished himself in the Assembly of the Clergy and the Estates General. Most important, his great endowments have been recognized by the king who called him to the royal council, thereby effecting a reconciliation between the ruler and the Queen Mother because of their mutual confidence in the Cardinal.[130] Among Richelieu's contributions to the life of the state, Morgues cited improved finances, wider prosperity, the maintenance of peace and order, and an increase in commerce and naval strength. In conclusion, he insisted that Richelieu rather than the authors of the ultramontane pamphlets was the true Christian. "He is most faithful to the Church because he cannot accept your theology which is not that of Jesus Christ . . . . That of violence, slander, and calumny cannot be that of the law of grace since it is not in the spirit of men but of devils."[131] Such writings as yours, Morgues said, have cost us two kings whose blood may call down divine

[129] *Ibid.*, p. 672.   [130] *Ibid.*, pp. 673-74.   [131] *Ibid.*, p. 677.

wrath upon the lands where these detestable deeds were planned. Furthermore, "If the disorder that you have aroused continues, the Holy Father will remove from the community of the faithful those who cause such disturbances which are capable of effecting a schism in the Church . . . . They are well known, but even if they were not known to men they must fear the justice of God who punishes . . . principally those who have abused his holy name by using it to promote defamations, calumnies, violence, murders, civil wars, and all the disorders that they bring, pitting Catholics against each other and dividing their loyalties."[132]

These were the key arguments with which Richelieu justified his policies for the benefit of France. He seems genuinely to have believed that his stance in support of Christian monarchy was closer to the principles of Catholicism than that of his foreign critics. They might be as politically motivated as he, Richelieu admitted, but they speciously justified their objectives with a cloak of religion whereas he and his sovereign worked straightforwardly for the benefit of France and the Catholic faith. Both Louis XIII's personal piety and Richelieu's position as Cardinal of the Church qualified them to develop a state policy that would redound to the benefit of Christian monarchy and Catholicism, whereas their critics were not only doing disservice to France but were violating the principles of true religion and endangering the unity of Catholic Christianity itself. For French readers whose loyalties to their monarchy and Catholicism were quite fused, these must have been very cogent arguments in support of Richelieu's policies.

Expressions of ultramontane opinion by the Jesuits continued to harass Richelieu throughout the year 1626. In one episode, that involving Father Garasse, Richelieu and his policies were involved only tangentially, yet it was important because it called forth support for him from none other than Saint-Cyran, the later Jansenist leader. Garasse had published a number of works that were known chiefly for their bad taste, violent tone, and caustic criticism, often concerning mere trivialities. In order to demonstrate his ability to produce a serious treatise, he published his *Somme théologique* late

---

[132] *Ibid.*, p. 679.

in 1625.[133] Although approved by the Dominicans, this work was marred by inexact statements and references as well as near heresies. On March 2, 1626, the Rector of the Faculty of Theology brought it to the attention of that body which appointed a committee to consider it. When their report was submitted, delaying tactics by Garasse's friends prevented a decision until later in the year. Meanwhile, Saint-Cyran who was on intimate terms with Richelieu and supported him in the factional in-fighting at court anonymously published his *Somme des fautes et faussetez capitales contenues en la Somme théologique du père François Garasse.*[134] For our purposes, the only pertinent portion of this work is its dedicatory epistle to Richelieu which extravagantly praises the Cardinal and his foreign policy. It is a coincidence, said Saint-Cyran, that two erroneous works should appear simultaneously, one attacking the king and his principal ministers, the other God's majesty and the rules of the Church. The first (doubtless the *Admonitio*) had been adequately answered; therefore he would reply to the second, that of Garasse. The epistle, however, sang the praises of Richelieu at considerable length. The key to his success, Saint-Cyran claimed, was his ability to achieve a proper admixture of religious and secular motivation in shaping policy, for "he who stands highest in government and is obliged to be equally loyal to the state and religion must possess an extraordinary power of judgment to preserve complete integrity in the service that he owes God and his king."[135]

[133] *La Somme théologique des veritez capitales de la religion chréstienne,* Paris, 1625. On this work, see Prat, Vol. IV, 491-512. C. Nisard, *Les Gladiateurs de la république des lettres aux XVe, XVIe et XVIIe siècles,* Paris, 1860, Vol. II, section on François Garasse, Chap. 9. H. Fouqueray, *Histoire de la Compagnie de Jésus en France des origines à la suppression (1528-1762),* Paris, 1925, Vol. IV, Chap. 4. A. Przyrembel, *La Controverse théologique et morale entre Saint-Cyran et le père Garasse,* Paris, 1917.

[134] *La Somme des fautes et faussetez capitales contenues en la Somme théologique du père François Garasse de la Compagnie de Jésus,* Paris, 1626. On this phase of Saint-Cyran's career see J. Orcibal, *Les Origines du jansénisme,* Paris, 1947, Vol. II, 486-88. On the publication of the *Somme des fautes,* see Orcibal, Vol. I, 299.

[135] Dedicatory epistle, n.p. All other quotations given here from this work are from the dedicatory epistle.

When the highest member of the Council of State is a great church-man, he said, citing Richelieu's position as Cardinal, his religious qualities, his various publications, and his standing among theologians, "with what dexterity of judgment he acts and speaks when the interests of religion require that he somehow temper the decisions that are deemed necessary to the state, and the interests of the state on the other hand require that he temper decisions that are necessary to the Church and religion." And he compared Richelieu to Moses who combined authority and wisdom in the sacred and secular spheres.

Moses was also, like Richelieu, subjected to criticism and calumny by an ungrateful people who instead should have prayed for their king and all in his council because they were inspired by God and could not be disparaged without sacrilege. It was not, said Saint-Cyran, that he would make kings and their ministers equal to God; he merely wished to silence criticism by subjects who, no matter how learned, were more ignorant of public matters and their motivation than the simplest things in nature.

> If ever there were occasions to apply the commandment that prohibits judgment by individuals, that is, their undertaking to do on earth what the Son of God will do only at the end of the world, it is in these important matters where the slightest liberty of speech is accompanied by great offence which disturbs civil peace and opens the door to factions by the great and sedition by the people. It would be better to submit for a time to evil and to tolerate disorder, if any, and to attempt to deter it by prayer, patience, and judicious silence which would have greater effect in promoting the public good than these pamphlets whose authors attempt to discredit the state and those who direct it with their counsel . . . . Because God divided men in civil life among various orders, those of highest rank regard persons who pursue a private and solitary life as having nothing in common with them, which causes their virtues and actions to be so different that what is good and fitting for the first is bad and improper for the others.

Those who merely write books in their cells, Saint-Cyran maintained, lack this special knowledge "which is dependent on God's
providence and renders him homage and service by governing the
peoples and realms of the earth." Hence the errors of those who
criticize policy. You may seem to prefer an alliance with the Huguenots to one with Spain, said Saint-Cyran entering the slightest suggestion of dissent, but appearances are deceiving. The great should
not be disturbed by criticism and often must wait for their fame
and reward.

Richelieu was understandably delighted with this unsolicited
justification of his position and policies. Many of the ideas in the
dedicatory epistle were so similar to his that they might have been
taken from the *Catholique d'estat*. Of particular note was Saint-
Cyran's emphasis upon Richelieu's loyalty to both church and state
and the religious orientation of his policies. He also indicated complete willingness to leave the mysteries of state to the constituted
authorities and approved of different standards of justice in public
and private affairs. That Saint-Cyran, a man of deep religious convictions, would commit himself to paper in this vein is but another
illustration of the widespread belief at this time that Richelieu's
policies embodied a religious good and that his insistence upon a
special standard of justice in matters of state accorded with Christian morality.

As if to confound the problems of Richelieu who was striving to
maintain a steady course in the midst of various controversies, in
February 1626 one of the most extreme ultramontane publications
of the period appeared in Paris, the *Tractatus de Hæresi* by the
Italian Jesuit, Antonio Santarelli.[136] The work at once caused a stir
in ecclesiastical and judicial circles in spite of the efforts of the local
Jesuits to keep it out of sight. The statements that at once caught
the eye of French readers occurred in chapters 30 and 31 where
Santarelli reiterated Cardinal Bellarmine's theory of the pope's indirect power over kings and relentlessly pushed it to its logical con-

[136] *Tractatus de Hæresi, Schismate, Apostasia, sollicitatione in sacramento
poenitentiæ, et de potestate Romani Pontificis in his delictis puniendis*, Rome,
1625.

clusions. Among his propositions were the following.[187] The pope holds both the spiritual and temporal swords from God; the spiritual he exercises directly but he wields the temporal only in certain instances. All princes govern their states under commissions from the pope; in case of necessity the pope may govern states or appoint executors to take the place of their temporal rulers. The pope may punish any secular ruler on earth even with the death penalty, not only for heresy or schism but any other great crime or negligence. He may depose princes, appoint new ones, divide states, and absolve subjects from their oaths of allegiance. Santarelli's assertion of the supremacy of the spiritual over the temporal in all matters of judgment could hardly have been more complete. Needless to say, such statements were certain to arouse controversy in an atmosphere that was already charged with animosity and friction between Gallicans and ultramontanes.

The agitation concerning Santarelli's book merged with that concerning other offending works but outdid them all in violence.[138] The major participants were those that were always found in such frays: the Parlement of Paris, the Faculty of Theology, the papal nuncio, the Jesuit leaders, and, of course, Richelieu. On March 13, the Parlement condemned Santarelli's work as seditious, ordered it to be burned, and summoned the Provincial of the Jesuits and other members of the order to appear in court for a hearing on the matter.[139] On the following day, the venerable Father Coton and three other high-ranking members appeared before the Parlement, were subjected to intensive interrogation, and were presented with three articles which specified direct divine authorization of kings and denied papal authority to dispense subjects from their oaths of al-

---

[187] These occur in Chap. 30. Chap. 31 gives supporting arguments of a doctrinal nature.

[138] Many authors have described the Santarelli affair in detail; I give only certain essentials. See Prat, Vol. iv, Bk. 26, Chaps. 2-4. E. Puyol, *Edmond Richer*, Paris, 1876, Vol. ii, Chaps. 13, 14. M. Houssaye, *Le Cardinal de Bérulle et le Cardinal de Richelieu*, Paris, 1875, Chap. 4. H. Fouqueray, *op.cit.*, Vol. iv, Chaps. 6, 7. V. Martin, "L'Adoption du gallicanisme . . . ," *Revue des sciences religieuses*, vii (1927), 205-25, 373-401, 545-78.

[139] *Mercure français*, Vol. xi, 88-90, second pagination. *Mercure jésuite*, 840-41.

legiance.[140] Two days later, the Jesuit leaders signed a declaration denouncing Santarelli's statements concerning kings, their authority, and their states, admitting direct divine authorization, and promising to accept any censure of Santarelli's book that might be made by the Assembly of the Clergy, the universities, or the Sorbonne.[141] They remained silent, however, concerning the pope's indirect power. While the Parlement continued to pursue the Jesuits, the Faculty of Theology framed its condemnation which proved to be the most sweeping of all and rapidly became the focal point of the controversy. Instead of a general denunciation, the Faculty on April 4 issued a censure of Santarelli's book which included its most offensive propositions and condemned them as "new, false, erroneous, and contrary to the word of God, rendering the Supreme Pontiff's dignity odious and opening the door to schism, derogating the sovereign authority of kings which is held from God alone, preventing the conversion of infidel and heretic princes, disturbing the public peace and disrupting realms, states, and republics. In brief, it dissuades subjects from the obedience that they owe their sovereigns and incites them to factions, rebellions, seditions, and attempts on the lives of their rulers."[142]

From this point onward, the controversy entered a broader phase which needs only to be summarized. The specific bone of contention was the Faculty of Theology's strongly Gallican pronouncement which was certain to arouse hostility in Rome and ultramontane circles generally. Spada reacted violently and sharply criticized Richelieu for not preventing the Faculty's action, whereupon the Cardinal found himself caught between fires from the Parlement, the Sorbonne, the French Jesuits, the papal nuncio, and the ultramontane faction at court. An intermediary to negotiate with all parties was needed and both he and the pope appealed to Bérulle to accept this thankless task. As for Richelieu, rising opposition to him at court plus his gradual reorientation toward the *dévot* faction

---

[140] *Mercure jésuite*, 844.

[141] *Mercure français*, Vol. XI, 90-91, second pagination. *Mercure jésuite*, 844-45.

[142] *Mercure français*, Vol. XI, 98, second pagination. *Mercure jésuite*, 853-54.

caused him to wish for nothing more than an amicable settlement of the controversy. Extremely complex negotiations continued throughout the remainder of the year, punctuated by condemnation of Garasse's *Somme théologique* by the Faculty of Theology on September 16[143] and a comprehensive royal decree on November 2 ordering all parties to cease their disputes concerning the royal authority.[144] This, of course, settled nothing and left all parties dissatisfied. Richelieu thereupon determined to bring the matter to an end by a show of force. On January 2, 1627, the Bishop of Nantes carried a *lettre de cachet* to the Faculty of Theology ordering cessation of all deliberations concerning Santarelli's book. The Bishop also stated that the king wished to know whether the learned doctors continued to uphold their earlier condemnation of the work, whereupon a large majority agreed to rescind it in the hope of framing another.[145] As for the Parlement, it was silenced by a decree of

---

[143] The book was condemned as containing "many heretical, erroneous, scandalous, and foolhardy propositions, many badly cited, corrupted and distorted passages from Holy Scripture and the Fathers, and innumerable buffooneries that are unworthy of being written or read by Christians or theologians." *Mercure français*, Vol. XII, 529-30.

[144] The decree forbade "all subjects of any profession, position, or condition whatsoever to write, treat, or dispute in the affirmative or negative regarding propositions concerning the power and sovereign authority of His Majesty and other kings and sovereigns without express permission of His Majesty by letters patent, on pain of being punished as seditious and disturbers of the public peace." *Mercure français*, Vol. XII, 335. This was reiterated by letters patent on December 13. *Ibid.*, Vol. XII, 14-19, second pagination. Richelieu's extremely difficult position throughout these negotiations is clearly indicated in Maxim CLVIII of his well known *Maximes d'État et fragments politiques*. Here he states that although the Parlement's action against Santarelli's book was to be praised, the jurists should be restrained because they might exasperate the Jesuits to the point where they would create a situation that would be impossible to control. "And the reason for this recommendation comes down to this, that the Jesuits must not be reduced to the point where they might bring themselves to act in desperation, for in that case there might appear a thousand mad and devilish souls who, under the pretext of mistaken zeal, would be capable of undertaking evil acts that could be curbed neither by fire nor other penalties." *Maximes d'État et fragments politiques du Cardinal de Richelieu*, G. Hanotaux, ed., p. 803. In *Mélanges historiques*, Paris, 1880, Vol. III.

[145] *Mercure français*, Vol. XII, 21-29, second pagination.

the Council of State on January 29 which evoked all discussion of royal authority to the council, quashed all earlier acts by various bodies, specifically prohibited consideration of Santarelli's book by the Parlement, and specified that a group of "Cardinals, prelates, and others" would be chosen to frame a condemnation of the work.[146] Since no such body was ever appointed, this ended the affair.

In this way, the celebrated dispute over Santarelli's book passed into history. It is clear that the outcome was a major victory for the Jesuits and the ultramontanes generally. The condemnation by the Faculty of Theology had been rescinded; all major mouthpieces of Gallicanism had been silenced, and no further action was taken. Thus the doctrine of indirect papal power over kings and all that it implied were allowed to stand. The episode gives clear evidence of the great power of the supporters of ultramontanism both in France and abroad and the corresponding strength of the conviction that all things political should be subject to judgment by theologians. In this context, any independent ethic of state policy was automatically excluded. As for Richelieu, developments in foreign and domestic affairs as well as his fear of acquiring additional enemies induced him to yield to the mounting pressures and to allow the dispute to lapse without a categorical solution. He had stated his position in the *Catholique d'estat* and other works and could afford to bide his time.

The relevance of the Santarelli episode to the Valtelline question may seem remote but was very clear to contemporary French observers. To them it was no accident that the most penetrating criticisms of French foreign policy came from the same quarters that insisted upon papal supremacy over kings. Not only were the ultramontane forces abroad chiefly in alliance with France's enemies; the pope's indirect power over temporal rulers also provided a solid theoretical basis for the claim that theologians might judge and condemn French policy. Consequently, many patriotic Frenchmen viewed all ultramontane writings, especially those that criticized royal acts, as hostile to the independence of their state and

[146] *Ibid.*, Vol. XII, 31-34, second pagination.

bent on destroying it. The latter position is clearly delineated in the *Raisons pour les condemnations,* whose author lists himself simply as a "French Catholic."[147] This strongly Gallican and royalist tract grouped together the *Admonitio, Mysteria politica, Quæstiones quodlibeticæ,* and the books of Garasse and Santarelli as purveyors of seditious and destructive doctrine. Recalling earlier treasonable acts by many ultramontane-oriented factions, the author maintained that if their teachings were accepted in France, "the realm would be subjected to wretched foreign domination, the person of the king and the entire royal household would be exposed to continual danger, and the subjects would be in perpetual apprehension."[148] The major purpose of the work, however, was to demonstrate that political ultramontanism was erroneous on religious grounds, and as proof he cited the Sorbonne's condemnation of Santarelli's book as contrary to the word of God. This showed that the doctors were "not only good theologians but very good and faithful servants of their king and master."[149] As a Catholic, the author's main stumbling block, of course, was the fact that the papacy itself upheld the ultramontane allegations. In order to establish their doctrinal falsity, he was forced to distinguish between the papacy and the Church Universal and to insist that only the latter was infallible—an advanced Gallican position which indicates the difficulties that faced all Catholic writers who would challenge papal supremacy over kings.[150] It also indicates the problems that confronted all Catholics who denied that theologians might judge state policy. In order to extricate themselves doctrinally, the proponents of even a partially autonomous political ethic were forced to develop alternative bases of argument while remaining within the canons of Catholic Christianity. Such was particularly incumbent upon Richelieu who believed that he could serve his God while simultaneously guiding the fortunes of the French state and fulfilling his role as a Prince of the Church.

[147] *Raisons pour les condemnations cy-devant faictes du libelle Admonitio, du livre de Santarel, et autres semblables. Contre les Santarelistes de ce temps et leurs fauteurs, Par un François Catholique,* n.p., 1626.
[148] *Ibid.* (p. 5).   [149] *Ibid.* (p. 9).   [150] *Ibid.* (pp. 13-16).

Throughout the Valtelline episode, as we have seen, Richelieu made extensive efforts to justify his policies from the twin stand-points of French state interests and those of Catholic Christianity. Even after the Treaty of Monçon terminated hostilities with the Spanish, the Cardinal felt it necessary to reiterate his assertion that French military and diplomatic actions relative to the Valtelline had in no way compromised the Catholic cause. Later in 1626, after the Treaty of Monçon had been concluded, there appeared an important pamphlet, the *Discours sur plusieurs poincts importans de l'estat présent des affaires de France,*[151] which was a veritable apologia of the Cardinal's policies and certainly was officially inspired. Regarding the outcome of the Valtelline affair, the author claimed that it had not prejudiced the position of Catholicism in Europe for two reasons: Richelieu had so skilfully directed French policy that he avoided a dangerous cleavage between political and religious interests, and he had even benefited the papacy in ways that the pope did not understand but that would be made clear in the future.[152] So anxious was Richelieu to avoid criticism on the religious count that he claimed to have understood the long-range interests of the papacy better than Urban VIII. Years later, after France had entered

[151] N.p., 1626. Reprinted in Hay du Chastelet, *Recueil* . . . , with modifications. I cite the edition of 1626. On the nature and significance of this work, see Deloche, pp. 406-11.

[152] As for the peace of Italy, concerning which no one is free of passion, who cannot but admire his industry in dexterously guiding such an important matter which seemed certain to end by creating a breach between religion and the state. We nevertheless saw with what judgment in this treacherous matter he successfully seconded Your Majesty's intentions to maintain and preserve the integrity of both without the slightest prejudice to either. It also seemed that his profession would cause him to follow completely the desires of His Holiness who, although he upheld only those that are suitable to the common father of Christians, nevertheless was not well informed concerning the deeds of those who always cover their acts with a pretext of religion and sought things that might (contrary to his intention) have tarnished the honor of France. He [Richelieu] resisted this courageously, knowing that whereas the present brings hatred, the future will provide rewards, and that the cause of these, although distasteful to His Holiness, would be approved by him as worthy of praise and redounding to the good and the repose of Italy and strengthening the authority of the Holy See. (*Discours*, pp. 16-17.)

the Thirty Years' War, Jean de Silhon, a member of the French Academy and one of the more important intellectuals supporting Richelieu, wrote an *Apologie du traité de Monçon*[153] which reexamined the diplomacy of the Valtelline episode and concluded that Louis XIII had sought to support and preserve the Catholic faith even at the expense of state interests.

> True reasons of state do not clash with the maxims of religion, and the same Authority that established the distinction between the secular and ecclesiastical powers directed that they be joined by bonds of friendship and aid each other. Although a wise prince should not permit this harmony to be broken nor the bounds that separate them to be blurred, in the straits into which Christianity has fallen and the multiplicity of factions of different religions that are tearing it asunder, the king has not only taken care to identify the interests of the Catholic faith and to protect sacred persons and places from the attacks of those who might violate them; it may even be said that he has sometimes foregone advantages that he might in good conscience have seized and for the good of religion has restricted himself in affairs of state where he might justifiably have been more relaxed if he had not always believed that any small disadvantage which he assumed would be amply compensated by Him who does not suffer that an offering made in his name goes without reward and that God would not only bless the justice of his arms and the equity of his conduct but would also reward his piety and zeal for holy things.[154]

These repeated assertions that Richelieu's foreign policy benefited both the French state and the Catholic faith amply indicate the difficulty of justifying his policies to Catholic opinion and his convic-

[153] *Divers Mémoires concernant les dernières guerres d'Italie. Avec trois Traitez de feu M. de Silhon, qui n'ont point encore esté vûs*, Paris, 1669. Vol. I of this collection contains the *Apologie du traité de Monçon*. On the basis of internal evidence, this work was written after France's entry into the Thirty Years' War. Taken as a whole, the publication is an extensive justification of French foreign policy over a period of years.

[154] *Apologie*, pp. 104-06.

tion that this must be done at all costs. They also indicate that Richelieu firmly believed in the viability of his role as Christian statesman.

During the years 1624-1627, Richelieu relied chiefly upon his group of expert pamphleteers to plead his cause before the bar of public opinion. Such men as Fancan, Sirmond, Ferrier, Morgues, and several others penned reasonably competent statements of the theoretical arguments with which he attempted to convince the literate public of the necessity, justice, and religious benefits of his policies. As the years advanced, however, Richelieu increasingly abandoned his pamphleteers in favor of professional writers of major intellectual stature. That this process was under way before 1627 is indicated by the publication in that year of the *Recueil de lettres nouvelles*, edited by Nicolas Faret.[155] This extensive compilation was dedicated to Richelieu and has rightly been called by Professor Adam a glorification of the Cardinal and an effort to develop a mystique of reason of state.[156] The contributors whose letters touch upon political matters include such names as Faret, Guez de Balzac, Jean de Silhon, and François de Cauvigny, sieur de Colomby—all future members of the French Academy. Aside from the extravagant praise accorded the Cardinal, the political concepts that are most frequently encountered in this volume are similar to those that we have noted many times: the special knowledge of the king and his ministers relative to the mysteries of state, the varied benefits of enlightened leadership, and the necessity of effective controls in all areas of human endeavor.

Two of these authors deserve special attention: Guez de Balzac and Jean de Silhon. Richelieu and Balzac seem to have enjoyed reasonably close personal relations from an early date and by 1620 were engaged in active correspondence. Balzac repeatedly praised Richelieu for his many abilities and sent him manuscript copies

---

[155] This work passed through several editions. My references are to the Paris edition of 1639.

[156] A. Adam, *Histoire de la littérature française au XVIIe siècle*, Paris, 1948, Vol. I, 214-15.

of letters that would later make him famous.[157] In a letter to Richelieu dated December 25, 1625, which was included in Faret's *Recueil*
and was repeatedly published, Balzac stated the following concerning the Valtelline negotiations which were then well advanced: "I
have observed that the Italians have exhausted every stratagem without gaining advantage over anyone and that these subtle men who
think they may dictate to all and are masters of reasons of state have
been unable to defend themselves against you except with passion
and anger. They complain only that you have persuaded them to
do all that they were resolved not to do."[158] Balzac concluded the
letter on his favorite note by praising the Cardinal: "Because of
your prudence, there will be no more rebellions among us nor
tyranny among men. All the cities of the realm will be secure for
upright persons. Innovations will be accepted only in colors and
fashions of dress. The people will leave liberty, religion, and the
public good in the hands of their superiors, and from legitimate
government and complete obedience will come that felicity which
political leaders seek and is the objective of civil life."[159] It is clear
that Balzac genuinely admired Richelieu's abilities as administrator
and leader of men. Richelieu, for his part, apparently wished to
make use of Balzac's literary talents in his program of publicizing
and defending his political ideals. Balzac was at this time working on
his book, *Le Prince*,[160] which was published four years after Faret's
Recueil, and there is reliable evidence that Balzac undertook the

[157] Balzac wrote very laudatory letters to Richelieu on May 15, 1620, and
September 4 and 16, 1622. *Lettres du sieur de Balzac*, Paris, 1624, pp. 25-30,
140-42. My citations are to the critical edition edited by H. Bibas and K. T.
Butler, Paris, 1933, Vol. I. The letters are also in Balzac, *Œuvres*, Paris, 1665,
Vol. I, 4-8. In October 1622 Richelieu wrote to Balzac thanking him for the
manuscript copies of his letters. *Lettres . . . de Richelieu*, Vol. I, 734-35.
[158] *Les Œuvres de Monsieur de Balzac*, Paris, 1627, pp. 16-17, in Vol. II of
the edition by Bibas and Butler.
[159] *Ibid.*, p. 21. This letter was published separately in 1626, at the head of
the *Œuvres* in 1627, and in the *Recueil* of Faret in 1627. It also appears in the
Œuvres, Paris, 1665, Vol. I, 8-11, and in later editions of the *Recueil*.
[160] Faret's *Recueil* contains a letter from Silhon to M. de Marca, President
of the Parlement of Navarre, in which Silhon says that he is sending de
Marca certain portions of Balzac's *Prince*. *Recueil*, pp. 371-82.

project at the Cardinal's request.[161] When completed, the book set forth important views on reason of state which will be considered below.

For our purposes, by far the most important missive in Faret's *Recueil* is Jean de Silhon's "Lettre à l'Evesque de Nantes."[162] It seems that the Bishop who was a doctor of the Sorbonne and a famous preacher had read Silhon's first publication, a theological study entitled *Les Deux Veritez* which appeared in 1626,[163] and had written to Silhon praising it and asking for more. In his response, Silhon extensively outlined his plans for a third part of the work. Although this addition was never published in its projected form, Silhon's proposal is valuable as an indication of his thinking during the first years of Richelieu's ministry. Essentially, Silhon planned to continue the effort that he had begun with his *Deux Veritez*: to combat atheism, rationalism, and heresy, and to offer proofs of the absolute truth of Catholicism. In fact, Silhon early in his career had made it his lifelong objective to uphold the Catholic faith in its fundamentals and applications, and followed this plan in his publications, first in religious doctrine and later in political thought.[164] That the latter area was already one of his major concerns in these years is shown by his extensive consideration of it in

[161] At the head of the *Œuvres de Monsieur de Balzac*, Paris, 1627, an introductory letter by Silhon contains the following. After stating that Balzac had been ill and should devote all his spare time to his *Prince*, Silhon added that the letters in the volume may seem to lack certain things. "But all these truths will appear in good time in the work which the king through your mouth, Monseigneur, commanded Monsieur de Balzac to undertake and which a year of leisure will complete. In it he will show everyone that in order to have [before us] the image of a perfect prince, it was necessary for us to wait for the reign of as great a monarch as our own." P. 12 in the edition by Bibas and Butler. The letter is included in Balzac's *Œuvres*, Paris, 1665, Vol. II, Pt. 2, 178-80. On Balzac's relations with Silhon, see R. Kerviler, *Jean de Silhon*, Paris, 1876, pp. 19-21.

[162] Pages 450-508 of the first edition of the *Recueil*. My citations are to the edition of 1639. This letter was also published separately under the title *Lettre du sieur de Silhon à Monsieur l'Evesque de Nantes*, n.p., n.d.

[163] *Les Deux Veritez de Silhon, l'une de Dieu et de sa Providence, l'autre de l'immortalité de l'Ame*, Paris, 1626.

[164] Kerviler, pp. 8-9.

his letter to the Bishop of Nantes. Because of the strength of Silhon's religious convictions and his increasing association with men who were close to Richelieu, it is important to examine the manner in which he proposed to treat reason of state.

During the mid-1620's, Silhon could not boast of such intimate relations with Richelieu as those enjoyed by Guez de Balzac. Silhon gained genuine favor only at a later date. Both men nevertheless were well aware of the fact that the Cardinal's policies presented in full force the problem of just government and reason of state. Balzac did not publish his ideas on the subject until 1631 when his *Prince* appeared. In the meantime, his friend and associate, Silhon, planned to treat its central issue, the relations of politics and morals, in his addition to his *Deux Veritez*. Sensing that the crux of the matter from a practical standpoint was the maintenance of a proper balance between advantage and justice, Silhon proposed the following:

I shall take the opportunity to combat Machiavelli's maxim, so fundamental to his *Prince*, that one may use unjust means to attain any good, [which is] contrary to that of St. Paul who says that damnation is fitting for those who do evil in order to achieve good. In explaining these two maxims, I shall show the balance that I propose between the maxims of state and those of conscience. It is a science that is no less necessary to a minister of state who would govern well than is the sun to natural life to sustain it. Although those who recognize no good but utility and no honesty except in appearances are always pernicious, those who have unblemished souls sometimes cause no fewer disasters because of their scruples of conscience. For all that, this important science has become, through some untold misadventure, the most sophisticated science of all. Among those who claim to understand it, some plunge into extreme injustice like Machiavelli and his sect . . . while others lean a little too far toward the other extremity and do not sufficiently extend the limits of that which the public interest renders legitimate . . . . It seems to me that there is a mean between that which conscience permits and affairs require. Those who discuss this mean merely add precepts which tend toward the position that they favor, and do not relate them to the universal truths upon which their justice depends, diminishing knowledge of their applicability to events.[165]

Clearly, Silhon had gone to the heart of the problem, the divergence between necessity and justice, and felt the need to relax the limitations of morality in the conduct of political affairs. As the best means of handling this dangerous procedure, he suggested that each matter be examined from the standpoint of its essence rather than its surface appearances:

> Since this science consists of dextrously joining the useful and the just and continually resisting evil under any guise that it may assume, one must perfectly understand the conditions of the latter and distinguish between what is evil by nature and what is merely accessory to it. Arsenic is intrinsically a very violent poison but quicksilver is sometimes a poison and sometimes a remedy according to its preparation. There are things whose essence is corrupted by an inherent evil and are forbidden as such; others are merely associated with evil because they are prohibited or lessen the authority of the ruler. The first are the subject of natural laws, the second of positive .... Natural laws are constant, but positive laws are subject to change and cease to apply in certain instances. Since laws govern only in accordance with the intention of the legislator, one should interpret his intention and search for the causes that occasioned their making, whether they have ceased or continue, and whether the laws have become injurious or useless.[166]

This flexibility in the application of positive law was admitted by many writers, but Silhon extended it much further by applying it to matters of higher law in a passage that shows the clear influence of probabilism:

> In doubtful cases, he [the minister of state] will always choose what is safest and most advantageous to his master even though

[165] *Lettre*, pp. 406-07.   [166] *Ibid.*, pp. 408-09.

169

the least probable, provided that it is truly probable. In this, he combines two maxims, one of conscience and the other of prudence. Conscience permits us to select from two probable opinions that which we prefer, while prudence directs us . . . to choose that which is the most profitable. The reason for conscience is that although we are always obliged to adhere to known truths, this is so difficult a quest and falsehood imitates the appearance of truth so artfully that it is often least present where its seems to be. The reason for prudence is so natural that it is known to all.[167]

This remarkable statement graphically illustrates how a man of strong religious convictions and considerable theological learning could relax the restrictions of Christian morality upon human conduct in the political sphere by applying the techniques of probabilism. Very early in his career, Silhon, the defender of the Catholic faith, felt that the nature of European politics required an accommodation of theological principles to the dictates of necessity, and he found in probabilism a convenient mechanism which enabled him to accomplish this while remaining within the bounds of orthodoxy.

The remainder of Silhon's letter to the Bishop of Nantes touches briefly upon several important questions that consistently confronted rulers and statesmen. He would comment, he said, on Tacitus' dictum that great actions may cause private misfortunes but redound to the public good, Louis XI's saying that he who does not know how to dissimulate does not know how to reign, and whether the subjects' lives and goods may be sacrified by the ruler in case of necessity.[168] The ultimate sanction for royal policy he found in direct di-

---

[167] *Ibid.*, pp. 412-13.

[168] *Ibid.*, pp. 415-18. Unfortunately, Silhon discusses neither Tacitus' maxim nor the problem of the subjects' lives and goods, but he expresses grave doubts concerning dissimulation. "The abuse of them [dissimulation and equivocation] is so great and they are so important to human relations and society that it would have been better if no one had begun such dangerous practices. It may develop that we no longer comprehend one another and that speech, which was given men to express their thoughts, will be understood only in misconceptions and truth will be found only in contradictions." *Ibid.*, pp. 416-17.

vine authorization of the sovereign and implied that no ecclesiastical authority had the right to interfere in secular affairs.[169] His outline ended on the note that "the minister of state, in order to be both faithful and useful to his master, must perfectly understand the concurrence of the maxims of conscience and those of state."[170] This may best be achieved, he said, when power is wielded by a great churchman for then the state is guided both by a council of state and a *conseil de conscience*, as at present under Cardinal Richelieu.

This extensive proposal by Jean de Silhon is ample evidence that thinking men during the first years of Richelieu's ministry were troubled by the problem of reason of state and ardently desired its solution. Both Silhon and Balzac were undoubtedly familiar with the many pamphlets that had been published for the purpose of justifying Richelieu's policies, but they realized that the broader connotations of the matter required further consideration. Essentially, Richelieu and his pamphleteers based their argument on the concept of coordinate, interlocking but distinct church and state. France was a Christian state in its traditions, nature, and mission, and was led by its Cardinal-Minister in such manner that his policies were ultimately of political and religious benefit to France and Europe alike. If questionable procedures were used, they were dictated by the condition of European politics and were the special province of those who alone understood the mysteries of state. These in turn permitted France's rulers to govern according to a special ethic of state policy which was not to be questioned by those outside official circles. All this was accepted as morally sound by many men of strong religious convictions, as is evidenced by their continued support of the Cardinal during these years. The position suffered from limitations and unresolved problems, however, in part because it reflected current French policy and because of the nature of the tracts in which it was presented. Richelieu himself seems to have realized this; hence his turning to more sophisticated writers who might give reason of state a broader treatment and incidentally make use of the type of argumentation that had been developed by non-French thinkers before he came to power. In comparison

[169] *Ibid.*, pp. 418-23. [170] *Ibid.*, p. 424.

with their treatises, the writings of the French pamphleteers, while vividly reflecting the traditions of the realm and the beliefs of its leaders, were relatively restricted productions and neglected many of the inherent problems of politics and morals. Such was the position of French thought concerning reason of state as Richelieu turned his major attention from the Valtelline to internal affairs.

PART III

INTERNAL AFFAIRS, STATE-BUILDING, AND ATTENDANT CONTROVERSIES, 1624-1632

RICHELIEU'S ADVERSARIES: THE NOBILITY AND THE HUGUENOTS, 1624-1629

U ntil the Treaty of Monçon temporarily solved the Valtelline question, Richelieu was chiefly occupied with the direction of foreign policy, but at the same time he was forced to contend with many troublesome developments within the realm which hampered his efforts to strengthen the French state system. As the years advanced, he realized that further ventures abroad must be preceded by a major effort to eliminate or at least to contain the sources of resistance at home. In internal affairs, the Cardinal's many undertakings were consistently directed toward one major, comprehensive end: state-building. Indeed, all his acts on many fronts may be subsumed under this single head. For this purpose, he was determined to introduce new order and controls into various phases of French life, and the most effective means of doing so was to strengthen the royal power and to apply it to the task of disciplining the French nation. From the standpoint of existing law, the royal authority was more than ample to permit Louis XIII and his First Minister to effect any needed measures. Since the crown embraced all public power and was defined in terms of divine right sovereignty, it was not difficult to find legal justifications for the great majority of Richelieu's innovations. Many, however, ran counter to accepted traditions and were increasingly resented by those whose way of life was disrupted. Divine right sovereignty might attribute comprehensive discretionary power to the ruler, but ingrained ways of thought and conduct on all levels of French society were such that many of Richelieu's contemporaries regarded his authoritarian program of state-building as tyrannical. For this reason, his domestic as well as his foreign policies required justification according to the canons of reason of state.

Two major objectives of Richelieu's many-sided effort to strengthen the French state within its borders were, first, to increase the effective power of the administrative system and institutions of government, and second, to ensure that all elements of the population were in every sense the king's loyal subjects. Regarding the first, the necessary foundations had been laid before he became First Minister in that the royal administration extended throughout the entire realm. Richelieu merely sought to make the existing system more efficient by staffing it with his creatures, controlling its operations, and adding certain elements which increased effective power at the center. All this was entirely within the sphere of royal competence. On the other hand, to make meaningful the concept that all Frenchmen were equally subject to the crown regardless of their positions in the social hierarchy was considerably more difficult because of the complex character of French society. During this period, the social structure of France resembled that of the medieval realm much more than the post-revolutionary state of modern times. The French jurists of the sixteenth century had completed the separation of status under the ruler from tenure of lands, thereby ending the sharp limits that subinfeudation had placed upon the king's contacts with those below him and in effect making all persons the "subjects" of the crown. In this sense, all were subjects of His Majesty regardless of wealth, lands, or privileges.[1] This legal factor, however, did little to change relations within the social structure which was very complex indeed. French society was subdivided into innumerable highly self-conscious units which occupied specific positions in the social hierarchy, enjoyed corresponding privileges, and adhered to distinct ways of life. Especially among the nobility, family ties, class-consciousness, and their code of honor were all-powerful in determining social relationships and even attitudes toward royalty. Furthermore, innumerable men of quality, wealth,

[1] W. F. Church, *Constitutional Thought in Sixteenth Century France*, Cambridge, Mass., 1941, pp. 185-91 and generally Chap. 4.

and influence developed clienteles of followers who were tied to their benefactors by bonds of interest and personal fidelity. All these factors made for sharp fragmentation of French society into innumerable units which were the object of correspondingly diverse loyalties: loyalty to family, social estate, professional unit, and clientele, not to mention further loyalties to one's province and one's church. In this situation, loyalty to the king and the state was but one of several. Although it was generally regarded as the most binding, never in this period did it entirely supersede all others. And in many situations, loyalty to the state yielded to more immediate ties and obligations. This was a major source of what Richelieu believed to be the chronic indiscipline of the French, and his only means of neutralizing it was to ensure that loyalty to the crown *always* took precedence over all others. Only in this way could he make meaningful the concept that all were equally subject to the state.

From 1624 to 1629, Richelieu's major problems on the domestic front consisted of checkmating noble conspiracies and reducing the political power of the Huguenots. These two movements were distinct in themselves but were related and in many ways similar. Their major difference, of course, lay in the religious sphere and all that it implied, but beyond that the parallelisms are striking. Both owed their inception to nobles who, for all their mixed motives, were characterized by a common desire to force concessions from the crown. In this sense, the Huguenot rebellion (which was not supported by a large percentage of the French Calvinists) paralleled the aristocratic conspiracies. Furthermore, Richelieu's reactions to both were remarkably similar. Although he willingly embarked upon hostilities against the Huguenots for the purpose of combatting heresy, his major concern both in reducing La Rochelle and restricting the activities of the nobility was generally the same: to eliminate foci of resistance within the realm which hampered the expansion and exercise of state power and to demonstrate that all Frenchmen, Catholic and Huguenot, noble and commoner, must be docile and loyal subjects of the crown. For this reason, similar arguments were used to justify his actions in both instances. After the resolution of the Huguenot problem, a major crisis occurred at the French court concerning the proper policy to follow in both foreign and domestic affairs. The *dévot* faction advocated peaceful foreign relations, amelioration of internal conditions, and religious proselytizing, whereas Richelieu favored an aggressive foreign policy and the requisite sacrifices and controls at home. This historic struggle was not resolved until the Day of Dupes when Richelieu's triumph ensured his power and essentially determined royal policy for the remainder of the reign—a fact that was not lost on his contemporaries and partially explains the outburst of publication in his favor at that time.

Richelieu's attitude toward the nobility was ambivalent in that it reflected both his aristocratic mentality and his desire to subject all elements of French society to the power of the state. Priding himself on his noble blood, he held the nobility in high esteem, believed that it made important contributions to the life of the nation, and was willing to allow it to preserve its privileged position. He was also sympathetic with its problems and sought to alleviate them with various measures, a few of which were put into practice.[2] He was adamant, however, in his insistence that all nobles, even the greatest, must refrain from meddling in matters of policy and must remain in their stations as loyal subjects of the crown. This unmitigated subservience to the state was hardly understood by the great nobles of Richelieu's time, largely because of the very different traditions and mode of life within the noble order. The quality of nobility they believed to be shared by all members of the second estate including the king himself—an assumption that gave meaning to the tradition, so prized by the great nobles, that the king was merely *primus inter pares*. The jurist Charles Loyseau, in discussing

---

[2] For an able, comprehensive treatment of Richelieu and the nobility, see O. A. Ranum, "Richelieu and the Great Nobility: Some Aspects of Early Modern Political Motives," *French Historical Studies*, III (1963), 184-204. Some of Richelieu's attempts to alleviate the problems of the nobility are discussed in G. Zeller, "Une notion de caractère historico-social: la dérogeance," *Cahiers internationaux de sociologie*, XXII (1957), 40-74. (Reprinted in G. Zeller, *Aspects de la politique française sous l'ancien régime*, Paris, 1964.) M. Bataillon, "L'Académie de Richelieu, Indre-et-Loire," *Pédagogues et juristes. De Pétrarque à Descartes*, IV (1963), 255-70.

the question whether a mere petty nobleman on the land were as noble as the king, said that although it was "odious, insolent, and blasphemous" to compare a subject to the king, the proposition was true in itself because the quality of nobility was held absolutely and not in degree.[3] And the literature of the period gives ample evidence that from this standpoint the king was but the highest ranking member of the order.[4] Consequently, the great nobles regarded their ties with their sovereign not as those of king and subject but as personal relationships that were made meaningful by mutual obligations of honor and fealty. Service of the king was therefore a personal and voluntary matter. Great nobles might pride themselves on being "loyal subjects and servants of the king," as appears in so many contemporary documents, but they instinctively regarded themselves as very special persons who served in their individual capacities and were much more than mere undifferentiated subjects. They served the king rather than the realm or the state and could not understand why he preferred the counsel of upstart ministers. Many could not forget that personal ties between ruler and nobles had been unusually meaningful in the immediate past because of Henry IV's cultivation of the friendship of individual noblemen—a practice that was increasingly discarded by Louis XIII.

This concept of service as a personal and voluntary matter had very important influence upon social and political relationships. For many a high-ranking nobleman, advancement at court depended upon his success in attaching himself to a greater noble, a minister of state, or a member of the royal family, that is, participation in a powerful person's clientele. And the highly unpredictable ebb and flow of favor from the great often caused their less successful followers to transfer their loyalty from one influential personage to another. Such seemed entirely proper, especially if it merely involved changing one's immediate ties from one member of the royal family to another. Many ambitious nobles felt entirely justified in at-

[3] *Traité des ordres et simples dignitez*, Chap. VI, Nos. 1, 2. First published in Paris, 1613.

[4] This is ably discussed in F. E. Sutcliffe, *Guez de Balzac et son temps: littérature et politique*, Paris, 1959, Chap. 3.

taching themselves to Gaston d'Orléans, the center of so many intrigues, since he was not only Louis XIII's brother but also heir to the throne until 1638. Their personalized concept of service, loyalty to their order, and the clientele system all go far to explain the repeated noble conspiracies against Richelieu whom many regarded as a tyrant and a menace to their way of life. In this context, it was but a further step for a given nobleman who had fallen from grace to seek honorable employment abroad. During the chaotic years 1613 and 1614, both the young Bassompierre and the Marquis de Beauvais-Nangis, having momentarily last favor with the Queen Mother, seriously contemplated such a move.[5] They abandoned the idea, however, upon regaining the Regent's good graces. Much later, after Bassompierre had won a marshal's baton, he was implicated in the plots preceding the Day of Dupes. Upon being advised of his imminent arrest, he sought advice from the aged Duke of Epernon who said that if he, like Bassompierre, were fifty years old instead of almost eighty, he would not remain in Paris an hour. And he offered Bassompierre financial assistance to enable him to flee. Bassompierre, however, said that he had served the king for thirty years and would not now seek another career abroad. Since he was innocent, he was certain to be pardoned.[6] The result was that he was arrested and incarcerated in the Bastille for twelve years, gaining his release only after Richelieu's death.

Although the nobles' personalized concept of service and fidelity seemed to justify participation in factions that opposed royal policy and even transference of their allegiance to foreign princes, well-established French law decreed that such actions were punishable as *lèse-majesté*. As early as the Ordinance of Villers-Cotterets (1539), Francis I defined this most serious offense as "conspiring, plotting, or moving against our person, our children, or against the state (*république*) of our realm."[7] This was reiterated in more elaborate form in the Ordinance of Blois (1579)[8] and in still greater detail in

---

[5] *Journal de ma vie: Mémoires du Maréchal de Bassompierre*, de Chantérac, ed., Paris, 1870-1877, Vol. I, 366. *Mémoires du Marquis de Beauvais-Nangis*, Monmerqué and Taillandier, eds., Paris, 1862, pp. 139-40.

[6] *Bassompierre*, Vol. IV, 131-33.   [7] Isambert, Vol. XII, Pt. 2, 590.

[8] *Ibid.*, Vol. XIV, 424.

the royal declaration of May 27, 1610.[9] Although this legislation made use of general, comprehensive terminology in defining *lèse-majesté*, the crime was considered to consist of overt or covert acts against the person of the king, members of his family, or the safety of his realm. The concept remained personalized in that it was centered upon the king; the more impersonal idea of treason against the state did not assume major importance in French law until the Revolution. Richelieu expanded the definition of *lèse-majesté* to include the composition, publication, and distribution of defamatory libels concerning political matters. Because of his recommendations to the Assembly of Notables of 1626-1627 and their favorable action, the Code Michaud (1629) added these offenses to the long list of crimes that were subject to the penalties of *lèse-majesté*.[10] In this way the Cardinal sought to equate loyalty to the king with acceptance of his policies for the benefit of the state. Furthermore, in the factional strife that was so frequently directed against himself, Richelieu did not hestitate to accuse the followers of the Queen Mother and Gaston d'Orléans of *lèse-majesté*. The members of the royal family itself were untouchable, but the followers of all but Louis XIII found themselves guilty of crimes against the state in the course of serving the Queen Mother and the heir to the throne. The period presents no clearer instance of the disparity between the nobles' concept of personal loyalty and Richelieu's efforts to make allegiance to the state both supreme and exclusive. Even he, however, was capable of reversing the condemnation of an offending nobleman when his loyalty was assured, provided that his talents served the Cardinal's purposes. During the Huguenot uprisings, the Duke of Rohan, a very able military man, was declared guilty of *lèse-majesté* in the first degree, yet he was later restored to favor and given command of a French army in the Valtelline.

The first serious threat from the factious nobility arose in 1626 during the intrigues that surrounded the marriage of Monsieur (Gaston d'Orléans) and burgeoned into the Chalais conspiracy. The two most important victims of this episode were Marshal d'Ornano

[9] *Ibid.*, Vol. xvi, 6-8.
[10] *Ibid.*, Vol. xvi, 275-76. See n. 34 and text.

and the Marquis de Chalais, both of whom had in fact plotted against the crown and, given the condition of French society, had jeopardized the safety of the state. Ornano seems to have advised Gaston to undertake bold action against his royal brother, and Chalais evidently laid plans for the assassination of Richelieu. There was more than a suggestion that Louis XIII might be killed, after which Gaston would ascend the throne and marry Anne of Austria. Noble support for the conspiracy reached formidable proportions. That both Ornano and Chalais were guilty of *lèse-majesté* as it was defined seems certain. When Louis XIII learned of the matter and considered arresting Ornano, he sought the advice of Richelieu and Schomberg who answered that in such cases it was impossible to obtain mathematical proofs of guilt. The king should therefore forestall the threat to his realm by taking strong measures in advance of the crime. Because factionalism and rebelliousness were so widespread and because of continuing danger from the Huguenots and Spain, there were no other means of preserving the safety of the king and the state.[11] Here appears once more the idea that in political affairs a special standard of justice without proofs of guilt was both necessary and justified. Ornano was subsequently arrested on the charge that his seditious advice to Gaston had impaired relations between him and the king and might ruin the heir to the throne.[12] Within a matter of weeks, Ornano died in prison of natural causes. Richelieu greatly regretted this untimely death because he wished to bring Ornano to trial, doubtless as an example to other conspirators.[13] In view of the record, it seems certain that he would have been convicted. In 1643, after Richelieu's death, there appeared a violent pamphlet, *Le Maréchal d'Ornano, martyr d'état*, which purported to exculpate Ornano. Its argument was

[11] Richelieu, *Mémoires*, Vol. VI, 36-41.

[12] *Mercure français*, Vol. XII, 267, 280.

[13] *Lettres*, Vol. VII, 951. When Ornano died in prison, there were rumors that he succumbed to poisoning at Richelieu's order. It seems, however, that Ornano was a doomed man because of his acts but died a natural death. J. Charay, "Une énigme historique: Comment mourut le maréchal J.-B. d'Ornano?" *Revue du Viverais*, LXI (1957), No. 2, 49-63.

then very familiar: Richelieu had equated loyalty to the state with loyalty to himself and had eliminated princes, laws, and rights in exercising personal tyranny. Ornano "perished under the fury of a minister for merely attempting to preserve the rights of the monarchy."[14] Had this argument been applied to certain later acts of Richelieu, it would have been more convincing, but in 1626 he had not yet achieved the heights of power that he later obtained. It seems clear that the decision to arrest Ornano was as much Louis XIII's as the Cardinal's. The episode is important chiefly as dramatic evidence of the dangers that confronted both king and minister, and the consequent necessity of their using extraordinary expedients to forestall sedition.

In the case of Chalais, there seems to have been ample evidence of his guilt. Even so, Louis XIII, doubtless at Richelieu's suggestion, created a special criminal court at Nantes for the trial, the first of many such tribunals in the period. The court was staffed chiefly from the Parlement of Rennes but included certain royal officers as well.[15] This practice of appointing *ad hoc* tribunals to try great cases was unusual but entirely within the judicial prerogatives of the crown. The commission to the judges to try Chalais mentioned his conspiracy, its divisive effects within the royal family, his plan to take up arms, and accused him of "*lèse-majesté* in the highest degree, plotting and agitating against the state, and disrupting the public peace."[16] A verdict of guilty was quickly reached on the basis of the evidence and the letter of the law, and Chalais was executed forthwith in spite of many appeals for clemency. Richelieu's role in the affair is not entirely clear but he seems to have strongly influenced the king in favor of firmness. In a memoir that he wrote shortly after the execution, he clearly described the dangers of such conspiracies as well as the difficulty of controlling them and the reasons why the king should exert every effort to do so. "If the principal authors of this conspiracy were done away with," he

---

[14] *Le Maréchal d'Ornano*, p. 7.
[15] *Mercure français*, Vol. XII, 387-89.
[16] *Ibid.*, Vol. XII, 394.

wrote, "it seems that they would not attain their objective, but it is impossible to annihilate all of them because they include so many persons of quality whom we cannot think of punishing.[17] The relatives of those who are punished will always be ready to embolden them, and the women will not lose their discontent and their fury.[18] Messieurs de Vendôme are still in prison. If they are freed they will raise the devil; if they are executed their children will resent it. Saint-Ursin and the other princes will always be the same and could not be changed even if we gave them half the state."[19] Rarely had the dilemma that confronted Louis XIII and Richelieu been presented so clearly. The plots, Richelieu continued, were directed chiefly against himself, but if he were sacrificed to such machinations Louis XIII would lose a servant who was most devoted to the interests of the king and the state. This would injure the king because it would demonstrate to all that he was not strong enough to protect those who serve him and to combat the interests of the great who constantly attempt to lower the king and lessen royal power. It would even convince others that they should place no confidence in the king's protection and should seek safety elsewhere, all of which was impossible to combine with effective service to His Majesty and the state.[20] It was this inexorable reasoning that simultaneously convinced Louis XIII of the necessity of rigorous justice and associated Richelieu's person and policies with the fortunes of the state.

Two additional measures of Louis XIII and Richelieu against the nobility and their way of life occurred in 1626: an edict against duelling (February) and a royal declaration ordering the destruc-

---

[17] César, Duke of Vendôme, and his brother, the Grand Prior, were legitimized natural sons of Henry IV and Gabrielle d'Estrées, and were arrested in June 1626, for their part in the Chalais conspiracy. The Grand Prior died in prison in February 1629, possibly of poison. The Duke was freed after four years of detention.

[18] Intrigue by the great ladies of the court was invariably a major element of the noble conspiracies. The Duchess of Chevreuse was a prime mover in the Chalais affair.

[19] *Lettres*, Vol. ii, 266-67.

[20] The entire memoir is printed in the *Lettres*, Vol. ii, 265-68.

tion of fortresses that were not on the frontiers (July).[21] Both were for the purpose of increasing royal control over the nobles, were clearly within the scope of the royal authority, and were supported by extensive precedents. The most dramatic resulting episode was the trial and execution of Henri de Montmorency, Count of Bouteville, and his cousin, the Count des Chapelles, who participated in a famous duel in the Place Royale, a piece of bravado in open defiance of the king and his edict. This time the accused were tried before the Parlement of Paris with the usual legal formalities. Because of Bouteville's family heritage—he was a cousin of the Duke of Montmorency—and the importance of duelling to the noble code of honor, many of the most prestigious nobles in France petitioned Louis XIII for clemency. The Prince of Condé put his finger on the essential point when he wrote the king that Bouteville "had erred because of the error of the custom of your realm which causes honor to consist of perilous actions. It was this concept of glory rather than any specific intent to disobey you that brought him to this disobedience. If, in order to maintain the law that Your Majesty has made and because of the need of examples, it is necessary for you to punish these guilty ones, please do so, Sire, in such a way that does not destroy their being nor bring shame to their name."[22] And he urged imprisonment for life. The Duke of Montmorency also wrote to the king, recalling the services of his house to the monarchy and appealing for clemency.[23] In answer, Louis XIII and Richelieu wrote simultaneous letters to the Duke, arguing that justice must take its course if the royal authority were to be preserved.[24]

[21] Isambert, Vol. xvi, 175-83, 192-94. On Richelieu's efforts to stop duelling and his limited success, see R. Herr, "Honor versus Absolutism: Richelieu's Fight against Duelling," *Journal of Modern History*, xxvii (1955), 281-85.

[22] *Mercure français*, Vol. xiii, 420. This volume of the *Mercure* is a major source for all aspects of this episode.

[23] *Ibid.*, Vol. xiii, 421-22.

[24] Louis XIII wrote that if he pardoned Bouteville he would violate his oath relative to duelling and would be criticized for allowing infraction of his edicts, thus lessening his authority. Also, he would lose further noblemen to the evil of duelling. Justice must therefore take its course. *Mercure français*, Vol. xiii, 422-24. Richelieu wrote that under any other circumstances "in

After the Parlement condemned Bouteville and des Chapelles to death as guilty of *lèse-majesté* for violating the edict against duels, a delegation of great ladies headed by the Princess of Condé and including Bouteville's wife appealed to Louis XIII for mercy. In answer, he said, "I am as afflicted by their loss as you, but my conscience forbids my pardoning them."[25] The episode demonstrates that Louis XIII was determined to fulfill his duties as divinely authorized monarch as he understood them and to preserve his authority even at the expense of more humane values. His actions were clearly within the royal prerogative and required no other justification, but the widespread reaction against enforcing his edict in this instance vividly demonstrates the extensive psychological adjustments that were required before the nobles could view themselves simply as subjects of the crown.

The Assembly of Notables of 1626-1627 witnessed further efforts on Richelieu's part to augment royal control over the nobles and their rebellions. Having wrestled with foreign and domestic problems as First Minister for more than two years and having reached a moment of *détente* in both areas, the Cardinal called the assembly in order to gain support for his long-range plans for strengthening the state. These included a wide variety of reforms in financial, administrative, military, and other affairs. That he exerted every effort to render the gathering a success is attested by the care with which he prepared for it in advance, directed its discussions and implemented its decisions.[26] In his prepared agenda, rebellion by the nobles and crimes against the state occupied an important position,[27] and during the session on December 2, both Richelieu and Marillac made it clear that they hoped for more effective means of suppressing such uprisings. Marillac, who was Keeper of the Seals, said that although ample proofs of guilt were had in the Chalais

---

which the interest of his state is not involved," the king would have granted Montmorency's request. *Lettres*, Vol. II, 479-80.

[25] *Mercure francais*, Vol. XIII, 450.

[26] This is demonstrated in J. Petit, *L'Assemblée des notables de 1626-1627*, Paris, 1936.

[27] *Lettres*, Vol. II, 321-23.

conspiracy, these were often lacking because of the secrecy sur-
rounding such deeds. In similar instances without such proofs, it
would be entirely legal to move against the conspirators on the basis
of mere conjecture.[28] And Richelieu, in discussing the condition of
state finances, said that although economies were desirable, the
safety of the state justified any necessary expenditures and extraordinary expedients.[29]

Richelieu's tactic in obtaining acceptance of increased controls
over factious nobles was to propose a reduction of the penalties for
disobedience but speedier application of them in practice.[30] Whether
he intended any leniency may be doubted, since his marginal comment on this proposal reads: "Kings are kings only as long as their
authority is recognized and they demonstrate their favor. They are
unable to ensure the effects of these unless they are strictly obeyed,
since disobedience by one individual is capable of arresting the
course of a plan whose effects will benefit the public. Obedience is
the true characteristic of the subject."[31] In any case, the notables
decided in favor of retaining the older ordinances in all their rigor
and asked for their enforcement, thereby giving Richelieu the support that he sought for additional restraints.[32] The most effective
means of implementing these was to expand the definition of *lèse-
majesté*. After considerable discussion, the notables agreed to all the
Cardinal's major proposals on this score.[33] As they eventually appeared in articles 170 to 178 of the Code Michaud, the following
were punishable as capital offenses if done without royal permission: contacting ambassadors of foreign powers, recruiting troops,
maintaining more arms than necessary for protection, accumulating
war materials, casting cannon, entering into leagues, fortifying cities
and strong points, calling assemblies, leaving the realm, and writing,

[28] [P. Ardier], *L'Assemblée des notables tenue à Paris és années 1626 et
1627*, Paris, 1652, p. 35.

[29] *Ibid.*, pp. 39, 41. *Lettres*, Vol. ii, 300, 302.

[30] *Lettres*, Vol. ii, 321. Ardier p. 149.

[31] *Lettres*, Vol. ii, 321.

[32] Petit, pp. 196-97.

[33] The proposals are in the *Lettres*, Vol. ii, 322-23. The discussion is outlined in Ardier, pp. 149-156.

publishing, or selling seditious libels.[34] These sweeping provisions seemed to cover all aspects of noble conspiracies but in fact they merely expanded and made more specific the provisions of earlier ordinances and added nothing new except the prohibition of unlicensed publications. They were, however, quite sufficient for the Cardinal's purposes.

Richelieu also sought the notables' approval of his plans to implement the edict calling for the destruction of castles not on the frontiers. In this instance, the discussion touched only upon certain provinces and was kept under control by Richelieu who doubtless wished to proceed with the demolition according to plans of his own devising. He received general approval of the destruction which he proceeded to carry out through the remainder of the reign.[35] Not all of Richelieu's acts during the assembly were contrary to the interests of the nobility, however. The members of the second estate presented an elaborate petition which asked for many concessions: assignment of certain offices in church and state exclusively to nobles, places of importance in local administration, extensive authority in the military establishment, schools for military training of young noblemen, and various financial favors.[36] A few of these were incorporated into the Code Michaud and indicate that Richelieu was genuinely concerned with the plight of the nobility, but he agreed to none that allowed them to participate by their own right in governmental affairs on any level. This was reserved entirely for the king and his ministers.[37] On the basis of the record, it seems that Richelieu went far in persuading the notables to approve measures that were designed to subject the second estate to indefeasible royal controls. All were within the scope of the royal prerogative but ran counter to many elements of the nobles' traditional way of life. Reason of state in this instance therefore involved the violation not of legal rights but social values.

[34] Isambert, Vol. xvi, 274-76. These articles closely follow the Cardinal's proposals. *Lettres*, Vol. ii, 322-23.

[35] Petit, pp. 151-63.

[36] *Mercure français*, Vol. xii, 40-52, second pagination.

[37] Details are given in Petit, pp. 219-20.

The policies of Louis XIII and Richelieu relative to the Huguenot uprisings present much that is irrelevant to a study of reason of state. Indeed, it may be questioned whether these episodes should be characterized as rebellions by the Huguenot minority or Catholic crusades under the leadership of the Most Christian King, since they partook of the characteristics of both. The great majority of contemporary publications that touched on the movements were marked by extreme partisanship rather than solid reasoning. Undoubtedly there was much hatred, bad faith, and outright fear on both sides. Certain essentials are nevertheless clear. The Huguenots were subjects of the French monarchy and always regarded themselves as such, even while resisting and plotting against their sovereign. They were subjects who were differentiated from the great majority, however, in that they held extensive special privileges which had been conceded them by the crown. After the Edict of Nantes, their formal statements of political theory were invariably royalist. As much as the Gallican Catholics, the Huguenots accepted divine right sovereignty and attributed corresponding power to the ruler.[38] Far from deterring them from rebellion, however, the position provided them with a certain justification for overt acts against the crown. The Huguenots' special privileges stemmed from the Edict of Nantes and several later "treaties" between the ruler and his Protestant subjects at the conclusion of successive revolts. Technically, these were not treaties in the usual sense but unilateral concessions on the part of His Majesty who granted and renewed special privileges at his discretion. Whether the king was bound to observe them was highly debatable. Legally, of course, he was not, since he was responsible to no earthly power and his concessions to his subjects had no force except that which he gave them. Morally, however, there was a strong case that he was bound to observe his promises to his subjects as well as foreign princes. And since the Huguenots could easily point to unfulfilled and violated royal concessions, they

---

[38] C. Mercier, "Les Théories politiques des calvinistes en France au cours des guerres de religion," *Bulletin de la Société de l'histoire du protestantisme français*, LXXXIII (1934), 389-95. A. Galland, "Les Pasteurs français Amyraut, Bochart, etc., et la royauté de droit divin," *ibid.*, LXXVII (1928) 14-20.

invariably assumed the position that they were merely loyal subjects who were revolting not against their king but for what was rightfully theirs because of specific royal actions and the ruler's obligation to keep his word.

A famous instance of this was the controversy over Fort Louis, the royalist stronghold that was erected in 1621 in a commanding position near La Rochelle and continually threatened the independence and commerce of the city. Demolition of the fort was promised in connection with the Treaty of Montpellier (1622), together with a stipulation requiring destruction of all new fortifications that were in Protestant hands.[39] The Duke of Rohan faithfully carried out the latter, but Fort Louis remained intact and was almost immediately strengthened for use against the Rochellese.[40] In March 1623 a petition was presented to the Royal Council by the two Huguenot General Deputies who were resident at court, requesting fulfillment of various provisions of the treaty and the destruction of the fort, but this was denied by the king.[41] Rohan and Soubise subsequently pointed to the failure to destroy the fort as one of the many justifications of their revolt in 1625. The Treaty of Paris which ended this uprising early in the following year stated that although Fort Louis was not to be destroyed, it would never be used to threaten "the security and freedom of commerce" of La Rochelle.[42] This was accompanied by a verbal promise of destruction which,

[39] The treaty of Montpellier specified that all new fortifications that were held by the Huguenots should be destroyed, leaving only the earlier ones intact. *Mercure français*, Vol. VIII, 840-41. The destruction of Fort Louis was not mentioned in the treaty, but a promise to this effect was given the Huguenot leaders. E. Benoît, *Histoire de l'Édit de Nantes*, Delft, 1693, Vol. II, 410. The fact that this promise was made is accepted by all later writers and is even admitted in Richelieu's *Mémoires*, Vol. VII, 219. Cf. Rohan, *Mémoires*, Amsterdam, 1644, pp. 183, 187-88.

[40] *Mercure français*, Vol. VIII, 851. A year later, Fort Louis was a major stronghold. *Ibid.*, Vol. IX, 448.

[41] *Ibid.*, Vol. IX, 451. Benoît, Vol. II, 66, second pagination.

[42] *Mercure français*, Vol. XI, 120, second pagination. It is noteworthy that Fancan, an ardent partisan of accommodation with the Huguenots, strongly advocated granting them satisfaction by destroying Fort Louis. S. R. Gardiner, "Un Mémoire inédit de Richelieu relatif aux Huguenots," *Revue historique*, I (1876), 228-38. This memoir is now attributed to Fancan.

to no one's surprise, was not fulfilled. The issue was still unsettled when Richelieu embarked upon his massive campaign against the city, at which time the Huguenots again instanced it as an example of Catholic bad faith.

Richelieu, for his part, distrusted and despised the Huguenots as heretics and troublemakers within the realm. That he hated them for their heresy is evident from his religious writings, yet he generally advocated peaceful means of effecting their return to the Catholic fold and realized the dangers of renewed warfare between religious factions.[43] Of greater moment to him as director of royal policy was the troublesome position of the Huguenots as checks upon royal power. In his well-known instructions to Schomberg during his first ministry (1616), he argued that their uprisings were punished not for religious reasons but as pure rebellion.[44] His patience with the Huguenots was put to its severest test during 1625 when Rohan and Soubise chose to revolt while he was thoroughly occupied with the Valtelline affair. This convergence of challenges tested his statesmanship to the utmost and its lesson was not lost on him, for, as he wrote to Louis XIII in May of that year, "As long as the Huguenots retain their position in France, the king will never be master within the realm nor will he be able to undertake any glorious action abroad."[45] That he was determined to reduce their political power is evident. Regardless of the special problems that their religion presented, Richelieu was adamant that the Huguenots, like all other Frenchmen, were subjects of the crown and must recognize that the sovereign guided his relations with them according to the canons of reason of state.

It was during the Huguenot rebellion of 1625-1626 that Richelieu's spokesmen first applied the doctrine of reason of state to the rela-

[43] See Pt. 1, n. 222, 223, and text. The ablest recent study of Richelieu's projects relative to eliminating the Calvinist heresy is P. Blet, "Le Plan de Richelieu pour la réunion des protestants," *Gregorianum*, XLVIII (1967), 100-129. Blet shows that Richelieu had a consistent, extensive plan for peaceful conversion of the Huguenots and pursued it intermittently throughout his entire ministry, although with small success.

[44] Cf. Pt. I, n. 225, 226, and text.

[45] *Lettres*, Vol. II, 83.

tions between Louis XIII and his subjects. This was notably apparent in a long pamphlet, *Response au Manifeste du sieur de Soubize*, which appeared in 1625 and was incorporated into the *Mercure français*.[46] Although it was attributed to Jérémie Ferrier, there is considerable evidence that it was written under the close supervision of Richelieu himself.[47] The section which argues the relevance of reason of state to the king-subjects relationship discusses the question that was so extensively agitated by the Huguenots at this time, whether the king was bound to keep faith with his subjects. The Manifesto of Soubise charged that "the king has been persuaded to accept a maxim unworthy of a Christian prince, that he is not obliged to keep faith with his subjects, much less with heretics."[48] In answer, the author of the *Response* argued that kings, unlike all others, are bound by their special position and obligations of office to place service of the state above all other considerations:

The virtues of kings differ from those of ordinary individuals in that the former must be guided by the interests and laws of their states; otherwise these would not be virtues but most dangerous errors. One would not say that the king does not love his children and is not a good father to them if he does not divide the realm among them. He may not do so according to the laws, for in submitting to them he is not only king but becomes something more, if possible, because to be king places him above men but to submit to the laws raises him above himself. Of these laws, the most important are those of majesty, sovereignty, and the government of the people; he should be more heedful of these laws than his own life. Likewise, one would not call the king cruel if he does not pardon all criminals, for he should not do so. One would not call him unjust if he extends the boundaries of his state; he should do so because of reason of state and the laws of majesty, and because as soon as he touches the sceptre he swears a solemn oath, solely because he takes it in his

[46] Vol. XI, 221-335.
[47] Deloche, pp. 263-66.   [48] *Mercure français*, Vol. XI, 241.

hand, to devote all his strength to the preservation and growth of his rule. Whoever doubts this truth is very ignorant in politics.[49]

Because of the sovereign's all-embracing obligation to serve the state, his policies must be determined by circumstances rather than his commitments:

> An individual is bound promptly to carry out what he promises; the king is bound to do so only if it pleases him, and it should please him only when it can be done without harming his state. The justice of sovereignty places it above ordinary justice in such matters. To be a most just, loyal and faithful king is to avoid all harm to his state . . . . We must remember that the promise made by the sovereign to the state when he assumed direction of it limits all promises that he may subsequently make. When the interest of the state is involved, we must return to first principles and recall that the law of the state compels him to prize it above all his individual acts. Such is the glory of kings and the security of governments.[50]

On the basis of the foregoing, the author reached the all-important conclusion that "the king keeps the promises that he makes to his subjects but in a manner and with a justice other than that [which he would use] if they were not his subjects. For in keeping his word to them, he must preserve their safety and that of the state."[51] That is, the circumstances of politics were more binding upon the ruler than his moral obligation to keep faith with his people. As an example of this, the author insisted that Louis XIII's violation of his promise not to disturb Protestantism in Béarn was necessitated by developments in that area.[52] Again Richelieu was arguing that the nature of politics and the unique obligations of the sovereign were such that circumstances justified policies which ran counter to the general principles of morality and would not be permitted among individuals. The subjects were bound by the canons of Christian

[49] *Ibid.*, 242-43.   [50] *Ibid.*, 243-44.   [51] *Ibid.*, 247.
[52] *Ibid.*, 247-49.

morality but the Most Christian King was exempt from them to the extent that was required for effective fulfillment of his divinely assigned role. In this manner, Richelieu sought to convince the Huguenots that reason of state freed Louis XIII from his obligation to keep faith with them in all instances.

The Treaty of Paris which ended this revolt essentially restored the *status quo ante* and was ratified on February 5, 1626.[53] In answer to petitions by the Huguenot deputies, it was confirmed by a more extensive royal edict which was registered by the Parlement of Paris on April 6.[54] The preamble of the edict makes it clear that it was strictly a royal concession which had been solicited "with every submission that subjects may render their king to pardon them and forget the past."[55] More important than the provisions of the peace, however, was the intense dislike of the settlement among the ardent Catholics of the period. As a practical politician, Richelieu realized that his policies required further justification, particularly because the Valtelline affair remained unsettled and the royal court contained many persons who resented any accommodation with the Huguenots. Ferrier's *Response au Manifeste du sieur de Soubize* had answered the Huguenots' charge of duplicity, and the Cardinal now sought to defend his actions before his Catholic critics. For this purpose he made use of a brief work by one Dryon, a minor pamphleteer of the period, whose *Discours au Roy sur la paix qu'il a donnée à ceux de la religion prétenduë réformée* stated the case for peace with the Huguenot minority and was published with Richelieu's approval, appearing in the *Mercure français*.[56]

In essence, Dryon's position was that the peace of the realm was more important than religious proselytizing and doctrinal unity. Echoing the arguments of the earlier *politiques*, he insisted that the crying need of France was peace, and the only means of securing it was to enforce the king's edicts relative to religious pacification. Warfare for religious purposes is self-defeating, he said, since it fails

---

[53] *Ibid.*, 119-20, second pagination.

[54] *Ibid.*, 127-39, second pagination.   [55] *Ibid.*, 128, second pagination.

[56] *Ibid.*, Vol. XII, 437-50. Richelieu's request that Dryon publish his tract is mentioned on p. 425.

to convert the Huguenots and merely strengthens their heresy. The pope may be for war against the Huguenots, but he is so envenomed against all heretics that he has lost his perspective, said Dryon, quoting a famous passage from Cardinal d'Ossat's letters relative to papal views on reason of state.[57] For this reason, Dryon claimed, again quoting d'Ossat, "secular princes obey and humor the pope up to a certain point, but when he touches their states and their reputations, they have reason to dissociate themselves from his acts."[58] And he cited Henry IV's alliance with England and protection of Geneva as entirely justified although opposed by the papacy. As for the Huguenots, Dryon continued, they do not seek to throw off royal sovereignty but revolt merely for matters pertaining to their religion. Enforcement of royal edicts will therefore preserve peace, he said, citing the promise to destroy Fort Louis and implying that this should be done.[59] Most important, it is not heresy that limits royal absolutism but rebellion and war. In peace the king is strongest; therefore peace even with the heretics in his realm strengthens his rule and is to be preferred to the chaos of religious strife. Through this simple but forceful reasoning which reflected decades of French experience with religious upheaval, Dryon concluded that peace and effective royal absolutism were more important to the state than doctrinal unity which could be achieved only at immense cost, if at all. Papal recriminations and threats of excommunication might be ignored, he added, once more quoting from Cardinal d'Ossat to the effect that God's judgments are based on truth and are always correct whereas the popes' reflect opinion and may be wrong.[60] He concluded logically by denying papal supremacy over kings. In this manner, Dryon and Richelieu through him attempted to convince Catholic opinion that the safety of the state was to be preferred to religious unity and that reason of state justified accommodation with heretics even in a Christian monarchy.

The last and most extensive conflict between Louis XIII's government and the Huguenots, that of 1627-1629, produced only a limited number of developments relative to reason of state. Essentially, both

[57] *Ibid.*, 440. See Pt. I, n. 119 and text.
[58] *Ibid.*, 441.   [59] *Ibid.*, 445.   [60] *Ibid.*, 448-49.

parties continued to adhere to the positions that they had taken in earlier struggles of this nature. Throughout the Huguenots maintained that they were merely loyal subjects who were fighting for the privileges that had been conceded them by earlier royal edicts and peace settlements, and they justified their rebellion by citing continual violation of these promises. Their claims were extensively set forth in such key documents as the *Manifeste contenant les causes et raisons qui ont obligé ceux de la ville de La Rochelle de prendre les armes et se joindre à celles du Roy de la Grande Bretagne* and the *Manifeste du Duc de Rohan*.[61] As was stated in the Oath of Union which was subscribed to by the towns that followed the Duke of Rohan in open revolt,

> We solemnly protest before God that we wish to live and die in the obedience, subjection, and fidelity that we owe the king who is the legitimate and natural prince that God has given us. We feel bound to this duty by the laws of our consciences, and this with the benefits of his edicts, warrants, declarations, and general and specific concessions that were made for the security and maintenance of the reformed churches in this realm. Inasmuch as the enemies of his state and our peace have violated and infringed them and continually strive to do so, we declare and protest to you that we will use all the courage and strength that God has given us to ensure that they are faithfully maintained and observed.[62]

And the oath added that the King of England had sent forces to aid the Huguenots merely for this purpose.

The royal government, of course, refused to recognize the legitimacy of these claims. As for the king's promises to his subjects, these were mere concessions that were made at royal pleasure; coercion of the ruler to observe them was out of the question:

> It is the glory of kings, the security of governments, and the salvation of the people never to demand from their king any

[61] Excerpts of these are printed in the *Mercure français*, Vol. XIV, 51-104 and 224-305, together with extensive criticisms from the royalist standpoint.
[62] *Ibid.*, 310.

promises whatsoever that may lessen his authority. The means of restricting the people to their duty and consequently saving them from the ruin that sedition brings is to convince them that they should never attempt to secure anything by force of arms or illicit means but should seek their safety and guidance from their kings. Otherwise, inevitable ruin follows when they attempt to be kings themselves and to control and govern themselves as they please. These reasons of state concern you—you who nourish rebellion in the heart of your city. Take care that in importuning the king to order the demolition of Fort Louis at La Rochelle His Majesty's righteous indignation does not order it to be preserved as long as you are rebels and bad subjects.[63]

Clearly, the Huguenots' argument that they were merely revolting for what was rightfully theirs carried no weight with the royal administration. As the year 1627 advanced and the rebellion grew in scope, Louis XIII accused the Duke of Rohan and all the towns that had followed him in revolt of *lèse-majesté* and ordered that they be tried by the Parlement of Toulouse.[64] Although this denied the Duke's traditional privilege of trial before the Parlement of Paris in the presence of his peers, the royal administration took the position that Rohan had forfeited this privilege by rebellion. His crime was so obvious that proofs of guilt might be dispensed with, and prompt punishment would have a chastening effect upon other rebels in the area.[65] The trial was duly held, and the Parlement of

---

[63] *Ibid.*, 77. This is from the commentary on the *Manifeste contenant les causes et raisons qui ont obligé ceux de la ville de La Rochelle de prendre les armes et se joindre à celles du Roy de la Grande Bretagne.*

[64] *Mercure français*, Vol. XIV, 319-23. The commission is dated October 14, 1627.

[65] The reasoning supporting this is set forth in a "Recueil Sommaire des Raisons de la Resolution prise par le Roy d'envoyer au Parlement de Toulouse la Commission pour faire le Procez au Duc de Rohan, le declarant decheu du Privilege de Pairie," Bibliothèque Nationale, Fonds Français, 18429, fols. 47-52. The main contentions are (1) there is no written basis of such a privilege, but even if there were it would be forfeited by rebellion, (2) privileges granted by the state can never be used to prevent punishment of crimes against the state, (3) if the peerage is a fief, confiscation does not have to wait for con-

Toulouse condemned Rohan and his followers in two separate decrees early in 1628.[66] From this point onward, the dispute was adjourned to the battlefield. At the capitulation of La Rochelle, the Huguenot deputies sued for peace and threw themselves upon the mercy of Louis XIII who informed them:

> I pray God that it is with your hearts that you honor me and that it is not the extremity to which you are reduced that causes you to use these words. I well know that you have done everything in your power to throw off the burden of obedience to me. I forgive your rebellions. If you are my good and faithful subjects, I shall be a good prince to you, and if your actions conform to the protestations that you have made to me, I shall hold to what I have promised you.[67]

These memorable words of Louis XIII epitomized the relationship that Richelieu sought to establish between the king and his subjects throughout the realm. All discretion and freedom of action lay with the ruler, and his subjects had no choice but to submit to any policies that he might adopt. Even the execution of his promises to his subjects depended on his pleasure. That Richelieu succeeded in reducing the Huguenots to a position of unquestioning obedience is demonstrated by the success of the Peace of Alais (1629) and their nonparticipation in the rebellions that occurred later in the reign. Even the most serious, those of Gaston d'Orléans and his followers, failed to attract a following among the Huguenots, a fact that won them the gratitude of both Louis XIII and Richelieu.[68]

---

demnation because proofs are not required in cases of manifest guilt, (4) peerage is merely a granted privilege and may be revoked, (5) precedents for trial of peers are varied and uncertain; therefore it is best to have the case tried in the province where the crime was committed, and (6) condemnation by a local court will strike terror and be a salutary example for many remaining rebels.

[66] *Mercure français*, Vol. xiv, 45-57, second pagination. The decrees are dated January 22 and 29, 1628.

[67] *Ibid.*, 696, second pagination.

[68] On August 8, 1632, Richelieu wrote to Marshal de La Force, a Calvinist, that Louis XIII was very satisfied with the loyalty of the adherents to La Force's religion. *Lettres*, Vol. iv, 341.

RICHELIEU'S ADVERSARIES: FACTIONS OF THE GREAT, 1629-1632

In January 1629, five months before the Peace of Alais terminated the resistance of the Huguenots, Richelieu submitted to Louis XIII a lengthy *Advis donné au Roy après la prise de La Rochelle, pour le bien de ses affaires.*[69] This was one of the most important of many memoirs with which the Cardinal sought to guide and instruct his royal master. Richelieu's purpose at this juncture was to press the case for his many-sided program of state-building and incidentally to demonstrate his own indispensability to its fulfillment. Essentially, he was indicating the measures that Louis XIII must adopt if he would strengthen the French monarchy and state system, both at home and abroad. "Now that La Rochelle is taken," he wrote, "if the king wishes to make himself the most powerful monarch on earth and the most esteemed of princes, he should consider before God and carefully and secretly examine with his faithful servants what personal qualities are required of him and what should be reformed in his state."[70] For this purpose, extensive efforts must be made to increase effective royal power in both foreign and domestic affairs. In the latter area, Richelieu urged the king to end the Huguenot menace by reducing their remaining cities in the south, destroy all strongholds except those on the frontiers and others that might serve to overawe rebellious urban centers, lessen the burden of taxation on the lower classes, discontinue the *paulette* (an annual payment by holders of venal offices making them fully heritable) when it terminated a year hence, prevent encroachment by the Parlements upon royal sovereignty, ensure obedience by great and small, appoint wise and capable bishops, repurchase the alienated royal domain, and increase the royal revenue by one-half.[71]

This ambitious program was well conceived for its purpose, the strengthening of the state, but much of it was never realized, chiefly because of the crown's fiscal weakness. Regarding France's posture

---

[69] This document is printed in Richelieu's *Mémoires*, Vol. IX, 14-59, and in the *Lettres*, Vol. III, 179-213. My citations are to the *Lettres*.

[70] *Lettres*, Vol. III, 179-80.   [71] *Ibid.*, 180-81.

in foreign affairs, Richelieu insisted that her chief enemy was Spain but that outright war with her was to be avoided as far as possible. Instead, Louis XIII should strengthen France's military resources and her defensive position by increasing her power on the sea, fortifying cities and strongholds on all her borders, and establishing gateways into enemy territory for possible later use.[72] That Richelieu, who desperately sought to neutralize Hapsburg power, should advocate such limited measures graphically indicates the military weakness of France at this time and the handicaps that he experienced in directing French foreign relations. In his eyes, much remained to be done before France might assume her proper position in the affairs of nations.

Returning to domestic problems, Richelieu made clear that one of his major concerns was to control the great nobles and to limit their seditious activity. In this area, he approached his recommendations with great caution, as if to emphasize the importance and difficulty of the matter. Regarding Monsieur, Richelieu simply urged keeping him satisfied by giving him everything that he might desire, provided that it was not prejudicial to the state.[73] The king's lack of an heir sharply increased the dangers of noble factions, Richelieu warned; Louis should therefore do everything possible to avoid needlessly offending the great. He should even feign an appearance of favoring them and should assume the onerous burden of supporting them so as to prevent their lending their services to other princes.[74] That Richelieu who gloried in the majesty of Louis XIII should recommend that he stoop to these measures speaks volumes concerning the continuing danger from the nobility. Richelieu emphasized, however, that Louis XIII must exert greater effort to enforce his laws, including those that touched the nobles, and he specifically mentioned the edict against duelling. The laws concerning crimes against the state must be applied with extraordinary severity, he insisted, for otherwise the state cannot survive.[75]

For our purposes, one of the most significant passages of the *Advis* is that in which Richelieu lectured his sovereign on the differences

[72] *Ibid.*, 181-82.   [73] *Ibid.*, 184.   [74] *Ibid.*, 188-89.
[75] *Ibid.*, 192-93.

between his moral obligations as a man and as king. "The sins of kings as kings," he said, "differ from those that they commit as mere men. As men, they are subject to all that God imposes upon human beings, but as kings they are bound to use their power strictly for the purposes for which they received it from heaven, and moreover, without abusing it by extending their rule beyond the limits prescribed for them."[76] Although their authority is bounded by the rights of others, Richelieu continued, the primary duty of kings is to wield their power for the benefit of their states without regard to personal or humanitarian considerations. They should subject their states to the strict rule under which they belong and rigorously punish all crimes so as to forestall greater ones. Failure to fulfill this imperious role is a sin against the divinely established order of things, for "although as a man he may seem a saint, he will nevertheless be condemned as king."[77]

For this all-important reason, kings govern according to a morality which differs from that of other Christians:

> A Christian cannot be too quick in forgiving an insult or pardoning an offense, nor a king, governor, or magistrate quick enough in punishing them when the crimes concern the state. This distinction is crucial but the reason for it is clear and is based upon a single principle.
>
> God does not leave punishment in the hands of individuals, because with this pretext any man might follow his passions and disturb the public peace. On the contrary, He placed punishment in the hands of kings and magistrates according to the rules that He prescribed for them because, if [salutary] examples and chastisements were lacking, any injustice and violence might be committed with impunity against the public tranquility.
>
> Men's salvation occurs ultimately in the next world, and it is therefore not surprising that God wishes men to leave to Him the punishment of the wrongs that He scourges with his judgments in eternity. But states have no being after this world.

[76] *Ibid.*, 193.   [77] *Ibid.*, 194.

Their salvation is either in the present or nonexistent. Hence the punishments that are necessary to their survival may not be postponed but must be immediate.[78]

This is one of Richelieu's clearest statements of the necessity and justice of a special ethic of state policy, one that was practical and worldly but entirely appropriate to the Most Christian King when seeking the betterment of Christian France. Through this reasoning, Richelieu sought to clarify for his sovereign the difference between public and private morality and to provide a rationale for the harsh rule and occasionally immoral policies that both knew to be requisite to strengthening the French state.

Why did Richelieu find it necessary to include such observations in his recommendations to the king? The answer lies in Louis XIII's concept of royal authority and his view of his role as sovereign. There is ample evidence that Louis XIII was well aware of his duties as divinely authorized monarch and was determined to fulfill them to the letter. Although vacillating and occasionally weak-willed, he resolutely insisted that he was master and meant to be obeyed. Furthermore, he was strongly religious and thoroughly cognizant of the sacerdotal qualities of his office. Richelieu had no need to instruct his royal master in these matters. Louis XIII's resultant concept of just government, however, did not include such sophisticated refinements as the concept of reason of state and a special morality of politics. He thought merely in terms of his sovereign authority and his obligation to strengthen royal power and govern effectively. As an orthodox Christian of not overly subtle mentality, he found it difficult to comprehend that he might justifiably undertake measures that violated traditional moral and legal values. For this reason, Richelieu, both as First Minister and a Cardinal of the Church, sought to ease Louis' conscience regarding the justice of measures that were necessary to the advancement of state power. Repeatedly in the *Advis*, Richelieu stressed the personal qualities and attitudes that were requisite to a king if he were to be well

---

[78] *Ibid.*, 195. Cf. the similar views in Richelieu's *Instruction du chrétien*, in Pt. I, n. 220 and text, and in the *Catholique d'estat*, Pt. II, n. 69, 73, and text.

served, and he capped these by providing a rationale that went far to justify measures that were politically necessary but morally questionable.

The year 1629 witnessed rapid accentuation of the conflict between Richelieu and the *dévot* faction concerning the proper orientation of royal policy, a conflict that was not resolved until the Day of Dupes. Under the leadership of Cardinal Bérulle (until his death on October 2) and Michel de Marillac, the Keeper of the Seals, the *dévots* enjoyed strong support even from members of the royal family and advocated a policy that was opposed to Richelieu's in all essentials. The immediate cause of renewed friction was the resumption of anti-Hapsburg hostilities. Almost immediately after the fall of La Rochelle, Richelieu and Louis XIII embarked upon an Italian campaign that was occasioned by the disputed Mantuan succession. And after returning to southern France to crush the remaining strongholds of the Huguenots and destroy their political power, Louis XIII and Richelieu in the following year undertook more extensive hostilities in northern Italy for the purpose of supporting France's allies and neutralizing Hapsburg military advances. The reduction of the Huguenots to political impotence understandably pleased the *dévots* who would have preferred the total extirpation of Calvinism, but Richelieu's resumption of his anti-Hapsburg foreign policy quickly alienated all who favored peaceful relations with Catholic Spain and the restoration of religious uniformity, not to mention their desire to improve the crown's finances and to alleviate the widespread distress among the lower classes. As Bérulle wrote to Richelieu on February 21, 1629, "It is said . . . that we are beginning an interminable war in the midst of public necessities and the people's misery, and that under the pretext of [taking] Casal we wish to enter the Milanese. This is publicly and vociferously criticized even by avowed enemies of the King of Spain."[79]

[79] Bérulle, *Correspondance*, Vol. III, 449. The fundamental study of the struggle between Richelieu and the *dévots* over policy matters is G. Pagès, "Autour du 'grand orage': Richelieu et Marillac, deux politiques," *Revue historique*, CLXXIX (1937), 63-97, which I follow in this section. See also R. Mousnier, *La Vénalité des offices sous Henri IV et Louis XIII*, Rouen [1945],

The *dévot* faction at the royal court was a large, ill-defined group that enjoyed powerful support in high places. Cardinal Bérulle, who was a confidant of the Queen Mother, opposed Richelieu's policies for religious reasons and worked for all that would advance the interests of international Catholicism: peace with the Hapsburgs, persecution of heresy in France and throughout continental Europe, and the conversion of England. Marillac, the spokesman for the *dévots* in the royal council, was an ardent Catholic of mystical bent who thoroughly agreed with Bérulle's criticism of Richelieu's foreign policy on religious grounds. But as Keeper of the Seals, Marillac was also painfully aware of the financial weakness of the royal government as well as the poverty and chronic unrest throughout the nation, and feared that the crown was too weak to support the burden of a major war. He also seems to have been genuinely disturbed by the condition of the peasantry and urged amelioration of their lot by lightening or at least not increasing the burden of taxation. That popular unrest was widespread is attested by the fact that almost every year witnessed one or more major uprisings against the local authorities in various areas of France. The rebels' grievances invariably centered upon the fiscal demands of the crown, and so intense was feeling against them that the lesser nobility and minor officials often supported the revolts.[80] It seems, therefore, that the *dévots* opposed intensification of the war and sought a reorientation of foreign policy for very plausible reasons. If they misjudged the extent of the Hapsburg threat to France, they at least consistently advocated measures which reflected much that was best in contemporary French ideals.

The climax of the struggle between Richelieu and the *dévots* occurred in 1630 in a series of well-known, dramatic incidents that need not be recounted here. Throughout, Richelieu repeatedly ap-

---

pp. 610-14. V. L. Tapié, *La France de Louis XIII et de Richelieu*, Paris, 1967, pp. 192-207.

[80] Pagès, p. 72. Cf. B. Porchnev, *Les Soulèvements populaires en France de 1623 à 1648*, Paris, 1963, Pt. 1. R. Mousnier, "Recherches sur les soulèvements populaires en France avant la Fronde," *Revue d'histoire moderne et contemporaine*, v (1958), 81-113, and *Fureurs paysannes*, Paris, 1967, Pt. 1.

prized Louis XIII of the dangers and uncertainties of his anti-Haps-burg policy while simultaneously insisting that it was essential to the safety of the state and the king's reputation. After the fall of Pignerol to the French, an event which Professor Pagès rightly regarded as a key moment of decision, Richelieu on April 13, 1630, dictated a memoir to the king setting forth the alternatives in unmistakable terms:

> If the king decides for war, it will be necessary to abandon all thought of repose, economy, and reorganization within the realm. If on the other hand peace is desired, it will be necessary to abandon all thought of Italy in the future and nevertheless to assure peace as far as possible under conditions that can only be uncertain, and to be satisfied with the present glory that the king will have because of forcibly maintaining the Duke of Mantua in his state against the combined power of the Empire, Spain, and Savoy.[81]

Shortly after this key document was penned, Louis XIII's foreign policy was openly debated in the royal council. Marillac cogently argued the case for peace, pointing to the personal risks to the king who lacked an heir, the misery of the lower classes, and the desirability of eliminating the remnants of heresy. Richelieu's counter-arguments were contained in another important memoir which he composed in mid-May:

> The arguments presented by the Keeper of the Seals make it clear that one cannot wage war without great inconvenience. This is true not only of this particular occasion but all others, since war is one of the scourges with which it pleases God to afflict men.
>
> But it does not follow from this that one must make peace under weak, base, and shameful conditions, because in this way one would be exposed to disadvantages much greater than those of the present war.
>
> The aversion of the lower classes toward war does not deserve

[81] Pagès, p. 85.

consideration as a reason for making such a peace, since they are often sensitive to and complain of necessary evils as readily as those that may be avoided, and they are as ignorant of what is useful to a state as they are excitable and quick to bewail the ills that they must endure in order to avoid greater ones.

Whoever would make peace under onerous conditions would not preserve it for long, would lose his good name forever, and would expose himself to future wars of long duration. [Under these circumstances,] it is certain that no one would fear to attack us, given the limited constancy and firmness that we would have demonstrated on this occasion when we enjoy advantages that we cannot have at another time. All foreign nations would regard an alliance with us as useless because of our unreliability and would think that they can no longer find security except with Spain from whom they would willingly endure any oppression in order to escape evil Spanish designs, from which they would not believe us capable of protecting them.[82]

In this remarkable memoir which Richelieu dictated in the midst of intense factional strife appear many of the fundamental preconceptions that underlay his foreign policy. He did not shrink from war as did Marillac, since it was a prime necessity to building state power and the prestige of the monarchy. He was willing to assume the inevitable risks because an aggressive foreign policy was the only means of neutralizing threats from abroad and advancing state interests. Already in the early phases of his program of state-building, Richelieu seemed caught in an unending spiral in which the survival of the state in a situation of international rivalry necessitated armed combat which in turn engendered further rivalry. As for the sacrifices that war entailed, these must be accepted since war was a scourge of God and could not be avoided. Most remarkable was his disdainful attitude toward the lower classes who ultimately paid for the wars with their lives and goods. Their complaints and sufferings might be ignored, the Cardinal insisted, since they invari-

[82] *Lettres*, Vol. III, 665-66.

ably bewailed their lot without comprehending its causes. They were completely ignorant of the mysteries of state and requirements of high policy, and should not resist the sacrifices that their superiors required of them. This approach to the problems and hardships of the lower classes characterized Richelieu throughout his entire life. That he regarded the exploitation of the peasantry and urban proletariat as thoroughly justified for reasons of state is amply demonstrated by his increasing the burden of taxation and merciless suppression of popular uprisings.

This far-reaching struggle between Richelieu and the *dévots* proceeded to its well-known denouement in the celebrated Day of Dupes when the orientation of official French policy was determined for the remainder of the reign. For our purposes, Louis XIII's decision in Richelieu's favor quickly produced two important results which influenced the development and implementation of reason of state: first, the governmental policies and pamphleteering that stemmed from the flight of Gaston d'Orléans and his mother and another insurrection by leading members of the nobility, and second, a major outburst of formal publication by writers of the period in Richelieu's favor. These developments will be analyzed in that order.

The immediate effect of Louis XIII's decision at the Day of Dupes was the disgrace of the leaders of the *dévot* faction. Michel de Marillac who headed the group after the death of Bérulle in 1629 was deprived of the seals and imprisoned at Chateaudun where he died on August 7, 1632. Three months earlier, his half-brother, the Marshal de Marillac, was executed after a lengthy and dramatic trial which will be discussed below. Marshal Bassompierre was imprisoned in the Bastille and remained there without trial until after Richelieu's death.[83] The Duke of Guise, who had good reason to distrust the justice of the French courts when political matters were involved, sought refuge in Italy, never to return.[84] A number of lesser opponents of Richelieu and his policies suffered similar treat-

[83] See n. 5, 6, and text.
[84] Richelieu, *Lettres*, Vol. iii, 803 and Vol. iv, 169.

ment. Such actions may seem unjustified and arbitrary in the extreme, but it should be remembered that throughout the seventeenth
century, persons and policies were so intimately allied that it was
impossible to criticize given measures without undermining the
position and prestige of their proponents as well. In an age when
men staked their fortunes and often their very lives upon royal
approval of policies which they supported, it is understandable that
the victors should resort to very high-handed tactics against their
defeated rivals. Indeed, this was often done with the ruler's consent, as occurred after the Day of Dupes. The association of a given
policy with the reputation of its proponents extended to the king
himself, and when Louis XIII decided in favor of Richelieu, he
placed his seal of approval upon the Cardinal's conduct of foreign
and domestic affairs as meeting the requirements both of royal
prestige and state interests. From this position it was but a short
step to equate opposition to Richelieu's policies with *lèse-majesté*.

Much more disturbing to Louis XIII and Richelieu than the fate
of a few high-ranking officials and noblemen was the flight of Gaston d'Orléans and the Queen Mother in 1631 to Spanish-held territory. For members of the royal family to seek refuge with France's
most powerful enemy was extremely dangerous to the safety of the
state because they retained the sympathies of many important persons and were capable of disrupting Louis XIII's control over his
subjects as well as his relations with foreign powers. Gaston d'Orléans was especially to be feared because he was heir to the throne
and enjoyed a large if indeterminate following within the realm.
A French nobleman might feel justified in offering his services to
a foreign prince, but for the heir to the reigning monarch to seek
refuge with France's greatest rival threatened to disrupt the entire
state because of the vital significance of the royal family to the
functioning of the system of government. French opinion concerning the justice of the self-imposed exile of Gaston and his mother
was sharply divided, and there soon occurred an outburst of pamphleteering unequalled since the height of the Valtelline controversy.
During 1631, the year of decision for Gaston and Marie, it was said
that pamphlets supporting them against Richelieu arrived in Paris

"*par pacquets*,"[85] a fact that forced Louis XIII to take a strong public stand against his mother and brother.[86] Both sides enlisted the aid of able writers, although the supporters of the crown invariably enjoyed the advantage. The result was a lively discussion of the issues that stemmed from the Day of Dupes and its aftermath. Although the debate was extensive and touched upon many matters, for our purposes it is not as significant as the polemics that accompanied the Valtelline episode. Both Richelieu's supporters and critics devoted more attention to personalities than issues. They were also more concerned with domestic problems than foreign. And after Gaston and Marie quit the realm, there was no denying that they had disobeyed royal orders, compromised their loyalty to the French monarchy, and were in a potentially treasonable position. The major issue relative to reason of state, therefore, was the nature of the actions that were taken against them and their followers and the consequent implementation of the concept of *lèse-majesté*.

On March 30, 1631, Louis XIII issued a declaration against all who had advised Gaston to leave the realm, followed him abroad, or raised troops in his behalf as guilty of *lèse-majesté*.[87] This was registered in the Parlement of Dijon on the following day. On April 1, Gaston published a letter to the king in which he attempted to explain his flight as caused by mistreatment of himself and his mother, and protested his continuing loyalty.[88] On April 30, however, he issued from Nancy a much longer letter to the king which is usually called Gaston d'Orléans' Manifesto.[89] This important document was doubtless written by some of Gaston's followers but he openly assumed responsibility for it. The entire tract is a lengthy diatribe against Richelieu and his policies which Gaston claimed were ruining the state. Richelieu was usurping the royal authority, denying access to the king even by members of the royal family, and making himself effectively sovereign by controlling the armed

[85] *Mercure français*, Vol. XVII, 195.

[86] *Ibid.*, 374-75.

[87] *Ibid.*, 146-52. P. Hay du Chastelet, *Recueil de diverses pièces pour servir à l'histoire*, n.p., 1635 (pp. 302-05). Hereafter referred to as Hay, *Recueil*.

[88] *Mercure français*, Vol. XVII, 153-69; Hay, *Recueil*, pp. 294-302.

[89] *Mercure français*, Vol. XVII, 202-59; Hay, *Recueil*, pp. 319-49.

forces, restricting the king's movements, and even dismissing officials that he had appointed. Richelieu personally held Brouage, Le Havre, and many other strongholds, did not hesitate to usurp the functions of innumerable officers of the crown, and involved the realm in useless foreign wars. The crime of *lèse-majesté*, said Gaston in a telling passage, is no longer defined as a criminal attempt against the king or his state but merely consists of insufficient enthusiasm for, and failure to give blind obedience to, all the Cardinal's policies. And in support of this contention Gaston cited the banishment and imprisonment of many well-known personages. When Richelieu formerly did these things without benefit of justice, "it was under the pretext of serving you and the interests of the state, but now he openly proceeds in this fashion against all who do not serve him to his liking or oppose his undertakings."[90] Continuing, Gaston accused Richelieu of accumulating great wealth and unmercifully increasing taxes. He thrives on discord within the royal family, has forced the heir to the throne into exile, and has ruined many officials by poisoning the king's mind against them. Gaston concluded by vividly describing the poverty and misery in the countryside[91] and appealing for more humane treatment of the Queen Mother, after which he reiterated his devotion to Louis XIII and his state.

This brief summary of Gaston d'Orléans' Manifesto, which falls far short of the virility and cogency of the original, suffices to indicate the tenor of the arguments that Richelieu's critics marshalled

[90] *Mercure français*, Vol. XVII, 224; Hay, *Recueil*, p. 331.

[91] Not a third of your subjects in the countryside eat ordinary bread; another third lives only on bread of oats, while the other third has not only been reduced to mendicity but languishes in such lamentable need that some die of hunger while others subsist only on acorns, grass, and similar things like beasts. Of these, the least to be pitied are those who eat only the offal that they gather from slaughterhouses. I have seen these miseries with my own eyes in many places since leaving Paris. It is a prodigious and shameful calamity for this state and an evil augury. God grant that the sobs that it tears from the hearts of these wretches, whose plaintive voices rise to Heaven, will not provoke its ire and will cause it to fall only on the head of the Cardinal, the sole cause of their misery. (*Mercure français*, Vol. XVII, 254-55.)

against him. While protesting their complete loyalty to the sovereign, they attributed all responsibility for France's woes to the Cardinal's pernicious policies and influence. The logical riposte, of course, was that these policies were those of the royal government only because Louis XIII had approved them. This was the essence of the king's official answer to Gaston, a document which was unquestionably written by Richelieu and very effectively justified his position.[92] In it, Louis XIII began by denouncing the evil and disruptive counsel of those who had persuaded Gaston to leave the realm. The criticisms of royal policy that were contained in the Manifesto did not merit a detailed answer, Louis said, but as king he insisted upon making one point: the document was an attack upon his dignity and sovereignty because of the bad impression of his government that it gave his subjects and foreigners alike. All who seek to undermine the sovereign authority of princes do so by attacking their ministers. "I know the qualities and capacity of those whose services I employ, and God has given me the grace to understand my affairs better than those who mistakenly attempt to interfere by discussing them. It is neither for you nor them to censure my actions and those of the men whom I employ in my service. You have no power over them; on the contrary, it is up to me to cause your followers to be punished if they do wrong."[93] As for his devotion to duty and contributions to the good of the real, Louis was entirely confident that they were above reproach. For this reason, he said, "It is insufferable that cowardly and infamous persons should have the audacity to seek to diminish the honor that is due me because of them and to be so presumptuous as to write that I am a prisoner without knowing it, which is to heap upon me the worst possible insult. Now that you understand their crimes and are undeceived as you should be, I hope that you will be the first to beg me to inflict upon them the extraordinary punishment that they have so often deserved."[94]

[92] Printed in the *Mercure français*, Vol. xvii, 260-65; Hay, *Recueil*, pp. 350-53, and the *Lettres*, Vol. iv, 177-81. Avenel regarded this as one of the most "beautiful" letters that Richelieu ever wrote. *Ibid.*, Vol. iv, 167.
[93] *Mercure français*, Vol. xvii, 261.
[94] *Ibid.*, 262.

After reciting his accomplishments since 1624, Louis continued:

> On all these occasions I have been served with such fidelity and
> courage by my Cousin, Cardinal Richelieu, and his counsel has
> been so useful and advantageous to me that I can only demon-
> strate to everyone my complete satisfaction with the signal
> services that he has rendered and constantly continues to render
> my person and my state. I would not strive, as I do, to merit
> the name of "Just" if I did not reward them, and if instead of
> seeking to censure what I have done for him, as do those who
> envy the success of my policies, I should increase still further
> my favors to him as occasions present themselves, entirely con-
> fident that I cannot entrust the things that concern me to better
> hands than his. You should realize once and for all that I have
> complete confidence in him and that in all that has happened
> he has done nothing except at my express command and with
> complete fidelity. All his acts oblige me to tell you that he
> merits as much praise as your followers attempt to cast blame
> upon him, contrary to every truth. And I shall regard as said
> and done against myself all that you shall say and do against
> him whose services render him so commendable and dear to
> me.[95]

Conditions of life in the realm, Louis insisted, were not as bad as
Gaston claimed. High policy, furthermore, required great expenditures:

> Your followers maliciously exaggerate the misery and need of
> my poor people who are the object of my concern in all things.
> They seem not to understand that the necessary and unavoid-
> able expenditures which I have had to make in order to avoid
> abandoning not only my allies but my entire realm have been
> immeasurably increased by the pernicious advice that they have
> given you. For your actions and your two departures from the
> state have greatly hindered my affairs, as everyone knows and
> all the dispatches that I receive from my ambassadors clearly
> indicate.[96]

[95] *Ibid.*, 263-64.   [96] *Ibid.*, 264.

Continuing to the end the fiction that Gaston's followers were responsible for his misconduct rather than the prince himself, Louis concluded:

> I pray God that He will give you as good counsel as you have received bad until now, and that you will be dissuaded from conspiring under my authority against the good and the peace of this state, as I have always urged upon you. Then you will find me entirely disposed to forget the past and to demonstrate to you that I wish to remain your most affectionate brother,
>
> LOUIS[97]

Louis XIII's remarkable letter to his brother enabled Richelieu to present an unanswerable defense of his policies by giving them the sanction of royal approval. So effective were his arguments that the discussion might have ended there had Richelieu not felt the need of further publication to influence public opinion. Almost immediately he arranged for the appearance of a pamphlet by Jean Sirmond, *La Défense du Roy et de ses ministres, contre le Manifeste que sous le nom de Monsieur on fait courre parmi le peuple.* Its official inspiration was obvious and it was incorporated into the *Mercure français.*[98] Actually, Sirmond's tract is chiefly important because of its emphasis upon the dire consequences of undermining the king's dignity and reputation. Taking the position that Gaston's Manifesto was in reality directed against Louis XIII rather than Richelieu, Sirmond argued that it was an attack upon the monarchy itself because the royal authority ultimately depended upon acceptance of the myth of divinely authorized kingship:

> It is a great crime to attempt to blemish the reputation of kings which is the only basis of their existence and greatness. Since they are of the same condition as other men in all that concerns their natural lives, their power rests only upon acceptance of the idea that they are the anointed of the Lord, created by God to govern the earth, and that we are naturally born to obey

[97] *Ibid.*, 265.
[98] *Ibid.*, 265-336. Also in Hay, *Recueil*, pp. 353-89. In both collections it appears immediately after Louis' letter to Gaston.

and are persuaded of this by our love and fear of their power which renders them awesome to us. It causes us passively to permit the sending of our fathers, children, and friends to their deaths without a murmur, submitting to all that the kings' commands require of us. Not only kings themselves are thus revered but also all their officials from the highest to the lowest.[99]

Such a statement from the pen of one of Richelieu's most important pamphleteers clearly indicates the great significance that he attached to the ideology of monarchy and why he regarded attacks upon the reputation of the king or his ministers as *lèse-majesté*. As for the arbitrary imprisonments and banishments from the court that were cited in Gaston's Manifesto, Sirmond argued that all were justified because the victims, in various ways, were guilty of offenses against the safety and reputation of the state which took precedence over all individuals. The Cardinal had not usurped royal authority, Sirmond insisted, pointing to many more powerful ministers in earlier reigns. Otherwise the tract presents little but raucous denial of Gaston's allegations and praise of Richelieu's acts. It concludes on the expected note that slander and calumny are self-defeating and have no place in a well-ordered monarchy.

The most immediate answer to Sirmond's pamphlet was published by none other than Mathieu de Morgues who had formerly written in Richelieu's favor.[100] During the aftermath of the Day of Dupes, Morgues moved rapidly toward Marie de Medici and soon became one of her staunchest and most faithful supporters. Upon learning that Paris was unsafe for him, he fled to a retreat in the Cévennes where he wrote his *Très-humble, très-veritable, et très-importante Remonstrance au Roy* which was published in August 1631.[101] This tract, his first in a long series that vehemently criti-

[99] *Mercure français*, Vol. XVII, 268.
[100] See Pt. II, n. 121-32 and text.
[101] Reprinted in Morgues, *Diverses Pièces pour la défense de la Royne Mère du Roy très-chréstien, Louis XIII*, n.p., 1637, Vol. I, 1-109. My citations are to this edition. The circumstances under which Morgues wrote this work are indicated in G. Fagniez, "Mathieu de Morgues et le procès de Richelieu," *Revue des deux mondes*, CLXII (1900), 558.

cized Richelieu and his policies, was one of his most significant works in this period because it occasionally transcended personalities and discussed fundamental issues. Bitterly denouncing Richelieu as the chief cause of France's many troubles, Morgues appealed directly to Louis XIII who alone could rectify the situation. After describing the pitious state of the peasantry in many provinces and decrying the Cardinal's enormous ambition, Morgues continued:

Sire, you are the sovereign judge of all your people. God has given you the sword of justice as well as of war. False witnesses, produced by those who control your affairs and report to you as counsel before a court, are those who now condemn men although you sometimes order their arrest. I say sometimes because I know that arrests and imprisonments are often made without your knowledge. If you are informed, evidence is falsified and favorable information suppressed . . . . In order to magnify matters of small importance, they allege the safety of your person and your state; they enter the formidable charge of *lèse-majesté* in the highest degree and say that your authority will be lost if those whom they wish to destroy are not condemned. If the sovereign courts remonstrate against edicts that oppress the people, if frontier provinces point to their privileges which Your Majesty has confirmed, if they oppose the introduction of changes that will ruin them, all are reduced to questions of authority. Petitions are called rebellion; no mention is made of kindness, clemency, or justice, only severity, rigor, and force. No one points to the people's misery, the disorder caused by war, the ravages of disease, the extent of famine . . . . They try to persuade you that it is good policy to lose the hearts of men in order to preserve the body of your state, as if it could survive without that which gives it life and strength for your service.[102]

This statement aptly summarizes the widespread view among Richelieu's opponents that his influence was transforming the French monarchy into an outright tyranny whose main quality was sheer coercive force. Fundamentally, Morgues was appealing for re-

[102] *Très-humble . . . Remonstrance*, pp. 42-44.

turn to a more traditional type of monarchy, one in which the aristocracy exercised a major role, the rights of all persons and groups were respected, justice was the order of the day, and royal power, although absolute, was exercised with restraint:

> Our good kings, your predecessors, understood what all earlier political writers maintain and the histories of all the world's governments confirm, that monarchies untempered by aristocracy are of short duration because they first become suspect and then odious to the people who readily criticize them. Our kings wished to avoid both this reputation and its effect. They knew that the laws of their state and the submission of the French permit them to dispose of their subjects' lives and goods and even to create new taxes, offices, and regulations according to need. That these innovations might be more readily accepted according to justice, the kings voluntarily allowed them to be examined and verified by the sovereign courts, both to clear the kings' consciences before God and to preserve their reputation among men. They none the less reserved the right to use the absolute authority that is indicated by these words which they included in all letters patent and edicts, *tel est notre bon plaisir.* Good princes like you content themselves with writing these words on parchment to demonstrate their power, but they never make use of all their sovereign authority which should be exercised with caution, preferably according to customary usage so that he who holds it may be loved and revered. Murmurs arise against a ruler who acts otherwise and criticisms of his government make their appearance, inclining men little by little to rebellion. Forgive me if I disclose to you this most important truth. I would not love your person or your state if I were to hide it.[103]

This was as far as Morgues dared to go in voicing outright criticism of Louis XIII whom he seems genuinely to have admired. The fault, he insisted, lay entirely with Richelieu who reduced everything to expressions of authority, thereby violating the traditional and more

[103] *Ibid.,* pp. 77-79.

humane values that Morgues associated with Christian monarchy. Richelieu's treatment of the Queen Mother and Gaston d'Orléans sufficed to convince Morgues that the Cardinal was a tyrant obsessed with power and capable of disrupting the entire realm if it served his purposes, and Morgues' constant theme was the injustice of their persecution. In public affairs, however, the greatest calamity in Morgues' eyes was the continual warfare upon which Richelieu had embarked:

> It is most important that Your Majesty examine the aims of those who would undertake purposeless wars and refuse to terminate them . . . . This is abominable before God and punishable under justice in all the states of the globe. Sire, good and wise kings are persuaded to undertake war only because of necessity and wage it solely to establish peace in their states or gain it for their allies. When peace is proposed and the occasion arises for giving or receiving it without loss of reputation, it must be embraced as a daughter of God, sister of justice, mother of abundance, guardian of piety, and the most treasured gift that heaven may send earth or kings may give their subjects . . . . Nothing disturbs him [Richelieu] like fear of peace, because a tormented mind fears tranquility more than confusion. Arrest his ambition, his avarice, and his violence, Great King. Call to yourself those who by natural right should be near you and merit it because of their virtue . . . . Realize the condition of your finances and the position of your arms; relieve your poor people, and God will give you perfect health, peace of mind, peace at home and abroad, a better council than you now have, faithful officials, an obedient realm, and will crown you with all manner of benedictions.[104]

It was on this note that Morgues concluded his passionate appeal to Louis XIII to rid himself of Richelieu and return to an ideal monarchy in which the exercise of power was limited by moral, legal, and ethical values and respect for the rights of individuals. Whether such a monarchy as Morgues envisaged actually existed

[104] *Ibid.*, pp. 100, 109.

at any time in French history may be questioned; it was widely believed to have prevailed for a brief moment under the good king Louis XII. But it is noteworthy that the tradition survived into the Age of Absolutism and sharply differed from Richelieu's ideal in which the state and its interests assumed priority over all else and were even endowed with a special morality. From Morgues' standpoint, it seemed all too evident that Richelieu's emphasis upon power and discipline, his subordination of all persons (even members of the royal family) to the state, and his imposition of great sacrifices upon the realm for the support of foreign wars were creating the most disastrous of tyrannies.

Meanwhile, Marie de Medici had fled the realm and sought refuge in Spanish territory. On July 21, she issued a letter to the king in which she attributed her flight to Richelieu's persecution of her in so violent a manner that it resembled imprisonment of a common criminal.[105] Louis XIII's answer, also made public, did little but deny her accusations and reiterate the Cardinal's complete integrity and indispensability.[106] After this exchange, which completed the revelation of the discord within the royal family, Richelieu again felt it wise to enlist the aid of a pamphleteer to justify his position. The result was the *Discours d'un vieil courtisan désintéressé sur la lettre que la Reyne Mère du Roy a écrite à sa Majesté après estre sortie du Royaume.*[107] This tract is essentially a point-by-point refutation of the Queen Mother's letter, in which the author easily demonstrated that her flight to Spanish territory placed her in a completely untenable position. The author also practically equated disobedience of the Cardinal with the same toward the king:

---

[105] Printed in the *Mercure français*, Vol. xvii, 343-48, and Hay, *Recueil*, pp. 389-92.

[106] *Mercure français*, Vol. xvii, 348-50. Hay, *Recueil*, p. 393. Richelieu may have written this letter but evidence is lacking.

[107] N.p., 1631. Reprinted in the *Mercure français*, Vol. xvii, 350-70 and in Hay, *Recueil*, pp. 453-64. It was possibly by Achille de Sancy who was one of Richelieu's secretaries and had a major role in compiling his *Mémoires*. The official inspiration of this pamphlet is evident throughout.

Those who attack ministers of state spare the person of the king on paper but actually censure and offend him. She [Marie de Medici] says that she is not obliged to obey the Cardinal, not daring to say that she is not bound to obey the king, and calls it obeying the Cardinal, which is [the same as] obeying the king, so as to use this pretext to disguise the constance and guilt of her disobedience.[108]

Richelieu's apologists were clearly edging toward identifying his will, although not his authority, with that of the king. The author of the tract maintained with complete logic that the good of the state was superior to the interests of any individual, even the Queen Mother:

The king is aware of the devotion that he owes his mother and does not fail to render it to her .... But he also does not neglect the devotion that he owes his state, from which he cannot deviate for any reason whatsoever. If every man's first duty is to his country, how much greater is the duty of the king who has a fundamental relationship with the state?[109]

As a general proposition, this was undoubtedly accepted by all of Richelieu's contemporaries, but it implied a subordination of individuals to state interests that was deplored by such writers as Mathieu de Morgues.

While this debate was proceeding, Richelieu, with the thorough support of Louis XIII, was tightening the noose about Gaston d'Orléans, Marie de Medici, and all who had followed them into exile. On July 22, Louis issued a royal ordinance giving Gaston's officers and domestics fifteen days in which to choose between continuing to serve him and reentering the realm. The choice was to be definitive, and if they elected to remain with Gaston, they might not return to French territory without being prosecuted as spies and disturbers of the public peace.[110] And on August 13, Louis XIII

[108] *Mercure français*, Vol. xvii, 352.
[109] *Ibid.*, 354.
[110] *Mercure français*, Vol. xvii, 372-74. Hay, *Recueil*, pp. 394-95.

completed his break with his mother and brother by issuing a declaration which stated that all who had left the realm with them were guilty of *lèse-majesté* and would be prosecuted accordingly.[111] Included were all who had advised Gaston and Marie to quit the realm, followed them, or aided them by levying troops. Their property of all types was to be confiscated and local authorities were ordered to proceed against them with force. It should be noted that one of the stated reasons for this severe measure was to forestall an increase of the following of Gaston and Marie because of "the credence that some of our subjects might give their pretended complaints, writings, and manifestos which are full of impostures that they continue to publish against us, our government, and our principal ministers."[112] Richelieu was doing all possible to check the influence of subversive publications. These royal declarations struck only the followers of Gaston and Marie while the latter remained untouched, but it was clearly Richelieu's objective to subordinate them to the power of the crown and to reduce them to the position of subjects regardless of their membership in the royal family.

Throughout the remainder of 1631 and well into 1632, the pamphleteers continued their polemics concerning the fragmentation of the royal family and Richelieu's role in the affair. The most important spokesmen for the Cardinal were Jean Sirmond, Achille de Sancy, and Paul Hay du Chastelet, among whom the latter was rapidly increasing his favor with the Cardinal. By far their most energetic opponent was Mathieu de Morgues who joined Marie de Medici in the Spanish Netherlands and poured forth a steady stream of tracts in answer to Richelieu's defenders. The intricacies and progress of the debate are largely irrelevant to this study; it suffices to indicate the fundamental positions which the antagonists assumed concerning the Cardinal's exercise of royal power and its impact upon the realm. Essentially they did little but develop certain implications of the arguments that we have already examined. Richelieu's apologists, secure in the knowledge that Louis XIII thoroughly approved of the Cardinal's policies and made them those of the

[111] *Mercure français*, Vol. xvii, 377-89. Hay, *Recueil*, pp. 395-402.
[112] *Mercure français*, Vol. xvii, 385-86.

crown, easily defended his position by appealing to the fact of royal approbation and the doctrine of divine right sovereignty. Morgues, on the other hand, could do little but criticize the effects and injustices of official policy and entreat Louis XIII to cast off Richelieu and his pernicious influence. A few key quotations will suffice to indicate the tenor of the exchange.

One of the more important pamphlets, probably by Hay du Chastelet, argued in the clearest terms that it was impious to question kings and that their ministers, the instruments of their power, shared in the sovereign's immunity from criticism:

> It is a type of sacrilege to debate the prince's judgment and to seek to examine whether he did good or evil to anyone. The position of kings would be very debased and lowered if they were obliged to render an account of their acts; one should admire their effects rather than searching for their motives. We should believe that God does not raise them to such great preeminence without giving them grace proportionate to their offices . . . . Therefore, do not debase with vile language the reputation of those whom the king prizes for their merits and the outstanding services that he has received from them; try to imitate rather than slander them. Do not write so freely and speak so lightly of princes who, no more than God, do anything contradictory and whose thoughts are not measured by the judgment of their subjects . . . . It is much more honorable and less perilous for you simply to obey their will than to scrutinize and boldly judge their intentions.[113]

Clearly, Richelieu's defenders aimed to unite obedience to the Cardinal with subjection to the king. Jean Sirmond went even further in his effort to approximate king and Cardinal:

> Ministers are to the sovereign as its rays are to the sun. Even the imagination has difficulty distinguishing between them. All the fine protestations which some make that they criticize only

---

[113] [P. Hay du Chastelet], *Discours au Roy, touchant les libelles faits contre le gouvernement de son Estat*, n.p., 1631. In Hay, *Recueil*, pp. 440-53. The quotation is on p. 442.

the bad conduct of those who direct policy under the prince, without lessening the respect that they owe him, are pure illusions.[114]

Changing the metaphor, Achille de Sancy, the supposed author of one of the ablest royalist tracts of the period, compared the relationship of Richelieu to Louis XIII with that between Moses and God. As God commanded his people through Moses, so the Cardinal acts for the king over his subjects:

> The Cardinal has never failed, as concerns all the great things that the king has effected through him, to follow with respect to the king, the image of God, the example of Moses toward God himself.[115]

Such eulogistic treatment of a royal minister was unknown in earlier French history. In their desire to shield Richelieu from criticism, his apologists not only pointed to his support by Louis XIII but endowed him with an immunity from censure which approximated that of the king himself. As they repeatedly maintained, when an author "criticizes the conduct of affairs, it is the king that he attacks, reproaches, and decries, no matter what fraudulent and useless protestations he may make to the contrary."[116]

This confusion of king and Cardinal goes far to explain how and why Richelieu sought to equate criticism of his policies with *lèse-majesté*. Indeed, some of his supporters openly argued in favor of this novel defense of his conduct of affairs. After stating that ministers were almost indistinguishable from their royal masters, Sirmond recalled that in England it was considered *lèse-majesté* to attack either the king or one of his ministers, and implied that this should be followed in France.[117] In answer, Mathieu de Morgues

---

[114] J. Sirmond, *Advertissement aux provinces sur les nouveaux mouvemens du Royaume*, Paris, 1631. In Hay, *Recueil*, pp. 472-517. The quotation is on pp. 506-07.

[115] [Achille de Sancy], *Response au libelle intitulé très-humble, très-veritable, et très-importante Remonstrance au Roy*, n.p., 1632. In Hay, *Recueil*, pp. 567-659. The quotation is on p. 583.

[116] *Ibid.*, p. 581.   [117] Sirmond, *Advertissement*, p. 507.

cryptically retorted that this made Richelieu king.[118] Morgues'
charge that Richelieu exaggerated the nature of many crimes by
labelling them *lèse-majesté*[119] undoubtedly contained an element of
truth, and the Cardinal's supporters could ill afford to allow the
accusation to go unanswered. To defend his tactics with well-sub-
stantiated legal arguments would have been very difficult, given
the limited number of relevant precedents and the vague definition
of the offense. The Cardinal's pamphleteers therefore once more
took the easy path by placing responsibility for Richelieu's actions
squarely upon the king. In answer to Morgues' statement that the
Cardinal was using the charge of *lèse-majesté* as a means of judicial
tyranny, Sancy merely replied, "As if the king could not identify
and lacked the judgment to discriminate between a small fault and
the most grievous and punishable of all, the crime of *lèse-majesté*.
This is to speak of the king with little respect or truth."[120] Once more,
royal acquiescence was held to be sufficient to establish the justice of
Richelieu's measures.

Regarding the actual conduct of policy, Richelieu's pamphleteers
maintained that the crying need within the realm was the preservation of order and the suppression of all potentially disruptive factions, a role that the First Minister was exerting every effort to
fulfill. With the Queen Mother and Gaston d'Orléans clearly in
mind, Jean Sirmond wrote:

> No matter who causes the trouble, there is no obligation so great
> nor consideration so just that it should prevent forestalling the
> beginning and arresting the progress of the evil influence of the
> persons from whom it comes or from whom one suspects that
> it comes. I make no exception in this; it is subject to none. Let
> no one plead natural law nor close blood relationship in this
> instance. What God sometimes does against the original order

---

[118] Morgues, *Advertissement de Nicocléon à Cléonville, sur son Advertissement aux provinces*, n.p., 1631. In Morgues, *Diverses pièces pour la défense
de la Royne Mère du Roy très-chrestien Louis XIII*, n.p., 1637, Vol. 1, 353-437.
The reference is to p. 417.

[119] See n. 102 and text.   [120] [Sancy], *Response*, p. 611.

of things for the good of the universe the prince who represents Him may do for the good of the realm.[121]

This assumption concerning the supremacy of the state and its interests caused Sirmond to draw the logical conclusion that the ruler's obligation to preserve his state might cause him to override all other values in human society:

> From this one may conclude that nothing may be neglected in matters of state, that delays are most perilous, and when it is a question of preserving the public peace this consideration outweighs all others: the safety of the state is the supreme law.[122]

The argument could be carried no further. For Richelieu and his spokesmen, even rumored criticism of royal policy might be interpreted as presaging resistance to the crown, and the First Minister, acting with royal approval, might take any manner of preventive measures, since they were justified by the overriding, all-embracing necessity of preserving the state.

Likewise in foreign affairs, the Day of Dupes gave Richelieu and his supporters the inestimable advantage of royal approbation of his policies and reduced his critics to petitioning an unsympathetic sovereign. True, a strong case might still be made against Richelieu's foreign policy because of the great sacrifices and risks that it entailed, but from this time forward the position of the *dévots* was merely a basis of criticism and theoretical alternative. This appears vividly in an important, anonymous defense of Michel de Marillac which was written shortly after his arrest.[123] In recounting the factional strife before the Day of Dupes, the author stated:

[121] Sirmond, *Advertissement*, p. 501.

[122] Sirmond, *La Vie du Cardinal d'Amboise, en suite de laquelle sont traictez quelques poincts sur les affaires présentes*, n.p., 1631. In Hay, *Recueil*, pp. 402-39. The quotation is on p. 433.

[123] *Apologie pour le sieur [Michel] de Marillac, garde des sceaux de France, contre un libelle diffamatoire publié sous le titre d'Entretiens des Champs-Elysées*. Bibliothèque Nationale, MS. FR. 18461. Internal evidence indicates that this pamphlet was written soon after the appearance of the *Entretiens* in 1631. The *Apologie* seems never to have been published, although it circulated widely in manuscript as is indicated by the presence of four copies in the Bibliothèque Nationale. The *Entretiens des Champs-Elysées* was a bizarre

The Cardinal desired war and feared peace in which the accustomed course of the laws, order, and justice would have deprived him of any pretext to be so thoroughly occupied, to absorb so completely the mind of the King, and to advance measures that are occasioned by the expenses of war. The Keeper of the Seals, on the other hand, desired peace and did all in his power to achieve it by sure and honorable means. He perceived the needs of the Church and religion, the great misery of the people, the disorder of justice, the extraordinary measures that were daily necessary to raise money, the risks that the King incurred to his health, the frequent uprisings of the people, and the universal discontent. This is why he desired peace, contrary to the Cardinal.[124]

Such argumentation illustrates both the convictions and the frustrations of Richelieu's critics after Louis XIII's decision against them. Indeed, no alternative position was open to them as long as they were unwilling to direct their strictures against the king himself. Occasionally, it is true, they questioned the aura of sanctity with which the royalists endowed their ruler. In answer to Hay du Chastelet's statement that it was sacrilege to debate the prince's judgment and to examine whether he did good or evil,[125] Morgues replied:

He must be regarded as mad if he means that it is sacrilege to question whether the prince does good or evil to anyone, since these are not articles of religious faith, nor moral, nor natural. To do good or evil to someone are facts which one may question without mortal sin, much less sacrilege.[126]

Much more typical of Morgues' pamphleteering, however, is the following passage which reveals the sincerity of his appeals to

---

attack upon the *dévot* faction, their foreign policy, and particularly the Marillac brothers. It was probably written by Hay du Chastelet and appears in his *Recueil*, pp. 212-49.

[124] *Apologie*, fols. 123a-123b.   [125] See n. 113 and text.

[126] Morgues, *Charitable Remonstrance de Caton chréstien à Monseigneur l'éminentissime Cardinal de Richelieu*, n.p., 163. In Morgues, *Diverses pièces*, Vol. I, pp. 220-352. The quotation is on p. 294.

Louis XIII as well as the frustrations of his position as an exile with a sense of mission:

> Open your eyes and ears; behold the misery of your people and listen to the voices of your older and faithful servants. He who listens only to one man is always deceived. The minister who wishes to be alone is surely presumptuous; there is great likelihood that he is a traitor . . . . Remember that you are king in order to render justice and that your people cannot hope for it from you as long as you deny it to your mother and brother . . . . Do not wait until the extreme misery of France makes you hated because of those who are its causes, but stop them before the evil is beyond remedy . . . . Listen to your peace-loving counselors. Yours are not united in loyalty to you but are in league to support each other. God wishes you to reign with peace, justice, and wisdom without the assistance of this man who thinks that supreme power has no instrument but the agility of his small mind which is more capable of disruption than solutions . . . . He cannot be useful to you because he is not agreeable to God from whose grace flow all good thoughts and actions.[127]

Morgues' desperate effort to reorient royal policy by appealing to the king against the Cardinal is evident. On the contrary, Richelieu's spokesmen, confident that they were defending officially approved policy, did not hesitate to insist that all prescribed sacrifices were necessary for the good of the state. Indeed, Sirmond doubtless reflected the Cardinal's personal view when he insisted that the misery of the people was exaggerated. They should be glad that taxation was not as heavy as it had been under the worst of the Merovingians and during the Hundred Years' War.[128] Sancy, however, took a more reasoned position. After admitting that all wars cause great disruption and human suffering, he continued:

---

[127] Morgues, *Le Génie démasqué du Cardinal de Richelieu*, n.p., n.d. (written in 1632). In Morgues, *Diverses pièces*, Vol. i, 439-55. The quotation is on pp. 453-55.

[128] *La Vie du Cardinal d'Amboise*, pp. 437-38.

But there are necessary wars without which it is impossible to have peace. When opposing ambitious and aggressive neighbors, too much fear of war causes one to give way because of weakness, whereas the reputation of one's arms may by itself preserve peace. Let us weigh the gains and the harm that we have incurred from the wars that the king has undertaken because of the Cardinal's advice, and which God through his grace has successfully and gloriously terminated for His Majesty. The people's misery is a disadvantage that passes; a year of peace restores everything. But the gain that has accrued to the king in these wars is permanent. He has restored his reputation through Christendom and has brought fear of his arms to those who in the future would do him violence. This realm, which was divided by factions and was, according to our Lord's warning, menaced with desolation and ruin, is now united under a single authority.[129]

Sancy was evidently bent upon justifying Richelieu's foreign policy as the necessary accompaniment of the type of rule that had brought power, prestige, security, and discipline to the realm. Although sacrifices were required of the populace—he clearly underestimated these—the benefits of war far outweighed its disadvantages which would be more than counterbalanced by Richelieu's program of state-building.

While this debate between Richelieu's spokesmen and critics was proceeding, one of the most dramatic and notorious of all the trials of political prisoners by special commission during the reign took place, that of the Marshal de Marillac. His close ties with his now imprisoned brother and his small part in the intrigues prior to the Day of Dupes were the substantive reasons for his prosecution, although other charges were necessary to meet the test of legality. There is no doubt that Richelieu exerted great pressure upon the judges for a conviction. Regarding his own personal rights, the Cardinal might insist that "the laws do not consider a man guilty

---

[129] [Sancy], *Response*, p. 571.

when he is not convicted of his crime, and whatever conjectures there may be, the laws permit him to justify himself when there are no incontrovertible proofs against him."[130] But when the offense or suspected offense concerned political matters, particularly opposition to himself and his royally approved policies, he readily resorted to arbitrary imprisonment and manipulation of the trials of the accused. In the case of Marillac, Richelieu's eagerness for a conviction resulted chiefly from factors that were entirely beyond the Marshal's control and had nothing to do with the charges against him: the intransigence and continued machinations of Marie de Medici and Gaston d'Orléans in enemy territory, Richelieu's fear of an uprising with foreign aid for the purpose of reversing the results of the Day of Dupes, and the Cardinal's need of a salutary example to give pause to other conspirators.[131] The result was a trial that followed accepted judicial procedures but seemed to many to be a conspiracy rather than a rendering of justice.

Richelieu's influence was clearly evident in the choice of judges and the physical arrangements for the trial. In its final form, the special, hand-picked commission of twenty-four judges included the jurist and councillor of state, Cardin Le Bret, who in 1632 published an important treatise which included a comprehensive analysis of *lèse-majesté*,[132] Paul Hay du Chastelet who served as *maître des requêtes de l'hôtel du roi* and kept Richelieu closely informed concerning the proceedings, and the Marquis de Châteauneuf who had replaced Michel de Marillac as Keeper of the Seals. The proceedings were initiated at Verdun, but after many delays and a letter from Hay du Chastelet informing Richelieu that the judges were

---

[130] *Lettres*, Vol. IV, 58. Richelieu made this statement in regard to the Queen Mother's accusations against him, which he dismissed as unfounded calumnies.

[131] This is the conclusion of the best book on the subject, P. de Vaissière, *Un Grand Procès sous Richelieu: L'Affaire du Maréchal de Marillac (1630-1632)*, Paris, 1924.

[132] See n. 170, 274-279, and text. It is noteworthy that the privilege to publish this work is dated Dec. 10, 1630, shortly after the Day of Dupes and well before Marillac's trial. Because of Le Bret's close association with the royal administration, his ideas on *lèse-majesté* and his hatred of opposition to the crown were undoubtedly well known to Richelieu.

in no mood to condemn the Marshal,[133] the trial was moved to Richelieu's own house in Rueil, doubtless to render the judges more susceptible to his desires. And after the completion of the trial, the records of the proceedings were destroyed by royal order. Together, these circumstances indicate great pressure upon the commission to produce a verdict of guilty.

The formal charges that were brought against Marillac included peculation of funds for the royal army, embezzlement of monies that were to be used for construction at Verdun and elsewhere, abusive exercise of authority over local bodies, and the vague accusation of *lèse-majesté*. Against the first three, which were all too common in this period, Marillac offered a carefully documented defense and in fact fought his accusers every inch of the way. As for the charge of *lèse-majesté*, he merely dismissed as entirely unfounded—a position that proved to be sound. When he finally faced his judges on April 28, 1632, he extensively questioned the fitness of the commission to sit in judgment on his case and dramatically denounced Hay du Chastelet because he was the personal enemy of the Marillac brothers and had perjured himself by falsely swearing that he had not written some impious Latin verse against them. When Hay proved unable to deny the charge, he was asked to retire after which he admitted his guilt and was debarred from the panel of judges. His action so displeased Louis XIII that he ordered Hay's arrest, but after a brief incarceration he was freed by Richelieu and was not only restored to favor but also published a lengthy defense of the commission's verdict.[134] Meanwhile, the remaining judges

---

[133] De Vaissière, pp. 138-40.

[134] The essential facts concerning Hay du Chastelet's actions are well established, although various authors have relied upon different sources. One is the account in the *Relation veritable de ce qui s'est passé au iugement du procez du Mareschal de Marillac*, n.p., 1633. In Morgues, *Pièces curieuses en suite de celles du sieur de S. Germain, contenant plusieurs pièces pour la deffence de la Reyne Mère du Roy très-chrestien Louis XIII et autres traitez d'Estat sur les affaires du temps, depuis l'an 1630 jusques à l'an 1643*, n.p., 1644. This *Relation* is invariably attributed to Morgues who was thoroughly hostile to Hay du Chastelet. It is reprinted in the *Journal de Monsieur le Cardinal Duc de Richelieu, qu'il a fait durant le grand Orage de la Cour, és Années 1630 et*

terminated the trial with a vote of thirteen for death against ten for lesser punishments. Only one judge upheld the charge of *lèse-majesté*, but the slight majority in favor of the death penalty sufficed to seal Marillac's doom. The decree of condemnation was duly issued,[135] and the Marshal was executed on May 10, maintaining his innocence to the last and showing great steadfastness before his fate.

In spite of the clear personal risks to anyone who might publicly criticize the conduct of Marillac's trial, a few voices were raised in protest. All, it should be noted, protected themselves by remaining anonymous or publishing from the haven of the Spanish Netherlands. During the trial, a French jurist composed a long, legalistic denunciation of the procedures that were used to ensure an adverse decision.[136] Because no one came forward to accuse Marillac, he said, the commissioners rounded up various witnesses and practically forced them to testify. As for Marillac himself, he was originally allowed to give evidence in self-defense, but a decree of the royal council forbade its use at the trial. Of the accusations against the Marshal, many were false and none provided a basis for the charge of *lèse-majesté*. The author concluded that such proceedings placed in question the king's justice and even the reputation of the monarchy. And before the end of the trial, one Dicée, writing from Brussels, published a strong appeal to the judges to end the farcical proceedings and return to the true ways of justice.[137] "The interpretation of the law that they seek to impose upon you is only too

---

1631, Paris, 1652, Vol. ii, 5-99. The key paragraph from this source is quoted as authoritative in Pellisson and d'Olivet, *Histoire de l'Académie française*, Paris, 1858, Vol. i, 167-68, and in de Vaissière, p. 205. The Latin poetry in question is in the *Journal*, Vol. ii, 107-09. R. Kerviler, "Paul Hay du Chastelet," *Revue de Bretagne*, XXXIV (1873), 202-17, relies on different sources, chiefly from Hay du Chastelet himself, and gives a more favorable interpretation of his actions but is unable to deny the essentials. (Reprinted in Kerviler, *La Bretagne à l'Académie française au XVIIe siècle*, Paris, 1879.)

[135] See n. 141 and text.

[136] *Discours de droit sur le Factum de M. le Mareschal de Marillac employé en sa production*, n.p., n.d. The dating is based on internal evidence.

[137] *Lettre escripte aux Iuges, et Commissaires, du Mareschal de Marillac*, n.p., 1632. Signed: Dicée, à Bruxelles, ce 8 avril, 1632.

apparent. It is the Marshal's head that they want from you. They would willingly bring you the decree completely prepared, and if his enemies use greater forbearance in speaking to you, it is because no matter what precautions they may have used to make sure of you, they fear that you would be horrified by the true names of the things they seek."[138] The judges, he continued, were painstakingly selected from various courts. Their interests and connections were considered. Offices and other rewards were offered them, and occasionally coercion was applied—all in an effort to determine the verdict.[139] Such proceedings were not only a travesty of true justice but encouraged the use of force by those in authority, made the judges a party to the crime, and opened the way to all manner of abuses and insecurity throughout the realm. Without naming Richelieu, Dicée maintained that all these evils stemmed from pernicious influences at court, and urged the justices to resist them for the sake of preserving the monarchy.

It is noteworthy that Richelieu's contemporaries never challenged the authority of the crown to order the trial of great cases by *ad hoc* panels of judges. The claim was occasionally advanced that a given defendant enjoyed the right to be tried in one of the permanent courts, such as the Parlement of Paris, but the belief that the king was the source of all judicial authority in the realm effectively precluded any questioning of his power to authorize the trial of offenders in any manner that he might choose. Instead, the writers who criticized such proceedings concentrated upon their abuses: the ways in which Richelieu pressured the judges to condemn the accused, the resulting violations of true justice, and the dangers of such practices to the realm generally. Within this focus occurred the most important debate on Marillac's trial, that between Mathieu de Morgues and Paul Hay du Chastelet. Writing shortly after the event, Morgues published his *Relation veritable de ce qui s'est passé au iugement du procez du Mareschal de Marillac.*[140] The major portion of this tract consists of a vivid and highly sympathetic account of the final phase of Marillac's trial and his execution, both

[138] *Ibid.*, p. 2.   [139] *Ibid.*, pp. 7-8.
[140] N.p., 1633. On this work, see n. 134.

of which are described in considerable detail. In this instance, Morgues was satisfied to let events speak for themselves although his manner of treatment leaves no doubt that his sympathies lay entirely with the accused. No charge was made against Richelieu except the transparent statement that Marillac was the victim of a conspiracy. As a piece of writing from a partisan standpoint, Morgues' description of the events of less than two weeks is very effective. This is followed in the pamphlet by the decree of condemnation which stated that the Marshal was convicted of "crimes of peculation, embezzlement, levying monies, exactions, falsification of receipts, and oppression of the king's subjects,"[141] but significantly omitting the charge of *lèse-majesté*.

Almost immediately, Hay du Chastelet, at Richelieu's request, replied by publishing his *Observations sur la vie et la condemnation du Mareschal de Marillac.*[142] This long and labored tract attempts to justify the death sentence by giving extensive information concerning Marillac's financial dealings and showing that there were many precedents for capital punishment in such instances. The forced nature of his argumentation becomes apparent in the final section where he comments on Morgues' account of Marillac's last wishes. Regarding the Marshal's exhortation to his nephew that "after God he should serve the king,"[143] Hay argued that "the service of God and the king are indistinguishable"[144] and Marillac could have been moved to take this position only by hostility to his sovereign:

> How should we judge a Catholic speaking of his king, reputed to be the most just, pious, and Catholic ruler ever to hold the sceptre, who recommends serving him with the proviso, 'after God?' What can we assume but that such a man had conceived a most malicious opinion of his prince's ardor and piety and that his desire to render him suspect, a secret hatred, desire

[141] *Relation veritable*, p. 50. The decree is also printed in the *Journal* of Richelieu, Vol. II, 99-105. The essentials are given in the *Mercure français*, Vol. XVIII, 84-85.

[142] Paris, 1633. In Hay, *Recueil*, pp. 783-858.

[143] *Relation veritable*, p. 38.   [144] *Observations*, p. 854.

for vengeance and conspiracy formed against him under the pretext of a cabalistic piety had rendered this man so verbose in death that he took pains to indicate in his last words a distinction between serving the king and serving God?[145]

Mathieu de Morgues, of course, could not let this go unanswered. The first part of his riposte, *La Verité deffendue*[146] which he wrote at once but did not publish until 1635, offered a point-by-point defense of Marillac. Understandably, Morgues could not refrain from dwelling upon Hay's perjury and dismissal from the trial, concluding that he was unfit even to discuss the case.[147] As for Hay's charge that it was inadmissible to serve the king only after God, Morgues merely replied that in this Marillac had taken the true Christian position.[148] No other comment was necessary. The second portion of the tract vehemently restates all the usual charges against Richelieu's foreign and domestic policies in more impassioned manner than heretofore, doubtless because of developments in the interim. In this inconclusive fashion, the controversy over the injustice of Marillac's condemnation was allowed to subside, but not before the pertinent issues had been fully explored.

Long before this exchange concerning Marillac's trial ended, the inequities to which special tribunals lent themselves when such a man as Richelieu was First Minister were subjected to even more penetrating criticism by another pamphleteer, Jacques d'Apchon, seigneur de Chanteloube, or simply Father Chanteloube after he joined Bérulle's *Oratoire*. Chanteloube followed Marie de Medici into exile and, more than Morgues, was her favorite spokesman and adviser, writing most of her appeals to Louis XIII.[149] Because of two letters in which he defended the Queen Mother and incidentally attacked Richelieu,[150] he was condemned on June 14, 1631, by a

---

[145] *Ibid.*, pp. 854-55.

[146] N.p., 1635. In Morgues, *Diverses pièces*, Vol. II, 3-90.

[147] *La Verité deffendue*, pp. 55-58.

[148] *Ibid.*, p. 61.

[149] This phase of Chanteloube's life is ably sketched in G. Fagniez, "Mathieu de Morgues et le procès de Richelieu," *Revue des deux mondes*, CLXII (1900), 569-75.

[150] *Lettre au Roy*, n.p., 1631. *Lettre au Cardinal de Richelieu*, n.p., 1631.

special tribunal in the Arsenal in Paris. Being of a fiery temperament, he seized the occasion to denounce the procedures of such special courts in his *Lettre du père Chanteloube aux nouvelles chambres de justice* which he signed and dated as of Brussels, August 14, 1632.[151] In this vigorous and cogent tract, Chanteloube left no doubt where the fault lay:

> He [Richelieu] hands over innocent men and these judges concoct crimes for them; he orders arrests and they proclaim them; he condemns and they execute them. Votes are counted, weighed, and bought. Those of upright men who might prevail serve for little, but their defeated and persecuted virtue receives more acclaim than the ignorance with which they are confronted.[152]

Richelieu's tendency to equate opposition to himself with *lèse-majesté* understandably stirred Chanteloube's wrath:

> Today it is generally accepted that it is just to imprison anyone because of the slightest wish of a favorite (for all know that these acts do not come from the king). Every suspicion is cause for imprisonment; every imprisonment is authorized by the judges. Every pretext is a crime; every crime is subject to condemnation; every condemnation is for not less than life. Whoever displeases a favorite is put in prison, and whoever is in prison must be executed to justify the act of him who caused him to be imprisoned. Are these maxims of state or of hell?[153]

And Chanteloube implored heaven to protect the king and his people and to punish only the perpetrator of such injustice.

Broadening his analysis, Chanteloube considered the problem of warning the king against bad counsel and impending disaster to both himself and his state. When every criticism is persecuted as subversion, how can a loyal subject move to inform the king of the dangers of his present course?

---

[151] In Morgues, *Pièces curieuses*. Unlike Morgues, Chanteloube always signed his pamphlets.

[152] *Lettre*, p. 4.   [153] *Ibid.*, p. 25.

What remedy is there for this but to warn him of it? What advice, either by the spoken or written word? How is it possible with words when the mere appearance of being capable of this has been the cause of so many banishments and imprisonments? And how by writings addressed to the king if you call calumny and disruption of the state all that is said and written against the true disturber, even though it is for the honor of the king and the good of his service? If every opinion that one gives the king and every truth that one tells him concerning any subject are called calumny and judged punishable by death, what other means remain for any public or private person whatsoever to save or relieve in any fashion the king and the state?[154]

The cogency of these questions and their relevance to Richelieu's persecution of his political opponents as enemies of the state are obvious. For many of his contemporaries, Richelieu's identification of his policies with the good of the state merely laid the groundwork for his personal tyranny. In conclusion, Chanteloube praised the dispensing of justice as a reflection of the sovereign's power and God's, and insisted upon the necessity of its freedom from coercion. This might be assured only if the magistrates would quit the special tribunals and return to the traditional practices of their profession.

Such penetrating criticism understandably aroused Richelieu's ire to fever pitch, and he made every effort to lay hands on his critics. In the edict of March 30, 1631,[155] Chanteloube was named with several others as guilty of *lèse-majesté* for counselling the Queen Mother to leave the realm. And in the following year, Morgues' *Remonstrance au Roy* and *Caton chrestien* were burned in Paris and their author condemned to death and hanged in effigy.[156] At the same time, Richelieu dispatched two special envoys to the Spanish Netherlands to work through official channels for the extradition of

---

[154] *Ibid.*, p. 26.

[155] See n. 87 and text.

[156] P. Henrard, "Mathieu de Morgues et la maison Plantin," *Bulletin de l'Académie royale des sciences, des lettres et des beaux-arts de Belgique,* 2ᵉ série, xxxxix (1880), 549.

Morgues and Chanteloube for trial.[157] The effort came to naught because of the refusal of Marie de Medici and the local authorities to give over the two pamphleteers to certain death. In all subsequent correspondence with the Queen Mother, Richelieu insisted that she give up the two men as a precondition to negotiations for a reconciliation, but she steadfastly refused. Marie de Medici and Chanteloube both died in exile, while Morgues returned to France only after Richelieu's death.

The most famous trial and execution of a political prisoner during the year 1632, that of the Duke of Montmorency, was of an entirely different character. Montmorency, who was Governor of Languedoc and scion of one of the most prestigious noble houses in France, allowed himself to be persuaded to participate in an extensive conspiracy in support of Gaston d'Orléans and aided him militarily when he reentered the realm in mid-June. That Montmorency, like many other great nobles of the period, viewed his loyalties to his superiors in thoroughly personal terms is illustrated by the fact that he considered seeking service with Gustavus Adolphus of Sweden in case his venture failed. Even before Gaston made his fateful move, however, Louis XIII and Richelieu had tightened the definition of *lèse-majesté*. On April 5, a royal decree was issued against all persons who might receive or shelter any officers or servants of Marie de Medici or Gaston d'Orléans or who would protect such officers or servants if they reentered the realm. Beginning one day after publication of the edict, all who did so would be prosecuted as "rebellious, disobedient subjects and guilty of *lèse-majesté*."[158] When Gaston reentered the realm with military support, he immediately published a manifesto in which he answered the charge of rebellion by insisting that his sole purpose was to save the French state by ridding it of the pernicious influence of Richelieu who was "a disturber of the public peace, enemy of the king and the royal family, destroyer of the state, usurper of all the best offices in the realm,

---

[157] P. Henrard, *Marie de Medicis dans les Pays-bas*, Paris, 1876, pp. 271-79.
[158] *Mercure français*, Vol. XVIII, 74-75. Hay, *Recueil*, pp. 686-87. The decree of July 22, 1631, concerning Gaston's officers and domestics did not define their offense as *lèse-majesté*. See n. 110 and text.

tyrant over a great number of persons of quality whom he has oppressed, and generally all the people of France whom he has over-burdened."[159] Such was undoubtedly the major purpose of the revolt, although Montmorency personally seems to have felt little resentment against the Cardinal. Jean Sirmond, writing at Richelieu's request, as usual took the position that Gaston's move was in fact a rebellion against the king. "It is against your king that they [Gaston's advisers] cause you to resort to arms . . . . It is against him whose actions you should not examine because God caused you to be born merely as a Frenchman and a subject, and even though he might reign with results and effects far removed from those that cause him to be admired by everyone."[160] In any case, the treasonable nature of the Duke's actions was clear, and on August 12 Louis XIII issued a blanket declaration condemning all who were aiding Gaston directly or indirectly as rebels and guilty of *lèse-majesté*.[161] This was quickly followed by the skirmish at Castelnaudary where Montmorency was wounded and captured by loyal forces.

The exalted position and great prestige of their prisoner embarrassed Louis XIII and Richelieu. Instead of ordering his trial by a special commission, the king issued a declaration accusing Montmorency of *lèse-majesté* and giving jurisdiction over the case to the Parlement of Toulouse,[162] which, significantly, had refused to follow the Duke in supporting Gaston's rebellion. This assignment of litigation violated Montmorency's right to trial by peers in the Parlement of Paris but probably had little effect upon the outcome. After extensive interrogation, the court experienced little difficulty in reaching a verdict of guilty. Because of the Duke's exalted rank, famous name, and attractive personal qualities, large numbers of influential persons in France and a few beyond her borders appealed to Louis XIII for clemency. In a laudatory letter, the Duke of Angoulême even begged the king to demonstrate his likeness to God by

[159] *Mercure français*, Vol. XVIII, 505.
[160] *Le Bon Génie de la France à Monsieur*, n.p. [1632]. In Hay, *Recueil*, pp. 680-86. The quotation is on pp. 680-81.
[161] *Mercure français*, Vol. XVIII, 530-36. Hay, *Recueil*, pp. 692-97.
[162] *Mercure français*, Vol. XVIII, 545-52. Richelieu, *Journal*, Vol. II, 110-19.

such an act of mercy,[163] but to no avail. There is evidence that Richelieu attempted to increase Louis XIII's animosity toward Montmorency,[164] but in this instance the king seems to have been convinced that the Duke must pay the supreme penalty. When the Marshal de Chastillon entreated Louis XIII to pardon Montmorency, he answered that "he would not be king if he yielded to his feelings for individuals."[165] On October 30, the Parlement of Toulouse decreed that Montmorency was guilty of *lèse-majesté* in the highest degree and ordered his execution.[166] Like so many others in this period, he met death with great fortitude. The stated official view of the affair was that the Duke suffered the death penalty not only because he was guilty but also because it "would give pause to the worst persons, restricting them to the duty and obedience that they owe their king."[167] The trial and execution of Montmorency caused a sensation throughout France and dramatically showed how the supremacy of the state was forcibly replacing older loyalties and values.

OUTBURST OF PUBLICATION IN RICHELIEU'S FAVOR, 1631-1632

Although there was widespread criticism of Richelieu's "tyranny" following the Day of Dupes, an important segment of French opinion strongly favored the type of rule that he and Louis XIII were forging. This was demonstrated by the appearance of a remarkable number of formal treatises in support of royal absolutism during the years 1631 and 1632. A limited number of pamphleteers, especially those who wrote from abroad, continued to speak for the many who were disturbed by the First Minister's high-handed tactics, but a large majority of the full-scale works on politics to appear at this time gave either implicit or explicit support to his actions. There

---

[163] *Mercure français*, Vol. xviii, 826-27. Richelieu, *Journal*, Vol. ii, 229-31.
[164] *Lettres*, Vol. iv, 355-59.   [165] *Mercure français*, Vol. xviii, 842.
[166] *Ibid.*, 836-38. Richelieu, *Journal*, Vol. ii, 223-28.
[167] *Mercure français*, Vol. xviii, 845-46.

is no doubt that this outburst of commendatory publication partially resulted from Richelieu's triumph at the Day of Dupes when his continued domination of official policy was given the stamp of royal approval. Many writers and publishers correctly assessed the episode as a crucial watershed after years of vacillation and viewed the moment as opportune for the issuance of works favorable to strong monarchy. Among the authors who published major treatises at this time, the following are the most important: the professional writers Guez de Balzac[168] and Jean de Silhon,[169] the jurist Cardin Le Bret,[170] the famous diplomat Philippe de Béthune,[171] Charles de Noailles, Bishop of Saint-Flour,[172] and two other writers whose works concerning Louis XIII's claims to territories beyond the French borders will be discussed below, Charles Hersent[173] and Jacques Cassan.[174] French publishers also sensed that the tide of opinion was turning in Richelieu's favor, and they seized the opportunity to issue several additional works that supported absolutism.[175] Richelieu's known desire for a following among the intel-

[168] *Le Prince*, Paris, 1631. My references are to the version in the *Œuvres*, Paris, 1665, Vol. II.

[169] *Le Ministre d'Estat*, Paris, 1631. (The second and third parts of this work were not published until 1643 and 1661.) Also, *Histoires remarquables, tirées de la seconde partie du Ministre d'Estat, avec un discours des conditions de l'histoire*, Paris, 1632.

[170] *De la Souveraineté du Roy*, Paris, 1632. The privilege for publication of this work is dated Dec. 10, 1630, but it was not printed until March 1632. My references are to the version in the *Œuvres*, Paris, 1689.

[171] *Le Conseiller d'Estat, ou Recueil des plus générales considerations servant au maniment des affaires publiques*, Paris, 1633. The date usually given for this work is 1632, but I have been unable to find any edition before 1633. The privilege is dated July 28, 1632. On the authorship of this work, see n. 296, 297, and text.

[172] *L'Empire du juste, selon l'institution de la vraye virtu*, Paris, 1632. The privilege for publication of this book is dated August 14, 1631.

[173] *De la Souveraineté du Roy à Metz . . .*, Paris, 1632.

[174] *La Recherche des Droicts du Roy et de la Couronne de France sur les Royaumes, Duchés, Comtés, Villes et Pays occupés par les Princes estrangers . . .*, Paris, 1632.

[175] Works by Colomby, Cabot, and Boitet de Frauville fall into this category. The *Discours de l'autorité du Roy* by François de Colomby was reissued in Paris in 1631. This edition is usually listed as the first, but this is erroneous.

lectuals, his increased control of the press, and the eagerness of writers for the favor of the great undoubtedly influenced many to publish at this time, yet the sum total of the movement cannot be attributed solely to official pressures and interested motives if only because governmental controls were inefficient and the authors represented many walks of life. Certain writers undoubtedly chose this path as a possible route to recognition in high places, but none, it should be noted, can be shown to have altered his views significantly in favor of absolutism at this juncture. Instead, they should be regarded as proponents of strong monarchy and supporters of the regime who, because of key developments at the pinnacle of the state system, now found it opportune to express their convictions in published form. The fact that royal policy and statements of opinion moved simultaneously in the direction of absolutism is but another illustration of the vital relationship between political practice and ideology in this period.

Of the many formal treatises that made their appearance shortly after the Day of Dupes, one of the most important for our purposes is *Le Prince* of Guez de Balzac, both because of his ideas concerning reason of state and the controversy to which they gave rise. As we have noted, Balzac was in correspondence with Richelieu for more than a decade before 1631, the year when *Le Prince* was first published, and had undertaken the work partially at Richelieu's request.[176] During the interim, Balzac had acquired a certain renown in literary circles, although not without controversy, and he now

---

Lelong gives the date 1623 for this work, and the Library of the University of Texas owns a copy with that date. Comparison of the two editions shows that they are absolutely identical except for a new title page in the later. This undoubtedly means that a number of copies of the 1623 edition were publisher's remainders and were offered for sale again in 1631, with a new title page. Also, two strongly absolutist works were published posthumously at this time, doubtless by publishers who found the market favorable: Vincent Cabot, *Les Politiques*, Toulouse, 1630, and Claude Boitet de Frauville, *Le Prince des Princes, ou l'Art de regner, contenant son instruction aux sciences et à la Politique, contre les orateurs de ce temps*, Paris, 1632. Cabot died in 1620 and Boitet de Frauville in 1625.

[176] See Pt. II, n. 157-161, and text.

brought forward his *Prince* as his intended masterpiece. Although the work focuses upon Louis XIII as the ideal ruler rather than upon his minister, Balzac also intended it to eulogize Richelieu's policies and their benefits. This he made clear in two letters to Richelieu, dated August 4, 1630, and March 3, 1631, which were always printed with *Le Prince*.[177] In the first, Balzac informed Richelieu of his intention to send him a portion of *Le Prince* and addressed him in these terms: "After the king, you are the perpetual object of my mind. I hardly ever divert it from the course of your life, and if you have followers more assiduous than me and who perform their duties to you with greater ostentation and show, I am certain that you have no more faithful servant nor one whose affection springs more from the heart and is more ardent and natural."[178] Balzac also declared that one of his major purposes in life was to defend Richelieu's policies against their critics: "I would wish . . . that you might witness the success with which I defend the public cause, the manner in which I refute false reports that are circulated, and how I silence those who speak disparagingly of your affairs. It is certain that they could not be more flourishing, the success of the king's arms more glorious, the peace of his subjects more assured, nor your administration more judicious."[179] Upon receiving the first part of *Le Prince*, Richelieu wrote Balzac praising the work and saying that while his earlier writings had merit, in this one he outdid himself.[180] It is evident that Balzac was making every effort to please the Cardinal. For these reasons, the treatise may be regarded as partially inspired by him and embodying the version of reason of state that Balzac, who avidly desired Richelieu's favor, believed it necessary to support.

In his second letter to Richelieu, Balzac informed him that the completed *Prince* would be delivered to him by the Bishop of Nantes. This second missive was even more laudatory of Richelieu's

---

[177] In Balzac, *Œuvres*, Paris, 1665, Vol. I, 322-35. Unless otherwise noted, this is the edition of the *Œuvres* that is cited. Also in *Œuvres*, Paris, 1854, Vol. I, 189-205; Hay, *Recueil*, pp. 551-66.

[178] *Œuvres*, Vol. I, 323.   [179] *Ibid.*, 325.

[180] *Lettres*, Vol. IV, 116-17.

policies than the first and assumed the form of a true panegyric. In fact, it went even further and maintained that the reverence due the sovereign must be accorded all who served him: "All who approach kings should seem to us purer and more resplendent because of the radiance that they receive from them. The respect that we give them should extend even to their livery-servants and valets, and all the more to their affairs and their ministers."[181] Balzac was evidently in sympathy with Richelieu's attempts to associate himself with the power and majesty of the crown and to equate criticism of his policies with *lèse-majesté*. In view of this, it is not surprising that Balzac himself sought the protection of the crown and attempted to forestall his critics by charging them with disloyalty: "There are those who accuse me . . . of flattery because I try in certain passages to tell the truth with embellishment. I do not wish to do anyone a bad turn, but be assured, Monseigneur, that these persons are more the enemies of my subject than my book and are more hostile to the prince than to his spokesman."[182] Also, "Whoever finds my prose excessive does not understand the duty of a subject and does not have the opinion that he should have of his prince."[183] Balzac's mention of his rhetorical style, which today seems very stilted and contrived, raises the question of the accuracy of his statements as representative of his thought.[184] Indeed, Balzac himself hinted that his readers might experience difficulty in this respect when he wrote, "I frankly admit that consideration of such exalted virtue [of the prince] has given me thoughts that I could not expect from the mediocrity of my mind, and I have been so extraordinarily enraptured by them that I often did not recognize what I had just written."[185] The inspirational nature of many of his statements still confronts the reader who would distinguish between content and hyperbole. Nevertheless, in the main it seems that his arguments may be taken at face value even when they seem most extravagant.

[181] *Œuvres*, Vol. I, 330.   [182] *Ibid.*, 328.
[183] *Ibid.*, 330.
[184] Sainte-Beuve went so far as to assert that Balzac's writing was all rhetoric and contained no ideas whatsoever. *Causeries du lundi*, Paris, 1857, Vol. XII, 23. This is untrue, as many later studies have shown.
[185] *Œuvres*, Vol. I, 327.

An example is his account of the worship and deification of the late Roman Emperors, a practice that he implied should prevail in France.[186]

In their essentials, Balzac's political ideas differed little from those of the more ardent proponents of divine right sovereignty, although he expressed them in exaggerated form.[187] Throughout the *Prince*, he presented an idealized Louis XIII, eulogizing his way of life, his virtues (positive and negative), his prudence, and above all his piety. These qualities found their most important expression in the king's admirable deeds in both foreign and domestic affairs, Balzac argued, and he waxed lyrical in praising the reduction of La Rochelle and Louis XIII's liberation of small Italian states from the yoke of Hapsburg tyranny. It was the king's renovation of the French state, however, that Balzac regarded as Louis' greatest achievement. With some justice, he wrote: "I can hardly believe my own eyes and impressions when I consider the present and recall the past. It is no longer the France that until recently was so torn apart, ill, and decrepit. No longer are the French the enemies of their country, slothful in the service of their prince and despised by other nations. Behind their faces I see other men and in the same realm another state. The form remains but the interior has been renewed."[188] The cost of national revival had been high, Balzac admitted, but the benefits more than outweighed the sacrifices: "In recent years, expenses have truly been great but they have been

---

[186] *Ibid.*, Vol. I, 329.

[187] Among the better works on Balzac's political ideas are J. Denis, "Balzac: première ébauche du XVIIᵉ siècle et de Bossuet," *Mémoires de l'Académie des sciences, arts et belles-lettres de Caen*, 1866, pp. 301-58. J. Declareuil, "Les Idées politiques de Guez de Balzac," *Revue du droit public et de la science politique en France et à l'étranger*, XIV (1907), 633-74 (reprinted separately). L. Delaruelle, "Le 'Prince' de Guez de Balzac et son actualité pour le public du temps," *Revue d'histoire littéraire de la France*, XXXXIX (1949), 13-20. P. Watter, "Jean-Louis Guez de Balzac's *Le Prince*: A Revaluation," *Journal of the Warburg and Courtauld Institutes*, XX (1957), 215-47. F. E. Sutcliffe, *Guez de Balzac et son temps: littérature et politique*, Paris, 1959. For a full listing, see B. Beugnot, *Jean-Louis Guez de Balzac: Bibliographie générale*, Montreal, 1967.

[188] *Œuvres*, Vol. II, 50.

necessary. The people have paid handsomely but it is their ransom that they have purchased. No sacrifices are too great for the deliverance of our *patrie* which is now free, nor for the peace of our posterity to whom we will bequeath no troublesome legacy."[189]

Because Balzac believed that France owed her very survival to her sovereign, he willingly attributed him absolute power—absolute, that is, with only intangible limitations. "Here is a man," he said, "who knows how to place the limits of his virtue upon his power which has none."[190] And like all writers of this period who upheld the literal interpretation of divine right, Balzac believed that the king was uniquely inspired by the Deity:

> If we may believe those who have the honor of approaching the king and observing his inner life and the motivation of his acts, he is so fortunate in what he conceives and judges so accurately the most mysterious things that it seems certain that he does not view them as we do but is guided by a purer light than that of ordinary reason. Most of his great decisions have been sent to him from heaven. Most of his resolutions stem from a superior prudence and are inspired immediately by God rather than propositions made by men.[191]

For this reason, Balzac implicitly accepted the argument of the most advanced absolutists that the king's acts were *ipso facto* just, and he invariably forestalled potential criticism of this position by insisting that Louis XIII's conscience effectively disallowed any tyrannical acts. "His conscience is so sensitive that it cannot suffer anything that weighs upon it or removes it ever so slightly from perfect equity .... He judges the works of others but is a tyrant, so to speak, over his own and never forgives himself as he sometimes forgives others."[192] Self-restraint, therefore, was the only fundamental limitation upon the king's discretion. "He is far from extending his sovereign authority beyond bounds because he confines himself to civil justice. He is far from doing what is forbidden because he abstains from what is permitted."[193] Ultimately, only the canons of

---

[189] *Ibid.*, 63-64. [190] *Ibid.*, 21. [191] *Ibid.*, 85.

[192] *Ibid.*, 88. [193] *Ibid.*, 35.

Christian justice guided and limited his acts, but his submission to the intangible principles of higher law sufficed to ensure the justice of his rule:

> His justice guides and directs his valiance. The latter might overturn all if the former did not sustain all, for without this counterweight no one would be secure in his station. Christianity, which he genuinely professes, limits the reach of his courage, masters the pride of spirit which is born in heroes, and enchains, so to speak, his ambition and boldness which undoubtedly would achieve marvelous things if they operated with full liberty and the entire extent of their power. He never takes the wealth of others, knowing that God placed it under his special protection by one of the commands of the Decalogue. He does not steal because he lives under laws that do not even permit him to wish to do so; he is far from acting tyrannically because he does not believe it lawful to conceive of unjust desires.[194]

It is evident that Balzac had complete confidence in the king's inherent sense of justice and the dictates of his conscience. The equity of his actions, for Balzac, was assured by the ruler's divine inspiration and his adherence to the canons of the Catholic faith. The essential justice of his policies therefore stemmed less from his acquiescence to external limitations of established law than from his personal, inward compliance with comprehensive but intangible principles. Balzac's confidence in the inherent justice of all royal decisions had very important bearing upon his view of reason of state and explains why he was willing to approve even very questionable measures which the king, in his wisdom, might undertake for the general good. It should be remembered that Balzac and thousands like him desperately feared a return to the chaos and civil war of earlier generations, and were convinced that only strong and occasionally arbitrary monarchy was capable of providing the needed discipline and control over the nation. The ideal combination of equitable and irresistible rule he believed he had found in the absolutism of France's Christian monarch who simultaneously

[194] *Ibid.*, 99.

adhered to the principles of justice and prevented the outbreak of sedition. "His power today is such that if three rebels assemble against the state he has four means of scattering them . . . . They raise their hands to strike and find themselves apprehended; they plan ere long to share the realm and find themselves reduced to a room in the Bastille."[195]

For Balzac and all others who advocated coercion of potential rebels, the most practical problem was the extent to which the rights of individuals might be violated for the preservation of the state. Specifically, the practice of preventive arrest of suspected persons who had committed no crime raised issues that went to the heart of the problem of reason of state. In Balzac's case, all major elements of his thought caused him to favor detention of potential offenders as a legitimate necessity. His fear of rebellion and willingness to submit to any type of rule that would preserve the status quo,[196] plus his extreme confidence in the justice of royal policies and his reverence for the monarch which reached religious proportions all caused Balzac to believe that the Christian king literally could do no wrong. It is with such factors in mind that one should read the key passage of *Le Prince* which sets forth Balzac's view of reason of state and became the focal point of much later controversy:

> To tell the truth, it seems to me entirely reasonable to anticipate certain crimes that cannot be punished after they are committed and not to defer remedying the evil until the criminals have become masters of their judges. It is true that because of

[195] *Ibid.*, 61.

[196] In his letter of March 3, 1631, to Richelieu, Balzac said:
I am far from criticizing the government of my country and disliking what takes place above my head. I am always satisfied with the current integrity and the wisdom that is presently utilized. I never speak against the pilot who guides me and do not seek innovations to which I would probably become accustomed with difficulty, no matter how good they might be. I endure tyranny and desire equitable administration. If my superiors are vexatious, I am docile and patient; when they are as they should be, I give them gratitude and love. I meet evil with silence and discretion, but I never tire of saying good of those who should do it or of praising laudable things. (*Œuvres*, Vol. 1, 330.)

foolish pity we always favor those who rebel against princes, because in all cases the more powerful party is regarded as the more offensive and injury is assumed to arise from strength rather than weakness. The people will not believe that a conspiracy against the king has occurred until he is dead. However, I do not advise rulers to allow themselves to be killed in order to justify this distrust of them nor to fall into traps that are set for them in order to prove that they have no reason to fear. They may forestall the danger, even by executing those whom they suspect; it is an excusable severity. But it is also a kindness, impossible to praise sufficiently and most appropriate to kings, to accomplish the same end without executing anyone.

Upon a mere suspicion, a minor misgiving, a dream that the prince may have had, why should he not be permitted to detain his rebellious subjects and put his mind at ease merely by punishing them with their own safety? Why should not a faithful servant joyfully suffer detention which, by providing proof, would demonstrate his fidelity, contradict the calumny of his accusers, and appease the anxiety of his master?

Is it not better to prevent crimes by the innocent than to be reduced to the sad necessity of punishing the guilty? Are not acts of this type exercises in clemency? Do they not usually result in the preservation of persons who would ruin themselves? If such simple means had been used to combat the evils that menace the state, the liberty of a single individual would not so frequently have ruined an entire realm. If the instigators of our rebellions had been quickly seized, not only would they have been saved but an infinite number of other lives would have been spared, as well as all the blood that was spilled during the civil wars. If the bad winds had been contained, the sea would not have become agitated; if kings had enough prudence, they would have little need of justice.

I mean that punctilious and scrupulous justice which will not condemn crimes that are afoot because they have not yet been committed, which waits until the rebels have ruined the state before it may legitimately move against them, and which observes the terms of the law but allows all laws to perish. This highest equity is supreme injustice, and it would be a sin against reason in this case not to sin against the forms. If the virtues did not succor each other, they would be imperfect and defective. Prudence must modify justice in many things. Prudence should prevail when justice would move too slowly and never be complete, and prudence must prevent crimes whose punishment would be either impossible or dangerous. Justice is rendered only according to the actions of men, but prudence has its rights over their thoughts and secrets. It extends into the future; it concerns the general welfare; it provides for the good of posterity. And for these it must everywhere make use of means which the laws do not ordain but necessity justifies, and which would not be entirely good if they were not for a good end.

Public utility often benefits from injury to individuals . . . . Life is redeemed by abstinence, suffering, and even the loss of a part that is willingly sacrificed to save the whole. Although the king has preserved the dignity and reputation of the crown on occasions when others would have thought it necessary to do anything to save the state, although even in the greatest extremities he has attempted if possible to avoid using disagreeable remedies, although in a word he is infinitely sensitive to the misery and complaints of his people, he has been unable to avoid weakening them while curing their ills and taking from their blood and treasure the means of achieving their own salvation. But we should willingly endure brief pain that brings long prosperity. We may not honorably seek relief from a burden that we share with our master, and when the prince puts forth great effort and does not spare himself, it is just that the subjects exert themselves on their part and that no one in the realm remain indolent or cowardly while he labors and risks his life.[197]

This very significant passage gives a full statement of Balzac's understanding of reason of state, supporting arguments included. In the perpetual conflict between individual rights and collective se-

[197] *Ibid.*, Vol. II, 61-63.

curity, he clearly prized the latter much more than the former and willingly approved of any measures that the king might deem necessary for the safety of the state. Balzac's mention of the ruler's prudence indicates his awareness of the controversy over the subject among his contemporaries, but unlike many, he had no difficulty relating it to higher values. For Balzac, the king's prudence was merely his special faculty to make rational decisions according to necessity and opportunity, combining judgment with courage and always for a laudable end.[198] The latter proviso was fundamental to Balzac's thought because for him it meant that even the most arbitrary acts of the ruler would accord with Christian morality. For this reason, Balzac never espoused the secularized prudence of Machiavelli. The fundamental differences between the two writers relative to purposes and values meant that Balzac, even when approving very high-handed measures by the king, never fell into the position of the astute Florentine.[199] Always Balzac insisted that royal government was by definition consonant with Christian principles. This he believed to be true even of Louis XIII's execution of potential rebels, as he attempted to explain in a revealing passage:

> He has perhaps diminished France by two or three heads which were required for the preservation of the public peace, for his clemency has not always overcome his justice . . . . Posterity, however, will find very few examples of this in his history. He has used his sovereign authority only against those who would usurp it and has caused his thunderbolts to fall only upon those who would wrench them from his hands. He has consented to the execution of criminals only when there remained only this means of arresting their crimes. He does not kill or take pleasure in seeing killed even the enemies of the state, but tries as far as he can to make them good citizens and subjects.[200]

Even arbitrary executions were therefore justified in Balzac's eyes, both because they were necessary to the safety of the state and because they were decreed by the all-wise, divinely inspired monarch.

[198] Chap. 16 of *Le Prince*.
[199] This point is emphasized in Sutcliffe, pp. 186-88.
[200] *Œuvres*, Vol. II, 60-61.

Balzac's uncompromising equation of royal policy with Christian justice at least had the merit of consistency, even though it raised many doubts in the minds of his contemporaries. On the theoretical level, however, it had the advantage of enabling Balzac to reject the contention of many political writers that the preservation of the state required kings and their ministers to operate according to a higher standard of justice than that in force among the people. Instead, Balzac specifically denied the existence of two levels of justice and subordinated all human activity simply to the canons of Christianity:

> In our religion, reason and equity must keep the discretion of kings within bounds, as rivers and mountains fix those of realms. Kings must equate the unjust with the impossible. And as God is not imperfect because of his inability to sin, so kings do not lack power because they can do no wrong. Is it fitting that small faults be punished but great ones honored, that the enormity of the deed justify the crime and the criminal, and that a poor man who tries to gain a living in his bark at sea be called a pirate and despised by all while another who does the same with a powerful fleet be called Emperor and praised by everyone?

> It surely is not fitting. We should absolutely reject the saying of the tragic poet, so frequently sung in theaters and so familiar to a celebrated tyrant, that in matters of state and rulership it is lawful to violate principles which must be observed in other things. After considering this maxim and examining it closely, I have found that it makes little sense and is more absurd than dangerous. For if it is true, as the ancients thought, that certain evils are a part of tyranny as small numbers are of large, and tyranny causes the ruin and dissolution of the body politic, how is it possible to preserve the body politic and part of justice while destroying it all? Or to admit the greatest degree of evil while excluding its principles and elements? Or to hope to retain life in a fingertip when the body is already dead and broken to pieces? Whoever speaks in this manner surely does not under-

stand or agree with himself. He seems to appear to prohibit something but in reality permits anything, and says without meaning to do so that one should be on one's guard against becoming a perjurer, sacrilegious person, or parricide, but that legitimately one may be all three at once and thus be innocent because of the extent and nature of one's crimes.[201]

For Balzac, one level of justice for the Christian king and another for his Christian subjects was an absurdity. So complete was his confidence in the justice of royal policy that he ignored the possibility of its violating the Christian principles that bound all men. Or, stated differently, the Christian monarch, because he was Christian, was always justified in what he might do for the common good. Balzac thus circumvented the problem inherent in two levels of justice by insisting upon a unique standard, that of Christianity, and simply denying that the king would violate it. The logic of his position was more sound than that of the proponents of differing standards of justice for public and private affairs, but it rested upon the dubious assumption that political necessity would never require the king to do wrong and that his policies were *ipso facto* just. For this reason, Balzac was forced to admit the legitimacy of almost any measure that might be required for political survival:

> A drowning man seizes anything he can, be it a drawn sword or a hot iron. Necessity divides brothers and unites strangers. It unites Christian and Turk against Christian; it excuses and justifies all that it creates. The law of God has not abrogated natural law. Self-preservation is the most pressing if not the most legitimate of duties. In extreme peril one disregards propriety, and it is no sin to defend oneself with one's left hand.[202]

Such were the essentials of Guez de Balzac's view of reason of state. His was a simplistic position which found its basis and implementation in a single, comprehensive assumption: the inherent justice of all acts of the Christian king. For this reason, he had no trouble with such refinements as the definition of prudence and

[201] *Ibid.*, 101-02.   [202] *Ibid.*, 114.

two levels of justice. He simply approved of all that the king deemed necessary to the good of the state. In his specific argumentation, Balzac did not hesitate to appeal to natural law and the dictates of necessity but never with the intent of contravening Christian principles. In all these respects—with the notable exception of his denying any distinction between public and private morality—Balzac's thought closely resembled Richelieu's. Both men occasionally came close to arguing that the safety of the state justified all that was necessary for its preservation, but they never meant that the safety of the state was the supreme law to the exclusion of Christian morality. Both were convinced that the purposes of Christian monarchy might be fulfilled without violating the precepts of higher law. Even so, both ended by justifying many highly arbitrary measures whose justice was questioned by a significant number of their contemporaries.

Contrary to Balzac's hopes and expectations, his *Prince* did not bring him the rewards and renown that he so coveted. The learned community did not receive the book with any enthusiasm, and it found only a minor response in literary circles. More disappointing was Richelieu's reaction, apparently because of the second of the appended letters to him. With incredible ineptitude, Balzac devoted most of the final section of this missive to detailing the animosity and friction between Richelieu and the Queen Mother.[203] Balzac's purpose was to congratulate the Cardinal for overcoming this impediment and demonstrating anew his indispensability to the conduct of royal policy, but this public discussion of his bad relations with an important member of the royal family offended Richelieu who was ultra-sensitive to such matters. Partially for this reason, Balzac never succeeded in winning the rewards and recognition that he sought from the First Minister.

To cap his difficulties, Balzac experienced trouble with the ecclesiastical censors at the Sorbonne. For reasons that are not entirely

---

[203] *Ibid.*, Vol. I, 331-33. A. Adam, *Histoire de la littérature française au XVIIe siècle*, Paris, 1948, Vol. I, 256 shows that Richelieu also had personal reasons for disliking Balzac. In any case, he never succeeded in gaining his anticipated rewards from Richelieu.

clear, two versions of the *Prince* were published simultaneously in 1631. Balzac's own explanation of this unusual procedure was that one version was modified according to earlier recommendations from the Sorbonne, but that the other was mistakenly submitted to the censors for official examination.[204] This may be correct, although it is possible that Balzac who was very sensitive to criticism used this stratagem to meet the strictures that resulted from censorship. In any event, on January 2, 1632, the learned doctors asked Balzac to change several passages to which they took exception.[205] The only one of importance relative to reason of state is that translated in the previous quotation. The original version of it was as follows:

> Vne personne qui se noye se prend indifferement à tout ce qu'elle rencontre, fust-ce vne espée nuë ou vn fer ardent. La Necessité divise les freres et vnit les Estrangers; Elle accorde la Chrestien avec le Turc contre le Chrestien; *Elle excuse et justifie tout ce qu'elle fait.* La Loy de Dieu n'a point abrogé les Loix naturelles. *La conseruation de soy-mesme est le plus ancien de tous les deuoirs*: Dans vn extreme peril, on ne regarde pas de si prés à la bien-seance, et ce n'est pas pecher que de se deffendre de la main gauche.[206]

The italicized portions were declared false when conceived in general terms, as well as dangerous, especially when thus linked together. And it was added regarding the second that man's obligation to God

---

[204] The various editions of Balzac's *Prince* have been extensively studied in the following. H. Bibas, "L'Edition originale du *Prince*," *Bulletin du bibliophile et du bibliothécaire*, 1938, pp. 536-44. L. Wilmerding, "*Le Prince* by Guez de Balzac: Note on a Paris Printing, 1631," in *Bookman's Holiday: Notes and Studies Written and Gathered in Tribute to Harry Miller Lydenberg*, New York, 1943, pp. 489-97. H. Bibas, "Les Editions du Prince de Guez de Balzac au XVIIe siècle," *Bulletin du bibliophile* . . . , 1946, pp. 530-43. D. Fulton, "Printings of *The Prince*, 1631," *Bulletin of the New York Public Library*, LXIII (1959), 318-19.

[205] The censored passages and the objections to them are given in C. Du Plessis d'Argentré, *Collectio judiciorum de novis Erroribus*, Paris, 1728, Vol. II, Pt. 2, 364-65. Its information is identical with that in the censor's copy in the Bibliothèque Nationale.

[206] *Le Prince*, Paris, 1631, p. 373.

is more weighty and stringent than his self-preservation. Balzac always insisted that he was willing to alter his writings according to the theology of the Sorbonne, but in this instance his compliance was minimal. All editions of 1631 and 1632 contain the censored passages unchanged. Beginning in 1634, the second passage was altered to read: "La conseruation de soy-mesme est la plus pressant, sinon le plus legitime de tous les devoirs." The modification was slight but significant. The first censored passage, however, remained intact and was repeated, together with the new version of the second, in all later editions. It is noteworthy that Balzac's statements regarding reason of state were censored on theological grounds only in the rare instances when he seemed to place political interest and necessity above higher law. Otherwise, the doctors at the Sorbonne offered no criticism of his view of reason of state.

Before the Sorbonne completed its censorship of the *Prince*, the book gave rise to an extensive and significant pamphlet controversy which lasted throughout the winter of 1631-1632. Not only was Balzac frankly partisan in his uncritical support of Richelieu; his justifications of royal policy were such that they were very unlikely to go unchallenged in this age of strident controversy. All who took part in the debate remained anonymous, but its major participants seem to have been none other than Balzac himself and Mathieu de Morgues, with a brief incursion by Father André de Saint-Denis. The latter had previously engaged in polemics with Balzac over literary matters and now saw fit to enter the lists again. The major debate, however, occurred between Morgues who attacked the *Prince* on a variety of grounds and Balzac who sought to defend even his most extravagant justifications of absolutism. Because of Morgues' self-appointed role as spokesman for the opposition to Richelieu, it was in the nature of things that he should find much to criticize in Balzac's *Prince*. Not surprisingly, his most penetrating strictures were directed toward Balzac's understanding of reason of state.[207]

---

[207] On the basis of internal evidence, the controversy took place in the following order. (1) [Morgues], *Discours sur le Livre de Balzac entitulé Le Prince, et sur deux Lettres suivantes. En Decembre, 1631*, n.p. This work is generally attributed to Morgues. (2) [Balzac], *Apologie pour le Livre de Monsieur de*

Mathieu de Morgues initiated the controversy with his *Discours sur le Livre de Balzac entitulé Le Prince, et sur deux Lettres suivantes,* an elaborate pamphlet which gives evidence of considerable thought. Immediately he seized upon one of the most questionable elements in Balzac's eulogy of Louis XIII. In an unguarded moment, Balzac had written that the king could not accuse himself in the confessional without slandering himself because he had never lost the innocence conferred by baptism. If he prostrated himself before his confessor, this was merely to confirm him in his present state rather than to cleanse him of his sins.[208] This inordinate elevation of the king to a spotless condition was condemned by the Sorbonne[209] and challenged by Morgues who easily showed the fallacy of Balzac's encomium by arguing that no man, however saintly, can

---

Balzac, entitulé Le Prince, n.p., 1632. The tenor of this pamphlet is such that it seems patently from Balzac's pen. (3) [André de Saint-Denis], *Response à l'Apologie du Prince de Balzac,* n.p., 1632. This is definitely by Father André de Saint-Denis, as is proved by a reference on page 5 to his earlier controversy with Balzac. (4) [Balzac], *Replique à la Response de l'Apologie du Prince de Monsieur de Balzac,* n.p., 1632. The author of this pamphlet claims that he also wrote the *Apologie*; thus it seems to be Balzac. (5) [Morgues], *Defense du Discours sur le Livre intitulé Le Prince. Contre l'Apologie de I. P. En Fevrier, 1632.* N.p. The author says that he also wrote the *Discours*; it therefore seems to be by Morgues. In all cases, literary style and manner of argumentation support these attributions. As for the entire controversy occurring during December, January, and February 1631-1632, this seems possible because of the rapidity with which these works were composed. In the *Replique,* Balzac says that he wrote the *Apologie* in three or four days and the *Replique* in a single day while the *Response* was being hawked in the streets. Morgues also was quite capable of rapid composition in the heat of controversy.

[208] *Œuvres,* Vol. II, 34.

[209] In its original form, part of this passage read: "Bien qu'on le voye assez souvent prosterné devant son Confesseur, et toute sa Majesté humiliée aux pieds d'un de ses Subjets, qu'on ne s'imagine pas pour cela que l'habitude qu'il a à pecher luy rende plus familiere ceste action; car, humainement parlant, et dans la rigueur de nostre justice, s'il ne se calomnie soy mesme, il ne peut s'accuser de mal faire." *Le Prince,* Paris, 1631, p. 116. The Sorbonne objected to this because it unduly exalted the prince by making him faultless. D'Argentré, Vol. II, Pt. 2, 365. Balzac then changed the latter part of the passage to read: "Car humainement parlant, et dans la rigueur de nostre justice, il semble qu'il n'ait pas perdu son innocence."

escape human imperfection and that Louis' participation in the confessional should be regarded as indicating his religiosity and reverence for God rather than weakness. It should therefore increase popular respect for the king rather than the reverse, which Balzac seemed to fear. Although the ruler was above the censure of men, there was no need to praise him in this fashion.[210] In this instance, Morgues seems clearly to have had the better of the argument and Balzac to have been led astray by his own rhetoric.

Morgues reserved his sharpest barbs for Balzac's analysis of reason of state. In a vehement passage, he railed against Balzac's justification of arbitrary execution of suspected rebels:

> He writes that "he does not advise rulers . . . to allow themselves to be killed." "They may," he says, "forestall the danger even by executing those whom they suspect." What? Merely suspect? Balzac adds nothing more. "It is," he decrees, "an excusable severity." In which of God's commandments or admonitions of the Apostles did he find such an important truth? In what morality or political knowledge if not peradventure in that of Machiavelli whom he canonizes as a saint? In what life of a moderate and just prince such as ours are to be found any examples of such a disastrous and barbarous doctrine? Kill suspected persons? And what if they have committed no crime? What if they are falsely suspected? What if that "prudence which penetrates the thoughts and secrets of men" but is neither divine nor infallible is mistaken, who will recall to life the men unjustly killed?[211]

The king's mind, Morgues continued, may easily be poisoned by calumny against his best servants, as too many examples show. And if they are executed? In this event the remedy is worse than the disease because the king becomes a criminal merely in order to gain certainty. This is a maxim of tyranny and can only fill the land with fear. Enemies of the prince will be everywhere, and there will be conspiracies without end. "This is where your Christian prudence

---

[210] *Discours*, pp. 16-18.   [211] *Ibid.*, pp. 30-31.

leads; this is what your cruel and murderous eloquence may produce."[212]

For similar reasons, Morgues decried Balzac's justification of arbitrary imprisonment:

> As he permits killing on suspicion, he encourages imprison-
> ment "upon a minor misgiving, a mere dream." May innocent
> men therefore be deprived of contact with their wives and chil-
> dren, their friends' conversation, the pleasure of their lands
> and houses, the free breath of air and of life? For a fancy?
> For a dream? Balzac finds it reasonable. But he does not con-
> sider how miserable would be the sovereign who conducted
> himself according to these laws, how dangerous it would be if
> the prince were thought to allow himself to be swayed by these
> inhuman opinions . . . and how his friendship would be as
> feared as his hatred, with everyone continually in suspense and
> fearful for his liberty, knowing that it depended only on a
> fancy or a dream.[213]

Clearly, Morgues felt that Balzac's concept of just government was
wrong on both moral and practical grounds and could only bring
ruin. Both Balzac and Morgues, it should be noted, firmly believed
in Christian monarchy and divine right sovereignty, but they
strongly disagreed concerning the measures that the ruler might
undertake for the preservation of the state, especially when lives
were involved. Balzac, the man of lofty abstractions and fear of disorder, would willingly sacrifice individuals for what he believed to
be the best interests of the whole, whereas Morgues held that the
king should not violate the rights of his subjects even while exercising absolute power. In a sense, Morgues' position was the more
complex and difficult to implement. From a practical standpoint, he
doubtless had the edge of the argument when he wrote that the
most secure foundation of royal power was the people's confidence
in the ruler's justice and that this would soon be dissipated if he
were to apply Balzac's recommendations concerning arbitrary im-

[212] *Ibid.*, pp. 33-34.   [213] *Ibid.*, p. 34.

prisonments and executions.[214] But when Morgues directly faced the problem of preventive arrest, he was forced to admit its legitimacy and occasional necessity, doubtless because he knew that to deny this to the sovereign would offend Louis XIII. After praising the king's generally accepted reputation for justice, Morgues added:

> He does nothing unusual nor does he use absolute power without great and potent reasons and very just and important considerations. If he is sometimes obliged to secure the persons of some of his subjects, even though the reason is not made public, it is nevertheless assumed that this is grounded in most valid and just reasons, and not minor misgivings or dreams. Even those who are arrested, if they believe and claim themselves innocent, nevertheless do not criticize his majesty's justice . . . but complain only of the junction of time and circumstance and some hidden misfortune which provided the king with a just and reasonable cause for detaining them.[215]

Even Morgues, therefore, admitted the legitimacy of arbitrary imprisonment if it were decreed by a just and equitable ruler. The differences between Morgues and Balzac concerned neither the definition of sovereignty nor the necessity of justice to legitimate government but only the measures whereby the latter might be implemented in case of necessity. Their dispute was therefore limited to means rather than ends, but the former were of crucial importance to the many who, like Morgues, felt the impact of royal policy and feared that the French government was becoming not only absolute but arbitrary.

Upon reading these criticisms of his work, Balzac immediately seized his pen and replied with his *Apologie pour le Livre de Monsieur de Balzac, entitulé Le Prince* in which he vehemently defended all his earlier positions. In his opening pages, he reiterated the charge that his critics were not only wrong about his book but were enemies of the state and fomenters of sedition. This he applied to the author of the *Discours,* accusing him of being both misguided and disloyal, possibly even in the pay of the King of Spain.[216] Patriotism

[214] *Ibid.*, pp. 35-37.   [215] *Ibid.*, pp. 37-38.   [216] *Apologie*, pp. 3-5, 7.

was indeed Balzac's first line of defense. Criticism of Louis XIII, Balzac continued, was unjustified for the simple reason that he was perfect. Morgues' statement that the king, although elevated, remained imperfect, Balzac condemned because it ignored the special knowledge and miraculous powers that had been divinely bestowed upon the ruler.[217] On this basis Balzac fully maintained his earlier assertion that Louis XIII retained the complete innocence conferred upon him by baptism and could not admit to sin in the confessional without needlessly degrading himself. And as proof he again cited the special qualities and powers with which the king was endowed at his coronation and were evidenced by his enlightened and miraculously successful policies.[218] Balzac's position was indeed simple. Any assertion that the king was not perfect he met with the query: "Is this the way to be French and a faithful servant of the king? Is it not to be ignorant of what one treats and malicious to the utmost point of extreme madness?"[219]

Regarding arbitrary imprisonments and executions, Balzac not only maintained his earlier position but added certain refinements. Reason of state is above the law, he said, and in carrying out extraordinary measures for the preservation of the state the prince is limited only by his pleasure.[220] Yet in another sense, such procedures are legal because the purpose of the law is merely to foster the general good. For this reason, arbitrary execution of those who plot against the ruler's life is justified:

The law permits and reason decrees it, and whoever acts otherwise in these matters is responsible for the prince's life to the people whom he would plunge into war and dissension by his death. When I say that the law permits it, let no one think that I am mistaken. For the law is merely that which prevents external ills and commands strict observation of whatever may redound to the relief of the people and the state that is protected .... One should not be concerned with the interests of individuals when the safety of a province or a realm is at

---

[217] *Ibid.*, pp. 15-16. [218] *Ibid.*, pp. 40-49. [219] *Ibid.*, p. 42.
[220] *Ibid.*, p. 66.

stake, for they can no more survive when their head is removed than the rest of the body when it has lost this part . . . . It would be better for whole cities and provinces to be completely ruined than for the prince to die because of failure to observe this maxim. Cities and provinces may be restored, but a dead prince cannot be reborn.[221]

In this statement, Balzac showed more clearly than ever before how crucial he believed the king to be to the life of the realm. For Balzac, the ruler's survival was literally synonymous with that of the state. Not only individuals but whole provinces might be sacrificed for the preservation of the whole; he alone was essential. One could go no further in justifying any measure that might be necessary for his protection.

At this point, Father André de Saint-Denis decided to enter the fray with his *Response à l'Apologie du Prince de Balzac*. This tract struck a different note and was more satirical than argumentative, although it left no doubt that its author had little sympathy with Balzac's position. Of course he denied Balzac's dictum that to criticize his work was to deprecate the monarchy. The king's interests and Balzac's eloquence are not inseparable, said Father André, and he found it entirely possible to criticize the *Prince* while praising the monarchy of Louis XIII.[222] On many key points, however, Father André did little but support the position taken in Morgues' *Discours*. Regarding the disputed question of the king and the confessional, he simply referred to the *Discours* as an adequate treatment of the subject.[223] And he summarily dismissed Balzac's arguments in favor of arbitrary executions as an affront to the well-known moderation and clemency of Louis XIII.[224] Balzac, however, could not allow even this mild reproof to go unanswered and immediately responded with his *Replique à la Response de l'Apologie du Prince de Monsieur de Balzac*. With unblushing conceit, he reiterated his association of his *Prince* with the prestige of the French crown in the most self-congratulatory terms: "Kings contribute renown to

[221] *Ibid.*, pp. 68-70. [222] *Response*, pp. 4-5. [223] *Ibid.*, p. 29.
[224] *Ibid.*, pp. 36-38.

all who approach them. Their names are majestic and their valets are princes, but their purple is not so dazzling and the gold of their crowns and diadems has no rays so luminous that they cannot benefit from those of eloquence."[225] Balzac claimed acquaintance with many virtues, but modesty was not one of them. As for arbitrary executions, he simply reiterated his earlier arguments which allowed the king unlimited discretion in such matters:

> If the king is master of his subjects' lives, as he undoubtedly is, and without any formalities may send us to our deaths, why should he not have as much power over a man whom he suspects of plotting against him and is already criminal in thought? . . . This proposition is bold but reasonable, and those who regard the public as something holy and respect the head as its most sacred part find this reasoning to accord with the law of peoples and of nature.[226]

Balzac concluded by expressing the hope that his critics would leave him in peace and would cease to arouse the populace concerning things that they did not understand.

Mathieu de Morgues nevertheless insisted on having the last word with his *Defense du Discours sur le Livre entitulé Le Prince*. To counter Balzac's claim that his critics were the enemies of Louis XIII, Morgues brought forth what he believed to be the perfect retort. The doctors of the Sorbonne had recently found errors in Balzac's *Prince* but were entirely loyal; why could not others assume the same position?[227] The argument was unanswerable. Likewise, Morgues had the best of the dispute concerning the king and the confessional. All men, even the most saintly, he said, are subject to error, and it is entirely possible to incur mortal sin after baptism. The author of the *Apologie*, Morgues claimed with some justice, had not answered this fundamental truth but had merely hurled invectives.[228] Again Morgues had little difficulty presenting a conclusive case. The longest section of his tract he once more devoted to the central issue of the controversy, Balzac's justification of arbitrary

---

[225] *Replique*, p. 17.   [226] *Ibid.*, pp. 30-31.   [227] *Defense*, pp. 20-21.
[228] *Ibid.*, pp. 12-15, 38-39.

executions, and marshalled a variety of counterarguments. Quoting Scripture, Morgues maintained that the divine authorization of kings placed upon them a great obligation to rule justly, that is, according to divine law. Thus kings by their nature were not permitted to persecute the innocent. [229] This proposition, of course, was accepted by all proponents of the divine right of kings, Balzac included, but he and Morgues violently disagreed concerning its practical applications. To the argument in the *Replique* that kings might execute their subjects without benefit of any formalities, Morgues scornfully replied: ". . . as if princes were not bound by religion and conscience, and as if good reasons of state might in any way be contrary to those of divine and natural justice."[230] Balzac's approval of executions only on suspicion of present or future offenses, Morgues vehemently insisted, was a barbarous doctrine with no limits whatsoever and opened the way to Asiatic despotism, the worst of tyrannies.[231] All France should abominate its proponents, not only for proclaiming such scandalous precepts but also for urging them upon Louis XIII, "who is known as the Just, and to whose surname and entire life, full of piety, kindness, and moderation, there is nothing more contrary and dissimilar than these Scythian atrocities and Turkish principles of Balzac's followers."[232]

On this note the debate ended.[233] Both men doubtless believed that they had established their positions beyond dispute. Their areas of agreement within the broad spectrum of divine right sovereignty were, in fact, more substantial than those of controversy, but the latter centered upon the key problem of reason of state, justifiable royal policy, and was of such moment that the two men were aroused to a violent polemic which remained unresolved because of their divergent views of the legitimate exercise of royal power in dangerous

[229] *Ibid.*, pp. 48-49.   [230] *Ibid.*, p. 49.   [231] *Ibid.*, p. 55.
[232] *Ibid.*, p. 60.

[233] Morgues' *Response à la seconde lettre que Balzac a fait imprimer avec son Prince*, n.p., 1632 (in *Diverses pièces*, Vol. 1, 457-95) adds nothing to his discussion of reason of state. In the first part of the tract, Morgues reiterates his position concerning two key matters of controversy: arbitrary executions, and the king and the confessional, making the same points as in his *Discours*. The remainder of the tract is devoted to a defense of the Queen Mother.

situations. Balzac believed that the supreme duty of the Christian king was self-protection, even at the expense of his subjects, since his life was synonymous with the survival of the state and the general good, whereas Morgues favored a more traditional view of the limitations which Christian justice placed upon the sovereign's discretion when fulfilling his obligations to his people. In the course of the confrontation, neither Balzac nor Morgues conceded one iota to his opponent. Instead they sharpened their barbs and laid bare the essentials and ultimate implications of their respective positions, thereby starkly revealing the nature and pitfalls of reason of state.

Considerably different was the treatment of reason of state in Jean de Silhon's *Ministre d'Estat*,[234] which was published in the same year as Balzac's *Prince*. Silhon, it will be recalled, had early in his career made it his primary objective to defend the Catholic faith, both in its essential doctrines and its applications to human affairs, especially the political.[235] Because of the breadth of his perspective and the quality of his writing in this and later periods, Silhon should be rated as one of the ablest of the professional writers who consistently supported Richelieu. Silhon's ties with the Cardinal had been gradually strengthened in recent years, partly by the publication of his *Panégyrique à Mgr le Cardinal de Richelieu* in 1629, which praised Richelieu's campaigns against the Huguenots in La Rochelle and southern France as indicative not only of his abilities as a statesman but also his mission as Catholic champion.[236] Two years later, shortly after the Day of Dupes, Silhon brought out Part I of his *Ministre d'Estat*, his first major treatise on political matters. Unlike Balzac's *Prince*, Silhon's *Ministre* was generally well received by the literary world.[237] The work is a straightforward exposition of

---

[234] *Le Ministre d'Estat, avec le veritable usage de la Politique moderne*, Paris, 1631. This is the first part of this work only. The second and third parts were published in 1643 and 1661.

[235] See Pt. II, n. 164 and text.

[236] *Panégyrique à Mgr le Cardinal de Richelieu, sur ce qui s'est passé aux derniers troubles de France*, Paris, 1629.

[237] Kerviler, *Jean de Silhon*, pp. 27-29. At the request of President de Mêmes for specific examples of the precepts that were contained in the *Ministre*, Silhon

Silhon's concept of the perfect minister and repeatedly points to Richelieu as fulfilling his ideal. In the *Advertissement*, Silhon states that while he praises various great men, past and present, where praise is due, and holds that the glory of recent successes has accrued principally to the king, this does not dim the brilliance of Richelieu's merits and achievements. "I do not think that anyone will find it strange that I praise a man who has rendered such great and well known services to the king, who has deserved so well of the state and religion, and who is infinitely esteemed by our neighbors and even by those who do not love us."[238] Praise of Richelieu is constant throughout the work and leaves no doubt that Silhon's purpose was to produce a major defense and justification of the Cardinal's policies.

In discussing the necessary attributes of his ideal minister, Silhon contended that a genuine understanding of the science of government and its implementation, reason of state, was as rare as it was difficult. The precepts of thinkers were often no more than deceptive and dangerous platitudes, he said, and arguments from the experience of other rulers might be deficient, although he qualified this by urging that a knowledge of history was essential to statesmen.[239] More important to the proper conduct of policy, he insisted, was a knowledge of the principles of morality. Although this was essentially a matter of personal conviction, it vitally affected the life of society because it was the source of its most important virtue, justice. Justice Silhon defined simply as equitable relations with one's neighbor, giving and receiving according to one's due. Rules of justice, he said, had been incorporated into laws and customs and were enforced by the authority of the crown, but a man of principle must be guided by something higher, namely, his own conscience and ultimately the doctrines of Christianity, the final measure of all

published his *Histoires remarquables tirées de la seconde partie du ministre d'Estat*, Paris, 1632. This work contains six discourses which recount various historical events to illustrate Silhon's generalizations concerning political matters. It unfortunately contributes nothing significant to an understanding of his ideas.

[238] *Advertissement*, n.p.   [239] *Ministre*, Bk. I, Discourse 2.

good things.[240] This, Silhon continued, is the meaning of the saying that those who command should be better than those who obey. Not only should they have superior intelligence; they should also acquire greater dexterity in matters of government by developing and applying their superior virtues. Although these qualities were frequently lacking in sovereigns, Silhon conceded, he immediately added that Louis XIII possessed them to the full. He was sent by God to end disorder and serve as a model of perfection. Most important, he had chosen a First Minister who lacked all significant vices and was a paragon of reason and virtue.[241]

In view of Silhon's evident conviction that politics should be conducted in accordance with the principles of justice and equity, he might be expected to place sharp limits upon the legitimate use of royal power. On the contrary, the key section of his book where he discussed the proposition, "A Minister should Regulate his Conduct only According to the Interest of the Prince, Provided that He never offend Justice,"[242] placed greatest emphasis upon the minister's obligation to defend the interests of the state:

> Let the minister remember that the principle of his conduct and the primary motive of his actions should be the good of the state and the interests of the prince, that he has no other law to follow nor path to take, and that he is never permitted to deviate from it, provided that he never offends justice which is a rule that should always be inviolable and is never subject to exception or denial. Individuals may relinquish their rights in many things and voluntarily suffer losses in order to do noble deeds. In this, they risk only what is theirs; they lose only that over which they are masters and proprietors, and the loss that they incur is sufficiently compensated by the glory of the good that they do. But princes (and this touches ministers even more), instead of being noble when they abandon the interests of their states, become imprudent. They are unjust if they sacrifice that which is not theirs and has been placed in their hands as a sacred

[240] *Ibid.*, Discourse 3.   [241] *Ibid.*, Discourse 4.
[242] The title of Discourse 11 in Bk. 1.

trust by the people who surrendered it. And since the first obligation of ministers is to prevent those who have given them their liberty and placed themselves under their domination from becoming miserable, it is certain that ministers injure their dignity and sin against their own character if they permit the loss of a right of their state or the diminution of some part, and that their subjects may justly oppose this and refuse to consent to it without crime.[243]

For Silhon, therefore, the justice of ministers was chiefly evident in their performing their sacred duty to defend the rights of the crown and preserve the state. They fulfilled their great responsibilities essentially by protecting and making good the monarchy's rights according to justice and law. Applying this to specific matters of policy, Silhon considered the problem of rival claims to various territories and urged that all recognized titles be regarded as valid, although they should be limited by the rules of prescription. Thus the French might legitimately keep Metz, Toul, and Verdun even though they had been unjustly occupied. Likewise the French still had valid claims to Flanders, Milan, Naples, and Navarre because these claims were well known and had never been compromised by treaty. On the other hand, it was pushing things too far to go back to the successors of Charlemagne.[244] And again he included the usual praise of Richelieu's superb performance in defending the interests of the French state as well as its greatness and glory.

While insisting that the limits of law and justice restricted the minister's freedom of action, Silhon nevertheless conceded that there were different ethical standards in public and private affairs, as the above quotation makes clear. Indeed, when he contrasts the thoroughly practical role of ministers with the canons of rightful conduct among individuals, his words are reminiscent of Richelieu's *Advis* of 1629, a document almost certainly unknown to Silhon.[245] It was impossible, he maintained, for ministers to be limited to the traditional concepts of morality when defending the rightful inter-

[243] *Ibid.*, pp. 99-100. [244] *Ibid.*, pp. 100-104.
[245] Cf. the quotation n. 78 and text.

ests of the state because of the latter's enormous significance to the whole population. "Concerning the habits and conduct of individuals, charity requires us to give them the most honorable complexion and favorable interpretation possible. But when it is a question of the good of the state and the interests of princes, one should judge differently."[246] Effective protection of the rights of the state therefore warranted the use of questionable measures, all in the interest of political justice. With this qualified and not entirely consistent argument from legality and necessity, he felt that he had succeeded in delineating both the duties and the competence of ministers without breaking the fundamental tie between politics and morals.

Throughout this discussion of ministers' rightful policy, Silhon was strongly influenced by the Aristotelian doctrine that the man of reason is endowed with superior virtue, raising him far above the commonality.[247] And this position bore directly upon Silhon's concept of political prudence because of the further Aristotelian teaching that moral virtue is the necessary accompaniment of all true prudence.[248] Within this framework, Silhon was able to interpret prudence as the faculty of a very select few to direct policy both according to the exigencies of the moment and the requisites of higher values, and throughout his book he made it clear that he regarded Richelieu as a man of these exceptional capacities. Reason predominated over emotion in both his private life and his direction of public affairs, and his superior virtues provided the foundation of his essential morality. The result was that the Cardinal had attained the highest order of intelligence and moral qualities, in which even his sense of nobility and passion for glory were subordinate to virtue and reason. As evidence of this, Silhon found it sufficient to recount the record of enlightened policies and concrete achievements that the Cardinal had to his credit.[249] Moreover, it is crucially important to note that it was this concept of political prudence which enabled Silhon to attribute such wide discretionary power to the First Min-

[246] *Ministre*, p. 108.
[247] This point is made repeatedly in Bk. I, Discourse 4.
[248] *Ibid.*, beginning of Discourse I, in Bk. II.
[249] *Ibid.*, Bk. II, Discourse 5.

ister without fear that he would violate the canons of morality. By definition, the Cardinal was a man of reason and superior virtue; he could therefore be trusted to wield great power with complete justice. Silhon consequently advocated the widest latitude for Richelieu when determining proper policy, both in domestic and foreign affairs.[250] The latter area was especially sensitive and required maximum flexibility, he urged, because the passions of princes are determined chiefly by their interests:

> Let ministers rest assured that the majority of princes feel neither hatred nor friendship except for [reasons of] propriety, and that they are impassioned only by those things that their interests occasion. There is, therefore, no friendship so dear to them as the least of their affairs, and no relative that they would not abandon if it would benefit them and not expose them to misfortune. The beautiful sentiments of thankfulness and gratitude are only for individuals and the common people; they hardly ever appear among princes. It is traffic and not friendship that is practiced among them; the laws of trade enter their treaties more readily than those of philosophy. Interest is the only tie that binds them, and since reason of state does not teach good and noble ways, it is no surprise that they ordinarily cannot owe or recognize good.[251]

This view of interstate relations understandably moved Silhon to approve the use of artifices, deceptions, and other ruses in defending one's rights. "Although it is always condemned in speech and conversation . . . let us conclude that on these occasions, distrust is the mother of security, and in order to avoid deception, one must be prepared as though one might be."[252] For Silhon, such measures were merely the necessary accompaniments of effective policy for proper purposes. He was certain that in the hands of a virtuous First Minister they would be used only with justice and for rightful ends.

[250] This is specifically applied to foreign affairs in Bk. II, Discourse I, and to domestic matters in many other sections of the work.
[251] *Ibid.*, pp. 257-58.   [252] *Ibid.*, p. 110.

Silhon's confidence that Richelieu's policies were just and equitable was based upon his assumption that a man of superior reason and virtue would govern according to the canons of religious morality, but this did not in his eyes require subordination to the papacy. In fact, he devoted a major portion of his book to a vehement, biting denunciation of the evils and corruption in Rome and papal interference in French affairs.[253] Recognizing the reverence that was due the Church and the pope as spiritual head of Christendom, Silhon insisted that he held fast to eternal Christian doctrines and was a true believer, but he condemned all efforts of the popes to exercise influence in the temporal sphere and argued for complete institutional independence of Church and state. Not that Richelieu could not simultaneously serve both: as a great Prince of the Church and First Minister of the state he had benefited both enormously, Silhon argued, pointing to the campaigns against the Huguenots. But Richelieu also knew when to arrest ultramontane interference, as exemplified by the Santarelli affair:

> He alone found the means of pacifying the Sorbonne which was in an uproar over the matter, of reuniting this body politic which had been torn asunder, of restoring misguided opinions, of satisfying the pope, and saving our liberties and the rights of the crown. This action was so necessary that without it our affairs would never have resumed their advantageous and difficult course, and I dare assert that it could have been done only by a First Minister of the state, a Prince of the Church, a great theologian, and an excellent politician all in one man.[254]

Here Richelieu is again presented as the ideal Christian statesman who sought to benefit both church and state, although within the framework of Gallicanism. Clearly Silhon believed that the Christian mission of the French state was adequately served by her Cardinal-Minister.

In sum, Silhon's *Ministre d'Estat* portrays Richelieu as a Christian statesman whose intellect, superior virtue and religious principles en-

[253] *Ibid.*, Bk. II, Discourses 10-16. See also the *Advertissement.*
[254] *Ibid.*, conclusion of Discourse 10 in Bk. II.

sured the justice of his policies. Partially following the canons of classicism, Silhon presented the Cardinal as a man of such superior abilities that he might be entrusted with the fortunes of the French monarchy and all that it represented. Silhon's knowledge of the contemporary political scene caused him to recognize that ministers must break with traditional morality when defending state interests, but he always insisted that political prudence must be accompanied by justice consonant with its purposes. A moralist himself, Silhon regarded the Cardinal as the epitome of the qualities that were required of a Christian statesman who would serve his master equally in the realms of practical affairs and higher objectives. For this reason, he was willing to allow Richelieu very wide discretion in guiding the fortunes of Christian France. That this fusion of pragmatism, idealism, and Christian morality provided one of the most effective defenses of Richelieu's policies is attested by the success of Silhon's work and the appearance of parallel arguments in many later writings.

Among the many authors who published treatises supporting Richelieu shortly after the Day of Dupes, by far the most important jurist was Cardin Le Bret whose *De la Souveraineté du Roy* appeared in 1632. Le Bret's extremely long career included service during the reigns of Henry IV, Louis XIII, and the minority of Louis XIV, always with distinction.[255] He held a number of important posts including that of *avocat général* to the Parlement of Paris and was a councillor of state during Richelieu's entire ministry. It is therefore not surprising that the two men cooperated in many matters and gave each other their mutual support. Richelieu made use of Le Bret's legal talents on a number of occasions and sent him on several delicate missions both within the realm and abroad. Also, we have noted that he was one of the judges in the trial of Marshal de Marillac and voted for the death penalty.[256] During Le Bret's long

[255] The best works on Le Bret's life and ideas are G. Picot, *Cardin Le Bret et la doctrine de la souveraineté*, Paris, 1948, and V. I. Comparato, *Cardin Le Bret: "royauté" e "ordre" nel pensiero di un consigliere del '600*, Florence, 1969.
[256] See n. 132-35 and text.

career he was widely known for what he was—an able jurist who
strongly favored royal authoritarianism and even arbitrary measures
when necessary to preserve order in society, but always within what
he considered to be the limits of legality. Because his publications
dealt with matters of law rather than policies and personalities, they
could not be as patently favorable to Richelieu as the more theoretical
works of Balzac and Silhon. But Le Bret's discussion of many legal
questions leaves no doubt that he should be grouped among Richelieu's supporters.

Le Bret's *De la Souverainetté du Roy*, his most important work
of political and legal doctrine, stands in the direct line of evolution
from Bodin who first developed the concept of sovereignty to the
absolutists who wrote under Louis XIV. Essentially, the writers who
contributed to this metamorphosis of ideas adopted Bodin's definition of the powers of the sovereign but relaxed further and further
the legal and moral limits upon his discretion. A summary of Le
Bret's views in this single treatise will suffice to indicate his exact
position in the process. He opened his work by reiterating the fundamental proposition that the king personally held in perpetuity all
public authority in the realm directly from God and was responsible
only to Him for his acts.[257] Surprisingly, Le Bret felt it necessary
to add that neither the pope nor the Emperor acted as intermediary
in this process of ordination.[258] More to the point was Le Bret's insistence that the ruler did not hold his sovereign power, much less
the realm at large, as a personal possession but according to the
stipulations of fundamental law.[259] As for the exact content of the
sovereign authority, Le Bret viewed it as comprehensive indeed
since it embraced all essential public functions—administration,
adjudication, legislation, and taxation—and suffered few positive
limitations. All administrative power, he insisted, was held solely
by the king; therefore all officials of any type whatsoever, including

---

[257] *De la Souveraineté*, Bk. I, Chap. I. My citations to given sections are
to book and chapter. Those to specific quotations are to the *Œuvres*, Paris,
1689.
[258] *De la Souveraineté*, Bk. I, Chaps. 2, 3.
[259] *Ibid.*, Bk. I, Chap. 4; Bk. IV, Chap. 19.

those who benefited from venality, had no authority in their own right and were merely his instruments, acting in his name.[260] Le Bret even went very far in ascribing to the crown administrative control over the French Church, since he, like the great majority of his professional colleagues, was a strong Gallican.[261] Likewise all judicial authority in the realm Le Bret vested strictly in the king. Even such august bodies as the Parlements exercised no jurisdiction in their own right but only delegated power, and he made it clear that the king and his council were superior to the Parlement of Paris.[262] All legislation also, he maintained, following Bodin, was the work of the sovereign alone. If the Parlements opposed certain new laws or changes in old ones, this was mere counsel and in no way touched the king's monopoly of legislative authority "because the king alone is sovereign in his realm and sovereignty is no more divisible than a point in geometry."[263] As for taxation, this was an undoubted right of the crown, said Le Bret, insisting that the king might dispose of his subjects' property according to need.[264] He made no mention whatsoever of consent and was clear that all levies were assumed to be just. All basic governmental powers were therefore, for Le Bret, royal monopolies and suffered no significant institutional limitations. It goes without saying that this position was very congenial to Richelieu who, during his years as First Minister, found it necessary to resort to coercive measures in all these areas.

It should not be assumed from this that Le Bret favored a type of rule approaching the seventeenth century concept of despotism. His fundamental position was simply that all governmental authority was held by the crown and should be exercised within the limits of higher law and in a manner consonant with the requirements of the general good. In his opening paragraph, the best definition that he could find for royalty was "supreme power granted to one man, giving him the right to command absolutely and having as its

---

[260] *Ibid.*, Bk. ii.   [261] *Ibid.*, Bk. i, Chaps. 10-18.

[262] *Ibid.*, Bk. ii, Chaps. 2, 3.

[263] *Ibid.*, p. 19. Many authors have quoted this passage and given it undue significance whereas it merely reiterates the Bodinian idea of indivisible legislative sovereignty.

[264] *Ibid.*, Bk. iii, Chap. 7; Bk. iv, Chap. 10.

only purpose the peace and utility of the public."[265] And the best means of achieving this end, Le Bret felt, was to urge that the sovereign's absolute authority be wielded with moderation. In practice, this required a high degree of cooperation between the various governmental organs, not because of any sharing of authority but because such procedures ensured maximum benefit and observance of traditional values. Thus, in administration, no official or constituted body held any intrinsic authority of its own, but royal cooperation with the provincial estates and the Estates General usually redounded to the general good.[266] In the all-important matter of adjudication, all was done either by the king in person or by his agents in his name; nevertheless the king should normally allow the courts to function in their traditional manner and even submit his own cases to them for trial.[267] The king's legislative power was complete in that he held all authority to create, change, and interpret the laws of the realm, but there was great value in the process whereby the Parlements remonstrated against unjust or inopportune laws. Approval by the courts also ensured the acceptance and observation of new legislation by all concerned.[268] And in the most sensitive area of all, taxation, Le Bret again maintained that while the crown enjoyed the power to tax the subjects for all necessities of state, the ruler should follow the course of moderation, carefully measuring the people's sacrifices against possible benefits and preferably collecting only the established levies. He should never take a man's property for his own personal use but only for the public advantage:[269] "One should not measure this right of sovereignty by the grandeur and absolute power of the prince but rather the principle of royalty which directs kings to benefit all their subjects and never injure anyone."[270] Clearly, Le Bret believed that the most advantageous system of government was one in which the sovereign held absolute power but respected the traditional rights and functions of established

[265] *Ibid.*, p. 1. [266] *Ibid.*, Bk. IV, Chap. 12.
[267] *Ibid.*, Bk. III, Chap. 11; Bk. IV, Chap. 3.
[268] *Ibid.* Bk. I, Chap. 9; Bk. II, Chap. 9.
[269] *Ibid.*, Bk. III, Chap. 7; Bk. IV, Chap. 10.
[270] *Ibid.*, p. 161.

social and institutional bodies and was guided by a strong sense of justice.

This ideal of voluntary self-limitation by an absolute ruler was the heart of Le Bret's ideological position, but there remained at least the theoretical problem of tyranny by an unjust ruler and active resistance by the subjects. The question was central to reason of state, and Le Bret was sufficiently pragmatic to discuss it even in a work of legal theory. Fundamentally he urged his readers to assume that the French kings' sense of justice sufficed to negate the possibility of tyranny:

> Our kings have always had the good fortune not to fall into this abuse; on the contrary, they have always governed their realm with complete benevolence and moderation . . . rarely have they given their people cause to complain of their rule. If some of them have been obliged to resort to extraordinary remedies, they were forced to this by necessity whose power is so absolute that none can claim to be free of it in his rule.[271]

Le Bret's mention of necessity shows that he recognized at least the possibility that circumstances might force the king, however unwillingly, to violate the principles of justice, and he carefully examined this question in one section of his work.[272] Royal commands contrary to divine law, he said categorically, should not be obeyed. Likewise all that involve unjust persecution of innocent persons, even with an appearance of justice, for these are its opposite. Such instances, however, Le Bret viewed as resulting from the ruler's purely personal tyranny and for no other purpose. But when the safety of the state was involved, this significantly changed the picture and the subjects should readily obey:

> Since such extraordinary things happen but rarely, under the rule of tyrants, I shall speak no more of them and shall pass on to another case, to wit, whether one must obey commands which, even though they seem unjust, have for their objective the good of the state, as when the sovereign prince orders the

---

[271] *Ibid.*, p. 2. [272] *Ibid.*, Bk. II, Chap. 9.

killing of someone who is notoriously rebellious, factious, and seditious. My opinion is that in such instances one should obey without scruple.[273]

Readers of this passage in 1632 must have been vividly reminded of recent events. Le Bret went on to list preventive war as a similar instance of questionable policy which must be accepted because of its benefit to the state. And he cited St. Thomas to the effect that the subjects should wage war at their ruler's command without inquiring into the justice of the enterprise. Le Bret's assumption that the king would simultaneously adhere to the principles of justice while ruling for the benefit of the state caused him to approve such measures as wars, increased taxes, and arbitrary executions. One must therefore conclude that he accepted the essentials of reason of state.

Le Bret made his fundamental authoritarianism and hatred of subversion more evident in his lengthy and thorough analysis of the crime of *lèse-majesté*.[274] This section of his treatise is remarkable both for its very inclusive definition of the offense and its rarity in the legal manuals of the period. In fact, Le Bret's treatment of *lèse-majesté* was a landmark in the history of the concept since it was by far the most important analysis of the subject to be published by a jurist while Richelieu was attempting to articulate the doctrine of crimes against the state.[275] Le Bret seems to have sensed the importance of the matter to his analysis of royal sovereignty and state interests, for he said, "I would not consider that I had brought my work to complete perfection if I did not demonstrate in this place

---

[273] *Ibid.*, p. 60.   [274] *Ibid.*, Bk. IV, Chap. 5.

[275] Treatments of *lèse-majesté* are surprisingly rare in this period. In all other legal manuals that appeared during Richelieu's ministry, the crime is merely analyzed in summary fashion, as one of the *cas royaux*. An earlier work on the subject is [Pierre de Belloy], *De l'Authorité du Roy, et crimes de lèze majesté, qui se commettent par ligues, designation de successeur, et libelles escrits contre la personne et dignité du Prince*, n.p., 1587. This, of course, was the work of a strong royalist writing against the Catholique League. Belloy bases his position largely on Roman rather than French legal precedents and makes many of the points that are reiterated by Le Bret. Thus the latter's work was not entirely original but was nevertheless unique in the period.

the nature of such a wicked act and the penalties that it deserves as its punishment."[276]

Le Bret listed three general categories of *lèse-majesté*: slander against the prince, attacks on his life, and conspiracy against his state. In implementing all three, he relied extensively on Roman history and legal precedents, clearly attempting to apply the highly developed concept of treason in Roman Law to French political practice. His discussion of slander as an offense against the monarch is especially noteworthy in view of the importance that Richelieu attached to the matter. Slander of the prince approaches sacrilege, said Le Bret, "because sovereign princes being vicars of God, his living images, or rather gods on earth as Holy Scripture calls them, their persons should be respected by us as divine and sacred things . . . so that one may say that when one insults the king, one insults God himself."[277] And Le Bret insisted that this offense included "not only the slanders that are published against His Majesty because of envy, hatred, or animosity but also those that are meant as taunts and raillery which have always been as severely punished as the others."[278] His examples make it clear that almost any type of criticism, whether serious or in jest, was included in this most serious crime against the sacred dignity of the crown. In view of this reading of the law, it is not surprising that Richelieu's most vehement critics such as Mathieu de Morgues and Father Chanteloube published their tracts abroad.

Regarding outright attacks on the life of the prince, Le Bret expressed unimaginable horror at the thought of such a lamentable event which would bring disaster to the entire realm. "For since the prince is the spirit that animates the body of the state, holds its members together, preserves peace among all his subjects, and causes justice to reign," the loss of the prince would leave nothing but "confusion, disorder, brigandage, violence, and sedition which would end in the ruin and complete destruction of the state. This is why it may be said that this crime embraces all the other more horrible evils that men may commit."[279] A more comprehensive

[276] *De la Souveraineté*, p. 140.
[277] *Ibid.*, p. 140.   [278] *Ibid.*, p. 140.   [279] *Ibid.*, p. 141.

definition of *lèse-majesté* could hardly be imagined. Le Bret evidently realized that such a sweeping interpretation might unjustly be turned against innocent persons merely on the basis of suspicion, and as a jurist he insisted that guilt must be established. But he also admitted that this might be based on long-harbored intent and efforts to carry out a plot that never occurred.

As for attacks upon the state, Le Bret in this instance was able to cite the Ordinance of Blois and later legislation which defined the offense as treating with foreigners, leaving the realm without royal permission (which Le Bret would limit to high-ranking officials and nobles), and levying troops without royal authorization. The nature of the guilt in each case, plus instances of each in the immediate past, were clear to his contemporaries. He then went on to detail the extensive punishments that were meted out in cases of *lèse-majesté*. Not only the perpetrators of the deed but their descendants, associates, and friends suffered severe penalties, as did all who followed the leaders of the conspiracy. This included not only individuals but entire communities and cities. Again contemporaries had little difficulty recalling recent examples. The use of astrology and the casting of horoscopes for political purposes he similarly condemned because they involved penetration into the mysteries of state and the secrets of God who controls all earthly matters, including the lives of sovereigns and realms. Finally, slander and attacks upon the officers and magistrates of the crown were considered *lèse-majesté* because the monarch was the ultimate target of such actions. In such instances, however, Le Bret urged lighter punishments, not for humanitarian reasons but because the more exalted rank and greater prestige of the monarch required that his personal enemies be subjected to severer penalties.

This rigorous suppression of all offenses against the crown Le Bret believed to be entirely in accord with the canons of higher law and his ideal of just government because the prince, in carrying out such measures, was only fulfilling his divinely prescribed duty. The final chapter of Le Bret's treatise emphasized king's subjection to God and the fact that more than all others they were bound to obey divine law because they set the most influential example for their subjects. God not only raises princes and states but also sends avengers against those who offend Him, said Le Bret, citing examples from ancient history and Gustavus Adolphus' successful campaign against the Emperor. On the other hand, if kings follow God's will and benefit their subjects, "God will always be on their side, will cause all their enterprises to prosper, and will always render them victorious and triumphant."[280] Louis XIII thoroughly fulfilled this ideal, Le Bret maintained, praising Louis' personal qualities and listing his recent successes in both foreign and domestic affairs. Le Bret concluded by expressing the hope that Louis XIII would continue to follow the ways of God, "that is, always pious, just, and merciful, so that, adding to the honor of so many generous acts that he has happily concluded, he will continue to work for the elimination of the many disorders and abuses that gradually undermine the foundations of this monarchy and prevent the people's enjoying the fruits of so many victories that he has gloriously won over his enemies both within and without the realm."[281] Although Le Bret's extensive justification of royal policy was couched in legal terms, it leaves no doubt that he thoroughly approved of Richelieu's authoritarian and often arbitrary measures as well as his efforts to suppress all opposition. The fact that these positions were upheld in the published work of a responsible jurist goes far to demonstrate both the flexibility of relevant law and the extent to which Richelieu could find a legal basis for reason of state.[282]

The final two treatises that deserve mention as part of the extensive pro-administration publications of 1631-1632 are Philippe

---

[280] *Ibid.*, p. 181.   [281] *Ibid.*

[282] At Richelieu's request, the jurist-archivists Pierre Depuy and Jacques Godefroy assembled massive collections of legal documents with which Richelieu might support his actions against the enemies of the crown, both foreign and domestic. For our purposes, the most important of these collections concerned earlier uses of the charge of *lèse-majesté* and French claims to border territories. To my knowledge, these materials, particularly those on *lèse-majesté*, have never been adequately examined. On these matters, see Pt. IV, n. 88, 204-218, and text.

de Béthune's *Conseiller d'Estat*[283] and Charles de Noailles, *L'Empire du juste*.[284] Both are of interest only because they treat a relatively narrow aspect of reason of state, the ruler's use of stratagems and other questionable measures, and the extent to which such practices were justified. The two books, it may be noted, approach the problem from very different standpoints, yet both admit not only the necessity but also the justice of immoral measures under certain conditions. Noailles, a member of the famous noble family of that name, was Bishop of Saint-Flour and later Rodez. He was active in the Assembly of the Clergy and was one of the earliest members of the Company of the Holy Sacrament.[285] His intellectual position was that of a theologian and very strong absolutist combined, and his very lengthy book was ultralaudatory of Louis XIII. Approaching all political matters through religious doctrine, Noailles grounded absolutism upon Christian precepts and interpreted it strictly as rule according to divine law. This permitted him to go beyond many comparable writers when he not only stressed the divine authorization of kings but also insisted that their laws were based on right reason and were therefore a participation in eternal law.[286] The law was not simply the work of the king; the king who rules according to reason and justice *is* the law and superior to any written code.[287] "Good kings are always over their people as reason is above the other faculties, that is to say, an animate and living law, authorized by nature and its Creator."[288] The royal science, it followed, was a participation in divine knowledge, and Noailles did not hesitate to assert that the king as legislator enjoyed the same relation to God as Moses.[289]

This comprehensive concept of the king as a living law determined Noailles' approach to matters of policy. True prudence for him was

---

[283] *Le Conseiller d'Estat, ou Recueil des plus générales considérations servant au maniment des affaires publiques*, Paris, 1633. This book is often listed as first published in 1632, the date of its privilege.

[284] *L'Empire du juste, selon l'institution de la vraye vertu*, Paris, 1632.

[285] R. Allier, *La Cabale des dévots*, Paris, 1902, p. 17.

[286] *L'Empire*, pp. 171-73.   [287] *Ibid.*, pp. 209-11.

[288] *Ibid.*, p. 176.   [289] *Ibid.*, Bk. II, Chaps. 20, 21.

simply rule for the public good according to the principles of Christian charity.[290] Ultimately, therefore, the nature of policy depended upon its essence, as determined by the king's intentions. In a lengthy chapter, he applied this approach to the problem of stratagems, cunning, and the like.[291] His basic position was that there is an absolute difference between divine and mundane knowledge. True prudence, as previously defined, was a participation in divine knowledge and absolutely good, whereas cunning (*astuce*), ruses, and similar measures were merely worldly knowledge and therefore absolutely bad. After examining Scriptural examples, he concluded that "the wisdom of this world is to disguise one's heart with ruses, distort one's meaning with words, cause the false to seem true and true to appear false."[292] Its devotees seek vain honors, exact undue vengeance, and override all others. "The wisdom of the just, on the contrary, is to feign nothing through ostentation, express oneself clearly, love truth as it is, avoid deceit, freely gratify others, endure evil more readily than inflict it, refuse to seek vengeance for insults received, and to believe that calumny is the reward for the love of truth. But this simplicity of the just is ridiculed because the wise of this world believe that the virtue of purity and integrity is folly."[293]

With such a rigid position, Noailles might be expected to condemn outright all questionable policy measures, but he seems to have realized that the necessities of government in this world required rulers to compromise the purity of his ideal. In any case, he reluctantly opened the door to ruses and stratagems within certain limits. On the authority of Aristotle and St. Ambrose, he answered in the affirmative the question whether stratagems may *aid* true prudence. If the intent is not vicious and they serve the public utility, he said, they may be tolerated.[294] Specifically, they may be used against all potential rebels: the brave because they may seek undue liberty, the wise because they may use their ability to plot against authority, and the just because the people may wish them to be given greater power. "Princes should not neglect to use artifices against

[290] *Ibid.*, Bk. II, Chap. 14.

[292] *Ibid.*, p. 329.

[294] *Ibid.*, pp. 333-34.

[291] *Ibid.*, Bk. II, Chap. 30.

[293] *Ibid.*, pp. 329-30.

these foxes, because it is unjust to abandon rulers to such appre-
hensions and more reasonable . . . that temporal wisdom should
not be denied them if the end is just and it does not derogate
from the principles of true prudence which is founded on charity."[295]
Noailles doubtless felt that he was preserving his position intact by
allowing questionable measures as a limited adjunct to true prudence
and only for a good end, but this qualification of his ideal represented
a significant concession to the requirements of political necessity.

Entirely different was the treatment of this question in Philippe
de Béthune's *Conseiller d'Estat*. The book was published anonymously during this period, and its authorship remained uncertain
until much later. There was a widely accepted tradition that it was
written by Eustache Du Refuge whose popular *Traité de la cour*
and other works were likewise published anonymously at this
time.[296] All internal evidence in the *Conseiller* is such that it could

---

[295] *Ibid.*, p. 335.

[296] The *Conseiller d'Estat* is usually attributed to Philippe de Béthune on
the basis of a statement by his grandson, Henri de Béthune, in the Paris edition of 1667 (with a different title and considerably revised) that the work
was by his grandfather. This attribution is accepted by Lelong and all modern
authorities. Before 1667, however, the book was always published anonymously
and was variously attributed to Jean de Silhon, President Jeannin, and especially Eustache Du Refuge. There is considerable evidence that Du Refuge's
authorship was widely accepted at that time. The *Conseiller* was published
by Richer in 1633 in two different versions. In the first, the editor disclaims
any knowledge of the book's authorship but mentions that it may have been
written by Du Refuge. This is omitted in the later version which merely states
that the work was originally not meant for publication and that the manuscript bore the title, *Recueil des plus générales considerations servant au
maniment des affaires publiques*. Several manuscript copies of the work, bearing this title, exist: Bibliothèque Nationale, Fonds Français, Nos. 19048, 19049,
19050, and 17461 (the latter incomplete and with another title), and Bibliothèque de l'Arsenal, Nos. 2336 and 2864. In the manuscript catalogues of these
libraries, all are listed either as anonymous or are attributed to Du Refuge,
three on the basis of notations on the manuscripts. Also, Du Refuge is listed
as the author in C. Sorel de Souvigny, *La Bibliothèque française*, Paris, 1664,
p. 61. Barbier attributes the work to Béthune but also lists the edition of 1665
(with a slightly different title) as by Refuge, even though the two works are
identical. Surprisingly, this error is repeated in L. André, *Sources*, Vol. VII,
158. The similarity of the *Conseiller* to Du Refuge's other works, such as his
Traité de la cour and his *Géographie historique* which were also published

have been written by either Béthune or Refuge, since it contains few specifics and both men had extensive political experience, especially in diplomacy. It may well have been written considerably before Richelieu came to power in 1624, and there is evidence that it circulated widely in manuscript before it was published.[297] In any case, its publication at this juncture is further evidence of the increasing popularity of absolutism in literate circles after Richelieu's dramatic triumph.

The *Conseiller d'Estat* was intended only as a general, systematic treatment of all matters pertaining to government, a manual for rulers and statesmen and incidentally the casual reader. It brings together much information on all the usual topics in such works: types of monarchy, religion in the state, legislation, taxation, wars, and many other subjects, and analyzes them briefly with a copious sprinkling of general observations and historical examples. The author's approach is strictly that of a man of practical affairs; even the accepted norms of justice and religious morality are handled in thoroughly pragmatic fashion. His consideration of reason of state, that is, permissible stratagems, is part of the section on the prince's reputation and how best to preserve it. For this purpose, prudence is the prime requisite, the author maintains, and prudence always follows the dictates of interest. "The prince will be well enough aware that in all deliberations concerning his condition, interest is the argument and the motive that prevail and cause all decisions to favor the quarter in which it shows itself. For this reason the prince should not rely upon friendship, alliance, league, or other tie unless interest is associated with it."[298] Prudence, therefore, was

---

anonymously, is striking. All are mere manuals which bring together many precepts from various uncited authors for the reader's convenience. The clear parallelisms between these works plus the many contemporary attributions of the *Conseiller* to Du Refuge cause me to believe that he wrote it, but in the absence of definitive proof I have allowed the traditional attribution to Béthune to stand.

[297] The *Conseiller d'Estat* refers to nothing that occurred after 1610. The large number of manuscript copies listed in the previous note would seem to indicate extensive circulation of the book.

[298] *Conseiller*, p. 390.

merely the ability to master situations promptly by taking firm measures, avoiding undue risks, pursuing one's aims, leaving little to chance, and maintaining secrecy.[299]

With such a practical approach to political prudence and justifiable policy, the author might be expected to allow all stratagems that might prove effective, but at this point he fell back on the recommendations of another author whom he did not identify but who was obviously Lipsius. In his chapter on artifices (*finesse*), the author of the *Conseiller* at once made public advantage his criterion of justice. "It is always the prince's duty to procure the public good. The safety of the people is the supreme law according to which the prince should regulate all his actions."[300] In implementing this position, he closely followed Lipsius' three categories of princely offenses, but with a significant difference.[301] Lipsius' first two categories which he recommended and tolerated respectively were incorporated into the *Conseiller* almost without change, but its author departed from Lipsius' objections to his third classification, the greatest offenses against virtue, law, and justice. Instead of prohibiting them as Lipsius had done, the *Conseiller* permitted even these if they were necessary to the safety of the state. As examples he cited arbitrary, secret execution of suspected persons without trial, confiscation of subjects' wealth, revocation of privileges that had been granted to individuals or groups, and preventive war.[302] "All these things are in themselves unjust, but this injustice is counterbalanced by public necessity and utility. Necessity, as is said, knows no law, and the prince who is reduced to this extremity should be able not only to command according to the laws but even over the laws themselves. The only requirement is that the prince not create this necessity and oppression himself, to satisfy his own covetousness and ambition, for instead of gaining a reputation for wisdom, he would cause himself to be considered unjust and an inhuman tyrant."[303] The latter proviso was standard in the thought of the period, even among the most ardent absolutists, be-

---

[299] *Ibid.*, Pt. II, Chap. 7.

[300] *Ibid.*, p. 399.

[301] See Pt. I, n. 136-140, and text.

[302] *Conseiller*, pp. 402-03.

[303] *Ibid.*, pp. 403-04.

cause of their concern for the "image" of their ruler. Otherwise, the author of the *Conseiller* built his position upon a few authoritarian maxims and regarded public necessity as sufficient justification of any policy whatsoever.

Many other works that appeared in the years immediately following the Day of Dupes might be examined, but these will suffice to indicate the views of reason of state that were advanced to vindicate Richelieu's policies. The great divergence of opinion among the Cardinal's supporters is evident, extending as it did from Charles de Noailles' strict moralism to the utterly mundane outlook of Philippe de Béthune, with Guez de Balzac, Jean de Silhon, and Cardin Le Bret occupying positions between the two extremes. In their implementation of political prudence, however, it should be noted that all but Béthune preserved its ties with higher principle, thereby maintaining the relevance of morality to politics. And among the positions taken by the other four writers, it is Silhon's which seems closest to that of the Cardinal himself. This is indicated not only by the increasing favor that Silhon enjoyed as the years advanced; it is also apparent in the similarity of their views. To all who knew him, Richelieu regarded himself as a man of superior intelligence, outstanding ability, and nobility of purpose, all of which he believed to place him far above the commonality and even his own associates, and in combination with his firm religious beliefs amply endowed him with the qualities of a great Christian statesman. His occasional use of arbitrary measures was forced upon him by political necessity, but it was also legitimized by the unique nature of his vast responsibilities, the special morality of politics, and his own superior knowledge of such matters. On all these counts, Silhon's picture of the ideal minister paralleled the Cardinal's view of himself. It was therefore in the nature of things that Richelieu and his supporters should believe that he must be allowed great latitude in directing official policy, and it was from this standpoint that he conducted his massive program of state-building during the remainder of his life.

PART IV

THE CLIMAX, 1630-1642

RICHELIEU'S FOREIGN AND DOMESTIC POLICIES: THEIR NATURE, OBJECTIVES, AND IMPACT

T HE rapid appearance of many important works favoring absolutism and reason of state soon after the Day of Dupes may be said to have inaugurated Richelieu's final and most significant period of leadership as First Minister. For our purposes, the years between his triumph over the opposition in 1630 and his death twelve years later may be treated as a single unit because they witnessed the climax of his efforts in state-building and his final articulation of reason of state. During these crucially important years, Richelieu wielded royal power in such fashion that he more than Louis XIII was the true ruler of France. Although he was entirely dependent upon royal favor and was repeatedly forced to maneuver against opposition at court, he succeeded in retaining Louis XIII's support in all major matters of policy. In spite of their very dissimilar personal characteristics, the two men inevitably drew closer together because of their common belief in divine right absolutism and their parallel objectives in state-building. Indeed, it was Richelieu's indispensable ability to implement his sovereign's intense desire to be a true absolute monarch in the best sense that ensured the Cardinal's favor until the end. As the dominant partner, however, Richelieu became more autocratic as time advanced, both because it was he who fashioned official policy and because he greatly strengthened his personal control over the royal administration. He dominated the meetings of the royal council, now reduced in size, and built a very extensive following among the myriad office-holders under the crown. The king's ministers and councillors were Richelieu's creatures, and his clientele extended throughout the vast administrative apparatus and even into the military establishment. He even built a territorial basis of power by acquiring control over such cities as Le Havre and Brouage and building the town and chateau of Richelieu near his family seat in Poitou. From this position of strength, he directed official policy subject to royal approval which was consistently forthcoming. The period consequently witnessed the climax of Richelieu's massive effort in state-building, both by strengthening royal power at home and entering into all-out war abroad. And these developments were accompanied by extensive efforts to justify many of his measures which large numbers of his contemporaries regarded as tyrannical. The result was further elaboration of the concept of reason of state. The arguments that he and his supporters now put forward essentially extended those that they had previously evolved, but their contentions acquired a new cogency and were presented in more sophisticated and comprehensive fashion, in part because of the nature of accompanying events. Since the evolution of royal policy and political thought occurred simultaneously on many fronts, it is necessary to depart from strict chronology in treating the major developments of the period and to examine the Cardinal's actions and the relevant discussions of reason of state in topical fashion.

As the period progressed, Richelieu gave increasing attention to foreign affairs largely because of Imperialist successes in the Thirty Years' War and the consequent deterioration of France's diplomatic position. He was, however, extremely reluctant to enter into full-scale war against the Hapsburgs because of the well-known weaknesses of the French military system, and preferred to implement his foreign policy with brief campaigns and the pressures of diplomacy. In his *Advis au Roy* of January, 1629, he had urged mere limited, covert action against the Spanish:

Abroad, we must perpetually strive to arrest the course of Spain's progress. And contrary to that nation's aim to increase her dominion and extend her frontiers, France should seek only to fortify herself and to build and open gateways for the purpose of entering into the states of her neighbors so as to be able to protect them from Spanish oppression whenever the opportunities for this may present themselves.[1]

[1] *Lettres*, Vol. III, 181. See Pt. 3, n. 72 and text.

This was followed by two Italian campaigns in 1629 and 1630, the second of which was crucial in determining the future orientation of French foreign policy.[2] Meanwhile, Ferdinand II was rapidly approaching the zenith of his power. His utter defeat of Christian IV of Denmark and the collapse of all organized opposition to the Imperialists was followed by his Edict of Restitution which, if it had been consistently applied, would have effected a minor revolution in the tenure of properties and power among the German principalities. Richelieu understandably sought to neutralize these Imperialist gains by diplomatic means. He renewed the French alliance with the Dutch and then sent Father Joseph and Brulart de Léon to the Electoral Assembly of Regensburg where they effectively strengthened the anti-Hapsburg stance of several Electors. Soon the dramatic Day of Dupes occurred when Louis XIII definitively chose to support Richelieu's foreign policy. The king's decision undoubtedly stemmed from his conviction that the Hapsburg threat must be met and that the Cardinal alone was capable of directing the tortuous and dangerous policy which this entailed. The nature of the undertaking was quickly demonstrated by the Treaty of Bärwalde which cemented the French tie with Gustavus Adolphus and accorded him a large annual subsidy while stipulating that he should not disturb Catholicism in any areas that he might conquer. Gustavus' unexpected and dramatic successes almost forced a reversal of French policy before his death at Lützen, but subsequently the utter rout of the anti-Imperialist forces at Nördlingen and extensive defection of France's allies among the German princes finally forced Richelieu to take the step that he had resolutely avoided—outright war against the Hapsburgs. That all his major, active allies at this key moment were Protestant did not deter him, since it was impossible for him to proceed on any other basis. On May 19, 1635, a French herald-at-arms, standing in the *Grand' Place* at Brussels and following the time-honored ritual, formally declared war on the King of Spain in the name of the Most Christian King of France, Louis XIII.[3]

[2] See Pt. 3, n. 81, 82, and text.
[3] *Procès-verbal du heraut envoyé au Cardinal Infant luy dénoncer la guerre,*

Almost immediately the official *Déclaration du Roy, sur l'ouverture de la guerre contre le Roy d'Espagne* was issued and was verified in the Parlement of Paris on June 18, 1635.[4] This was quickly followed by the clarifying *Manifeste du Roy contenant les justes causes que le Roy a eues de déclarer la guerre à l'Espagne,*[5] which was drawn up by Father Joseph and approved by Richelieu. These two documents present in the clearest terms the official justification of France's entry into the Thirty Years' War and are invaluable for that reason. The *Déclaration* insisted that the French kings had always sought peace with Spain, as exemplified by the Spanish marriages, whereas the Spaniards, in pursuing their goal of universal monarchy, had repeatedly shown bad faith and had injured French interests by renewing hostilities in the Valtelline, proceeding against the Duke of Mantua, conspiring with the Duke of Lorraine, giving support to the rebellious French nobles and Huguenots so as to turn France against herself, embarking on anti-French acts in Germany, seizing the Elector of Trier who was under French protection, and making hostile preparations in Flanders which served as a base for perpetual war against the French. Furthermore, the Catholic religion "has always been the mask with which they [the Spanish] have sought to hide the injustice of their undertakings."[6] For these reasons, the French must actively seek to liberate all peoples under Spanish domination, especially those in the Low Countries which should be created a sovereign state under French protection.

All these points except that concerning the independence of the Low Countries were repeated in the *Manifeste*, but this later, explanatory document dwells much more extensively upon religious considerations, thereby reflecting Father Joseph's great concern for

---

in *Mercure français*, Vol. xx, 928-32. Also in the *Gazette* for 1635 and in Hay, *Recueil*, edition of 1643, pp. 909-12.

[4] In *Mercure français*, Vol. xx, 933-48. Also in the *Gazette* for 1635, pp. 335-44 and in Hay, *Recueil*, edition of 1643, pp. 912-21.

[5] Paris, 1635. Also in *Mercure français*, Vol. xx, 948-59. On Father Joseph's role in preparing this document, see Fagniez, *Le Père Joseph et Richelieu*, Vol. ii, 265-66.

[6] *Mercure français*, Vol. xx, 938.

this aspect of French foreign relations and his desire to counteract criticism from ultramontane sources both at home and abroad. For many observers, France's alliances with several Protestant powers and her entry into war against the Hapsburg champions of Catholicism were questionable in the extreme. In answer, Father Joseph wrote:

> Regarding this matter, the King is certain that all the princes of Europe and all persons of sound judgment, who will hear the Spaniards' complaints against His Majesty concerning recent events in Germany, will recognize the more clearly his equitable conduct. For all know the reasons why the King of Sweden came armed into Germany and that the King [of France] had no hand in it. But he was later obliged to oppose the injustices of the Spaniards who, in their desire to render the Empire hereditary in the House of Austria, made such a show of the inordinate pretensions of their monarchy over all Christendom as well as their hostilities against all princes on all occasions that we clearly see that the pretext of religion, which they have always sought to use, now serves them only as a cloak to hide their illicit ambitions.[7]

Here was reiterated the favorite argument of Richelieu's supporters that the Spanish were guilty of duplicity in claiming that their foreign policy supported the Catholic cause, whereas their true objective was merely self-aggrandizement. The King of France, on the contrary, Father Joseph held to be immune to such criticism, and he deplored the writing and publishing in Spanish territory of libels that contained "calumnies and abominable propositions against the honor and lives of persons whom divine and human law declare sacred."[8] For the intention of the King was merely to insure the preservation of peace, justice, and the true faith:

> His Majesty . . . protests before Christendom and declares, calling upon God to witness his heart and the sincerity of his intentions, that it is not his fault that the Church is not promptly

---

[7] *Ibid.*, 957-58.   [8] *Ibid.*, 958.

delivered from the miseries and calamities that have been brought down upon it by those who began and now continue the troubles in Italy and who have incited war between Catholics . . . . However, His Majesty hopes that God, who is the scrutinizer of hearts and holds those of kings in his hand, will protect the King's good cause and will continue to bless with his goodness his just intentions that seek from this war only an honorable, sure, and durable peace which may be general, in which piety and justice may regain strength, and which cannot but be greatly weakened by the disunity and misunderstanding of those who should be its protectors. This His Majesty most ardently desires for the augmentation of God's glory and the easing of the burden of taxation that he has had to impose on his subjects for their preservation which is as dear to him as his own life, a life that he has often exposed and will always most willingly expose on all occasions when it is a question of the honor of the Divine Majesty, the peace of this state, and the preservation of his good neighbors and allies.[9]

In their essentials, these documents merely reiterate the arguments that Richelieu and Father Joseph repeatedly set forth throughout the period to justify their foreign policy. Although many of their statements concerned specific grievances, it is evident that their position was grounded upon the assumption that the nature and purposes of the French state were fundamentally religious and that the cause of religion might therefore be served by acts in support of French interests. For this reason, it is not surprising that Richelieu and Louis XIII should seek divine intervention in favor of the French cause when, after the first years of armed conflict, the burden of war upon the French people was becoming calamitous and the much hoped for peace, which alone might solve the realm's most pressing problems, was as elusive as ever. In December 1637, Louis XIII, doubtless acting in concert with Richelieu and Father Joseph, approved the famous declaration committing the Kingdom of France to the protection of the Virgin.[10] The preamble of the docu-

[9] *Ibid.*, 958-59.   [10] Richelieu, *Lettres*, Vol. v, 908-12.

ment dwelt in magisterial terms upon the special favor that had been divinely bestowed upon Louis XIII among princes:

> God who raises kings to the throne of their grandeur, not content to have given us the inspiration that He accords all the princes of the earth for the guidance of their peoples, has sought to take such special care of both our person and our state that we cannot examine the success of the course of our reign without seeing therein as many marvelous effects of his mercy as mishaps that might have ruined us.[11]

After recalling the success of the French monarch in quelling internal disorders, suppressing the Huguenot rebellion, reestablishing Catholicism in many areas where it had been destroyed, and giving effective aid to his allies, the declaration continued:

> So many evident graces require that, in order not to defer their acknowledgment and without waiting for the peace that will doubtless come to us from the same hand from which we received these graces—peace that we ardently desire in order to cause the people who have been committed to us to experience its benefits—we feel ourselves obligated, prostrating ourselves at the feet of the Divine Majesty whom we adore in Three Persons, the Holy Virgin and the sacred cross in which we revere the fulfillment of the mystery of our redemption through the life and death of the Son of God, to dedicate ourselves to the greatness of God through his Son, lowered unto us, and to the Son through his Mother, raised unto Him, and under her protection we especially place our person, our state, our crown, and all our subjects, in order to secure by this means that of the Holy Trinity through her intercession . . . .
>
> These reasons moving us thereunto, we have declared and declare that, taking the most holy and glorious Virgin as the special Protectress of our realm, we particularly dedicate to her our person, our state, our crown, and our subjects, beseeching her to consent to inspire in us such holy rule and to defend this

[11] *Ibid.*, Vol. v, 908-09.

realm with such solicitude against the encroachments of our enemies that, whether it suffers the scourge of war or enjoys the benefits of peace, we beseech God with all our heart that it never leave the ways of grace which lead to those of glory.[12]

As evidence of this commitment of France to the protection of the Virgin, special services were authorized throughout the realm and the clergy were urged "to admonish all our people to give particular devotion to the Virgin, to implore her protection so that, under such a powerful Patroness, our realm may be protected from the machinations of its enemies, it may long enjoy a firm peace, and God may be served and revered so piously that we and our subjects may blissfully attain the final end for which we were all created."[13] Such a document literally breathes the spirit of religiosity and devotion which underlay Richelieu's dedication to the French state and his conviction that his policies in the interests of France were in accord with higher values.

Among Cardinal Richelieu's chief supporters, the career of Father Joseph most dramatically demonstrates the fusion of religion and politics in contemporary thought and the ways in which it might be implemented in practice. Indeed, Father Joseph's position was in many respects more clear-cut than that of the Cardinal himself. Much as their contemporaries might question the morality of Father Joseph's political activity, they had little reason to doubt the sincerity of his faith. He has authoritatively been identified as a true Christian mystic, although not of the highest type since his mysticism was of the active, energetic mode rather than the contemplative.[14] His work for the advancement of Catholicism adequately demonstrates the fulness of his convictions. A Provincial of the Capuchin Order, he collaborated with the high-born Antoinette d'Orléans to found the Filles du Calvaire as a model for other orders and remained its spiritual director throughout the rest of his life. The religious well-being of its members was always one of his prime concerns and was the object of much effort on his part, including

[12] *Ibid.*, Vol. v, 909-10.   [13] *Ibid.*, Vol. v, 912.
[14] H. Bremond, *Histoire littéraire du sentiment religieux en France depuis la fin des guerres de religion jusqu'à nos jours*, Paris, 1923, Vol. ii, 174-86.

the composition of important religious tracts. In addition, he doggedly sought to promote a crusade against the Turk, sent out missionaries to many areas of the globe, and worked for discipline and reform in the Gallican Church. Much of this he pursued while at court, actively engaged in implementing Richelieu's foreign policy.[15]

That Father Joseph felt no fundamental inconsistency between his religious convictions and his diplomatic efforts in behalf of the French monarchy is evident from the record of his life, if only because of his persistent support of both causes. Always dedicated to the advancement of his faith, he was likewise Richelieu's right-hand man in the conduct of diplomacy during the better part of the latter's ministry. In fact, Father Joseph did not hesitate to stoop to very questionable methods if they served French interests. At Regensburg in 1630, his support of the Catholic princes of the Empire, including Maximilian of Bavaria, against the Emperor was influential in preventing their agreement on key issues and had much to do with the continuation of the war. Regarding French support of Gustavus Adolphus, Father Joseph admitted that it might temporarily endanger the Catholic faith but found it to be justified by necessity. "One must utilize such things as poisons, of which a little serves as an antidote but too much kills."[16] Maximilian of Bavaria understandably objected to the French tie with the Swedish king, but Father Joseph held that the interests of Catholicism were protected by the Treaty of Bärwalde and regarded Gustavus as an unwitting instrument of God, working for the cause of France and the true faith.[17] Somewhat different justifications were set forth by Richelieu and Father Joseph after the Treaty of Frankfort (September 9, 1633) allied France with the Protestant German-Swedish League of Heilbronn. In their protestations to their Protestant allies, the Cardinal and the Capuchin argued that war between different religions was to be avoided like the plague, that Protestant and Catholic powers should unite against the Hapsburgs who aimed to dominate all

---

[15] The best works on Father Joseph's political and religious activities are still those of Fagniez and Bremond, cited above, and L. Dedouvres, *Le Père Joseph: Études critiques sur ses œuvres spirituelles*, Paris, 1903.
[16] Fagniez, Vol. 1, 566.   [17] *Ibid.*, Vol. 1, 575.

states of both faiths, and that France had no ambition in Germany but fought merely for the peace and equilibrium of Europe.[18]

Although Richelieu and Father Joseph indulged in many questionable diplomatic maneuvers and adjusted their arguments to the sensitivities of their hearers, they nevertheless held to a consistent position regarding the justice and necessity of their anti-Hapsburg policy. The Capuchin in particular regarded himself as a champion of both Catholicism and the Christian state, and viewed his efforts in behalf of his faith and the French monarchy merely as twin phases of his life-long mission. Thoroughly aware of the French crown's time-honored tradition of serving the Church—a tradition that stemmed from Clovis, reached its zenith in the time of Charlemagne and the crusades (*Gesta Dei per Francos*), and was far from dead during the reign of Louis XIII—Father Joseph found it only natural to associate his battle for the faith with support of the French state. Conditions in Europe during his time were such that the advancement of French interests necessitated war against the Catholic Hapsburgs. So be it, he felt, and energetically devoted himself to undermining the latter's position while convincing himself that the courts of Vienna and Madrid were merely using the Catholic cause to cloak their essentially selfish designs. Father Joseph's diplomatic efforts in behalf of Richelieu were therefore in support of Catholicism within the French national framework, although he simultaneously sought its advancement abroad through foreign missions and other means. His ultimate objective was French supremacy over a pacified Europe which would support a crusade against the Turk and guarantee the peace of all nations while advancing the cause of the true faith. In spite of his immersion in the intricacies of diplomacy, he never lost sight of these essentially religious ends.[19]

Toward the end of his life, it is true, he experienced some disillu-

[18] *Ibid.*, Vol. II, 145-52.

[19] This is the conclusion of Fagniez, Vol. II, 433-39, which is still the best treatment of the subject. It is apparent that I cannot accept the view in A. Huxley, *Grey Eminence*, New York, 1941, where Huxley thoroughly distorts Father Joseph's understanding of his political activity.

sionment with his accomplishments and the type of life that he had lived. In 1635, three years before his death, he spoke the following before a group of his Calvarians:

> I myself have experienced, as punishment for my mistakes and my misuse of the time allotted to me, no longer having the leisure to meditate on the interior life, always distracted by multitudinous occupations, the evil of not being united with God and not giving possession of my soul to the spirit of Jesus that He may guide it according to his will, and how necessary for this it is to be in the company of the good where all may be strengthened and give each other mutual support.[20]

This, however, was little more than the disappointment of an old crusader who felt his years and opportunities slipping away. After his death, controversy over his political morality continued unabated, but at least one funeral oration, pronounced at the time, put the matter in Father Joseph's own perspective.[21] To those who criticized the Capuchin for spending too much time at court and in political activities, the orator answered that nothing in Father Joseph's religious vocation prohibited this and in fact it was approved by St. Thomas, St. Bernard, St. Francis, and many others. Furthermore:

> Is not God the Creator of the state as well as religion? Were not the priesthood and royalty formerly united? Is the train of princes a peril to virtue? Is piety incompatible there? If a man who greatly values both cannot live at court without being damned, alas! What has become of so many men who knew only the externals of those two things and passed their lives there? . . . Does the religious vocation dispense subjects from

---

[20] Quoted in Bremond, Vol. II, 191. Huxley (pp. 286-87) lifts this quotation out of context and distorts its meaning.

[21] Funeral oration for Father Joseph, "prononcée au Monastère des Religieuses du Calvaire au Faubourg Saint-Germain, par le R. P. Georges de Paris Le Juge, prédicateur Capucin," in Bibliothèque Nationale, Fonds Français 23067, fols. 6b-15b. This funeral oration directly approaches the question of the morality of Father Joseph's political activity. The other funeral oration for Father Joseph in the manuscript, by the R. P. Léon, avoids this issue and concentrates entirely upon Father Joseph's work in religion.

the natural obligation that they owe their prince? And does it deny him the services that he may require of them on occasions that are justified and beneficial to his state? Who can better inform him of the qualities and affinities that he should have with God, whose image he is, than one who has devoted years to contemplation of the divine Prototype?[22]

One by one, the orator answered the many criticisms of Father Joseph's diplomatic activities by the simple device of insisting that he always sought to protect the Catholic religion in all negotiations regardless of the doctrinal position of the other party. "The deceased was a good Christian and a good Frenchman .... Never did he separate reason of state from that of the Church."[23] The orator concluded: "Continue your negotiations in Paradise with the King of Kings who holds in balance and judges all peoples' interests. Entreat Him to favor the monarchy of the First Son of the Church, the peace of Christendom, and our propensity for glory."[24]

Richelieu's motivation in directing French participation in the Thirty Years' War was in many ways similar to Father Joseph's. The two men could hardly have cooperated so thoroughly and remained on such intimate terms if they had not been essentially agreed concerning both the methods and the objectives of this most dangerous commitment to the goddess Fortuna. Historians, however, continue to place a variety of interpretations upon the Cardinal's motives and their implications concerning his spectrum of values. His devious and deceptive diplomacy, his alliances with heretic powers for practical advantage, his imposition of great sacrifices upon the nation, and the evolution of the war itself have combined to cause many authorities to view Richelieu merely as a man of power, a Machiavellian statesman who would stoop to any illegal or immoral measures that might benefit French interests.[25] The logical concomitant of this view of French policy is the dictum, often repeated, that the first three periods of the Thirty Years' War constituted its religious phase whereas the entry of the French in

[22] *Loc.cit.*, fol. 11a.   [23] *Ibid.*, fol. 12a.   [24] *Ibid.*, fol. 15b.
[25] See Introduction.

1635 on the side of the Protestant powers transformed it into a purely secular struggle because confessional interests were now subordinated to those of the state. This impression of a thoroughly secularized French policy is enhanced by its pragmatic, *ad hoc* character, since Richelieu, unlike Louis XIV, was unable to plan his moves well in advance of their execution and was forced to meet developments as they occurred, often in the midst of unexpected pressures at home and reverses abroad. Given the chaotic state of French finances, continuing opposition to him in high places, and the weakness of the French military system, not to mention the ebb and flow of the fortunes of war, he was continually forced by factors beyond his control to adjust means to possibilities, often in very unscrupulous fashion. For years he relied upon diplomacy, subsidies to his allies, and limited campaigns when seeking French advantage, and only in 1635 did he commit French fortunes to the battlefield. Throughout the remainder of his life he nevertheless conducted secret negotiations with the Count-Duke Olivares, his opposite number in Madrid, for the restoration of peace.[26] Too much should not be read into these efforts, since they may have stemmed in part from Richelieu's view that unremitting diplomacy itself served as a weapon and an instrument for the advancement of state interests. Both ministers had pressing reasons for desiring peace and undoubtedly longed for it, but both insisted upon peace with advantages that the other would not concede. Richelieu in particular refused to desert his Protestant allies. Both ministers charged the other with bad faith, with some justice. If nothing else, this phase of Richelieu's diplomatic activity shows that the issues which divided the two greatest Catholic powers were so fundamental and their sense of rivalry and antagonism so keen that peace could be achieved only by a military solution.

The flexibility and opportunism of Richelieu's diplomacy and conduct of the war should not blind us to his larger objectives. These did not include a massive offensive against Hapsburg territory

---

[26] A. Leman, *Richelieu et Olivarès: Leur Négociations secrètes de 1636 à 1642 pour le rétablissement de la paix*, Lille, 1938. Cf. Hauser's comments on this book, *Revue historique*, CLXXXX (1940), 132-33.

—indeed, such was beyond the capacity of the French military system at that time—and he certainly did not seek to acquire any "natural boundaries" such as the Rhine for the French monarchy.[27] Instead, his posture was essentially defensive against Spanish encirclement which he sought to counteract by acquiring strategic areas on France's most vulnerable frontiers and building a coalition of anti-Hapsburg states, large and small. He also advocated the acquisition of bridgeheads into Germany for potential thrusts against the enemy, but this was for the purpose of neutralizing Hapsburg power and protecting French territory.[28] This general position, in fact, Richelieu had urged upon Louis XIII as early as the *Advis* of January, 1629, when he proposed the following:

> In foreign affairs, you must have a continuing plan to stop the advance of Spain. Although that nation's objective is to increase its dominion and extend its boundaries, France should seek only to strengthen herself internally and to build and open gateways [on her borders] in order to be able to enter into the states of her neighbors and protect them from Spanish oppression when the occasion arises .... You must consider fortifying your position at Metz and advancing as far as Strasbourg if possible so as to gain a gateway into Germany. This must be done with great discretion and with quiet and clandestine methods. You must build a great citadel at Versoix to overawe the Swiss, have an open door into that country, and put Geneva in the position of being one of the outworks of France .... You must consider [taking] the Marquisate of Saluzzo, either through an understanding with the Duke of Savoy by giving him greater conquests in Italy if his mercurial disposition causes him to return to Your Majesty's service, or by taking advantage of the bad relations between him and the subjects of the Mar-

---

[27] G. Zeller, "La Monarchie d'ancien régime et les frontières naturelles," *Revue d'histoire moderne*, VIII (1933), 305-33.

[28] G. Zeller, "Saluces, Pignerol et Strasbourg. La Politique des frontières au temps de la prépondérance espagnole," *Revue historique*, CLXXXXIII (1942-1943), 97-110. Reprinted in Zeller, *Aspects de la politique française sous l'ancien régime*, Paris, 1964, pp. 115-27.

quisate to reconquer it . . . . We may think of Navarre and the Franche-Comté as belonging to us, since they are contiguous to France and easy to conquer whenever we have nothing else to do. This, however, should not be bruited about since it would be imprudent to consider it if these more important matters had not succeeded and because it could not be done without causing open war with Spain, which must be avoided as far as possible.[29]

Richelieu's hesitations as well as the nature of his long-range plans for the defense of the French state and the advancement of its interests are evident in this key document. Although the course of events caused him to alter his plans according to the fortunes of war and other circumstances, his fundamental approach to the problems of French foreign policy remained substantially unchanged.

Richelieu's intellectual stature, moreover, was such that he was much more than a mere diplomat and war minister using every means at his disposal to defend French interests. He was also a statesman of comprehensive views and looked beyond immediate crises to a general peace with mutual guarantees of security as the only solution to Europe's ills. Such he knew to be particularly necessary in Germany where the fragmentation of political power opened endless vistas of armed conflict. Richelieu's assertion that France should serve as the protector of smaller states, which is contained in the *Advis* of 1629, was but part of his effort toward a general peace that would guarantee a secure equilibrium in interstate relations. Of course, it should not be forgotten that such a peace settlement would have increased France's security and strengthened her diplomatic position through the simple process of protecting her Protestant allies, especially those in Germany, from Hapsburg encroachment, yet Richelieu was sufficiently astute to realize that a Europe-wide system of sovereign states was the only viable alternative to Hapsburg universalism. Even before the entry of France into active hostilities in 1635, Pope Urban VIII, who unremittingly

[29] *Lettres*, Vol. III, 181-82. For the principal recommendations of the *Advis* concerning domestic matters, see Pt. 3, n. 69-78 and text.

worked for peace between France and the Hapsburgs, realized that the latter's unwillingness to meet French demands for a general peace settlement constituted a major obstacle to ending the war.[30] And on May 8, 1635, eleven days before the French declaration of war, Father Joseph wrote to d'Avaux: "The King's true intention is to make at the earliest possible date a general peace with mutual guarantees for the future, which [thereby] should become a golden age like the time of Augustus. The means that he employs to this end is to support all types of good negotiations and overtures to peace with several armies."[31] This view of France as the protector of the smaller European states against Hapsburg encroachment and as the proponent of universal peace under French leadership was widely reflected in the pro-Richelieu tracts of the period.[32]

The best recent scholarship, that of Fritz Dickmann, abundantly substantiates this interpretation of Richelieu's foreign policy. Dickmann succeeds in demonstrating that Richelieu was fundamentally a man of principle, always seeking to define the boundaries between power and just policy, and invariably conscious of the demands of the latter.[33] Using a variety of newly discovered sources, particularly the instructions of 1643 to the French representatives at the peace

[30] Instructions to Bolognetti, Papal Nuncio to France, April 1, 1634, in A. Leman, ed., *Recueil des instructions générales aux nonces ordinaires de France de 1624 à 1634*, Paris, 1919, pp. 167-68, 191-96.

[31] A. Leman, *Urbain VIII et la rivalité de la France et de la maison d'Autriche de 1631 à 1635*, Lille, 1920, p. 520.

[32] See n. 369, 374, 421, 480.

[33] M. Braubach and K. Repgen, eds., *Acta Pacis Westphalicae*, Series 1: *Instruktionen*. Vol. 1: *Frankreich, Schweden, Kaiser*, F. Dickmann, K. Goronzy, E. Schieche, H. Wagner, E. M. Wermter eds., Münster, 1962. F. Dickmann, "Rechtsgedanke und Machpolitik bei Richelieu. Studien an neu endeckten Quellen," *Historische Zeitschrift*, CLXXXXVI (1963), 265-319. F. Dickmann, *Der Westfälische Frieden*, Münster, 1965 (2nd edn.). The article in the *Historische Zeitschrift* is especially important for our purposes. Dickmann's reinterpretation of Richelieu's motivation and fundamental principles has been widely accepted. Cf. reviews by H. Rowen, *Journal of Modern History*, XXXIII (1961), 53-56, and G. Livet, *Revue historique*, CCXXVIII (1962), 481-83 and CCXXXV (1966), 199-201. For a criticism of Dickmann, see K. von Raumer, "Westfälischer Friede," *Historische Zeitschrift*, CLXXXXV (1962), 596-613.

negotiations at Münster[34]—instructions which were written after Richelieu's death but embody his mature views and objectives—Dickmann shows that Richelieu consistently sought to follow accepted legal principles in his conduct of negotiations. This was most evident in his handling of French policy relative to the German states, the most complex area and yet the most crucial in his eyes. Interference in the affairs of other sovereign states Richelieu disliked on principle, yet he found ample precedents for intervention in areas where the ruler's authority was limited, his subjects enjoyed the right of resistance, and they openly solicited French aid. Under such circumstances, direct negotiation with an enemy's subjects was accepted diplomatic practice in Richelieu's period and went far to justify his building an anti-Hapsburg faction among the German princes and pressuring them to support French interests. It also legitimized Richelieu's policy of seizing strong points and establishing bridgeheads into enemy territory. These were not, in his eyes, permanent annexations but bases of maneuver for the protection of French soil against the omnipresent Hapsburgs and the creation of favorable conditions for a permanent peace.[35]

Richelieu understandably sought to capitalize upon the conflicting legal rights to innumerable small territories on France's German frontier and interpreted them to French advantage. Many of these areas had been held by earlier French kings, and Louis XIII's rights to them were part of the royal domain and therefore inalienable. French claims to these small but strategic holdings were based in law, and their reversion to the French crown merely restored the rightful order of things. Such was Richelieu's reasoning when pressing French claims to border areas and encouraging several ranking jurists to justify such actions.[36] Of course Richelieu was an interested party to such procedures, but he should not for this reason be accused

[34] Printed in *Acta Pacis Westphalicae*, Vol. 1, 58-123.
[35] Cf. H. Weber, "Richelieu et le Rhin," *Revue historique*, ccxxxix (1968), 265-80. Weber accepts Dickmann's interpretation and applies it to Richelieu's Rhine policy.
[36] These are treated in n. 198-244 and text.

of mere specious propagandizing to justify an essentially Machia-vellian policy. Instead, he was acting within the terms of the law, the only relevant law that was known in his time. No alternative legal procedures were available to him, and he believed that he was entirely justified in attempting to make good the sacred, inalienable rights of the French crown. Dickmann shows that Richelieu con-sistently followed such precepts in his actual conduct of diplomacy on many different occasions and under a wide variety of circum-stances.[37] He concludes that Richelieu's ultimate aim was collective security based on a general peace which would be guaranteed by all major and minor signatories. The only solution to Europe's ills, particularly the threat of Hapsburg domination and perpetual war, was the creation of a community of sovereign states in which France might hold first place and whose security would be preserved by mutually binding engagements and respect for law.

Fundamentally, therefore, Richelieu appears as a man of principle whose values were those of right rather than might. True, he fre-quently implemented his policies with highly questionable tactics, most notably the Protestant alliances and various Machiavellian maneuvers which scandalized his more scrupulous contemporaries, but in retrospect the majority of these measures seem to have been forced upon him by the circumstances of European political align-ment and religious division, and should not be taken to denote an utterly pragmatic view of just policy. Like many principled states-men who must work within the limitations of adverse conditions that are thrust upon them, Richelieu was forced to make compro-mises and to resort to means which he himself found distasteful. His frequent consultation of jurists and theologians regarding the legiti-macy of many of his measures and his extensive campaign to mold public opinion in his favor indicate that he was disturbed by the implications of some of his tactics and would have preferred a sim-pler, more Catholic-oriented foreign policy. Such, however, was impossible to combine with the defense of French interests against the Hapsburgs, given the prevailing alignment of the European

---

[37] "Rechtsgedanke . . . ," pp. 284-308.

powers and their religious orientation. Hence the necessity of utilizing questionable means toward a laudable end.

Richelieu's political principles, moreover, were profoundly relevant to, and influenced by, the strength of his religious convictions.[38] Like Father Joseph, his chief aide in conducting French foreign policy, the Cardinal thoroughly believed in the mission of the Church and held that the true interests of Christianity might be served by working for the cause of Christian France. Not only was Richelieu a Prince of the Church with the firm, orthodox faith of the professional ecclesiastic; his religious tracts and active proselytizing, his efforts toward monastic reform, and his consistent defense of Catholicism in his negotiations with Protestant powers reveal a man with a strong sense of mission. That a man of such substance should devote his great talents and energies to serving the state he found in no way incongruous. For him the religious qualities and legitimate interests of the French monarchy were but concomitant elements of a sacred institution whose preservation had been committed to his hands. Like many of his contemporaries, he held that church and state were divinely sanctioned, coordinate institutions, each supreme in its sphere, and that the French state enjoyed an autonomy, rights, and powers which rested upon a firm foundation of natural law.[39] But above all it was a Christian state whose nature and interests were inseparable from those of religion. He therefore believed that the twin objectives of French foreign policy should be to increase French advantage and to establish a just and lasting peace throughout Christendom. Under these conditions, war against the Hapsburgs was at least in part for religious purposes. The peace, which Richelieu so ardently desired and was achieved only after his death, was later hailed in France as a religious good.[40] In his de-

[38] See Pt. 1, n. 220-35 and text.

[39] This is developed by J. Lecler, "Politique nationale et idée chrétienne dans les temps modernes," *Études: Revue fondé en 1856 par les pères de la Compagnie de Jésus*, ccxiv (1933), 692-96, and "Les Principes de Richelieu sur la sécularisation de la politique française," *Cahiers d'histoire publiés par les Universités de Clermont, Lyon, Grenoble*, iv (1959), 46-52

[40] H. Weber, "Friede und Gewissen," in *Forschungen und Studien zur Geschichte des Westfälischen Friedens*, Münster, 1965, pp. 85-108.

fense of specifically French interests and his search for collective security, Richelieu may have anticipated the modern European community of secularized sovereign states, but for him the fusion of religion and politics stemmed both from his personal convictions and the nature of the state whose ends he served. Reason of state, for him, was therefore grounded upon legal, moral, and religious values which provided the guides and determined the objectives of his foreign policy.

As France became increasingly involved in the Thirty Years' War, Richelieu's domestic policies necessarily assumed second place to his conduct of foreign affairs. As early as April 1630, he had made clear to Louis XIII that an active anti-Hapsburg policy, with its attendant drain upon the resources of the realm, would force postponement of domestic reforms and cause the war effort to assume priority over all else.[41] With Louis XIII's decision in Richelieu's favor at the Day of Dupes, and especially after 1635, the shaping of high policy revolved chiefly around foreign relations, yet Richelieu was simultaneously able to pursue his program of state-building on many fronts. The strengthening of the state within its borders he believed necessary not only to discipline the French and to channel their energies into the most profitable pursuits but also to provide the indispensable material support of hostilities against the Hapsburgs. For this purpose, a wide variety of increased controls over many elements of French society were deemed necessary by Richelieu who conceived of state-building as increasing the effective power and prestige of the crown with attendant benefits to the nation at large. A majority of these measures fell strictly within the royal prerogative to create and strengthen the instruments of government and were therefore immune to criticism on the basis of legality. When Richelieu reformed the administration by reorganizing the royal councils, redefining the functions of the secretaries of state, and establishing a newly powerful system of intendants; when he undertook a variety of mercantilist measures, strengthened the army, built a navy, and even when he sharply increased taxes and resorted to a host of fiscal

[41] See Pt. 3, n. 81 and text.

expedients, he was acting within the limits of the sovereign authority of the crown as it was understood by him and the great majority of his contemporaries. The issue, therefore, was not Richelieu's legal right, as agent of Louis XIII, to do these things for the purpose of implementing royal power. Rather, it was the impact of these and similar measures upon various institutions, groups, and classes, and the extent to which their traditional rights and privileges were violated.

In his effort to strengthen the crown and make the resources of the realm, that is, the lives and goods of the subjects, available to the war effort, Richelieu inevitably rode roughshod over many rights, privileges, and immunities that bore the sanction of tradition and, in certain instances, accepted law. Richelieu's only means of achieving his ends, however, was to increase royal control over all elements of the population, and any attempt to accomplish this in the highly fragmented, hierarchically structured society of his time was certain to clash with a host of vested interests and accompanying prerogatives. Even so fundamental a matter as the supremacy of loyalty to the crown over all other loyalties in the state presented unavoidable difficulties, although Richelieu and Louis XIII understandably made this the cornerstone of their concept of authoritarian rule. Such was implicit in their views concerning taxation, the function of government which contemporaries most noticed and resented. Generally, Richelieu held to the simplistic position that taxes were owed to the crown as a matter of royal sovereignty and discipline of the populace, according to the needs of the state. And Louis XIII, speaking before a deputation from the Parlement of Paris which was resisting the raising of royal revenue for war purposes early in 1637, dissociated his personal desires from public necessity and based taxation squarely on the latter: "The money that I ask is not for gambling or foolish expenditure. It is not I who speaks; it is my state. It is the need that all have of it. Those who contradict my orders do me more harm than the Spanish." And for emphasis he repeated, "It is not I who speaks; it is my state."[42]

[42] H. Griffet, *Histoire du règne de Louis XIII*, Paris, 1758, Vol. II, 818-19. Quoted in V. L. Tapié, *La France de Louis XIII et de Richelieu*, Paris, 1967, p. 327.

Acting upon this all-encompassing necessity of defending the French state, Richelieu pursued a host of expedients which inevitably caused many of his contemporaries to accuse him of tyranny. His great power, his use of sheer force on many occasions, his ingratitude, and his enormous ambition were among the charges most frequently leveled against him,[43] but in his defense he could always plead the support of Louis XIII and above all the necessity of strong, even violent measures for the good of the state:

> It is to be desired that benefits rather than punishments restrain men within the bonds of their duties, but the malice and misery of the human race are so great that a prince may deem himself fortunate if there is a single year of his reign when he is not obliged to secure the public good by means that are offensive to individuals . . . . Such actions are the fruits of true justice, fruits so glorious that those who achieve them would not have been able to refrain from doing so without committing injustice and cowardly outrage against the principle of the public interest.[44]

During a period of outright war, such an elastic principle was easily extended to justify almost any measures that Richelieu might deem necessary for the safety of the state. For the sake of brevity, we shall examine only the more controversial aspects of his domestic policies and their impact upon the more important established institutions and social classes.

The Parlement of Paris was by far the most important institution within the royal administration to feel the weight of the Cardinal's wrath. Because of its long tradition as guardian of the laws and protector of the interests of the realm, the Parlement held that it had both the right and the duty to make its influence felt in purely political matters by refusing to enregister royal legislation and sending up remonstrances to the highest authorities, often the king himself. The process frequently resulted in compromise, caused innu-

---

[43] E.g., *Callomnies dont on charge de Cardinal [de Richelieu], et ses iustes deffenses*, Bibliothèque Nationale, Fonds Français, No. 10455, *passim*. Another copy of this tract: No. 15644, fols. 474-586.

[44] *Callomnies*, fols. 65a, 74a.

merable delays, and acted as a severe check upon the implementation of royal policy. During Richelieu's ministry, the Parlement frequently resisted financial edicts, the creation of new offices, and such extraordinary judicial measures as the *grands-jours*, the appointment of special tribunals to try great cases, and many of Richelieu's moves against Gaston d'Orléans and his followers. Much of this was self-interested in the extreme, but it must be admitted that the Parlement frequently had legal tradition on its side. Louis XIII, Richelieu, and their supporters, of course, adhered to the contrary position which was equally valid at law, namely, that the crown possessed a monopoly of judicial authority and the Parlement enjoyed only such competence as the sovereign permitted it. The Parlement was merely a court for trying cases between subjects and had no right to interfere in political matters of any kind. The two views inevitably produced a series of clashes between the court and the Cardinal whose years as First Minister were punctuated by such coercive measures as *lettres de jussion*, repeated *lits de justice*, and the exile of important magistrates from Paris.[45]

During the siege of La Rochelle, the Parlement resisted all efforts of the royal administration to secure the necessary funds for operations against the Huguenots. The magistrates were particularly incensed by royal edicts creating new venal offices within the royal administration. Their opposition was detested by Richelieu who was doing his utmost to eliminate the Huguenot threat to royal power, and on November 15, 1627, a letter which bore Louis XIII's name but was probably dictated by Richelieu was dispatched from the royal encampment before La Rochelle to Mathieu Molé, the Procureur General who consistently upheld the Parlement's position.[46] This letter denounced the court's opposition in the strongest

[45] These developments are summarized in E. Glasson, *Le Parlement de Paris: son rôle politique depuis le règne de Charles VII jusqu'à la Révolution*, Paris, 1901, Vol. I, 133-75. The most important sources are M. Molé, *Mémoires*, Paris, 1855, Vols. I, II, and the *Mémoires* of Omer Talon.

[46] Molé, *Mémoires*, Vol. I, 478-82, and Avenel, *Lettres*, Vol. II, 717-21. The editors of Molé's *Mémoires* ascribe this letter to Louis XIII himself, but Avenel shows that it was written by a secretary who imitated Louis' handwriting and argues that it must have been dictated by Richelieu.

terms and insisted that there was no difference between the edicts that were registered in the king's presence and those that were merely submitted to the Parlement. Otherwise the sovereign's authority would be inferior to that of the court, which, said Louis, "can have no force nor substance but within mine."[47] Peaceful remonstrances were permissible, but no other manifestation of opposition would be tolerated. Several weeks later, Michel de Marillac, then Keeper of the Seals, also wrote to Molé accusing the Parlement of "establishing a throne above that of the king."[48] And Marillac added: "I believe that order consists of ensuring that complete obedience is rendered the sovereign courts by all below them and the king by all below him."[49] Molé, however, countered with the following:

> Kings command whatever they please, but it is not necessary for the execution of their commands to establish a new order, new officers, and new laws, but rather to follow the traditional ones and to assign to each [officer] what belongs to him according to the function of his office. Then all in general and each in particular will render due obedience and the just orders of the prince will be most readily followed, especially by his officers who have no power but that which His Majesty has conceded to them, and whose greatest glory is to obey.[50]

Such conditional obedience was anathema to Richelieu. Marillac subsequently wrote to Molé in a more conciliatory manner, and the dispute was eventually resolved by compromise concerning the edicts in question.

On January 15, 1629, Louis XIII held a *lit de justice* during which Marillac requested the registration of several edicts as well as his "Code Michaud," and argued the monarchy's position in the clearest terms:

> We are all agreed that the King should do nothing unjust; he knows it and believes it himself. No matter how much he may be above the laws, he nevertheless is willing to be below reason.

[47] Molé, Vol. 1, 479. [48] *Ibid.*, 490-93. The quotation is on p. 491.
[49] *Ibid.*, 492. [50] *Ibid.*, 498.

But the nub of the question is, who will be judge of the King's actions, to say whether they are just or not? If we make the subjects or officers of the King his judges, it is up to them to limit his acts and declare them just or unjust. The King is no longer King but under the tutelage of his officers, and sovereignty is dependent upon them. It is to open the door to factions in the state and to give the proponents of change and innovation a means of constantly criticizing the actions of the King and compromising his state. It is therefore true that the King alone is judge of the justice of his acts. He renders an account of them to God alone, and as each of us loves the state and public peace, so should he hold firm to this resolution.[51]

This view that the king was the sole judge of his actions and policies rested upon a long and venerable tradition. In the context of seventeenth century absolutism, it was essential to the doctrine of reason of state since it permitted the ruler great latitude in the rightful exercise of his sovereign power and all but implied that his policies were *ipso facto* just. In his speech, Marillac did not hesitate to present the logical corrollary, namely, that the Parlement, for all its prestige as the highest court in the land, should never examine matters of state. These were reserved for the royal council.[52] The clear implication was that only the king and his ministers should determine both the necessity and the justice of royal policy. Marillac's Code Michaud placed important restrictions upon the Parlement's right of remonstrance but had little practical effect in limiting the magistrates' acts or pretensions.[53]

[51] *Mercure français*, Vol. xv, 19-20, second pagination.

[52] *Ibid.*, Vol. xv, 23-25, second pagination.

[53] Article 1 decreed that all laws which had been formulated before 1629 should be applied by the courts whether registered or not. Remonstrances concerning these laws were permitted for six months, but at no time should the courts refuse to apply them. Article 53 limited remonstrances concerning new legislation to two months and required that all such laws be applied without modification, whether registered in the royal presence or not and regardless of any remonstrances. Isambert, *Recueil*, Vol. xvi, 225-26, 239. The Parlement's response was that no legislation was valid unless registered by the appropriate courts, "according to the order at all times observed concerning the laws of the realm." *Ibid.*, Vol. xvi, 344-45.

The Parlement, of course, continued its attempts to influence royal policy. When Louis XIII issued a declaration condemning those who had followed Gaston d'Orléans into exile as guilty of *lèse-majesté*, the court refused to register the act, whereupon a decree by the royal council once more forbade consideration of political matters by the magistrates "on pain of deprivation of their offices and greater measures if necessary."[54] Subsequently, several ranking members of the Parlement were temporarily exiled from Paris. The struggle continued intermittently for years in this vein. During a royal audience on January 5, 1636, the Chancellor, speaking for Louis XIII, expostulated:

> Consider who you are and who is King; what disproportion there is between his condition and yours! You have no authority but that which he concedes to you; you nevertheless use it to oppose his prudence and his affairs, and it seems that you seek to find fault with the government of the state . . . . For this the King prohibits your assembling and [orders you] to execute his will punctually, to receive the officers that will be appointed, and to prove your obedience to him by your actions.[55]

Even when the Spanish were besieging Corbie in 1636, the Parlement had the temerity to resist Richelieu's countermeasures. In answer, he prepared an allocution which Louis XIII delivered before certain of the magistrates:

> I would never have believed that I might have the occasion to send for you because of the matter that brings you here. It is not for you to trouble yourself with the affairs of my state, and you could not have thought of what was done this morning in the present conjuncture without great ill will . . . . I forbid you to continue your deliberation and to seek to be my tutors by interfering in affairs of state.[56]

[54] Molé, Vol. II, 50-52. The quotation is on p. 51. The decree is dated May 12, 1631.

[55] Talon, *Mémoires*, Paris, 1838, p. 49.

[56] Richelieu, *Lettres*, Vol. v, 541-42. During the later years of his ministry, Richelieu fell into the habit of speaking to the Parlement through the mouth

Finally, in 1641, Louis XIII and Richelieu determined to end the magistrates' opposition to royal policies. This was effected in a *lit de justice* on February 21, when an elaborate ordinance was registered.[57] After reciting the virtues and necessity of strong rule, its restoration by Henry IV, the setbacks that it received during the Regency, and its reinstitution under Louis XIII, the document asserted the necessity of limiting the Parlement's competence for the good of the realm. For this purpose, consideration of all matters of government and administration of the state was denied the court which was limited to dispensing justice between subjects. Remonstrances concerning tax edicts alone might be made by the Parlement, but these should be registered without change upon receipt of a royal order. All other legislation regarding matters of government was to be registered without debate or consideration of any kind. The measure effectively checkmated the Parlement's efforts to influence Richelieu's policies and was a victory of absolutism and reason of state, but the Cardinal's death in the following year meant that his triumph was short-lived.

Among the many quasi-autonomous organs with which Richelieu clashed, by far the most powerful was the French wing of the Roman Catholic Church. This greatest and most prestigious corporation in the realm enjoyed extensive privileges and immunities, performed innumerable administrative functions, and possessed vast properties upon which the Cardinal cast a covetous eye. Inevitably its uniquely favored position placed limitations upon certain elements of Richelieu's state-building. It is not that he was merely a partisan of state power at the expense of the Church. In the perennial strife between Church and state, Richelieu consistently assumed a middle ground and preferred accommodation to controversy. Repeatedly he sought a *via media* in the chronic quarrels between Gallicans and ultramontanes, never yielding completely to either faction and avoiding

---

of the king. Instances of this are found in the *Lettres*, Vol. v, 392-93, 429-30, 727-28, 758-59.

[57] Molé, Vol. II, 500-510. Isambert, Vol. XVI, 529-35.

close association with both. It may be argued that such a policy was forced upon him by the precariousness of his tenure of power. Given the intense factionalism within the realm and France's complex relations with other Catholic states and with Rome, he could maintain his position only by riding the waves of controversy and steering an extremely tortuous course toward his various objectives. More accurate, however, is the view that his *via media* merely reflected his profound belief that Church and state were independent and co-operating powers, each autonomous in its sphere.[58] Thoroughly conscious of the historic mission of the French Church, Richelieu believed it to be absolutely essential to the organization and functioning of the nation. He dreamed of a reformed, purified Church that would more effectively fulfill its great role, and attempted by various means to strengthen its position in France. In his writings, he sought the conversion of heretics and provided guides for the faithful; as administrator he took measures to improve the level of competence among the higher clergy and attempted extensive reform of the massive Benedictine Order. He enjoyed the intimacy of many of the most religious men of his time and supported the inspired work of St. Vincent de Paul and many others, both at home and abroad. Indeed, it may be said that Richelieu's efforts to strengthen the French Church should be viewed not only as evidence of his personal convictions and reverence for the Church of which he was a prince; it also indicates his great concern for the religious life of the realm. In this sense, his attempts to strengthen the Church were part of his program of state-building, the building of Christian France.

On the other hand, Richelieu did not hesitate to bring great pressure upon the French Church and individual clergymen when he deemed it essential to the implementation of his policies. Again, his justification was that neither autonomous institution should en-

---

[58] J. H. Mariéjol, *Henri IV et Louis XIII*, Paris, 1905, Bk. III, Chap. 9. (E. Lavisse, ed., *Histoire de France* Vol. VI².) V. Martin, "L'Adoption du gallicanisme politique par le clergé de France," *Revue des sciences religieuses*, VIII (1928), 1-23. L. Willaert, *Après le concile de Trente: La Restauration catholique, 1563-1648*, Tournai, 1960, p. 400.

croach upon the other's domain, and he consequently showed no hesitation to use force against what he believed to be clerical inter-ference in affairs of state. Especially after the Day of Dupes, he re-fused to brook the typical *dévot* opposition to his policies. The most famous instance of this was his treatment of Father Caussin who became Louis XIII's confessor in March 1637.[59] Caussin believed that in purely civil matters he had no role in counselling the king; spiritual concerns were his chief domain. But between these two categories lay innumerable mixed matters, affairs of state that were also matters of conscience, and he was determined to exhort his royal charge to follow moral dictates in this area.[60] His convictions regard-ing royal policy, as it happened, paralleled the *dévot* position and opposed Richelieu on three basic counts: the split within the royal family, the immense, unjustifiable burden of taxation upon the populace, and most importantly, the iniquity of a war against Spain in alliance with heretic powers.[61] After a dramatic interview with the king on December 8, 1638, when Father Caussin leveled all these charges against Richelieu and implored Louis XIII to abandon such policies for the good of his soul, Richelieu forced his sovereign to choose between his First Minister and his confessor. Louis made the inevitable choice, and Father Caussin was exiled first to Rennes and then to Quimper where he was kept under strict surveillance until the end of the reign. He was replaced by the aged, scholarly, pliable Jacques Sirmond who strictly abstained from discussing political matters.

On a very different level was the project that was attributed to Richelieu to set himself up as head of the French Church, in con-trol over its institutional functioning and leaving only doctrinal matters to the papacy. This ambitious plan was extensively rumored during the later years of the reign and took the form of Richelieu assuming the title, Patriarch of the Gauls, and threatening schism

[59] H. Fouqueray, *Histoire de la Compagnie de Jésus en France des origines à la suppression (1528-1762)*, Paris, 1925, Vol. v, 89-106.

[60] C. de Rochemonteix, *Nicolas Caussin, confesseur de Louis XIII, et le Cardinal de Richelieu*, Paris, 1911, Chap. 4.

[61] Cf. *Lettres*, Vol. v, 805-13.

after the manner of Henry VIII. Sufficient evidence survives to indicate that this ominous proposal was taken seriously both in France and Rome, and much discussion of it occurred in official circles.[62] It may be doubted that such a plan involving outright schism was ever precisely formulated, and in any case Richelieu never pressed it to conclusion. The consensus now seems to be that he merely sought to use the threat of schism as a weapon with which to extract concessions from the papacy.[63] In fact, by 1640 the issues at stake reached the point where they were considered in Rome by a special Congregation for French Affairs.[64] In the midst of worsening relations with Rome and ever-increasing military expenses, the Cardinal did not hesitate to conduct a "war of nerves" even against the pope. If constant, devious diplomacy was effective against secular princes, why not use it also against the Supreme Pontiff? Richelieu consequently threatened schism but went no further. In his efforts to gain concessions, especially of a monetary nature, he did not hesitate to brandish this most formidable weapon from his extensive arsenal when he thought it was necessary for the good of the state, but in the process he undoubtedly made many enemies and added further to his reputation for tyranny.

The most specific source of friction between Richelieu and the French Church was the Cardinal's repeated demands for ever-larger subsidies from the clerical estate. Even before his ministry, the traditional ten-year grant of 1,300,000 *livres* annually had frequently proved insufficient to meet royal needs, and the Assembly of the Clergy had fallen into the habit of granting extraordinary *dons gratuits* during periods of emergency. Although these grants were invariably used for the purpose of prosecuting war against the here-

[62] The best treatment of this matter is found in J. Orcibal, *Les Origines du jansénisme*, Paris, 1948, Vol. III, 108-46. Orcibal, however, relies too extensively upon the *Mémoires* of Charles de Montchal, Archbishop of Toulouse, who was extremely hostile to Richelieu. This viewpoint is reflected in Orcibal's text.

[63] Orcibal somewhat reluctantly comes to this conclusion. Cf. P. Blet, "Jesuites et libertés gallicans en 1611," *Archivum Historicum Societatis Iesu*, XXIV (1955), 169-75.

[64] P. Blet, "La Congrégation des affaires de France de 1640," *Mélanges Eugène Tisserant*, Vatican City, 1964, Vol. IV, 59-105.

tics, they were agreed to only after a great deal of hard bargaining between the Assembly and the agents of the crown. In 1628, Richelieu experienced considerable difficulty in obtaining an extraordinary subsidy of 3,000,000 *livres* toward the expenses of the siege of La Rochelle. The declaration of war against Spain brought a much heavier drain upon the royal treasury and further demands upon the clergy, although now for a different purpose. As early as 1632, Le Bret had written that all landed property of the church in France was subject to the crown and that the ruler might require subsidies from the clergy according to the dictates of necessity.[65] As for Richelieu, he consistently took the position that the clergy were a part of the realm and should assume their share of the burden when the state was in danger—a position which he was determined to make good. Immediately after the declaration of war against Spain in 1635, he brought great pressure upon the Assembly of the Clergy to grant a very large *don gratuit* for the support of the royal armies. Under the leadership of Charles de Montchal, Archbishop of Toulouse, a large faction in the Assembly strongly resisted the royal demands, but Richelieu and his spokesmen repeatedly pressed the argument that the clergy were a part of the state and as interested in the success of the war as any other body. In the present emergency, they should therefore consent to a handsome subsidy to support the war effort.[66] After months of negotiation, the Assembly agreed to a *don gratuit* of 3,792,000 *livres*. The Assembly of the Clergy of 1635-1636 is therefore notable as the first in history to grant a greatly increased extraordinary subsidy for a purpose other than war against the heretics.[67] To this extent, Richelieu succeeded in establishing the precedent that the wealth of the French Church might be used for the defense of the realm against any and all enemies regardless of religious considerations.

The climax of Richelieu's friction with the French Church over

[65] Le Bret, Bk. I, Chaps. 12, 13. Le Bret cites Roman law and French precedent in support of his position.

[66] P. Blet, *Le Clergé de France et la monarchie*, Rome, 1959, Vol. 1, 460, 463.

[67] *Ibid.*, 477.

its contributions to state expenses occurred during the last years of his ministry. As French involvement in the Thirty Years' War continued year after year and governmental deficits rose alarmingly, Richelieu determined to secure greatly increased financial support from the clerical estate, if possible, without calling together the Assembly of the Clergy. In 1639, the jurist Pierre Dupuy who had long been in Richelieu's service published a variety of statements to the effect that the crown might tax clerical wealth without the consent of its holders.[68] And in the same year, Richelieu launched a campaign to amass extensive funds from the clergy by enforcing the dormant but entirely legal *droit d'amortissement*. This ancient royal right permitted the crown to levy a handsome payment whenever the church acquired landed property which thereupon fell into mortmain. Although such collections had fallen into disuse, prescription did not hold against the royal prerogatives. Louis XIII was entirely within his rights when on April 19, 1639 he issued a declaration ordering enforcement of such payments on all lands that the church had acquired since 1520.[69] This was followed on May 21 by royal letters creating a sovereign chamber to execute the order. The commission included the jurist Le Bret, whose views we have noted and who estimated that the French Church held one-third of all landed wealth in the kingdom,[70] and d'Hémery, an aggressive, high-ranking finance officer who later became a Superintendent of Finance.[71] In enforcing their claims upon ecclesiastical property, the

[68] In his *Traitez des droits et libertez de l'église gallicane. Preuves des libertez de l'église gallicane*, 2 vols., n.p., 1639. This work was strongly condemned by high-ranking spokesmen for the clergy. G. Demante, "Histoire de la publication des livres de Pierre Dupuy sur les libertés de l'église gallicane," *Bibliothèque de l'Ecole des Chartes*, v (1843), 589. See n. 345 and text.

[69] Isambert, Vol. xvi, 503-05. J. Tournyol du Clos, *Les Amortissements de la propriété ecclésiastique sous Louis XIII*, Paris, 1912, pp. 23-25, 35-36. This work contains much information on *amortissements* and negotiations between Richelieu and the clergy, but strongly reflects Montchal's strong anti-Richelieu bias. Generally, I follow the account given in P. Blet, *Le Clergé de France et la monarchie: Étude sur les assemblées générales du clergé de 1615 à 1666*, Rome, 1959, Vol. I, Bk. II, Chap. 7.

[70] *De la souveraineté*, Bk. I, Chap. 14.

[71] Tournyol du Clos, p. 45.

commission did not hesitate to resort to seizures and other arbitrary measures which caused great criticism of Richelieu but failed to produce the expected revenue. Subsequently, the matter was considered in a series of conferences between Richelieu and several groups of ranking ecclesiastics, in which the latter seemed to agree to a levy of 6,000,000 *livres* or one-third of the revenues of all benefices for three years. These commitments were not binding, however, and Richelieu reluctantly agreed to a special session of the Assembly of the Clergy.

This most dramatic of such gatherings during the reign held its first session at Mantes on February 25, 1641. Richelieu's choice of Mantes for the Assembly undoubtedly reflected his desire to control its actions, since the city lay within the diocese of the ultra-royalist Bishop of Chartres. Richelieu also attempted to dictate the choice of delegates to the Assembly, but failed in his effort to exclude such spokesmen for the opposition as the Archbishops of Toulouse and Sens. In the opening session, the representatives of the crown, Brûlart de Léon and d'Hémery, made it clear that the royal administration not only demanded an extensive subsidy from the clergy but also claimed the right to tax them without their consent. The king had permitted the present meeting merely to enable it to arrange for the previously agreed contribution "although he might, with complete justice and because of immemorial right, after the example of the kings his predecessors, tax the goods and revenues of the clergy as far as he, in his conscience, believed and found it necessary."[72] There followed the usual months of negotiation, with the Bishop of Chartres supporting the claims of the crown and the Archbishop of Toulouse leading the opposition. Richelieu repeatedly demanded his 6,000,000 *livres* but was met by extensive and very effective resistance. On May 30 he determined to use force,[73] and on June 3 d'Hémery read before the Assembly a royal order expelling the Archbishops of Toulouse and Sens, and the Bishops of Evreux, Maillezais, Bayas, and Toulon who were required by *lettre de cachet*

[72] Instructions to Brûlart de Léon and d'Hémery, signed by Louis XIII. *Lettres*, Vol. vi, 754. Cf. Blet, *Le Clergé de France*, Vol. i, 494.
[73] *Lettres*, Vol. vi, 801-06. Cf. Blet, p. 510.

to return immediately to their dioceses. Such action, although within the king's rights, appeared even to many of Richelieu's supporters as an abuse of power. He had overcome the opposition, however, and subsequent negotiations with the Assembly proceeded smoothly. On August 14 a contract was signed requiring the clergy to pay 5,500,000 *livres*. Meanwhile, Pope Urban VIII condemned such attacks upon ecclesiastical property, but the Parlement refused to register the bull as an infringement of royal rights. In answer to the pope's action, Richelieu undoubtedly held true to his own position when he urged Chancellor Séguier to assert to the nuncio: "As all Christians are obligated to recognize the spiritual power of the pope as a matter of conscience, they are also obligated to recognize the temporal power of the king according to the same principle."[74] Again, the Cardinal's fundamental concept of two cooperating but autonomous powers enabled him to defend the sovereign rights of the crown, as he interpreted them. In this instance, they involved the disputed matter of taxing ecclesiastical wealth, and Richelieu was able to make good his claim only by a show of force. He had in effect established the principle that the church must contribute to the needs of the state when it was in danger, but his measures, although within the law, were viewed by many of his contemporaries as tyrannical abuses of power.

Like the clergy, the great nobility of France felt Richelieu's heavy hand increase in power as the reign progressed. After the execution of the Duke of Montmorency, Richelieu continued to pursue his objective of reducing the great nobles to the status of subjects of the crown, invariably insisting that loyalty to the state took precedence over all other ties in French society. In assuming this position, Richelieu had the letter of the law as well as the weight of monarchical tradition on his side, yet the high nobility continued to adhere to a way of life that implied only a conditional obedience to their sovereign. The great difficulty that they experienced in regarding themselves as mere subjects of the crown like all others has already

[74] *Lettres*, Vol. vi, 877.

been analyzed.[75] It should be added that as the concept of reason of state received further implementation and was increasingly associated with royal policy, the ideological gulf between the nobles and the monarchy widened. The means-end justifications of official policy were arguments from necessity and were essentially pragmatic, whereas the noble code was sentimental and idealistic. Instinctively the nobles regarded their code of personal honor, virtue, and heroism as higher and more laudable than manipulation of governmental processes, especially if the latter entailed dishonesty, dishonor, and mere practical advantage. They looked down on the whole ethic of reason of state because it seemed to stand on a lower moral plane than their own social ethic.[76] From this standpoint, there is little wonder that the nobles' spirit of independence remained in full force during Richelieu's last years and continued to plague him until the end.

Richelieu, on his part, continued to prize the noble ethic and even had the interests of the nobility at heart, but he was determined that they should serve the state and its purposes as loyal subjects of the crown. Extensive mechanisms were available to him for keeping the nobility in check. His favorite device, apart from outright coercion, was to accuse noble offenders of the crime of *lèse-majesté*. On the assumption that royal approval of his policies equated them with the safety, interests, and prestige of the monarchy, Richelieu brought the charge against many who resisted or criticized his policies, and even, on occasion, some who failed to implement them effectively. And when it is recalled that he habitually ordered the trial of great cases before hand-picked panels of judges, it is evident that he controlled a formidable engine for making effective his will. The result was a series of accusations against a large number of his critics and enemies.

Against one group of offenders, however, Richelieu eventually

[75] See Pt. III, n. 1-10 and text.

[76] This is ably shown in Mary C. Kahl, "Political Drama on the Eve of the Fronde," Ph.D. dissertation, Harvard University, 1969. See especially pp. 153-55.

found it expedient to press the charge of *lèse-majesté* with considerable circumspection, not because of legal considerations but because of their special relations with the royal family. These were the followers of Gaston d'Orléans who remained heir to the throne during all but the last five years of the reign. We have noted how Gaston and then the Queen Mother fled to Spanish territory in 1631 after the Day of Dupes, and how their followers were repeatedly declared guilty of *lèse-majesté* later in the year.[77] After the defeat and capture of Montmorency, Gaston returned to France, and at Béziers, on October 1, 1632, signed a capitulation in which he yielded on most of the disputed points. In this agreement, which was negotiated by Bullion, Superintendent of Finance, Gaston pledged complete submission and acquiesced in the punishment of those who had accompanied him into exile, although exceptions were made of the Duke d'Elbeuf and Gaston's domestics.[78] But on November 6, one week after the execution of Montmorency, Gaston again fled the realm and joined the Queen Mother in Brussels, this time remaining abroad for two years. On November 12, while at Montereau, he wrote to his royal brother stating that he had completely accepted the terms of the earlier agreement, even though it required him to give "the basest submission that Your Majesty might wish from the least of your subjects,"[79] only on condition that he might be influential in saving Montmorency's life. He had made this clear to Bullion and even the Duchess of Montmorency; the execution of the Duke was therefore a stain on his honor. In his answer, dated November 25, Louis XIII stated that the condemnation of Montmorency was entirely legal in view of his crimes, and that as king he was determined "to do that which nature and blood require of me, with the same care that all divine and human laws oblige me to take above all else for the good of my state, and to prevent the desolation and ruin of my poor people caused by these miserable revolts."[80] Again the direct clash of personal honor and loyalty to the state.

[77] See Pt. III, n. 87, 110, 111, and text.
[78] *Mercure français*, Vol. XVIII, 774-78.
[79] *Ibid.*, 873. The letter is on pp. 869-75.
[80] *Ibid.*, 877. The letter is on pp. 876-78.

Early in 1633, Richelieu continued to press home his charges of *lèse-majesté* against Gaston's followers. On January 14, the Parlement of Dijon declared the Duke d'Elbeuf as well as Puylaurens, Coudray, Montpensier, and Goulas guilty of *lèse-majesté*, decreed the confiscation of their property, and ordered their execution in effigy.[81] This was duly carried out. And on January 19, a royal declaration was framed for the purpose of tightening legislation against royal officials who were guilty of *lèse-majesté*, specifically President Le Coigneux who had left his office in the Parlement of Paris and repeatedly accompanied Gaston abroad. The declaration stated that Article 28 of the Ordinance of Moulins (1566), which gave those condemned by default five years in which to present themselves for clearance, did not apply to royal officials. This, it was stated, should have been clear from Article 183 of the Ordinance of Blois (1579) which forever deprived those condemned of *lèse-majesté* by default of their offices, titles, dignities, etc., but the king wished to apply this specifically to Le Coigneux whose office was thereby suppressed because he had given Gaston bad advice "so contrary to the good and the peace of our realm that there is no one who does not believe that without God's help and the good and gracious counsel of our principal ministers complete subversion of this state is to be feared."[82]

But as time advanced and it became obvious that Gaston could not be enticed back to France by such harsh measures, Richelieu

[81] *Ibid.*, Vol. xix, 47-48.

[82] *Ibid.*, 69. The declaration is on pp. 68-74. The date usually assigned to this document is April 12, 1633, when it was registered by the Parlement of Paris. But January 19 is given in the version in Bibliothèque Nationale, Fonds Français 18424, fols. 2-4. When it was submitted to the Parlement on January 31, the court resisted the declaration because it suppressed an office in that body, and a *lit de justice* was required to force its registration on April 12. Molé, *Mémoires*, Vol. ii, 168-70. It may be noted that Le Bret, in the edition of his *Œuvres* that was published in 1642, added a discussion of this declaration at the end of his chapter on *lèse-majesté* in his *Souveraineté du Roy*. In this addition, Le Bret compared French and Roman law concerning the treatment of offending officeholders, and concluded that the French was the more lenient. This addition appears in no other edition of Le Bret's *Œuvres*. The articles of the Ordinances of Moulins and Blois that were amended by the declaration of 1633 are in Isambert, Vol. xiv, 196-97, 424.

altered his tactics. This seemed particularly necessary in view of the legal and theological tangles that were created by Gaston's marriage to Marguerite, sister of the Duke of Lorraine, a union that Louis XIII and Richelieu were determined to have annulled. On January 16, 1634, Louis XIII issued a long royal declaration in which he reviewed the successes of his government, especially in foreign affairs, asserted that Gaston's absence abroad was the major remaining source of trouble, and attempted to entice him back to France by promising amnesty for his followers if he and they would return to France within three months. Le Coigneux and a few others were exempted from the amnesty.[83] Secret negotiations followed, in which Puylaurens took a major part. Finally, on October 8, Gaston and many of his followers, weary of their long exile, fled Brussels and dramatically appeared without warning at the gates of La Capelle on the frontier. On October 21, Louis and Gaston met at Saint-Germain en Laye and were reconciled in an emotion-filled scene, whereupon Puylaurens was immediately pardoned. Before the end of the month, Louis XIII issued a royal declaration forgiving all of Gaston's hostile acts although without accepting his marriage. Louis then pardoned all who had accompanied Gaston into exile regardless of their rank and quality—all, that is, except Le Coigneux who was again denied amnesty. The king restored to all others their properties, offices, honors, etc., and in the strongest terms forbade any future prosecution of them because of past offenses.[84] In this way, the great majority of the charges of *lèse-majesté* against Gaston's followers were dropped. Gaston and Richelieu were soon reconciled, at least in public, although the Cardinal sought to control the heir to the throne by marrying Puylaurens to one of his many nieces. Richelieu even went so far as to make Puylaurens a duke and peer of France, but such successes did not arrest his appetite for intrigue and on February 14, 1635, he was arrested and imprisoned at Vincennes where he died on July 1. As for Le Coigneux, he remained in disfavor until the end of the reign when his fortunes were dramatically reversed. On June 26, 1643, he was not only pardoned but

[83] *Mercure français*, Vol. xx, 25-38. Cf. the *Gazette* for 1634, pp. 23-24.
[84] *Ibid.*, Vol. xx, 877-79.

was reinstated in his office in the Parlement and took an active part in affairs during the regency.[85] Gaston, on the other hand, remained under Richelieu's strict surveillance until the latter's death. In 1636, he did not hesitate to insist that Gaston dismiss all trouble-makers in his entourage who were giving him bad advice,[86] and later in the same year, after a show of independence by Gaston, Richelieu, through a series of letters signed either by himself or the king, administered severe reprimands to the restless duke.[87] These lengthy and intricate developments adequately indicate how Richelieu adapted the charge of *lèse-majesté* to the exigencies of the moment but eventually succeeded in subjecting even the brother of the king to severe controls.

Political prudence may have forced Richelieu to treat the members of Gaston d'Orléans' clientele with especial leniency, but such was not the case with any other offenders among the nobility. On numerous occasions the Cardinal found it expedient to bring the charge of *lèse-majesté* against many high-ranking persons for a variety of reasons. Furthermore, it should be noted that in this area of activity, as in so many others, Richelieu took care to provide himself with expert advice and information. Among his large corps of professional aides were several who were thoroughly familiar with the legal intricacies of the crime of *lèse-majesté*. Most important were the archivist-jurists Pierre Dupuy and Théodore Godefroy who compiled extremely extensive manuscript collections of data concerning all major trials of persons accused of *lèse-majesté* from the depths of the Middle Ages until well into Richelieu's ministry.[88] It goes without saying that this information was readily available to the Cardinal. Likewise Chancellor Séguier, in his enormous manuscript library, possessed records of all such trials of both lay and ec-

---

[85] Molé, *Mémoires*, Vol. III, p. 84 n.1.

[86] *Lettres*, Vol. v, 712.

[87] *Ibid.*, 695-97, 711-14.

[88] E.g., Bibliothèque Nationale, Fonds Français 18428-18429, 18433, Nouveaux Acquêts 3360, and Bibliothèque de l'Arsenal 2831-2832. It is interesting to note that after 1642 Dupuy compiled a list of all persons who were arrested and executed during Richelieu's ministry. Bibliothèque Nationale, Collection Dupuy 625.

clesiastical offenders.[89] The Galland brothers also took care to make such compilations.[90] And it may be significant that the version of Le Bret's *Souveraineté du Roy* which was published in 1642 contained new emphasis upon the crime of *lèse-majesté*, doubtless reflecting the Cardinal's views.[91] Further research would uncover additional evidence concerning his efforts to use the charge of *lèse-majesté* as a major weapon for combatting offenses against the state and its interests. For our purposes, an analysis of certain great cases will suffice to indicate the manner in which he used both the charge and arbitrary imprisonment to implement his concept of reason of state.

After Louis XIII declared war against Spain, May 19, 1635, and all the attendant dangers of open warfare threatened the French state, the crisis in French affairs went far to justify such procedures and Richelieu acted accordingly. In dealing with known traitors, such as Louis Clausel, Lord of La Roche, he did not hesitate to bypass the usual judicial forms. Clausel, who began his career as an intimate of the Duke of Rohan and subsequently served as a Spanish agent, contacted the Duke in 1635 while he was in command of the French forces in the Valtelline. Through Clausel, the Spanish offered the Valtelline itself to Rohan if he would desert Louis XIII. Rohan had Clausel seized and notified Richelieu, sending incriminating documents, whereupon Richelieu immediately assumed direction of every step of the affair which he considered to be of prime importance.[92] He had Clausel condemned by default at Châlons on October 18, 1635, and even supplied the judgment against him. The document included the proposition that the crisis in French foreign

[89] E.g., Bibliothèque Nationale, Fonds Français 18425, 18431.

[90] E.g., Bibliothèque Nationale, Fonds Français 18424.

[91] At the beginning of his chapter on *lèse-majesté*, Le Bret added a statement that rebellion and other offenses against the crown had become so frequent that he wished to analyze *lèse-majesté* so as to show the enormity of the crime and the punishments that it deserved. See n. 82 for his additions at the end of this chapter. None of these additions appeared in any other edition of the work.

[92] *Lettres*, Vol. v, 304, 308.

relations justified dispensing with the customary judicial formalities.[93] After the condemnation, Lasnier who was intendant of the French army in the Valtelline interrogated Clausel according to a plan supplied by the Cardinal. Clausel was executed after torture on November 10. The procedures were extralegal but were justified, Richelieu held, by the evident danger to the state.

Very different was the case of Adrien de Montluc, Count of Cramail and Prince of Chabanais. Cramail, a military man of some ability, had been in the anti-Richelieu faction before the Day of Dupes and was imprisoned briefly thereafter. In 1635 he accompanied Louis XIII to his army in Lorraine but meanwhile criticized Richelieu's plans by insisting that the French were no match for their enemies in Lorraine and Flanders, and urging the necessity of peace. Richelieu, fearing Cramail's influence with the king, had him imprisoned in the Bastille on October 23, 1635, where he remained in protective custody until after Richelieu's death.[94] In this case, no charges were brought. The Cardinal's purpose, he wrote to Chavigny, was merely to prevent any dangerous actions by Cramail. "No harm will be done to him; he will be held there only to prevent his doing so . . . . I admit that I believe this necessary because, if in this time of adversity the acts of such men are not checked by some noteworthy punishment, they will grow marvellously, and wherever

[93] His Majesty, because of this and many other acts against his service and the good of his state which the said Clausel has done in the past in Spain, Flanders, Germany, England, Savoy, and other places, and being unable to bring him to France for judgment according to the customary forms of justice because of the hostile armies that are near the place where he is held, nor also to leave such a crime unpunished nor longer keep a person accustomed to such practices and schemings and who, from one day to another, is capable either of escaping as he already did in Geneva or otherwise extensively doing disservice to the state, His Majesty declares the said Clausel attainted and convicted of seeking to remove the said Duke of Rohan from his obedience and to turn sovereign princes from his friendship and alliance in order to league them with declared enemies of the state. (*Ibid.*, Vol. v, 322.) The plans of interrogation and judgment are given on pp. 319-22.

[94] *Ibid.*, Vol. iii, 757, n.1; Vol. v, 215, n.1, p. 252, n.1, p. 305, n.4.

this man goes, envenomed as he is, the king may well believe that he will do him wrong which he is obliged to prevent by an innocent remedial measure."[95] Richelieu then dictated a long memorandum for Louis XIII, justifying the detention of Cramail by arguing in the following vein. "If one does not check factions, crushing them at birth when their beginning is so weak that those who are unaware of their nature do not realize that they should be feared, they will grow and gain strength in an instant in such manner that it is impossible later to resist their violence."[96] After citing Cramail's faults, the advantages of the similar detention of Bassompierre, the adverse influence of rumors on diplomacy, and the fact that such prudent measures were authorized by Scripture, Richelieu appealed to Louis XIII's superior strength of character and sense of responsibility: "To govern states and guide and maintain armies with discipline, one must have a certain manly virtue which is never found in common men, and without which, nevertheless, neither states nor armies may be well governed nor preserved intact."[97] Finally: "If the prince in whose state there are men bold enough to slander his conduct, mutter against his rule, defame those whom he employs to administer his affairs, and retard his plans by such conduct does not severely punish them, he does wrong in the eyes of God, and withdrawing the means whereby those who faithfully serve him do so with effect, he risks his own destruction."[98] With such extensive argumentation did Richelieu think it necessary to justify to the scrupulous Louis XIII a measure which the Cardinal, because of his vast experience with plots and factions, believed justified by political prudence and reason of state.

One of the most interesting instances of Richelieu's use of the charge of *lèse-majesté* was that which he brought against Bernard de Nogaret, Duke of La Valette, the son of the aged and fiercely independent Duke of Epernon and heir to his father's title. La Valette was a man of considerable military experience and, although married to one of Richelieu's cousins, shared his father's hatred of

[95] *Ibid.* Vol. v, 317.
[96] *Ibid.*, 330-31.   [97] *Ibid.*, 334.   [98] *Ibid.*, 334-35.

the Cardinal. He drew Richelieu's wrath for his failure at the siege of Fontarabie during the summer of 1638. Fontarabie was a Spanish stronghold only a short distance inside the Spanish border on the Gulf of Gascony, and Richelieu, who seriously needed a victory at this point to compensate for recent reverses and had assured Louis XIII of a favorable outcome of the undertaking, counted heavily upon its success. La Valette was made Lieutenant General of the French army but was under the supreme command of the Prince of Condé, the first prince of the blood, whom La Valette also detested. With such divided counsels among their leaders, it is not surprising that the French failed to achieve their objective. During the first part of the siege, they succeeded in opening the way for an assault, but extensive foot-dragging for which La Valette was partially responsible postponed decisive action until the arrival of Spanish counterforces. In September, the latter raised the siege by attacking the French who fled in utter rout, leaving Condé's headquarters in the hands of the enemy. Richelieu was aghast. He wrote to Chavigny: "I am incensed by it; it pierces my heart and I can tell you nothing further of it."[99] And to Louis XIII: "Yesterday I was so dazed by this blow that I no longer felt the pain of my illness. Today I feel it [the blow] the more as I consider its cause and results . . . . When I become aware of Your Majesty's views, no time should be lost in doing what will be necessary to check the course of the consequences of this accident which pierces my heart."[100]

As evidence accumulated concerning La Valette's negligence, Richelieu moved rapidly to render the duke responsible for the debacle. Condé and many others thoroughly cooperated in supplying incriminating information, and the Cardinal was soon able to com-

[99] *Lettres*, Vol. VI, 181.
[100] *Ibid.*, Vol. 183. Richelieu sought to disguise the extent of the French debacle before Fontarabie by ordering Renaudot to print in the *Gazette* that the French had lost only 500 to 600 men killed and as many prisoners, with 10 cannon, and to add that the French had taken as many prisoners from the Spanish during the present year and had caused them to lose more at sea. Richelieu to Chavigny, September 22, 1638. *Lettres*, Vol. VI, 189. All this was duly printed in the *Gazette*, September 30, 1638, pp. 565-66.

pile a series of weighty accusations. To the more routine charges of incompetence, failure to obey orders, and the like, he significantly added:

> Since the passions of individuals cannot take precedence over public interests without crime, it is certain that jealousy cannot be the cause of this without deserving severe punishment, more or less rigorous according to the degree of harm that the state may incur from his desires, and this cannot be ignored without abandoning public interests and enabling all the evil men of this realm to undertake all that their malice may suggest to them to thwart its success. Thus, whatever the Duke of La Valette may say, he deserves the severe punishment that is actively sought for him by the Prince of Condé, solely because of the interests of the state.[101]

This is a remarkable recognition by Richelieu of the chronic divergence of personal and political loyalties and the consequent difficulties that he encountered in establishing the supremacy of loyalty to the state, which he accused La Valette of subordinating to his passions. The Cardinal, of course, kept Louis XIII fully informed of all developments and secured the king's complete cooperation in building a case against La Valette. In writing to the duke's brother, the Cardinal of La Valette who had forsaken the cross for the sword and held an important French command in Italy, Richelieu maintained that he merely wished justice to take its course,[102] but in fact he did everything possible to obtain a conviction. The Duke of La Valette soon realized the hopelessness of his position and prudently fled to England where he remained until after Richelieu's death.

Undaunted, the Cardinal continued to press for condemnation of the duke who, he claimed, had been negligent, sullied the royal honor, and frustrated official policy. After much incriminating evidence had been assembled, an extraordinary, enlarged session of the Council of State was held at Saint-Germain en Laye on February 4, 1639. The assembly included not only the usual members of the council but also other officials, great nobles, all the presidents of the

[101] *Lettres*, Vol. VI, 207.   [102] *Ibid.*, Vol. VI, 185-86, 214-16.

Parlement, and various others, and was presided over by the king.[103] After information was given concerning La Valette's conduct, Louis XIII asked for the presidents' opinions, whereupon the First President objected to such procedure and requested that the matter be referred to the Parlement, since La Valette was a duke and peer of the realm and should be tried by that body according to customary usage. The Chancellor heatedly answered that the king had the authority to assign the trial to any body that seemed appropriate to him, and that the precedent of trying peers before the Parlement had been departed from on many occasions.[104] At this, the justices were startled, but after various sallies and further objections it was agreed that La Valette should be prosecuted. After the session, the king recalled the First President and four others and said to them:

> You always disobey me. I am very displeased with you and despise those who say that I can try dukes and peers only in the Parlement. They are ignorant and unworthy of their offices. I do not know whether I shall assign them any others. I wish to be obeyed, and I give you to understand that all privileges are founded only on bad usage. I do no wish to hear them spoken of.[105]

On the same day the Council of State ordered the Procureur General to issue a warrant for La Valette's arrest, interrogation, and the confiscation of his property.

Finally, on May 24, a similar session of the Council of State was held for the trial of La Valette on the accumulated charges. After presentation of the evidence, most of the judges agreed to condemnation. The major exception was President Bellièvre who argued that La Valette was being tried for a military offense that was outside the jurists' competence and that there was insufficient evidence to

---

[103] Omer Talon, *Mémoires*, ed. Petitot, Paris, 1827, Vol. I, 187.

[104] *Ibid.*, p. 188. Cf. Bibliothèque de l'Arsenal, MS. 2832, fol. 209b. This manuscript contains extensive documents on the La Valette affair and is more complete than Bibliothèque Nationale, Fonds Français 18424 which includes many of the same materials.

[105] Bibliothèque de l'Arsenal, MS. 2832, fol. 213b.

justify capital punishment.[106] To this the Chancellor answered that La Valette had besmirched the honor of the king. After many other opinions had been expressed, the king himself spoke, saying that it was not a question of La Valette's cowardice but of disobedience and failure to follow orders to attack when his forces were sufficient for him to do so.[107] This persuaded the assembly, and a decree of the Council of State was issued condemning the Duke of La Valette of *lèse-majesté* for abandoning His Majesty's service at the siege of Fontarabie and leaving the realm without the king's permission.[108] The duke was ordered executed in effigy, which was done at the Place de Grève on June 8. In this fashion, Richelieu made military negligence a crime of *lèse-majesté*. La Valette's punishment may seem unduly severe, but all who were involved in the affair knew full well that many who were so condemned lived to regain royal favor. Richelieu's objective in this instance was to punish a failure to implement royal policy, to vindicate the king's honor, and to subordinate the personal hostilities of great nobles to state interests, thereby ensuring the supremacy of loyalty to the state. As for La Valette, he remained in England until 1643 when he returned to Paris, now Duke of Epernon, and was completely absolved. After an inquest into his offenses by a special commission that was appointed by the Regent, the Parlement considered the matter and quashed all earlier decisions against the duke even though they had been made by the Council of State in the presence of the king.[109] Epernon was even made Governor of Guyenne, a post long held by his father. In this manner, another of Richelieu's intended victims was exonerated and rehabilitated.

The most famous case involving the charge of *lèse-majesté* late in the reign of Louis XIII was that which led to the execution of Cinq-Mars and de Thou. In this instance there was no doubt concerning the guilt of the accused according to contemporary law, but Richelieu's handling of the case and the complex circumstances in which

[106] *Ibid., fols.* 220a-224b.
[107] *Ibid.,* fol. 226. Cf. Talon, *Mémoires,* Vol 1, 195-96.
[108] Bibliothèque de l'Arsenal, MS. 2832, fols. 228a-230b.
[109] *Ibid.,* fols. 239b-242b.

it occurred reveal much concerning both the problems that beset him even in the last year of his life and the lengths to which he would go in manipulating the judicial process. Cinq-Mars, as is well known, was a young, dashing nobleman of good family who rapidly made an extreme impression upon the aging and infirm Louis XIII.[110] Originally put forward by Richelieu who thought he could control him, Cinq-Mars soon gained such favor that he was appointed Grand Master of the Horse at the age of nineteen and soon began to exert extensive influence over the king, threatening even to displace the Cardinal. Intense rivalry between the two men quickly developed. Cinq-Mars retaliated against Richelieu's efforts to control him by plotting with the Cardinal's enemies for his removal, possibly by assassination, and in any case for the reversal of his foreign policy. Their objectives were to rid France of Richelieu's leadership and at the same time to make peace with Spain. This extensive plot included the Duke of Bouillon who held Sedan, several other nobles, and Gaston d'Orléans himself, with de Thou serving as intermediary. A proposed treaty with Spain was drawn up in the presence of Gaston and was copied in final form by Cinq-Mars. The document provided for peace between France and Spain and called for the return to Gaston of all French strong points that were in Spanish hands, together with adequate military support. No hostile action against Louis XIII was contemplated; only his foreign policy was to be reversed. The conspirators succeeded in communicating the treaty to Olivares who signed it on March 13, 1642.

Richelieu, whose spies were everywhere, soon learned of the treaty although he seems not to have secured a complete copy of it. He had sufficient evidence, however, to convince Louis XIII that a dangerous conspiracy was afoot and persuaded the reluctant monarch to order the arrest of the principals. On June 11, Cinq-Mars was imprisoned at Montpellier and de Thou at Tarascon. Bouillon was seized a few days later. Gaston, as usual, quailed before such

---

[110] The best modern works on the trial of Cinq-Mars and de Thou are P. de Vaissière, *La Conjuration de Cinq-Mars*, Paris, 1928, and J. Imbert, ed., *Quelques procès criminels des XVIIᵉ et XVIIIᵉ siècles*, Paris, 1964, Chap. 5. See also Avenel in the *Lettres*, Vol. vi, 642-48, 942-43, and many later bits of information in his footnotes.

forceful acts and divulged details of the plot, admitting complicity but placing the blame on Cinq-Mars. In fact, Gaston cooperated so thoroughly that he was later spared the pain of appearing as a witness at the trial of Cinq-Mars and de Thou. As for Richelieu, he was determined to ensure the condemnation of both men because of their offenses and as a salutary example for others, and he quickly assumed control of the affair. While gathering evidence from Gaston and elsewhere, he took care to prepare a judicially sound case, for as he wrote to Chavigny, "It is one thing to be certain of a crime and another to be able to prove it in justice."[111] He even felt it necessary to inform the major royal officials and to prepare public opinion. On July 26 he sent Chavigny to the king with a draft of an official statement to be published with royal approval.[112] Louis XIII, still somewhat reluctant but convinced of the necessity of prosecuting the principals to the plot as well as defending his foreign policy, wrote Richelieu on August 4 giving him complete support in all that he might do to obtain a conviction,[113] and on the same day Richelieu

[111] Richelieu to Chavigny, July 13, 1642. *Lettres*, Vol. vii, 24. This memorandum deals extensively with judicial procedures and arrangements.

[112] *Lettres*, Vol. vii, p. 52.

[113] The complete letter is as follows:

My Cousin. I judge that it is so important for my person, for those of my children, and for the good of my state completely to clarify the proofs of the crime of the Duke of Bouillon and of the Lord of Cinq-Mars that I have felt obliged to order M. the Chancellor to proceed to Lyon, so that if you think it appropriate he may confer with you and, with his knowledge and the experience that he has had in similar affairs, may prepare procedures that may place this one in the posture that I desire. I urge you to join with him in all that may be done in conscience and to resolve all that you believe to be for the good of my service. I rely entirely upon your judgment, and I have been much too fortunate until now in the unqualified confidence that I have had in you not to continue to give you evidence of it on this occasion. I urge you to do all that you can to hasten your recovery, for I never felt such impatience to see you.

Louis

This letter is printed in Comte de Beauchamp, ed., *Louis XIII d'après sa correspondance avec le Cardinal de Richelieu*, Paris, 1909, pp. 436-37, where it is listed as in the Archives of Chantilly and is given the date, August 3. However, the copy that is in the Bibliothèque Nationale, Fonds Français, MS. 18431, fol. 400, is in the king's hand and is dated August 4.

issued, over the king's signature, a public statement explaining and justifying his actions.[114] After reviewing the circumstances that seemed to indicate the existence of a plot, the document upheld the necessity of preventive imprisonment: "Having given us ample reason to be suspicious of him [Cinq-Mars], the interest of our state (which we have always held dearer than our life) obliged us to secure his person and those of his accomplices."[115] *After* these men were arrested, it was explained, their treasonable dealings with Spain were uncovered. The involvement of Gaston d'Orléans in the affair was made clear, and Richelieu even placed the following in the mouth of the king: "We shall keep an eye on his conduct and shall act toward him as the good of our state will require, without however abandoning our good nature of which he has always received proofs."[116] The document concluded on the note that the gravity of the matter required dissemination of this information so that all persons in authority might protect the state from subversive activity. It was duly sent to the parlements, city councils, commanders of the French armies, ambassadors abroad, and others. Surely this represented a major triumph of Richelieu and his policies even over the hesitations of the king.

Rapidly the machinery of royal justice ground onward under Richelieu's guidance. Cinq-Mars and de Thou were transferred to Lyon for interrogation and trial, while Richelieu as usual secured the appointment of a special panel of judges. The commission was headed by Chancellor Séguier who could be counted on to secure the desired verdict,[117] and was drawn chiefly from the royal council and the Parlement of Grenoble. Richelieu himself took up residence in Lyon during the proceedings and kept in close touch with them throughout. Interrogation quickly established Cinq-Mars' guilt, but de Thou's role was not made clear until he was tricked into a con-

---

[114] *Lettres*, Vol. VII, 71-75. Also in the *Gazette* for 1642, August 27, pp. 791-95, and Hay, *Recueil* (edition of 1643), pp. 971-73.

[115] *Lettres*, Vol. VII, 73.

[116] *Ibid.*, 74.

[117] "If the Chancellor's thoughts concerning crimes of *lèse-majesté* are held [by the commission] as seems reasonable, all will go well." Richelieu to Chavigny, August 5, 1642. *Lettres*, Vol. VII, 77.

fession. In his case, capital punishment for mere complicity and nonrevelation was based on an ordinance that dated from the reign of Louis XI. After his association with the plot became evident, he explained his conduct in these very pathetic and revealing terms:

> If you ask me why I did not inform the king of my knowledge of the treaty with Spain, as my duty required of me, I shall ask you to consider the reason that caused me to keep silent. It would have been necessary to make me an informer of a political crime against Monsieur, the king's only brother, and against M. de Bouillon and M. le Grand [Cinq-Mars] who were all more powerful and superior in standing to me. I would certainly have failed in this accusation, not being in a position to verify it with any proof. I would therefore have appeared as a slanderer, and my honor which will always be dearer to me than my own life would have been irretrievably lost.[118]

Again, we see a conflict between personal loyalties and obligation to the state. In reaching a verdict, all judges approved the death penalty for Cinq-Mars, but two declared for a lesser punishment for de Thou, whereupon Richelieu immediately asked Séguier for their names.[119] On September 12, Cinq-Mars and de Thou were condemned for the crime of *lèse-majesté*, the one for treasonable activity and the other for participation in the same.[120] Execution quickly followed. As for the Duke of Bouillon, he was spared on condition that he surrender Sedan to the French crown.[121]

Throughout the proceedings, Richelieu clearly manipulated the processes of justice. He secured the arrest of the principals, chose the panel of judges, closely checked the interrogations, asked for the names of the judges who wished to spare de Thou, and undoubtedly destroyed many relevant documents after the records of the trial were transferred to his personal archives. That his personal resentments played a large part in determining the course of events is obvious. All his actions he nevertheless believed entirely justified

---

[118] Imbert, p. 95, quoting Griffet.   [119] *Lettres*, Vol. VII, 125.
[120] Isambert, *Recueil*, Vol. XVI, 546-47.
[121] *Mercure français*, Vol. XXIV, 567.

as long as he retained full support of the king and was working for the good of the state. The royal monopoly of judicial authority was the king's to share with whomever he chose, and Richelieu knew that his many interventions before and during the trial were but applications of the royal prerogative. If he seemed to violate traditional legal procedures, he believed this to be necessitated by the unique nature and responsibilities of the state. Not only was the charge of *lèse-majesté* fully justified; it was also legitimate to obtain convictions for this offense by quasi-arbitrary means. In this instance, however, Louis XIII's sentiments rebelled against giving Richelieu full support—doubtless more for personal than legal reasons—and the Cardinal constantly felt uneasy in spite of the king's repeated assurances. Even after the execution of Cinq-Mars and de Thou, Richelieu found it advisable to justify his actions to his sovereign. For this purpose he composed a series of memoranda in which he mustered all his best arguments and, in effect, threatened to resign if Louis did not approve his actions.[122] Regarding the widespread impression that he did not follow the accepted canons of justice, he said:

> In such affairs of great importance, legitimate suspicion should almost take the place of proofs, or approximate them, principally when it is merely a question of innocent remedies, such as exile from the court. Even more so, that which concerns the reputation of the state should be held to be true even when it is not precisely known, because the governing and security of great states very often requires precautions that dispense with the forms that are observed in the course of ordinary justice.[123]

Again the assertion that public necessity justified otherwise illegal measures appears, to which he added: "Great states need from time to time rigorous, not to say violent, examples to confine everyone by fear to his duty."[124] And in defending these policies which were predicated upon a special morality in governmental concerns, he fell back upon his supreme argument: "I believe, before God, that all

[122] *Lettres*, Vol. VII, 163-70, 173-78.   [123] *Ibid.*, 167.
[124] *Ibid.*, 167.

that I have proposed to him [Louis XIII] is entirely necessary to preserve the prosperity of this state."[125] That Richelieu was entirely sincere in viewing governmental policy in this light seems unquestionable, as was Louis XIII's full agreement with the Cardinal's actions, at least in principle. Inevitably, Louis XIII once more yielded to Richelieu's insistence upon full support for his policies which both men held to be necessary for the preservation of the French state.

Richelieu's attitude toward political offenses by members of the clergy, the nobility, and the professional classes was partially tempered by his respect for their superior positions in the social hierarchy, but the same cannot be said of his view of the lower elements of the population. The great mass of peasants and artisans at the base of the social pyramid he simply lumped together as the *peuple*, and like all persons of quality in his age, he despised them as base and servile. Fully aware of the fact that the entire nation lived on their labors, Richelieu consistently echoed the predominant view that the "people" should be content to remain in their divinely appointed stations and willingly contribute their services, goods, and even their lives to the support of the whole. From this position it followed that the lower classes were by nature and tradition obligated to make all sacrifices that their governing superiors might require of them for the preservation of the state. This included increased exactions according to need, as determined by their rulers who alone understood the mysteries of state. Resistance in this context was both treasonable and contrary to the natural order of things. The crown was therefore thoroughly justified in utilizing its monopoly of judicial and coercive power to suppress any rebellion or threat of the same within the lower strata of society.

Taxation was by far the most important burden that the royal government imposed upon the unprivileged majority, and in almost every instance the popular uprisings of the period were sparked

[125] Richelieu to Chavigny, November 5 or 6, 1642, in which Richelieu gave Chavigny arguments to use in defending the Cardinal's actions before the king. *Lettres*, Vol. VII, 171.

by real or imagined increases in the levies that were demanded by royal agents.[126] Richelieu, on his part, fully recognized the great inequities in the prevailing system of tax collecting and the difficulty of remedying its endemic abuses,[127] but the great expenses of state-craft, especially after the declaration of war, caused him merely to urge his aides to make the best of a bad situation. On September 2, 1639, he wrote to Bouillon: "I have no doubt whatsoever that you are thoroughly correct in the things that you do to find money, since necessity compels more than you might wish .... However ... it is impossible in these times to do only things agreeable to the people. One should merely take great care to do only those that displease the least."[128]

As the cost of continual warfare mounted, the burden of taxation was correspondingly increased and the period witnessed repeated uprisings in the cities and the countryside. Not a year of Richelieu's ministry passed without major trouble in some corner of the realm, although in all fairness to the Cardinal it should be noted that such revolts were endemic both before and after his tenure of power. During the period after 1635, the intensity of the revolts was more than matched by the determination of the royal government to suppress them. Usually the task was assigned to such local authorities as the governors and their subordinates, but if they were unable to control the situation the Cardinal reluctantly sent in the troops needed to suppress the revolt. Such was done in June 1636 in the face of a strong insurrection in Angoumois, and it is to be noted that Louis XIII thoroughly approved of the procedure.[129] Similar measures were used in the following year when the Duke of La Valette was recalled

[126] For all their differences, the two most outstanding authorities on popular uprisings in the seventeenth century—Boris Porchnev and Roland Mousnier—agree concerning the primary role of royal taxation in causing rebellion. B. Porchnev, *Les Soulèvements populaires en France de 1623 à 1648* (French trans.), Paris, 1963. R. Mousnier, "Recherches sur les soulèvements populaires en France avant la Fronde," *Revue d'histoire moderne et contemporaine*, v (1958), 81-113, and *Fureurs paysannes*, Paris, 1967.

[127] R. Mousnier, ed., *Lettres et mémoires adressés au chancelier Séguier (1633-1649)*, Paris, 1964, Vol. 1, 235-46 (text and notes), 273-74, 294.

[128] *Lettres*, Vol. vi, 515.   [129] *Ibid.*, Vol. v, 485-90.

from the Spanish front with a large contingent of royal forces and was sent against a powerful uprising of *croquants* in Périgord. On June 13, 1637, Richelieu wrote to Louis XIII that this *canaille*, numbering 5,000 to 6,000 men, would soon be reduced *à la raison*.[130] La Valette easily crushed the insurgents, whereupon the Cardinal wrote to him in the following revealing terms:

> The condition to which you have reduced the *croquants* is so advantageous to the service of the king and so glorious for you, that although I have already indicated to you the joy that I feel because of such a fortunate success, I nevertheless cannot let the Marquis de Duras return to the place where you are without again showing it to you by these lines. He will especially tell you of His Majesty's satisfaction with your conduct on this occasion [and] how grateful he is to you for the manner in which you have acted . . . . I hope that you will be as fortunate against the Spanish as you have been against these miserable rebels.[131]

By far the most serious and dramatic popular uprising during Cardinal Richelieu's war years was the rebellion of the *nu-pieds* in Normandy in 1639. The story of the revolt has often been told and need not be repeated here,[132] save as it illustrates this phase of Richelieu's reason of state. Traditionally one of the most heavily taxed of all the provinces, Normandy was repeatedly subjected to new levies by Richelieu as the war dragged on. Resistance reached the boiling point in the summer of 1639, when the local authorities rapidly lost control in the face of a massive, coordinated rebellion which spread to most of the province and was especially extensive in the city of Rouen. Because of continuing French operations

---

[130] *Ibid.*, 786.

[131] *Ibid.*, 792-93. Letter dated June 22, 1637. Cf. Porchnev, p. 83.

[132] This revolt has been extensively studied. A. Floquet, *Histoire du Parlement de Normandie*, Rouen, 1840-1842, Vols., IV, V, and Floquet's edition of the *Diare ou journal du chancelier Séguier en Normandie après la sédition des nu-pieds (1639-1640)*, Rouen, 1842. See also Porchnev, Pt. II, and Mousnier, *Fureurs paysannes*, Pt. I, Chap. 5. The most extensive recent examination of the revolt is M. Foisil, *La Révolte des nu-pieds et les révoltes normandes de 1639*, Paris, 1970.

against her enemies abroad, Richelieu was momentarily unable to intervene. On August 28 he wrote to Superintendent Bouthillier: "I am aware of the disorders in Rouen, but I do not know the remedy, it being impossible to find the soldiers that are needed, unless we sacrifice all the affairs of the king and abandon France to the foreigners."[133] But as the revolt grew in strength and intensity, the Cardinal's hand was forced. Sensing that the Parlement of Rouen and the Norman nobility had not done all possible to stem the rebellion and might even have encouraged it in various ways, Richelieu determined to treat the uprising as "a matter of state of the greatest importance and to cause it [i.e., its suppression] to serve as an example."[134] He quickly dispatched Colonel Gassion, an expert professional soldier, with 4,000 men and 1,200 horse to Normandy. After occupying Caen, Gassion fought a crucial and extremely bloody battle near Avranches, destroying the main force of the *nu-pieds*, after which he occupied Rouen and gradually reestablished royal control over the province. Richelieu wrote Gassion: "You could give the king no greater satisfaction than you have done in the subjugation of the rebels in Normandy,"[135] and promised him a promotion.

For the royal administration, punishment of the province and prevention of future trouble were as important as its momentary subjection. For this purpose, Richelieu chose Chancellor Séguier and a large commission that was chiefly composed of members of the royal council. Séguier was given extremely extensive powers— so extensive, in fact, that he literally became a temporary viceroy for the region.[136] Supreme administrative, military, and judicial authority were bestowed upon him personally. All local officials were subjected to his commands; he might give final judgment against offenders by mere verbal order without a hearing or other legal formality. Even Colonel Gassion reported to him daily for orders. Unique in the history of the French Chancellorship, such undiffer-

---

[133] *Lettres,* Vol. VI, 500.

[134] From *Reg. de l'hôtel de ville de Rouen,* November 15, 1639. Floquet, *Histoire,* Vol. IV, 644.

[135] Letter dated Dec. 26, 1639. *Lettres,* Vol. VIII, 360.

[136] Floquet, *Histoire,* Vol. IV, 662-64; *Diare,* p. 2.

entiated powers truly reflected the royal authority itself, and Séguier's vast if temporary prerogatives clearly indicate Richelieu's determination to make an example of Normandy after her defiance of royal control. After rejecting the pleas of François de Harlay, Archbishop of Rouen, for clemency, Séguier entered the city with his extensive following and immediately began to punish all parties that he held responsible for the uprising. His first act was to suspend all local administrative, military, and judicial officials, including the Parlement of Rouen which was given four days in which to leave the city. Full publicity of these measures was assured when the decrees against the authorities in Rouen were published in the *Gazette*.[137] At one point, Séguier even suggested destroying Rouen's *hôtel de ville* but was overruled by Richelieu who, however, approved all his other acts.[138]

In the absence of the suspended Parlement of Rouen, the jurists and councillors who had followed Séguier to the city were designated the sovereign court of the area. This commission proceeded to judge innumerable of the accused, but Séguier, not to be outdone, personally decreed the punishment of many major offenders without the formality of a trial. And when the commission's judgments seemed overly lenient to the Chancellor, he did not hesitate to order further executions on the basis of personal decision.[139] Punishments, including banishment, numbered in the hundreds. The possessions of Rouen were incorporated into the royal domain, and the impoverished city, already exhausted by rebellion, occupation by Gassion's troops, and a massive indemnification of local financiers, was subjected to an incredible fine of 1,085,000 *livres* which was collected by a variety of new taxes.[140] To bring an end to the reprisals and the occupation of their city, large numbers of leading citizens signed a declaration in which they assumed personal responsibility for its continued loyalty and submission, at the peril of their lives. Having

[137] *Gazette* for 1640, pp. 17-44.
[138] Floquet, *Histoire*, Vol. v, 5-6. Foisil, p. 299.
[139] Floquet, Vol. v, p. 23. Cf. *Diare*, p. 226. Foisil, pp. 300-11.
[140] Floquet, *Histoire*, Vol. v, pp. 30-34. Foisil, p. 314.

reduced Rouen to impotence, Séguier then traveled throughout Normandy and imposed similar measures in such places as Caen, Bayeux, and Coutances. Only in 1641 did Rouen regain its Parlement, now divided into two separate chambers which sat alternately in six-month sessions, thereby requiring the creation and sale of many new offices which further enriched the royal treasury.

Thus ended the most formidable popular uprising against the crown during the reign of Louis XIII. Throughout the entire affair, there is no doubt that Richelieu and Louis XIII thoroughly approved of ultra-rigorous measures against the rebels. Séguier regularly reported his actions to the Cardinal,[141] and the latter eagerly seconded the Chancellor's procedures. Early in January 1640, Richelieu wrote to Séguier: "I repeat to you that I see nothing to do in Rouen and Normandy but what you have planned. In carrying this out, I urge you always to remember that we cannot make too great an example in this instance."[142] On January 14, Séguier sent Louis XIII a memorandum in which he asked for royal approval of his handling of Rouen's revenues and privileges, his arbitrary execution of rebels, and his arming certain citizens who had assumed responsibility for the city's continued loyalty. In each instance, Louis XIII entirely approved the Chancellor's actions.[143] And after he had completed his mission, the king rewarded him with vast confiscated properties in Normandy, but Séguier magnanimously declined the offer.[144] It is evident that Louis XIII, Richelieu, and their chief aides were entirely in agreement concerning the necessity and justice of all measures that might be needed to keep the lower classes under control. The supremacy of the state must be preserved at all costs and justified any measures, judicial or coercive, that were necessary to maintain order and obedience. But in a broader sense, Richelieu's harsh treatment of the "people" was merely an extension of his policies and his ideology which both required and justified the subjection of all classes as far as necessary to the good of the state.

[141] Bibliothèque Nationale, Fonds Français 18432, fols. 9-10, 15-16, 28.
[142] *Diare*, p. 215n.1. Cf. *Lettres*, Vol. VII, 253.
[143] *Diare*, pp. 386-91.   [144] *Ibid.*, pp. 448-49.

RICHELIEU AND PUBLIC OPINION

Although Cardinal Richelieu enjoyed relatively greater security as First Minister after the Day of Dupes, he continued and even expanded his efforts to influence public opinion in favor of his policies. He knew that his augmentation of absolutism at home and his anti-Hapsburg policy abroad were anything but noncontroversial for large numbers of Frenchmen, and he consequently sought to publicize a variety of justifications of his extensive program of statebuilding. Especially vulnerable to criticism was his foreign policy, as he was well aware. Richelieu was one of the first statesmen in the history of France to mount a massive publishing campaign in his favor, yet the requisite means and governmental authority were available to him and, in a sense, merely awaited his masterful mind to utilize them for this purpose. In an age which, for all its intellectual diversity, was fundamentally ideological, it was both habitual and legal for the royal government to exercise control over the various organs and bodies that might influence opinion, particularly in the political sphere. During his final period of power, Richelieu both extended and formalized his control over such agencies, and correspondingly benefited from their support. As we have noted, he gradually came to rely less upon the polemics of pamphleteers and more upon the formal treatises of jurists, historians, and men of letters generally. His pamphleteers remained active until the end of his life, however, and continued to meet the major *ad hoc* criticisms of his policies, as will be shown in due course, but he knew that learned opinion might be more effectively influenced by the works of recognized authorities. For this reason, he sought to gain the public support of as many outstanding professional writers as possible.

Richelieu also made extensive use of the two established instruments for disseminating information concerning current affairs, the *Mercure français* and the *Gazette*, and succeeded in making them mouthpieces for the official view of political developments. The *Mercure* continued under the direction of Father Joseph until his death in 1638 when it was taken over by Théophraste Renaudot who had adequately demonstrated his loyalty as director of the *Gazette*. Founded in 1631, the *Gazette* was not the first "newspaper" in the capital, but Renaudot, with a powerful assist from Richelieu, rapidly crushed his competitors and gained a monopoly over the dissemination of news.[145] Understandably, Richelieu and even Louis XIII made certain that the *Gazette* presented the interpretation of events that was most favorable to royal policy and interests. Richelieu not only assigned certain writers to aid in the redaction of key issues; he personally collaborated in the writing process and frequently submitted entire articles, insisting that they be published without change.[146] At his orders, the issue of June 4, 1633, was extensively revised after it had been partially distributed.[147] And Louis XIII occasionally reserved to himself the writing of articles, especially those that reflected upon the conduct of members of the royal family.[148] In this way, King and Cardinal kept a tight rein upon the dissemination of information concerning all matters of policy.

Richelieu's efforts to control Renaudot's *Gazette* reflect his concern for public opinion, as far as it existed in his time, but his most important maneuver to win and institutionalize the support of thinkers

[145] F. Dahl, "Découverte d'un journal parisien antérieur à la Gazette de Renaudot," in Dahl, *Les Débuts de la presse française: nouveaux aperçus*, Paris, 1951, pp. 17-38.

[146] E. Hatin, *Histoire politique et littéraire de la presse en France*, Paris, 1859, Vol. I, 105-06. Hatin, *Bibliographie historique et critique de la presse périodique française*, Paris, 1866, p. 7. Instances of Richelieu dictating the contents of the *Gazette* are found in the *Lettres*, Vol. v, 51, 945; Vol. vi, 134, 176, 189; Vol. vii, 92; Vol. viii, 81, 105, 147, 156. Richelieu's relations with the *Gazette* are examined in a forthcoming work by Howard M. Solomon, *Public Welfare, Science, and Propaganda in Seventeenth Century France: The Innocent Inventions of Théophraste Renaudot*.

[147] Hatin, *Histoire*, Vol. I, 176-77, 463-65.

[148] Louis XIII wrote the account of the negotiations between Richelieu and the Duke of Lorraine which led to the Treaty of Charmes because of Gaston d'Orléans' relations with the Duke. (*Gazette* for 1633, pp. 400-04.) Louis also wrote the account of Gaston d'Orléans' return to France in 1634. (*Gazette* for 1634, pp. 442-44, 458-60.) Both were slightly modified before publication in the *Gazette*, probably at Richelieu's request. *Lettres*, Vol. iv, 485, 623-24. Cf. L. Delavaud, "Quelques collaborateurs de Richelieu," in *Rapports et notices sur l'édition des Mémoires du Cardinal de Richelieu*, Paris, 1907-1914, Vol. ii, 130.

who counted was his founding of the French Academy. The story of his transforming an informal gathering of men of letters into an official organ of the state is well known and clearly reflects his ability to seize upon all available instrumentalities so as to further his personal interests and to benefit France simultaneously. Richelieu's major objective in this instance was undoubtedly the perfection of the French language and the production of good literature, but he expected to reap political rewards as well. After the founding of the Academy in 1635, he held tight control over its membership and expected both obedience and service from that body. He did not hesitate to request individual members to review his speeches and theological works, and he even went so far as to order the production of poems and plays, some of which embodied frank justifications of his policies.[149]

In the political sphere, there is no doubt that Richelieu hoped that the Academy would afford him extensive ideological support, both through the publications of its members and the association of a prestigious institution with all that he represented. Indeed, the political complexion of the Academy's membership clearly indicates his intentions. The more important political writers among the new Academicians included none other than our old friends Paul Hay du Chastelet, Jean Sirmond, Jean de Silhon, and Guez de Balzac. All expressed opinions favorable to Richelieu in official sessions of the institution. Hay du Chastelet was one of the most active early members, taking a major part in framing the Academy's statutes and organizing many of its activities. He succeeded in obtaining the group's approval of his massive *Recueil de diverses pièces pour servir à l'histoire*, an officially sponsored answer to many criticisms of Richelieu's policies.[150] Jean de Silhon, whose lengthy *De l'immortalité de l'ame* (1634) had greatly pleased Richelieu,[151] joined

[149] Delavaud, pp. 71-79. Adam, *Histoire*, Vol. 1, 225-26. E. W. Najam, "*Europe*: Richelieu's Blueprint for Unity and Peace," *Studies in Philology*, LIII (1956), 25-34.

[150] Pellisson and d'Olivet, *Histoire de l'Académie française*, Paris, 1858, Vol. 1, 48.

[151] *De l'immortalité de l'ame*, Paris, 1634. This very lengthy work expands the themes of his earlier *Deux Veritez* (see Pt. II, n. 163 and text), combat-

Jean Sirmond in reading political discourses in support of the Cardinal's foreign policy before the assembled members.[152] The most reluctant was Guez de Balzac who, after initial raillery at the very idea of an Academy, accepted membership. He appeared before the body only once, in 1636, to read part of his *Aristippe* which he had

---

ting rationalism and skepticism and offering logical proofs of traditional Christianity. The book is dedicated to Richelieu, and in the dedicatory epistle Silhon presents Richelieu as a model Christian statesman: "Never did a man better join God's law which he observed so faithfully with that of the state over which he was so great a master." (Dedicatory Epistle, n.p.) On the French alliances with Protestant powers:

> The King's piety is so well known and his zeal for holy things has carried his renown and odor of sanctity so far that one cannot doubt that he does not truly feel all that adversely affects religion and that it cannot receive a wound that he does not feel, nor suffer in any way that does not affect him. He has encompassed its interests with a comprehensive protection; his concern for it extends wherever his name is honored and his power revered. The main point of his alliance with the Swedes and the necessary tie of this relationship are the liberty of conscience that Catholics should have in all places where the Swedes will conquer. He has opened his arms equally to all the Catholics of Germany; he has given them all security not only for their religion but also for their wealth and their states, and in this way has sought only their own tranquility and has merely required of them that they remain neutral in a war that is only a war of state and allow the interested parties to settle the quarrel. (*Ibid.*)

On the sacrifices that Richelieu's policies required of the people:

> The sick dislike the beverages that should cure them and the hand that should give them salutary pain. They should appreciate that one does not for this reason blame the physicians who order these remedies and make these cures. It is the destiny of things here below and the common law of nature that one does not obtain good with good; one does not gain without loss; and nothing is created without being preceded by corruption. You [Richelieu] are unable to change this order; you cannot give another destiny to things. And if as a man, a Christian, and a Prince of the Church you regret the people's suffering which you attempt to limit and over which you sometimes shed tears that you cannot contain, you are obligated as principal Minister of State, called by God and chosen by the King, to a function so necessary to France and so beneficial to Christendom to work for the public good even though it is costly to individuals, when it cannot be otherwise, and to imitate the sun which does not cease to send its hot, fiery rays in summer to ripen the harvest even though some traveler may be inconvenienced and some other creature may be impaired by it. (*Ibid.*)

[152] Pellisson and d'Olivet, Vol. 1, 116-17.

originally undertaken for the Cardinal.[153] Two author-members who were only secondarily interested in politics, Nicolas Faret and François de Colomby, had earlier expressed opinions of which the Cardinal thoroughly approved.[154] Later additions to the Academy also indicate that Richelieu kept a tight rein on its composition. Louis Giry, who received his chair in 1636, subsequently aided in the defense of Richelieu's ecclesiastical policies.[155] And in 1639, François de La Mothe le Vayer and Daniel Priézac were added to the roster of "Immortals." Both men wrote important works in support of Richelieu before and after their election to the Academy, and Priézac lived to publish one of the most important justifications of all that the Cardinal stood for.[156] Such evidence makes clear that Richelieu assigned the Academy a very important role in his campaign to influence public opinion in his favor. The extent to which his new Academicians defended him against the attacks of his critics will be indicated in subsequent pages.

The first debate concerning the Academy's services to Richelieu occurred immediately in 1635 between Paul Hay du Chastelet and Mathieu de Morgues. The latter thereby became the earliest critic of the new institution in its political role. The occasion was the appearance of Hay du Chastelet's massive *Recueil de diverses pièces pour servir à l'histoire* which assembled within a single volume dozens of documents and earlier pro-Richelieu tracts, many of which we have previously considered.[157] In the history of the polemics of the period, the publication of Hay's *Recueil* was a major landmark, since it was an officially sponsored exposition of the Cardinal's position on many key issues and sought to refute the widespread criticism of his policies through sheer weight of argumentation. Richelieu also undoubtedly had in mind the preservation of extensive

---

[153] *Ibid.*, Vol. I, 115-17, 149, 390-92. Guez de Balzac wrote a long letter to Hay du Chastelet praising his preface to his *Recueil*. R. Kerviler, *La Bretagne à l'Académie française au XVIIe siècle*, Paris, 1879, p. 56.

[154] For Faret, see Pt. II, n. 155, 156, and text. For Colomby, see the same notes and Pt. III, n. 175.

[155] See n. 352. [156] See n. 479-501 and text.

[157] See Pt. II, n. 65, 123, 151; Pt. III, n. 87-89, 92, 98, 105-07, 110, 111, 113-15, 122, 123, 142, 158, 160, 161, 177; Pt. IV, n. 3, 4, 114.

justifications of his policies for the benefit of future generations of readers. His sponsorship of the *Recueil* and his approval of the positions taken in it are clear. He assumed all the expenses of publication,[158] and Hay secured official approval of the work by the newly founded French Academy, as has been noted. In addition, there is major evidence of official inspiration in Hay's own contribution to the volume, a long introductory *Au Lecteur*[159] of more than one hundred pages which stated its purpose and summarized the major arguments of its contents. We may be certain that Richelieu read and approved this portion of the *Recueil*.

In his preface, Hay du Chastelet at once upheld the key association, even the near-identity, of King and Cardinal in matters of policy: "Cardinal Richelieu's virtue is so blended with the good fortune and admirable success of the King's affairs that the hand, the instrument, and the product of an artisan have less interrelationship than is evident between the fine actions of such a noble master and the skill of such a faithful servant."[160] After singing Richelieu's praises in extremely extravagant language,[161] Hay then turned upon the Cardinal's critics and singled out Mathieu de Morgues for special condemnation. Asserting that Morgues had sold his pen to the Spanish,[162] he quoted several of Morgues' major criticisms of

[158] Deloche, *Autour de la plume* . . . , p. 492.

[159] Published separately under the title, *Discours d'Estat sur les escrits de ce temps auquel est faict response à plusieurs libelles diffamatoires publiez à Bruxelle par les ennemis de la France*, n.p., 1635. My references are to the version in the *Recueil*.

[160] *Au Lecteur*, p. 4.

[161] We are well aware of his constancy in the face of machinations both against the state and himself; we are well aware that he stands firm as a rock which great storms wash over but do not disturb . . . . We also constantly recognize that he anticipates our difficulties, and that by using public power against them with such skill and courage he is like the hand behind a buckler which receives and deflects the most dangerous blows that come from our enemies. But we are also aware that if the defense of religion and our allies takes us beyond our borders, if our arms, the final arbitors of strife between princes, protect us from the bad faith of our neighbors, all our undertakings gain renown by their glorious and humane effects. (*Ibid.*, p. 7.)

[162] *Ibid.*, p. 10.

French policy. The French alliance with the Turks allowed Frenchmen to abandon their religion. France "no longer has any religion but that of the state, founded on the maxims of Machiavelli."[163] The French are fickle, disloyal, rash, and untrue to themselves. And they have abandoned God, that is, justice in all things. In answer, Hay vehemently denounced the emotionalism and untruth of such statements and then brought forth his supreme defense. It was not Richelieu who was the true target of Morgues' criticisms but Louis XIII and the *patrie*:

> It is France against which his mouth, reeking with injustice and rebellion, seems to cry so loudly at the same time that he accuses her of having neither stability, judgment, faith nor religion . . . .
> If one must regard one's *patrie*, however ungrateful she may be, with love and reverence; if her glory should be the principal foundation of the happiness of the lives of the virtuous; and if one cannot be loyal to a person who is not loyal to his country, what trust merits, or rather, of what condemnation is this wretched and perfidious slanderer not deserving?[164]

Continuing, Hay inveighed against Morgues' tracts as extremely dangerous to the peace and harmony of the realm, and incidentally paid tribute to his ability as a pamphleteer by asserting that no earlier century had produced such an expert in the art of calumny.[165] The remainder of this lengthy diatribe traces Richelieu's noble lineage, examines the major criticisms of Richelieu (particularly those of Morgues and Chanteloube), and summarizes the arguments of the various tracts in the volume. Hay concluded on the note that Richelieu had found France weak, dishonored, and despised, and had given her order and stability and raised her to new heights among nations by his divinely inspired leadership:

> He readily acknowledges, however, that his wisdom, his conduct, and his success come only from heaven; he attributes all their honor to this principle and recognizes that his mind has been merely an organ obeying the independent directives of

---

[163] *Ibid.*, p. 11.   [164] *Ibid.*, p. 13.   [165] *Ibid.*, pp. 16-17.

Him who governs and sustains all. It is also from God, as from an inexhaustible source of light and justice, that we expect to see produced further truths that will confound slander and lies, and will teach all to respect in the person of the Cardinal the choice that his [God's] providence has made for our recovery. How great a joy it would be to me if this work might be considered a ray of his glory! How happy my hand would be if it were worthy of unveiling the great statue that we owe him! But whatever destiny comes to this long defense that I have made of his name, it cannot be tiresome to upright persons. One will always speak too little of the merits of this great minister, and the calumny of those who believe they have destroyed him will never be sufficiently condemned. The multitude of so many different things rather than the argument of each has expanded this work which would be limitless if I had undertaken to describe all the virtues of the Cardinal and all the vices of his enemies.[166]

Morgues understandably could not let this blast go unanswered, and he quickly published his *Iugement sur la préface et diverses pièces que le Cardinal de Richelieu prétend de faire servir à l'histoire de son crédit*.[167] Initially resorting to ridicule, he wrote: "I confess that I have never seen so many follies *in folio*, and I believe that the Cardinal's writers . . . thought that by throwing this heavy mass at our heads they would stagger us."[168] Repeatedly he denied that he had sold his pen to the Spanish and insisted that he remained entirely loyal to Louis XIII although in exile.[169] After reiterating his usual charges against Richelieu, Morgues argued that to criticize the Cardinal was to defend the King against encroachment upon his power, and it was Hay who was guilty of *lèse-majesté*.[170] Such statements were nothing new to Morgues, but he now added to his barbs a denunciation of the political role of the newly founded French Academy. This body he confused with the

---

[166] *Ibid.*, pp. 111-12.
[167] N.p., 1635. In *Diverses pièces*, Vol. ii, 93-182. My references are to this version.
[168] *Iugement*, p. 94.   [169] *Ibid.*, pp. 150-57.   [170] *Ibid.*, pp. 103-05.

contributors to Renaudot's *Gazette*, an error that may easily be explained by Morgues' absence in exile:

> In truth, I have never seen a man more unfortunate in his eulogies than His Eminence who has never been esteemed by an upright man nor praised by an able and learned writer. He has recognized his poverty, and in order to overcome it he has established a school or rather an aviary of Sappho, the Academy which is in the house of the Gazetteer, that is, the father of lies. There assemble a great many poor zealots who learn to compose frauds and to disguise ugly acts and make ointments to soothe the wounds of the public and the Cardinal. He promises some advancement and gives small favors to this rabble who combat truth for bread.[171]

If Morgues confused the contributors to the *Gazette* with the members of the Academy, it was partially because both groups consistently wrote for the purpose of defending Richelieu's policies. No matter. The burden of his charge was that those who published in support of the Cardinal constantly distorted the truth in order to gain his favor. Referring to Hay, Morgues continued: "The chief of this infamous band is a man who is the more wicked as he rebels against wisdom. He neither sins nor is blinded by ignorance nor handicapped by poverty, but is pushed by ambition and tyrannized by fear."[172] Or again: "It is apparent that the lord Hay has worked more to appease the Cardinal and to gain repute among the ignorant than to satisfy his conscience and gain esteem among the wise."[173] Morgues, of course, claimed that he would lift the veil of falsehood which distorted all such writings as those in Hay's *Recueil*, and in later years he continued to charge that the members of the *"Académie Gazetique"* poured forth all manner of compositions merely to flatter the Cardinal.[174] Whether Morgues or the Academicians were

---

[171] *Ibid.*, p. 95. Pellisson and d'Olivet, Vol. 1, 400-04, shows that Renaudot did in fact conduct small discussion groups at the headquarters of the *Gazette* and that there are good reasons why Morgues confused the two groups of writers.

[172] *Iugement*, pp. 95-96. [173] *Ibid.*, p. 97.

[174] The opening paragraph of Morgues' tract, *L'Ambassadeur chimerique*

nearer the truth only the historian can judge, and any decision must at best be relative. Neither party was venal. Morgues had no more sold his pen to the Spanish than the Academicians were the mindless, fawning tools of Richelieu, and both undoubtedly were essentially honest in their public statements of their views. For our purposes, their writings are valuable chiefly as extensive if fragmentary expositions of their respective positions in a debate which had ramifications that even its major participants did not realize. But in examining the course of the controversy, it must be remembered that Richelieu's great power, enormous wealth, control over official bodies and the press, and access to all manner of rewards and favors gave him a very substantial advantage over his critics.

FRENCH INTERESTS AND TERRITORIAL CLAIMS

It was inevitable that Richelieu's foreign policy should be the subject of the most extensive political controversy during his later years as First Minister. After Louis XIII placed his stamp of approval upon the Cardinal's anti-Hapsburg policy at the Day of Dupes, and especially after the French declaration of war against Spain in 1635, military and diplomatic considerations necessarily overshadowed all other elements of his program of state-building. With the commitment of the nation to war, the issues were clearly drawn and forced many thinking men to make choices that they had heretofore avoided. The ever-increasing drain upon the resources of the realm and France's alignment with the Protestant powers were in themselves sufficient to give rise to wide-ranging debate, since many of Richelieu's contemporaries violently objected to his moves on both

---

ou le chercheur de dupes du Cardinal de Richelieu, n.p., 1635, a satire, contains the following: "M. Jean Sirmond . . . will have in his train five or six zealots of the *Académie Gazetique* . . . above all they will be instructed in praising Monseigneur the Cardinal-Duke, and to this end they will learn all the poems, epigrams, elegies, acrostics, anagrams, sonnets, and other pieces composed by the Latin and French poets of our time, so as to distribute everywhere this beautiful merchandise." In *Pièces curieuses*, Vol. ii, p. 2 (individual pagination).

counts. The resulting polemics touched upon a great variety of issues and went to the heart of the problem of reason of state. They therefore require a detailed examination that must be topically structured, partially in violation of chronological order.

One of the most important political concepts to acquire new cogency during the period was the idea that the state was an objective, identifiable entity with interests and therefore a morality of its own. This view that the interests of the state determined the legitimacy of measures for its benefit was essential to the idea of a special morality of politics—so essential, in fact, that Friedrich Meinecke limited his treatment of the growth of reason of state under Richelieu to this single consideration.[175] Needless to say, this completely distorts the Cardinal's much more complex and religiously grounded position. The idea of state interests as such was by no means his personal invention and was extensively accepted in France before he became First Minister.[176] It seems simply to have been the natural, indeed inevitable, by-product of European interstate relations and the rivalries of self-styled sovereign powers. As we have noted, one of the earliest full-scale treatments of this concept from the standpoint of French interests was the anonymous *Discours des princes et estats de la Chrestienté plus considerables à la France, selon les diverses qualitez et conditions* of early 1624, therefore antedating Richelieu's appointment as First Minister.[177] A survey of the prevailing European scene, the work examined the interests of the various European powers, large and small, with special reference to their bearing upon French policies. Interest the author defined as diplomatic, military, economic, and/or strategic advantage, all of which he viewed in strictly practical terms, quite apart from any legal or moral considerations except as these impinged upon matters of expediency.

Richelieu, of course, directed his foreign policy for the advance-

---

[175] *Machiavellism*, Chap. VI.

[176] This is evident in many tracts in the *Recueil des pièces les plus curieuses qui ont esté faites pendant le règne du Connestable M. de Luyne*, n.p., 1628, and the *Recueil de quelques discours politiques, escrits sur diverses occurrences des Affaires et Guerres estrangers depuis quinze ans en çà*, n.p., 1632.

[177] See Pt. II, n. 30-32 and text.

ment of French interests, and he extensively used diplomacy itself as a weapon for promoting the French cause. For these purposes he required vast amounts of exact information if he were to succeed in gaining advantage over France's natural enemies, the Hapsburgs. This information he received from a group of highly trained professionals who provided him with memoranda concerning any and all political developments on the European scene. Understandably, these memoranda were entirely pragmatic and were limited to surveying specific matters and suggesting corresponding policies. They were the First Minister's indispensable tools, but they were far from embodying his total view of French policy and its justifications. An excellent illustration of this is found in the work of Paul Ardier, one of the abler functionaries who advised Richelieu on foreign affairs. An expert on the relations between the European powers, Ardier furnished Richelieu with memoranda which embodied extensive data concerning current diplomatic developments and their roots in the immediate past.[178] One of the most important treatises of this type was the *Mémoire sur les affaires générales de la Chrestienté du mois d'avril 1633*,[179] which was probably by Ardier and certainly by one of Richelieu's key aides. The work proposed to survey "the greatness and power of the states of each prince, his forces, means, alliances, interests, and his conduct," all from the standpoint of France "as far as it accords with the good of the state."[180] Beginning with the Valtelline on which Ardier was very well versed, the author traces recent diplomatic developments among the European powers, always for the purpose of indicating the most advantageous policy for France.[181] Again the approach is purely pragmatic and devoid of other considerations.

[178] Delavaud, pp. 199-213. On Ardier's career and work for Richelieu, see C. Piccioni, *Les Premiers Commis des Affaires Etrangères au XVIIᵉ et XVIIIᵉ siècles*, Paris, 1928, pp. 77-91.

[179] Printed in Molé, *Mémoires*, Vol. IV, 166-223. My references are to this version. On this work, see Delavaud, pp. 217-21.

[180] *Mémoire*, pp. 166-67.

[181] An example of this is his treatment of the problem of maintaining peace in the Italian peninsula.

The interests of France, opposed in all things [as they are] to those of

For Richelieu, such memoranda were no more than necessary aids in his conduct of French foreign policy, but his ruthless methods and those of other rulers and statesmen increasingly convinced some observers that the interests of states were the primary and perhaps the sole factors governing their foreign relations. This viewpoint gave rise to a small but growing literature on the subject as the century progressed. One of the earliest and ablest of such works was the Duke of Rohan's *De l'Interest des princes et des Estats de la Chrestienté*, which he probably completed in the year 1634.[182] It seems that Rohan, after his restoration to favor, not only sought important military assignments (which were given him only to a limited extent) but also hoped to influence Richelieu to under-

---

Spain, are also [opposed] in this matter, for France should always seek peace among the princes of Italy, because by being united they may present a counterweight to the power of Spain for the safety and preservation of their states and their liberty and sovereignty. In addition, it is very difficult in case of war in Italy for the King not to take part in order to forestall the advantages that the Spanish may gain from it, from which His Majesty will always encur great expense with little or no profit. The experience of past events sufficiently demonstrates how much the Italian wars have cost France in men and money, so that His Majesty, following the example of the former king by whose authority an accord was made between Pope Paul V and the Republic of Venice at the time of the interdict, should energetically make use of his name and his influence to arrest the course of the dispute between these two powers, both of whom are worthy of respect, the first because of his dignity and the second because of the powerful tie between this crown and the Republic. Furthermore, it is to the interest of the Church that Christian princes remain at peace with the common father and to the interest of the Most Christian King to keep them at peace. (*Mémoire*, pp. 188-89).

[182] Meinecke, p. 165. Rohan's *Interest des princes* was first published in the *Mercure français*, Vol. xx, 46-126, in its discussion of the events of 1634. This version is similar to all later printings except that Rohan's name is nowhere mentioned and the dedication to Richelieu is lacking. The work was published in Paris in 1638, with Rohan's *Parfaicte Capitaine* and independently in 1639. Many editions of the *Interest* contain a preface by Jean de Silhon, but this was written as an introduction to the *Parfaicte Capitaine* and has nothing to do with matters of political interest. Meinecke devotes almost his entire treatment of the concept of state interests in France to analyzing Rohan's ideas and finds essential parallelisms between his position and Richelieu's. I cannot accept this interpretation of Richelieu's ideals and motivation.

take a much more aggressive policy against Spain. For this purpose he wrote his *Interest des princes* which he dedicated to Richelieu, stating that although the Cardinal was not mentioned in the entire treatise, he was present throughout because his policies came under discussion and spoke for themselves. And Rohan protested complete devotion and loyalty to Richelieu, obviously hoping to win his attention and influence his thinking on diplomatic and military matters.

Like the two similar treatises that we have examined, Rohan's work analyzes the interests of the major and minor European states and the ways in which their relationships might be turned to French advantage. Taking the position that European diplomacy had become polarized about the two predominant powers, Spain and France, Rohan first examines many pertinent factors such as geographical position, efficiency of governments, military strength, and religious orientation—all from a purely pragmatic standpoint as they affected French interests. The second part of the treatise analyzes various historical episodes—wars, treaties, diplomatic struggles, successions to power—as illustrations of his earlier exposition of the constants in politics. His essential viewpoint, however, is adequately set forth at the beginning of his Introduction:

Princes rule peoples, and interest rules princes. An understanding of this interest is as influential over princes' actions as the latter are over the people. The prince may be deceived and his council may be corrupt, but interest alone is forever sure. According to [whether] it is well or badly understood, it preserves or ruins states. And since it always has gain or at least preservation as its objective, it must change with the times in order to be successful. For this reason, to examine well the interests of today's princes, it is not necessary to go back very far, but merely to cast one's eyes upon current affairs. For this, one must establish as fundamental that there are two powers in Christendom which are as the two poles from which stem the pressures for peace and war upon other states, to wit, the Houses of France and Spain. That of Spain, being suddenly aggran-

353

dized, has not been able to hide her intention to make herself supreme and to cause a new monarchy to rise in the West. That of France forthwith sought to play the role of counterpoise. The other princes have attached themselves to one or the other according to their interests. But inasmuch as they [their interests] have been well or badly followed and have caused the ruin of some [princes] and the greatness of others, I resolved to demonstrate in this treatise, first, what are the true interests of these two great powers and the others that seem in some manner to depend upon their protection. After that, I shall show how these true interests have not been followed, either because they were not well understood by the prince or because they were misrepresented to him by the corruption of his ministers.[183]

For Rohan, therefore, a given state's interests were all-determinative in shaping its foreign policy, and he treated all pertinent factors, including moral and religious principles, in precisely this vein. He achieved the separation of politics and morals simply by ignoring the relevance of the latter (except its practical implications). For all his strict Calvinism, Rohan advocated pure expediency and advantage as the only meaningful basis of foreign policy,[184] and it was with this type of argument that he attempted to influence Richelieu. The latter, however, continued to follow his own counsels and actively entered the Thirty Years' War only after all alternatives had been exhausted. Rohan's book is significant not for its positive influence but for its frankly secular and pragmatic view of French state interests and the appropriate means of implementing them. That his viewpoint was gradually gaining acceptance is illustrated by the repeated adaptations of his book later in the century.[185]

[183] *Mercure français*, Vol. xx, 46-47.

[184] Meinecke, pp. 180-89, attempts to reconcile Rohan's Calvinism with his purely pragmatic view of state interests and policy. The explanation seems to me to be unduly forced.

[185] The first revision of Rohan's work was made in 1647 by an anonymous author. The manuscript is in the Bibliothèque Nationale, Fonds Français, No. 4253, and is entitled *Traité succinct des vraies Maximes des Princes et Estats de l'Europe*. The date of this manuscript is indicated by a reference to Charles I of England on p. 81, and is confirmed by a statement on p. 120 of the

If the publication of Rohan's *Interest des princes* in the *Mercure français* indicates Richelieu's willingness to make use of a tract that supported his policies regardless of the author's broader ideological position, the same may be said of his relations with a writer of an utterly different stamp, François de La Mothe le Vayer.[186] This very learned skeptic and Pyrrhonist first made public his doubts concerning the entire range of political philosophy in his *Dialogue traictant de la politique sceptiquement*, which appeared in 1631.[187] Combining great erudition with devastating skepticism, La Mothe

Maximes, edition of 1666, listed below. The *Traité* involved much rewriting of Rohan's work, systematized it, added to it, and brought it up to date. In 1665, a further revision was published in Cologne under the title, *Maximes des princes et estats souverains*. In this version, the unnamed editor published the *Traité* in its entirety but made extensive further additions in the form of *Remarques* after many of the treatments of individual states, again bringing the work up to date. Thus the *Traité* and the *Maximes* were frankly based on Rohan. In 1666, another work, the *Interêts et Maximes des princes et des Estats souverains*, was also published at Cologne. Internal evidence, on p. 30, shows that it could not have been written before 1663. This work, by an unknown author, also surveys the interests of the European powers but differs significantly from Rohan and his annotators in that it is basically legal in nature and emphasizes precedents and the legal claims of various states against each other. Finally, Courtilz de Sandras published his *Nouveaux Interêts des Princes de l'Europe, où l'on traite des Maximes qu'ils doivent observer pour se maintenir dans leurs Estats, et pour empêcher qu'il ne se forme une Monarchie Universelle*, Cologne, 1685. This is a reexamination of prevailing conditions in Europe but the author owes much to Rohan and returns to the latter's purely pragmatic view of state interests and policy. On this work see B. A. Woodbridge, *Gatien de Courtilz*, Baltimore, 1925, pp. 26-34, and Meinecke, Chap. x. The many editions and variants of these works adequately indicate their popularity.

[186] On La Mothe le Vayer, see R. Kerviler, "François de La Mothe le Vayer, 1583-1672," *Revue historique et archéologique du Maine*, v (1879), 28-74, 162-97, 259-329; vi (1879), 5-57. (Also published separately.) F. L. Wickelgren, *La Mothe le Vayer: sa vie et son œuvre*, Paris, 1934. R. Pintard, *Le Libertinage érudit dans la première moitié du XVIIe siècle*, Paris, 1943, 2 vols.

[187] In *Quatre dialogues faits à l'imitation des anciens, par Orasius Tubero; Cinq autres dialogues du mesme autheur faits comme les precedents à l'imitation des anciens*, Frankfort, 1606. Both the place and date are fictitious. It seems that the first four dialogues were first published in 1630 and the other five in 1631. The *Dialogue traictant de la politique sceptiquement* is in the second group, pp. 239-325.

le Vayer opened the work by arguing the impossibility of applying high-minded political ideals in practice, and then insisted that "you can also regard as certain that it [politics] has no reasons of state so certain that they do not have their counterreasons, nor maxim so well taken and extensive that does not have its antiaxiom."[188] He thereupon passed in review a great number of precepts concerning all phases of government—the types of states, power, sanctions (including divine right), policies, justice, war, etc.—and found apparently valid counterpropositions for all. His conclusion seemed the negation of all principle:

> This pretended science of the state, with which many so pride themselves, has no principles so certain that the least encounter with affairs, the least accident of fortune, or the least change in circumstance does not easily disprove them, nor any thesis or proposition so constant that, with very small application of mind, one cannot easily form an antithesis and an entirely opposed or contrary maxim.[189]

And he advocated retreat to the countryside into the realm of philosophy.

Richelieu found no appeal in Pyrrhonism of this nature but was apparently impressed by La Mothe le Vayer's learning and talent for argumentation. Be that as it may, the two men soon made contact and La Mothe le Vayer's next publications took the form of two tracts in support of the Cardinal's foreign policy. In his *Discours sur la bataille de Lutzen* which was printed in the *Mercure français*,[190] La Mothe le Vayer meditated on the death of Gustavus Adolphus, comparing him with the heroes of antiquity and arguing that unlike the conquerors of the ancient world his work would not disappear with him because of the continuing strength of the pro-French North German Confederation and Swedish leadership. Soon after appeared La Mothe le Vayer's *Discours sur la proposition de trefve au Pays Bas en 1633*, which was likewise incorporated into

---

[188] *Dialogue*, p. 256.   [189] *Ibid.*, p. 310.

[190] *Discours sur la bataille de Lutzen*, Paris, 1633. Also in *Mercure français*, Vol. XVIII, 707-21, and La Mothe le Vayer, *Œuvres*, Paris, 1662, Vol. I, 192-99.

the *Mercure*.[191] This tract set forth the following reasons why the Dutch, who were allies of the French, should not accept the Spanish offer of a truce during negotiations at The Hague. The Dutch had won their independence through war and were continually dependent upon it because the Spanish had never renounced their claim to rule the Dutch and could not be trusted. A truce would cause further disintegration of the anti-Spanish alliance. The Dutch should follow the example of the Romans who built all on war; Dutch acceptance of the truce would be equivalent to renunciation of their success and greatness. Clearly, these two pamphlets offered merely pragmatic justifications of Richelieu's foreign policy and nothing more. As such, they were deemed valuable contributions to the *Mercure français*, but at this point in his career La Mothe le Vayer went no further. He had lent his pen to Richelieu's support, doubtless in the hope of gaining recognition and other rewards, but only later did he attempt to grapple with the problem of reason of state.[192]

The tracts of Ardier, Rohan, and La Mothe le Vayer treat only pragmatic and operational matters of a type that must always be central to the conduct of foreign affairs and were exploited by Richelieu to the full. Equally significant for him and many of his most important supporters was the other side of the coin, namely, legal and moral principle. Regarding the legality of his actions, it should be noted that one element of his policy for the advancement of French interests was his effort to capitalize upon the claims of the French crown to territories beyond the borders of the realm. In handling this delicate matter, the Cardinal made extensive efforts to give his actions a basis in law. True, the conflicting claims to many of these areas were susceptible to very divergent interpretations, but it should be remembered that the chaotic body of inherited law provided the only known basis of legal right and was therefore synonymous with it. For this reason, rulers and statesmen who sought to ground their policies upon law and justice were perforce required to take seriously the claims and counterclaims that were

[191] *Discours sur la proposition de trefve au Pays-Bas en 1633*, in *Mercure français*, Vol. XIX, 224-39, and the *Œuvres*, Vol. I, 200-06.
[192] See n. 470-76 and text.

based upon a myriad of precedents and legal traditions. Many French writers of the period consequently produced massive tomes for the purpose of establishing French titles to disputed areas. The basic problem, of course, lay in the fact that the body of legal precedent extended well over a millennium, and it was extremely difficult to determine a reasonable and conclusive position in any given dispute.

One of the most moderate French writers to discuss the matter was Jean de Silhon. As we have indicated, Silhon held that the French kings had valid claims to Metz, Toul, Verdun, Flanders, Milan, Naples, and Navarre, but they should not attempt to make good the losses that had been suffered by Charlemagne's successors.[193] Other French writers, on the contrary, took a much more extravagant position. By extending the fundamental law which prohibited the alienation of the royal domain to territories beyond the borders of the realm, they were able to make the most sweeping claims for the French crown. The royal domain, they frequently maintained, was sacred and inalienable and rightfully included the entire empire of Charlemagne, since the French kings were his successors. And occasionally they went back to Clovis or even ancient Gaul, bounded by the Rhine, Alps, and Pyrenees. Such arguments were far removed from the realities of seventeenth-century politics, but the nature and extent of the literature on the subject demonstrates great concern for legal right on the part of Richelieu and his supporters.[194]

When examining this literature and its relevance to Richelieu's foreign policy, it is essential to determine whether a given author wrote under official sponsorship or was merely developing his own views, possibly in the hope of gaining recognition in high places. A few writers, such as Christophe Balthasar and Charles Hersent, seem to have worked independently of any official directives. Balthasar was a minor provincial jurist who served as *avocat du roi à*

---

[193] See Pt. III, n. 244 and text.
[194] For general treatments of this literature, see W. Mommsen, *Richelieu, Elsass und Lothringen*, Berlin, 1922, pp. 387-406. Albertini, pp. 146-59. Dickmann, "Rechtsgedanke . . . ," pp. 284-308. Dickmann's treatment is the most recent and by far the best.

Auxerre and later turned Calvinist. In 1625, he published a lengthy work in which he compiled historical events and legal precedents in an effort to demonstrate that the French crown still had valid rights over such Spanish territories as Sicily, Naples, Milan, Flanders, Roussillon, Navarre and other areas to the north and east.[195] The work was well received but had no immediate progeny. Charles Hersent, a cleric, lived a very agitated life, in and out of the Oratoire, and in repeated trouble with his superiors. In 1627 he was made Chancellor of the cathedral church in Metz and in that capacity published five years later his book which purported to set forth the legal basis of French sovereignty over the bishopric and its dependencies.[196] His reasoning was simple, although supported by extensive precedents and argument. Going back to the Kingdom of Austrasia, he insisted that Metz was first ruled by the Merovingians, and all later claims to the area stemmed from theirs. Charlemagne inherited these rights which then passed legally, if not actually, to the Kings of France. When developments in recent centuries seemed to discredit any effective current French claims, Hersent simply discounted these by citing earlier precedents from the first and second races of kings. In this way he sought to establish Louis XIII's sovereignty over the area rather than the mere protection which the local authorities recognized. His book was one of several of its type to appear in 1632, but it seems not to have won the recognition that its author sought. Disgruntled, Hersent later caused a major furor by publishing a tract which purported to reveal Richelieu's plan to set himself up as Patriarch of the Gauls.[197]

Unlike Balthasar and Hersent, a large majority of those who

[195] *Traité des usurpations des Roys d'Espagne sur la Couronne de France depuis Charles VIII. Ensemble un Discours sur le commencement, progrez, declin et démembrement de la Monarchie Françoise, droicts et prétentions des Roys Très-Chrestiens sur l'Empire,* Paris, 1625. An expanded version with the same title was published in Paris in 1626.

[196] *De la Souveraineté du Roy à Mets, pays Metsin, et autres villes et pays circonvoisins: qui estoient de l'ancien Royaume d'Austrasie ou Lorraine. Contre les prétentions de l'Empire, de l'Espagne et de la Lorraine, et contre les maximes des habitans de Mets, qui ne tienent le Roy que pour leur Protecteur,* Paris, 1632.

[197] See n. 348 and text.

wrote in support of French claims to territories beyond her borders were operating under the sponsorship of the crown. Among these authors, it was long believed that Jacques de Cassan, although an able jurist and royal councillor, had no official capacity until Professor Zeller discovered a letter from Louis XIII, dated June 15, 1627, ordering Cassan to search out the King's rights to various territories currently held by foreign princes.[198] Cassan's book, whose long title adequately indicates its purpose,[199] was directed squarely against Hapsburg suzerainty over many areas of Europe. The first portion attempts to establish French claims to such Spanish territories as Castille, Aragon, Portugal, Navarre, Sicily and Naples, Milan and others, while the second does the same for many imperial holdings to the north and east. Again Cassan's basis of argument is simple: he merely goes back to Charlemagne and occasionally Clovis, and bases French claims upon inheritance of Merovingian and Carolingian rights. All their territories were legally "parts of the French kingdom and subordinate to it."[200] Cardin Le Bret, whose work also appeared in 1632 and has previously been examined,[201] was sufficiently close to the royal administration throughout his long career to warrant the assumption that he reflected the official viewpoint. In fact, Le Bret was appointed in 1624 to head an important commission to investigate French rights over the three bishoprics, to be discussed below. In his key work, *De la Souveraineté du Roy*, Le Bret developed the concept of the inalienability of the royal domain as the basis of French claims to foreign territories.[202] Although his argument is more moderate and specific than Cassan's,

[198] G. Zeller, "La Monarchie d'ancien régime et les frontières naturelles," *Revue d'histoire moderne*, VIII (1933), 317.

[199] *La Recherche des droicts du Roy et de la Couronne de France: sur les Royaumes, Duchez, Comtez, Villes et Païs occupez par les Princes estrangers: Appartenans aux Roys Tres-Chrestiens, par Conquests, Successions, Achapts, Donations, et autres titres légitimes. Ensemble de leurs droicts sur l'Empire, et des devoirs et homages deubs à leur Couronne, par divers Princes estrangers,* Paris, 1632. The title of Cassan's book seems to indicate that it was written expressly to fulfill the request in Louis XIII's letter.

[200] *Ibid.,* p. 3.

[201] See Pt. III, n. 255-282 and text.

[202] *Souveraineté,* Bk. III, Chaps. 1, 2; Bk. IV, Chap. 8.

Le Bret goes almost as far in maintaining French titles to Hapsburg lands. More dubious is the official role of Louis Chantereau-Lefebvre. A learned jurist and historian, he was also a very able administrator. In addition to being royal councillor, he was from 1633 to 1636 Intendant of Lorraine and the Bishoprics of Metz and Toul, and in 1634 he was made a member of the Sovereign Council of Nancy. During all this time and several later years he was engaged in extensive research into French claims over the Duchies of Lorraine and Bar. A part of his findings were published in a massive volume in 1642.[203] The work is basically genealogical and attempts to show with a wealth of documentation that the House of Lorraine was not descended from Charlemagne whose rights therefore devolved upon the King of France. In this instance, there is no evidence of official sponsorship, the work having been published after its author left high office, but his earlier activity leads to the presumption that he at least reflected and sought to strengthen the official position.

Among Richelieu's aides in searching out French claims to foreign territories, by far the most important were Pierre Dupuy and Théodore Godefroy. These very able archivist-jurist-historians served the crown during the better part of their careers by reorganizing the official archives, writing innumerable legal memoirs and longer treatises on currently important matters, and undertaking many related activities at the request of their superiors in the royal administration. In 1615, on the recommendation of the very able Procureur General, Mathieu Molé, Dupuy and Godefroy were appointed to make an inventory of the neglected but priceless docu-

---

[203] *Mémoires sur l'origine des maisons et duchés de Lorraine et de Bar-le-Duc*, Paris, 1642. This work consisted of three parts, but only the first was published in this volume. The title of the first part: *Considérations historiques sur la généalogie de la Maison de Lorraine*. (The work is usually listed under this title.) The second and third sections: *Mémoires concernant les Droicts de la Couronne de France sur le Duché de Lorraine*, and *Mémoires des droicts de proprieté, mouvance et souveraineté appartenans au Roy et à la Couronne de France sur le Duché de Bar*. Both of these works are in manuscript in the Bibliothèque Nationale, with many others of Chantereau-Lefebvre on royal rights. In the preface to the printed work, he mentions that the third portion was written in 1634. The privilege also mentions his long research.

ments in the Trésor des Chartes.[204] Here they spent years compiling their inventory and generally bringing order out of chaos.[205] Their resulting familiarity with the fundamental records of French history gave them an erudition unequaled in the period. In the nature of things, both men moved easily from compiling an inventory in the Trésor des Chartes to assembling documentary evidence concerning a host of royal rights over both foreign and domestic lands, although there is no evidence that they did so before Richelieu assumed direction of affairs. The Cardinal immediately realized the value of legal evidence in current disputes, and in November 1624, secured the appointment of a commission headed by Le Bret and including Dupuy to investigate the usurpation of lands under Louis XIII's protection in the Bishoprics of Metz, Toul, and Verdun.[206] The commissioners were instructed to search out "the usurpations and acquisitions made by foreigners of the lands, seigneuries, and houses that are in the areas of the King's obedience and protection . . . , and to provide documents to His Majesty's procurators so that such usurpations and alienations may neither jeopardize nor prejudice the rights and duties that belong to him because of his protection and sovereignty."[207] Although Le Bret headed the commission, Dupuy did much work assembling the inventories of titles to lands in the three bishoprics.[208]

The exact year when Dupuy and Godefroy embarked upon more extensive, officially sponsored research into such matters is not known, but Godefroy was active in government service in 1628, and Dupuy received a commission in December 1629, to investigate

[204] Molé, *Mémoires*, Vol. 1, 58-61.

[205] Two descriptions of conditions in the Trésor des Chartes by Dupuy are given in Molé, *Mémoires*, Vol. 1, 530-32. Dupuy, *Traitez touchant les droits du Roy*, Paris, 1655, pp. 1013-14. H.-F. Delaborde, "Les Travaux de Dupuy sur le Trésor des Chartes," *Bibliothèque de l'École des Chartes*, LVIII (1897), 126-54. Also printed separately.

[206] The letters patent appointing Le Bret, de Lorme, and Dupuy are printed in Dupuy, *Traitez*, pp. 591-97. On the work of this commission, see G. Zeller, *La Réunion de Metz à la France*, Paris, 1926, Vol. II, 230-36.

[207] Dupuy, *Traitez*, p. 594.

[208] Letter of Dupuy to Le Bret, *Traitez*, pp. 597-98.

French titles to foreign territories.[209] By this time, it would seem that their work of this nature was well advanced, for by 1630 they produced one and possibly two treatises on French rights over Aragon and Navarre.[210] On February 15, 1631, Richelieu wrote to both men thanking them for their treatise on Navarre and asking them to complete similar studies of Lorraine and other areas.[211] On October 27, they jointly replied that they had submitted reports on Navarre, Genoa, Aragon, Naples, and Sicily, and had others on Flanders and Artois, Milan, Burgundy, Provence, Brittany, Anjou, Avignon, Mâcon, Auxerre, etc., as well as the claims of the Kings of England and France upon each other's territories, and would send them to the Cardinal at his request.[212] This unpublished letter is included in a manuscript which appears to be in part an interim report for the year 1631, listing projects yet to be undertaken and emphasizing the great extent of necessary research.[213] On November 16, Richelieu wrote thanking them for their letter concerning the state of their investigations,[214] and on November 25 he again wrote, thanking

---

[209] Dickmann, "Rechtsgedanke . . . ," p. 297.

[210] Avenel, the editor of the *Lettres*, refers in Vol. VII, 666, to the following two manuscripts by Dupuy and Godefroy. *Droits du Roy sur le Royaume d'Arragon, de Navarre, contre le Roy d'Espagne, 1630. Traité du droit légitime que le Roy a sur tout le Royaume de Navarre.* The latter may be the treatise that Richelieu referred to in his letter of February 15, 1631.

[211] *Lettres*, Vol. IV, 93. Also in *Bulletin de la Société de l'Histoire de France*, 1851-1852, pp. 304-06.

[212] Bibliothèque de l'Arsenal, MS. 4741, pp. 325-26.

[213] *Ibid.*, pp. 319-636. The title of this manuscript does not indicate its entire contents: *Réunions à la couronne, acquisitions, droitz du Roy sur Lion, Languedoc, Rivière d'Andaye, Guyenne, Gascogne, Charrolois, Dombes, Boybelle, Bourbonnois, Auvergne, etc.* In addition to much information on royal rights over areas within France it contains a long list of foreign realms, duchies, marquisates, and seigneuries under the heading, "Des Droitz du Roy, soit en demandant ou en deffendant, pour la propriété, Iurisdiction, et droit de féodalité aux Royaumes de . . . ." Pages 343-44 list the following bodies of information to be consulted: genealogies, the Inventory of the Trésor des Chartes, peace treaties, discourses, remonstrances, memoirs written by Dupuy (600 volumes), various histories, registers of the ordinances of the Parlement, etc.

[214] *Bulletin*, cited in n. 211.

them for their memoirs on Brittany and Flanders, adding that the King had seen them and was pleased.[215]

In later years, Godefroy was repeatedly sent on missions that involved the handling of documents. After the conquest of Lorraine in 1634, he was ordered to Nancy to investigate legal titles to various parts of the Duchy and brought back to Paris twelve great coffers of documents, the cream of the holdings of the Trésor des Chartes of Lorraine.[216] And on December 6, 1636, Richelieu issued elaborate instructions to Godefroy to attend the projected peace conference at Cologne and to be fortified with documents concerning a long list of France's outstanding territorial and diplomatic claims.[217] It is evident that the varied activities of Godefroy and Dupuy in support of the crown's legal rights extended over many years and were directly related to matters of policy. A selection of their reports was published in 1655, after Dupuy's death, by his brother Jacques under Pierre Dupuy's name,[218] but it is known that these were chiefly by Godefroy. The majority of such tracts by both men remained in manuscript, doubtless for official use only, and are to be found in the appropriate collections in Paris.

Although the relationships of these writers—Balthasar, Hersent, Cassan, Le Bret, Chantereau-Lefebvre, Dupuy, and Godefroy—with the royal administration varied greatly in individual cases, their works contain remarkably similar arguments in support of French

---

[215] *Ibid.* Also *Lettres*, Vol. IV, 209-10. All four of these letters mention money matters, Dupuy and Godefroy asking for payment and Richelieu making different promises each time. Apparently Dupuy and Godefroy were very poorly remunerated for their services.

[216] Molé, *Mémoires*, Vol. II, 347-48. Dupuy, *Traitez*, p. 1015. A. Digot, *Histoire de Lorraine*, Nancy, 1856, Vol. V, 242-44. Godefroy's expenses during this journey were not remunerated.

[217] *Lettres*, Vol. V, 705-07.

[218] This work is referred to in n. 205-08, 216. Its full title is: *Traitez touchant les droits du Roy Très Chrestien sur plusieurs estats et seigneuries possédées par divers princes voisins et pour prouver qu'il tient à juste titre plusieurs provinces contestées par les princes estrangers. Recherches, pour monstrer que plusieurs provinces et villes du royaume sont du domaine du Roy. Usurpations faites sur les trois eveschez Mets, Toul et Verdun: et quelques autres traitez concernant des matières publiques*, Paris, 1655.

claims to foreign territories. All were in basic agreement concerning the legitimacy of Louis XIII's titles to much of Europe and the reasons for their validity, and the common approach to the matter in this literature goes far to indicate its general acceptance among French thinkers of the period.[219] All built upon the indisputable fundamental law of the French monarchy, the inalienability of the royal domain. Le Bret was typical when he wrote that the royal domain was sacred and not subject to the rules of prescription, even after the hundred-year period stipulated in certain sections of Roman Law. "Usurpation cannot achieve any prescriptive right to retain them [confiscated lands], especially when the dispute is between two sovereign princes who hold their power only from God and the sword."[220] Likewise, all agreed that treaties which alienated portions of the realm, such as the Treaty of Madrid between Francis I and Charles V in 1526, were invalid because the king had no authority to diminish the rights, powers, and perquisites of the crown.[221] The actual claims of the French to formerly held territories these writers implemented with varying degrees of thoroughness, chiefly by tracing the genealogical and therefore legal transfer of titles over the centuries from Clovis, Charlemagne, and other rulers as the case might be. The labors of Dupuy and Godefroy differed from those of the others only in being more extensive and more thorough, planning as they did to compile genealogical, legal, and historical data to establish French claims to seven realms, five duchies, eleven counties, and an indeterminate number of seigneuries and other miscellaneous territories.[222] For all their remoteness, French claims

[219] The best recent survey of the basic concepts in these works is in Dickmann, "Rechtsgedanke . . . ," pp. 284-95.

[220] *Souveraineté*, p. 96.

[221] *Ibid.*, p. 255.

[222] In the manuscript referred to above in n. 212, 213, the more important territories to which Dupuy and Godefroy planned to establish French rights were: the kingdoms or former kingdoms of Navarre, Castille, Aragon, Sicily, England, Burgundy, and Lorraine; the Duchies of Milan, Bar, Burgundy, Anjou, and Brittany; the Counties of Flanders, Artois, Mâcon, Auxerre, Provence, Avignon, Venaisan, Nice, St. Paul, Ast, Roussillon, and Sardagne. Also the Marquisate of Pontamousson [sic], the Principalities of Orange, Sedan, and Piedmont, and many seigneuries.

to these areas, once held, continued valid, for as Cassan wrote, "These are sound titles, firm and constant rights which are derived from the justice of the most sacred laws and the most legitimate power of reason."[223] He added, doubtless in all seriousness, that French titles over so much of Europe made the King of France supreme over all others:

> The greatest monarchs who rule today in Europe are subordinate to the Kings of France . . . , and the monarchies and most powerful states over which they exercise sovereign power are but bits and diguised pieces of the Realm of France which the violence of the years and the blows of fortune have removed from the legitimate rule of our kings, but without depriving them of their rights, since justice, the guide of the crowns of princes and the guardian of the world, continues to preserve them in her temple, complete and inviolable.[224]

The clear implication was that the Kings of France might legitimately use force to regain their lost territories. Even the judicious Le Bret could write: "We should hope that God will some day open the way to our noble prince to recover from his enemies all the lands that they have usurped with so much injustice."[225]

For our purposes, it is essential to determine at least in general terms how Richelieu viewed these legal rights of the French crown and to what extent they influenced his foreign policy. The importance of the issue relative to any estimation of Richelieu's political morality is obvious. Did he use French claims to foreign territories merely as specious arguments with which to justify an essentially Machiavellian anti-Hapsburg policy, or did he regard legal right as a matter of principle which should be a major force in determining his actions and objectives? And if the latter is true, as I believe it to be, what was the exact matrix of principle and expediency that characterized his handling of French foreign relations?[226] One as-

[223] *La Recherche*, Dedicatory epistle, n.p.
[224] *Ibid.*, p. 3.   [225] *Souveraineté*, p. 97.
[226] Of the authorities listed above in n. 194, Mommsen and Albertini regard Richelieu's use of French claims to foreign lands merely as a means of imple-

pect of the problem of which we may be certain is that Richelieu invariably made reference to French claims to foreign territory whenever they seemed relevant to current affairs. His preoccupation with such rights extended throughout his entire career as First Minister and leads to the presumption that he believed them to be extremely significant to his defense of French state interests. His first such venture was Le Bret's inquest of 1624-1625 into the usurpation of lands under Louis XIII's protection in the Bishoprics of Metz, Toul, and Verdun. The ordinances and attached inventories which were drawn up by the commission established the extent of the usurped lands and other rights, reported them to the king, and provisionally decreed that French rights in the bishoprics should be inviolate.[227] The procedure foreshadowed in many essentials Louis XIV's later chambers of reunion. Although the work of Le Bret's commission had no immediate practical effect except to worsen the chronically bad relations between Duke Charles IV of Lorraine and Louis XIII, its actions indicate the importance that Richelieu attached to the rights and perquisites of the French crown.[228]

The work of Dupuy and Godefroy in furnishing documentary materials to those in charge of governmental affairs is not known in detail, but the correspondence of Mathieu Molé, the Procureur General, shows that during much of the year 1628 he and Michel de Marillac, the Keeper of the Seals, were keenly interested in the inventory which Dupuy and Godefroy were compiling in the Trésor des Chartes and repeatedly asked them for documents with which to defend the King's rights, both in domestic and foreign affairs.[229] After the Day of Dupes and the flight of Gaston d'Orléans first to Lorraine and then to Flanders, Richelieu's own correspondence with Dupuy and Godefroy understandably reflected his concern for tra-

---

menting a Machiavellian policy, whereas Dickmann finds that the Cardinal was primarily a man of principle who combined respect for legality with the realities of practical politics.

[227] The ordinances and certain relevant documents are published in Dupuy, *Traitez*, pp. 599-680.

[228] Cf. Zeller, *La Réunion de Metz à la France*, Vol. II, 235-36.

[229] Molé, *Mémoires*, Vol. I, 525-42.

ditional French rights over these areas.[230] Because of the machinations of Gaston and the Queen Mother in these provinces, Richelieu's newly strong position in his post as First Minister, and the general hardening of his anti-Hapsburg policy in the early 1630's, the simultaneous appearance of books by Hersent, Cassan, and Le Bret in 1632 seemed merely to reflect and confirm royal policy. During these years, Richelieu continued to avoid outright war with the Hapsburgs, but Lorraine was more vulnerable, partly because of traditional French rights over the area and the ill-advised policies of the Duke. The French conquest of the duchy in 1634 was followed, as we have noted, by the creation of a sovereign council at Nancy, one of whose members was Chantereau-Lefebvre, and Godefroy's massive confiscation of documents from the local Trésor des Chartes.[231] When Chantereau-Lefebvre published in 1642 his elaborate volume documenting French rights over Lorraine, it seemed again to confirm and implement French policy.

Richelieu's concern for French rights over foreign territories is also evident in his handling of French relations with the European powers generally. Even after France actively entered the Thirty Years' War, Richelieu continued to maintain diplomatic contacts with the Hapsburgs in an effort to secure an advantageous peace. The most revealing elements of this diplomatic sparring were those that centered about preparations for the projected peace conference in Cologne—a conference which was actively sought by Pope Urban VIII and officially approved by the French, Spanish, and Imperialists, but never met because the warring powers could not agree upon

[230] See n. 211-15 and text. In the *Lettres*, Vol. VII, 680, Avenel refers to one of their manuscripts on Flanders, dated 1631. Letters from Molé to Dupuy in 1632 clearly show their active concern for French rights over Lorraine. Molé, *Mémoires*, Vol. II, 160-68.

[231] See n. 203, 216, and text. After the French conquest of Lorraine, Richelieu continued to be concerned about specific French legal rights in the area. A letter from Godefroy to Molé, dated October 25, 1638, indicates that Molé had asked Godefroy to furnish him with information concerning royal *vs.* ducal rights over the appointment of ecclesiastics in the duchy. Molé, *Mémoires*, Vol. II, 404, n. 2.

the necessary preliminaries.[232] On December 6, 1636, Richelieu ordered Godefroy to be prepared to leave for Cologne within fifteen days and to take with him a large body of documents with which to support French interests.[233] Richelieu's listing of the matters under consideration excellently illustrates his method of combining legality with war-time diplomacy. Lesser items which Godefroy was to document included the legitimacy of French occupation of the Pignerol, the rights of the Duke of Mantua to his lands, and the freedom of the Duke of Parma and the German Electors to ally themselves with France regardless of any Imperial supremacy.[234] As for the all-important matter of Lorraine, Godefroy was to justify French retention of the duchy because of the rebellion of Charles IV, a vassal of France, and because of the many French rights over the three bishoprics. In order to demonstrate the solidity of the French claims to the area, Godefroy was to obtain documents which showed how feeble were Spanish and Imperial titles to lands which *they* had usurped. And Richelieu added the following very revealing guideline: even if the Spanish were to restore the Palatinate and Wurttemberg to their former rulers, France should not be expected to do the same for Lorraine because the French enjoyed an entirely different right to the latter area.[235] Clearly, for Richelieu the rights of the crown were not something expendable with which to purchase immediate advantage. And when Godefroy analyzed possible French answers to the demands that he expected the Spanish and

[232] A Leman, *Richelieu et Olivarès: Leur négociations secrètes de 1636 à 1642 pour le rétablissement de la paix*, Lille, 1938, *passim*.

[233] *Lettres*, Vol. v, 705-07.

[234] Specifically, Godefroy was instructed to document the following positions. The Duke of Savoy might alienate the Pignerol to France without prejudicing Imperial rights because France formerly held the area legally. The Duchies of Mantua and Montferrat legally belonged to the Duke of Mantua, a fact which proved the injustice of Spain's plan to take them. Neither the pope nor the Emperor could dispossess the Duke of Parma because he took up arms on the side of France. The German Electors, and especially the Elector of Trier, were free to place themselves under French protection.

[235] *Lettres*, Vol. v, 707.

Imperialists to make at Cologne,[236] he sharply differentiated between France's obligations to her allies and the crown's legal rights, giving far greater weight to the latter.[237] Although Louis XIII and Richelieu prided themselves on their fidelity to their allies, they readily subordinated such obligations to the preservation of regalian rights. These alone were sacred and inalienable, not subject to the fortunes of war and diplomacy. Dupuy undoubtedly reflected the official position when he wrote concerning the alienation of French regalian rights over the Duchy of Bar: "These rights are the true marks of royalty, which should always reside in the person of the prince who cannot separate them from himself nor alienate any part of them; they are imprescriptable in whole and in part. Among these rights, the most precious are those that are on the frontiers and over border areas."[238]

It is evident that attention to the legal rights of the crown was an integral part of Richelieu's foreign policy. In practice, of course, he did not attempt to make good French claims to Charlemagne's empire and was restricted to the potentialities of the seventeenth-century political scene, but this did not negate the significance of legal tradition in his eyes. Like his contemporaries, Richelieu regarded Louis XIII's regalian rights as the essence of royal authority which it was the First Minister's chief duty to defend. He knew no more laudable approach to the advancement of state interests, and on this important count he may be called a man of principle as well as expediency. It has even been maintained that he sought only those foreign territories that belonged to France of right.[239] Whether this

[236] *Demandes que l'Empereur et le Roy d'Espagne pourront faire au Roy dans la Conférence establie pour la paix générale*, in Dupuy, *Traitez*, pp. 546-47.

[237] *Examen des moyens d'accommodement sur lesdites demandes, ibid.*, pp. 547-52. This viewpoint is fundamental to the treatises that Godefroy wrote in preparation for the Congress of Cologne. Some of these tracts are printed in Dupuy, *Traitez*, pp. 553-88. Most of them were written early in 1637.

[238] Dupuy, *Traitez*, p. 553.

[239] L. Batiffol, "Richelieu et la question d'Alsace," *Revue historique*, cxxxviii (1921), 161-200. See especially p. 170. Dickmann cites Batiffol with approval in his discussion of this matter. "Rechtsgedanke . . . ," pp. 298-308. I essentially agree with Dickmann's position.

was thoroughly axiomatic with the ever-resourceful Cardinal may be questioned, but there is no doubt that legal claims bulked large in his approach to foreign policy. His chief aide, Father Joseph, regularly received and reviewed the tracts that Dupuy and Godefroy prepared to support French claims abroad.[240] The best exposition of Richelieu's mature position, however, is contained in a document which embodies his final instructions concerning peace negotiations and was published by Professor Dickmann.[241] After reviewing French claims to Navarre, Catalonia, Roussillon, Flanders, Hesdin, the two Burgundies, Milan, and Naples, the last part of this memorandum examines the difficult question whether the French should sacrifice any of their ancient rights as part of the price of a lasting peace.[242] The issue was clearly one of legality and right *vs.* expediency and practical advantage. After examining the ways in which French rights to foreign territories might be renounced, Richelieu recalled that all such rights were legally inalienable, adding that he accepted this maxim and would sin against the public interest if he doubted it. The only valid alienations were those that were absolutely necessary to prevent the ruin of the state.[243] In this instance alone, when all might be lost, were renunciations to be considered. But even under such extreme circumstances the French would be legally justified in reconquering the lost areas if the victors followed the Spanish example of advancing from conquest to conquest rather than observing the terms of peace.[244]

Moving on to the problem of achieving a firm peace settlement, Richelieu took the position that it was better to sacrifice potential gains than to secure them at the price of renouncing traditional French rights. Such renunciations were certain to cause future trouble; they would ruin the reputation of the minister who made or counselled them and would be condemned by posterity. As an aside, Richelieu added that he would willingly risk his own reputation by recommending such a peace if it benefited the state, since

---

[240] Fagniez, *Le Père Joseph et Richelieu*, Vol. II, 268, n. 1.

[241] *Acta Pacis Westphalicae*, Series 1: *Instruktionen*, Münster, 1962, Vol. 1, 159-89.

[242] *Ibid.*, pp. 182-89.   [243] *Ibid.*, pp. 185-86.   [244] *Ibid.*, pp. 186-87.

individuals must sacrifice their personal interests to those of the state. In the present situation, however, he was convinced that the only firm peace was one in which France would retain her ancient rights plus any new conquests and create two leagues of princes, one in Germany and the other in Italy. Only such a combination of restraints might forestall Spanish violation of the settlement.[245] Respect for legal rights plus the necessary coercive arrangements were therefore the essentials of Richelieu's formula for perpetual peace. And these in turn lay at the root of his concept of collective security which he felt must be based upon mutual guarantees, binding all signatories.[246] It is evident that throughout his diplomatic activity for both the advancement of French state interests and the creation of a durable peace, the element of legal right was of primary importance in Richelieu's thought and practice. He consistently defended legality, built upon it, and believed it essential to the peace of Europe. In this, he was a man of principle as far as the exigencies of politics and war permit to any statesman.

THE DEBATE ON RICHELIEU'S FOREIGN POLICY

During this final period of Richelieu's ministry, the polemics concerning the justice of his foreign policy gradually assumed a different character. The published tracts of the 1630's give evidence of an increasing polarization of thought for and against the Cardinal, with extreme partisanship on both sides. Especially after the French declaration of war against Spain in 1635, opinion was thoroughly divided between praise and condemnation of his policies—a not unusual situation in time of war and national crisis. The arguments that were used by both his supporters and critics were essentially unchanged, but they were now presented with a new sense of immediacy. A limited number of these tracts will be analyzed in order to indicate the tenor of the debate and the final positions that were assumed by the participants.

[245] *Ibid.*, p. 188.
[246] Cf. Dickmann, "Rechtsgedanke . . . ," pp. 308-12.

In 1634 a lengthy work, *L'Homme du Pape et du Roy*, appeared, probably by Jean Sirmond.[247] It was written in answer to an earlier tract by Juan Antonio de Vera y Figueroa, Count of La Roca, the Spanish ambassador to Venice.[248] In this work, La Roca not only attacked French foreign policy from the Spanish viewpoint but also criticized Pope Urban VIII for not exerting all pressure upon Richelieu to alter his foreign policy. In answer, Sirmond sought to justify the actions of both Louis XIII and Urban VIII by setting forth a remarkably secular view of the war. First, he reiterated the usual charges against the Spanish: they used religion to cloak their selfish national interests and attempted to make a religious war of one that was for essentially secular purposes.[249] Individual rulers may have their personal religious convictions, said Sirmond, praising Louis XIII's piety,[250] but the treaties into which they enter with other sovereigns concern only their interests and have no relevance to religion:

> As if the treaties of sovereign princes were not ordinarily simple ties of interest which have nothing in common with religious sentiment. Leagues establish civil communication between wills and forces, and not the opinions and beliefs of those who form them. Faith in no way enters into these relationships. Those that the Most Christian King has made with certain others have as their objective only the preservation of the oppressed princes of the Empire, the restoration of their property, the preservation of their rights, the pacification of their lands . . . and the reciprocal freedom of communication between the crowns of

[247] *L'Homme du Pape et du Roy, ou Reparties véritables sur les imputations calomnieuses d'un libelle diffamatoire semé contre Sa Sainteté et Sa Majesté Très-Chrestienne*, Brussels (?), 1634.

[248] *Al Pio, al Grande, al Beatissimo Padre Urbano octavo: Lodovico Zambeccari Servitore, et humillima creatura di vostre Beatudino, Salute 1635*. Bibliothèque Nationale, Fonds Français 23153, fols. 204-19. I have not found a printed copy of this work, but Sirmond's references leave no doubt that this is the tract that he answered. Lelong suggests that La Roca used the pseudonym "Zambeccari" because of the tract's violent criticisms of both Urban VIII and French foreign policy. *Bibliothèque historique de la France*, Vol. II, 862.

[249] *L'Homme du Pape et du Roy*, pp. 9-19, 24.

[250] *Ibid.*, pp. 57-62.

France and Sweden. What can one find to criticize in that? Where are the laws that prohibit it? I know of none. In this matter, examples should have the force of law. The histories of all peoples and all centuries mention an infinite number of good and wise princes who have allied themselves, some with infidels and others with heretics, without ever having been criticized for it. One reads almost nothing else.[251]

And Sirmond illustrated his point by recalling such acts as Charles V's alliance with Henry VIII and the sack of Rome.[252] Sirmond would defend French and papal policies simply by arguing that alliances were irrelevant to religion, and on this basis he claimed to be both *l'homme du pape et du roi*. Neither Richelieu nor Urban VIII accepted this simplistic and secularized view of foreign policy, but Sirmond's tract indicates that it was slowly gaining acceptance and was, in fact, one of the viewpoints that was expressed in support of the Cardinal's foreign policy in his own entourage.

The increasing polarization of thought concerning Richelieu's foreign policy is nowhere more evident than in the debate that took place in the years 1635-1636 between Hay du Chastelet and Sirmond, the Cardinal's partisans, and Mathieu de Morgues, his chief critic. In 1635, Hay published his *Recueil de diverses pièces*, as we have noted, bringing together a large selection of the more important pro-Richelieu pamphlets and commenting upon the whole in a lengthy introduction, his last political tract.[253] Essentially, he merely summarized the arguments in the various pamphlets and reiterated the justifications of Richelieu's policies that were upheld by his most intimate and knowledgeable supporters. Morgues' answer in his *Iugement sur la préface*[254] was similarly unoriginal. His total condemnation of Richelieu's actions is adequately indicated by such queries as these:

We would be delighted to know the secret of the rupture with the Duke of Savoy . . . what hidden design underlay the war in

[251] *Ibid.*, pp. 62-64. [252] *Ibid.*, pp. 75, 101-10.
[253] See n. 157-166 and text. Du Chastelet died in 1636.
[254] See n. 167-171 and text.

Italy; what happened at the Diet of Ratisbon and whether the Cardinal negotiated in good faith; whether, at the moment when the Emperor was disarming, His Eminence called the King of Sweden into Germany and under what terms . . . the undertakings against the Empire, the extraordinary assistance that he gave the Dutch and the Swedish to ruin the House of Austria and render the Queen Mother wretched . . . the machinations to make Wallenstein a traitor after the death of the King of Sweden; the latter's aims and [proposed] division of Europe; Wallenstein's tragic end; the efforts to forestall peace in Germany; the negotiations in Constantinople.[255]

Such massive, emotional condemnation allowed no rational analysis of the principles or practices of the Cardinal's policies. Morgues had repeatedly made his points in earlier pamphlets and doubtless felt that uncritical castigation was the only instrument remaining to him. Soon after publishing the *Iugement*, therefore, Morgues penned a series of satirical pieces in which he sought to overwhelm the Cardinal through sheer weight of ridicule and invective.[256] His reason for resorting to satire he indicated in his *Catholicon françois*. Criticism of the Cardinal, he claimed, was dangerous: "To say it, even to think it is a crime against the state unless the enigma slithers along under raillery."[257] Morgues knew whereof he spoke. On June 3, 1635, the Chambre de l'Arsenal in Paris condemned him to death for plotting against the safety of the state and the Cardinal's life, when in fact his only offense was criticism of royal policy.[258] Be that as it may, his satirical works struck home on several counts. The *Ambassadeur chimérique* is an able, derisive account of an imaginary ambassador traveling from one capital to another, promising all

[255] *Iugement*, pp. 98-99.
[256] *L'Ambassadeur chimérique ou le Chercheur de dupes du Cardinal de Richelieu. Le Catholicon françois, ou Plaintes de deux chasteaux rapportées par Renaudot, Maistre du Bureau d'Adresse. Satyre d'Estat, ou Harangue faite par le Maistre du Bureau d'Adresse à son Eminence le Cardinal de Richelieu, et le Remerciment dudit Cardinal.* Perroud assigns all these works to the year 1636. All are included in *Pièces curieuses*; I have used these versions.
[257] *Catholicon*, p. 5.
[258] Fagniez, "Mathieu de Morgues et le procès de Richelieu," pp. 566-67.

things to all persons in authority, twisting facts, and constantly seeking to undo all other powers, including his own allies. Morgues' specifics were sufficiently close to the truth to give a certain appearance of veracity to his invective. And in his *Catholicon françois* he repeated many of these charges, adding such caustic comments as this concerning Richelieu's apparent manipulation of religion for political purposes:

> You make use of religion as your preceptor Machiavelli showed the ancient Romans doing, shaping it, turning it about one way after another, explaining it and applying it as far as it aids in the advancement of your designs. Your head is as ready to wear the turban as the red hat, provided the Janissaries and the Pashas find you sufficiently upright to elect you their emperor.[259]

Such satire made thoroughly enjoyable reading for many of Richelieu's contemporaries, but it did little to advance understanding of the true issues.

Once more Jean Sirmond stepped into the breach, this time with his *Advis du françois fidelle aux malcontents nouvellement retirés de la Cour*.[260] The tract was an appeal to the great of the realm, particularly Gaston d'Orléans and the Count of Soissons, who had left the court and were stirring up trouble for Louis XIII and Richelieu in the midst of a major war. Sirmond's denunciation of such disruptive tactics was a familiar one: the dissidents were placing their personal interests above those of the state, whereas the latter should always take precedence:

> They forget the concerns of their master, or rather they completely subject them to their own individual concerns and distort all public affairs according to their own interests and aims which they cover with the name of princely affairs. And under this disguise they follow their own wishes, to which they subordinate the interests of the prince and the state. They are not troubled when, if it serves their purposes, they make and break alliances,

---

[259] *Catholicon*, p. 51.
[260] N.p., 1637. Perroud also assigns this work to the year 1636.

make war and peace, fill offices and give orders at will, not for the public good but to accomplish their own designs.[261]

The problems that confronted Louis XIII and Richelieu because of such opposition were formidable and Sirmond was merely reflecting the concerns of his superiors, yet his only recourse was to urge Gaston and the others to submit to royal authority. This included, Sirmond was careful to note, complete acceptance of Richelieu's policies, since the Cardinal wielded power with royal approval. Through this simple logic, he gave Richelieu's actions all the sanctity of the royal prerogative, a position that he and others had developed earlier. Therefore to attack the minister *was* to attack the king, said Sirmond, instancing Edward II and Richard II of England.[262] Bad counsel, even deception of the ruler did not alter the legal situation, since the king was still sovereign: "I admit that the prince may be deceived or badly advised. But it is none the less the prince who commands. It is the prince persuaded."[263] Even if changes were desirable, Sirmond added, momentarily abandoning a key maxim of reason of state, bad means such as revolts should never be used for a good end: "One must join good methods to good objectives, and what is good in itself must be achieved by good means."[264] Like many of Richelieu's apologists, Sirmond would allow questionable means toward a good end only to the governing authorities; all others were limited by conventional morality. In any case, he concluded, respectful remonstrance was the only legitimate means of criticism. In no way whatsoever should dissidents "injure the sovereign authority and disturb the public peace."[265] The circle was complete: King and Cardinal alone determined official policy and must be obeyed, whereas all others should be submissive subjects regardless of any misuse of power.

Mathieu de Morgues answered this restatement of pro-Richelieu absolutism with a well-argued reiteration of its opposite in his *Derniers advis à la France par un bon Chrestien et fidele citoyen*.[266]

---

[261] *Advis*, p. 6.   [262] *Ibid.*, pp. 12, 14.   [263] *Ibid.*, p. 13.
[264] *Ibid.*, p. 19.   [265] *Ibid.*, pp. 21, 24.
[266] N.p., 1636. I have used the version in the *Pièces curieuses*.

His opening passage condemned the Cardinal's foreign policy as utterly disastrous:

> His anger has brought the Goths into the state; his madness has called the Poles, Cossacks, Croats, and Hungarians into France and has brought us enemies, wars, and disorders such as France has never seen since her beginning. He causes foreigners to complete the pillage that he began in France and brings seizures, massacres, and desolation to all areas that he does not control.[267]

This Morgues followed with a vivid description of the miseries of all elements of French society—the royal family, the princes of the blood, clergy, nobility, officials, and common people—*and* an appeal to all, from the King to the lowest peasant and city dweller, to rise up and forcibly remove the cause of France's ills:

> All good Frenchmen, open your eyes to see what a miserable condition you are in; open your minds to foresee the great desolation that menaces you. Do not permit a puny man, sick in body and mind, to tyrannize over the bodies and minds of so many sane persons, nor an apostate monk [Father Joseph], his principal counsellor, to treat you as galley-slaves. Cast off these two evil instruments. If the King, prevented by artifices that are too strong, does not break his chains and yours, boldly loosen them; you will not lose the respect that you owe the sovereign by saving his person, his state, and yourselves. Not only will you protect your lives from death, your goods from pillage, and your friends from oppression; you will acquire great glory before men and much merit before God. All these benefits will reach you when you courageously remove the true cause of all your ills.[268]

The divergence between the views of Morgues and Sirmond of Richelieu and his policies was total. Their debate had long ago passed the point of rational analysis and ended in a complete polarization of positions regarding means, ends, and their implementation.

[267] *Derniers advis*, p. 98.   [268] *Ibid.*, p. 108.

For Morgues, Richelieu's reason of state and accompanying procedures were morally reprehensible and brought unmitigated disaster, while for Sirmond the Cardinal could do no wrong. Such were the end-positions to which both men adhered throughout the remainder of Richelieu's life. Although both continued to publish tracts reiterating their convictions, neither subsequently added anything significant to his earlier contentions.

The mid-1630's also witnessed the appearance of a number of pro-Richelieu treatises by lesser writers, both lay and ecclesiastical, arguing the compatibility of state interests and true religion—the issue that was rapidly becoming the main focus of political discussion throughout France. Unlike Sirmond and Morgues, these publicists did not debate specific points but simply presented a massive, unqualified case for the justice of official policy according to religious morality. Invariably the king is lauded to the skies and Richelieu is praised as his incredibly able and inspired instrument. One of the most straightforward works of this type was the book by Pierre Blanchot, whose very title indicates its nature and purpose.[269] Blanchot was a layman, a lesser provincial jurist, *avocat du roi* at Arnay-le-Duc in Burgundy, but it is noteworthy that his work received clerical approval.[270] It was written before 1632, the date of his death, but was not published until 1635. Three comparable tracts of varying length and similar argumentation also appeared in the same period.[271] All the latter were by clerics and carried Blanchot's extravagances even further.

[269] *Le Diurnal des Roys et Conseillers d'Estat, où sont les maximes extraictes de l'Escriture*, Lyon, 1635.

[270] At the end of the book: Approved by Fr. Bern Mollaison, "licentié théologien en l'Université de Paris" and "Lecteur Iubilé" at the Convent of the Cordeliers in Lyon.

[271] Hélie Poirier, *Discours panégyrique du bonheur de la France sous le règne de Louis le Juste*, Paris, 1635. *Deux Discours pour le Roy, faits en avril, 1632, par M.D.B.*, Paris, 1635. D.P.C., *Le vray Prince et le bon sujet contenant l'unique méthode pour bien gouverner les peuples par les veritables maximes de religion et d'estat, les qualitez qui doivent accompagner un prince*, Paris, 1636. Both anonymous works are dedicated to Richelieu. The latter may have been written in answer to Jansenius' *Mars Gallicus*, but I have found no proof of this.

At the outset, Blanchot stated that his purpose was to "confirm the opinion which you [the king's councillors] share with upright men, that those who say that maxims of state are contrary to religion have erred. For I shall demonstrate by my discourse that they are founded on Scripture, both the Old and New Testament, for otherwise this would be a tyrannical type of state which could not long subsist."[272] Specific examples and political truisms are to be avoided, he said, because circumstances constantly change. "This is why one must constantly seek guidance from the Holy Spirit in order to recognize the heart of the matter and to answer questions when they are presented. One will obtain this guidance if he is devoted to Her who is its Dispenser, the Virgin Mother of God and the Temple of the Holy Spirit."[273] In implementing this position, Blanchot proposed a regime of enlightened, absolute royalism. God created man in his own image, endowing man with special powers and a sense of justice, but among men He gave special knowledge and power to the king, the image of God. The king by definition therefore sets the standard for all others below him; such is the first support of monarchy.[274] The others are his good councillors who should be able, devoted servants and work solely for the glory of the king, the laws of the state which are made and enforced by the king according to circumstances and the canons of justice, and his good relations with his allies and confederates regardless of their religion.[275] The latter item Blanchot undoubtedly included because of the nature of Richelieu's foreign policy. Repeatedly applying such epithets as *ange du grand conseil* and *cet ange incarné* to the Cardinal, Blanchot defended his alliances with heretic powers to the hilt. Such measures are dictated both by self-preservation and Christian duty, he insisted. Is it not required of all to befriend and succor one's neighbors regardless of their beliefs? Scripture gives many examples of this on both the personal and political levels, from the parable of the good Samaritan to the alliance of the Romans and

[272] *Diurnal*, dedicatory epistle, "Aux Courtisans." N.p.

[273] *Diurnal*, *loc.cit.*   [274] *Ibid.*, Chap. 1.

[275] Chaps. 4-6 treat the royal councillors and officials, Chap. 7 the laws, and Chap. 8 the king's alliances.

the Machabees. Not that the king should entirely trust his heretic allies; with them he should always be on his guard. But true religion permits and entirely justifies such mechanisms.[276]

Blanchot then turned logically to defining a just war and found three types to be sanctioned by Scripture: war against the infidel, against a ruler who has mistreated one's ambassadors, and to resist aggression. In waging such wars, he continued, all manner of ruses and stratagems are justified, but the best ruse of all is to have God and right on one's side, that is, to fight for a just cause, for God alone gives victory.[277] The justice of the king's policies, however, should never be questioned by the subjects whose only legitimate role is one of complete obedience. As reapers gather the harvest under the sun, so should subjects obey their prince. Holy Scripture teaches that obedience should be "without distinction or exception, signifying by the term absolute that the king's command is absolute, without criticism or contradiction."[278] God gave the power of life and death over rebels to kings "because being chosen and called by God and anointed and consecrated, they are undeniably aided by the Holy Spirit."[279] Again citing Scripture, Blanchot maintained that the Holy Spirit inspired the King and his council in their decisions so that even if the king were to command something contrary to religion, "I would obey . . . because I believe and know very well that he will not and cannot proceed . . . without the aid of the Holy Spirit which presides in this body . . . . If we must obey the king in the spiritual sphere as far as it is within his power, so much the more [we should obey him] in the temporal over which his power is particularly applied."[280]

In this way, Blanchot extended the divine sanction and inspiration of monarchy beyond the king even to his councillors, and there is no doubt that Blanchot developed the position in order to present the strongest possible defense of Richelieu's policies. The equation of Louis XIII and his First Minister, and the justification of their common policies, especially in foreign affairs, could be carried no

[276] *Ibid.*, Chap. 8.
[277] *Ibid.*, Chaps. 12, 17.
[278] *Ibid.*, pp. 70-71.
[279] *Ibid.*, p. 71.
[280] *Ibid.*, pp. 72-73.

further. It followed, of course, that all opposition by the subjects should be met with the greatest possible dispatch. In one of his final chapters, Blanchot analyzed various means of handling treason and traitors.[281] The best, he said, was for the ruler to beseech God twice daily for protection, since God provides this through the Holy Spirit and preserves good princes. But since we are dealing with human affairs and should not tempt Providence, the prince should assume that every man is a fierce beast of prey seeking liberty, and that traitors wear sheep's clothing, insinuating themselves into the king's good graces in order to strike more quickly. The remedy, of course, was immediate seizure of the guilty, after which consideration might be given the method of punishment. The latter should be prompt, degrading, and an object lesson for others. All such measures stemmed entirely from the prudence of the prince, Blanchot added, entirely ignoring the issue of legal justice.

In this fashion, Blanchot posited not a legal but a religious basis of absolute monarchy. Although a minor publication in its time, his work is a valuable, representative example of argumentation predicated upon the religious bases of the state and shows how religious precepts might be used to justify any and all measures that the king and his minister, in their superior wisdom, might deem necessary for the good of the state. For Blanchot, divinely inspired reason of state was synonymous with good government, since the acts of king and minister were *ipso facto* just. That the position was widespread among Richelieu's supporters is evident from its appearance in many similar writings during this period of his ministry.[282]

[281] *Ibid.*, Chap. 15.

[282] See n. 271. The following are examples. "If the eyes of God are on the just and his ears attentive to their prayers, where would his ancient mercies be if He did not see in our king the image of his justice as well as his power, and if He did not harken to the wishes of this just one who lives of the faith and in the faith of the Son of God?" *Deux discours* . . . , p. 59. Also: "It is true that with the aid of Him for whom kings reign, he [Louis XIII] has become absolute within and arbitor without his state, that he has weakened the erring, suppressed the rebellious, aided the oppressed, and checked the violence of those who put their trust in their chariots and their horses, that is, their arms. But it is also true that in all this he is the cooperator and coadjutor of God, and that his grace has not been useless to him since he has made the

By far the most resounding controversy of the mid- and later 1630's concerning Richelieu's foreign policy was that which was precipitated by the *Mars Gallicus* of the renowned Jansenius whose political views closely paralleled those of the *dévot* faction. The dispute began innocently enough with the publication in 1634 of Besian Arroy's book, *Questions décidées sur la justice des armes des Roys de France*, which was written for the express purpose of defending the French alliances with Protestant powers.[283] Arroy was a minor theologian who studied at the Sorbonne, became lecturer on divinity at the church in Lyon in 1634, and was later appointed Archbishop of Lyon. Although he wrote a variety of religious and historical works, he was not an able writer and is remembered chiefly because he was partially instrumental in stirring Jansenius to action. In his political tracts, Arroy did little but reiterate in mechanical fashion many of the usual justifications of Richelieu's policies, yet his works have a certain value as statements of this position. Whether Richelieu personally accepted all of Arroy's more extravagant assertions may be doubted, but he was quite willing to permit their publication in support of his foreign policy.

For the reader's benefit, Arroy summarized his defense of Richelieu's alliance system at the outset under these heads: (1) Louis XIII is not only sovereign but his sovereignty is superior to that of all other rulers; (2) his intentions are just because he fights to preserve the peace of the realm and religion, and to defend his friends and allies; and (3) the legality and justice of his claims ensure that he fights a just war.[284] The body of the work consists of exhaustive implementation of these positions. Regarding Louis XIII's superior sovereignty, Arroy reiterated the accepted doctrine of direct divine

---

most of it." *Ibid.*, p. 108. The anonymous work, *Le vray Prince et le bon sujet . . .* , is almost 1,000 pages in length, treats many of these same topics, and is extremely extravagant in its praise of absolutism grounded in religion.

[283] *Questions décidées sur la justice des armes des Roys de France, sur les alliances avec les hérétiques ou infideles et sur la conduite de la conscience des gens de guerre*, Paris, 1634. Although Arroy chiefly discussed political problems, his major authority was St. Thomas Aquinas. On Arroy's book, see Jover, pp. 60-71.

[284] *Questions décidées*, pp. 12-16.

right of kings but with a new twist. "Kings are the images of God on earth. They reign by his divine power and have no power but from Him."[285] But after comparing God to the sun whose rays strike earthlings unequally, Arroy continued: "Likewise, sovereign power moves from God to monarchs with greater or lesser abundance according to their nearness to Him and the extent to which they dispose themselves to receive it or erect barriers to weaken it."[286] As evidence of the superior degree of divine favor that was enjoyed by Louis XIII, Arroy cited the coronation with holy oil from the sacred ampula, the resulting corporeal and spiritual changes in the ruler, his power to cure scrofula, his title of Most Christian, and the Salic Law which, while not itself divine law, was based upon it.[287] As for the justice of the present war, Arroy argued that the Salic Law gave Louis XIII rightful title to all lands held by Charlemagne, cited the inalienability of the royal domain, the justice of French claims according to the law of peoples, and then detailed French claims to the Empire, Flanders, Artois, Milan, Sicily, Lorraine, Spain, Portugal, Castille, Aragon, Catalonia, Majorca, and Navarre![288] After all this, Arroy concluded, Louis XIII's intentions must be just. He nevertheless added a final section defending French alliances with heretic powers with the following arguments. They are justified by Biblical precedents. Even a heretic may be of service if he is used for a good cause. Where heretics are tolerated by law, they may enter into contracts and other agreements. St. Thomas says that even infidels may do good. Alliances with them do not involve a union of religions and so will not benefit heresy. The latter should be extirpated but this will occur only if God wills it; we can best serve Catholicism by serving the king.[289] And Arroy added the usual prohibitions against enquiring into royal policy. The book, in sum, presents a mishmash of arguments that were very disparate but were widely accepted in various forms among Richelieu's supporters, including the strongly Gallican Faculty of Theology which approved its publication.

Such assertions were apparently too much for Jansenius, and he

[285] *Ibid.*, p. 17.   [286] *Ibid.*   [287] *Ibid.*, pp. 21-84.
[288] *Ibid.*, pp. 89-189.   [289] *Ibid.*, pp. 190-200.

at once replied with his *Mars Gallicus,* his most important political tract, which he published in 1635 under the pseudonym, Alexandre Patricius Armacanus, theologian.[290] Successive editions of the work appeared in 1636 and 1637, but it was only after a French translation by Charles Hersent appeared in the latter year[291] that Richelieu arranged for the publication of officially inspired rebuttals. The fact that he allowed two years to elapse before seeking to counteract the influence of this expert and cogent critique of his foreign policy indicates his much greater sense of security as Louis XIII's First Minister than he enjoyed a decade earlier, yet the appearance of the French translation of Jansenius' work he found sufficiently disturbing to warrant extensive replies.

As might be expected, Jansenius' approach to the legitimacy and justice of royal policy was based squarely upon the unqualified supremacy of religious values, specifically those inherent in both the doctrine and interests of international Catholicism. His position therefore was simple and uncompromising—much more so than that of Richelieu and his supporters—and his criticism of the Cardinal was correspondingly penetrating. It undoubtedly held a wide appeal for many thoughtful readers. In his preface, Jansenius at once asserted that all true Catholics deplored the French policy of warring against the defenders of Catholicism in alliance with heretics, and cited Arroy's book as a horrible example of specious justification. Instead, Jansenius maintained, he would seek the truth concerning the present state of affairs, for truth is superior to all mortals, even princes. "I well know that we should respect and fear kings, but I also well know that we are not less bound by the truth. Besides, this shameful flattery which causes us to hide their vices and faults that are clear to everyone cannot be called fear or respect. It is more respectful to expose and criticize them with modesty and

---

[290] *Alexandri Patricii Armacani, theologi Mars gallicus, seu de justitia armorum, et federum regis galiae libri duo,* n.p., 1635.

[291] *Le Mars François ou la guerre de France, en laquelle sont examinées les raisons de la justice prétendue des armes et des alliances du Roy de France, mises au jour par Alexandre Patricius Armacanus, théologien, et traduites de la troisième édition par C.H.D.P.D.E.T.B.,* n.p., 1637.

discretion, as Christian charity commands."[292] Jansenius also was careful to note that he was criticizing actions, not persons, but he unflinchingly maintained that while men might dissimulate and defend externals in human affairs, they remained troubled in their consciences. Such hypocrisy Jansenius found not only offensive but morally wrong, for truth and conscience must always agree.

Having taken this rigid but theologically sound position, Jansenius presented an elaborate point-by-point refutation of Arroy's defense of French foreign policy. The first portion of Jansenius' work discounted Arroy's arguments in support of the superior sovereignty and greater prestige of Louis XIII among the sovereigns of Europe. Carefully examining the coronation and anointment at Reims, the royal touch, the title of Most Christian, and the Salic Law, Jansenius admitted their significance but denied that they gave the King of France any superiority over other rulers. As for French claims to Charlemagne's empire, he found these specious, both because the various provinces of the early empire were not closely united under a single crown and because the subsequent titles of various rulers to many portions were valid on the basis of prescription. Any war that was fought for such reasons was manifestly unjust, he claimed, particularly one that benefited heresy. And tipping his hand, he rejected the familiar French argument that the Spanish used religious proselytizing to cloak their territorial ambitions. Is it not better, he asked, to extend the true faith and Spanish dominion than to wage war which benefits heresy merely because of some fancied danger that the French will be oppressed by a superior power?[293]

Jansenius thereupon went to the heart of the matter by examining and rejecting the habitual French justifications of their alliances with heretic powers. The century has witnessed endless questioning of truth in all fields, especially moral and religious, he lamented, citing Arroy's book as particularly offensive because it not only sought to defend but purported to justify alliances that injured the faith and benefited heresy. On the contrary, Jansenius proposed to examine the matter in the pure light of religious truth and justice.

[292] *Ibid.*, Preface, n.p.   [293] *Ibid.* (p. 113).

"One needs but a small ray of God's grace to distinguish what is just from what is not, what is true from what has only its appearance, what is pious from that which is mere irreligion and hypocrisy."[294] Biblical precedents are irrelevant to the present situation, he claimed. It is a simple matter of principle.

Standing foresquare on this dogmatic but unchallengeable position, Jansenius then set forth his critique of Richelieu's foreign policy as injurious to the true faith. After dwelling at length upon the widespread notion that heresy and rebellion went hand in hand,[295] he asserted that the primary objective of the Swedes and the Dutch was religious in that they sought above all else to advance their heresy by injuring the Spanish, the defenders of Catholicism. The predominant motive force in the present conflict was therefore religious, and the war was in this sense a true war of religion.[296] For this reason, the French soldiers who were sent against the Spanish risked eternal damnation if they followed orders. "It means nothing to reply that subjects must obey without scruple the commands of their king even though they have the appearance of injustice, for there are some so obviously unjust that neither the power of kings nor the authority of doctors who support them may justify them. This is what caused St. Gregory of Nazianzus to say *Be faithful to the king but first to God*, and the Apostle, *We must obey God rather than man*."[297] Certain theologians, Jansenius continued, say "the king did it; it is therefore just . . . but immutable truth condemns some crimes aloud in the souls of those who commit them."[298] Clearly, the argument of the extreme absolutists that the ruler's acts were *ipso facto* just carried no weight with Jansenius. He even claimed personal knowledge of disobedience by French soldiers who refused to fire on their coreligionists in Germany and the Low Countries. "For even the ignorant and the lower classes can easily see that this is not a war of state but of religion and rebellion, and

[294] *Ibid.* (p. 193).
[295] *Ibid.*, Bk. II, Chaps. 2-8. Jansenius cited the Dutch and the Bohemians as outstanding examples.
[296] *Ibid.*, Bk. II, Chaps. 10, 12.
[297] *Ibid.* (pp. 258-59). Italics in the original.
[298] *Ibid.* (p. 259).

that it is not waged for the defense of some rights but to maintain a dastardly perfidy which can no more be sanctioned by Catholic kings and soldiers than theft, sacrilege, or adultery."[299] The clear implication was that French policy was utterly contrary to immutable Christian principles and that all true believers should resist it.

Continuing, Jansenius examined the many ways in which Louis XIII was both directly and indirectly responsible for damage to the Catholic faith. Indirectly, the case was clear.[300] The King of France may not actively seek the destruction of churches and the faith, but such are the results of his policies in Germany and the Low Countries because he supports those who perpetrate such deeds. Interests of state do *not* justify the policies that aid and abet such disasters:

> Let the King of France and all good Catholics consider whether the interests that are alleged to justify the alliances which have been made with heretics are so important that the Catholic Church and even Jesus Christ, her Bridegroom, are more compelled to suffer sacrilege and ruin of the Catholic religion than France [is obliged] to break these alliances and refuse the aid that they have brought. Do they believe that a secular, perishable state should outweigh religion and the Church? ... Should not the Most Christian King believe that in the guidance and administration of his realm there is nothing that obliges him to extend and protect that of Jesus Christ, his Lord? ... Would he dare say to God: Let your power and glory and the religion which teaches men to adore You be lost and destroyed, provided my state is protected and free of risks?[301]

And Jansenius expatiated at length on the religious nature and obligations of the Most Christian King. Directly as well, French policies favored the spread of heresy, Jansenius claimed, asserting that anything which enabled non-Catholic rulers to extend their dominions injured the faith. The provisions in French treaties guaranteeing protection for Catholics in conquered areas were worthless, since these same treaties aided the expansion of heretic power and per-

[299] *Ibid.* (pp. 259-60).   [300] *Ibid.*, Bk. ii, Chaps. 13-24.
[301] *Ibid.* (pp. 293-94).

mitted diversity of religion, the worst thing on earth.[302] And Jansenius concluded his work with a multitude of citations, chiefly scriptural, in support of his position. His attack upon Richelieu, although the latter was unnamed, was clear when he deplored the burden of kings who "heed the counsels of men more readily than those of God, because the former give indication of immediate gain whereas the latter offer nothing but expectation and hope."[303] Instead of yielding to the blandishments of dissimulating, self-seeking ministers, kings should commend themselves to God and forever reign for the benefit of his Church.

Such was the consistent, single-minded, expert critique with which Jansenius sought to discredit Richelieu's foreign policy and war for the benefit of the French state. From his dogmatic, uncompromising viewpoint, Jansenius' denunciation was indeed devastating, and there is no doubt that it found a sympathetic response among the many of Richelieu's contemporaries who placed religious values above all else. Of course, it may easily be shown that Jansenius quite ignored such practical, mundane problems as the nature of the interstate relations that confronted Louis XIII and Richelieu as well as the counterarguments from the religious nature and purposes of the French state itself. He simply asserted that Catholic kings should seek first and always the Kingdom of God by supporting the cause of international Catholicism. In essence, Jansenius' argumentation was remarkably similar to that of the Jesuit *Admonitio* a decade earlier—a similarity which reflects one of the rare points of agreement between Jansenist and Jesuit during the century. The continuing preponderance of religious considerations in political thinking has no better illustration in the period. And it was undoubtedly for this reason that Richelieu felt constrained to provide the reading public with a series of rebuttals.

Richelieu and his supporters fully realized that any convincing answer to the *Mars Gallicus* must argue the justice of the French cause from the standpoint of religious morality rather than mere advantage. For long, both the French and the Spanish had defended their respective policies in this manner, but more than a decade of

[302] *Ibid.*, Bk. II, Chaps. 25-30.   [303] *Ibid.* (p. 445).

debate had fully demonstrated that their common loyalty to the Church of Rome and its doctrines did not ensure agreement concerning the conduct of politics. Christian morality was by definition universal and exclusive, yet the French and Spanish both claimed to observe it while prosecuting utterly divergent and mutually antagonistic foreign policies. Clearly the problem of higher law and its relevance to government was involved, and many observers began to feel that such different interpretations of Christian justice by two nations that claimed to adhere to identical religious ideals must reflect some fundamental differences between the two peoples themselves. Could it be that one nation was more genuinely Christian than the other? Richelieu seems to have been intrigued by the idea that the French and Spanish, for all their common religious principles and loyalties, differed in the nature of their piety. Soon after the appearance of the *Mars Gallicus*, La Mothe le Vayer published a tract in which he sought to explain the chronic hostilities between the French and Spanish by pointing to the natural differences that separated the two peoples.[304] The accidents of geography and climate, he urged, accounted for many of their divergent traits of character and served as perpetual sources of friction.[305] Since this natural basis of enmity was ineradicable, he continued, one must examine the record without prejudice in order to determine the extent to which each people has followed the precepts of justice. The

[304] *Discours de la contrariété d'humeurs qui se trouve entre certaines nations, et singulièrement entre la françoise et l'espagnole, traduit de l'italien de Fabricio Campolini, Veronais*, Paris, 1636. In La Mothe le Vayer, *Œuvres*, Paris, 1662, Vol. I, 157-91. My citations are to this version. The work is dedicated to Richelieu with an extremely flattering dedicatory epistle. It is not a translation from the Italian but La Mothe le Vayer's own.

[305] The French are gay, open, hospitable, generous, religious, unceremonious, and good horsemen, but inconstant, full of wit, talkative, slanderous toward their compatriots when abroad, unable to endure hunger and the other inconveniences of war, fighting more with strength of body than of mind and with more ferocity than deception or plan. Completely opposite, the Spanish are melancholy, dissembling, inhospitable, avaricious, superstitious, and obtrusively polite, but steadfast, poised, taciturn, esteeming each other when abroad, good in infantry, able to endure hunger, thirst, and all the hardships of war, achieving more by the head than the hand, and doing more by ruse and stratagem than pure force. (*Discours*, p. 167.)

bulk of his treatise therefore merely recited the innumerable instances in which the Spanish had covered their aggression with a cloak of religion. For more than a century it had been but a monstrous chronicle of war, bloodshed, and terror throughout Europe and the New World. By comparison the greater justice of French policy he found self-evident.

There is no evidence that Richelieu solicited this explanation of the endemic Franco-Spanish hostilities and the greater justice of the French cause. In any case, shortly after the appearance of the French translation of the *Mars Gallicus*, he personally requested Denis Cohon, Bishop of Nîmes, to write a tract on the different qualities of French and Spanish piety.[306] Bishop Cohon was one of

---

[306] *En Quoy la Piété des François diffère de celle des Espagnols dans une profession de mesme Religion.* (Written early in 1638.) In E. Griselle, ed., *Documents d'histoire*, Paris, 1911, Vol. II, 547-66. Cohon's authorship of this tract seems certain, but various writers continue to ascribe it to La Mothe le Vayer, apparently because no one has realized that only a single work is involved and that the texts which are attributed respectively to Cohon and La Mothe le Vayer are identical. Attribution of the work to La Mothe le Vayer resulted from the following circumstances. It was published anonymously in Paris in 1658, with a notice by the editor to the effect that although the tract was an anti-Spanish work that was written under Louis XIII at the order of Cardinal Richelieu, it was equally appropriate to current French foreign policy in view of the recent French alliance with England against Spain. Both the tract and the notice were incorporated into the third edition of La Mothe le Vayer's *Œuvres*, Paris, 1662, Vol. I. Modern works that discuss La Mothe le Vayer's pamphleteering in support of Richelieu attribute the tract to La Mothe le Vayer on the strength of its inclusion in the *Œuvres*. Wickelgren (pp. 128-32) accepts La Mothe le Vayer's authorship, although noting that the work departs from his usually dispassionate, rational style and shows much more emotion than was his wont when criticizing the Spanish. The attribution to La Mothe le Vayer is preserved in A. Cioranescu, *Bibliographie de la littérature française du dix-septième siècle*, Paris, 1965-1966. On the other hand, there is conclusive evidence that the tract was the work of Bishop Cohon. The Bibliothèque Mazarine's MS. 2001 contains a complete copy of the work which is introduced by the listing: "Traitté composé par M. Cohon Evesque de Nismes après en avoir reçu l'ordre de Mons. le Card. de Richelieu," and ends with the statement, "Commencé le 28 Janvier 1638 que je receu l'ordre et achevé le 7 febvrier suivant." The entire tract is printed in E. Griselle, ed., *Documents d'histoire*, Paris, 1911, Vol. II, 547-66. A comparison of this text with that in La Mothe le Vayer's *Œuvres* immediately reveals that the two are identical. As for the provenience of the manuscript in the Bibliothèque Maza-

Richelieu's friends and his staunch supporter in the Assembly of the Clergy.[307] His treatise, which he wrote in less than two weeks, was similar to La Mothe le Vayer's in surveying the historical record of Spanish policy and emphasizing the falsity of Spanish claims to uphold the cause of Catholic Christianity. French kings since Pepin and Charlemagne, he insisted, had consistently supported the papacy, whereas Charles V and Philip II habitually resisted it and placed advantage above all else. "It is in this way that reason of state prevailed in the minds of these princes over that of religion. This did not, however, prevent their having some good and pure sentiments [in matters] other than political considerations, but in any event one cannot deny that the temporal has always prevailed over the spiritual in the principal acts of their government."[308] The tract then discusses the different objectives of the French and Spanish in making alliances with heretics and infidels. Such alliances are licit and are made by all parties, even popes, he said, but the French, unlike the Spanish, take care to preserve the rights of Catholicism in all such transactions. The Spanish even have the temerity to criticize the most Christian king in the world, Louis XIII, who has repeatedly been favored by God and whose policies have been more advantageous to true religion than those of all his predecessors.[309] Cohon believed that this last point completed his case, but his tract did little but repeat stock arguments and apparently failed to please Richelieu, since it remained unpublished until well after his death.

---

rine, the Abbé François Duine, who did more research on Cohon than any other modern scholar and was thoroughly familiar with his handwriting, states categorically that "Ce traité est écrit de la main même de Cohon." F. Duine, *Un Politique et un orateur au XVIIe siècle. Cohon, Evêque de Nîmes et de Dol. Essai de bibliographie avec documents inédits*, Rennes, 1902, p. 46. Duine's familiarity with Cohon's extensive manuscript remains is adequately indicated in his study, "Avant Bossuet. Cohon: Evêque de Nîmes et de Dol, précepteur des neveux de Mazarin, prédicateur du roi," *Bulletin de la commission historique et archéologique de la Mayenne*, XXIII (1907), 407-28; XXIV (1908), 55-116, 141-86. (Also printed separately.) It seems clear therefore that this tract was the work of Bishop Cohon rather than La Mothe le Vayer in spite of its inclusion in the latter's *Œuvres*.

[307] *Lettres*, Vol. V, 328-29.   [308] *En Quoy la Pieté* . . . , p. 557.
[309] *Ibid.*, p. 563.

The Cardinal had failed to find a justification of French foreign policy in the superior qualities of French piety. As an answer to the *Mars Gallicus*, Cohon's pamphlet was indeed inadequate. Bessian Arroy, whose book had sparked Jansenius' effort, also composed an answer which appeared in 1639 and lamely reiterated his earlier contentions concerning the anointment of French kings during their coronation, the holy ampula, the royal touch, their title of Most Christian, and their precedence over the Kings of Spain.[310] His book added nothing of value and neglected to discuss the main point at issue—French alliances with heretic powers in a war against Spain—possibly because the subject had already been dealt with by the man who was by far the ablest writer to answer Jansenius' challenge.

This was Daniel de Priézac, a provincial jurist who had succeeded by sheer ability in establishing himself in the highest circles in the capital. Beginning as a very brilliant student of law at the University of Bordeaux and then teaching the subject with great success at the same institution, his renown spread throughout Europe and in 1635 he was brought to Paris by none other than Chancellor Séguier who secured his appointment as a councillor of state. In 1638, the year after the appearance of the French translation of the *Mars Gallicus*, Priézac published his *Vindiciæ Gallicæ adversus Alexandrum Patricium Armacanum theologum*[311] which was on all counts the ablest and most significant French response to Jansenius' work. In 1639 appeared a French translation of Priézac's book by Jean Baudoin,[312] and early in the same year Priézac was made a member of the French Academy, at least partially in recognition of his success in answering the *Mars Gallicus*. Priézac's close ties with the royal administration

---

[310] *Le Mercure espagnol, ou Discours contenans les responses faites à vn libelle intitulé Mars François, fabriqué par un sujet des Espagnols, se donnant le nom supposé d'Alexandre Patrice Armacan, et à faux le tiltre de Théologien: Ensemble les remarques de la Religion, prétexte des Espagnols, dans l'avant discours, et un rapport entre les François et les Espagnols, à la fin de ce Livre. Pour la gloire des Roys de France et de la nation Françoise*, n.p., 1639.

[311] Paris, 1638.

[312] *Défence des droits et prérogatives des Roys de France*, Paris, Chez Pierre Rocolet, Imprimeur et Libraire ordinaire du Roy, 1639. My citations are to this edition.

and his appointment to the Academy are sure indications that his book presented the official view and had the Cardinal's approval.[313] Also, very fortunately, his work analyzes elements of the doctrine of reason of state which were implicit in the concept but were rarely examined by the writers of the period. Priézac's book therefore is one of the most valuable studies of reason of state to be published with Richelieu's sanction during the later years of his tenure of power.

To Jansenius' charge that the French, through their alliances with heretics and open warfare against the Hapsburgs, were aiding the cause of heresy and destroying both Christianity and the Church, Priézac answered by placing great emphasis upon the Christian character of the French state and the consequent religious justifications of royal policy. In fact, the greater part of his well-constructed volume he devoted to this theme, which he rightly considered the most effective answer to Jansenius. At the outset, Priézac struck the desired note by emphasizing the great services of the French kings to the Christian cause: "He is blind who does not see Christianity's great debt to them; he is ungrateful who seeing them does not praise them; he is mad who resists when one extols them."[314] The Spanish may be Christians like ourselves, he continued, but they merely cloak their conquests with a cover of religion, "the most deceptive in effect and the most plausible in appearance."[315] But truth and justice, Priézac insisted, give the lie to the self-appointed censors of our kings and exonerate "these illustrious defenders of the glory of the French, these heroes of history in which the memory of their name is forever dear. Can we hear, without our ears being offended, so many falsehoods and calumnies against these immortal demigods?"[316]

In developing his defense of French foreign policy, Priézac not only stressed the Christian character of the French kings and their

[313] The privilege of the French translation of Priézac's work is dated February 18, 1639. Four days later he was nominated to the French Academy.
[314] Priézac, *Defence*, p. 5.
[315] *Ibid.*, p. 7.　　　　[316] *Ibid.*, p. 18.

state but reached the point of claiming that the French monarchy was the most genuinely Christian in all Europe. First, he took up once more the much disputed religious attributes of the French rulers—the miraculous effects of their anointment during the coronation, the resulting inward changes in the rulers' abilities and character, the holy ampula, and the royal touch—and reiterated the most thoroughgoing traditional interpretation of these accompaniments of kingship, all for the purpose of upholding the sanctity and quasi-divine character of the long line of French monarchs.[317] More important to his justification of royal policy was his examination of the French kings' titles, "Most Christian" and "Eldest Son of the Church" in relation to the Spanish "His Catholic Majesty." His approach was not to deny the significance of these titles but to ask whether they were deserved. In answering this question, Priézac devoted almost a third of his volume to examining innumerable historical events, recent and remote, in order to demonstrate the great and heroic deeds of the French for religion and the Church over the centuries in war and peace, within the realm and abroad, arguing that the record was without equal. On the contrary, he claimed, the Spanish had been thoroughly hypocritical in their actions, always seeking to extend their dominions under the guise of religious proselytizing.[318] The Kings of Spain therefore hardly deserved to be called "Catholic" whereas the French line had truly served the interests of the Church. Again Priézac's exaggerations are evident, but the weight that he ascribed to religious factors is crystal clear.

Turning to the much more practical matter of the French alliances, Priézac built his case squarely upon the constant, insatiable aggression of the Hapsburgs and their desire for universal monarchy. The deeds of earlier Hapsburg rulers, especially Charles V, he recounted with relish, whereupon he insisted that France, because of her central geographical position, was the natural defender of the oppressed and the only effective barrier to Hapsburg universal dominion. Thus it was France's appointed role to preserve justice

[317] *Ibid.*, Chaps. 2-5.   [318] *Ibid.*, Chaps. 6-14.

by protecting the weak.[319] And this in turn had direct bearing upon the sanctity of Louis XIII's alliances with other anti-Hapsburg powers:

> We are entirely certain that our treaties with our allies are not contrary to the laws of nature or divine or human law. As for the first, which is natural law, we well know that it permits us to defend our allies, our goods and our lives with all manner of arms without distinction [according to] religion, to the point that in case the state is threatened with ruin, it is an act of prudence to sustain it with foreign help if this cannot be done otherwise.[320]

More extensive was Priézac's insistence that divine law likewise sanctioned treaties with heretics for defensive purposes, and here he cited at length the usual Biblical precedents.[321] Again, Priézac took great care to demonstrate that French policy did not violate higher law. "What evil has he [Louis XIII] done by having ties and counsel with Protestants and promising to aid them under certain conditions? Surely, since he did this for the defense and security of his state, *in this case justice and good faith are inviolate.*"[322]

Regarding the French alliance with the Dutch, Priézac simply maintained that it was to the mutual interest of the two threatened powers.[323] Answering Jansenius' charge that Louis XIII supported the Dutch as rebels against the Spanish, thus favoring both heresy and sedition, Priézac countered: "In the aid that we give them, we do not consider them as heretics and enemies of our faith but only as our friends, neighbors, and allies. For in this we are concerned only with the public good and generally that of all Christendom."[324] While maintaining that the French were conducting their foreign policy in accordance with Christian principles, Priézac was nevertheless approaching the position that alliances were made without regard to religion, at least when mutual defense against aggression was their objective. And in fact he proceeded to demonstrate this

---

[319] *Ibid.*, Chap. 18.   [320] *Ibid.*, p. 309.   [321] *Ibid.*, Chaps. 20-22.
[322] *Ibid.*, pp. 313-14. Italics in the original.
[323] *Ibid.*, Chap. 24.   [324] *Ibid.*, p. 370.

irrelevance of religion at length by recounting such instances as Spanish aid to the Huguenot rebels, appeals by the German Protestant princes to the French kings for aid against the Hapsburgs, and many others. Since all powers seem to conduct their foreign policy in this fashion, he concluded, blame should fall on all or none, but not the King of France alone.[325] Such was Priézac's common-sense answer to Jansenius, which distinctly reflected European realities.

> Extreme necessity . . . rejects no type of help, and without offending one's conscience or scruples, one may make alliances with infidels. The reason is that in this one merely enters into communication of purposes, supplies, and forces, but not religion. For in reality, faith is not exchanged, and these alliances concern only the security of peoples, the preservation of states, and the public tranquility.[326]

Such an assertion went far toward separating foreign policy from religious concerns. That Priézac viewed the alliances in question merely as instruments for the preservation of the state according to the exigencies of necessity is clear, and to this extent he recognized the secularization of policy. This does not mean, however, that he suddenly divorced acts of government from religious values. He merely recognized that in case of dire emergency, that is, aggression from abroad, both natural and divine law condoned alliances with enemies of the true faith as necessary practical expedients. The fundamental objectives of policy and the religious nature of the state whose defense was entrusted to the ruler retained for him their religious orientation and values.[327]

A lesser theorist would have terminated his argumentation at this point, but Priézac realized that he had touched upon the most controversial element of the rationale of reason of state—the issue of means and ends. Although the problem was central to any justifica-

---

[325] *Ibid.*, Chap. 28.   [326] *Ibid.*, pp. 401-02.

[327] At this point in his argument, Priézac once more attempted to demonstrate that Charles V and Philip II cloaked their true designs with religion, whereas the French kings since Clovis generally worked for the benefit of the true faith. This was his answer to Jansenius' charge that the French were indirectly aiding the spread of heresy. *Ibid.*, Chaps. 29, 30.

tion of official policy, few writers of the period faced it as directly or discussed it as extensively as Priézac. His analysis of the matter is therefore one of the most valuable elements of his book. Regarding Louis XIII's objectives in waging war against the Hapsburgs, Priézac insisted that Louis sought not to extend his dominions at the expense of his neighbors but to protect the oppressed, preserve his realm and the public good, and always to defend the interests and glory of religion. If accidents of war occurred, he was not responsible because his intent was pure: "He seeks peace by means of war, and if in waging it something happens contrary to his desires, it is not a crime of will but of necessity whose laws are most harsh and commands most cruel."[328] For Priézac, therefore, a just war was by definition one that was for a just cause regardless of the requisite suffering and bloodshed. Citing St. Augustine, he wrote:

> A war is just when the intention that causes it to be undertaken is just . . . . The will is therefore the principal element that must be considered, not the means. For one should always relate actions to objectives and not weigh what has been done by the good or bad that has resulted. Thus the will, which seeks and hopes for some good as its objective, does not sin, and he who intends to kill the guilty sometimes faultlessly sheds the blood of the innocent.[329]

Such reasoning went far to justify any and all means, provided the intended end was good. Priézac was completely aware of the implications of his position but merely wrote off any undesirable concomitant effects as the unfortunate dictates of necessity. In fact, he pushed his means-end argumentation to the point of insisting that rulers were morally bound to adopt questionable methods if they increased the general welfare:

> According to the opinions of theologians, when there is something that may be of great benefit to us and all the public, it is not just that we neglect it because of the harm that others might accidentally incur. If it were necessarily otherwise, one could

[328] *Ibid.*, p. 447.   [329] *Ibid.*, pp. 448-49.

not wage a just war against offenders, and all military justice would vanish, to the great loss of the public utility. This would also deny religion the means of self-defense against its enemies because of some Christians who might innocently and unwillingly find themselves in the enemy's camp.[330]

In taking this position, Priézac clearly adopted the logic and justifications of holy war, which he thereupon applied to Louis XIII's policies for the good of the French state. The only essential was the ruler's proper objective—to benefit his state and his faith simultaneously regardless of the means used:

> As for the Most Christian King's intention, it surely is most equitable and just. He ably directs his arms with his bloody hand, but with an innocent will and a conscience without blemish. While he wages war, it [his conscience] preserves and maintains his rights in the midst of battle, and he deliberately does nothing whatsoever that may injure religion or sacred things. Therefore, he who does nothing illicit even though he has the power shows by this that he never had the intention of doing so.[331]

This was the means-end argumentation with which Priézac sought to justify Louis XIII's use of war for both the defense of the realm and the cause of religion. With a devout king whose faith was intact and whose conscience was clear, all would ultimately be for the best.

Priézac was quick to add, however, that subjects should never inquire into their ruler's motives. In answer to Jansenius' charge that French Catholics might not in good conscience fight alongside the heretic Dutch, Priézac emphatically reiterated the absolutist position that kings were lieutenants of God and were endowed with superior understanding of the mysteries of state. "It in no way belongs to those who are born to obey to insinuate themselves into affairs of state and to scrutinize its principal maxims, nor to inquire why the prince undertakes war. They should be receptive to what they are

[330] *Ibid.*, pp. 450-51.   [331] *Ibid.*, pp. 452-53.

told and do it without objection instead of curiously asking why and for what purpose each thing is done and ordered."[332] Priézac was not saying that the king's acts were *ipso facto* just but only that his subjects should assume so. This was followed by a lengthy eulogy of Cardinal Richelieu who, although not mentioned by name, was clearly the object of his adulation.[333]

The final note of Priézac's book was fittingly religious. It is God rather than man, he insisted, who determines the fate of states, but in the divine order of things France has been assigned a special position. She owes much to Clovis but even more to St. Remigius who converted Clovis and made the French monarchy Christian, promising that France would never fall under foreign domination as long as her kings remained true to the faith. The saint's words have proved prophetic, he added, for France, unlike Spain, has never been conquered by other peoples. Surely this is an evidence of divine favor:

> Only France has not been subject to all these changes, and God, according to his promises, seems to have established her to last until the end of the world . . . . He so solidly founded and built our beautiful monarchy that the bond with which she has been secured and strengthened for so many centuries can be broken only with the destruction of those who would break it. Even more: the glory and conservation of the Christian Empire seem to be so clearly tied to, and absolutely dependent upon, her endless survival that if the predictions of the oracles are to be believed, *Roman greatness will not perish as long as there are Kings of France, for it will always be supported by them and preserved by their help.*[334]

Such was the argumentation with which Priézac replied to Jansenius' denunciation of Richelieu's foreign policy in the name of Catholic Christianity. Whether Priézac succeeded in identifying the cause of France with that of universal Christendom may be doubted, but it is clear that he regarded France as a Christian state and built

[332] *Ibid.*, p. 455.   [333] *Ibid.*, Chap. 33.
[334] *Ibid.*, pp. 486-87. Italics in the original.

upon this position when justifying all measures that might benefit her in any way. His constant theme was that France enjoyed a special place among Christian nations and that Louis XIII, the most devout of monarchs, always sought the good of the faith. Priézac's strong French patriotism had a profoundly religious cast and was focused upon the ruler who both symbolized and actively practiced the precepts of Catholic Christianity. In a crisis situation it was both his right and his duty to defend the realm and the values that it embodied; all measures including war, bloodshed, and alliances with heretics were justified because of the ruler's high intent and the justice of his cause. The means-end logic of reason of state was quite intact in Priézac's thought and in his eyes thoroughly vindicated current French policy. That questionable means might vitiate even the highest ends never occurred to him, since he believed that right, justice, God and the true faith were on the side of Christian France. Priézac's treatise therefore stands as one of the ablest and most thoroughgoing statements of the complex yet coherent rationale which Richelieu and his supporters believed to justify his policies. Few new ideas are found in Priézac's synthesis, but he argued his case with a new thoroughness and cogency. After much acrimonious and searching debate, the concept of reason of state was attaining a degree of maturity.

The controversy over the *Mars Gallicus* was at least partially responsible for one of Richelieu's most arbitrary acts in his later years, the arrest and imprisonment of Saint-Cyran. As so often, religion and politics in this instance were thoroughly intertwined. We have noted how Saint-Cyran in his early career was a staunch royalist, as exemplified by his *Question royalle* which was written at the suggestion of Henry IV.[335] Subsequently, when Richelieu was Bishop of Luçon, the future abbé became his close friend and agent, frequently sending him information concerning intrigues and other occurrences at the royal court.[336] He also arranged for the publication

---

[335] See Pt. I, n. 24-30 and text.
[336] The most extensive expert treatment of the relations of the two men is J. Orcibal, *Les Origines du jansénisme*, Paris, 1947, Vol. II, Chaps. 10, 11.

of Richelieu's important *Instruction du chrétien*. And after Richelieu became First Minister, Saint-Cyran went to great pains in his writings to defend the Cardinal against all calumnies, apparently with complete sincerity. Especially important was his *Somme des fautes*[337] which was published in 1626 at the height of the controversy over the *Admonitio* and similar ultramontane attacks upon French foreign policy. In his dedicatory epistle to Richelieu, Saint-Cyran equated criticism of the Cardinal with denunciation of Louis XIII— a position that pleased Richelieu no end. Like so many *dévots*, Saint-Cyran therefore began his career as a staunch supporter of Richelieu and so remained for years, apparently with few qualms of conscience.

In time, however, a number of episodes plus the evolution of his political and religious views completely altered his relations with the all-powerful First Minister. Like his mentor, Bérulle, Saint-Cyran gradually became more and more critical of Richelieu's foreign and domestic policies as inimical to the best interests of the nation. At the crisis of the Day of Dupes, the abbé was patently among the losers, since the Queen Mother appointed him Bishop of Bayonne at the height of her intended coup.[338] With the disappearance of the other leaders of the *dévot* faction, its headship seemed to devolve upon Saint-Cyran, although he never exercised it openly. His opposition to Richelieu's efforts to secure the annulment of Gaston d'Orléans' marriage was well known as was his friendship with Jansenius, the author of the hypercritical *Mars Gallicus*. Fundamentally, Saint-Cyran had come to abhor any suggestion that religion was being made to serve political ends. For this reason he even denounced Louis XIII's declaration placing the realm under the protection of the Virgin.[339] In view of these developments,

---

A. Adam, *Du Mysticisme à la révolte: les jansénistes du XVIIᵉ siècle*, Paris, 1968, Pt. 2, Chaps. 3, 4 follows Orcibal in certain respects but differs from him concerning some elements of Richelieu's motivation. I find myself closer to Adam's position.

[337] See Pt. II, n. 134-35 and text.

[338] Orcibal, Vol. II, 496.

[339] Regarding this famous event, he said, "There is nothing more capable of offending God than causing religion and piety to serve politics." *Ibid.*, Vol. II, 553.

it is not surprising that Richelieu found Saint-Cyran highly suspect. His religious views contributed even more significantly to his downfall. His growing influence over the convictions and deportment of the residents of Port-Royal and important persons in high places typically gave rise to intense factionalism both for and against him. His enemies claimed that his extreme emphasis upon self-abnegation and difficult morality, as well as his criticism of the Church, discounted the sacraments and monastic vows and seemed to favor illuminism. Especially important was the well-founded charge that he insisted upon contrition rather than attrition in the confessional —a position that Richelieu found particularly galling since he had defended to the hilt the sufficiency of attrition in his *Instruction du chrétien*.[340] Richelieu was painfully familiar with the potential for strife and disruption of disputes concerning such matters, and both as Cardinal and First Minister he was determined to avoid such a dangerous eventuality. Therefore, after a report by Father Joseph who thoroughly shared his views on foreign policy and the need of nipping ecclesiastical discord in the bud, Richelieu ordered Saint-Cyran's arrest. On May 14, 1638, he was confined in the Chateau of Vincennes.

Interrogation of the prisoner was conducted strictly along doctrinal lines, although factionalism continued to sway large numbers of interested observers. After it became clear that a case could not be made against him, Saint-Cyran was moved to better quarters in the chateau but was neither released nor brought to trial. Meanwhile, Richelieu was composing his own refutation of the doctrine of contrition. His *Perfection du chrétien*, which was not published until 1647, contained the strongest reaffirmation of the sufficiency of attrition.[341] Because of the various disruptive forces, political and religious, which Saint-Cyran represented, Richelieu regarded him as "more dangerous than six armies"[342] and was determined to keep him confined regardless of any demonstrable guilt. Once again the Cardinal took the position that the good of the state—in this case

[340] See Pt. I, n. 231-35 and text.
[341] Richelieu, *La Perfection du Chrétien*, Paris, 1647, Chaps. 9, 10.
[342] Richelieu to Condé. Cited in Orcibal, Vol. II, 517.

the benefits of his foreign policy and preservation of ecclesiastical peace—justified arbitrary persecution without reference to strict legality. In this instance, large numbers of influential persons made clear their sympathy with the victim but failed to bring about his release. Saint-Cyran outlived Richelieu but only long enough to enjoy eight months of freedom after his persecutor's death. The episode once again vividly illustrates the inextricable fusion of religious and political motivation that characterized Richelieu's understanding of reason of state.

During Richelieu's last years as First Minister, his policies of state-building seemed to give rise to endless controversies concerning religious matters, both doctrinal and institutional. We have already noted such dramatic episodes as his expulsion of recalcitrant members of the Assembly of the Clergy at Mantes, Jansenius' attack on his foreign policy, and his imprisonment of Saint-Cyran. In addition, as if to complete the circle, the thorny and ultrasensitive problem of Gallicanism once more reared its head. Although the resulting controversy involved a variety of issues, the most important for our purposes was a thoroughly practical one, royal control over the greatest corporation of the realm and exploitation of its resources for purposes of state. As the war became more and more burdensome and the Cardinal experienced ever-increasing difficulties in financing the campaigns of the royal armies, he inevitably cast a covetous eye toward the vast properties of the Church. Rumors that he sought to become Patriarch of the Gauls and even contemplated schism were rife for years.[343] Although Richelieu was decidedly not a doctrinaire Gallican and had on more than one occasion moved to combat the position,[344] he was willing to permit his supporters to propagandize the independence of the French Church from Roman controls in order to give weight to his demands upon the institution. A firm believer in coordinate and mutually independent church and state within their respective spheres, the Cardinal also believed that the French Church

[343] Orcibal, *Origines*, Vol. III, Appendix 4. See n. 62, 63, and text.
[344] V. Martin, "L'Adoption du gallicanisme par le clergé de France," *Revue des sciences religieuses*, VIII (1928), 1-23.

should bring aid and succor to the state in its hour of need, yet he was also aware of the extensive and dangerous opposition which any blatant enunciation of the principles of Gallicanism might provoke.

It was with such factors in mind that Richelieu permitted Pierre Dupuy, together with his brother Jacques, to publish late in 1638 a large folio volume entitled *Traitez des droits et libertez de l'Eglise gallicane*. This was quickly followed by a second volume, *Preuves des libertez de l'Eglise gallicane*.[345] The first reprinted a large number of earlier treatises, many by French jurists of ultra-Gallican views, while the second contained a vast quantity of official acts by French kings, assemblies of the clergy, parlements, universities, and other bodies that were hostile to Roman jurisdiction and administrative controls. Both volumes were published anonymously and without privilege, although Dupuy's very close relations with the Cardinal warrant the assumption that he approved of them. To forestall the expected critical reaction, Richelieu obtained on November 20, 1638, a decree by the royal council condemning both volumes on the ground that they had been published without privilege. They nevertheless continued to circulate, and on February 9, 1639, eighteen bishops in Paris met and framed a letter, to be addressed to all high-ranking clergy in France, denouncing the publications in the strongest terms as pernicious, heretical, schismatic, impious, contrary to the word of God, and most injurious to the Holy See. In answer, Dupuy composed a response in which he charged that the bishops sought to destroy the king's sovereignty. He decried the patience of those who acquiesced in the extension of papal power over the ruler and expressed the fear that this would ruin the monarchy and France. On March 24, 1640, the Parlement of Paris condemned the bishops' letter and prohibited its publication.

The controversy over Dupuy's volumes remained privy to those who were immediately concerned, but such was not the case with the affair of the *Optatus Gallus* which resounded throughout high

[345] The best account of the controversy to which these works gave rise is still G. Demante, "Histoire de la publication des livres de Pierre Dupuy sur les libertés de l'Eglise gallicane," *Bibliothèque de l'École des Chartes*, v (1843-1844), 585-606.

governmental and ecclesiastical circles.[346] It seems that Charles Hersent, the former Oratorian who had written in support of Louis XIII's claims to Metz,[347] became disgruntled because of his failure to win recognition and rewards in high places, and retaliated against the Cardinal by attacking him in manner that was certain to cause trouble. Early in 1640, Hersent anonymously published a tract of 39 pages entitled *Optati Galli de cavendo schismate . . . , liber paræneticus,*[348] which restated the ultramontane position concerning papal supremacy in the strongest terms and accused Richelieu of working for schism. Not only did Hersent uphold the usual ultramontane assertions that popes were supreme over kings, that all disputed matters were subject to papal jurisdiction, and that the King of France had no right to tax the Church; he also indicated that Richelieu sought to become Patriarch of the Gallican Church. The tract at once provoked a controversy which was the last thing Richelieu wanted, and he immediately initiated measures to discover the author's identity and to have the work condemned. The author he seems not to have found, but he quickly obtained condemnation of the tract by the Parlement of Paris and the local ecclesiastical authorities. On March 23, the Parlement, at Richelieu's request, condemned the work as denying the king's divinely bestowed authority to legislate concerning temporal matters and to request aid from the clergy for the preservation of the state. The decree also stated that the tract offended by placing in doubt the liberties of the Gallican Church and fomenting sedition. For these reasons, it was ordered burned by the hangman, and all printers and booksellers were forbidden to distribute it on pain of *lèse-majesté.* Upon hearing of the decree, Richelieu at once sent a letter of congratulation to Molé, the First President of the Parlement.[349] The order was duly carried out on March

[346] This is discussed in Orcibal, *Origines,* Vol. III, 132-36; Fouqueray, Vol. V, 412-14; and Martimort, pp. 121-25.

[347] See n. 196.

[348] The complete title is: *Optati Galli de cavendo schismate, ad illustrissimos ac reverendissimos Ecclesiæ gallicanæ primates, archiepiscopos, episcopos, liber paræneticus,* n.p., 1640.

[349] The texts of the decree and Richelieu's letter are in Molé, *Mémoires,* Vol. II, 487-89. Molé shows that the decree followed Richelieu's instructions almost to the letter.

28, and on the same day the Archbishop of Paris, the bishops of his province, and sixteen other archbishops and bishops who were in the capital condemned the work and prohibited the reading or keeping of it by the clergy under their jurisdiction.[350]

Such condemnations were routine for Richelieu, but he knew that they were far from satisfying public opinion and consequently arranged for a series of published refutations. All emphasized the necessary and natural cooperation of church and state, and denied that the Cardinal was contemplating schism. One of the first to appear was a lengthy work by a doctor of the Sorbonne and royal preacher, Isaac Habert, entitled *De Consensu hierarchiæ et monarchiæ*,[351] which the academician Louis Giry soon issued in French translation.[352] The official inspiration of the work is obvious, and it was, in fact, one of the ablest responses to Hersent's polemic. At the outset, Habert set forth as his basic position the time-honored Gelasian theory of divinely appointed and independent church and state. "These are two powers that God separated by limits which He himself established for them, both supreme, absolute, and independent."[353] He then denied the possibility of schism by arguing at length that it was mere rumor without foundation and listing the many acts of loyalty of the French kings, including Louis XIII, to the papacy. Schism made no sense, he argued, either to king or pope. As for Richelieu, he had given too many proofs of his virtue and fidelity to religion to resort to such a move.[354] The liberties of

---

[350] Fouqueray, Vol. v, 413.

[351] *De Consensu hierarchiæ et monarchiæ, adversus paræneticum Optati Galli, schismatum fictoris, libri sex*, Paris, 1640. I omit consideration of several answers to the *Optatus Gallus*. For example, the work by the Jesuit, Michel Rabardeau, *Optatus Gallus de cavendo schismate . . . benigna manu sectus*, Paris, 1641, was written at Richelieu's request and was one of the more extensive and virulent answers to Hersent's tract, but it adds little of significance for our purposes. On Rabardeau's relations with Richelieu, see P. Blet, "Jesuites gallicans au XVIIe siècle?" *Archivum historicum Societatis Iesu*, xxix (1960), 65-68.

[352] *De l'Union de l'Eglise avec l'État, ouvrage composé en Latin contre le livre d'Optatus Gallus, par M. Habert . . . mis en françois par Louis Giry*, Paris, 1641.

[353] *Ibid.*, p. 17.   [354] *Ibid.*, pp. 172-73.

the Gallican Church Habert found to be entirely justified, since they stemmed from the independence of both powers and their non-encroachment upon each other. Regarding the most important practical issue, royal insistence upon financial aid from the French Church, Habert merely pointed to the clergy's natural obligation to support the state in which they lived according to its needs. The king defends *both* the church and the state, he argued; thus the ruler has the right to expect assistance from the clerical estate when the preservation of all is at stake.

In this simple, straightforward manner, Habert effectively upheld the financial obligations of the clergy to the French state and easily discounted the idea of schism. Parallel arguments appeared in another officially inspired answer to the *Optatus Gallus*, Jean Sirmond's *Chimère deffaicte*.[355] Richelieu would never seek to become Patriarch, Sirmond maintained, because such a move would bring him no advantage. On the contrary, it would divide Catholics and weaken the realm, thereby favoring the designs of the Huguenots and Spain.[356] Sirmond's most conclusive argument he found in Louis XIII's well-known piety and many acts for the benefit of the Catholic faith, which he recounted at length. He even claimed that Louis habitually subordinated all gains that might accrue from reason of state to the dictates of his faith and the interests of the Church:

> Piety always takes first place in all his deliberations. Whatever benefit and advantage [may stem from] reason of state, which is the sovereign law over [all] others, he subjects it to that which right decrees [consonant] with heaven. Is it credible that a prince of this type, the only object of whose actions is the glory of God, would ever undertake anything prejudicial to the Bride of God?[357]

It is evident that Richelieu's apologists believed the soundest response to ultramontane criticism to be reassertion of the religious nature of both the French state and official policies for its benefit.

---

[355] [Jean Sirmond], *La Chimère deffaicte, ou Refutation d'un libelle séditieux tendant à troubler l'Estat, sous prétexte d'y prévenir un schisme*, Paris, 1640.
[356] *Ibid.*, pp. 46-53.   [357] *Ibid.*, p. 41.

Such writings as these set forth the essentials of the official position but, as Richelieu well knew, they could not satisfy the opposition or still ultramontane criticism. Rather than leave the controversy unresolved, he yielded to the need of a more conciliatory treatment of the complex relations between church and state, with special reference to the Gallican liberties, and commissioned Pierre de Marca, both a prelate and councillor of state, to undertake this thankless task. De Marca's resulting treatise, the *De Concordia sacerdotii et imperii*,[358] was one of the most labored and in certain respects the least significant of the entire controversy, important only as an instance of Richelieu's varied attempts to meet clerical criticism. De Marca stated at the outset that his purpose was not to analyze current, reciprocal relationships between church and state but to show their history so as to establish a factual basis for the respect due to both. The result was an extremely lengthy but able work which set forth innumerable precedents for the sovereignty and independence of church and monarchy, each in its sphere, in the hope of achieving a reconciliation. Building upon the divinely authorized absolutism of both king and pope, de Marca upheld the latter's supremacy over councils and went far toward accepting papal infallibility. But he also, as spokesman for the Gallican liberties, required the assent of the French king and clergy before papal legislation ran in France. The position contained clear incompatibilities. He resisted the extension of the *régale* to the entire realm, as demanded by Gallicans, but he favored use of the *appel comme d'abus* in jurisdictional disputes. In these and other areas he attempted, by adopting a moderate Gallican position and drawing a series of fine distinctions, to erase major areas of friction between church and state. Repeatedly he emphasized the natural and necessary cooperation of the two powers, and roundly denied the idea of a French patriarchate or schism.

De Marca's book was well received, as much for its viewpoint as its erudition, and in fact he was as successful as any writer of the

---

[358] *De Concordia sacerdotii et imperii, seu libertatibus ecclesiæ gallicanæ libri quatuor*, Paris, 1641. On de Marca and this work, see F. Gaquère, *Pierre de Marca (1594-1662). Sa vie. Ses œuvres. Son gallicanisme*, Lille, 1932.

period in delineating compromises between mutually incompatible positions. Guez de Balzac, who no longer felt attracted to Richelieu, wrote de Marca on August 6, 1641, praising his efforts for reconciliation in church-state controversies and saying that the work was based on truth and performed a great service.[359] Genuine ultramontane opinion, however, remained unsatisfied, and on April 7, 1642, the work was placed on the Index of Prohibited Books.[360] The publication of de Marca's book may be said to have ended the controversy, not through the resolution of all issues but the termination of polemics. As for the patriarchate and project of schism which had sparked the debate, rumors of these persisted until Richelieu's death, although it seems that he never genuinely intended such a move and merely used it as one of his arsenal of weapons with which to pressure the papacy.[361]

For our purposes, the chief value of the controversy lies in the extensive reiteration of some of the Cardinal's fundamental views concerning the justice of his policies. Even in the final years of his ministry when he felt the security of consistent royal support, he continued to be extremely sensitive to the charge that he was injuring the Church and its faith. His officially inspired rebuttals simply restated the now-familiar position that since the monarchy was absolute in its sphere and responsible for the safety of the state, the king might rightly expect financial support from the members of the first estate of the realm. Royal policy which was predicated upon this assumption was entirely justified because of the supremacy of the state and the requisite loyalty of all subjects to it in its sphere. But the supreme consideration for Richelieu and his supporters was the all-important religious nature of the monarchy and the corresponding orientation of royal policy toward religious ends. This fundamental position received greater emphasis in these officially inspired tracts than ever before. Whether Richelieu genuinely believed Sirmond's assertion that Louis XIII subordinated all potential

---

[359] Balzac, *Œuvres*, Vol. I, 536-37.

[360] Gaquère, p. 190. It is noteworthy that during an illness in 1647, de Marca signed a complete retraction and agreed to correct the errors in his book, as dictated by the papacy. He never revised his work, however.

[361] Orcibal, *Origines*, Vol. III, 136-40, 144-46. Martimort, pp. 122-25.

benefits of reason of state to religious considerations may be doubted, but the fact remains that in this final confrontation with his ultramontane critics the Cardinal built his defense upon the monarch's piety and the religious justification of his policies. Rather than mere specious apology for the "tyranny" of a power-oriented First Minister, the contentions of his supporters should be taken at face value because they thoroughly coincided with his conception of France as a Christian monarchy.

Turning to the writers and pamphleteers who wrote from a more secular standpoint in defense of Richelieu's policies during the last years of his ministry, it is noteworthy that the chorus of praise increased to the point where a large majority of the published works on political matters praised the Cardinal in the most extravagant terms.[362] As time elapsed and Richelieu's accomplishments became clearer to his contemporaries, more and more observers felt constrained to take up their pens on his behalf and to defend him against his critics. True, there were occasional tracts, usually anonymous, that deplored the great cost of the war and attendant human misery, appealing to Louis XIII for relief,[363] but these were surprisingly few in the sum-total of publications during the last years of the reign. A selection of typical pro-Richelieu pamphlets will now be examined in order to indicate the various justifications that were put forward in support of his policies.

In 1640, Julius Furic du Run, a self-styled Breton nobleman, published a tract in which he sought to answer criticism of Richelieu by recounting his many contributions to strengthening the realm.[364] The bulk of the work consists of a long recital of the Cardinal's achievements, both in domestic and foreign affairs, in state-building.

[362] This may be easily established by examining such standard bibliographies as those of Lelong and André, as well as the *Catalogue de l'histoire de France.*

[363] E.g., *La Voix gémissante du peuple chrétien et catholique accablé sous le faix des désastres et misères des guerres de ce temps, adressée au Roy très chrétien par un françois désinteressé*, Paris, 1640.

[364] *Réflexions politiques du sieur Jul. Furic du Run sur le gouvernement de Monseigneur le Cardinal duc de Richelieu*, Paris, 1640.

Throughout, du Run gives evidence of strong patriotic sentiment and does not hestitate to denounce such obstacles to absolute rule as the nobles and the Parlement of Paris. Because Richelieu's policies necessarily touched many vested interests, he was certain to make many enemies, du Run said, adding this pregnant observation: "Having worked as extensively as he has for the glory of France, he can henceforth have no enemies other than those of the state."[365] Louis XIII's great achievement was to choose a first minister who combined loyalty to Christian principles with knowledge of the secrets of state:

> Although ordinary virtue would have experienced difficulty in joining the greatness of the prince with the happiness of his people, the key was nevertheless very simple for the king's prudence which alone understood the means of combining prosperity and glory in the same reign. As persons well disciplined and instructed in the truth of Christian maxims find no difficulty in revering God's judgments which they cannot understand, likewise, there are certain secrets of state which subjects are permitted to admire but not to elucidate, [since] kings have certain obscure designs which resemble prophecies and can be best understood only after their fulfillment.[366]

Once more appeared the typical structure of absolutist thought: unquestioning reverence by the subjects for the superior knowledge of king and minister of the secrets of state, all within a religious frame of reference. Even more succinct was du Run's conclusion: "Since M. the Cardinal has no objective in all his great designs other than the honor of God, the good of religion, and the glory of the state, he has accordingly been so fortunate as never to have been checked in the pursuit of them for any of his ends."[367] The Breton nobleman, like Richelieu's closest apologists, found a religious purpose and justification for his state-oriented policies. The position was carried further in another tract that appeared in the same year,[368] probably by a cleric, which argued that since God presides over the

---

[365] *Ibid.*, p. 2.   [366] *Ibid.*, pp. 12-13.   [367] *Ibid.*, p. 27.
[368] *Sainte défense pour Son Eminence. Au Roy*, Paris [1640].

counsels of princes, criticism is irreligious and contrary to the subjects' natural role in the divinely established order of things.

In the following year, there appeared a moderate, factual defense
of Richelieu, probably by Jacques Ribier, councillor of state.[369] Ribier
emphasized the Cardinal's specific accomplishments and insisted
that his greatest work lay in his bringing all elements of the population, including the nobles and the Parlement, under royal control,
thereby rendering Louis XIII absolute throughout his realm. As for
the war against Spain, Ribier argued that the purpose of war is
peace which is greatly desired by all. Therefore, after a victorious
peace, all elements of the realm will flourish, thanks to Richelieu.
The argument seems naive but expressed widespread expectations.
Very different was a highly philosophical anonymous defense of
Richelieu which appeared in the same year.[370] The author, evidently
well versed in the ways of abstract thought, found in Richelieu the
epitome of all that philosophers had always sought—a man of superior abilities who combined wisdom with success in practical
affairs. His union of virtue and achievement had not only restored
the rightful order of things within the state but had also brought
about the victory of true religion throughout the realm.[371] In this
sense, Richelieu worked for both the state and the truth:

> But how have you strengthened this power? You conducted
> yourself as a sage and philosopher; you did those things to render
> the monarchy indestructible that sages do to strengthen their
> sects; you worked for the state in exactly the same way that they
> work to establish the truth. As in learning it is necessary to
> support an opinion by destroying those that are contrary to it,
> likewise to carry out policy it is necessary to eliminate all power
> of enemies and rebels. This you have perfectly done according
> to the maxims of true wisdom.[372]

[369] *Discours de M.I.R.C.D.*, n.p., 1641. The initials probably stand for
"Jacques Ribier, Conseiller d'Estat." Ribier had already published his *Discours
sur le gouvernement des monarchies et principautez souverains*, Paris, 1630.

[370] *Panégyrique à Monseigneur le Cardinal duc de Richelieu, sur le sujet du
philosophe indifférent*, Paris, 1641.

[371] *Ibid.*, p. 13.   [372] *Ibid.*, pp. 21-22.

It was in this sense that the author concluded that Richelieu had retrieved the French from "those wretched centuries when the people were without repose and the prince without authority . . . . Through you, we are in a happier century, since you have the government of the realm in your hands and you direct affairs as the soul, the genius and the intelligence of this great body."[373] Praise of Richelieu evidently ran the gamut from the most pragmatic to the most idealistic.

In 1641 and 1642, Guillaume Boyer des Roches, a lawyer associated with the Parlement of Paris, published two pamphlets which sounded further notes in praise of Richelieu.[374] The first placed in the mouth of a German prince the beneficial effects of French foreign policy. It was for the purpose of protecting and restoring the rights of princes of the Empire who were subject to Spanish tyranny and had been dispossessed of their holdings, Boyer said. For this reason, France was in a morally sound position and was performing a service that was desperately needed by all Christendom. In his second tract, Boyer presented the most extravagant praise of Richelieu's virtue, methods, successes, and ideals, insisting that he fulfilled the concept of the perfect minister to the hilt. His greatest achievement was to realize that the interests of the state took precedence over those of any individual or group and to work for the general good. Many would suffer in consequence, Boyer conceded, and Richelieu would be subject to criticism no matter what measures he might adopt to this end. But it was sometimes necessary to exact sacrifices from certain elements of the population in order to preserve the state, and the minister must be above and immune to criticism when the good of all is his objective.[375] This viewpoint had

[373] *Ibid.*, pp. 22-23.

[374] *Le Coup d'Estat de l'Empire, envoyé par un prince alleman aux autres princes, Estats, Villes Imperiales et Anseatiques de l'Allemagne. Pour l'union de leurs forces aux desseins de la France, afin d'establir par ce moyen une paix générale en la Chrestienté*, n.p., 1641. *La Politique du temps. Discours panégyrique du gouvernement, contenant plusieurs belles Maximes d'Estat*, Paris, 1642.

[375] *La Politique du temps*, pp. 34-39.

been extensively developed in earlier writings by Richelieu's intimates, and its appearance in such a minor piece as Boyer's tract shows how widespread was its acceptance at the end of the reign.

These writings, selected from the various controversies and expressions of opinion during the last decade of Richelieu's ministry, should suffice to indicate the fundamental reasons why a growing number of his contemporaries approved of his foreign and domestic policies. At home, his great contribution in their eyes was his strengthening of royal power and his subordination of all dissidents in the complex social structure. It was widely realized that this restoration of "order" necessitated infringement of many traditional rights and privileges, but this seemed a small price to pay to avoid the turmoil and chaos that had plagued France during several previous generations. From this standpoint, the sacrifices and adjustments that were exacted by Richelieu's program of state-building were essential to the general good. Reason of state in internal affairs brought very tangible benefits to all. As for the Cardinal's foreign policy, this was viewed by his supporters as both necessary and justified by the political realities of international relations in an age when Hapsburg domination threatened the entire continent. The prevailing alignment of states left Richelieu no choice but to seek alliances with the Protestant powers. These ties, although questionable in themselves, were but instruments to a laudable end, the preservation and strengthening of the French state whose religious foundations and values remained intact. In this context, reason of state was but the necessary adjunct of a policy that enabled the Most Christian King and his Cardinal-Minister to defend the French state and fulfill its higher purposes.

RICHELIEU'S MAJOR APOLOGISTS DURING HIS LAST YEARS

It remains to consider the views of the five most important authors who wrote in support of Richelieu during the last years of his ministry. These were Louis Machon, Jean de Silhon, François de La Mothe le Vayer, Guez de Balzac, and Daniel de Priézac.[376] All but Machon had defended the Cardinal's policies in earlier writings and were maturing positions that they had previously delineated, but this does not mean that they were mere interested apologists. The remarkable diversity of their views and, more significantly, the increasing hesitations of several before some of the implications of reason of state indicate both their intellectual independence and the extent to which Richelieu succeeded in gaining the support of representative French literary talent during his final years. All had a common sympathy with his policies and objectives, yet they analyzed and justified these in very individualized fashion.

Louis Machon is remembered chiefly for his *Apologie pour Machiavelle* which he wrote at Richelieu's request. Machon was a member of a large family of jurists and administrators in Lorraine. Being a younger son, he was destined for the Church, was educated in Paris, and began his career as canon of the cathedral of Toul.[377] After a

[376] It will be noted that only one of these men, La Mothe le Vayer, was a member of the group that is usually called "libertine." Gabriel Naudé was the only other adherent of this small but congenial clique to write extensively on reason of state, but his works had no relations whatsoever to Richelieu and need not be considered. Naudé had certain limited contacts with the Cardinal, and the two men had many friends in common, such as the Dupuy brothers, Cardinal de Bagni, Mazarin, and others. However, Naudé's most important political treatise, *Considérations politiques sur les coups d'Estat*, was entirely apart from those that were in any way related to Richelieu's ideas or policies. Naudé himself stated that he wrote the book strictly at the request of his patron, Cardinal de Bagni, who found it very agreeable. *Mémoire confidentiel adressé à Mazarin par Gabriel Naudé après la mort de Richelieu*, A. Franklin, ed., Paris, 1870, pp. 6-10. Although it was written in 1631 and 1632 for de Bagni, the *Coups d'Estat* was not published until 1639 and then in an extremely small edition—only about a dozen copies, again for de Bagni. René Pintard has carefully examined the provenience of this work and has concluded that it was essentially Italianate in inspiration and can in no way be associated with Cardinal Richelieu. *Le Libertinage érudit*, Paris, 1943, Vol. I, 265-67; Vol. II, 614-15.

[377] On Machon, see R. Céleste, "Louis Machon, apologiste de Machiavel et de la politique de Richelieu," *Annales de la Faculté des Lettres de Bordeaux*, III (1881), 446-72, and "Louis Machon, apologiste de Machiavel et de la politique du Cardinal de Richelieu: Nouvelles recherches sur sa vie et ses

period of residence and advancement in that city, he was won over to Richelieu's policies which involved annexation of his native Lorraine. Machon apparently lent considerable aid to Dupuy and Godefroy when they were preparing the legal case for the French conquest of the province,[378] and he continued to cooperate with Dupuy when the latter gathered the materials for his compendious tomes on the Gallican liberties.[379] These contacts with men very close to Richelieu, plus his habit of frequenting the best libraries in Paris—including Richelieu's own—inevitably brought him to the attention of the Cardinal and Chancellor Séguier. In about the year 1641, Richelieu informally asked Machon to write a defense of Machiavelli and, in addition, to compile materials that might be used to defend royal rights over the French Church in disputes with the papacy. The result was two lengthy works, both of which Machon had the misfortune never to publish. His *Traité politique des différends ecclésiastiques*[380] took the form of an immense assemblage of legal materials concerning the king's prerogatives over the institution of the French Church, and was completed in 1648 but remained in manuscript, probably because it contained doctrinal errors. Machon's *Apologie pour Machiavelle,* our chief concern, experienced a more complex but ultimately similar fate. Machon apparently made rapid progress with the work, since he completed it in the form in which he intended to present it to Richelieu by 1643 and sought to publish it at that time.[381] The Cardinal, however, was dead, and rededication of the work to Séguier failed to secure the necessary approval. Much later, after the upheavals of the Fronde

---

œuvres," *ibid.,* v (1883), 67-132. Both were also printed separately. K. T. Butler, "Louis Machon's 'Apologie pour Machiavelle'—1643 and 1668," *Journal of the Warburg and Courtauld Institutes,* III (1939-1940), 208-27. Procacci, Pt. II, Chap. 4. Thuau, pp. 334-50.

[378] See n. 216-18 and text.

[379] See n. 345.

[380] *Traité politique des différends ecclésiastiques arrivés depuis le commencement de la monarchie jusques à présent tant entre les papes et les Roys de France que le clergé de leur royaume.* Bibliothèque Nationale, Fonds Français, 17617.

[381] Céleste, "Nouvelles recherches . . . ," p. 127.

in which Machon took an active part, he returned to the work, extensively expanding it and completing it in 1668. Both versions of the work remain in manuscript today,[382] but we shall examine that of 1643, since it was the one that Machon wrote for Richelieu and intended to submit for his approbation.

Machon's good fortune and his favor with the great rapidly declined after Richelieu's death, following which he lived an agitated and frequently poverty-stricken existence. Soon losing the support of Chancellor Séguier, he found none with Mazarin and turned against both men, writing against them with increasing vehemence. During the Fronde he supported both the Parlement and the nobles, and published miscellaneous Mazarinades in which he not only violently criticized Mazarin but also presented arguments contrary to those that he had incorporated into his *Apologie*. In fact, he repeatedly altered his position, favoring Richelieu before his death, then turning against Séguier and Mazarin, joining the Frondeurs, and finally abandoning the latter and arguing for peace.[393] Furthermore, he easily shifted his ground concerning fundamental matters of political morality, as may be demonstrated by examining some of his minor works. In 1641, he obtained permission to publish a *Sermon pour le jour de l'Assomption Notre Dame*[384] in which he both praised Richelieu's policies and insisted upon the closest union of politics and religion. Twenty-four years later, on the other hand, after many bitter experiences, he maintained that politics and morals are entirely different matters, each with its own type of reasoning and expertise, and should never be confused.[385] All this suggests that he was easily swayed by events and his own interests, and did not

---

[382] *Apologie pour Machiavelle en faveur des Princes et Ministres d'Estat*, Paris, 1643. Bibliothèque Nationale, Fonds Français, 19046-19047. *Apologie pour Machiavelle ou plustost la politique des Roys, et de la science des souverains, en faveur des ministres d'Estat*, Au Tourne, 1668. Bibliothèque de la Ville de Bordeaux, MS. 535.

[383] Céleste, "Nouvelles recherches . . . ," pp. 11-13.

[384] *Sermon pour le jour de l'Assomption Notre Dame, au retour de la procession générale establie par le Roy Louis XIII, surnommé le Juste, en l'an 1638*, Paris, 1641.

[385] *Discours pour servir de règle ou d'avis aux bibliothécaires*, ed. Daspit de Saint-Armand, Bordeaux, 1883, pp. 74-76.

scruple to advocate views that might find favor with the great—all of which gives his treatment of Machiavelli a certain significance as a reflection of what he believed the Cardinal's position to be.

Since it is undeniable that Machon undertook his defense of Machiavelli at Richelieu's suggestion, much has been made of this fact by writers who would represent the Cardinal as essentially Machiavellian.[386] The exact significance of Richelieu's solicitation of an apology for Machiavelli, however, is very difficult to determine, since Machon himself described the incident as resulting from a mere chance encounter in the Cardinal's own library.[387] On the other hand, there is no doubt that Machon possessed considerable erudition, as is evidenced by the multiplicity and accuracy of his references to a vast array of earlier writers.[388] Richelieu presumably was aware of Machon's extensive learning. Be that as it may, the key to the significance of Machon's *Apologie pour Machiavelle* would seem to lie in an analysis of the exact nature of his defense of the astute Florentine whose name was so frequently associated with reason of state.

The reader of Machon's *Apologie* is at once made aware of the fact that his primary objective was to demonstrate the conformity of Machiavelli's precepts with those of Catholic Christianity. Fully alive to the tradition that Machiavellism was the antithesis of Christian morality, Machon did his best to reconcile the two positions and to show that the Florentine's teachings concerning reason of state accorded with, or at least were not antithetical to, Christian principles. In fact, Machon repeatedly asserted that piety and religion were among Machiavelli's central concerns. As a cleric who was attempting to please Richelieu, Machon apparently felt this to be the surest means of winning recognition and support from the powerful Cardinal-Minister. In structuring his defense of Machiavelli, Machon quoted twenty-three of Machiavelli's more questionable maxims— thirteen from the *Discourses* and ten from the *Prince*—and then ex-

---

[386] E.g., A. Sorel, *L'Europe et la Révolution française*, Paris, 1893, Vol. I, 17. Orcibal, *Origines*, Vol. II, 490.

[387] In the preface to the Bordeaux manuscript. Butler, pp. 209-10.

[388] Butler, p. 213.

amined their exact nature and implications from the practical and ideological standpoints, always with an eye for their relevance to Christian values. His own position regarding each problem he usually supported by amassing parallel statements from a great array of "authorities," lay and ecclesiastical. This manner of composition causes his work to appear as a highly mechanical compilation, yet it succeeds in presenting a certain case for the compatibility of Christian morality and reason of state.

In defending many of Machiavelli's maxims concerning statecraft, Machon fell back upon the historically valid position that in many areas Machiavelli was merely recording events and showing the true condition of human affairs. His accounts of sordid political machinations did not mean that he advocated such measures in principle; he was merely being realistic and describing politics as they were. Machon, in fact, handled a majority of his twenty-three maxims from Machiavelli in this limited fashion. This approach had the advantage of enabling Machon to present Machiavelli simply as an astute observer who remained neutral concerning many questions of political morality. This, however, was neither Machon's primary purpose nor the major focus of his work. Instead, he was determined to demonstrate that Machiavelli's political precepts were not contrary to Christian principles. In his preface he insisted that Machiavelli abhorred irreligion, rejected perfidy, found unlimited ambition insufferable, and condemned vice, cruelty, and tyranny.[389] Machiavelli denounced calumny and slander with an ardor equal to that of the Church Fathers. He placed religion and piety above all else and made it the unique foundation of realms and states. He defended virtue and advocated rigorous justice. "In short, there is nothing religious in morality, nothing holy in politics, nothing sacred and revered among men that he does not preach and advocate with fervor, justice, and prudence."[390] And at the end of his book, Machon added a "Declaration and Protestation," stating that if he had made any statement contrary to Catholic, Apostolic, and

[389] *Apologie*, fol. G1. The pages of the Preface are lettered rather than numbered.
[390] *Ibid.*, fol. H1.

Roman doctrine, he condemned it forthwith and submitted his work to the judgment of the Church, protesting that he was and would remain its faithful and submissive servant.[391] Clearly, Machon believed that he was writing as an orthodox Christian in his effort to Christianize Machiavelli.

It was precisely those maxims of Machiavelli that were directly related to reason of state that received the most extensive treatment in Machon's work. This would seem a sure indication that he was aware of the contemporary debate concerning the justice of Richelieu's policies and sought to defend them while doing the same for Machiavelli. Early in his work, Machon examined two of Machiavelli's maxims which bore directly upon the place of religion in the state. The first was: "It is necessary to follow religion, although erroneous, because of reason of state, as [religion is] its [the state's] principal support."[392] In discussing this proposition, Machon limited himself to emphasizing the very close relationships between religion and the state. The latter, he insisted, found one of its chief props in the religious faith of its subjects. Religion provided stability and caused the people to accept subjection and do their duty. The prince should not tamper with the people's faith, merely allowing it to subsist in its extant form. As for its practical effects, said Machon, Machiavelli was correct when he accused the Christian princes of being less religious than the ancient pagans, especially the Egyptians and Romans who lived purer lives than modern Christian rulers. He was also correct in deploring the decline of religious fervor among the Christians, especially the Italians. With such arguments, Machon purported to defend Machiavelli's perspicacity as well as his orthodoxy, and simply presented him as reiterating the generally accepted fusion of church and state, regardless of the truth of the doctrine involved.

Machon was on firm ground when he posited the complete interrelation of religion and politics, a truism that was accepted by the great majority of his contemporaries, but he found it more difficult

[391] *Ibid.*, fol. 807.
[392] *Ibid.*, fol. 70. This is the fifth maxim in Pt. 1 of the book and is treated in fols. 70-127.

to defend his next maxim from Machiavelli which read: "It is neces-sary to accommodate religion to the state for its good and its preser-vation."[393] Although he was quick to assert that Machiavelli was thinking of the Romans who frankly followed this policy, Machon recognized that this was one of Machiavelli's more questionable posi-tions and the basis of much criticism of him.[394] The key to the mat-ter he found in the fact that religion is an essentially inward relation-ship between man and God whereas social and political ties are ex-ternal. This, plus the complete fusion of the sacred and the secular in human affairs, justified accommodating religion to the state:

> I do not know why it is blasphemous or sacrilegious to say that religion may be accommodated to the state, in view of the fact that these two matters are so closely allied, that one is merely interior and the other exterior, that the first concerns God and consciences whereas the second men and their purely moral actions, and that there is no ruler of a state without religion, nor religion without a state.[395]

This Machon followed with many examples from Scripture and history showing how men of principle accommodated religion to practical necessity and circumstance. Even Christ, he said, recog-nized certain Jewish customs, while St. Peter and St. Paul accom-modated their teachings to the people's ingrained habits and al-lowed many pagan practices to survive. "Why, therefore, should kings and sovereigns who are the anointed of the Lord and lieu-tenants of God on earth not be able to act as these great saints to establish the states that they hold from heaven and bring their peo-ple and subjects into the union, concord, and obedience that they owe?"[396] And this, in turn, was followed by a long list of earlier rulers who had adapted religious principles to practical necessity. Such, indeed, Machon found justified by the purposes of religion itself:

[393] *Ibid.*, fol. 128. This is Machon's sixth maxim and is discussed in fols. 128-98.
[394] *Ibid.*, fols. 132-33.   [395] *Ibid.*, fols. 138-40.   [396] *Ibid.*, fol. 165.

There never have been a church nor any nations of any kind that have not accommodated either their religion or that of others to the good, the glory, and the advancement of their states, because it is certain that there is not one [religion] that does not lead toward the same end, which is to seek one's salvation in the knowledge and adoration of a God, the Creator and Savior of men, the ceremonies of which are entirely external and are merely the polity and custom of the land in which one lives.[397]

Far from following Richelieu's critics who advocated the supremacy of religious morality over all things mundane, Machon assumed the opposite position in which religion might be accommodated to practical necessity for the good and the purposes of religion itself. This was possible to him only because of the relatively restricted role that he assigned to religion, reducing it to its barest essentials. He even went so far as to assert that since religion was a mere moral virtue of the individual, others such as faith, hope, and charity were of a higher nature and had more important social connotations which the prince should follow even while adapting religious practices to the public good.[398] Fundamentally, however, he based his position on the complete fusion of the sacred and profane in human affairs and the impossibility of rulers' living up to a super-human ideal:

I would gladly ask all these great zealots for religion and those blind despisers of the public good how they would go about causing the interests of religion to be separated from those of the state, and those of the state from those of religion, so that one might act independently of the other without their injuring each other. Men are completely within both religion and the polity; religion cannot subsist without the polity, nor the polity without religion, because in removing the polity you remove religion, at least that of which we speak. We seek to act like angels in one area and beasts in the other, [but] our nature is

[397] *Ibid.*, fols. 179-80.   [398] *Ibid.*, fols. 188-92.

not such; it is middling between the one and the other, and for better or worse it must be endured . . . . It would be easy for me here to act the contemplative and to parade a great many beautiful meditations on the purity and perfection of religion, and to show what it should be . . . . [But] I speak to men. Our lives are more action than speculation. We must see what we are capable of, and not what we should desire, for we are neither responsible nor guarantors for the impossible nor for things that are not within our power.[399]

In this way, Machon sharply reduced the supremacy of religious morality over royal policy while preserving the fundamental concept of the religiously grounded and oriented state.

Having taken this position, Machon easily turned to the topics that were so fashionable among the writers who were wrestling with the problem of reason of state—the justice and necessity of trickery, finesse, dissimulation, and an appearance of virtue on the part of the prince.[400] Machiavelli, he said, seemed to advocate all such measures, but the subject required careful exploration. Regarding trickery, he initially took the position that Machiavelli greatly abhorred it and merely described the ways in which rulers made use of it for immediate advantage. It is so ingrained in our nature and the very shape of our lives, said Machon, that men of all stripes in all ages have resorted to it. And again he presented long lists of leaders, including biblical figures and saints, who had indulged in the practice.[401] The essence of his position, however, he reserved for his final consideration when he asserted that not only is deceit permissible to a prince; the condition of human affairs is such that the ruler is *required* to use it if he would fulfill his obligations to the state:

I say with so many learned men that one may justly and legitimately deceive for the good and the preservation of the state, since he could not be excused who would permit its ruin and

---

[399] *Ibid.*, fols. 195-97.
[400] Machon treated these as maxim 10 in Pt. I and maxims 5, 6, and 7 in Pt. II.
[401] *Apologie*, fols. 315-50.

loss ... Is it more just and legitimate to gain by violence or by deceit? The same laws that authorize one do not condemn the other .... If he who deceives breaks his word, he who forces him to do so is unjust in obliging him to keep to things to which he is not bound. Kings are always each other's enemies; when they are not injuring one another, it is because they are unable to do so .... Since they do not depend upon themselves but upon their neighbors, their subjects, their enemies, and the many disruptions and civil wars that are constantly aroused against them, they must also be dependent upon times and events, that is, they must know how to make use of these and bend them to the benefit of their states. The wise man does not always walk at the same pace any more than he always takes the same road; he does not change but adapts himself. If it is necessary and within his power, he does what his enemy condemns. ... The clever sailor adjusts his sails according to the times and the winds ... all roads are good that lead straight to a safe haven. It is a great thing for a man to succeed well, and if the means were as praiseworthy as the end, they would be too glorious and belong only to God. In a word, everyone agrees that the prince may justly and legitimately deceive for the good and benefit of his state.[402]

For Machon, the ruler's great responsibilities and the nature of political affairs entirely justified any mechanism that might enable him to fulfill the obligations of his office.

Having developed this position, Machon easily disposed of such matters as finesse and dissimulation by finding them both honorable and necessary.[403] Machiavelli's maxim that the prince should preserve an appearance of virtue even though he lacked this quality Machon found somewhat more troublesome and analyzed at greater length.[404] Machiavelli's objective, Machon declared, was not to urge that the mere appearance of virtue was equal to its essence but to show that while the virtues of the prince and his subjects were the same, their resulting practices were entirely different.[405] All men,

[402] *Ibid.*, fols. 353-57.   [403] *Ibid.*, fols. 627-63.   [404] *Ibid.*, fols. 664-713.
[405] *Ibid.*, fols. 670-71.

kings and commoners, have the same relations with God, he maintained, but their virtues are applied in very different fashions among
men. For example, the prince might break his contracts and other
agreements for the general good, but such was not permitted to his
subjects.[406] The special functions and obligations of the ruler set
him apart from and above all others. And Machon added that in
any case an appearance of virtue was of value even without its substance, since the people are chiefly impressed by externals and the
tradition of equitable rule would thereby be perpetuated.

In Machon's examination of these propositions, he was developing an essential component of reason of state—two levels of morality which justified questionable actions by the ruler but denied them
to the subjects. The special ethic of politics he made clear in discussing the maxim, "It is permissible to break faith for the good of the
state and the safety of the republic."[407] At once he asserted that it
was impossible to keep faith, given the frailty of human nature and
the conditions of earthly existence. "In order to be exempt from
disavowal, it [an agreement] should not be subject to error; and
never to revoke a promise, one must never have erred."[408] Such was
manifestly impossible in human affairs, Machon insisted. If holy
vows to God might be revoked because of such circumstances as lack
of consent, so much the more should princes be permitted to break
their promises to mere men, particularly when the good of millions
was involved. Machiavelli praised fidelity to promises but believed it
impossible in practice; thus he adopted the common-sense position
that princes must preserve their liberty of action. "Let us then say
that the prince may break his faith and promises for the good of the
state and the safety of the republic."[409] Realizing that he had gone
far to justify any expedient policy, Machon pushed on to the logical
conclusion:

> A prince, a sovereign, and all the most powerful ministers of
> state should have no other aim nor guide to their duty than the
> safety of the people, the public utility, and the preservation of

[406] *Ibid.*, fols. 674-75.   [407] *Ibid.*, fols. 388-424.   [408] *Ibid.*, fol. 389.
[409] *Ibid.*, fol. 392.

the state. *Suprema lex salus populi*. These four words form the cube and base of all political laws; this oracle is the secret of human prudence, and this rule is the only one that should be common to all men. It is she that conveys innocence and requires that love of country be the aim of our moral virtue and the object of our earthly affections.[410]

Machon faced the problem of two levels of morality most directly and extensively in commenting on Machiavelli's maxim, "A prince should accommodate vices and virtues to his state." Apparently realizing the great importance of the doctrine of two moralities to reason of state and the difficulties that it presented, Machon devoted more space to this maxim than any other.[411] First, he felt it necessary to posit at length a thoroughly relativist concept of virtue. Far from adhering to any absolute standard, virtue for him was decidedly uncertain since it varied with circumstances and in any case was very rare in human society.[412] He then moved logically to a straightforward, thoroughgoing exposition of the superiority of the ruler's virtues over all others:

It is time to speak of the prince's advantages and privileges. His nature is human but his status raises him above, and separates him from, the commonality of others. His quality dispenses him from thousands of subjections that are inseparable from private persons and all who are under his scepter and his crown, there being nothing more certain than that the justice, virtue, and integrity of the sovereign function entirely otherwise than those of individuals. It has broader and more liberal ways because of the great, burdensome, and dangerous responsibility that it bears and conveys, which causes it to perform in a manner that would seem confused and disordered in another but is nonetheless necessary, upright, and legitimate in him. He must sometimes evade and dodge; a measure opportunely taken gains on the road rather than lengthening it. He is required to mingle prudence with justice, not always nor in all cases but when it is

[410] *Ibid.*, fols. 423-24. This is the conclusion of Bk. 1.
[411] *Ibid.*, fols. 444-583.   [412] *Ibid.*, fols. 445-508.

a question of necessity and the important and evident utility of the republic, that is, of the state and the prince which are things conjoined and inseparable. This obligation is natural to him and cannot be dispensed with because of any pretext whatsoever. He always does what he must when he achieves and increases the public good. *Salus populi suprema lex esto.*[413]

Applying this to those who made official policy, Machon continued: "This distinction is so just and reasonable that it is certain that princes and their ministers do many things which are considered good and praiseworthy but which nevertheless would be reprehensible and vicious, even punishable, in individuals."[414] Rarely before had the concept of two levels of morality been so explicitly stated. Machon hastened to add that the prince should indulge in such measures only for public reasons and never for personal,[415] but he then proceeded to support his position with the following arguments. "Because the prince is in his state what God is in heaven, the sun is in nature, and the soul is in the body,"[416] he *must* conduct himself unlike common men, for otherwise "Where would be his prudence? Where would be his quality of father and ruler of the people? Where would be the difference between the man and the sovereign? . . . How would he distinguish between his personal, private actions and those as king which concern the good of his state and the preservation of his subjects?"[417] The reasoning was powerful and quite in accord with contemporary assumptions concerning the monarch's superior qualities and supreme role in guiding all public affairs. In this context, Machon was entirely logical in emphasizing the superhuman, divinely bestowed virtues of the prince and their application to the problems of government through true prudence:

Who would dare deny the paternal love and more-than-human charity that they have for their people, their subjects, and their state? Let us therefore say that only the virtue of the prince is perfect, prudent, and charitable, and that protection depends

---

[413] *Ibid.*, fols. 508-09.
[414] *Ibid.*, fol. 513. Machon cites Montaigne in support of this statement.
[415] *Ibid.*, fol. 520.   [416] *Ibid.*, fol. 521.   [417] *Ibid.*, fol. 522.

on his being able to blend it with all the others so as to achieve the necessary results; that his prudence consists of being able to adapt it [his virtue] to the state; and that his charity is evidenced by the care, vigilance, and benevolence that he has for the good, the benefit, and the preservation of his people.[418]

All these positions, it should be noted, Machon supported with extensive references to the "authorities," especially Scripture and the Church Fathers. As a typical advanced absolutist, he concluded that the superior virtue of the ruler, when exercised with essentially unlimited discretion according to his unique insights, endowed him with the true prudence with which he alone might conduct justifiable policy for the general good.

Such were the positions that Machon developed in this remarkable treatise in which he simultaneously defended Machiavelli's precepts and Richelieu's policies by articulating the doctrines of divine right absolutism and reason of state. Even this incomplete examination of Machon's work indicates the complexities of his argumentation and many of the compromises that were required of those who would coordinate reason of state with Christian morality. Machon defended Machiavelli by presenting him as an acute, disinterested analyst of nefarious political practices, as a writer whose precepts were justified by depraved human nature and political necessity, and as a Christian who deplored the collapse of virtue among men and proposed measures that found their justifications in their benefit of the general good. All this, Machon believed, was entirely legitimate because in his view it accorded with the canons of Christian morality. In implementing this position, however, he not only upheld the ruler's divine authorization, inspiration, and vast discretion as did most of his contemporaries; at the same time he went far toward separating politics and morals by assuming a relativist position regarding higher values, interpreting religion as an inward thing whose outward manifestations might be accommodated to the needs of the state, and extensively developing the concept of two levels of morality which all but exempted the ruler

[418] *Ibid.*, fols. 539-40.

from Christian principles that bound ordinary men. All this enabled Machon to quote with approval the ancient maxim, *salus populi suprema lex esto*. His version of reason of state contained all requisite elements and more, but it was not an accurate reflection of Machiavelli's thought. Neither was it entirely in accord with Richelieu's view of the matter. Instead, it should be regarded as a valuable statement of the exaggerated absolutist view of divine-right sovereignty, reason of state, and the logical end-positions to which these doctrines might be pushed. Richelieu himself and his more representative followers hesitated before more than one of the precepts that Machon, in his desire to please the Cardinal, developed to the hilt. In the broadest sense, Machon's treatise is significant in that it presents further if ingenuous evidence that Richelieu and those who supported him grounded their political ideology upon the Christian nature of the state and thereby found religious justifications for policies that were undertaken for its benefit.

While Louis Machon was presenting in extreme form the ideology of reason of state, certain more important followers of Richelieu were elaborating and qualifying the position in various ways. Their handling of the concept varied greatly according to a variety of factors, such as each man's personal circumstances, his closeness to the Cardinal, his instinctive moral reactions to the impact of official policies upon the life of the realm, and his consequent views of means-end argumentation and all that it implied. Silhon, Balzac, La Mothe le Vayer, and Priézac are most representative of this group. All were members of the French Academy, the latter two having won acceptance into the ranks of the Immortals early in 1639. Consideration of their mature views of reason of state during the final years of the reign graphically reveals the extent to which these consistent supporters of the Cardinal continued to accept its fundamentals but also, in certain instances, recoiled before some of its implications. Their doubts stemmed both from disillusionment with the practical consequences of the doctrine and the moral problems that it presented. In certain instances these became evident only after Richelieu's death; for this reason we must give limited consideration to their relevant views after 1642. In no case, however, was there a sharp reversal of a given author's position; rather, their qualifications of reason of state can be shown to have stemmed from the logic of their earlier precepts. Even Guez de Balzac, who violently criticized the Cardinal after his death, was merely voicing sentiments that had been brewing in his mind for years, while Silhon and Priézac essentially did little more than carry their earlier views to fruition. The great diversity of their positions in their published works late in the reign and shortly thereafter dramatically demonstrates that they were fully capable of combining intellectual independence with staunch absolutism and that even among writers who stood high in Richelieu's favor there was no single, official view of reason of state.

During these years, Jean de Silhon was one of the most active members of the French Academy and likewise one who was closest to Richelieu. Upon the latter's death, Silhon transferred his allegiance to Cardinal Mazarin and became his secretary, traveling with him and writing in his support. Silhon consistently remained in the clienteles of the two First Ministers, but it should be noted that in spite of his continuing favor he retained his personal integrity and independence in the eyes of his contemporaries, remaining in royal service at considerable personal sacrifice.[419] He likewise continued to adhere to the religious orthodoxy that he had spelled out at length in such earlier works as his *Deux veritez* and *De l'Immortalité de l'ame*.[420] Repeatedly seeking to stem the destructive influence of skepticism, deism, and Machiavellism among his contemporaries, he presented a rationalized, orthodox defense of Christianity and sought at the same time to elaborate his views of the rightful relations between politics and morals in the Christian French state.

For our purposes, Silhon's most important publication during this period is Part II of his *Ministre d'Estat* which appeared in 1643 but was completed under Richelieu.[421] The work embodies Silhon's mature reflections concerning the problem of morals and politics in

[419] Pellisson, Vol. I, 279-83.   [420] See Pt. II, n. 163, 151.

[421] *Le Ministre d'Estat, avec le veritable usage de la politique moderne*, 2ᵉ partie, Paris, 1643. The privilege is dated November 21, 1642.

the light of Richelieu's policies. Understandably, the entire book is devoted to defending Richelieu's foreign policy, by far his most significant application of the doctrine of reason of state in this period. In his introductory *Au Lecteur*, Silhon indicates that he frankly if moderately presents the case for the French king in his war with Spain. While the Spanish have many good qualities, he added, their foreign policy is always based on *force et artifice*, and lacks the justice that accompanies French arms. His purpose was therefore to elucidate the essential justice of the French cause against Catholic Spain. In this way he believed that he was serving both his prince and his *patrie*.

In laying the groundwork for his case, Silhon fell back upon the accepted concept of divine-right monarchy and all that it implied concerning the fundamental justice of royal governance. God gives the power of justice to sovereigns, he said; they should therefore exercise it boldly over their subjects and in their relations with other princes. Such is not only the essence of royal rule; it also gives the prince the right to wage a just war and to ensure justice unto himself.[422] Having posited this basis for the rightful use of force in interstate relations, Silhon then developed certain criteria for the observation of justice in war.[423] Ideally, he said, a war is just, necessary, and for the good of the state only when the *honnête* and the *utile* are conjoined, but since this is not always possible, the prince should attempt as far as he can to preserve both the form and matter of justice in the following ways. (1) Rather than annihilate a defeated and disarmed army, he should follow the laws of war, *honnêteté* and *bienséance*. (2) The justice of a war should not be measured by its utility or success; such is the teaching of Machiavelli. Rather, its purpose and motivation should be the criterion. (3) A war should not be justified on religious grounds unless they are genuine; the Spanish have erred in this respect. Specious religious justification might enable the prince to use bad means toward a good end. The Crusades were waged primarily against the power, incursions, and barbarisms of the Moslems rather than the errors of Mohammed. (4) Justice requires that Catholic rulers keep their

[422] Bk. 1, Discourses 2, 3.   [423] Bk. 1, Discourse 4.

sworn promises even to heretic princes, since there are certain common precepts among men which all upright persons should observe. Religion does not destroy these; on the contrary, it reinforces them. If the papacy and other Catholic powers deny the necessity of keeping faith with heretics, they are merely following their own interests.

A mere listing of Silhon's recommendations at once reveals his overriding concern for justice in war and his need of carefully threading his way through a variety of considerations in order to demonstrate the justice of the French cause. Convinced as he was that right and morality lay with the French, he nevertheless was forced to maneuver among various alternatives when defending Richelieu's policies. To strengthen his case he added the further considerations of honor and pacific intentions to his arguments for the French side in the conflict. Princes must defend their honor and reputation, he insisted. The King of France could not honorably avoid war in this instance after the fall of Trier and the capture of the Elector who was under French protection.[424] For the same reason, Louis XIII was bound to honor his commitments to his allies.[425] The French king's intentions were likewise more honorable than those of the Spanish, since the French consistently sought peace whereas the Spanish were the aggressors and continually worked for perpetuation of the conflict—a position which Silhon attempted to uphold with a rather forced account of recent events.[426]

None of these arguments was new, and Silhon was merely marshalling them in support of what he believed to be the superior morality of the French cause. Taken together, they went far to implement and corroborate the moderate, religiously based version of reason of state that characterized the thinking of the men closest to Richelieu. One fundamental question, however, inevitably presented itself to Silhon and many who thought like him. Since justice was his main concern, what limits did it impose on the discretionary power of the ruler? Reason of state in the hands of a Christian prince seemed to go far toward justifying any and all acts that he might in good conscience deem essential to the general good.

[424] Bk. 1, Discourse 5.   [425] Bk. 1, Discourse 8.
[426] Bk. 1, Discourses 9, 11, 12.

Specifically, were there any remaining limits upon the sovereign's power over his subjects? And was there not a genuine risk that power so exercised might destroy individuals or at least debase their character and true worth? Fully aware that recent events rendered such speculation more than a mere rhetorical exercise, Silhon approached the issue from the standpoint of the honor of individuals and states respectively.[427] Personal honor he defined in the highest terms as merit, uprightness, and integrity, a manifestation of virtue which is the "final objective of man in this life."[428] It crowns all faculties and all operations of the soul; men prize it above all else. The reputation of the state, on the contrary, is inferior in that it may stem from causes other than virtue, such as success and power. In this perspective, personal morality was superior to public. Silhon thereupon asked whether the king, who might rightfully sacrifice his subjects' lives and goods for the public benefit, might also sacrifice their honor for the same reason. And he gave as an illustration the destruction of a man's reputation by causing him to appear guilty of a crime when he was innocent, thereby discharging the ruler's culpability upon a victimized subject.[429] To this question, Silhon answered categorically in the negative. The people, he reasoned, had transferred to their ruler many powers over themselves but not supremacy over their honor which stems from nature and is based upon personal virtue. Subjection to the ruler is owed in many areas but not in this. The power of kings is great, he said, but is not without limit. As kings have no right to oblige their subjects to violate the laws of *probité* and become perjurers, blasphemers, and adulterers, they must not dishonor them with false accusations. Silhon's argumentation in this instance patently differed from the usual justifications of divine-right monarchy and the inherent justice of the enlightened ruler's policies. Its presence in his work clearly indicates that one of Richelieu's closest followers firmly believed

---

[427] Bk. 1, Discourse 10, "De la différence qu'il y a entre l'Honneur des Particuliers et la Reputation des Estats, et si le Prince est maistre de l'honneur aussi bien que de la vie et du bien de ses sujets, quand la necessité publique le requiert."

[428] *Ibid.*, p. 157.   [429] *Ibid.*, pp. 160-64.

that justice and right not only were concomitant elements of reason of state in a Christian monarchy but also placed meaningful limits upon the royal discretion.

This qualification of royal absolutism was a minor element in Silhon's work, although a very significant one. He even carried it further by asking whether the subjects themselves had the right to sacrifice their honor for the public interest, thereby destroying their own reputations for the preservation of that of the prince and his policies.[430] Silhon recognized that the problem, couched in these terms, presented great difficulties. Reason of state, he admitted, both permits and rewards doing one's worst to one's enemy, but he quickly added that even war should be conducted according to *droit des gens*. Too frequently men debase their honor, "principally when this prostitution is covered by a special cloak, such as the service of the prince or the good of his affairs."[431] Again Silhon's reluctance to accept certain implications of reason of state is evident. Such debasement of persons, he lamented, was constantly occurring at court, where men readily sacrificed honor and virtue for wealth and power. But the remedy was simply to avoid falling into this trap, and he doggedly maintained that many lived upright lives and preserved their honor in the midst of the evils and temptations of the court. They were even rewarded for it, though infrequently.

This was Silhon's reasoned defense of Richelieu's policies and the ethic of reason of state. It is evident that his argumentation left many important questions unanswered and that he hesitated before some of the implications of reason of state as he knew it, particularly its potential for abuse of power and debasement of persons who might become its innocent victims. Whether Silhon had in mind any who had felt the heavy hand of Richelieu's "tyranny" is impossible to determine, but it is noteworthy that he entered this caveat in his last writing under the Cardinal and that it was in this area rather than broader policy matters that Silhon perceived the greatest risks. It is nevertheless clear that in spite of this nagging doubt, he continued to uphold the justice of the French cause as rooted in Christian morality, not only because its objectives accorded with justice and right

[430] *Ibid.*, pp. 164-72. [431] *Ibid.*, pp. 169-70.

but also because he believed that it might be implemented by justifiable means. This was his answer to the charge that reason of state permitted the ruler to utilize any measures provided they brought general benefit—a Machiavellian doctrine which he specifically repudiated. His insistence upon just measures appeared not only in his repeated emphasis upon the necessity of observing the laws of war; he also made this the basis of his criticism of Spanish efforts toward universal monarchy in the final portion of his book.[432] After extensively reviewing the growth of this policy from Ferdinand and Isabella through Charles V and Philip II to the Emperor Ferdinand, Silhon urged that the stated objective of the Spanish to arrest the spread of heresy may have been good but the means that they employed to this end were bad.[433] Ferdinand II in particular used force and bloody repression quite unjustifiably and sought to establish a basis of conquest through illegal seizures in Germany. These were immoral methods, Silhon concluded, and went far to justify the French entry into the war because, contrary to Spanish practices, the measures that were undertaken by the French were just and their objective was peace and justice for all parties. In this way, Silhon claimed that both the means and ends of French policy rested upon a sound moral foundation, and that Cardinal Richelieu had successfully avoided the trap, so intrinsic in reason of state, of adopting immoral means to a good end.

While Jean de Silhon was refining his views of reason of state and attempting to mitigate certain of its implications, Guez de Balzac was reversing his position much more dramatically, although for very different reasons. After his *Prince* failed to win him either Richelieu's favor or recognition among the *literati*, Balzac nevertheless continued to seek fame and fortune at the highest levels. Richelieu, unimpressed, refused him a sinecure in the church, dashing his hopes for a more comfortable existence. When the French Academy was founded, Balzac reluctantly accepted membership and appeared before the group once, to read parts of his *Aristippe*.[434]

[432] The subject of the entire Bk. III.
[433] Bk. III, Discourses 6, 7.   [434] See n. 153 and text.

His projected dedication of the work to the Cardinal receiving no favorable response, he retreated to his homestead on the banks of the Charente, never to see the capital again. His isolation was merely physical, however, and he continued to write and publish, and carried on an enormous correspondence with important persons throughout Europe. Evidently torn by conflicting emotions, his enormous vanity and egotism caused him continually to seek to increase his renown, particularly in literary circles, and he even had the temerity to manifest pretensions to a bishopric. On the other hand, he took comfort in avoiding the frustrations of the court, and above all he prided himself on preserving intact his intellectual independence and integrity as well as his large measure of idealism.

These circumstances partially explain Balzac's violent expressions of hostility toward Cardinal Richelieu, beginning immediately after the latter's death. In his correspondence with his intimate, Chapelain, after 1642, Balzac repeatedly and explicitly accused Richelieu of the most heinous tyranny.[435] His hatred of the Cardinal knew no bounds and seems genuine, and he took delight in exchanging criticisms of the former First Minister with his sworn enemy, Charles de Montchal, Archbishop of Toulouse.[436] Balzac blamed Richelieu for the many long, arbitrary imprisonments in the Bastile,[437] and above all he castigated him for continuing the war beyond all reason.[438] In all this, Balzac recognized the blatant shift in his own position, but could merely lament that he had earlier been duped into praising the Cardinal and insisted that he now unequivocally preferred the policies of the Regent.[439] Actually, his change of viewpoint was neither immediate nor total, since he had been moving away from Richelieu's position for some time and had developed certain doubts concerning his policies. In any case, Balzac now turned toward the new rising star, Mazarin, and again sought recognition and monetary reward. Repeatedly he urged Chapelain, acting through Silhon as intermediary, to intercede for him and secure him a pension or

---

[435] *Lettres de Jean-Louis Guez de Balzac*, ed. P. Tamizey de Larroque, in *Mélanges historiques*, Paris, 1873, pp. 409-10, 424, 461, 462.
[436] *Ibid.*, pp. 429-30.
[437] *Ibid.*, p. 410.   [438] *Ibid.*, p. 462.   [439] *Ibid.*, p. 543.

even a bishopric, although always protesting that he could subsist without aid and maintain his intellectual independence. He even rededicated his *Aristippe* to the new First Minister.[440] Mazarin, however, remained as obdurate as Richelieu, and after all such efforts failed, Balzac rededicated the ill-fated work to Queen Christina of Sweden, in which form it was posthumously published in 1658. In his last years, Balzac withdrew more and more unto himself, seeking solace in religion. He added two rooms to the Capuchin house at Angoulême, retreating there intermittently and working on such tracts as his *Socrate chrétien*. Although a friend and admirer of leading Jansenists, he had no affinity for their rigorous doctrines and instead developed a simple fideism, increasingly rejecting his earlier rationalism and the world in which he had lived his checkered career.[441]

The difficulty of establishing with certainty Balzac's view of reason of state at any given moment is well illustrated by his *Aristippe*.[442] Undertaken very early in his career, it became one of his favorite projects and he worked on it all his life. Consisting of seven discourses, it purports to present a picture of the perfect minister, his key role in affairs, his vital position as intermediary between the king and the nation, and the innumerable pitfalls and possibilities of misguided counsel that plagued the court. The work was apparently undertaken originally for Richelieu, and according to Balzac's own statement the Cardinal read and approved it, perhaps in its entirety.[443] After its various dedications and possible reworking, the book finally appeared in print four years after Balzac's death. It is therefore impossible to assign the *Aristippe* to any given period of his career, although the better part of it seems to have been completed before 1642.[444] Also, as always, Balzac's penchant for exag-

---

[440] *Ibid.*, pp. 474, 488, 566, 577.

[441] J. B. Sabrié, *Les Idées religieuses de J.-L. Guez de Balzac*, Paris, 1913. H. Busson, *La Pensée religieuse française de Charron à Pascal*, Paris, 1933, pp. 266-69.

[442] *Aristippe ou De la Cour*, Paris, 1658. In *Œuvres*, Paris, 1665, Vol. II, 125-90. My citations are to the *Œuvres*.

[443] *Aristippe, avant-propos*, p. 127.

[444] In a letter to Conrart, dated March 4, 1652, Balzac wrote: "Mon *Aristippe*

geration and fascination with his own rhetoric must be taken into account when analyzing the work. In it he nevertheless presented straightforward and significant observations concerning the problem of reason of state.

For our purposes, the most pregnant passages of the work occur in the sixth and seventh discourses. In the former, Balzac argued that Cato's idealism, which is here pictured as utterly doctrinaire and impractical, was entirely unsuited to the maneuvers and compromises that are essential to effective government:

> The world lost its innocence long ago. We live in the corruption of centuries and the decrepitude of nature. All is deficient; all is diseased in assemblies of men. If therefore you wish to govern effectively, if you seek to work successfully for the good of the state, accommodate yourself to the defect and imperfection of your material. Rid yourself of that importunate virtue of which your age is incapable. Endure what you are unable to reform. Conceal the faults that cannot be corrected .... It is fine, if possible, to satisfy the honor and dignity of the crown. But do not lose the crown in attempting to preserve its honor and dignity .... Remember that reason is of much less moment in politics than in morality, and that its latitude is much more extensive and freer without comparison when it is a question of making the people happy than when making individuals honest. There are maxims that are unjust by their nature but which their use justifies. There are foul remedies; they are nevertheless remedies .... Poison cures on some occasions, and in this instance poison is not bad.[445]

Such a statement closely resembles Balzac's most extravagant justifications of reason of state in his *Prince*.[446] But immediately in his

---

est entièrement achevé, et je vous advouë que c'est le cher et le bien-aimé de mes enfans." *Œuvres*, Vol. I, 930. On the other hand, in the *avant-propos* to the work, Balzac stated that Richelieu took no offense when he read the *seven* discourses. It would seem that the work was essentially completed before 1642 but may have been extensively retouched later.

[445] *Aristippe*, pp. 173-74.   [446] See Pt. III, n. 197 and text.

seventh discourse, which he devoted to the dangers of tyranny that might result from the influence of utterly unscrupulous ministers, he vociferously cautioned against the evils of such a regime:

> What shall we say of those unbearable servants who avenge their slightest quarrels with the arms and weapons of their master, who declare guilty of *lèse-majesté* all who do not prostrate themselves before them, and who, with bloody and cruel stillness, black with mourning and death, bring the people to despair and reduce upright men to incapacity to protect themselves save through revolt?[447]

Such ministers corrupt the ruler by urging the legitimacy of all measures of any kind, even those contrary to law, morality, religion, and the good of the people. If they wish to rid themselves of a member of the royal family, commit incest, break their word, or rely upon mere force in all things, they find many specious justifications and persuade the sovereign that he alone determines what is just and unjust. They replace the ruler's older, trusted advisers, persuade him to undertake new projects merely for his personal glory, and in innumerable ways render themselves indispensable. Such fearful developments subject the ruler himself to the tyranny of his ministers—a complete perversion of monarchy in which the king alone must rule according to law, morality, and above all the dictates of his divine mission. And Balzac concluded by urging all true kings to preserve their independence from ministerial influence and to reserve major areas of government to themselves.

These diverse elements in Balzac's *Aristippe* clearly indicate the tensions in his own thinking between the practical necessities of government in his own time and his determination to preserve the supremacy of moral values in political affairs. The dichotomy, however, is more apparent than real, since both elements were central to his concept of just and effective monarchy. The extent to which his evident fear of ministerial tyranny reflected any personal reaction to Richelieu's policies and great power is impossible to determine, particularly before 1642, although the bias of the *Aristippe* indi-

[447] *Aristippe*, p. 179.

cates that, at the very least, his thinking was potentially, and in some respects fundamentally, hostile to the Cardinal's acts. Be that as it may, extensive evidence exists showing Balzac's immediate, unabashed, violent revulsion against Richelieu immediately after his death. This appears not only in Balzac's correspondence but more extensively in his *Discours à la Reine, sur sa Régence,* with which he hailed the new regime.[448] The massive proportions of his criticism of Richelieu might, at first blush, be taken as another instance of his rhetorical extravagance, but Balzac assured his friend Chapelain, in a letter dated December 14, 1643, that the piece was not a panegyric but straightforward, measured, and deliberately moderate.[449] For once, it seems, Balzac's statements may be accepted at face value, at least in their specific content.

For all its lofty tone, Balzac's *Discours à la Reine* is a thoroughgoing critique of Richelieu's regime, especially his foreign policy, and a pained outcry for amelioration of conditions within the realm. Although the Cardinal is rarely mentioned—Balzac's stated intention was to blame the war for everything and to blame no one for the war[450]—his implications concerning responsibility are clear. Balzac opened his peroration by hailing the Regent in appropriately extravagant terms, praising her virtue, loyalty, and religiosity, and insisting that she alone might bring order and prosperity to the realm. Her piety was literally heaven-sent, an instrument of God, and ensured her success in all beneficent undertakings. Her clemency and mercy were at once made evident at the beginning of the Regency when she freed many political prisoners—surely a thrust at Richelieu.[451] Such statements as these clearly indicate the new orientation of Balzac's thought. Instead of advocating heroic deeds and prosecution of a just war for laudable motives, he now would replace all this with the Regent's piety and virtue as the major forces for betterment. "It is your virtue, Madam, from which we hope for

[448] *Discours à la Reine, sur sa Régence, fait en l'an* MDCXLIII, in *Œuvres,* Vol. II, 466-81.

[449] *Lettres,* p. 456.   [450] *Discours,* p. 471.

[451] *Ibid.,* p. 469. This is confirmed by a letter to Chapelain, dated September 14, 1643. *Lettres,* p. 410.

more than your armies, however victorious; than your alliances, however powerful and numerous; from your ambassadors, however wise and skillful. All their policies may be uselessly employed, whereas one of your sighs may succeed."[452] Such was his frame of reference that rejection of war as a viable instrument of just policy left him no alternative save pacification through divine intervention via the Regent.

Balzac's denunciation of the war that stemmed from Richelieu's foreign policy was so thorough that he echoed many of the criticisms that had been voiced by the Cardinal's *dévot* adversaries in the 1620's and 1630's. The condition of the lower classes he found abominable —so much so that he even discounted the glory that traditionally accompanied wars:

> The people, Madam, are made up of wretches and constantly present to your sight or imagination only infirmities and wounds, groans, and pain. They are not nourished by the momentous news that comes from your armies nor the great reputation of your generals. Their desires are more rude and their thoughts more tied to the earth. Glory is a passion that they do not know, that is too subtle and spiritual for them. They desire more wheat and fewer laurels. They often mourn the victories of their rulers and are chilled beside their bonfires because the benefits of war are never perfect nor victories complete, because mourning, losses, and poverty often accompany triumphs. No matter how great the success that accompanies our arms on the frontier and outside the realm, their renown abroad does not cure domestic ills. After facing the enemy on the frontier and abroad, everyone finds himself wretched at home. And the condition in which we are is not a true prosperity; it is a misery that is praised and in good repute.[453]

Moreover, the war was destroying all human ties, justice, equity, and religion:

> Age has not made the war better; it has not been converted from its ancient impiety. It continues to violate religion and pro-

[452] *Discours*, p. 475.   [453] *Ibid.*, p. 471.

fane altars. Disorder, license, and unpunished crimes still follow in its train; it still mocks justice and equity, kinship and compacts, and begins by breaking the most sacred ties that link men with each other. It was never more pitiless nor more cruel.[454]

Balzac's denunciation was total. He even added that the war partook of a fratricidal character because both parties adhered to the Catholic faith.[455] Initial responsibility for the conflict, he held, lay with the Spanish who had launched it in the affair of the Mantuan succession and the siege of Casal. But if the Spanish were the original guilty party, "a Frenchman who is no longer in this world did not wish to terminate it, and seeking to perpetuate our ills, in order to render his authority eternal, always merged his ambition with the justice of the cause of France"[456]—another transparent thrust at Richelieu whom he thus accused of prolonging all the evils of war for personal advantage.[457] As for justifications, "we should recall that necessity is a violent and imperious thing, that its counsels are absolute and unconditional, and that it justifies what it counsels."[458] There was no solution but to ignore the advice of those who advocate war:

Regardless of the specious likelihood with which its terms are colored, distrust rhetoric that seems to embellish precipices and abysses, rhetoric of fire and blood, counsellor of death and misery, ruinous to your state, and hostile to your person. It greatly extolls the reputation of your arms, your advantages over the enemy, and the dignity of your crown. But do not listen to it to the detriment of public opinion which assures you that the true dignity of the crown is the good of the realm and implores you to cease to conquer, to make no more conquests, and to put an end to your profitable successes. Since one victory always requires another, you are obliged to subsidize and nourish your conquests, your successes will never end our ill fortune, and gain increases poverty.[459]

[454] *Ibid.*, p. 472. [455] *Ibid.*, p. 477. [456] *Ibid.*, p. 474.
[457] This is confirmed in his letter to Chapelain, January 4, 1644. *Lettres*, p. 462.
[458] *Discours*, p. 478. [459] *Ibid.*, p. 476.

From every standpoint, he concluded, "there can be no public felicity without general peace."[460] War was a scourge of God, but peace
would likewise come from God through the Regent's piety. And he
terminated his *Discours* by describing the benefits of peace: the restoration of order, decency, humanity, Christian virtue, the honor
due each element of society, and the reunion of the royal family,
including Gaston d'Orléans whose true worth had been obscured
by "the violences and artifices of a hostile court."[461]

Tyrannical, self-interested, and misguided—such was Balzac's denunciation of Richelieu's reason of state. Clearly, the main target of
Balzac's barbs was the war's destructive impact upon conditions of
life and the very civilization of the realm, and his revulsion pushed
him to the point of denying war's traditional glory and even its
viability as an instrument of policy. Convinced as he was that war
could bring no good, he even went so far as to reject the concept
of a just war for a rightful cause and regarded its continuation, regardless of its objectives, as a crime against the true interests of the
state. In its place he would substitute the virtue and piety of the
Regent as the most effective force for good in the Christian monarchy that was France. How much of this was motivated by Balzac's
self-interest is impossible to establish, yet it seems evident that he
increasingly rejected reason of state at least in part for idealistic
reasons.

The evolution of François de La Mothe le Vayer's views on reason
of state was somewhat more complex. Through Richelieu's last years,
this well-known skeptic continued his active support of the Cardinal's policies, although without examining in print the fundamental
issue of morals and politics, except by implication. As we have noted,
his tracts in which he lauded specific developments in foreign affairs
were essentially works of circumstance that avoided the deeper
problems of political morality.[462] At the same time, his ambition for
recognition in high places increased. This he made clear in his

[460] *Ibid.*, p. 478.   [461] *Ibid.*, p. 481.
[462] See n. 187-92 and text.

Discours de l'histoire which was published in 1638.[463] In this work, he frankly used his criticism of the Spanish historian Sandoval's history of Charles V as a vehicle for justifying Richelieu's foreign policy. As he said, if the enterprises of Francis I are denounced, "should it not be feared that similar animosity might be directed against those in which your incomparable prudence is constantly admired, that all the good intentions of our great king might be wrongly interpreted, and that his most heroic acts might be similarly exposed to slander?"[464] And La Mothe le Vayer marshalled in the body of this lengthy work all the usual denunciations of the Spanish in such a way as to justify continuation of the war. The effort evidently pleased the Cardinal, and on February 14, 1638, its author was named to a chair in the French Academy.

La Mothe le Vayer's mounting ambitions were further indicated by his two major works during Richelieu's final years. Neither was officially sponsored by Richelieu, but both were dedicated to him and were patently motivated by La Mothe le Vayer's effort to gain increased favor with the all-powerful First Minister. The first, *De l'Instruction de Monseigneur le Dauphin*,[465] was the author's bid for the coveted post of preceptor to the Dauphin. It consists of brief, generalized treatments of a host of subjects needful to a prince: religion, justice, administration, various fields of learning, the arts, war, royal pastimes, etc., and despite its breadth contains nothing of value on our subject since it avoids all thorny issues and presents mere platitudes. Both Chapelain and Balzac criticized it as a string of commonplaces.[466] La Mothe le Vayer's other work, *De la Vertu*

---

[463] *Discours de l'histoire, où est examinée celle de Prudence de Sandoval, Chroniqueur du feu Roy d'Espagne, Philippe III, et Evesque de Pampelune, qui a escrit la Vie de l'Empereur Charles-Quint*, Paris, 1638. In *Œuvres*, Paris, 1662, Vol. I, 225-78. My citations are to the *Œuvres*.

[464] *Ibid.*, Dedicatory Epistle to Richelieu, p. 228.

[465] Paris, 1640. In *Œuvres*, Vol. I, 1-156.

[466] Wickelgren, p. 38. The similarity between La Mothe le Vayer's ideas in this work and those in Richelieu's *Testament politique* is indicated in L. Lacroix, *Quid de instituendo senserit Vayerius*, Paris, 1890, Chap. 5. Lacroix's explanation is that La Mothe le Vayer was very familiar with

des Payens, appeared in 1642,[467] and was part of the very extensive debate that stemmed from the rise of Jansenism.[468] Assuming the Cardinal's anti-Jansenist stance, La Mothe le Vayer attempted to reinforce it by arguing that the virtues of the ancient pagans were such that there was a strong probability of their salvation. The subsequent literary debate between La Mothe le Vayer and the great Arnauld demonstrated the weakness of the skeptic's theological position. These works identified La Mothe le Vayer as a partisan and supporter of Richelieu, but the latter's death brought a decline in his fortunes. When the preceptor to the Dauphin was finally chosen, the intellectual climate had changed and both the Regent and Mazarin rejected La Mothe le Vayer's candidacy. He was nevertheless made preceptor to Philip, the Duke of Anjou, in 1647.

From the early years of the Regency until he assumed his duties as preceptor to Monsieur, La Mothe le Vayer seems to have maintained only intermittent contact with the court. Simultaneously attracted by its honors and repelled by the way of life that it imposed upon all residents, he intensely disliked the personal servitudes of the life of a courtier and the consequent limitations upon his intellectual freedom and literary efforts.[469] The latter he pursued extensively during these years, as was evidenced by the number and rapidity of his publications. These touched upon a wide variety of subjects and incidentally revealed once more his Pyrrhonism which he had kept under cover when writing for Richelieu. His many works during this period, however, include only one item of significance for our purposes. This is a brief piece entitled "Du Commandement souverain," which he included in his *Petits Traitez en forme de Lettres escrites à diverses personnes studieuses* and was

---

Richelieu's ideas and easily incorporated them into this work—avoiding all controversial issues, we might add.

[467] In *Œuvres,* Vol. 1, 553-774.

[468] Wickelgren, Chap. 6, discusses the work well in this context. Cf. Pintard, Vol. 1, 520-23.

[469] Cf. his *De la Liberté et de la Servitude,* Paris, 1643, Chap. 5: "De la Servitude de la Cour."

first published in 1647.[470] In this short but succinct essay, it seems that La Mothe le Vayer for the first time directly grappled with one of the thorniest problems in reason of state, the two moralities. The proverb, *de méchant homme bon Roy*, he said, seems to divorce morals from politics. Recalling both Louis XI's well known maxim advocating dissimulation and the argument that the ruler's responsibilities are so different from those of individuals that what is vice for one passes for virtue in the other, he pointed to the fact that kings are not reproached for the disorders and injustices that accompany their conquests. Great vices are covered with a cloak of virtue, and it seems impossible to govern a state without injustice.

Having stated this experiential basis of the two moralities, La Mothe le Vayer then met the argument directly by simply denying its validity. "It must be held as a constant that true governance (*politique*) is never contrary to good morality."[471] Such is demanded by Christian politics:

> But even the Italians who make so much of reason of state, although it is essentially nothing but complete attention to interest, admit that it should never be used except in extreme necessity and when ordinary means may not be effective . . . . Except for such occasions, Christian politics obliges sovereigns to dissociate themselves from vice and to follow virtue as much and more than the rest of mankind. It teaches them that the most absolute commandments and the most despotic will never be the best and that *plenitudo potestatis nihil aliud saepe est, quam plenitudo tempestatis* . . . . A king should submit to reason and to God, to whom to obey is to reign . . . . A good prince is the father of his people and has all the tenderness for them

[470] The date usually given is 1648, but an edition of Paris, 1647 is listed in the annotated bibliography in La Mothe le Vayer, *Deux Dialogues faits à l'imitation des anciens*, ed. E. Tisserand, Paris, 1922. The "Du Commandement souverain" is in the *Œuvres*, Vol. II, 606-11, which I cite. It appears that this piece was written after Richelieu's death and before La Mothe le Vayer was made preceptor to Monsieur.

[471] "Du Commandement souverain," p. 606.

that one may have for children. Away then with all these dangerous maxims that a king can do only what is just because he is above the laws . . . . Let us beware of making good that infamous *si libet, licet*; and let us detest the damnable thought of Caligula, *Imperatoriae majestatis esse, ne vitus quidem alteri cedere.* Diogenes spoke much better than Anacharsis to Alexander who asked him [Diogenes] for some precepts for ruling well. It is impossible, he said to him, to do evil in such a profession and consequently to be a bad prince, since from the moment he goes about ruling badly the virtue of rulership is lost, and instead of reigning he tyrannizes.[472]

For La Mothe le Vayer, therefore, the fundamentals were simple. Christian monarchy required observation of fixed norms of conduct, since Christianity "gives sovereigns the rules of a just and reasonable command."[473] Although they were masters of their subjects' lives and goods, they should use this power only for the people's preservation. But above all, rulers should willingly follow the precepts of higher law and, indeed, were more bound by them than were ordinary men:

Our monarchs will be much better instructed when they are made to understand from their earliest years that the virtue which seems merely an honorable possession of the rest of mankind is utterly necessary to them [the rulers] in order to represent Him whose image they are, that they should be more just than other men because they dispense justice to others, and that they are the more obliged to respect the laws because, not being subject to them, they do not fear them. What glory it is to a king to abstain from sensual pleasure, he who may possess them all! To take pleasure in work, he who cannot be compelled to it! And neither to desire nor to take the goods of others, he who may appropriate all to himself at will! It is thus that Louis XII deserved to be named Father of the People, our annals showing us that he often refused taxes that his subjects had generously granted him.[474]

[472] *Ibid.*, pp. 606-07.   [473] *Ibid.*, p. 607.   [474] *Ibid.*, p. 608.

Mutual trust of ruler and subjects La Mothe le Vayer found the true basis of the greatness of states, exceeding even their power and glory:

> The extent of a ruler's domain will never give rise to a glorious reputation if his justice and other virtues do not support it, and no matter how small his state, he may make it the most eminent. . . . Why, said the little Greek king, would the Emperor of Persia be greater than I if he is neither more just nor better than I may be?[475]

Such a statement went far toward negating traditional sources of kingly glory and denying a major justification of arbitrary acts for reasons of state.

The circle seems largely complete in La Mothe le Vayer's brief but eloquent essay. For all his idealism, however, he was well aware of the improbability that his precepts would be followed in practice, and he ended his piece on a pessimistic note which reflected his antipathy toward the court and those around the ruler. "Truth is not sufficiently flattering to be admitted into the chambers of princes,"[476] he wrote. The courtiers are fawning creatures who yield to every glance and whim of the ruler, and are too spineless to give good counsel. And La Mothe le Vayer expressed his relief at his retreat from the court although great things were expected of the young Louis XIV. But even regarding the budding young monarch he expressed a cautionary reservation by recounting a legend of Alexander the Great. This ruler, he said, originally mocked those who counselled conquest of the East, observing that the brevity of life rendered dominion even over the whole world vain. But when some court philosophers urged that rule of the earth resembled that over heaven and was the surest means of getting there, he at once began to march.

La Mothe le Vayer evidently feared both bad counsel and the risks inherent in power and majesty, but he determinedly persevered in his idealism and continued to hope for equitable and morally sound rule. Although aware of the problems of effective government, he

[475] *Ibid.*   [476] *Ibid.*, p. 609.

was chiefly concerned with the ideal and was unwilling to compromise his principles which for him were the essence, the *sine qua non*. It is therefore significant that he questioned reason of state at its weakest point, the doctrine of two moralities. True kingship for him was by definition absolute monarchy in which the ruler rigidly followed Christian morality and restricted his policies accordingly. Although they used very different arguments and terminology, both Balzac and La Mothe le Vayer reached the point of insisting that Christian monarchy could be true to itself only by strict adherence to a single, universal standard of justice and that there were more effective as well as rightful means of government than the expedient use of force.

Of our four academicians, only Daniel de Priézac maintained his view of reason of state entirely unchanged during Richelieu's last years and the subsequent Regency. It is also significant that it was he who articulated the concept with greatest cogency both before and after 1642. We have noted how Priézac was discovered and brought to Paris by Chancellor Séguier and achieved his first major success in refuting Jansenius' *Mars Gallicus*.[477] Already a councillor of state, he was rewarded with membership in the French Academy on February 22, 1639, eight days after La Mothe le Vayer. During subsequent years, and in fact throughout the remainder of his life, he continued to enjoy high favor and close association with the powerful Chancellor, and was likewise active in the affairs of the Academy which Séguier took under his protection after Richelieu's death. Both Priézac's personal relations with the great and his intellectual temperament strongly inclined him toward authoritarianism in all walks of life, and it is not surprising that he despised and reacted violently against the disorders of the Fronde which he witnessed firsthand.[478] His publications during the Regency were few but significant. His religious views he expounded in *Les Privilèges de la Vierge, Mère de Dieu*, a lengthy work which appeared in three volumes in 1648, 1650, and 1651. A series of homilies of didactic

[477] See n. 311 and text.
[478] R. Kerviler, *Le Chancelier Pierre Séguier*, Paris, 1874, p. 565.

nature, the work treats a long series of topics concerning the Virgin from the strictly orthodox viewpoint. The work was well received, both for its content and style. Simultaneously he was working on his most important political treatise, the first volume of which was published under the title *Discours politiques* in 1652.[479] In this work which he dedicated to Chancellor Séguier, Priézac analyzed a lengthy series of topics including among many others the state, sovereignty, royalty, tyranny, and most important for our purposes, reason of state. Each chapter begins on a high theoretical plane, applying Aristotle's ideas as far as possible to the problem at hand and then attempting to grapple with its more practical implications, although Priézac very rarely descended from fundamental principles to the specific exigencies of government.

Priézac's forte lay in his ability to state in few words the essentials of positions that were accepted by many of his contemporaries but were rarely set forth in such meaningful language. The *res publica* he lauded as providing the very framework of human life on earth, the focus of existence, and the norms of achievement.[480] When discussing sovereignty, he listed all the accepted powers and attributes of the monarchy,[481] and his treatment of royalty placed due emphasis upon the virtues and divine origins of the monarchy.[482] When he reached the subject "majesty," however, he really extended himself regarding its divinity, its mystery, and the religious reverence that was its due:

> The source of the majesty of kings is so high, its essence so mysterious, and its strength so divine that it should not seem strange if, after the manner of celestial things, it is customarily revered by men without their being permitted to understand it. Its grandeur amazes them; its magnificence dazzles them; its pomp which resembles a perpetual triumph suspends all the power of their minds, and it seems that the same band which

---

[479] The general nature of this work is indicated by its original title, *Discours sur la politique d'Aristote*, which is given in the privilege.

[480] *Discours politiques*, Paris, 1652, Vol. 1, 25-26.

[481] "De la Souveraineté," *ibid.*, pp. 96-119.

[482] "De la Royauté," *ibid.*, pp. 120-41.

so gloriously encircles the monarch's head also ties our tongues in order to prevent our speaking of it. To discuss it [royal majesty] meanly is to injure it; one senses its secret movements much better than one expresses them; and it is not with imperfect speech but with religious silence that one should respect the features that the divine Hand imprints on the foreheads of those with whom He deigns to share his power.[483]

Rarely was the awesome quality of royal majesty so forcefully presented. And Priézac did not hesitate to insist that the cult of royal majesty partook of the qualities of a civil religion when he ascribed to it "that secret and revered gravity which moves between love and admiration, and, mingling veneration with fear, gives birth to a type of religion and civil cult."[484] The majesty of kings was "a gleam derived from the adorable majesty of God, a flash of his splendor, a refulgence of the glory that He earlier caused to shine on the face of the Prince of the Hebrews."[485] Inevitably, the only proper role of the subjects was reverence and silence before this awesome mystery: "The most respectful hommage that one may give kings is to revere them while closing one's eyes to the lightning that flashes from their crowns."[486] Regarding the powers, virtues, majesty, divinity, and religious reverence due to monarchy, Bossuet could go no further.

Priézac's fulsome description of royal majesty was but the logical concomitant of his fundamental concept of Christian monarchy. We have already noted how he made this the basis of his defense of Richelieu's policies against Jansenius' attack. In his later work, Priézac if anything carried this conception even further, elaborating it in all its essentials. Priesthood and royalty, the authorities in church and state, he recalled, were both divinely established and were therefore extensions of the authority of God himself:

---

[483] "De la Majesté," p. 142. Because of the excellence of Priézac's style, the accuracy of his terminology, and the logical progression with which he developed his arguments, it seems best to represent his ideas by extensively quoting from him.

[484] *Ibid.*, p. 143.   [485] *Ibid.*   [486] *Ibid.*, p. 144.

Although the priesthood and royalty are two different likenesses of the grandeur and glory of God, He bound them together with such exquisite and admirable means that they may not be separated without corrupting and violating his most perfect and vivid images . . . . Indeed, if religion is the basis, the foundation, and the guardian power of the state and the eternal flame that watches over its safety, the state is also the buttress, support, protection, and the defense of religion. The one and the other need to lend each other their strength and to cooperate in order to establish the realm of heaven on earth.[487]

Within this perspective, religion was fundamental to the nature, policies, and objectives of the state:

It is religion that embraces our felicity, gives us the decrees of the glory of heaven, and is the source of all justice, the principle, the means, and the end of divine and human law . . . . It is she that consecrates monarchs and renders the people obedient to laws, bold in enterprises, confident in peril, and quick to relieve the needs of the state, in their belief that it is serving God when they serve the prince that He has given them.[488]

And on this basis, Priézac concluded that religious values and objectives should both dominate and determine governmental policies:

It is this that should teach them to cause the state to serve religion and not religion to serve the state, for whoever would reverse this order and prefer political prudence to the wisdom inspired from on high would fall into the error of placing civil virtue above heavenly virtue which is the greatest gift that the God of virtues can make to men. Indeed, human things should not rule over divine; religion does not receive regulation from the state but gives it to the state, and this sacred trust of heaven was not placed in the hands of kings to be the instrument but rather the objective of their rule.[489]

[487] *Ibid.*, pp. 203-04.   [488] *Ibid.*, p. 206.   [489] *Ibid.*, pp. 207-08.

Such a statement may seem surprising and out of place in the writings of Priézac, the defender of official French policies. The subordination of religious morality to the secular interests of the state was precisely the focus of criticism by the *dévots* and many others who denounced the actions of those who wielded royal power, particularly in foreign affairs. The statement quoted above might have been made by any one of a wide variety of Richelieu's critics. Its presence in Priézac's writings, however, is extremely important to note because it conclusively demonstrates his overriding concern for Christian principles *and* his conviction that royal policies, including those undertaken for reasons of state, might be justified in these terms. The preponderance of Christian morality in the thought of the absolutists during this period has no better illustration.

Although Priézac insisted that priesthood and monarchy shared the same qualities and sanctions and should fully cooperate in their work for religious ends, he also maintained that their roles were not identical:

> As the same motion does not measure the revolutions of the heavens and the course of things on earth, so the same powers should not control things spiritual and temporal. The distance that separates them should be understood, and the tiara should not be confused with the diadem nor the sword of St. Peter with that of Constantine. If political justice is royal, the priesthood is also royal; they should therefore be allied but not merged, because in this great alliance the grandeur of royalty is preserved by the sanctity of religion and at the same time religion is defended by the power of royalty. It is undoubted that religion is the most active part of justice and even the second source from which it is spread throughout states; nevertheless without the temporal power its effects would most often be confined to the secret thoughts of consciences, without the strength to be manifest externally.[490]

The monarchy, therefore, was the instrument *par excellence* through which religious principles were made effective on the level of human

[490] *Ibid.*, p. 208.

affairs. This statement explicitly shows how insistent Priézac was upon the complete fusion of religious morality and royal justice, as applied in official policy. Again, the emphasis and cogency of his words leave no doubt concerning his convictions.

Priézac's entering wedge when justifying French policy within the prevailing conditions of European politics was his concept of holy war. Although Christ taught humility and passivity, he said, human actions should be judged not by their specific nature but by their intent:

> All actions differ according to the diverse natures of the things that provoke them, and those that the Christian religion proposes are objects of virtue at the sight of which hearts are enflamed with a holy ardor, blood and spirit are warmed in the veins, and those who fight under such high aspirations await their crown, not as pagans from the hand of a man but from that of God.[491]

This, of course, introduced a means-end mechanism although in the area least subject to debate, since there were very few French writers in the century who maintained that the use of force was unjustifiable under any circumstances. The weighting of ends, not means, was on all counts the prevailing viewpoint. And Priézac was careful to indicate that for him the ends which most extensively justified resort to force were religious, reflecting the nature and purposes of the state.

The most important section of Priézac's *Discours politiques* in which he discussed the exigencies of political necessity was a chapter which he entitled "Des Secrets de la Domination, ou de la Raison d'Estat."[492] In this very significant and relatively long chapter he examined what he called the secrets of government, that is, a knowledge of the various measures, including artifices and deceits, that were effective in preserving the sovereign's dominion over his subjects. These, in essence, were the stratagems through which the ruler retained the people's respect and maintained his effective power. The human material of the state being of such a refractory

[491] *Ibid.*, pp. 211-12.   [492] *Ibid.*, pp. 254-306.

nature, such measures were essential to effective rule, but Priézac quickly added that they were not justified merely by expediency and the ruler's self-interest: "Artifices should not be placed in the ranks of things illicit, for when artifices are honorable and the government's ruses serve the public and the security of the governors, then deceit is not merely innocent but beneficial to those who are deceived."[493] Again the ruler's objective was the criterion of judgment. Kings, Priézac continued, are not like magicians who rely upon illusion and fraud, but are to be compared with true philosophers who use the mysteries of their science to enhance its dignity and the admiration of those who do not understand it. The latter, he maintained, included the vast majority of the nation which was quite incapable of comprehending the mysteries of state, but he added that the ancients, particularly Aristotle, had provided intelligent observers with guides that might legitimately be utilized when attempting to fathom the motivation of the ruler. This special knowledge of government or royal science Priézac equated with reason of state, defining it as "that mysterious art of governing the people which is known only to those who have combined the light of prudence with long observation of causes, actions, and events."[494]

For Priézac, reason of state was therefore not a mere means-end rationality which justified any expedient measures but the sovereign's special, divinely bestowed understanding of the mysteries of state. Within this broader definition, there nevertheless remained the crucial problems of politics and morals and the two moralities, which Priézac was sufficiently astute to perceive and to discuss at length. Immediately upon approaching these issues, he placed the sovereign above all civil law:

> Surely, if civil government is a miniature image of the great polity of the universe, and if it follows that it is necessary to give the latter a superior virtue which is not tied to ordinary rules, it is also necessary that there be in the republic a universal reason which is freed from all ties of civil law and retains supreme authority over it.[495]

[493] *Ibid.*, p. 258.   [494] *Ibid.*, p. 260.   [495] *Ibid.*, p. 261.

Priézac firmly believed in the absolute necessity of a supreme authority in all spheres of life, an authority that would combine both superior wisdom and ultimate power. In this sense, he argued that reason of state is above civil law as divine law is above natural; in each case the former gives the latter its perfection. Thus in government there must be a superior intelligence, master of all others, to lead the people to higher things.

But immediately after placing the monarch above the limitations of civil law, Priézac took pains to guard against the possibility of lawless tyranny and qualified his position according to his view of legitimate rule in a Christian state:

> However, those who mistake the shadow for the substance are convinced that this maxim is nothing but a dispensation from common law, a privilege of sovereigns against equity, and a supreme right of a tyranny that has been rendered legitimate by time and the submission of the people. But in this they have shown that they are ignorant of the differences that exist between true reason of state and its likeness, which are undoubtedly as remote from each other as justice is from crime. The first is born of necessity which forces sovereigns to resort to means proportionate to the objectives of their rule, whereas the second draws its origins from the unrestrained license of tyrants who seek to cover their infamy with a good name and simultaneously acquire the power to violate all laws with some appearance of reason. The one is nothing more than a comprehensive justice, a strength of government, a sovereign power that applies the universal to the particular and, in a word, right reason, or at least the noblest and most excellent part of reason; the other on the contrary, always being separated from virtue, is not a reason of state but a crime of state and an instrument of tyranny. The one is more humble and modest, acknowledges divine reason as its superior, and even willingly suffers correction by natural reason which it respects as a gleam and trickle of the sovereign reason that governs the universe; the other, always proud and barbarous, despises all human and divine law,

distrusts integrity, resists nature, and wars against God himself. Finally, the one, proportioning its power to the public good, faith, and religion, is never without moral virtue and civil prudence; but the other admits no limitation and is never as satisfied as when it can break the barriers that have been placed between the justice and injustice of government.[496]

This very significant passage marvelously delineates Priézac's concept of legitimate rule in relation to reason of state. Fully aware of the continuing debate concerning both the concept and the phrase, he found it necessary and appropriate to set forth in the strongest terms his view of the just implementation of policy. His sharp distinction between true and false reason of state had appeared in earlier works, notably those of certain writers who were most insistent upon the supremacy of religious values and who found their closest affinity with the *dévot* faction.[497] The appearance of the same concept in Priézac's mature thought again strikingly indicates the fundamentally religious quality of his political thought. Although he restricted his argumentation to the level of principle, it is clear that he was fully aware of the practical import of his position regarding the requisites of everyday government in a Christian society.

For all his insistence upon the limitations of higher law, Priézac unhestitatingly attributed very great discretionary power to the sovereign in his formulation of policy. Reason of state Priézac held to be "imprinted and engraved in the heart and mind of the prince who makes use of it in great matters and things that cannot be reduced to common and ordinary reason."[498] It was therefore "a living and superior law [which] rules over all other laws, tempers them, corrects them, and when necessary abrogates and annuls them for a much more universal good."[499] Instead of following fixed norms and rules, reason of state should be allowed flexible accommodation to necessity. And this in turn permitted the ruler to depart from the laws and rationality of mere individuals: "Who does not know that the prince is the living law, and as a public person and representing

---

[496] *Ibid.*, pp. 262-64.

[498] *Discours politiques*, p. 264.

[497] See Pt. I, 83-93, n. 169-179.

[499] *Ibid.*, p. 265.

all the grandeur of rulership, is sometimes permitted to depart from the reason of individuals in order to preserve general reason in which are subsumed the majesty, strength and fate of the state?"[500]

Such was the chain of argumentation through which Priézac justified two levels of morality, one for the populace and a higher one for the prince. He clearly based his position upon his extremely exalted view of monarchy and the consequent freedom of maneuver that was necessary to rightful government. But once more Priézac realized the danger of lawless, irresponsible rule that was inherent in his position, and he hastened to qualify it accordingly:

> However, no matter how sovereign and absolute the power that true reason of state wields over written laws, it does not cause things that by their nature are unjust to be divested of their imperfection; it merely causes those that are not licit according to ordinary laws to be licit according to a higher principle on which depends the preservation and felicity of republics.[501]

Again he insisted upon the supremacy of higher values in any legitimate rule, but ultimately he was ultra-optimistic concerning the justice of government by a Christian prince who was allowed a great measure of discretion. Priézac followed these apostrophes with a long exposition of the stratagems that were used in the ancient world, as recorded by Aristotle and Tacitus, for the preservation of democracies, aristocracies, and monarchies, respectively. His implication was that all were justified because they contributed to the preservation of the state.

This was Priézac's position concerning the justice and legitimacy of questionable, even illegal, measures that were for the public good. Reason of state for him was but the ruler's superior knowledge of government that was necessary and appropriate to successful leadership in a Christian state. Because of the extremely exalted, superhuman qualities that he ascribed to the monarch, Priézac came close to admitting that acts of government which were done in good conscience and for a good cause were *ipso facto* just, yet he avoided

[500] *Ibid.*, pp. 267-68.   [501] *Ibid.*, p. 268.

the obvious risk in this reasoning by insisting that the Christian prince was by definition both bound and limited by higher law. Ultimately he was more concerned with ends than means, although he required that both conform to the precepts of Christian morality. And it is clear that he believed this approach to problems of policy to be entirely viable in a Christian state. The essentials of this position he had developed under Richelieu and now merely gave further articulation in a work that appeared ten years after the Cardinal's death. The position was manifestly one of great confidence in monarchy, and for this reason he believed it unnecessary to define in greater detail the precise methods by which a Christian prince might apply Christian morality in practice, yet the final impression is one of conviction that this was entirely feasible and even requisite to the successful survival of Christian France. Such was the view of reason of state that was developed by one of Richelieu's most learned and representative followers. His optimism concerning monarchy undoubtedly reflected preponderant sentiment during the early years of Louis XIV.

PART V

DESIGN FOR IMMORTALITY

RICHELIEU'S EFFORTS TO PERPETUATE THE
MEMORY OF HIS GREATNESS

ARDINAL RICHELIEU'S extensive efforts to influence opinion in
his favor were not limited to his contemporaries. Like so
many Frenchmen who participated in the dramatic political and military events of his time, he sought to project his image
and renown into the future for the edification and benefit of posterity. As the chief actor in a drama whose import and motivation
were extremely controversial and whose significance was admitted
by all, the Cardinal sought to preserve the record of his achievements
and to demonstrate to future generations the essential justice and
necessity of the policies that he had undertaken for the benefit of
the French state during this key moment in its ascent on the European scene. His ultimate objective undoubtedly was to perpetuate
his personal glory which he instinctively associated with justification of his policies during his years as First Minister, and for this
purpose he sought both to accumulate and even to manipulate the
materials of the history of the reign. He thus appears as one of the
most historically minded ministers in this self-conscious, memoir-
writing century. Indeed, when written records of his ministry were
concerned, it almost seems as though he operated with one eye
on the future. From the beginning of his political career, he took
care to amass extensive personal archives. His many masterful reports to Louis XIII, and even many of his letters to other important
personages, are models of clarity and seem to bear the stamp of a
man who was writing in part for posterity. He supported the extensive archival research of such experts as Dupuy and Godefroy partially
because their findings gave his policies historical perspective. The
shape of contemporary events he caused to be preserved by ordering
the composition of innumerable *relations*, many of which were

461

issued separately, published in the *Mercure français*, or mined by the editors of the *Gazette*. He even sponsored collections of pamphlets in his favor, notably that of Paul Hay du Chastelet. The works of historians who had the temerity to write concerning events of recent memory were also reviewed and corrected by the omnipresent Cardinal. Finally, he sponsored the extremely ambitious project which eventuated in the compilation known as his *Mémoires*, to be followed by his less extensive but more significant *Testament politique*. These many efforts on Richelieu's part adequately bear witness to his determination both to perpetuate knowledge of his many contributions to the growth of the French state and to vindicate the policies that he had undertaken for its benefit. In seeking to immortalize his personal glory, he necessarily reiterated his understanding of reason of state, incidentally providing us with important keys to his manner of thought and self-justification.[1]

The various writings with which Richelieu and his supporters sought to perpetuate his memory and justify his renown were many indeed, but for our purposes it will suffice to examine representative examples of the historical works that were composed at least partially for that purpose. These histories of the period, of course, were not products of Richelieu's pen but were written by his supporters, secretaries, and others who enjoyed varying degrees of personal intimacy with the First Minister. Among his many followers in the literary world were a number of quasi-official historians who purposely wrote in defense of the Cardinal and his policies. Such men as Charles Bernard,[2] Louis Guron,[3] Gabriel de Gramond,[4] Emman-

---

[1] The best general discussion of Richelieu's efforts to preserve the record of his ministry for posterity is L. Delavaud, "Quelques collaborateurs de Richelieu," *Rapports et notices sur l'édition des Mémoires du Cardinal de Richelieu préparée pour la Société de l'Histoire de France*, Paris, 1907-1914, Vol. II, 45-278.

[2] *Histoire de Louis XIII jusqu'à la guerre déclarée contre les Espagnols*, Paris, 1640.

[3] *Histoire du temps, ou les Trois Veritez historiques, politiques et chrestiennes*, Cologne, 1686.

[4] *Historiarum Galliae ab excessu Henrici IV libri XVIII quibus rerum per Gallos tota Europa gestarum accurata narratio continetur*, Toulouse, 1643.

uel Fernandez de Villareal,[5] and the ablest of all, Scipion Dupleix fall into this category. All used documents that were made available by the Cardinal, and several submitted to him their finished works for correction and approval. Of these authors, Louis Guron produced the work that is the clearest instance of tendentious, officially directed historical writing. Guron was a royal councillor, one of Richelieu's intimates, agents, and partisan supporters who wrote in his favor for financial reward. His book, which he composed immediately after the Day of Dupes, traces Richelieu's career from 1617 through that crucial episode in extensive detail, always in a manner favorable to the First Minister.[6]

Guron's work takes the form of a combined narrative and polemic whose stated purpose is to meet the many criticisms to which Richelieu had been subjected and to reveal the nefarious machinations of his enemies, particularly Gaston d'Orléans. To this end, Guron proposed to construct his treatment on the basis of "three truths" that lay at the root of reason of state and justified Richelieu's policies:

> But finally, all patience being exhausted and rightly so because of reason, three truths appear to disperse by their light the darkness of so many falsehoods and by their purity the blemish of so many calumnies.
> The first presents accurately what has recently taken place in this realm.
> The second shows that nothing has been done that was not required by reason of state, according to the judgment of political thinkers (*politiques*).
> And the third clearly demonstrates that reason of state, which has been followed in these instances, has its foundations not only in the reasoning of profane authors who do not always restrict what should be done for the public good to the rules

[5] *El politico cristiano o discorsos politicos de la vita y acciones del cardenal de Richelieu*, Pamplona, 1642. (French trans., Paris, 1643)
[6] It is not known why this book remained unpublished until 1686.

of conscience, but also in the Scriptures inspired by the Holy Spirit, in the doctrines of the Fathers and the dogma of theologians who do not believe that the power of princes extends beyond the limits of justice.[7]

This statement in a history of the period by a man who was one of Richelieu's intimates must be regarded as an accurate reflection of his thinking. Again the element of higher principle is held to be determinative. After the reader has perused his narrative in which these truths are made evident, Guron concludes, "it will be impossible not to understand, because of the justice of the acts of the king and his followers and the unjust methods of those who decry the conduct of so good a prince, that they [Richelieu's enemies] can have no objective other than interference with the course of his successes [which are] advantageous to the glory of God and most necessary to the good and repose of this state."[8] Once more, the association of political processes and God's purposes.

Scipion Dupleix was by far the ablest and most prolific of Richelieu's historian-apologists. Royal historiographer since the days of Luynes, he was also a militant Catholic and absolutist, firmly convinced that the only solution to France's ills lay in increased authoritarianism. His first published works, which dealt with earlier periods of French history, contain the most extravagant statements concerning the divine appointment and guidance of kings, their quality as God's representatives on earth, and the necessity of complete obedience to their commands,[9] as well as the preeminence of the Kings of France over all others and the superior virtues and achievements of their realm.[10] Since Dupleix enjoyed ready access to official documents and many other sources, he claimed to write accurate, unbiased history of a strictly factual nature, but as he approached his own century his partisanship became increasingly evident. In-

---

[7] Guron, *avant-propos*, no pagination.

[8] *Ibid.*, *avant-propos*.

[9] *Mémoires des Gaules depuis le Déluge jusques à l'établissement de la Monarchie Françoise*, Paris, 1619, Preface.

[10] *Histoire générale de la France*, Paris, 1621-1628, 3 vols., Vol. 1, Dedicatory Epistle.

deed, such was inevitable, since he regularly submitted his works to Richelieu who did not hesitate to alter their contents. The Cardinal was undoubtedly responsible for the changed treatment of Henry IV's foreign policy in the second edition of Dupleix's *Histoire de Henri le Grand*. The first edition, dated 1632, gave only limited attention to Henry IV's foreign policy in his last years, but the version that appeared in 1635 presents an expanded, unhistorical account of the first Bourbon king's foreign contacts and objectives, strongly implying that Richelieu was his successor and continuator in this important area.[11] Such evidence and the known fact that Richelieu reviewed Dupleix's works before publication caused him to be criticized as a mere slavish servant and willing mouthpiece of the Cardinal. The latter Dupleix undoubtedly was, but it would be unwarranted to dismiss his works as mere partisan propaganda in the guise of history. Rather, they should be viewed as officially guided and obviously tendentious accounts of recent events by an author who was thoroughly in sympathy with Richelieu's policies and philosophy of government.

From this standpoint, Dupleix's most important work was his *Histoire de Louis le Juste, treizième de ce nom, Roy de France et de Navarre*, which was first published in Paris in 1635.[12] Because it dealt with many recent events of his own making, we may be certain that Richelieu closely scrutinized the work before its publication. Here, then, is an excellent guide to the estimate of himself and his policies that the Cardinal wished to be preserved for posterity. The work is dedicated to Louis XIII whose three great accomplishments are listed as (1) defeating the Huguenots, ensuring their obedience, and destroying the factions of great nobles, (2) extending the boundaries of the realm for the first time since Charlemagne, and (3) rendering the royal authority absolutely sovereign, thereby assuring peace in the state and reducing high and low equally to obedience.[13] But after paying his respects to Louis XIII's major

[11] Delavaud, pp. 150-54.

[12] In 1648 Dupleix published a *Continuation de l'histoire du règne de Louis le Juste, treizième du nom*, but the writing of this postdates the reign.

[13] *Histoire de Louis le Juste*, Dedicatory Epistle, n.p. I cite the first edition.

achievements (for which Richelieu habitually if discreetly took credit), Dupleix made it clear that his work was written in praise of the Cardinal. After reviewing the failures of Louis XIII's earlier ministers, Dupleix continued:

> But since Cardinal Richelieu has had the government of the state in hand, all these defects have ceased because of the precise remedies that he has applied to them with superhuman prudence. For he has taken his measures so well, so skillfully adapted his projects to means, and means to the objectives that he has set for himself, that success has happily crowned his efforts. The King's plans have secretly been developed between him and His Majesty, deliberations maturely resolved, undertakings prudently directed and vigorously executed. Nothing has been spared in discovering the enemy's plans; army commands have been given only to captains of unwavering fidelity and great experience; never have money, provisions, munitions, or military discipline been wanting; and we have seen the greatest men who are criminals condemned and executed like any of the lowly.[14]

All this, of course, in contrast to the bungling of earlier ministers.

The most important portion of his book that Dupleix devoted strictly to Richelieu was the chapter that he inserted at the point where the Cardinal became First Minister.[15] Here Dupleix went all out in praise of his powerful patron. First listing the manifold abilities that were requisite to a strong and expert minister—judgment, reason, diligence, assiduity, knowledge and experience in affairs of state, uprightness, reputation, nobility of birth, eloquence, skill, courage, boldness, and many more—Dupleix found them all in Richelieu in abundance. He then traced the Cardinal's family tree, emphasizing the nobility and glorious deeds of his ancestors, and outlined his earlier career, insisting that his actions were vital to the reign whose history would show his greatness *without* any need of flattery.[16] This disarming statement he followed with a discussion of the delicate question whether all ministers should be

---

[14] *Ibid.*, Preface, p. 4.   [15] *Ibid.*, pp. 243-51.   [16] *Ibid.*, p. 249.

equal or one should have superior authority. The latter position, of course, he found preferable, not only because of its greater efficiency but also because it reflected the divine order of things:

> One does not discuss matters of state with them [the other ministers] to hear their reasons and sentiments; the decision should be made only between the prince and the general director so that the secret may not be divulged . . . . After all, since political government is organized after the model of the celestial hierarchy, no criticism of it can be made. For as God established an intelligence in each celestial sphere to activate it and cause it to revolve according to its natural course, so that which guides the movement of the primary body gives an impulse to all others and forces them to rotate every twenty-four hours. Thus each of our inferior ministers should carry out his particular function and daily account to the first with a full and punctual report.[17]

For Dupleix, and doubtless for Richelieu, such a parallelism was unchallengeable since it was but an extension of prevailing assumptions concerning the divinely established hierarchy among all created things. From this position it was but a step to the assertion that Richelieu himself was divinely chosen and inspired:

> God, by a singular grace toward this monarchy, has given us a Frenchman who sincerely and tenderly prizes his fatherland and deserves not only to be cherished and honored but also venerated, since His Royal Majesty himself honors him. It is this most illustrious Cardinal Richelieu, one of the most celebrated heroes that France has produced since the foundation of the Most Christian Monarchy. France receives the benefits of this with so much glory and more that it seems that since [the beginning of] his ministry it is easier for him to extend the boundaries of his state than earlier it was to defend them . . . . Even our enemies are astonished and confused by the prodigious advances of French arms, and all Europe admires it. Those who are envious of him are also forced to admit this truth, that never was

[17] *Ibid.*, p. 250.

France guided by such an excellent genius; and the course of history will furnish proofs of this as admirable as they are evident.[18]

The circle seems complete. Richelieu, through Dupleix, was reaching for the position that his acts, like those of a divinely appointed monarch, were *ipso facto* just, as the record would demonstrate.

Dupleix's treatment of the events of the reign, while not establishing that French affairs were guided by a true genius, consistently reiterated the official interpretation of all governmental undertakings. His narrative is very condensed and factual. Matters of policy are so handled as to demonstrate both the necessity and justice of key decisions. The argument is therefore from facts rather than theory, although always with a substratum of concern for justice. Approximately one-third of the entire work is devoted to the campaigns against the Huguenots, which are given all the characteristics of a crusade. Richelieu's anti-Hapsburg foreign policy is justified with the usual statements concerning Spanish supranational ambitions and French desire for peace, justice, and liberty for all. It is unnecessary to cite instances, since the reader is fully aware of the official position which both reflected and purported to justify Richelieu's policies. The same viewpoint is evident in Dupleix's treatment of key individuals in French political life. Those who supported Richelieu are consistently presented as working for the good of the French state, whereas those who opposed him did so for selfish reasons and sought to undermine the state and the monarchy. Cardinal Bérulle is described as a high-minded man of religion who lacked experience in political affairs and supported the faction of the Queen Mother without realizing the consequences of his partisanship.[19] Regarding the execution of the Marshal de Marillac, Dupleix insisted that the pleas of outstanding persons that peculation was common among military commanders merely hastened his condemnation, since the jurists held that frequency of a crime increases the neces-

[18] *Ibid.*, p. 251.
[19] *Ibid.*, p. 397. This is the view of Bérulle which is presented at greater length in Richelieu's *Mémoires*. See n. 42, 43, and text.

sity of its rigorous punishment.[20] These and other apologetic passages in Dupleix's work may have had a certain significance in the eyes of his contemporaries, but their arguments frequently seem somewhat forced.

It is not surprising that Dupleix's history of the reign was subjected to severe castigation by writers who opposed all that Richelieu stood for. Of these, Mathieu de Morgues' lengthy critique was the most important.[21] Morgues spared no effort in condemning Dupleix as incapable of writing sound history. Honesty, decency, and objectivity are the requisites of a true historian, he said, but Dupleix lacked all such qualities and instead merely wrote to win Richelieu's favor. "His history is a portrait of the passions of the Cardinal."[22] In addition to this sound criticism, Morgues indulged in his usual extensive invective and grouped many of his arguments around his customary defense of the Queen Mother, but his lengthy examination of Dupleix's treatment of events and persons thoroughly established his point that Dupleix's history was marred by a clear bias in favor of Richelieu's record, to the point of reflecting his animosities. Dupleix waited until 1645, three years after Richelieu's death, to publish his answer to these charges.[23] Accusing Morgues of being "ignorant in his corrections, criminal in his detractions, brutal in his passions, and barbarous in his diction and style,"[24] he likewise produced a work of invective in which he set forth a purported point-by-point refutation of Morgues' criticisms. His method was not always suc-

[20] *Ibid.*, p. 418.

[21] *Lumières pour l'histoire de France et pour faire voir les calomnies, flatteries et autres défauts de Scipion Dupleix*, n.p., 1636. Also in *Diverses pièces*, Vol. II, 219-386. I cite the latter version, which was used by Dupleix in writing his *Responce*.

[22] *Lumières*, p. 223.

[23] *Responce à Saint-Germain, ou les lumières de Mathieu de Morgues, dit Saint-Germain, pour l'histoire, éteintes par Messire Scipion Dupleix*, Condom, 1645. It is possible that Dupleix deliberately postponed his answer to Morgues until after Richelieu's death in order to be in a position to write more freely. In 1643 Dupleix published a revised edition of his *Histoire de Louis le Juste*. Two years later appeared his answer to Morgues' criticisms of the earlier version.

[24] *Responce*, p. 9.

cessful, since he often merely rejected Morgues out of hand or leveled an accusation at him. The chief value of the debate is its statement of differing concepts of justice within the monarchical framework.

In one of the rare instances in this exchange when the two men grappled with fundamental issues, Morgues quoted Dupleix as stating that "the King is responsible for his acts only to God and may honor those whom he chooses for reasons that please him.[25] To this Morgues answered:

> I am certain that His Majesty, who wishes to retain the title, Louis the Just, will not accept this rule. For justice is never derived from will and absolute power but from the law that decrees that men should be raised according to their merit, rewarded in number, and relied upon in moderation. A flatterer similar to Dupleix [once] said to Antigonus that all things are honest and just for kings. This wise prince answered that this was a precept for tyrants, whereas for good kings there is nothing that is honest but that which is honest nor just but that which is just. In reality, the sovereign is the protector and should be the first to apply what is equitable and honorable.[26]

Dupleix in turn replied to this barb that the rewarding of men was not a matter of justice but authority. The king *is* responsible only to God and may use his authority as he wishes. In granting recognition, the king should act according to the merits of the recipients rather than their number.[27] The exchange touched upon several points concerning which both men were agreed, but their divergent emphases indicate important shadings in their views of royal justice.

Regarding Richelieu himself, Morgues of course extensively reiterated his charges that the Cardinal was a narrow, tyrannical minister who was constantly stirring up trouble for his own benefit, ruining all who opposed him, and involving France in wars beyond her means. In answer, Dupleix could merely deny these accusations and reassert his contention that Richelieu had been a supremely able minister who undertook all for the good of the state. The opposition

[25] *Lumières*, p. 239.   [26] *Ibid.*, pp. 239-40.   [27] *Responce*, pp. 48-49.

of the two writers on these matters was total and irreconcilable. More debate was possible regarding Dupleix's views of important individuals in French affairs, and here Morgues repeatedly exposed Dupleix's reflection of Richelieu's prejudices. In fact, the better part of both pamphlets was devoted to this element of Dupleix's history. One interesting but unusual example is their handling of the Marshal de Marillac. Morgues wrote, "The historian makes himself the destroyer of the Marshal de Marillac's reputation to please him who was the murderer of his body."[28] In answer, Dupleix repeated his earlier assertion that the widespread nature of Marillac's proven peculation of funds necessitated unusually severe punishment. But he then added that since no edict or ordinance posited the death penalty for this offense, it was evident that the Cardinal's anger against the Marshal had accounted for his prosecution and condemnation, which, in fact, had been carried out in a manner contrary to traditional legal procedures. Dupleix admitted that he had not included these considerations in the first edition of his history, explaining that they were not in the materials that had been available to him and that he had not been permitted to go beyond them at that time. They were nevertheless incorporated into the latest edition (1643) of his work.[29] In this instance, Dupleix admitted (after Richelieu's death, to be sure) the limitations of his history in its original version and the arbitrary character of Richelieu's prosecution of one of his enemies. Such, however, was highly unusual in this debate, and in all major essentials both men continued to hold to their earlier positions. Although they disagreed concerning the proper applications of power for the good of the state, both worked within the concept of enlightened monarchy and differed only concerning its proper implementation. The value of their debate lies in its demonstration of the great flexibility of the monarchical tradition and the fact that both Richelieu and his opponents believed themselves to be on solid ground when advocating very different concepts of just policy and reason of state. It is patent that the Cardinal had no hesitation in grounding his personal glory and claims to greatness upon the more authoritarian version.

[28] *Lumières*, p. 353.   [29] *Responce*, pp. 211-12.

THE *MÉMOIRES* AND THE *TESTAMENT POLITIQUE*

The two most important works that present Richelieu's image in the form that he destined for posterity are his *Mémoires* and his *Testament politique*. Both were initiated by the Cardinal and were the object of his intermittent attention during the better part of his ministry. The very extensive debate concerning their authenticity—whether they were genuinely his works or merely secondhand compilations by his secretaries—is of secondary significance to the present study. Preponderant opinion, which is doubtless correct, holds that Richelieu conceived both works for the purpose of recording for future generations the nature and extent of his achievements, their necessity and justice, and his consequent personal glory. Of course they were written by his secretaries rather than the constantly preoccupied Cardinal, but this does not negate their value as guides to his more general views. On specifics they are often unreliable, but on broader matters, such as the official stance on events and their justifications, they may be accepted as accurately reflecting Richelieu's position. The reasons for this are to be found in the manner in which they were compiled and the character of the men who were entrusted with the projects. Richelieu may have supported and made use of many able writers, but his secretaries were not of that calibre. They were invariably mediocre men who readily limited their roles to unquestioning obedience and following orders. Willing instruments and no more, none was even a second-rate thinker who might be expected to interpose his ideas in an officially sponsored work.[30] In addition, all were sufficiently close to the Cardinal to be familiar with at least the general nature of his policies and ideals. When these are expressed in the two works, we may accept them as mirror-

---

[30] Even Achille de Harlay, Baron de Sancy, Bishop of St. Malo who has been dubbed the "Secretary of the *Mémoires*" and who wrote pamphlets in Richelieu's favor was a mind of this type. R. Lavollée, "Le Secrétaire des *Mémoires* de Richelieu," *Rapports et Notices*, Vol. I, 35-65, and "Les différentes étapes de la rédaction des *Mémoires*. Les manuscrits et les ouvriers des *Mémoires*," *ibid.*, Vol. II, 327-47. On the general intellectual calibre of Richelieu's secretaries, see M. Deloche, *La Maison du Cardinal de Richelieu*, Paris, 1912, pp. 100-139.

ing Richelieu's position, or at least that which he desired to be recorded for posterity. This would seem particularly true regarding matters of ideology which are our major concern.

The inspiration of Richelieu's so-called *Mémoires* lay in his desire to leave behind him a lengthy, comprehensive history of his ministry as part of his program of self-justification.[31] The project was never completed, doubtless because it proved too massive for the harried Cardinal and his secretaries, and was finally abandoned in very unfinished condition. The resulting "memoirs" consist of a collection of summaries of documents, letters, and fragments of all sorts with a limited amount of connective material and commentary, the whole arranged in chronological order so as to give an official history of the period. There is some evidence of Richelieu's traceable contributions, especially in the first part, but these are very limited and their sum-total is impossible to establish with precision. The work therefore cannot be quoted as stemming from his pen except in extremely rare instances, but his active sponsorship and the limited initiative of his secretaries warrant the assumption that it provides an accurate exposition of his views. Even if part of the work was compiled after his death, which is possible, the same estimate holds because his secretaries were invariably his devoted servants and remained loyal to their former master and his ideals. Of necessity, the work presents important justifications of Richelieu's policies which reflect his understanding of reason of state.

Richelieu's *Mémoires* present a very extended, detailed account of the major events of the reign by summarizing and/or paraphrasing a great variety of documents, many of an official nature.[32] The au-

[31] The best studies of the *Mémoires* are those in the *Rapports et Notices*, Paris, 1905-1922, 3 vols., plus P. Bertrand, "Les Vrais et les Faux Mémoires du Cardinal de Richelieu," *Revue historique*, CXLI (1922), 40-65, 198-227 (answered by R. Lavollée in *ibid.*, CXLII [1923], 229-32), and M. Deloche, "Les Vrais Mémoires du Cardinal de Richelieu," *Revue des questions historiques*, CIX (1928), 257-312.

[32] For the years 1600 through 1629, I have used the edition of the *Mémoires* published by the Société de l'Histoire de France, Paris, 1907-1931, 10 vols. For 1630 through 1638, I have used the Petitot edition, Vols. v-x, Paris, 1823. I identify the former with "S.H.F." and the latter with "P."

thors develop their case for the Cardinal's greatness by arguing from the facts and exigencies of policy and rarely touch upon ideological matters, or rather, the essentials of divine-right sovereignty and the necessity of its implementation by a powerful First Minister are taken for granted. It is noteworthy that this authoritarian view of royal power is consistently extended to encompass the divine choice and inspiration of the Cardinal himself. God, it is repeatedly maintained, has chosen Richelieu to guide France through this perilous era and even directed his efforts in framing policy. When approaching the problems that faced the royal government in 1628, the compilers of the *Mémoires* stated:

> Only the Cardinal, to whom God gave his benediction to serve the King and restore to his state its ancient renown and to his person the power and authority appropriate to royal majesty, which is the second majesty after the divine, found in his mind the means of solving all these problems, dispelling all this gloom, and bringing honor to his master from all this confusion.[33]

In commenting on Richelieu's relations with the King at the time of the Day of Dupes, the *Mémoires* insisted:

> The Cardinal is the one whom God makes use of to give his counsels to His Majesty, which [counsels] even his enemies do not dare oppose publicly. They oppose them with traitorous cabals. Wonderful dexterity is needed to unravel these machinations; the Cardinal is alone in cooperating with the King to this end. He thereby risks his life, and because of continual vigilance, sacrifices his health, setting at naught his own good and all worldly things, provided that he causes his master to emerge gloriously from these challenges, as God in fact gave him the grace to do.[34]

And on the occasion of Louis XIII's making Richelieu Duke and Peer (1631) in spite of continued criticism by his enemies, the com-

---

[33] *Mémoires*, Vol. VIII (S.H.F.), 2.
[34] *Ibid.*, Vol. VI (P.), 425-26.

pilers of the *Mémoires* did not hesitate to assert that "God not only preserves him and demonstrates his innocence but raises him, increases his renown, and causes the success of the designs that He inspires in him for the glory of His Majesty who esteems him for it and loves him the more."[35] Other examples might easily be cited. Surely these were much more than mere rhetorical flourishes by the Cardinal's secretaries. Instead, they seem to be genuine reflections of his strong sense of mission and his conviction that he was miraculously destined to devote his superior talents to advancing the cause of Christian France.

It was within this context that the authors of the *Mémoires* and Richelieu himself justified French foreign policy. Occasionally the reader is presented with direct statements arguing divine intervention in favor of the French, as in this passage concerning the major events of 1631:

> Thus we see during the course of this year the Spanish and the entire House of Austria and their supporters very far from their objectives, and God shifting to them the disasters that they attempted to inflict upon others. They wished to revive the war in Italy, and God set their own states ablaze with it. They attempted to usurp the Duchies of Mantua and Montferrat, and a foreign king left the depths of the north and made himself master of theirs. The Duke of Lorraine, a vassal of the King to whose liberality he and his family were personally obligated, rebelled against his overlord; he found himself reduced to such straits that without His Majesty's protection, his ruin was inevitable. The King was not honored by his closest relatives to the extent that both his royal dignity and the eminence of his virtue deserved; God destroyed the foundations on which they based their hopes and caused His Majesty's glory to shine forth beyond that of his ancestors.[36]

Usually, however, the case for Richelieu's foreign policy is presented merely in terms of Spanish injustice and the consequent justice of French resistance, culminating in their declaration of war.

[35] *Ibid.*, Vol. VI (P.), 575.   [36] *Ibid.*, Vol. VI (P.), 474-75.

On the occasion of the latter, the *Mémoires* repeat all the usual charges against the Spanish: their violation of all treaties since Vervins, their constant encroachment upon all neighboring states, their repeated support of hostile factions of nobles and Huguenots within the realm, their preparations for major campaigns against France from bases north and south, and their never-ending quest for universal monarchy. The French, on the contrary, served as the only major bulwark against Spanish conquests and had long remained on the defensive, merely meeting each threat as it arose. But after years of suffering insults for the sake of peace, the French were now forced by the course of events, their sense of honor, their determination to defend their allies, and their dedication to the cause of European liberty to declare war against Spain.[37]

The *Mémoires* are equally thorough in presenting official refutations of the principal charges against the justice of the French cause. The accusation that the French were responsible for the devastation of Germany was answered by insisting that:

> On the contrary, the King is so religious that when the King of Spain emboldened the inhabitants of La Rochelle with false hopes to resist his [Louis XIII's] authority and sent Gonzalès to Casal to dispossess the Duke of Mantua, His Majesty, foreseeing the evils that would result from this to Christianity, did not wish to undertake to rescue this prince without the theologians first declaring that God obliged him to do so and that the misery of this war would not be attributed to him since he was not its cause but entered it merely to defend a prince who was unjustly attacked.[38]

As for the French alliances with heretic rulers, Gustavus Adolphus entered Germany not at French invitation but because of Imperial aggressions; his alliance with France was made only after he found himself among enemies. For that matter, all princes make alliances with others without regard to religious differences.[39] And the charge that the French had misled the pope by concealing their damages

[37] *Ibid.*, Vol. viii (P.), 212-15, 307-08.
[38] *Ibid.*, Vol. x (P.), 149.   [39] *Ibid.*, Vol. x (P.), 149-53.

to the faith was answered by insisting that it was the Spanish who had originally misled the supreme pontiff into favoring their side in this intra-Catholic war. "But he [Louis XIII] did not take offense at this, the more so because to the services that his predecessors rendered the Holy See, he wished to add this: to believe that since he [Urban VIII] is Vicar of God on earth, he resembles Him in his conduct and, doing nothing but with intention for our good, is favorable and charitable to us even when we receive ill from him."[40] The position is consistently maintained, and every effort is made to show that French policy reflected Richelieu's determination to preserve justice among nations according to the canons of Catholic Christianity.

With the good of the French state defined in such terms and the direction of policy in the hands of a First Minister who was purportedly inspired from on high, the justice of his policies appeared undeniable and anyone who opposed them was by definition an enemy of the state. Indeed, all the Cardinal's critics and enemies are cast in this light, since "he had not a single enemy as an individual and had never offended anyone except in the service of the state, in which he was resolved never to flinch, come what might."[41] In other words, all who opposed him for any reason was "mal affectionnés à la France." Cardinal Bérulle is described as a man for whom Richelieu had great respect and was willing to support but who held to his views with complete rigidity because he believed they conformed to God's will.[42] His consequent errors in political matters are "demonstrated" by a lengthy review of his misguided efforts.[43] Richelieu was apparently claiming a superior type of divine guidance, at least in matters of government. The same errors, particularly opposition to the war, were shared by Michel de Marillac,[44] and the exile of Father Caussin from the court is justified by a long digression on the reasons why the clergy should not mix into politics.[45] Again Richelieu was claiming insight into governmental affairs beyond that of other men of the cloth. His conviction that he enjoyed superior if not

[40] *Ibid.*, Vol. x (P.), 155.
[42] *Ibid.*, Vol. x (S.H.F.), 102.
[44] *Ibid.*, Vol. vi (P.), 135, 147-48.
[41] *Ibid.*, Vol. v (P.), 431.
[43] *Ibid.*, Vol. x (S.H.F.), 82-103.
[45] *Ibid.*, Vol. x (P.), 206-22.

unique understanding of the mysteries of state and that he was doing all for the good of the state go far to explain his willingness to accuse those who opposed him of *lèse-majesté*, the contemporary version of treason. In the instances of Montmorency-Bouteville and the Duke of Montmorency, the compilers of the *Mémoires* found it sufficient to repeat the legal charges.[46] The cases against the Marshal de Marillac and the Duke of La Valette were of much more dubious legality and are consequently presented at much greater length, strictly from the official viewpoint and ignoring all evidences of arbitrary persecution.[47] Most interesting in this regard is the treatment of Gaston d'Orléans. The *Mémoires* categorically state that Gaston was guilty of *lèse-majesté* according to well-established law and cite precedents for its application to members of the royal family. But Louis XIII, with brotherly solicitude, promised to receive Gaston back into his good graces and to give him many favors, "merely giving him to understand that if he were deficient and set at naught the fraternal offers that he made him, he [Louis XIII] would be constrained to proceed against him according to the laws of the realm."[48] This was the closest that Richelieu ever came to subjecting the heir to the throne to the penalties of crimes against the state.

Confidence in divine favor for France is nowhere more evident in the *Mémoires* than in their accounts of Louis XIII's placing the realm under the protection of the Virgin, and the subsequent birth of the Dauphin. The narrative of the former is based upon the royal declaration of 1637, here paraphrased and expanded. In order to seek benediction of his work for the peace of Christendom and to relieve "the people who groan under the burdens of so many public and personal calamities,"[49] and in recognition of the many earlier favors and successes that had been divinely bestowed upon the realm, both

---

[46] *Ibid.*, Vol. vii (S.H.F.), 77-79; Vol. vii (P.), 217-19.

[47] *Ibid.*, Vol. vii (P.), 70-79; Vol. x (P.), 262-97, 488-500.

[48] *Ibid.*, Vol. vii (P.), 175-79. The quotation is on p. 179.

[49] *Ibid.*, Vol. x (P.), 143. Neither these words nor this sentiment is in the original declaration, which is in Avenel, *Lettres*, Vol. v, 908-12.

at home and abroad,[50] Louis XIII dedicated his person, his state, his crown, and his subjects to the protection of the Virgin and ordered appropriate observances throughout France "so that, under such a powerful patroness, the realm may be protected from all the endeavors of its enemies, it may long enjoy a sound peace, and God may be so piously served and revered that His Majesty and his subjects may successfully achieve the final objective for which we were all created."[51] Interestingly, the compilers of the *Mémoires* utilized this same account of royal piety almost verbatim when approaching that momentous event, the birth of the Dauphin. The intent was clearly to relate the two developments:

> This prayer of the King was well rewarded by divine benevolence; for in the midst of His Majesty's efforts and afflictions in this war, whose end he desired for the glory of God, the peace of Christendom, and the relief of his people to which he subordinated his own glory and the augmentation of his grandeur, God gave him the consolation of seeing the Queen successfully delivered and himself the father of a son who would one day be heir to his virtues and after him would sit on the throne of his fathers.[52]

Louis XIII at once sent word of the joyous event to the provinces, indicating that:

> As he had always recognized the good fortune, the advantages, and the glory that France had enjoyed since [the beginning of] his reign as so many effects of divine aid which had made his state the most flourishing and victorious in Christendom, he now unmistakably recognized by the birth of a Dauphin that God

[50] These are more extensively detailed in the *Mémoires* than in the declaration.

[51] *Mémoires*, Vol. x (P.), 146. This is a verbatim quotation from the conclusion of the declaration.

[52] *Ibid.*, Vol. x (P.), 533-34. It is interesting and possibly significant that the compilers of the *Mémoires* introduced more statements concerning the relief of the people from the burdens of war than were contained in the official documents that they used.

took pleasure in heaping benedictions on his person and his realm; and, in the plenitude of his joy at seeing one of his most ardent desires fulfilled, there was nothing that touched him more than the hope that he now held that this new favor of Heaven would be followed by all the others that he might desire for perfect prosperity in his realm.[53]

The position—royal devotion and expectation of further divine favors—was complete, and, although presumptuous, has the ring of sincerity. There seems every reason to accept these statements at face value. The intensity of the faith of the age and the strength of the monarchical ideal were amply demonstrated by the ensuing celebrations throughout France—celebrations which were duly noted in the *Mémoires* and were for the purpose of thanking the Creator for the Dauphin who was literally believed to be *Dieu-donné*.[54] Adherents to such an ideology readily believed that God provided special protection and favors to Christian France, particularly since Louis XIII was the most devout French king in recent centuries. The cause of France was therefore the cause of justice, and Richelieu's inspired leadership provided the policies that would lead her to victory and greatness. Such was the picture that the compilers of the *Mémoires*, and doubtless the Cardinal himself, sought to preserve for posterity.

In time, Richelieu's projected massive history of his ministry proved too extensive an endeavor even for his large and able corps of secretaries. Apparently despairing of ever seeing it completed, he turned his attention to directing another more manageable and doubtless more congenial record of his accomplishments, his famous *Testament politique*.[55] The *Mémoires* were not completely abandoned and were labored over by his secretaries throughout the re-

[53] *Ibid.*, Vol. x (P.), 535.

[54] *Ibid.*, Vol. x (P.), 535-37. In commenting on this event, the compilers of the *Mémoires* inserted the thought that many believed the birth of the Dauphin to augur the beginning of a period of general peace. Vain hope!

[55] Richelieu's shift of interest is indicated in the Dedicatory Epistle (certainly written by himself) to Louis XIII in the *Testament politique*. My citations are to the edition by Louis André, Paris, 1947.

mainder of the reign, new materials being added as they become available, but the *Testament politique* undoubtedly received greater attention from the Cardinal since he was determined to leave behind him a record of his achievements and accumulated political wisdom for both personal and altruistic reasons.[56] The procedures that were followed in compiling the *Testament* were essentially similar to those used for the *Mémoires*. The same great variety of documents and other sources was utilized, and the work of distilling essentials was done largely by the same personnel. Again, the work is the product of Richelieu's secretaries rather than his own pen, but he evidently gave the *Testament* much closer personal supervision than the *Mémoires*. Aside from the disputed matter of Richelieu's handwriting and that of his *secrétaire de la main*, it should be noted that certain portions of the *Testament*, notably the dedicatory epistle and the passages where he admits error, could only have been written or dictated by the Cardinal himself.[57] Also, it seems inconceivable that the general plan, many of the ideas and even some of the maxims could hardly have had any other source, although positive proof is lacking. The very lengthy debate concern-

[56] The following are the more important recent studies of the *Testament politique*. M. Deloche, "Le Testament politique du Cardinal de Richelieu," *Revue historique*, CLXV (1930), 43-76. E. Esmonin, communication in the *Bulletin de la Société d'histoire moderne*, Jan. 1937, 214-16, followed by comments by H. Hauser. A number of studies followed the publication of the André edition of the *Testament politique*, including the following. J. Stengers published a lengthy review of this edition in the *Revue belge de philologie et d'histoire*, XXVI² (1948), 650-60. R. Mousnier, "Le Testament politique de Richelieu," *Revue historique*, CCI (1949), 55-71, and Addendum in *ibid.*, CCII (1949), 137. E. Esmonin, "Observations sur le Testament politique de Richelieu," *Bulletin de la Société d'histoire moderne*, Dec. 1951-Jan. 1952, 7-14, followed by extensive commentary by R. Mousnier and V. L. Tapié. Esmonin's communication is reprinted, with additions, in his *Études sur la France des XVIIᵉ et XVIIIᵉ siècles*, Paris, 1964, pp. 219-32. Mousnier's comments in the *Bulletin* are of major significance. R. Pithon, "A propos du Testament politique de Richelieu," *Schweizerische Zeitschrift für Geschichte*, VI (1956), 177-214. J. Engel, "Zur Frage der Echtheit von Richelieus Testament politique," *Aus Mittelalter und Neuzeit: Festschrift Gerhard Kallen*, J. Engel and H. M. Klinkenberg, eds., Bonn, 1957, pp. 185-218.

[57] These points are made by Hauser in the discussion in the *Bulletin* (1937) listed in the previous note.

ing the authenticity of the *Testament* definitively ended with the publication of Gabriel Hanotaux's invaluable discovery, the document which he called *Maximes d'État et fragments politiques du Cardinal de Richelieu*, in 1880.[58] It may still be argued that more reliable evidence of Richelieu's specific views may be obtained by consulting the documents that his secretaries used in constructing the work rather than this single, *ex post facto* compilation, yet every consideration warrants the assumption that the *Testament* may justifiably be mined for the major concepts and policy recommendations that the Cardinal wished to leave behind him.

Although both the *Mémoires* and the *Testament politique* bear witness to Richelieu's crucial role in guiding the fortunes of France during his ministry, their differences are fundamental and reflect their divergent purposes. The *Mémoires* were intended to be a massive history of the reign in which events and developments in policy predominated and personalities were kept to a minimum. On the other hand, the *Testament politique* was deliberately reduced to the essentials of Richelieu's achievements during the reign and his policy recommendations for the future. As he stated in the dedicatory epistle to Louis XIII, the *Testament* was "conceived in the shortest and clearest terms of which I am capable, as much to follow my bent and customary manner of writing as to accommodate myself to the temperament of Your Majesty, who has always desired that one come to the point in few words and who gives as much credence to the substance of things as he distrusts the long discourses that most men use to express them."[59] The *Testament politique*, therefore is a highly personalized document which embodies the essence of Richelieu's views on a host of considerations that he thought necessary to transmit to his sovereign "for the regulation and guidance of your realm."[60] Indeed, in constructing the work, Richelieu claimed to have "no other motive than the interests of the state and the advantage of your person,"[61] although we may confidently add that he also

[58] In *Collection de documents inédits sur l'histoire de France, Mélanges historiques*, Paris, 1880, Vol. III, 705-808.
[59] *Testament politique*, p. 91.   [60] *Ibid.*, pp. 90-91.
[61] *Ibid.*, p. 92.

hoped to perpetuate his own renown. Based upon his accumulated experience and vast knowledge of the problems that he claimed to have handled so successfully, the work sets forth his mature political concepts and throughout bears the stamp of his personality as well as his sense of mission. It is literally a testament in which Richelieu, as elder statesman, consigned to his younger sovereign the essence of his superior knowledge of the mysteries of state, to use as he would. Specifically, Richelieu presented a plan of reform for the realm after the conclusion of the much-desired and confidently expected peace—a plan that allowed him to neglect foreign affairs and to concentrate upon those at home. Not doctrinal but practical and logical, it represents a distillation of his views concerning the best policies with which future rulers might meet France's many domestic problems, increase her strength, and thereby advance her interests and glory. It is a key source of Richelieu's understanding of reason of state.

The value of the *Testament politique* for our purposes is evident, since there is no doubt among ranking authorities that the work is an accurate guide to Richelieu's broader and more fundamental political concepts. In other words, his secretaries, with his guidance, succeeded in capturing and presenting his basic views on a variety of important matters, including those most disputed in his own time.[62] Somewhat more difficult is the problem of the audience for which the work was intended. Was it written solely for Louis XIII, or did the Cardinal envisage a larger body of readers, perhaps even its publication?[63] Internal evidence is inconclusive because it contains ele-

---

[62] In his introduction to the *Testament politique* (p. 67), Louis André briefly summarizes the encomiums that have been given the work from this standpoint. Even the ultra-scrupulous late Professor Esmonin said of the *Testament*, "One finds in it much of Richelieu's thought and even his spirit, but the composition and articulation are not his." *Bulletin de la Société d'histoire moderne*, Oct.-Nov. 1951, 43. See R. Mousnier's reconstruction of Richelieu's thought based upon the *Testament politique*, in *Revue historique*, CCI (1949), 55-71.

[63] M. Deloche, in the article cited in n. 56, argues for a broader audience whereas L. André, in his introduction to his edition of the *Testament politique*, insists that it was written for Louis XIII alone.

ments which indicate both solutions.[64] Beyond this, there is evidence that in 1641, Richelieu voluntarily showed the work to Archbishop Montchal of Toulouse.[65] The Cardinal evidently did not intend to reserve the work *solely* for the eyes of the King. Furthermore, Richelieu was certainly aware of the possibility, even the probability, that the *Testament* would be circulated after his death, since he was thoroughly familiar with the laxity of controls over official archives and manuscript libraries and the frequency with which pirated works appeared in print, even during their authors' lifetimes. To have restricted the work perpetually to future French kings Richelieu knew to be impossible in practice. Finally, the great amount of self-praise, both direct and indirect, in the work, plus Richelieu's known desire to perpetuate his fame and glory after his death would seem to indicate that he had future generations of readers in mind. On balance, it seems that although the *Testament* was written as a personal memoir to the King, Richelieu was constantly thinking of a wider audience in future reigns. The work would therefore appear to have been conceived as part, although a unique part, of his program of providing extensive literary records of his achievements and superior political insights for the edification of Frenchmen who, in later years, would reap the benefits of his program of state-building and revere him accordingly.

In the vast literary remains that Cardinal Richelieu left behind him, the *Testament politique* occupies a unique place in that it alone presents within the covers of a single work the essentials of

[64] In the debate between Professors Esmonin and Mousnier, the latter listed the major evidences of this. The criticisms of Louis XIII in the work would indicate that it was intended to remain secret, whereas Richelieu's mention of securing popular approbation would indicate the opposite. (*Bulletin de la Société d'histoire moderne*, Dec. 1951-Jan. 1952, 19.) Esmonin, citing a key phrase from the dedicatory epistle, expressed the opinion that the work was intended for publication. *Ibid.*, p. 11.

[65] The statement from Montchal's *Mémoires* is reprinted in L. André's edition of the *Testament politique*, p. 457. On the different views of this key source, held by Professors Esmonin, Mousnier, and Tapié, see their debate in the *Bulletin*, Oct.-Nov. 1951, 46, and Dec. 1951-Jan. 1952, 9-10, 14-18.

his social and political ideology.[66] For modern scholars it is invaluable because it sets forth in specific terms many of his fundamental assumptions that are merely implicit in other documents, such as the *Mémoires* and the innumerable records of his administrative and diplomatic activity. The French state he held to be a hierarchical, corporate, organic structure of individuals and groups which occupied specific stations within the whole and made corresponding contributions to its life and advancement. This rationalization of contemporary society was in turn grounded upon the fundamental assumption that human beings are by nature inherently unequal. Richelieu, like his fellow believers, may have held that all are equal in the sight of God, but he was at one with the great majority of his contemporaries in holding that on earth all men are limited not only by their varying aptitudes and abilities but also their assignment, usually by birth, to given stations in the social organism. Self-fulfillment for the vast majority was achieved by remaining in their assigned positions in the social hierarchy and fulfilling to the hilt their corresponding obligations to its corporate existence. Richelieu therefore believed in the essential rightness, nay, the divine institution, of French society as it stood, and held that a major purpose of monarchy was to perfect it by ensuring that each segment fulfill its prescribed function. This he attempted to do by eliminating abuses, making maximum use of available human material, and urging each element of French society to achieve its own special virtue. Much of the *Testament politique* is devoted to the reformation of classes, orders, institutions, and the scrupulous choice of officials according to their respective abilities, merits, and interests— all for the purpose of strengthening the state in its present form. Similarly, he strongly disapproved of any influence that might cause dissatisfaction with, or otherwise disrupt, the existing social structure and assignment of functions. For this reason he advocated re-

[66] It may be objected that the *Testament politique* slights foreign affairs, but this is true only of their many specific problems and intricacies. The work adequately indicates Richelieu's fundamental views, techniques, and objectives in this area.

ducing the number of educational institutions, especially those of higher learning, to the point where they would train only a small, select elite.[67] Otherwise an oversupply of the learned would create discontent and disobedience, cause all elements of the economy to languish, reduce the sources of men-at-arms, and fill the nation with wranglers who would disrupt families and destroy the peace of the realm.[68]

The major domestic function of monarchy was accordingly the preservation and surveillance of the established hierarchical order:

> As a whole can subsist only through the union of its parts in their natural order and positions, so this great realm cannot flourish if Your Majesty does not cause the bodies of which it is composed to continue in their order, the Church holding first place, the nobility the second, and the officials who lead the people the third.[69]

Richelieu placed great emphasis upon the role and significance of the clergy in the life of the realm, and urged major, extensive reforms within the first estate in regard to such matters as appointments, jurisdiction, discipline, and many others. Fully aware of the endemic abuses within the institutional functioning of the French Church, the Cardinal devoted much more attention to this order than any other in his *Testament politique*, not only as a loyal Prince of the Church but also because of his conviction that religion was

---

[67] *Testament politique*, pp. 204-07.

[68] As a body that has eyes in all its parts would be monstrous, so a state would be if all its subjects were learned. In it one would find as little obedience as pride and presumption would be common; traffic in letters would completely banish that in merchandise which fills states with riches; it would ruin agriculture, the true support of the common people, and it would quickly empty the nursery of soldiers who should be brought up in the ruggedness of ignorance rather than the politeness of learning; lastly it would fill France with wranglers more fitted to ruin families and disturb the public peace than to bring any benefit to states. (*Ibid.*, p. 204.)

[69] *Ibid.*, p. 256.

central to the life of the French state. His recommendations were therefore largely for the purpose of restoring the French Church to a condition which would enable it to provide the religious leadership that was the purpose of its very existence within the national framework. For this he advocated not only a host of institutional reforms but also the appointment of the best qualified personnel to high ecclesiastical office—at which point his aristocratic sentiment was made evident by his urging the recruitment of bishops from noble families in spite of the obvious inherent risks.[70] As for the nobility itself, which he called "one of the principal sinews of the state,"[71] Richelieu recognized its great financial difficulties and general deterioration, and it is noteworthy that he remained thoroughly sympathetic to the concept of honor that was generally held to be the peculiar virtue of the nobility. Its loss for the true nobleman was literally a fate worse than death.[72] And again Richelieu proposed a variety of measures that were designed to restore the nobility to its ancient lustre and to enable it to carry out its traditional functions, although strictly for the general good and in the service of the crown. The third estate he treated under two heads, first, royal officials, chiefly those of the judiciary, and second, the common people. Regarding the former, his major concern was to eliminate a variety of abuses which militated against the sound, competent administration of justice, and he recommended changes accordingly, although reluctantly admitting that the abolition of venality of office would create more problems than it would solve. Most necessary he believed to be the choice of justices of both adequate training and personal integrity, and once more he advocated the appointment of nobles whenever possible because of their superior sense of virtue and responsibility.[73] Again the emphasis was upon a high level of performance and contribution within the state system.

It was in the nature of things that Richelieu's aristocratic temperament should be most apparent in his comments on the common people. The following famous passage in the *Testament politique*,

[70] *Ibid.*, p. 153.   [71] *Ibid.*, p. 218.   [72] *Ibid.*, p. 220.
[73] *Ibid.*, pp. 237-38.

often quoted but frequently misinterpreted, clearly reveals his attitude toward the *peuple*:

> All political thinkers agree that if the common people were too comfortable, it would be impossible to hold them to the dictates of their duty. Their reasoning is that having less understanding than the other orders in the state [which are] much more cultivated and instructed, if they were not curbed by some want they would not easily remain within the conventions that are prescribed for them by reason and law. Reason does not permit them to be exempted from all burdens because, losing in this way all evidences of their servitude, they would also forget their stations, and if they were free of tribute they would believe themselves freed from obedience. They must be compared to mules which, being accustomed to burdens, are spoiled by long rest more than by work. But as this work should be moderate and the burden on these animals proportionate to their strength, so it is with regard to taxes on the common people. If they are not moderate, even though they might be useful to the public, they would still be unjust.[74]

This passage is usually taken to mean that Richelieu, the self-superior nobleman and powerful First Minister, not only despised the commoners but was more than willing to exploit them for any and all purposes of state. That he believed them to be inferior and obligated by law and social morality to support their betters and the entire royal establishment in its various ventures is clear, yet the burden of his argument is merely that measures should be taken to cause the lower classes to remain contentedly in their stations and make their contributions to the general good. Far from advocating exploitation of the downtrodden on principle, Richelieu was merely suggesting means to ensure the proper functioning of the social organism for the benefit of all, including the commoners themselves. This is evident in his immediately subsequent statement concerning the route taken by tax moneys: "That which kings take from the people returns to them, and they advance it only to draw upon it by enjoying

[74] *Ibid.*, pp. 253-54.

the peace and wealth that could not be preserved to them if they did not contribute to the maintenance of the state."[75] But even for such a worthy purpose, levies should be determined by ability to pay: "There is a certain point that may not be passed without injustice, common sense indicating to all that in this there should be a certain proportion between the burden and the strength of those who bear it."[76] A good king, Richelieu insisted, established the proper balance between the taxes that were indispensable for public necessities and those that were exorbitant, and he urged Louis XIII to rely more upon income from the *fermes générales* than levies from the poor. Surely the purpose of this brief but crucial bit in the *Testament politique* was merely to extend to the lower elements of the social hierarchy his recommendations concerning the policies that were both just and necessary to its proper functioning.

In addition to reform and increased contributions to the corporate life of the realm, Richelieu's treatment of the various segments of French society invariably emphasized another element: discipline. In fact, he believed intensified discipline to be indispensable to any improvement in the functioning of the social organism. Repeatedly in the *Testament politique* he decried the inconstancy and volatile nature of the French, their lack of respect for rules of any sort, their infinite capacity for intrigue, and their willingness to place their personal and corporate interests above all others, even those of the state. That what became known as the *frondeur* spirit was endemic in French life during this period is obvious from a glance at the record, and Richelieu understandably sought the remedy in increased discipline in all phases of French life. In the political sphere, he believed this to be absolutely essential to his program of state-building. The failures of earlier ministers he attributed largely to their inability to cope with the indiscipline and lack of respect for authority that were rampant throughout French society,[77] and he also knew that the monarchy was the only instrument that was capable of imposing any degree of order upon such a complex, fragmented, fric-

---

[75] *Ibid.*, p. 254.   [76] *Ibid.*

[77] This is made clear in the opening paragraphs of the *Succincte Narration. Ibid.*, pp. 93-95.

tion-racked social structure. Hence his determination to discipline the realm, by coercion if necessary, in order to enable it to achieve its true potential and greatness. In this sense, his severe treatment of certain offending persons, groups, and institutions he felt to be justified by the common interest.

Richelieu's most pressing problem of this type was what he regarded as encroachments upon the powers of the crown. Not only were certain groups predatory toward each other; some even had the temerity to usurp powers and functions of the monarchy itself— that sacred institution whose mission was leadership and discipline of all portions of the state. In the *Testament politique* he particularly criticized two bodies under this head: the Parlements and the great nobility. Regarding the first, Richelieu's recommendations were simple. The Parlements should be restricted to trying cases between subjects and debarred from interfering in matters of government because the magistrates were utterly ignorant of affairs of state.[78] Such would have eliminated at a stroke all restrictions that the Parlements habitually placed on royal legislation and taxation through remonstrances and refusal to enregister new laws, and the statement in the *Testament politique* obviously anticipates Richelieu's attempt to do precisely this in 1641.[79] As for the great nobles, their encroachment upon royal power was at once more devious and more dangerous. The paramount risk was that certain powerful, self-seeking individuals and factions at court would insinuate themselves into positions of influence and even determine royal policy, not for the public good but for their own benefit. To place private interests above public in this fashion Richelieu viewed as the greatest disaster:

> The public interests should be the unique objective of a prince and his councillors, or, at least, both are obliged to give them special consideration and to weight them more than [those of] individuals. It is impossible to conceive of the good that a prince and those of whom he makes use in his affairs may do if they religiously follow this principle, and one cannot imagine the evil that happens to a state when private interests take prece-

[78] *Ibid.*, p. 248. [79] See Pt. IV, n. 57.

dence over public and the latter are ordered according to the former.[80]

It need hardly be recalled that Richelieu fought against such intrigues at court throughout his entire ministry and knew first hand their great power. Their adverse impact upon royal policy had been so great in previous ministries that when he was called to the council in 1624, "personal interests were placed above public and, in a word, the dignity of the royal house was so debased and so different from what it should be because of the shortcomings of those who were then principally in charge of your affairs that it was almost impossible to recognize it."[81] Such a collapse of royal power at the hands of self-serving persons Richelieu found intolerable. Among the prime requisites of effective rule he included anticipation and control of such eventualities,[82] and he insisted upon immediate exile of such "public plagues" at the first hint of trouble and without regard to personal considerations,[83] since the life of the state itself was at stake: "The peace of the state is too important a thing to permit neglect of this remedy without being responsible for it before God. I have sometimes seen the court, in the midst of peace, so full of factions for lack of practicing this salutary advice, that they very nearly destroyed the state."[84] For these reasons Richelieu found it indispensable to suppress noble factions without regard to personal or legal considerations. Again the public good took precedence over all else.

Ability to discipline the various elements of French society, foresight relative to factional strife, and determination to subordinate all private interests to the public good were but a few of the necessary attributes of the ideal minister according to Richelieu. In a portion of the *Testament politique* whose evident purpose was self-justification, he listed the qualities that he believed necessary to a minister who would successfully guide the fortunes of the realm: judgment rather than audacity, prudence in all things, honesty before both God and man, willingness to endure great responsibility and criticism, courage and firmness, a sense of glory, constant appli-

---

[80] *Testament politique*, p. 330.   [81] *Ibid.*, p. 94.
[82] *Ibid.*, pp. 334-37.   [83] *Ibid.*, p. 367.   [84] *Ibid.*, p. 369.

cation to affairs, avoidance of the influence of women, a special talent for public affairs over and above private, and many more.[85] And in another section of the work he frankly related the proper choice of ministers to his broader concept that all ranking members of the social organism should occupy the stations to which their talents were best suited, insisting that the king's duty to choose the best qualified was one of his most important obligations before God.[86] With a seriousness that was too genuine for mock modesty, he recognized the great difficulty of finding all these attributes in a single individual and urged the king to search for him throughout the realm. And Richelieu even argued the superiority of ecclesiastics in such posts because they were distracted by fewer personal interests than laymen.[87] He also gave all the stock arguments in favor of a single, supreme minister rather than several of equal power, chiefly for reasons of efficiency, since "there is nothing more dangerous in a state than several equal authorities in the administration of affairs."[88] Richelieu's extensive self-approbation in these portions of the work is evident, and it is noteworthy that some of his supporters lauded him in precisely the same terms,[89] yet he undoubtedly believed that his superior knowledge of the mysteries of state warranted the inclusion of such observations in his personal testament to the king.

Great emphasis should be placed upon the fact that Richelieu regarded strong, effective rule of this type not as an end in itself but as a means to an end, namely, raising the state to higher things and leading it to its true objectives which he defined in fundamentally religious terms. At the outset of Part II of the *Testament politique,* which deals less with reform than the qualities and purposes of government, he used superlatives in positing that the firmest foundation and primary aim of monarchical rule was to establish the reign of God on earth:

The reign of God is the principle of the government of states, and, indeed, it is a thing so absolutely necessary that without

[85] *Ibid.,* pp. 289-305. [86] *Ibid.,* pp. 357-59. [87] *Ibid.,* pp. 363-64.
[88] *Ibid.,* p. 306. [89] E.g., Dupleix. See n. 15-17 and text.

this foundation there is no prince whatsoever who can reign well, nor state that can be successful and effective. It would be easy to compose whole volumes on so important a subject, for which the Scriptures, the Fathers, and all manner of histories provide us with an infinite number of precepts, examples, and exhortations that conduce toward the same end. But it is something so well known to everyone by his own reason, which tells him that he does not derive his being from himself but has God for his Creator and consequently his Director, that there is no one who does not sense that nature has imprinted this truth in his heart with characters that cannot be erased.[90]

In this passage, Richelieu seems to be groping for words to express how central and fundamental were the religious qualities and purposes of royal government. In any case, he at once proceeded to apply this position to both its spirit and operations. Regarding the former, the greatest influence for good was the example set by the sovereign himself, for "nothing is more useful to a holy institution than the good life of princes, which is a living law and more effectively compelling than all the laws that they might make to coerce toward the good that they wish to procure."[91] Richelieu believed in enforcing the law to the hilt, but he knew human nature sufficiently to realize that the standard of conduct set by the prince was as effective as any constraint: "His example is not less valuable in [securing] the observation of his will than all the penalties of his ordinances, no matter how great they may be."[92] He praised the laudable influence of Louis XIII's personal piety, chastity, and abstinence from blasphemy as most appropriate and beneficial to monarchical rule in Christian France. He also insisted that the King was obligated to convert to the true faith those in his realm who had rejected it, meaning the Huguenots, although only with peaceful means.[93] And he did not hesitate to relate the ultimate fate of states to the extent to which they and their rulers followed God's precepts:

So many princes have been lost, they and their states, for basing their conduct on precepts contrary to their knowledge [of God],

[90] *Testament politique*, p. 321.
[91] *Ibid.*, p. 322.
[92] *Ibid.*
[93] *Ibid.*, pp. 264-65, 322-24.

and so many have been filled with benedictions for having subjected their authority to that from which it was derived, in order to seek their greatness only in that of their Creator and to care more for his rule than their own, that I shall not expatiate further concerning a truth too obvious to have need of proof.[94]

Government according to higher law Richelieu held to be so essential to rulers of Christian states that nothing could be clearer and no more need be said. Accordingly, he applied the same reasoning to ministers whose integrity he measured by similar standards. Honesty among men may differ from that required by God, he admitted, and the law of God contains precepts other than those prescribed by honor among men.[95] The ideal minister should be well versed in both, but if he must be deficient in either, his weakness must be in earthly wisdom because knowledge of God's law is fundamental and without it he cannot understand more mundane matters. "In a word, the statesman must be faithful to God, the state, men, and himself"[96]—in that order. True to their mission, Christian kings and statesmen were bound to rule according to God's law and, in their leadership of men, literally to establish God's reign on earth.

Their chief resource in fulfilling this superlatively important obligation was their reason. Richelieu, who was both a believer and a rationalist, confidently held that man's reason not only demonstrated God's existence as Creator and Director but also enlightened men concerning the means to make his precepts effective in human society.[97] Man, he held, was created rational; accordingly he should do nothing contrary to reason, for otherwise he would go against his own nature and consequently his Creator. Reason also taught that those in authority should make maximum use of reason, the essence of their being, because their advantages over other men obliged them to be more beholden to their nature and purposes than those below them. "From these two principles it clearly follows that, since man is supremely rational he should cause reason to reign supremely, which requires not only that he do nothing without it but also

---

[94] *Ibid.*, pp. 321-22.   [95] *Ibid.*, pp. 291-92.   [96] *Ibid.*, p. 292.
[97] *Ibid.*, p. 321 and Pt. II, Chap. 2.

obliges him to cause all who are under his authority to revere and religiously follow it."[98] The picture of rightful government is clear. The devout ruler and his ministers, in establishing the reign of God, should follow the precepts of reason and thereby be true to themselves and their Creator. For Richelieu, this concept of just rule had vital practical consequences, since he interpreted it to mean both that royal policy should be reasonable and just and that nothing should be decreed that could not be enforced, "for otherwise reason would not reign supremely."[99] In this way he moved from divine law and human reason to the justice and necessity of forceful, effective rule. All decisions and projects should be rationally determined and then carried through with perseverance and vigor. "The government of realms requires a masculine virtue and unshakable constancy,"[100] he wrote. "In a word, nothing should divert one from a good undertaking unless some accident happens that renders it completely impossible, and nothing should be forgotten that may promote the completion of those that have been decided upon with reason."[101] Effective government was achieved by following the precepts of divine law through maximum application of human reason and successful pursuit of state goals, all for the purpose of attaining religiously defined objectives.

RICHELIEU'S CONCEPT OF REASON OF STATE

It is within this complex, logically articulated framework, so effectively presented in Richelieu's *Testament politique*, that we should attempt to understand his concept of reason of state. One valid interpretation of reason of state has already been indicated, namely, the rule of reason in political affairs. As we have noted, Richelieu insisted that kings and ministers, being men of superior intellect and power as well as divinely bestowed reason, should in-

---

[98] *Ibid.*, p. 325.   [99] *Ibid.*, p. 325.

[100] *Ibid.*, p. 327. Cf. p. 276: "One must have manly virtue and do all things by reason." Richelieu repeated this advice because he found Louis XIII lacking in these qualities. Also see Pt. IV, n. 97 and text.

[101] *Ibid.*, p. 328.

variably act according to reason in all matters of government. Reason of state in this sense was merely reason expertly applied to all matters of state.[102] The more specific and controversial meaning, however, has to do with a means-end rationality that is predicated upon the legitimacy of a higher morality of state policy at the expense of traditional legal and moral values. In his *Testament politique*, Richelieu discussed this problem most specifically in the chapter on rewards and punishments.[103] Pursuing his line of reasoning that kings and ministers must be absolutely uncompromising in disciplining all who would put personal interests above public, he argued that while both rewards and punishments were important to effective rule, only the latter were indispensable. Rewards might be neglected without material loss, whereas failure to punish offenders against the state frequently opened the way to further dissension and disruption. This type of neglect was therefore a "criminal omission."[104] Not only was severe punishment most effective in restricting potential offenders to their proper stations; life was more secure under a prince who strictly enforced the law than under one whose leniency opened the door to all manner of license. "To be rigorous toward individuals who glory in despising the laws and orders of the state is good for the public, and one cannot commit a greater crime against public interests than to be indulgent toward those who violate it."[105] For such misguided rule a prince was blamed by the wise and must render an account to God.

From this position, which the Cardinal argued with great vehemence, it was but a small and logical step to the assertion that the uniquely dangerous character of crimes against the state justified extraordinary, even extralegal measures for their punishment and prevention. In many respects he found that the criteria of justice which prevailed in private affairs could not be applied to public, again because of the special nature of the latter. Here he was approaching the problem of a special morality of politics and standard of justice

---

[102] Mousnier, "Le Testament politique de Richelieu," *Revue historique*, CCI (1949), 59.

[103] Pt. II, Chap. 5.   [104] *Testament politique*, p. 339.

[105] *Ibid.*, pp. 339-40.

DESIGN FOR IMMORTALITY

relative to crimes against the state. Regarding forgiveness he mustered his authorities and declared: "Theologians as well as political philosophers (*politiques*) are agreed and all acknowledge that in certain instances in which individuals would offend by not pardoning, those who are responsible for public government would be guilty if, instead of severe punishment, they made use of indulgence."[106] Therefore:

> In matters of crimes against the state one must close the door to pity and disregard the pleas of interested persons and the talk of the ignorant populace who sometimes criticize what is most beneficial to them and often thoroughly necessary. Christians should forget offenses that they receive as individuals. But magistrates are obliged not to forget those that concern the public: in fact, to leave them unpunished is rather to commit them over again instead of pardoning and remitting them.[107]

To this extent, Richelieu recognized and even insisted that certain fundamental moral precepts, specifically Christian charity, could not be observed when the fate of the state was at stake. That he was developing a position of two moralities is patent, although he sincerely believed that the great risks which indulgence entailed in the current French situation and his superior knowledge of affairs of state justified all such measures. The fact remains that he was partially separating politics from a single, comprehensive Christian morality. With similar reasoning he argued the necessity of bypassing traditional legal processes when combatting crimes against the state. Pursuant to his belief that laws were valueless unless enforced, he wrote:

> Ordinances and laws are entirely useless unless they are followed by enforcement which is absolutely necessary. Although in the course of ordinary affairs, justice requires authentic proofs, it is not the same with those that concern the state, because in such cases, that which may seem evident [only] because of dangerous

[106] *Ibid.*, p. 339.
[107] *Ibid.*, pp. 342-43. Cf. Pt. I, n. 220 and text; Pt. III, n. 78 and text.

conjectures should sometimes be held to be sufficiently clear, inasmuch as the factions and conspiracies that are formed against the public welfare are ordinarily handled with such cleverness and secrecy that one never has clear proof of them except when they happen, which cannot then be undone. It is necessary on such occasions sometimes to begin with enforcement, whereas in all others it is necessary to implement the law with witnesses or unchallengeable documents.[108]

This celebrated passage of the *Testament politique* is often quoted to indicate the extent to which Richelieu was willing to violate tradition and resort to a novel standard of political justice in developing his ethic of reason of state. There is no doubt that he and his contemporaries realized the seriousness of abandoning legal procedures and proofs of guilt when handling political crimes, although from the record it is clear that in practice Richelieu was as ruthless in manipulating judicial processes as he was adamant in rejecting appeals for mercy. He even believed that proofs of guilt might be dispensed with when the accused had merely violated such royal edicts as that against duelling.[109] All this seemed to many of his contemporaries to be ultrarigorous justice of unwarranted severity both because it ran counter to many French social and legal traditions and because it attributed a special ethical standard to a single category of crimes, those against the state. His major justifications were that such measures were indispensable to the preservation of the state and that they were authorized by the crown and were therefore legal. Richelieu, moreover, was fully aware of the risks of tyranny that were implicit in his position and immediately sought to qualify and defend it against attacks on this score:

These maxims seem dangerous, and in truth they are not entirely free of peril. But they will most certainly be found free of it if they [rulers] do not use extreme and inordinate punishments for offenses that can be verified only by conjecture. One

[108] *Ibid.*, pp. 343-44. Cf. Hanotaux, *Maximes d'État*, maxims LXXX, CXXIV. Also Pt. III, n. 11 and text; Pt. IV, n. 123 and text.
[109] *Testament politique*, p. 228.

may simply arrest their course with innocent measures such as the dismissal or imprisonment of suspected persons. Good conscience and the penetration of a judicious mind, which, being learned in the course of affairs, discerns the future through the present almost as surely as faulty judgments through the observation of things, shields this practice from a bad outcome. And at worst, since the abuse that may be committed in this way is dangerous only to individuals whose lives are not touched by such measures, it does not cease to be admissible, since their interests are not comparable to those of the public. However, it is necessary to take great pains on such occasions not to open the door by this means to tyranny, against which one will undoubtedly be protected if, as I said, one uses only innocent punishments in dubious cases.[110]

Richelieu was evidently aware of the dangers in his position, but he was confident that a superior minister (such as himself) could easily neutralize its risks by enlightened manipulation of justice and stopping short of the most arbitrary measures. And in any case the resultant injury was only to individuals whose interests were not comparable to those of the state. For these reasons he believed extralegal procedures to be both indispensable and safe in his hands and, by implication, those of his enlightened successors. Richelieu's rationale of reason of state fully conceded the necessity of a double standard of justice and its attendant severities as essential to effective rule for the general good, and he consistently held to this position, both in theory and practice, throughout his ministry.[111]

[110] *Ibid.*, p. 344. This passage in the André edition contains two very confusing misprints which are lacking in Hanotaux, *Maximes d'État*, p. 784 n. 4, where the same passage is reproduced.

[111] It is noteworthy that the passage in the *Testament politique* on the dangers of two standards of justice is considerably less straightforward relative to the necessity of such prosecution and its results than the parallel passage in the earlier *Maximes d'État*, edited by Hanotaux. The earlier version reads:

This maxim seems dangerous and in truth it contains something perilous which can be corrected only by the perspicacity of a judicious and penetrating mind which, being learned in the course of affairs, discerns the future through the present as certainly as faulty judgments through the

It should be emphasized that although Richelieu recognized the risks that were inherent in his position, he considered it in no way contrary to the justice and morality that were vital attributes of true kingship in a Christian monarchy. This he made clear in his discussion of the foundations and elements of royal power, both within the realm and in relation to the other princes of Europe. The esteem and respect of all he found to be the primary basis of effective royal power both at home and abroad. In fact, these were its only sure and satisfactory foundations, since all others—meaning coercion and force—gave rise to hatred of princes "who are never in worse condition than when they sink into public aversion."[112] And the major assurance of this all-important esteem and respect lay in the prince's good reputation:

> Reputation is so very necessary to a prince that he of whom one has a good opinion does more with his mere name than those who are not esteemed do with their armies. They [princes] are obligated to value their reputations more than their own lives, and they should risk their fate and grandeur rather than allow their honor to be compromised, being certain that the first diminution that occurs to a prince's reputation, however slight, is the most dangerous step that he may take toward his ruin.[113]

Richelieu did not hesitate to apply this precept to matters of practical policy, going so far as to insist that rulers should reject all gains that conflicted with their honor. "They are blind and insensitive to their true interests if they accept any of this nature."[114] Such a statement from the Cardinal who devoted all his energies to advancing the interests of the French state speaks volumes concerning his extreme weighting of the moral connotations of monarchy.

---

observation of things. But inasmuch as the consequence of this maxim is dangerous only to the individual, it does not cease to be admissible, since the loss to individuals is not comparable to [that of] the public safety, and the danger can fall only on some individuals whereas the public receives its benefit and advantage. This maxim is good for great minds and opens a door to tyranny to those that are mediocre." (Hanotaux, maxim cxxv, p. 785.)

[112] *Testament politique*, p. 373.   [113] *Ibid.*, p. 373.
[114] *Ibid.*, p. 374.

Of necessity, the best means of preserving the respect of all lay in the enlightened conduct of policy. Regarding the relations between the ruler and the mass of his subjects, Richelieu may have urged strict discipline and control, but he also knew that the sovereign must retain their support and even their love, and recommended salutary measures accordingly.[115] As for the king's relations with his fellow princes, Richelieu found it indispensable that he keep faith and observe sworn treaties, once his word was pledged:

> Kings should be wary of making treaties, but when they are made, they should religiously observe them. I well know that many political thinkers teach the contrary. But without considering at this point what the Christian faith may teach against such maxims, I maintain that since the loss of honor is greater than that of life, a great prince should risk even his person and the interests of his state rather than break his word, which he cannot violate without losing his good reputation and consequently the greatest strength of sovereigns.[116]

Again, the interests of the state were of less moment than the principles of princely honor. Richelieu even carried this doctrine into the extremely sensitive area of war for the national good. War, he wrote, is sometimes inevitable and necessary for such purposes as to regain lost territory, avenge an insult, protect one's allies, stem the progress and pride of a conqueror, and to forestall ills that threaten and cannot otherwise be met—all of which reflect the reasoning behind his anti-Spanish policy. But before undertaking outright war, he insisted, those in charge of state policy *must* determine its justice according to the most fundamental precepts of Christian morality:

> I maintain, and it is the truth, that there can be no successful war unless it is just, because, if it is not, even though the occasion for it may be favorable according to worldly precepts, it will be necessary to render an account for it before the tribunal of God. In considering this matter, the first thing that must be done when one is forced to resort to arms is thoroughly to examine the equity [of the cause] that brings one to this, which

[115] *Ibid.*, p. 450.   [116] *Ibid.*, p. 355.

should be done with theologians of the requisite capacity and honesty.[117]

No statement concerning the requisite justice of war and the means of establishing it could be more explicit. Its inclusion as a primary consideration in Richelieu's testament to his sovereign is ample evidence that both believed their anti-Spanish policy, including outright war against a fellow Catholic state, to be justified by the fundamental principles of Christian morality.

Richelieu's concept of royal honor, then, was comprehensive in that it embraced not only the code of upright conduct among men but also active adherence to Christian principles. And he was explicit that the counsels which he incorporated into his *Testament politique* accorded with this ideal. His statement to this effect may be regarded as confirming the fact that *all* his proposals concerning enlightened royal policy, even those that his contemporaries found most questionable, conformed to his concept of Christian monarchy and led to its fulfillment:

> Those who will mold their conduct according to the rules and principles contained in this present testament will undoubtedly acquire renown that will not have small weight in the minds of their subjects and neighbors, particularly if, being reverent toward God, they are also the same toward themselves, that is, truthful in speech and faithful in their promises, conditions so absolutely necessary to a prince's reputation that, as those who are deprived of them cannot be esteemed by anyone, so it is impossible for those who possess them not to be revered by everyone and given great confidence.[118]

The didactic purpose of the *Testament politique* is clear, as is Richelieu's affirmation that all his recommendations concerning just policy and reason of state conformed to his ideal.

To conclude our consideration of this most important work of Cardinal Richelieu, we can do no better than to reiterate the argument of his final chapter in which he placed great emphasis upon the obligations of kings and ministers to rule justly in the sight of

[117] *Ibid.*, p. 382.   [118] *Ibid.*, p. 374.

God, on pain of committing sin. He approached this all-important principle by analyzing the great differences between the obligations of private persons and those who were entrusted with governmental authority. The responsibilities of kings and ministers he found to be so great that by neglecting their duties they might easily commit more sins of omission than others might by commission.[119] For this reason, a man might be virtuous as an individual but a failure in high office. And Richelieu listed as possible faults of omission neglect to carry out most of his recommendations in the *Testament politique*, including the establishment on earth of "the reign of God, reason and justice all together."[120] His treatment of faults of commission is even more striking in its emphasis upon divine retribution: "If they [kings and ministers] use their power to commit some injustice or injury that they cannot do as private persons, they commit a sin as prince or magistrate that has its origin solely in their authority and for which the Kings of Kings will demand a most exact accounting at Judgment Day."[121] Because of their much wider impact, sins both of omission and commission by the public authorities were much more reprehensible than those by private persons who therefore might escape the damnation that awaited offending kings and ministers. This should surely give them pause, Richelieu continued, citing the example of Philip II of Spain who, when dying, said that he feared punishment for his sins as king more than those that he had committed as Philip. It would have been much more beneficial to himself and his subjects, Richelieu commented, had he kept his supreme obligations in mind at the height of his power rather than on his deathbed. And Richelieu concluded by urging this precept upon Louis XIII and promising that "there will never be a day of my life that I do not try to bear in mind that which I should have at the hour of my death concerning the public affairs of which it pleases His Majesty to unburden himself upon me."[122]

This was the picture of Richelieu's achievements, motivation, and ideology of government that he wished to be preserved for posterity. It was also his most thoroughgoing and significant answer to his

---

[119] *Ibid.*, p. 451.   [120] *Ibid.*, p. 452.   [121] *Ibid.*, p. 453.
[122] *Ibid.*, p. 454.

many critics. Throughout, the dominant note was that France was a Christian state, governed by a Christian monarchy, and that all elements of royal policy should accord with the precepts of justice and Christian morality. In the process of leading the state to its true objectives, harsh discipline, seemingly arbitrary punishments, subordination of all to the public good, and even a special morality of politics were required by the imperatives of government and the exigencies of circumstances. But the latter were mundane and transitory whereas the principles that the state served were transcendental and eternal. Richelieu therefore believed that all measures that were necessary and advantageous to the advancement of state interests were justified not only as requisite means to a laudable end but also by their consonance with justice and Christian principles. Personal and corporate sacrifices might be exacted by royal policy, but the objectives of the state and enlightened rulership were so superior to all other considerations that there was no comparison. That Richelieu had full confidence in the justice of his position and his resultant policies is evident from the consistency of his life, even to its final moments. His promise to Louis XIII at the end of the *Testament politique* he believed he had fulfilled, when, on his deathbed, as the viaticum was placed before him, he said, "My Master, there is my Judge who will soon judge me. I pray Him with all my heart that He will condemn me if I have had any intention other than the good of religion and the state."[123]

[123] L. Lalanne, "Un Récit inédit de la mort du Cardinal de Richelieu," *Revue historique*, LV (1894), 305. Griffet, Vol. III, 576 gives the following version: "There is my Lord and my God whom I shall soon receive. I protest before Him and call Him to witness that in all that I have undertaken during my ministry, I have never sought anything but the good of religion and the state." Evidence that when Richelieu was asked whether he forgave his enemies he uttered the oft-quoted words, "I have no enemies but those of the state," is less reliable. Griffet, *loc.cit.*, states that some said he said this but according to others he merely said, "Yes, with all my heart, as I pray God that He will pardon me." Cf. *Mémoires du Marquis de Monglat*, Petitot, ed., Paris, 1825, Vol. I, 397. In any case, it seems certain that on his deathbed Richelieu manifested continued confidence in the justice of his policies for the good of religion and the state. His belief that his only enemies were those of the state was incorporated into his *Mémoires*. See n. 41 and text.

CONCLUSION

THE foregoing pages should suffice to indicate the nature of the rich and momentous debate in which the concept of reason of state was forged under Richelieu's aegis. In order to indicate his central role in these polemics, it has been necessary to present the full framework of discussion, including the many criticisms to which he was subjected, his efforts to influence public opinion in his favor, and the great variety of writings that were published in his defense. Throughout, it is clear that the religious frame of reference and concern for Christian morality were all-important. At the opening of the period, the generally accepted concept of divine-right sovereignty contained the germ of reason of state, but responsible French thinkers experienced profound difficulties when attempting to expand the position to justify any and all measures that might be for the general good. This was to a large extent accomplished in the heat of controversy that was generated by Richelieu's policies. As First Minister, he was charged with the enormous responsibility of preserving and strengthening the French state in the face of extremely formidable obstacles. These included not only the massive Hapsburg challenge abroad but also endemic governmental weakness, social fragmentation, and factionalism at home which severely weakened the state and produced what he regarded as outright anarchy and treason. In pursuing his program of state-building, he was therefore obliged to resort to many high-handed measures against recalcitrant persons and groups within the realm and to embark upon a vigorous anti-Hapsburg foreign policy in spite of the fact that these actions ran counter to the interests and religious perspectives of many segments of French society. For this reason his policies required justification that could be meaningful only in terms of the ends to be achieved.

The first major episode of the debate was precipitated by the Valtelline affair. Here were set forth all the major arguments of both parties relative to the justice of Richelieu's foreign policy. It is noteworthy that at this point he enjoyed the support of such important clerics as Bérulle, Saint-Cyran, and Mathieu de Morgues, all of whom later turned against him, although for different reasons. In internal affairs, Richelieu believed it essential both to bring all elements of the population under effective royal sovereignty and to eliminate opposition to his policies. Indeed, he habitually associated the one with the other. For this reason, he eliminated the Huguenots' defenses, struck down dissident noblemen, and engaged in an all-out struggle against hostile factions at court. The conflict was resolved in Richelieu's favor at the Day of Dupes, after which there occurred a sharp increase in the number of publications in his favor. This was followed by the lengthy period of climax in which the Cardinal's foreign and domestic policies were the order of the day and required implementation with measures that caused his enemies to raise the cry of tyranny but also produced extensive justifications of his acts by a wide variety of writers. The latter, significantly, ranged from Richelieu's intimates among men of letters to minor pamphleteers who merely sought to praise the First Minister for his vigorous moves against disorder at home and the enemy abroad. The tide of opinion seemed increasingly to be flowing in Richelieu's favor. The developed concept of reason of state, as it was set forth in the major pro-Richelieu tracts late in the reign, varied widely from one publicist to another and was frequently supported by arguments that stemmed from compromise positions, but almost all had in common a means-end rationality which posited a special ethic of politics and was justified by the nature and purposes of the Christian state.

All this, it should be noted, took place in an ideological society whose very structure, ways, and ideals were derived from tradition and drew their strength from legal, moral, and religious values which reflected accepted canons of justice, right, and higher law. This fundamental cast of mind accounts for the intensity of the debate concerning reason of state, since the issues that it raised touched upon vital matters which ranged from personal and corporate interests to religious morality and immutable Christian principles. The cogency of the opposition to Richelieu's foreign policy, when grounded upon the supremacy of religious considerations and the interests of international Catholicism, has been noted, as well as the more complex but coherent arguments that were necessary to his defense. "Reason of state" inevitably became a censorious phrase for the many whose interests and/or fundamental values were compromised and a mechanism of justification for those who prized its apparent benefits and believed it essential to effective government.

This ideological cast of mind also accounts for Richelieu's extensive efforts to justify his policies by mobilizing public opinion in his favor. The authoritarian mentality of the age and the concentration of all governmental power in the ruler were predicated upon the assumption that the constituted authorities knew best how to guide all phases of life for the general good. From his vantage point as First Minister and leader of the nation second only to the sovereign, Richelieu found it both natural and necessary to instruct his contemporaries in the principles of monarchy and the measures that would bring it greatest advantage. He did not regard the writers who publicized his views and received his favors as mere propagandists on his behalf; rather, they were edifying and guiding the nation concerning the true purposes of the French state and the paths that would lead it to greatness. Only a chosen few, among whom the Cardinal believed himself the most knowledgeable, understood the mysteries of state and might direct political discussion according to official ideology. In this sense, Richelieu's efforts to channel public opinion in support of his policies was but part of his comprehensive program of state-building.

Throughout the many controversies concerning reason of state during his ministry, Richelieu adhered to a position that was both flexible and consistent. For him, the French state was a Christian state that was governed by a Christian monarch with the invaluable aid of an enlightened Cardinal-Minister. The mission of both men was to improve the general good by pursuing policies that would strengthen the state and fulfill its higher purposes. Because of prevailing circumstances, the imperatives of government required harsh measures at home and an anti-Hapsburg foreign policy—questionable means that were justified by the supreme importance of the state's higher ends. Not all of Richelieu's apologists, however, gave evidence of adhering to this comprehensive, high-minded position. As we have noted, many limited their efforts to urging the advancement of the French state's secular interests and went no further. Their writings have been examined both to indicate the full dimensions of the debate and to show the potentialities of the arguments that were used to justify French policies. Examples of this type of publication are found among the many tracts that Richelieu solicited from Fancan and Jean Sirmond, plus those of the Duke of Rohan and La Mothe le Vayer that appeared in the *Mercure français*. These authors wrote for specific purposes and used *ad hoc* arguments as the occasion required. Richelieu's willingness to make use of their writings in no way compromised his religiously oriented concept of the French state's objectives, since he viewed their tracts merely as instruments of policy, comparable to incessant diplomacy or increased taxation. It is the works of other men—the Mathieu de Morgues of the *Théologien sans passion*, the group that composed the *Catholique d'estat*, Jean de Silhon, Daniel de Priézac—that most accurately reflect the Cardinal's true position. This is readily apparent when comparing their views of reason of state with Richelieu's, particularly as it is set forth in his *Testament politique*.

All surviving evidence indicates that when Richelieu died he remained fully convinced of the justice of his policies and their consonance with Christian principles. His achievements along his intended lines were indeed substantial in that he succeeded in laying the foundations of the absolutism that triumphed later in the century when the French monarchy attained its historical zenith. The concept of reason of state, however, ultimately became something that he would have abhorred. Richelieu believed that he had forged a justification for extensive application of discretionary power to achieve the state's higher purposes, and the circumstances and ideology of his time persuaded many of his contemporaries that his position was sound, but the subsequent evolution of the nature and practices of the state itself inevitably gave reason of state a different meaning. With the further development of state power, its entry into new spheres of competence, and the expanding secularization of European culture generally, the ever-present exigencies of politics undermined and eventually destroyed the fusion of politics and religion that was so characteristic of Richelieu's era. In its place there arose a rationalization of political affairs according to mere state interests, increasingly divorced from moral and religious considerations. The result was the pragmatic, secularized concept of reason of state of modern times.

This separation of morals and politics was instinctively feared by a number of Richelieu's critics during his ministry. As his policies and their justifications became more arbitrary, many observers began to fear that his applications of power might be more than temporary expedients and that they would corrupt the entire effort toward national revival. In other words, unjust and immoral means would compromise and take precedence over admittedly laudable ends. The danger seemed confirmed when Richelieu and his supporters insisted that governments operated according to a special morality which exempted them from ordinary canons of justice. Such a position risked the negation of all immutable principle and the substitution of Machiavellian expediency in which power and success were self-justifying. Richelieu's known penchant for autocratic power and the nature of his foreign and domestic policies were sufficient to give credence to these fears. Partially for these reasons, a number of his more religious minded supporters gradually moved to the opposition. Bérulle and Marillac assumed leadership of the chronically hostile *dévot* faction, and Saint-Cyran made no secret of his doubts concerning Richelieu's foreign policy. Other examples might be cited. Toward the end of the reign, even some of the Cardinal's consistent apologists began to question the morality of some of his measures. Jean de Silhon had reservations concerning their impact upon individuals; La Mothe le Vayer discarded the doctrine of two moralities; and Guez de Balzac at least claimed to have seen the light after the event. Their misgivings varied greatly from man to man, but all shared a common antipathy for any special ethic of politics.

Later in the century, absolutism in action aroused further concern because of the willingness of the constituted authorities to rule in a manner that seemed to divorce politics from morals. After the death of Louis XIII, Mazarin essentially continued Richelieu's policies, causing the inevitable reaction to this type of "tyranny" to burst forth in the Fronde. Claude Joly, the ablest apologist for the rebellion, placed the blame for the uprising squarely upon the unprincipled rule of the two Cardinals. In a ringing denunciation of their practices, he called for return to government in accordance with true Christian morality:

> It is a very great error, against which kings should be warned, that politics and Christian piety are incompatible and that it is impossible to accommodate the laws of the state to those of the Gospel. This most dangerous opinion is sometimes insinuated into their minds and, in addition to the great damage that it does to their consciences, is particularly detrimental to a King of France because it is capable of causing him to do many things that would completely tarnish his beautiful name of Most Christian. I can hardly endure the words of one of our foremost magistrates who, when attending the King in the Parlement at the registration of some edicts . . . was asked his advice and answered . . . *that there is one conscience for affairs of state and another for personal matters.* These accursed maxims have crept in among the greatest jurists today and have rendered them ready to carry out all the desires of royal favorites. For this reason it may be said that this is a major cause of the ills that we suffer, since the ministers' injustice and oppression of the people for twenty or thirty years, in the name of the King whose authority they usurp, have occurred with the assistance of these officials . . . . From this have come all the uprisings that have violently agitated this state in recent years and are capable of destroying it if no decision is made to govern the people with greater justice and leniency than has been done in the past. Now I say that the maxim concerning the incompatibility of religion and politics is entirely false and cannot be true except *for those who seek to govern tyrannically . . . and who have no aim but to satisfy their ambition, cruelty and avarice. Such men undoubtedly . . . should violate divine and human laws, having*

neither faith nor promise beyond what is profitable to their designs, shed blood pitilessly in endless wars, and climb over dead bodies to make their gains. But the faithful minister who adheres to justice and equity undertakes war only to have peace and seeks to bring the blessings of Heaven and earth upon his prince; and the prince himself, who, being genuinely religious and truly submissive to the laws of the King of Kings, does not wish to incur the indignation and anger of this vengeful God, *conducts himself in a different manner and deftly joins the prudence of a serpent with the artlessness of a dove.*[1]

Joly's exhortations went unheeded, and the failure of the Fronde ensured the triumph of absolutism. During the first generation of Louis XIV's personal reign, the voices of criticism fell silent, but constant exploitation of the nation's resources and growing reverses in the chronic warfare of the period eventually rekindled observers' doubts concerning the justice of royal policy. Increasingly, responsible members of the highest social echelons found reason to censure Louis XIV's applications of reason of state.[2] One important focus of their criticisms was Louis XIV's apparent willingness to conduct official policy without regard to recognized canons of right and justice. This point of view was best expressed by Archbishop Fénelon, whose utter sincerity and fearless insistence upon the supremacy of immutable Christian principles over all men, including the King, caused him to write some of the most searching denunciations of Louis XIV and his policies ever recorded. True kingship, Fénelon held, must accord with law, justice, and Christian morality which the ruler should follow in all things, whereas Louis XIV's fundamental weakness was that he was not a true Christian. Such was the burden of Fénelon's famous *Lettre à Louis XIV*[3] which castigated the ruler for his immoral and disastrous government of the nation.

[1] *Recueil de Maximes véritables et importantes pour l'institution du Roy,* Paris, 1663, pp. 63-67. Italics in the original quotation.

[2] Cf. my essay, "Louis XIV and Reason of State," in J. C. Rule, ed., *Louis XIV and the Craft of Kingship,* Columbus, Ohio, 1969, pp. 362-406.

[3] In C. Urbain, ed., *Fénelon: Ecrits et lettres politiques,* Paris, 1920, pp. 143-57.

Louis XIV's enormous pride and thirst for glory were the antithesis of Christian humility and induced him to exploit the resources of the realm for personal benefit and to embark upon wars merely to increase his grandeur. Such procedures, Fénelon said, could be justified only by a double standard of morality which he found abhorrent:

> A poor wretch who steals a coin on the highway in his great need is hanged, but a man who makes conquests, that is, who unjustly subjugates a part of a neighboring state, is treated as a hero! . . . To take another's field is a great sin; to seize a province is an innocent and glorious act! Where are ideas of justice? Will God judge in this manner? . . . Is justice no longer justice when the greatest interests are involved?[4]

Fénelon completely rejected the idea, so fundamental to reason of state, that politics might legitimately be conducted according to its own distinctive criteria of justice and morality. Louis XIV's departure from unique and immutable Christian principles had led him to undertake a series of wars that had caused enormous suffering and brought ruin to the realm. Such were the fruits of Louis XIV's egocentric version of reason of state, Fénelon held, advocating that Louis return all his conquests to their former owners.[5] Such a recommendation is indicative of the large measure of utopian idealism that characterized Fénelon's thought and caused Louis XIV, the realist, to refer to his archbishop as "le plus bel esprit et le plus chimérique de son royaume."[6] Fénelon nevertheless spoke for many who feared that the growth of state power and its applications according to the canons of reason of state had utterly distorted the true principles of Christian monarchy.

These and many other critics of reason of state feared the divorce of political policy from traditional morality, a development that seemed to be gaining irresistible momentum. The alternatives, they knew, were either to seek a return to the supremacy of religious

---

[4] *Examen de conscience sur les devoirs de la royauté*, in Urbain, p. 55.

[5] *Examen*, pp. 55-56; *Lettre à Louis XIV*, p. 157.

[6] Quoted in P. Janet, *Fénelon*, Paris, 1924, p. 141.

principles over human affairs or to proceed with further secularization. All who opposed the implications of reason of state sought the former solution, but history was to decree otherwise. We now know that the major currents of political thought and practice were leading inexorably to the secular state of modern times and that reason of state evolved accordingly. The end-product, however, was a far cry from the concept that had been developed by Richelieu and his spokesmen. They genuinely believed that they had adumbrated a scheme of Christian politics which, in the hands of a devout king and minister, justified all measures that they might deem necessary to strengthen the Christian state. Richelieu's view of reason of state nevertheless involved compromise with traditional principles, most notably his insistence upon the doctrine of two moralities which opened the door to further deviations from his position and ultimately to modern secularism. But in his own time this was neither the intent nor the effect of his ministry. He did not secularize modern politics and should not be so judged. He believed himself to be a Christian statesman who was meeting the exigencies of politics with the best available means for the building of Christian France. It remained for others after him to develop the concept of reason of state of the modern world.

BIBLIOGRAPHY

MANUSCRIPTS

Bibliothèque Nationale
  Fonds Français 3743, 4253, 5874, 10455, 15644, 17461, 17617, 18424, 18425,
    18428-18429, 18431, 18432, 18433, 18461, 19046-19047, 19048, 19049, 19050,
    23067, 23153, 25666
  Nouvelles Acquisitions Françaises 3360
  Dupuy 625
  Baluze 147
Bibliothèque de l'Arsenal
  2336, 2831-2832, 2864, 4741

SOURCES: ANONYMOUS WORKS

*Considérations d'Estat sur le livre publié depuis quelques mois, soubs le
    tiltre d'Advertissement au Roy*, n.p., 1625.
Deux Discours pour le Roy, faits en avril, 1632, par M.D.B., Paris, 1635.
Dialogue d'entre le maheustre et le manant, n.p., 1594.
*Discours de droit sur le Factum de M. le Mareschal de Marillac employé
    en sa production*, n.p., n.d.
*Discours des princes et estats de la Chrestienté plus considérables à la
    France, selon les diverses qualitez et conditions*, n.p., 1624.
*Discours sur l'estat lamentable auquel sont réduites les trois ligues des
    Grisons*, n.p., 1622.
Discours sur la justice et science royalle, Paris, 1618.
*Discours sur plusieurs poincts importans de l'estat présent des affaires de
    France*, n.p., 1626.
Examen de l'Apologie du sieur Pelletier pour les pères Jésuites, Paris, 1625.
Exhortation à la Sainte Union des Catholiques de France, n.p., 1589.
*G. G. R. Theologi ad Ludovicum XIII Galliae et Navarrae regem chris-
    tianissimum Admonitio . . . .* Augustae Francorum, cum facultate
    Catholic. Magistrat., 1625.
Interêts et Maximes des princes et des Estats souverains, Cologne, 1666.
*La Voix gémissante du peuple chrétien et catholique accablé sous le faix
    des désastres et misères des guerres de ce temps, adressée au Roy très
    chrétien par un françois désinteressé*, Paris, 1640.

515

BIBLIOGRAPHY

Le Droit Divin qu'il faut obéir aux Roys: et notamment que les Roys des Fleurs-de-Lys ont esté choisis du Ciel, comme les Enfans aisnez d'iceluy, Paris, 1622.

Le Maréchal d'Ornano, martyr d'Estat, n.p., 1643.

Le Prince absolu, Paris, 1617.

Le Reveille-matin des françois, et de leurs voisins, n.p., 1574.

Le Vray Prince et le bon sujet contenant l'unique méthode pour bien gouverner les peuples par les véritables maximes de religion et d'estat, les qualitez qui doivent accompagner un prince, Paris, 1636.

Les Sentinelles au Roy ou Advertissement des dangeureuses approaches des forces Espagnoles pour bloquer le Royaume de France, n.p., 1621.

Manifeste des ducs et pairs de France, de Vendôme, de Mayenne, maréchal de Bouillon, marquis de Cœuvres et le président Le Jay, n.p., 1617.

Manifeste du Roy contenant les justes causes que le Roy a eues de déclarer la guerre à l'Espagne, Paris, 1635.

Manifeste pour le public au Roy, Paris, 1620.

Maximes des princes et estats souverains, Cologne, 1665.

Mysteria politica, Hoc est: Epistolae arcanae virorum illustrium sibi mutuo confidentium lectu et consideratione dignae, Antwerp, 1625.

Panégyrique à Monseigneur le Cardinal duc de Richelieu, sur le sujet du philosophe indifférent, Paris, 1641.

Quaestiones quodlibeticae tempori praesenti accommodae ad Illustrissimum S. R. E. Cardinalem de Rochelieu seu de Rupella, Negotiorum Status in Regno Galliarum, Supremum Praefectum . . ., n.p., 1626.

Raisons pour les condemnations cy-devant faictes du libelle Admonitio, du livre de Santarel, et autres semblables. Contre les Santarelistes de ce temps et leurs fauteurs, Par un François Catholique, n.p., 1626.

Sainte défense pour Son Eminence. Au Roy, Paris [1640].

Sapiens francus G. G. R. Theologi et Admonitoris regii nuper propter nimiam suam sapientiam innocenter combusti discipulus . . ., Paris, 1626.

Vindiciae contra Tyrannos, n.p., 1579.

SOURCES: TRACTS, TREATISES, MEMOIRS, CORRESPONDENCE, ETC.

Ammirato, S. *Discorsi sopra Cornelio Tacito*, Florence, 1594.

——. *Discours politiques sur les œuvres de C. Cornelius Tacitus, tirez de l'Italien de Scipion Ammirato* [French translation by J. Baudoin], Paris, 1618.

516

————. *Discours politiques et militaires sur Corneille Tacite, traduits, paraphrasez, et augmentez par Laurens Melliet*, Lyon, 1618.

[Ardier, P.]. *L'Assemblée des notables tenue à Paris és années 1626 et 1627*, Paris, 1652.

————. *Mémoire sur les affaires générales de la Chrestienté du mois d'avril 1633*, in Molé, *Mémoires*, Vol. IV, 166-223.

Arroy, B. *Questions décidées sur la justice des armes des Roys de France, sur les alliances avec les hérétiques ou infideles et sur la conduite de la conscience des gens de guerre*, Paris, 1634.

————. *Le Mercure espagnol, ou Discours contenans les responses faites à un libelle intitulé Mars François, fabriqué par un sujet des Espagnols, se donnant le nom supposé d'Alexandre Patrice Armacan, et à faux tiltre de Théologien: Ensemble les remarques de la Religion, prétexte des Espagnols, dans l'avant discours, et un rapport entre les François et les Espagnols, à la fin de ce Livre. Pour la gloire des Roys de France et de la nation Françoise*, n.p., 1639.

Aubery, A. *Mémoires pour l'histoire du Cardinal Duc de Richelieu*, 2 vols., Paris, 1660.

Balthasar, C. *Traité des usurpations des Roys d'Espagne sur la Couronne de France depuis Charles VIII. Ensemble un Discours sur le commencement, progrez, declin et démembrement de la Monarchie Françoise, droicts et prétentions des Roys Très-Chrestiens sur l'Empire*, Paris, 1625 and 1626.

Balzac, J.L.G. de. *Les Œuvres de Monsieur de Balzac*, Paris, 1627.

————. *Œuvres*, 2 vols., Paris, 1665.

————. *Lettres du sieur de Balzac*, Paris, 1624.

————. *Les Premières Lettres de Guez de Balzac, 1618-1627*, H. Bibas and K. T. Butler, eds., 2 vols., Paris, 1933-1934.

————. *Lettres de Jean-Louis Guez de Balzac*, P. Tamizey de Larroque, ed., in *Mélanges historiques*. Paris, 1873.

————. *Le Prince*, Paris, 1631.

————. *Apologie pour le Livre de Monsieur de Balzac, entitulé Le Prince*, n.p., 1632.

————. *Replique à la Response de l'Apologie du Prince de Monsieur de Balzac*, n.p., 1632.

————. *Aristippe ou De la Cour*, Paris, 1658.

————. *Socrate chrétien*, Paris, 1652.

Barbier, J. *Les Miraculeux Effets de la sacrée main des Roys de France*, *pour le guerison des malades, et pour la conversion des hérétiques,* Paris, 1618.

Baricave, J. de. *La Défence de la monarchie françoise et autres monarchies, contre les detestables et execrables maximes d'estat d'Etienne Junius Brutus, et de Louys de Mayerne Turquet, et leurs adherans,* Toulouse, 1614.

Bassompierre, F. de. *Journal de ma vie: Mémoires du Maréchal de Bassompierre,* de Chantérac, ed., 4 vols., Paris, 1870-1877.

Beauchamp, Comte de, ed. *Louis XIII d'après sa correspondance avec le Cardinal de Richelieu,* Paris, 1909.

Beauvais-Nangis, A. de. *Mémoires du Marquis de Beauvais-Nangis,* Monmerqué and Taillandier, eds., Paris, 1862.

[Belloy, P. de]. *De l'Authorité du Roy, et crimes de lèze majesté, qui se commettent par ligues, designation de successeur, et libelles escrits contre la personne et dignité du Prince,* n.p., 1587.

Bernard, C. *Histoire de Louis XIII jusqu'à la guerre déclarée contre les Espagnols,* Paris, 1640.

Bertrand, S. *Panégyrique royal,* Paris, 1628.

Bérulle, P. de. *Œuvres complètes,* 2 vols., Paris, 1644.

————. *Discours de l'estat et des grandeurs de Iesus, par l'Union ineffable de la Divinité avec l'Humanité,* Paris, 1623.

————. *Correspondance du Cardinal de Bérulle,* J. Dagens, ed., 3 vols., Paris-Louvain, 1937-1939.

[Béthune, P. de]. *Le Conseiller d'Estat, ou Recueil des plus générales considérations servant au maniment des affaires publiques,* Paris, 1633.

Bignon, J. *De l'Excellence des Roys, et du Royaume de France,* Paris, 1610.

————. *De la Grandeur de nos Roys, et de leur souveraine puissance,* Paris, 1615.

Binet, E. *Quel est le meilleur gouvernement, le rigoureux ou le doux?,* Paris, 1636.

Binville, C. B. de. *Les Vérités françoises opposées aux calomnies espagnoles,* Beauvais, 1635.

Blanchot, P. *Le Diurnal des Roys et Conseillers d'Estat, où sont les maximes extraictes de l'Escriture,* Lyon, 1635.

Blet, P., ed. *Correspondance du nonce en France Ranuccio Scotti (1639-1641),* Rome, 1965.

Bodin, J. *Les Six Livres de la République,* Paris, 1578.

——. *The Six Bookes of the Commonweal* [English translation], K. D. McRae, ed., Cambridge, Mass., 1962.

Boitet de Frauville, C. *Le Prince des Princes, ou l'Art de regner, contenant son instruction aux sciences et à la Politique, contre les orateurs de ce temps,* Paris, 1632.

Botero, G. *Della Ragion de Stato,* Venice, 1589.

——. *Raison et gouvernement d'estat* [French translation by G. Chappuys], Paris, 1599.

——. *Aggiunte di Gio. Botero . . . alla sua "Ragion di stato,"* Pavia, 1598.

Boucher, J. *De Iusta Henrici tertii abdicatione,* Paris, 1589.

Boyer des Roches, G. *Le Coup d'Estat de l'Empire, envoyé par un prince alleman aux autres princes, Estats, Villes Imperiales et Anseatiques de l'Allemagne,* n.p., 1641.

——. *La Politique du temps. Discours panégyrique du gouvernement, contenant plusieurs belles Maximes d'Estat,* Paris, 1642.

Braubach, M. and Repgen, K., eds. *Acta Pacis Westphalicae,* Series 1: *Instruktionen.* Vol. 1: *Frankreich, Schweden, Kaiser,* F. Dickmann, et al., eds., Münster, 1962.

Cabot, V. *Les Politiques,* Toulouse, 1630.

Casaubon, I. *Ephemerides,* 2 vols., Oxford, 1850.

Cassan, J. de. *La Recherche des droicts du Roy et de la Couronne de France,* Paris, 1632.

Caussin, N. *La Cour sainte,* Paris, 1624.

Ceriziers, R. de. *Reflexions chrestiennes et politiques sur la vie des Roys de France,* Paris, 1641.

——. *Reflexions chrestiennes et politiques sur la vie des Roys Henri IV et Louis le Juste,* Paris, 1642.

Chanteloube, J. d'A. de. *Lettre au Roy,* n.p., 1631.

——. *Lettre au Cardinal de Richelieu,* n.p., 1631.

Chantereau-Lefebvre, L. *Mémoires sur l'origine des maisons et duchés de Lorraine et de Bar-le-Duc,* Paris, 1642.

Charron, P. *De la Sagesse,* A. Duval, ed., 3 vols., Paris, 1820-1824.

Cohon, D. *En Quoy la Piété des François diffère de celle des Espagnols dans une profession de mesme Religion,* in E. Griselle, ed., *Documents d'histoire,* Paris, 1911, Vol. II, 547-66.

Coignet, M. *Instruction aux Princes pour garder la foy promise, contenant un sommaire de la philosophie Chrestienne et morale, et devoir d'un homme de bien,* Paris, 1584.

Colomby, F. de. *Discours de l'autorité du Roy*, Paris, 1623, 1631.

Coquille, G. *Œuvres*, 2 vols., Bordeaux, 1703.

Courtilz de Sandras, G. de. *Nouveaux Intêrets des Princes de l'Europe*, Cologne, 1685.

De Marca, P. *De Concordia sacerdotii et imperii, seu libertatibus ecclesiae gallicanae libri quatuor*, Paris, 1641.

De Thou, J. A. *Histoire universelle*, 11 vols., The Hague, 1740.

Dicée, *Lettre escripte aux Iuges, et Commissaires, du Mareschal de Marillac*, n.p., 1632.

Du Boys, H. *De l'Origine et autorité des Roys*, Paris, 1604.

Du Cugnet, P. *Le Véritable ou le mot en amy, de Messieurs les Princes, adressé à la Royne Mère*, n.p. [1624].

Dupleix, S. *Mémoires des Gaules depuis le Deluge jusques à l'établissement de la Monarchie Françoise*, Paris, 1619.

———. *Histoire générale de la France*, 3 vols., Paris, 1621-1628.

———. *Histoire de Henri le Grand*, Paris, 1632, 1635, 1639.

———. *Histoire de Louis le Juste*, Paris, 1635.

———. *Responce à Saint-Germain, ou les lumières de Mathieu de Morgues, dit Saint-Germain, pour l'histoire, éteintes par Messire Scipion Dupleix*, Condom, 1645.

———. *Continuation de l'histoire du règne de Louis le Juste, treizième du nom*, Paris, 1648.

Dupuy, P. *Traitez des droits et libertez de l'église gallicane. Preuves des libertez de l'église gallicane*, 2 vols., n.p., 1639.

———. *Traité de la majorité de nos rois, et des régences du royaume*, Paris, 1655.

———. *Traitez touchant les droits du Roy Très Chrestien sur plusieurs estats et seigneuries possédées par divers princes voisins et pour prouver qu'il tient à juste titre plusieurs provinces contestées par les princes estrangers*, Paris, 1655.

Du Refuge, E. *Traité de la cour*, Paris, 1616.

Du Vair, G. *Traité de la constance et consolation ès calamitez publiques*, J. Flach and F. Funck-Brentano, eds., Paris, 1915.

Duvergier de Hauranne, J. *Question royalle et sa decision*, Paris, 1609.

———. *La Somme des fautes et faussetez capitales contenues en la Somme théologique du père François Garasse de la Compagnie de Jésus*, Paris, 1626.

[Estampes, L. d']. *Cardinalium, Archiepiscoporum, Episcoporum caeter-*

orumque qui ex universis Regni Provinciis, Ecclesiasticis Comitiis interfuerunt, de Anonymis quibusdam et famosis Libellis Sententia, n.p., 1625.

———. *Déclaration de Messieurs les Cardinaux, Archevesques, Evesques, et autres ecclésiastiques, Deputez en l'Assemblée Générale du Clergé de France, tenue à Paris. Touchant certains Libelles, faicts contre le Roy et son Estat,* Paris, 1626.

Fancan, F. L. de. *La France mourante, ou Discours du Chancelier de l'Hospital au Chevalier Bayard, dit sans reproche,* n.p., 1623.

———. *Dialogue de la France mourante,* n.p., 1623.

———. *La Voix publicque au Roy,* n.p., 1624.

———. *La Cabale espagnole entièrement descouverte, à l'avancement de la France et contentement des bons françois,* n.p., 1625.

———. *La Ligue nécessaire,* n.p., 1625.

———. *Le Miroir du temps passé,* n.p., 1625.

———. *Advis salutaire sur l'estat présent des affaires d'Allemagne,* n.p., 1626.

Faret, N. *Des Vertus nécessaires à un prince pour bien gouverner ses sujets,* Paris, 1623.

———. *Recueil de lettres nouvelles,* Paris, 1627.

Faroul, S. *De la Dignité des Roys de France et du privilège que Dieu leur a donné de guerir les écrouelles,* Paris, 1633.

Fernandez de Villareal, E. *El politico cristiano o discorsos politicos de la vita y acciones del cardenal de Richelieu,* Pamplona, 1642.

Ferrier, J. *Le Catholique d'estat ou Discours politique des alliances du Roy très-Chrestien contre les calomnies des ennemis de son estat,* Paris, 1625.

———. *Advertissement à tous les Estats de l'Europe, touchant les maximes fondamentales du gouvernement et des desseins des Espagnols,* Paris, 1625.

———. *Response au Manifeste du sieur de Soubize,* n.p., 1625.

Flavigny, J. de. *La Briefve et Facile Instruction pour les confesseurs composée par Maistre Jacques de Flavigny Docteur en théologie, et grand-vicaire de Monseigneur l'Evesque de Luçon, par commandement de mondit Seigneur,* Fontenay, 1613.

Floquet, A., ed. *Diare ou journal du chancelier Séguier en Normandie après la sédition des nu-pieds (1636-1640),* Rouen, 1842.

Frachetta, G. *Discorso della ragion di stato,* in *L'Idea del libro di governi di stato et di guerra con due discorsi, l'uno intorno la Ragione di Stato, & l'altro intorno la Ragione di Guerra,* Venice, 1592.

———. *Curieux Examen des raisons d'estat et de guerre* [French translation by L. Melliet], in S. Ammirato, *Discours politiques et militaires sur Corneille Tacite, traduits, paraphrasez, et augmentez par Laurens Melliet,* Lyon, 1628, Discours 12.

Furic du Run, J. *Reflexions politiques du sieur Jul. Furic du Run sur le gouvernement de Monseigneur le Cardinal de Richelieu,* Paris, 1640.

Garasse, F. *La Somme théologique des veritez capitales de la religion chrestienne,* Paris, 1625.

———. *Mémoires,* C. Nisard, ed., Paris, 1840.

Gazette, for 1631-1643.

Gentillet, I. *Discours sur les moyens de bien gouverner et maintenir en bonne paix un royaume, ou autre principauté . . . Contre Nicolas Machiavel Florentin,* n.p., 1576.

[Godefroy, J.]. *Le Mercure jésuite, ou Recueil des pièces concernant le progrès des Jésuites, leurs escrits et différents depuis l'an 1620 jusqu'à . . . 1626,* 2 vols., Geneva, 1626-1630.

Godefroy, T. *Le Cérémonial français,* 2 vols., Paris, 1649.

Gramond, G. de. *Historiarum Galliae ab excessu Henrici IV libri XVIII quibus rerum per Gallos tota Europa gestarum accurata narratio continetur,* Toulouse, 1643.

Guron, L. *Histoire du temps, ou les Trois Veritez historiques, politiques et chrestiennes,* Cologne, 1686.

Habert, I. *De Consensu hierarchiae et monarchiae, adversus paraeneticum Optati Galli, schismatum fictoris, libri sex,* Paris, 1640.

———. *De l'Union de l'Eglise avec l'Etat, ouvrage composé en Latin contre le livre d'Optatus Gallus, par M. Habert . . . mis en françois par Louis Giry,* Paris, 1641.

Hay du Chastelet, P. *Discours au Roy, touchant les libelles faits contre le gouvernement de son Estat,* n.p., 1631.

———. *Les Entretiens des Champs-Elysées,* n.p., 1631.

———. *L'Innocence justifiée en l'administration des affaires,* n.p., 1631.

———. *Observations sur la vie et la condemnation du Mareschal de Marillac,* Paris, 1633.

———. *Discours d'Estat sur les escrits de ce temps auquel est faict response à plusieurs libelles diffamatoires publiez à Bruxelle par les ennemis de la France,* n.p., 1635.

522

————. *Recueil de diverses pièces pour servir à l'histoire*, Paris, 1635, 1643.

Hersent, C. *De la Souveraineté du Roy à Mets, pays Metsin, et autres villes et pays circonvoisins: qui estoient de l'ancien Royaume d'Austrasie ou Lorraine*, Paris, 1632.

————. *Optati Galli de cavendo schismate, ad illustrissimos ac reverendissimos Ecclesiae gallicanae primates, archiepiscopos, episcopos, liber paraeneticus*, n.p., 1640.

Isambert et al., eds. *Recueil général des anciennes lois françaises*, Paris, n.d., Vols. XIV-XVI.

Jansenius. *Alexandri Patricii Armacani, theologi Mars gallicus, seu de justitia armorum, et federum regis galiae libri duo*, n.p., 1635.

————. *Le Mars François ou la guerre de France, en laquelle sont examinées les raisons de la justice prétendue des armes et des alliances du Roy de France, mises au jour par Alexandre Patricius Armacanus, théologien, et traduites de la troisième édition par C.H.D.P.D.E.T.B.*, n.p., 1637.

Joly, C. *Recueil de Maximes véritables et importantes pour l'institution du Roy*, Paris, 1663.

La Mare, P. de. *Discours sur la justice et science royalle*, Paris, 1618.

La Maunyaie. *Panégyrique au Roy*, Paris, 1622.

La Mothe le Vayer, F. de. *Œuvres*, 2 vols., Paris, 1662.

————. *Quatre dialogues faits à l'imitation des anciens, par Orasius Tubero; Cinq autres dialogues du mesme autheur faits comme les précédents à l'imitation des anciens*, Frankfort, 1606 [i.e., n.p., 1630, 1631].

————. *Discours sur la bataille de Lutzen*, Paris, 1633.

————. *Discours sur la proposition de trefve au Pays-Bas en 1633*, in *Mercure français*, Vol. XIX, 224-39.

————. *Discours de la contrariété d'humeurs qui se trouve entre certaines nations, et singulièrement entre la françoise et l'espagnole, traduit de l'Italien de Fabricio Campolini, Veronais*, Paris, 1636.

————. *Discours de l'histoire, où est examinée celle de Prudence de Sandoval, Chroniqueur du feu Roy d'Espagne, Philippe III, et Evesque de Pampelune, qui a escrit la Vie de l'Empereur Charles-Quint*, Paris, 1638.

————. *De l'Institution de Monseigneur le Dauphin*, Paris, 1640.

————. *De la Vertu des Payens*, Paris, 1642.

————. *Petits Traitez en forme de Lettres escrites à diverses personnes studieuses*, Paris, 1647.

———. *La Politique du Prince*, Paris, 1654.

———. *Deux Dialogues faits à l'imitation des anciens*, E. Tisserand, ed., Paris, 1922.

Lancre, P. de. *Le Livre des princes*, Paris, 1617.

La Noue, F. de. *Discours politiques et militaires*, Lyon, 1595.

La Roche-Flavin, B. de. *Treze Livres des Parlemens de France*, Bordeaux, 1617.

Laval, A. de. *Desseins de professions nobles et publiques, contenans plusieurs traictés divers et rares*, Paris, 1605, 1612.

Le Bret, C. *De la Souveraineté du Roy*, Paris, 1632.

———. *Œuvres*, Paris, 1635, 1642, 1689.

Le Guay, G. *Alliances du Roy avec le Turc et autres, justifiées contre les calomnies des Espagnols et de leurs partisans*, Paris, 1625.

Leman, A., ed. *Recueil des instructions générales aux nonces ordinaires de France de 1624 à 1634*, Lille, 1920.

Le Normant, J. *L'Homme d'Estat françois vrayment Catholique*, Paris, 1626.

Le Roy, L. *Les Politiques d'Aristote, Paris*, 1568.

L'Hommeau, P. de. *Les Maximes générales du droict françois*, Rouen, 1614.

Lipsius, J. *Politicorum Sive Civilis Doctrinae Libri Sex*, Leiden, 1589.

———. *Les Six Livres des politiques, ou Doctrine civile de Iustus Lipsius* [French trans. by C. le Ber], La Rochelle, 1590.

———. *Monita et Exempla Politica*, Antwerp, 1605.

———. *Les Conseils et les exemples politiques de Iuste Lipse* [French trans. by N. Pavillon], Paris, 1606.

Loisel, A. *Institutes coustumières*, M. Reulos, ed., 2 vols., Paris, 1935.

Loyseau, C. *Œuvres*, Lyon, 1701.

———. *Traité des seigneuries*, Paris , 1608.

———. *Cinq Livres du droit des offices*, Paris, 1610.

———. *Traité des ordres et simples dignitez*, Paris, 1613.

Machon, L. *Sermon pour le jour de l'Assomption Notre Dame*, Paris, 1641.

———. *Discours pour servir de règle ou d'avis aux bibliothécaires*, D. de Saint-Armand, ed., Bordeaux, 1883.

———. *Apologie pour Machiavelle en faveur des Princes et Ministres d'Estat*, Paris, 1643. Bibliothèque Nationale, Fonds Français, 19046-19047.

———. *Traité politique des différends ecclésiastiques arrivés depuis le commencement de la monarchie jusques à présent tant entre les papes et les Roys de France que le clergé de leur royaume.* Bibliothèque Nationale, Fonds Français, 17617.

Marchant, F. *La Science royale*, Saumur, 1625.

Marillac, L. de. *Remonstrance du Mareschal de Marillac au Roy*, n.p., 1631.

———. *Requestes présentées à MM. les Commissaires de la Chambre Souveraine establie à Rueil*, n.p., 1632.

Marillac, M. de. *Examen du livre intitulé Remonstrance et Conclusions des gens du Roy et Arrest de la Cour de Parlement du vingt-sixiesme Novembre MDCX . . . sur le Livre du Cardinal Bellarmin*, n.p., 1611.

Marquez, J. *El Governador Christiano, deducido de la vidas de Moysen y Josue*, Salamanca, 1612.

———. *L'Homme d'Estat chrestien, tiré des vies de Moyse et Iosué Princes du Peuple de Dieu* [French trans, by D. Virion], Nancy, 1621.

Mémoires de la Ligue, 6 vols., Amsterdam, 1758.

Mercure d'estat ou Recueil de divers discours d'estat, n.p., 1634.

Mercure français.

Molé, M. *Mémoires*, A. Champollion-Figeac, ed., 4 vols., Paris, 1855-1857.

Molinier, E. *Les Politiques chrestiennes: ou Tableau des vertus politiques considerées en l'estat chrestien*, Paris, 1621.

Monglat. *Mémoires du Marquis de Monglat*, Petitot, ed., 3 vols., Paris, 1825.

Montaigne, M. de. *Œuvres complètes*, A. Armaingaud, ed., 12 vols., Paris, 1924-1941.

Montchal, C. de. *Mémoires, contenant des particularités de la vie et du ministère du Cardinal de Richelieu*, Rotterdam, 1718.

Morgues, M. de. *Déclaration de la volonté de Dieu sur l'institution de l'Eucharistie contre les erreurs de Pierre Du Moulin, ministre de la religion prétendue réformée*, Paris, 1617.

———. *Véritez chréstiennes au Roy très-chrestien*, n.p., 1620.

———. *Le Droict du Roy sur les subjects chréstiens, à ceux de la religion prétendue réformée*, Paris, 1622.

———. *Advis d'un théologien sans passion, sur plusieurs libelles imprimez depuis peu en Allemagne*, n.p., 1626.

———. *Très-humble, très-véritable, et très-importante Remonstrance au Roy*, n.p. [1631].

———. *Advertissement de Nicocléon à Cléonville, sur son Advertissement aux provinces*, n.p., 1631.

525

————. *Charitable Remonstrance de Caton chrétien à Monseigneur l'éminentissime Cardinal de Richelieu*, n.p., 1631.

————. *Discours sur le Livre de Balzac entitulé Le Prince, et sur deux Lettres suivantes. En Decembre, 1631*, n.p.

————. *Defense du Discours sur le Livre intitulé Le Prince. Contre l'Apologie de I. P. En Fevrier, 1632*, n.p.

————. *Le Génie démasqué du Cardinal de Richelieu*, n.p. [1632].

————. *Relation veritable de ce qui s'est passé au iugement du procez du Mareschal de Marillac*, n.p., 1633.

————. *La Vérité deffendue*, n.p., 1635.

————. *Iugement sur la préface et diverses pièces que le Cardinal de Richelieu prétend de faire servir à l'histoire de son crédit*, n.p., 1635.

————. *L'Ambassadeur chimerique ou le chercheur de dupes du Cardinal de Richelieu*, n.p., 1635.

————. *Satyre d'Estat, ou Harangue faite par le Maistre du Bureau d'Adresse à son Eminence le Cardinal de Richelieu, et le Remerciment dudit Cardinal*, n.p., 1636.

————. *Derniers advis à la France par un bon Chrestien et fidele citoyen*, n.p., 1636.

————. *Lumières pour l'histoire de France et pour faire voir les calomnies, flatteries et autres défauts de Scipion Dupleix*, Condom, 1645.

————. *Diverses Pièces pour la défense de la Royne Mère du Roy très-chréstien, Louis XIII*, 2 vols., n.p., 1637.

————. *Pièces curieuses en suite de celles du sieur de S. Germain, contenant plusieurs pièces pour la deffence de la Reyne Mère du Roy très-chrestien Louis XIII et autres traitez d'Estat sur les affaires du temps, depuis l'an 1630 jusques à l'an 1643*, n.p., 1643.

Mousnier, R., ed. *Lettres et mémoires adressés au chancelier Séguier (1633-1649)*, 2 vols., Paris, 1964.

Naudé, G. *Considérations politiques sur les coups d'estat*, Rome, 1639.

————. *Mémoire confidentiel adressé à Mazarin par Gabriel Naudé après la mort de Richelieu*, A. Franklin, ed., Paris, 1870.

Noailles, C. de. *L'Empire du juste, selon l'institution de la vraye virtu*, Paris, 1632.

Ossat, A. d'. *Lettres du Cardinal d'Ossat*, 5 vols., Amsterdam, 1708.

Palazzo, G. A. *Discorso del governo e della ragion vera di stato*, Naples, 1604.

————. *Discours du gouvernement et de la raison vraye d'Estat* [French trans. by A. de Vallières], Douai, 1611.

Pasquier, E. *Œuvres*, 2 vols., Amsterdam, 1723.

Pelletier, J. *Apologie ou Défense pour les pères Jésuites contre les calomnies de leurs ennemys*, Paris, 1625.

Poirier, H. *Discours panégyrique du bonheur de la France sous le règne de Louis le Juste*, Paris, 1635.

Priézac, D. de. *Vindiciae Gallicae adversus Alexandrum Patricium Armacanum theologum*, Paris, 1638.

————. *Défence des droits et prérogatives des Roys de France* [French translation by J. Baudoin], Paris, 1639.

————. *Les Privilèges de la Vierge, Mère de Dieu*, Paris, 1648.

————. *Discours politiques*, Paris, 1652.

Rabardeau, M. *Optatus Gallus de cavendo schismate . . . benigna manu sectus*, Paris, 1641.

Recueil des pièces les plus curieuses qui ont esté faites pendant le règne du Connestable M. de Luynes, n.p., 1622.

Recueil de quelques discours politiques écrits sur diverses occurrences des affaires et guerres étrangères depuis quinze ans en ça, n.p., 1632.

Ribadeneyra, P. de. *Tratado de la religión y virtudes que deve tener el Príncipe Christiano, para governar y conservar sus Estatos. Contra lo que Nicolas Machiavelo y los Politicos deste tiempo enseñan*, Madrid, 1595.

————. *Traité de la religion que doit suivre le prince chrestien et des vertus qu'il doit avoir pour bien gouverner et conserver son Estat, contre la doctrine de Nicolas Machiavel et des politiques de nostre temps* [French trans. by A. de Balingham], Douai, 1610.

Ribier, J. *Discours sur le gouvernement des monarchies et principautez souverains*, Paris, 1630.

————. *Discours de M.I.R.C.D.*, n.p., 1641.

Richelieu, Armand Jean Du Plessis, Cardinal de. *Lettres, instructions diplomatiques et papiers d'État du Cardinal de Richelieu*, D.L.M. Avenel, ed., 8 vols., Paris, 1853-1877.

————. *Mémoires*, Petitot, ed., 10 vols., Paris, 1823.

————. *Mémoires*, Société de l'Histoire de France, 10 vols., Paris, 1907-1931.

————. *Testament politique*, L. André, ed., Paris, 1947.

————. *Maximes d'État et fragments politiques du Cardinal de Richelieu*, G. Hanotaux, ed., in *Mélanges historiques*, Paris, 1880, Vol. III.

————. *Journal de Monsieur le Cardinal Duc de Richelieu, qu'il a fait durant le grand Orage de la Cour, ès Années 1630 et 1631*, 2 vols., Paris, 1652.

——. *Les Principaux Poincts de la Foy de l'église catholique, deffendus contre l'escrit addressé au Roy par les quatre Ministres de Charenton*, Paris, 1618.

——. *Instruction du chrétien*, Poitiers, 1621.

——. *Traité qui contient la méthode la plus facile et la plus asseurée pour convertir ceux qui se sont separez de l'église*, Paris, 1651.

——. *Traité de la Perfection du Chrestien*, Paris, 1646.

——. *Mémoire d'Armand du Plessis de Richelieu, évêque de Luçon, écrit de sa main, l'année 1607 ou 1610, alors qu'il méditait de paraître à la cour*, A. Baschet, ed., Paris, 1880.

Rigault, N. *Apologeticus pro rege christianissimo Ludovico XIII adversus factiosae Admonitionis calumnias, in causa Principum foederatorum*, Paris, 1626.

Rohan, Henri, duc de. *Declaration de M. le duc de Rohan, pair de France etc., contenant la justice des raisons et motifs qui l'ont obligé à implorer l'assistance du Roy de la Grande Bretagne, et prendre les armes pour la défense des Eglise réformées de ce Royaume*, n.p., 1627.

——. *De l'Interest des Princes et des Estats de la Chrestienté* [published with his *Parfaicte Capitaine*], Paris, 1638.

——. *Mémoires*, Amsterdam, 1644.

Roland, L. *De la Dignité du Roy, où est montré et prouvé que Sa Majesté est seule et unique en terre vraiment sacrée de Dieu et du ciel*, Paris, 1623.

Saint-Denis, A. de. *Response à l'Apologie du Prince de Balzac*, n.p., 1632.

[Sancy, A. de]. *Discours d'un vieil courtisan désintéressé sur la lettre que la Royne Mère du Roy a écrite à sa Majesté après estre sortie du Royaume*, n.p., 1631.

——. *Response au libelle intitulé très-humble, très-véritable, et très-importante Remonstrance au Roy*, n.p., 1632.

Santarelli, A. *Tractatus de Haeresi, Schismate, Apostasia, sollicitatione in sacramento poenitentiae, et de potestate Romani Pontificis in his delictis puniendis*, Rome, 1625.

Savaron, J. *Traité de la souveraineté du Roy, et de son Royaume*, Paris, 1615.

——. *De la Souveraineté du Roy*, Paris, 1620.

Silhon, J. de. *Les Deux Veritez de Silhon, l'une de Dieu et de sa Providence, l'autre de l'immortalité de l'Ame*, Paris, 1626.

——. *Lettre du sieur de Silhon à Monsieur l'Evesque de Nantes*, n.p., n.d.

——. *Panégyrique à Mgr le Cardinal de Richelieu, sur ce qui s'est passé aux derniers troubles de France*, Paris, 1629.

——. *Le Ministre d'Estat, avec le veritable usage de la Politique moderne*, Pt. i: Paris, 1631; Pt. ii: Paris, 1643.

——. *Histoires remarquables, tirées de la seconde partie du Ministre d'Estat, avec un discours des conditions de l'histoire*, Paris, 1632.

——. *De l'Immortalité de l'ame*, Paris, 1634.

——. *Divers Mémoires concernant les dernières guerres d'Italie, avec trois traités de feu M. de Silhon qui n'ont encore été vus*, 2 vols., Paris, 1669.

Sirmond, J. *Le Coup d'Estat de Louis XIII*, Paris, 1631.

——. *La Défense du Roy et de ses ministres, contre le Manifeste que sous le nom de Monsieur on fait courre parmi le peuple*, Paris, 1631.

——. *Advertissement aux provinces sur les nouveaux mouvemens du Royaume*, Paris, 1631.

——. *La Vie du Cardinal d'Amboise*, n.p., 1631.

——. *Le Bon Génie de la France à Monsieur*, n.p. [1632].

——. *L'Homme du Pape et du Roy*, Brussels [?], 1634.

——. *Advis du françois fidelle aux malcontents nouvellement retirés de la Cour*, n.p., 1637.

——. *La Chimère deffaicte, ou Refutation d'un libelle séditieux tendant à troubler l'Estat, sous prétexte d'y prévenir un schisme*, Paris, 1640.

Talon, O. *Mémoires*, Petitot, ed., 3 vols., Paris, 1827.

Urbain, C., ed. *Fénelon: Ecrits et lettres politiques*, Paris, 1920.

Vaure, C. *L'Estat chrestien, ou Maximes politiques, tirées de l'Escriture; contre les faulse raisons d'estat, des libertins politiques de ce siècle*, Paris, 1626.

Zuccolo, L. *Della Ragione di stato*, in *Considerazioni politiche e morali sopra cento oracoli d'illustri personaggi antichi*, Venice, 1621.

SECONDARY SOURCES: BOOKS AND BRIEF STUDIES

Adam, A. *Histoire de la littérature française au XVIIe siècle*, Vol. I, Paris, 1948.

——. *Sur le Problème religieux dans la première moitié du XVIIe siècle*, Oxford, 1959.

——. *Les Libertins au XVIIe siècle*, Paris, 1964.

———. *Du Mysticisme à la révolte: les jansénistes du XVIIe siècle*, Paris, 1968.

Albertini, R. von. *Das Politische Denken in Frankreich zur Zeit Richelieus*, Marburg, 1951.

Albrecht, D. *Richelieu, Gustav Adolf und das Reich*, Munich, 1959.

———. *Die auswärtige Politik Maximilians von Bayern, 1618-1635*, Göttingen, 1962.

Allier, R. *La Cabale des dévots*, Paris, 1902.

Aubery, A. *L'Histoire du Cardinal Duc de Richelieu*, Paris, 1660.

Aulard, A. *Le Patriotisme français de la Renaissance à la Révolution*, Paris, 1921.

Avenel, G. d'. *Richelieu et la monarchie absolue*, 4 vols., Paris, 1895.

Bady, R. *L'Homme et son "institution" de Montaigne à Bérulle, 1580-1625*, Paris, 1964.

Barzun, J. *The French Race*, New York, 1932.

Batiffol, L. *La Journée des dupes*, Paris, 1925.

———. *Richelieu et le roi Louis XIII: Les véritables rapports du souverain et de son ministre*, Paris, 1934.

Battista, A. M. *Alle Origine del pensiero politico libertino: Montaigne e Charron*, Milan, 1966.

Beame, E. M. "The Development of Politique Thought during the French Wars of Religion (1560-1595)," Ph.D. dissertation, University of Illinois, 1957.

Bénichou, P. *Morales du grand siècle*, Paris, 1948.

Benoist, C. *Le Machiavélisme*, 3 vols., Paris, 1907-1936.

———. *L'Influence des idées de Machiavel*, in *Académie de Droit International, Recueil des Cours*, IV (Vol. IX of the collection), Paris, 1926, pp. 131-306.

Benoît, E. *Histoire de l'Édit de Nantes*, 5 vols., Delft, 1693-1695.

Beugnot, B. *Jean-Louis Guez de Balzac: Bibliographie générale*, Montreal, 1967.

Bigne de Villeneuve, M. de la. *Traité général de l'État: Essai d'une théorie réaliste de droit politique*, 2 vols., Paris, 1929-1931.

———. *L'Activité étatique*, Paris, 1954.

Bitton, D. *The French Nobility in Crisis, 1560-1640*, Stanford, California, 1969.

Blet, P. *Le Clergé de France et la monarchie: Étude sur les Assemblées générales du clergé de 1615 à 1666*, 2 vols., Rome, 1959.

———. *La Congrégation des Affaires de France*, in *Mélanges Eugène Tisserant*, Vatican City, 1964, Vol. IV, pp. 59-105.

Bloch, M. *Les Rois thaumaturges*, Paris, 1924.

Bourgeois, E. and André, L. *Les Sources de l'histoire de France: XVIIᵉ siècle*, 8 vols., Paris, 1913-1935.

Bremond, H. *Histoire littéraire du sentiment religieux en France depuis la fin des guerres de religion jusqu'à nos jours*, 12 vols., Paris, 1916-1936.

Bulletin de la Société d'histoire moderne, Jan., 1937; Oct.-Nov., 1951; Dec., 1951-Jan., 1952.

Burckhardt, C. J. *Richelieu*, 4 vols., Munich, 1961-1967.

Burd, L. A., ed. *Il Principe by Niccolò Machiavelli*, Oxford, 1891.

Busson, H. *La Pensée religieuse française de Charron à Pascal*, Paris, 1933.

Castelli, E., ed. *Umanesimo e scienza politica*, Milan, 1951.

———. *Cristianesimo e ragion di stato*, Rome, 1952.

Chabod, F. *Giovanni Botero*, Rome, 1934.

———. *Scritti su Machiavelli*, Turin, 1964.

Charbonnel, J. R. *La Pensée italienne au XVIᵉ siècle et le courant libertin*, Paris, 1919.

Chénon, E. *Histoire générale du droit français public et privé des origines à 1815*, 2 vols., Paris, 1926-1929.

Cherel, A. *La Pensée de Machiavel en France*, Paris, 1935.

Chevillier, A. *L'Origine de l'imprimerie de Paris*, Paris, 1694.

Church, W. F. *Constitutional Thought in Sixteenth-Century France*, Cambridge, Mass., 1941.

———. "Louis XIV and Reason of State," in *Louis XIV and the Craft of Kingship*, J. C. Rule, ed., Columbus, Ohio, 1969, pp. 362-406.

Cognet, L. *Les Origines de la spiritualité française au XVIIᵉ siècle*, Paris, 1949.

———. *La Spiritualité moderne*, Paris, 1966. Vol. 1: *L'Essor: 1500-1650*.

Comparato, V. I. *Cardin Le Bret: "royauté" e "ordre" nel pensiero di un consigliere del '600*, Florence, 1969.

Couzinet, L. *"Le Prince" de Machiavel et la théorie de l'absolutisme*, Paris, 1910.

Croce, B. *Storia della età barocca in Italia*, Bari, 1929.

———. *Politici e moralisti del siecento*, Bari, 1930.

———. *Politics and Morals* [English translation], New York, 1945.

Dagens, J. "Le Machiavélisme de Charron," in *Studies aangeboden aan Gerard Brom*, Utrecht-Nijmegen, 1952, pp. 56-64.

Dahl, F. *Les Débuts de la presse française: nouveaux aperçus*, Paris, 1951.

Declareuil, J. *Histoire générale du droit français des origines à 1789*, Paris, 1925.

De Crue de Stoutz, F. *Le Parti des politiques*, Paris, 1892.

Dedouvres, L. *Le Père Joseph polémiste: ses premiers écrits, 1623-1626*, Paris, 1895.

——. *Le Père Joseph: Études critiques sur ses œuvres spirituelles*, Paris, 1903.

Deloche, M. *La Maison du Cardinal de Richelieu*, Paris, 1912.

——. *Autour de la plume du Cardinal de Richelieu*, Paris, 1920.

Desqueyrat, A. *L'Enseignement "politique" de l'Église*, 2 vols., Paris, 1960-1964.

Dethan, G. *Gaston d'Orléans: conspirateur et prince charmant*, Paris, 1959.

Dickmann, F. *Der Westfälische Frieden*, Münster, 1965.

Digot, A. *Histoire de Lorraine*, 6 vols., Nancy, 1856.

Duine, F. *Un Politique et un orateur au XVIIe siècle. Cohon, Evêque de Nîmes et de Dol. Essai de bibliographie avec documents inédits*, Rennes, 1902.

Du Plessis d'Argentré, C. *Collectio judiciorum de novis Erroribus*, 3 vols., Paris, 1728-1736.

Eckhardt, C. C. *The Papacy and World Affairs*, Chicago, 1937.

Engel, J. "Zur Frage der Echtheit von Richelieus Testament politique," in *Aus Mittelalter und Neuzeit: Festschrift Gerhard Kallen*, J. Engel and H. M. Klinkenberg, eds., Bonn, 1957, pp. 185-218.

Esmein, A. *Cours élémentaire d'histoire du droit français*, Paris, 1910.

——. "La Maxime 'Princeps legibus solutus est' dans l'ancien droit français," in *Essays in Legal History*, P. Vinogradoff, ed., Oxford, 1913, pp. 201-14.

Esmonin, E. *Études sur la France des XVIIe et XVIIIe siècles*, Paris, 1964.

Etter, E. L. *Tacitus in der Geistesgeschichte des 16. und 17. Jahrhunderts*, Basel, 1966.

Evans, W. H. *L'Historien Mézeray et la conception de l'histoire en France au XVIIe siècle*, Paris, 1930.

Fagniez, G. *Le Père Joseph et Richelieu*, 2 vols., Paris, 1894.

Febvre, L. *Au Cœur religieux du XVIe siècle*, Paris, 1957.

Féret, P. *La Faculté de théologie de Paris et ses docteurs les plus célèbres*, 12 vols., Paris, 1900-1910.

Ferrari, G. *Histoire de la raison d'État*, Paris, 1860.

——. *Corso sugli scrittori politici italiani*, Milan, 1863.

Fidao-Justiniani, J. E. *Richelieu précepteur de la nation française: La Réforme morale et la réforme de l'État*, Paris, 1936.

Figgis, J. N. *Studies of Political Thought from Gerson to Grotius*, Cambridge, 1907.

——. *The Divine Right of Kings*, Cambridge, 1914.

Floquet, A. *Histoire du Parlement de Normandie*, 7 vols., Rouen, 1840-1842.

Foisil, M. *La Révolte des nu-pieds et les révoltes normandes de 1639*, Paris, 1970.

Forschungen und Studien zur Geschichte des Westfälischen Friedens, Münster, 1965.

Fouqueray, H. *Histoire de la Compagnie de Jésus en France des origines à la suppression (1528-1762)*, 5 vols., Paris, 1910-1925.

Friedrich, C. J. *Constitutional Reason of State*, Providence, Rhode Island, 1957.

Gaquère, F. *Pierre de Marca (1594-1662). Sa vie. Ses œuvres. Son gallicanisme*, Lille, 1932.

Geley, L. *Fancan et la politique de Richelieu*, Paris, 1884.

Gerhard, D. "Richelieu," in L. Krieger and F. Stern, eds., *The Responsibility of Power*, pp. 84-106.

Giesey, R. E. *The Royal Funeral Ceremony in Renaissance France*, Geneva, 1960.

Gilmore, M. P. *Argument from Roman Law*, Cambridge, Mass., 1941.

Gioda, C. *La Vita e le opere di Giovanni Botero*, 3 vols., Milan, 1894-1895.

Givan, W. "The Politiques in the French Religious Wars (1560-1593): Advocates of Religious Toleration and Strong Monarchy," Ph.D. dissertation, Yale University, 1950.

Glasson, E. *Le Parlement de Paris: son rôle politique depuis le règne de Charles VII jusqu'à la Révolution*, 2 vols., Paris, 1901.

Göhring, M. *Weg und Sieg der Modernen Staatsidee in Frankreich*, Tübingen, 1947.

Gooch, G. P. *Politics and Morals*, London, 1935.

Goyau, G. *Histoire religieuse* (*Histoire de la nation française*, G. Hanotaux, ed., Vol. VI), Paris, 1922.

Griffet, H. *Histoire du règne de Louis XIII*, 3 vols., Paris, 1758.

Haeghen, F. van der, et al. *Bibliographie Lipsienne*, 3 vols., Ghent, 1886-1888.

Hanotaux, G. and La Force. *Histoire du Cardinal de Richelieu*, 6 vols., Paris, 1932-1947.

Hartung, F. and Mousnier, R. "Quelques problèmes concernant la monarchie absolue," in *Relazioni del X Congresso Internazionale di Scienze Storiche*, Vol. IV, Florence, 1955, pp. 1-55.

Hatin, E. *Histoire politique et littéraire de la presse en France*, 8 vols., Paris, 1859-1861.

———. *Bibliographie historique et critique de la presse périodique française*, Paris, 1866.

Hauser, H. *Le Principe des nationalités: ses origines historiques*, Paris, 1916.

———. *La Pensée et l'action économiques du Cardinal de Richelieu*, Paris, 1944.

Henrard, P. *Marie de Médicis dans les Pays-Bas*, Paris, 1876.

Holmès, C. E. *L'Eloquence judiciaire de 1620 à 1660: Reflet des problèmes sociaux, religieux et politiques de l'époque*, Paris, 1967.

Houssaye, M. *M. de Bérulle et les Carmélites de France, 1575-1611*, Paris, 1872.

———. *Le Père de Bérulle et l'Oratoire de Jésus, 1611-1625*, Paris, 1874.

———. *Le Cardinal de Bérulle et le Cardinal de Richelieu, 1625-1629*, Paris, 1875.

Hubault, G. *De Politicis in Richelium lingua latina libellis*, Paris, 1856.

Huxley, A. *Grey Eminence*, New York, 1941.

Imbert, J., ed. *Quelques procès criminels des XVIIe et XVIIIe siècles*, Paris, 1964.

Janet, P. *Histoire de la science politique dans ses rapports avec la morale*, 2 vols., Paris 1913.

———. *Fénelon*, Paris, 1924.

Johannet, R. *Le Principe des nationalités*, Paris, 1923.

Jover, J. M. *1635: Historia de una polémica y semblanza de una generación*, Madrid, 1949.

Kahl, M. C. "Political Drama on the Eve of the Fronde," Ph.D. dissertation, Harvard University, 1969.

Kantorowicz, E. H. *The King's Two Bodies: A Study in Medieval Political Theology*, Princeton, 1957.

Kelley, D. R. *Foundations of Modern Historical Scholarship: Language, Law, and History in the French Renaissance*, New York, 1970.

Kerviler, R. *Le Chancelier Pierre Séguier*, Paris, 1874.

———. *La Presse politique sous Richelieu et l'académician Jean de Sirmond (1599-1649)*, Paris, 1876.

———. *Jean de Silhon*, Paris, 1876.

———. *La Bretagne à l'Académie française au XVIIᵉ siècle*, Paris, 1879.

Krieger, L., and Stern, F., eds. *The Responsibility of Power*, New York, 1967.

Labrousse, R. *Essai sur la philosophie politique de l'ancienne Espagne*, Paris, 1938.

Lacour-Gayet, G. *L'Éducation politique de Louis XIV*, Paris, 1898, 1923.

Lacroix, L. *Quid de instituendo senserit Vayerius*, Paris, 1890.

Lanson, G. *Les Essais de Montaigne*, Paris, 1930.

Lecler, J. *The Two Sovereignties* [English trans.], New York, 1952.

———. *Toleration and the Reformation* [English trans.], 2 vols., London, 1960.

Lelong, J. *Bibliothèque historique de la France*, 5 vols., Paris, 1768-1778.

Lemaire, A. *Les Lois fondamentales de la monarchie française d'après les théoriciens de l'ancien régime*, Paris, 1907.

Leman, A. *Urbain VIII et la rivalité de la France et de la maison d'Autriche de 1631 à 1635*, Lille, 1920.

———. *Richelieu et Olivarès: Leurs Négociations secrètes de 1636 à 1642 pour le rétablissement de la paix*, Lille, 1938.

Lestocquoy, J. *Histoire du patriotisme en France*, Paris, 1968.

Levi, A. *French Moralists*, Oxford, 1964.

Livet, G. *La Guerre de trente ans*, Paris, 1963.

Lublinskaya, A. D. *French Absolutism: the Crucial Phase, 1620-1629* [English trans.], Cambridge, 1968.

Maravall, J. A. *La Philosophie politique espagnol au XVIIᵉ siècle* [French trans.], Paris, 1955.

Mariéjol, J. H. *Henri IV et Louis XIII (1598-1643)*, (*Histoire de France*, E. Lavisse, ed., Vol. VI²), Paris, 1911.

Maritain, J. *Primauté du spirituel*, Paris, 1927.

———. *Principes d'un politique humaniste*, New York, 1944.

———. *Man and the State*, Chicago, 1963.

Martimort, A. G. *Le Gallicanisme de Bossuet*, Paris, 1953.

Martin, H. J. *Livre, pouvoirs et société à Paris au XVIIᵉ siècle*, 2 vols., Paris, 1969.

Martin, V. *Le Gallicanisme et la réforme catholique*, Paris, 1919.

Maspétiol, R. *L'État devant la personne et la société*, Paris, 1948.

———. *La Société politique et le droit*, Paris, 1957.

Mastellone, S. *La Reggenza di Maria de' Medici*, Florence, 1962.

Mattei, R. de. *La Politica di Campanella*, Rome, 1927.

———. *Il Pensiero politico di Scipione Ammirato*, Milan, 1963.

McIlwain, C. H. *The Growth of Political Thought in the West*, New York, 1932.

Meester, B. de. *Le Saint-Siège et les troubles des Pays-Bas, 1566-1579*, Louvain, 1934.

Meinecke, F. *Machiavellism* [English trans.], New Haven, 1957.

Mesnard, P. *L'Essor de la philosophie politique au XVIe siècle*, Paris, 1951.

———. *Essai sur la morale de Descartes*, Paris, 1936.

Mirot, L. *Manuel de géographie historique de la France*, Paris, 1948.

Molien, A. *Le Cardinal de Bérulle*, 2 vols., Paris, 1947.

Mommsen, W. *Richelieu, Elsass und Lothringen*, Berlin, 1922.

Mongrédien, G. *10 novembre 1630: La Journée des dupes*, Paris, 1961.

Mousnier, R. *La Venalité des offices sous Henri IV et Louis XIII*, Rouen, 1945.

———. *Les XVIe et XVIIe siècles*, Paris, 1954.

———. *L'Assassinat d'Henri IV*, Paris, 1964.

———. *Problèmes de stratification sociale: Deux cahiers de la noblesse pour les états généraux de 1649-1651*, Paris, 1965.

———. ed. *Problèmes de stratification sociale: Actes du Colloque International (1966)*, Paris, 1968.

———. *Fureurs paysannes*, Paris, 1967.

———. *La Plume, la faucille et le marteau*, Paris, 1970.

Nisard, C. *Le Triumvirat littéraire au XVIe siècle: Juste Lipse, Joseph Scaliger, et Isaac Casaubon*, Paris [1864].

O'Connell, D. P. *Richelieu*, New York, 1968.

Olivier-Martin, F. *Histoire du droit français des origines à la Révolution*, Paris, 1948.

———. *L'Organisation corporative de la France d'ancien régime*, Paris, 1938.

Orcibal, J. *Les Origines du jansénisme*, 5 vols., Paris, 1947-1962.

Pagès, G. *La Monarchie d'ancien régime en France*, Paris, 1932.

———. *La Guerre de trente ans*, Paris, 1939.

Parrot, C. *Fancan et Richelieu: le problème protestant sous Louis XIII*, Montbéliard, 1903.

Pastor, L. von. *The History of the Popes*, Vols. 26-29, London, 1937-1938.

Pellisson, P. and d'Olivet. *Histoire de l'Académie française*, 2 vols., Paris, 1858.

Périnelle, J. *L'Attrition d'après le Concile de Trente et d'après Saint Thomas d'Aquin*, Le Saulchoir, 1927.

Petit, J. *L'Assemblée des notables de 1626-1627*, Paris [1936].

Piccioni, C. *Les Premiers Commis des Affaires Etrangères au XVIIe et XVIIIIe siècles*, Paris, 1928.

Picot, G. *Cardin Le Bret et la doctrine de la souveraineté*, Paris, 1948.

Pintard, R. *Le Libertinage érudit dans la première moitié du XVIIe siècle*, 2 vols., Paris, 1943.

Poinsenet, M. D. *La France religieuse au XVIIe siècle*, Paris, 1952.

Poirson, A. *Histoire du règne de Henri IV*, 4 vols., Paris, 1865-1866.

Porchnev, B. *Les Soulèvements populaires en France de 1623 à 1648* [French trans.], Paris, 1963.

Post, G. "Status Regis," in *Studies in Medieval and Renaissance History*, W. M. Bowsky, ed., Lincoln, Nebraska, 1964, pp. 1-103.

Pottinger, D. T. *The French Book Trade in the Ancien Régime*, Cambridge, Mass., 1958.

Prat, J. M. *Recherches historiques et critiques sur la Compagnie de Jésus en France du temps du Père Coton*, 5 vols., Lyon, 1876-1878.

Procacci, G. *Studi sulla fortuna del Machiavelli*, Rome, 1965.

Prunel, L. *La Renaissance catholique en France au XVIIe siècle*, Paris, 1921.

Przyrembel, A. *La Controverse théologique et morale entre Saint-Cyran et le père Garasse*, Paris, 1917.

Puyol, P. E. *Edmond Richer*, 2 vols., Paris, 1876.

Radouant, R. *Guillaume Du Vair, l'homme et l'orateur*, Paris, 1907.

Ramorino, F. *Cornelio Tacito nella Storia della Coltura*, Milan, 1898.

Ranum, O. A. *Richelieu and the Councillors of Louis XIII: A Study of the Secretaries of State and Superintendents of Finance in the Ministry of Richelieu, 1635-1642*, Oxford, 1963.

Rapports et notices sur l'édition des Mémoires du Cardinal de Richelieu, 3 vols., Paris, 1907-1914. (Important studies by Delavaud, Lavollée, etc.)

Rice, E. F. *The Renaissance Idea of Wisdom*, Cambridge, Mass., 1958.

Rochemonteix, C. de. *Nicolas Caussin, confesseur de Louis XIII, et le Cardinal de Richelieu*, Paris, 1911.

Rott, E. *Histoire de la représentation diplomatique de la France auprès des cantons suisses, de leurs alliés et de leurs confédérés*, 10 vols., Berne, 1900-1935.

Rouillard, C. D. *The Turk in French History, Thought and Literature (1520-1660)*, Paris [1939].

Sabrié, J. B. *De l'Humanisme au rationalisme: Pierre Charron*, Paris, 1913.

———. *Les Idées religieuses de J.-L. Guez de Balzac*, Paris, 1913.

Sainte-Beuve, C. A. *Causeries du lundi*, 15 vols., Paris, 1852-1862.

Saunders, J. L. *Justus Lipsius: The Philosophy of Renaissance Stoicism*, New York, 1955.

Schramm, P. E. *Der Koenig von Frankreich*, 2 vols., Weimar, 1939.

Sorel, A. *Europe under the Old Regime* [English trans.], Los Angeles, 1947.

Sorel de Souvigney, C. *La Bibliothèque française*, Paris, 1664.

Stankiewicz, W. J. *Politics and Religion in Seventeenth-Century France*, Berkeley, 1960.

Steinberg, S. H. *The Thirty Years' War and the Conflict for European Hegemony, 1600-1660*, New York, 1966.

Strowski, F. *Pascal et son temps*, 3 vols., Paris, 1906-1908.

———. *La Sagesse française*, Paris, 1925.

———. *Saint François de Sales: Introduction à l'histoire du sentiment religieux en France depuis la fin des guerres de religion jusqu'à nos jours*, Paris, 1928.

———. *Montaigne*, Paris, 1931.

Sturzo, L. *Church and State* [English trans.], Notre Dame, Indiana, 1962.

Sutcliffe, F. E. *Guez de Balzac et son temps: littérature et politique*, Paris, 1959.

Tapié, V. L. *La Politique étrangère de la France et le début de la guerre de trente ans (1616-1621)*, Paris, 1934.

———. *La France de Louis XIII et de Richelieu*, Paris, 1967.

Thuau, E. *Raison d'État et pensée politique à l'époque de Richelieu*, Paris, 1966.

Toffanin, G. *Machiavelli e il "Tacitismo,"* Padua, 1921.

Tommasini, O. *La Vita e gli scritti di Niccolò Machiavelli nella loro relazione col Machiavellismo*, 2 vols., Rome, 1883-1911.

Tongas, G. *Les Relations de la France avec l'Empire Ottoman durant la première moitié du XVIIe siècle*, Toulouse, 1942.

Tournyol du Clos, J. *Les Amortissements de la propriété ecclésiastique sous Louis XIII*, Paris, 1912.

Treasure, G. *Cardinal Richelieu and the Development of Absolutism*, London, 1972.

Vaissière, P. de. *Un Grand Procès sous Richelieu: L'Affaire du Maréchal de Marillac (1630-1632)*, Paris, 1924.

——. *La Conjuration de Cinq-Mars*, Paris, 1928.

Valentin, L. *Richelius, Scriptor Ecclesiasticus*, Toulouse, 1900.

Vanel, M. *Histoire de la nationalité française d'origine*, Paris, 1945.

Vaumas, G. de. *L'Éveil missionnaire de la France au XVIIe siècle*, Paris, 1959.

Vaunois, L. *Vie de Louis XIII*, Paris, 1961.

Viollet, P. *Le Roi et ses ministres*, Paris, 1912.

Weil, E. *Philosophie politique*, Paris, 1956.

Wickelgren, F. L. *La Mothe le Vayer: sa vie et son œuvre*, Paris, 1934.

Willaert, L. *Après le concile de Trente: La Restauration catholique, 1563-1648*, Tournai, 1960.

Woodbridge, B. A. *Gatien de Courtilz*, Baltimore, 1925.

Zanta, L. *La Renaissance du Stoicisme au XVIe siècle*, Paris, 1914.

Zeller, G. *La Réunion de Metz à la France*, 2 vols., Paris, 1926.

——. *Histoire des relations internationales*, Vol. II, Paris, 1953.

——. *Aspects de la politique française sous l'ancien régime*, Paris, 1964.

SECONDARY SOURCES: ARTICLES

Alfieri, V. E. "Politica e morale in Montaigne," *Studi in onore di Vittorio Lugli e Diego Valeri*, Venice, 1961, Vol. I, 1-12.

Aymonier, C. "Les Opinions politiques de Montaigne," *Actes de l'Académie nationale des sciences, belles-lettres et arts de Bordeaux*, XI (1937-1938), 213-37.

Bataillon, M. "L'Académie de Richelieu, Indre-et-Loire," *Pédagogues et juristes: De Pétrarque à Descartes*, IV (1963), 255-70.

Batiffol, L. "Richelieu et la question d'Alsace," *Revue historique*, CXXXVIII (1921), 161-200.

Battista, A. M. "Sull'antimachiavellismo francese del secolo XVI," *Storia e Politica*, I (1962), 413-47.

——. "Montaigne e Machiavelli," *Rivista Internazionali di Filosofia del Diritto*, XL (1963), 526-63.

Berthelot du Chesnay, C. "La Spiritualité des laïcs," *XVIIe siècle*, Nos. 62-63 (1964), 30-46.

Bertrand, P. "Les Vrais et les Faux Mémoires du Cardinal de Richelieu," *Revue historique*, CXLI (1922), 40-65, 198-227.

BIBLIOGRAPHY

Bibas, H. "L'Édition originale du *Prince*," *Bulletin du bibliophile et du bibliothécaire* (1938), 536-44.

———. "Les Éditions du *Prince* du Guez de Balzac au XVIIᵉ siècle," *ibid.*, 1946, 530-43.

Bibas, H. and Butler, K. T. "Balzac et Marie de Médicis: un document perdu," *Revue d'histoire littéraire de la France*, XXXVIII (1931), 88-92.

Blesnick, D. W. "Spanish Reaction to Machiavelli in the Sixteenth and Seventeenth Centuries," *Journal of the History of Ideas*, XIX (1958), 542-50.

Blet, P. "Jésuites et libertés gallicanes en 1611," *Archivum historicum Societatis Iesu*, XXIV (1955), 165-88.

———. "Jésuites gallicans au XVIIᵉ siècle?" *ibid.*, XXIX (1960), 55-84.

———. "Le Plan de Richelieu pour la réunion des protestants," *Gregorianum*, XLVIII (1967), 100-29.

Bowen, W. H. "Sixteenth Century French Translations of Machiavelli," *Italica*, XXVII (1950), 313-19.

Butler, K. T. "Louis Machon's 'Apologie pour Machiavelle'—1643 and 1668," *Journal of the Warburg and Courtauld Institutes*, III (1939-1940), 208-27.

Cardascia, G. "Machiavel et Jean Bodin," *Bibliothèque d'humanisme et Renaissance*, III (1943), 129-67.

Céleste, R. "Louis Machon, apologiste de Machiavel et de la politique de Richelieu," *Annales de la Faculté des Lettres de Bordeaux*, III (1881), 446-72.

———. "Louis Machon, apologiste de Machiavel et de la politique du Cardinal de Richelieu: Nouvelles recherches sur sa vie et ses œuvres," *ibid.*, V (1883), 67-132.

Certeau, M. de. "Politique et mystique: René d'Argenson (1596-1651)," *Revue d'ascétique et de mystique*, XXXIX (1963), 45-82.

Charay, J. "Une Énigme historique: Comment mourut le maréchal J.-B. d'Ornano?" *Revue du Viverais*, LXI (1957), No. 2, 49-63.

Chaunu, P. "Le XVIIᵉ siècle religieux: Reflexions préalables," *Annales: Économies, Sociétés, Civilisations*, XXII (1967), 279-302.

Choné, J. "La Spiritualité sacerdotale," *XVIIᵉ siècle*, Nos. 62-63 (1964), 112-32.

Church, W. F. "The Problem of Constitutional Thought in France, from the End of the Middle Ages to the Revolution," *IXᵉ Congrès International des Sciences Historiques: Études présentées à la Commis-

sion Internationale pour l'histoire des assemblées d'États, Louvain, 1952, pp. 173-86.

———. "Cardinal Richelieu and the Social Estates of the Realm," *Album Helen Maud Cam*, Louvain, 1961, Vol. II, 263-70.

———. "Publications on Cardinal Richelieu since 1945: A Bibliographical Study," *Journal of Modern History*, XXXVII (1965), 421-44.

———. "The Decline of the French Jurists as Political Theorists, 1660-1789," *French Historical Studies*, V (1967), 1-40.

Cognet, L. "La Spiritualité de Richelieu," *Études franciscaines*, III (1952), 85-91.

Darricau, R. "La Spiritualité du prince," *XVIIᵉ siècle*, Nos. 62-63 (1964), 78-111.

Declareuil, J. "Les Idées politiques de Guez de Balzac," *Revue de droit public et de la science politique en France et à l'étranger*, XIV (1907), 633-74.

Dedouvres, L. "Le Père Joseph polémiste," *Revue des questions historiques*, LXI (1897), 137-65.

———. "Le Père Joseph diplomate," *Revue d'histoire diplomatique*, XII (1898), 80-98.

Delaborde, H. F. "Les Travaux de Dupuy sur le Trésor des Chartes," *Bibliothèque de l'École des chartes*, LVIII (1897), 126-54.

Delaruelle, L. "Le 'Prince' de Guez de Balzac et son actualité pour le public du temps," *Revue d'histoire littéraire de la France*, XXXXIX (1949), 13-20.

Deloche, M. "Les Vrais Mémoires du Cardinal de Richelieu," *Revue des questions historiques*, CIX (1928), 257-312.

———. "Le Testament politique du Cardinal de Richelieu," *Revue historique*, CLXV (1930), 43-76.

Demante, G. "Histoire de la publication des livres de Pierre Dupuy sur les libertés de l'église gallicane," *Bibliothèque de l'École des Chartes*, V (1843), 585-606.

Denis, J. "Balzac: première ébauche du XVIIᵉ siècle et de Bossuet," *Mémoires de l'Académie des sciences, arts et belles lettres de Caen*, 1866, pp. 301-58.

Dickmann, F. "Rechtsgedanke und Machtpolitik bei Richelieu. Studien an neu endeckten Quellen," *Historische Zeitschrift*, CLXXXXVI (1963), 265-319.

Dowdall, H. C. "The Word 'State,'" *Law Quarterly Review*, xxxix (1923), 98-125.

Duine, F. "Avant Bossuet. Cohon: Évêque de Nîmes et de Dol, précepteur des neveux de Mazarin, prédicateur du roi," *Bulletin de la commission historique et archéologique de la Mayenne*, xxiii (1907), 407-28; xxiv (1908), 55-116, 141-86.

Dupont-Ferrier, G. "Le Sens des mots 'patria' et 'patrie' en France au moyen âge et jusqu'au début du XVIIe siècle," *Revue historique*, clxxxviii (1940), 89-104.

Fagniez, G. "L'Opinion publique et la polémique au temps de Richelieu, à propos d'une publication récente," *Revue des questions historiques*, lx (1896), 442-84.

――――. "L'Opinion publique et la presse politique sous Louis XIII, 1624-1626," *Revue d'histoire diplomatique*, xiv (1900), 352-401.

――――. "Mathieu de Morgues et le procès de Richelieu," *Revue des deux mondes*, clxii (1900), 550-86.

――――. "Fancan et Richelieu," *Revue historique*, cvii (1911), 59-78, 310-22; cviii (1911), 75-87.

Febvre, L. "Aspects méconnus d'un renouveau religieux en France entre 1590 et 1620," *Annales: Économies, Sociétés, Civilisations*, xiii (1958), 639-50.

Fernández de la Mora, G. "Maquiavelo, visto por los tratadistas políticos españoles de la Contrarreforma," *Arbor*, xiii (1949), 417-49.

Fulton, D. "Printings of *The Prince*, 1631," *Bulletin of the New York Public Library*, lxiii (1959), 318-19.

Galland, A. "Les Pasteurs français Amyraut, Bochart, etc., et la royauté de droit divin," *Bulletin de la Société de l'histoire du protestantisme français*, lxxvii (1928), 14-20, 105-34, 225-41, 413-23.

Gardiner, S. R. "Un Mémoire inédit de Richelieu relatif aux Huguenots," *Revue historique*, i (1876), 228-38.

Gilmore, M. P. "Authority and Property in the Seventeenth Century: The First Edition of the *Traité des seigneuries* of Charles Loyseau," *Harvard Library Bulletin*, iv (1950), 258-65.

Grente, G. "Richelieu, homme d'église," *Le Correspondant*, August 10, 1932, 321-35.

Hassinger, E. "Das Politische Testament Richelieus," *Historische Zeitschrift*, clxxiii (1952), 485-503.

Henrard, P. "Mathieu de Morgues et la maison de Plantin," *Bulletin de l'Académie royale des sciences, des lettres et des beaux-arts de Belgique*, second series, XXXXIX (1880), 542-88.

Herr, R. "Honor versus Absolutism: Richelieu's Fight against Duelling," *Journal of Modern History*, XXVII (1955), 281-85.

Kantorowicz, E. H. "*Pro patria mori* in Medieval Political Thought," *American Historical Review*, LVI (1951), 472-92.

———. "Mysteries of State: An Absolutist Concept and Its Late Medieval Origins," *Harvard Theological Review*, XLVIII (1955), 65-91.

Kerviler, R. "Paul Hay du Chastelet," *Revue de Bretagne*, XXXIV (1873), 66-79, 155-69, 202-17, 306-20. (Reprinted in Kerviler, *La Bretagne à l'Académie française au XVIIe siècle*, Paris, 1879).

———. "François de La Mothe le Vayer, 1583-1672," *Revue historique et archéologique du Maine*, V (1879), 28-74, 162-97, 259-329; VI (1879), 5-57.

Kükelhaus, T. "Zur Geschichte Richelieus. Unbekannte Papiere Fancans," *Historische Vierteljahrschrift*, II (1899), 18-38.

Lalanne, L. "Un Récit inédit de la mort du Cardinal de Richelieu," *Revue historique*, LV (1894), 302-8.

Lecler, J. "Politique nationale et idée chrétienne dans les temps modernes," *Études*, CCXIV (1933), 385-405, 546-64, 683-702.

———. "Les Principes de Richelieu sur la sécularisation de la politique française," *Cahiers d'histoire publiés par les Universités de Clermont, Lyon, Grenoble*, IV (1959), 46-52.

Lekai, L. J. "Cardinal Richelieu as Abbot of Citeaux," *Catholic Historical Review*, XLII (1956), 137-56.

Malvezzi, A. "Papa Urbano VIII e la questione della Valtellina," *Archivio storico lombardo*, VII (1958), 5-113.

Martin, V. "L'Adoption du gallicanisme politique par le clergé de France," *Revue des sciences religieuses*, VI (1926), 305-44, 453-98; VII (1927), 1-51, 181-225, 373-401, 545-78; VIII (1928), 1-23, 173-95, 361-97.

Maspétiol, R. "Qu'est-ce que l'État?" *Revue politique et parlamentaire*, CCV (1951), 343-51.

———. "Le Droit et l'État au XVIIe siècle," *Revue des deux mondes*, March 1, 1964, 39-51.

———. "Les Deux Aspects de la 'raison d'État' et son apologie au début du XVIIe siècle," *Archives de philosophie du droit*, X (1965), 209-219.

Massaut, J. P. "Autour de Richelieu et de Mazarin. Le Carme Léon de Saint-Jean et la grande politique," *Revue d'histoire moderne et contemporaine*, VII (1960), 11-45.

Mattei, R. de. "Il Problema della 'Ragion di Stato' nel Seicento," *Rivista Internazionale di Filosofia del Diritto*, XXVI (1949), 187-210; XXVII (1950), 27-38; XXVIII (1951), 333-56, 705-23; XXIX (1952), 406-24; XXX (1953), 445-61; XXXI (1954), 369-84; XXXIII (1956), 439-49; XXXIV (1957), 166-92; XXXV (1958), 680-93; XXXVI (1959), 517-43; XXXVII (1960), 553-76; XXXVIII (1961), 185-200.

――――. "Il Problema della 'Ragion di Stato' nei suoi primi affioramenti," *ibid.*, XXXXI (1964), 712-32.

Mercier, C. "Les Théories politiques des calvinistes en France au cours des guerres de religion," *Bulletin de la Société de l'histoire du protestantisme français*, LXXXIII (1934), 225-60, 381-415.

Meuvret, J. "Comment les français du XVIIᵉ siècle voyaient l'impôt," *XVIIᵉ siècle*, Nos. 25-26 (1955), 59-82.

"Missionnaires catholiques à l'interieur de la France pendant le XVIIᵉ siècle," *XVIIᵉ siècle*, No. 41, 1958.

Momigliano, A. "The First Political Commentary on Tacitus," *Journal of Roman Studies*, XXXVII (1947), 91-101.

Mommsen, W. "Richelieu als Staatsmann," *Historische Zeitschrift*, CXXVII (1922), 210-42.

Montbas, H. de. "Richelieu et l'opposition pendant la guerre de trente ans (1635-1638)," *Correspondance historique et archéologique*, XX (1913), 201-16.

Mousnier, R. "Le Testament politique de Richelieu," *Revue historique*, CCI (1949), 55-71, and Addendum in *ibid.*, CCII (1949), 137.

――――. "Comment les français du XVIIᵉ siècle voyaient la constitution," *XVIIᵉ siècle*, Nos. 25-26 (1955), 9-36.

――――. "Recherches sur les soulèvements populaires en France avant la Fronde," *Revue d'histoire moderne et contemporaine*, V (1958), 81-113.

――――. "L'Évolution des institutions monarchiques en France et ses relations avec l'état social," *XVIIᵉ siècle*, Nos. 58-59 (1963), 57-72.

Nabholz, H. "Die öffentliche Meinung in Frankreich und die Veltlinerfrage zur Zeit Richelieus," *Jahrbuch für Schweizerische Geschichte*, XXVI (1901), pp. 1-67.

Najam, E. W. "*Europe*: Richelieu's Blueprint for Unity and Peace," *Studies in Philology*, LIII (1956), 25-34.

Nicolaï, A. "Le Machiavélisme de Montaigne," *Bulletin de la Société des amis de Montaigne*, third series, No. 4 (1957), 11-21; Nos. 5-6 (1958), 25-47; No. 7 (1958), 2-8; No. 9 (1959), 18-30.

Oesterich, G. "Justus Lipsius als Theoretiker des Neuzeitlichen Machtstaates," *Historische Zeitschrift*, CLXXXI (1956), 31-78.

Orcibal, J. "Richelieu, homme d'église, homme d'État, à propos d'un ouvrage récent," *Revue d'histoire de l'église de France*, XXXIV (1948), 94-101.

Pagès, G. "Autour du 'grand orage': Richelieu et Marillac, deux politiques," *Revue historique*, CLXXIX (1937), 63-97.

Perroud, C. "Essai sur la vie et les œuvres de Mathieu de Morgues, abbé de Saint-Germain, 1582-1670," *Annales de la Société d'agriculture, sciences, arts et commerce du Puy*, XXVI (1863), 205-383.

Pinon, R. "La Politique de Richelieu," *Le Correspondant*, CCCXII (1928), 828-39.

Pintard, R. "L'Influence de la pensée philosophique de la renaissance italienne sur la pensée française. État des travaux relatifs au XVIIe siècle," *Revue des études italiennes*, I (1936), 194-227.

Pithon, R. "A propos du Testament politique de Richelieu," *Schweizerische Zeitschrift für Geschichte*, VI (1956), 177-214.

———. "Les Débuts difficiles du ministère de Richelieu et la crise de Valteline, 1621-1627," *Revue d'histoire diplomatique*, LXXIV (1960), 298-322.

———. "La Suisse, théâtre de la guerre froide entre la France et l'Espagne pendant la crise de Valteline (1621-1626)," *Schweizerische Zeitschrift für Geschichte*, XIII (1963), 33-53.

Post, G. "The Theory of Public Law and the State in the Thirteenth Century," *Seminar*, VI (1948), 42-59. Reprinted in Post, *Studies in Medieval Legal Thought: Public Law and the State, 1100-1322*, Princeton, 1964.

Préclin, E. "Edmond Richer (1559-1631). Sa vie. Son œuvre. La Richérisme," *Revue d'histoire moderne*, V (1930), 241-69, 321-36.

Ranum, O. A. "Richelieu and the Great Nobility: Some Aspects of Early Modern Political Motives," *French Historical Studies*, III (1963), 184-204.

Rathé, C. E. "Innocent Gentillet and the first 'Anti-Machiavel,'" *Bibliothèque d'Humanisme et Renaissance*, XXVII (1965), 186-225.

Raumer, K. von. "Zur Problematik des Werdenden Machtstaates," *Historische Zeitschrift*, CLXXIV (1952), 71-79.

————. "Westfälischer Friede," *ibid.*, CLXXXV (1962), 596-613.

Singleton, C. S. "The Perspective of Art," *Kenyon Review*, XV (1953), 169-89.

Strowski, F. "Les Lois fondamentales du royaume au temps de Montaigne," *Revue des travaux de l'Académie des sciences morales et politiques*, 1950, 1er semestre, pp. 91-101.

Tapié, V. L. "Comment les français du XVIIe siècle voyaient la patrie," *XVIIe siècle*, Nos. 25-26 (1955), 37-58.

Teall, E. "The Seigneur of Renaissance France," *Journal of Modern History*, XXXVII (1965), 131-50.

Tentler, T. N. "The Meaning of Prudence in Bodin," *Traditio*, XV (1959), 365-84.

Vaulgrenant, Général de. "Le Vœu de Louis XIII," *Revue d'histoire de l'église de France*, XXIV (1938), 47-58.

Vigier, O. "L'Influence politique du père Joseph. Négociations avec les princes d'Allemagne et la Suède," *Revue des questions historiques*, L (1891), 430-98.

Watter, P. "Jean-Louis Guez de Balzac's *Le Prince*: A Revaluation," *Journal of the Warburg and Courtauld Institutes*, XX (1957), 215-47.

Weber, H. "Friede und Gewissen," in *Forschungen und Studien zur Geschichte des Westfalischen Friedens*, Münster, 1965, pp. 85-108.

————. "Richelieu et le Rhin," *Revue historique*, CCXXXIX (1968), 265-80.

Weil, E. "Philosophie politique, théorie politique," *Revue française de science politique*, XI (1961), 267-94.

Weins, E. "Fancan und die französische Politik, 1624-1627," *Heidelberger Abhandlingen zur mittleren und neueren Geschichte*, XXI (1908), 1-141.

Wilmerding, L. "*Le Prince* by Guez de Balzac: Note on a Paris Printing, 1631," in *Bookman's Holiday: Notes and Studies Written and Gathered in Tribute to Harry Miller Lydenberg*, New York, 1943, pp. 489-97.

Zeller, G. "La Monarchie d'ancien régime et les frontières naturelles," *Revue d'histoire moderne*, VIII (1933), 305-33.

————. "Saluces, Pignerol et Strasbourg. La Politique des frontières au temps de la préponderance espagnole," *Revue historique*, CLXXXXIII (1942-1943), 97-110. (Reprinted in Zeller, *Aspects de la politique française sous l'ancien régime*, Paris, 1964.)

————. "Une Notion de caractère historico-social: la dérogeance," *Cahiers internationaux de sociologie*, XXII (1957), 40-74. (Reprinted in *Aspects de la politique française sous l'ancien régime*.)

INDEX